Ty Cobb Enjoying Health and Wealth--Or Does He, Really?

The Country Squire

TY COBB, GREATEST COMPETITOR IN BASEBALL HISTORY.

WEALTHIEST OF THE RETIRED BALL PLAYERS — LIVES QUIET LIFE OF A COUNTRY SQUIRE NOW IN ATHERTON, CALIF. FAVORITE SPORT IS GOLF — SHOOTS IN THE YOUNG EIGHTIES.

GEORGIA PEACH, WHO RETIRED IN 1928 AFTER 23 YEARS, LED AMERICAN LEAGUE BATTERS 12 TIMES — NINE IN A ROW, STOLE 96 BASES ONE YEAR AND LED LEAGUE IN BASE THEFTS 10 TIMES.

Ty Cobb Unleashed

The Definitive Counter-Biography of the Chastened Racist

. . . .

Howard W. Rosenberg

Tile Books

TILE BOOKS
howieanson@yahoo.com

Library of Congress Cataloging-in-Publication Data

Rosenberg, Howard W.
    Ty Cobb Unleashed : The Definitive Counter-Biography of the Chastened Racist / by Howard W. Rosenberg
        p.   cm.
    Includes index.
    ISBN 978-0-9725574-4-3
    1. Cobb, Ty, 1886-1961.   2. Baseball players—United States—Biography
I. Title.
    GV865.C
    796.357'092—dc23   2017-903704

Colorization of cover graphics by Willie Brown (wbrown189@windstream.net)
Cover design by Gary Palmatier
Printed and bound in the United States of America

The author invites corrections of all types, and possible additions.

On the cover (from left to right): Cobb, Lou Costello, Bud Abbott and Joe DiMaggio

Contents

To Ty Cobb.

The Greatest of them all.

With cordial regard.

Douglas Mac Arthur.

In loving memory of my parents
Melvin Rosenberg, December 25, 1928, to January 26, 2013
Sydell Rosenberg, December 4, 1929, to February 8, 2017

who also made possible my four prior books:

Cap Anson 1: When Captaining a Team Meant Something: Leadership in Baseball's Early Years

Cap Anson 2: The Theatrical and Kingly Mike Kelly: U.S. Team Sport's First Media Sensation and Baseball's Original Casey at the Bat

Cap Anson 3: Muggsy John McGraw and the Tricksters: Baseball's Fun Age of Rule Bending

Cap Anson 4: Bigger Than Babe Ruth: Captain Anson of Chicago

Potpourri of Quotes By or About Ty Cobb

"And Cobb himself said nothing about race or no one recorded him saying anything about race until 1952 when he told the *Sporting News* 'the Negro should be accepted wholeheartedly and not grudgingly. The Negro has the right to play professional sports and who's to say he has not.' That gives me chills when I say that."
– 2015 Simon & Schuster Cobb biographer Charles Leerhsen on MSNBC.com, May 19, 2015

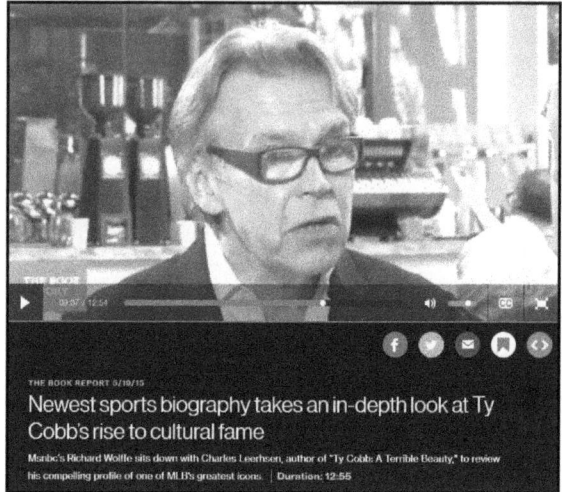

Newest sports biography takes an in-depth look at Ty Cobb's rise to cultural fame

Msnbc's Richard Wolffe sits down with Charles Leerhsen, author of "Ty Cobb: A Terrible Beauty," to review his compelling profile of one of MLB's greatest icons. | Duration: 12:55

"And did you ever notice that the morals of dogs are much better than those of men?"
– Cobb to kennel editor Frank F. Dole of the *New York Herald Tribune*, July 1924

"He has lived his strangely fascinating and fiery life, as always a law unto himself."
– *Detroit News* sports editor Harry G. Salsinger, in the third-to-last paragraph of a more than 50-part newspaper serial, December 1924

"Ball players eat too much, except when they are working under me. Two meals is enough for any man in active training."
– Cobb to Davis J. Walsh of the International News Service, March 1925

"Cobb fought his way through a ball game, brawled on the field, battled his way in and out of fights off the field, got himself kicked out of many a ball park by an irate umpire, put the fear of God into opposing basemen by his mere methods of riding into a bag with his spikes knee high."
– Anonymous writer doling out some exaggerations, as printed in the *San Diego Union*, October 9, 1927

"In batting, fielding, base running, together with diamond strategy and tactics, Mr. Cobb was a star of the first magnitude. As a penologist, he is still groping along the abandoned paths of terrorism."
– *St. Louis Post-Dispatch* editorial page, October 2, 1931

"I know it sounds silly but I must have the sausage."
– Cobb to J. Carter "Scoop" Latimer, sports editor of the *Greenville News* in South Carolina, 1940 letter

"Ty Cobb could do everything and spike you too. But there has only been one Babe [Ruth]."
– *Hearne Democrat (Tex.)* humor columnist Cayce Moore, August 1941

"Ty has mellowed with age and he often tells me he regrets some of the things he did when he was playing ball. But hell, that was what made Cobb great. If you got in his way he'd cut you down."
– former teammate Ossie Vitt to Emmons Byrne of the *Oakland Tribune*, September 1945

"As a hitter, he qualified for the Hall of Fame, but as a writer he should be admitted to the hall of shame."
– Bob Cooke, sports editor of the *New York Herald Tribune*, February 1952

"Love him? I hated him the way everybody else in the game did. Cobb was the meanest man who ever wore a uniform. But that has nothing to do with the fact he was so much the greatest player who ever lived it's not even close."
– Al Schacht, the famous baseball clown and 1919-21 major leaguer, to Gayle Talbot of the Associated Press, March 1955

"I'm always made out to be a louse."
– Cobb to Newspaper Enterprise Association reporter Pat Parrish, February 1960

"If Cobb had come west with the '49ers [in the days of the California gold rush], it is possible that he would have ended up owning most of the west – or with a bullet hole in his head. But he would have loved every minute of the battle."
– Hal Wood, longtime West Coast sports editor of United Press/United Press International, July 1961

1. *A Dodger No More*

What to make of the persona of Hall of Famer Tyrus Raymond "Ty" Cobb is one of the great unsettled subjects of baseball history. As reflected in newsprint, his combination of notoriety and fame for his aggressiveness on the diamond are unmatched. By far his most positive actions came in his last 15 years when the narrative was etched, but too late to rehabilitate him. Also during that period, he was harming his reputation by drinking heavily; at times he likely drank heavily to ease what in 1960 he called his "hellish pain" physically. A witness to his drinking that year and in 1961 was Alvin J. "Al" Stump, the co-author of his innocuous 1961 book who, posthumously, wrote a scathing article. Cobb's great off-the-field positives were philanthropic, toward building a hospital and in creating a college scholarship fund. While this book will present new analysis of him for his playing style too, other revelations, baseball racial ones, can start the ball rolling:

Cobb was clearly a racist, for having been personally opposed to the integration of organized baseball, at least as of the early 1940s. A pair of 1946 news columns to that effect indicate that he was a supporter of so-called institutional racism. The writer in both instances was one of the highest-paid sportswriters of the 1940s: *Boston Herald* sports columnist Elijah W. "Bill" Cunningham. As of 1941, his annual salary was $26,000, close to $500,000 in today's dollars.

A second revelation of mine, and a relatively short one to tackle, is that Cobb had been offered the position of interlocutor in the Honey Boy Minstrels in the offseason of 1912-13, an act led by his friend George Evans. But Cobb reportedly "declined, saying: 'My wife won't let me.'" That quote appeared in the *Lexington Leader* in Kentucky in September 1912, in an article written by its news editor. I could not figure out which newspaper may have reported that first. Similarly that December, a week before Evans's act was slated to appear in Santa Fe, N.M., the *Santa Fe New Mexican* stated, "Should Cobb be able to overcome his wife's

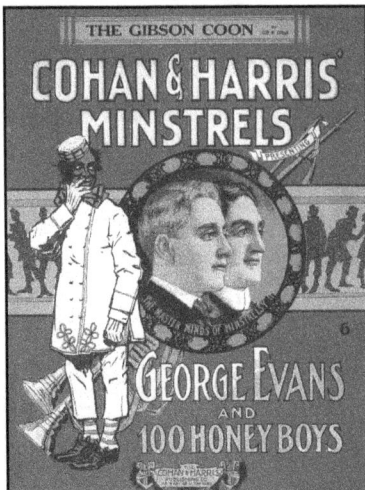

THE GIBSON COON
COHAN & HARRIS MINSTRELS
GEORGE EVANS
AND
100 HONEY BOYS

TY COBB MAY COME HERE WITH MINSTRELS

Has Been Offered Position by "Honey Boy" George Evans—Corbett Was Once With the Company.

Ty Cobb, the famous centerfielder of the Detroit American league team, may be a member of George Evans's "Honey Boy" minstrels when they make their initial appearance before an El Paso audience at the El Paso theater on December 21 and 22.

objections to him entering the hist[r]ionic realm, he will probably appear in the olio [variety show section of the performance] with a monologue, preceding that of the 'Honey Boy,'" Evans. "He will also appear for a brief period in the first part, 'The Floral Bower,' in the role of interlocutor." As described in 1913, The Floral Bower "was the name given by the artists to the exquisitely beautiful opening part, which introduces the well-known minstrel favorites seated in the usual semi-circle on a terraced dais."

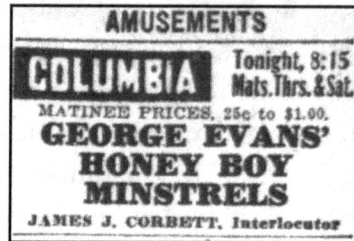

AMUSEMENTS

COLUMBIA Tonight, 8:15 Mats.Thrs.&Sat.

MATINEE PRICES, 25c to $1.00.

GEORGE EVANS' HONEY BOY MINSTRELS

JAMES J. CORBETT, Interlocutor

The earliest speculative Cobb-minstrel report that I found is from 1911. A report from Pittsburgh in the *Atlanta Constitution* stated that Cobb "will be a minstrel during the winter, according to an announcement made here last night." Evans was on especially good terms with Cobb as of 1912. In the previous four seasons, he had awarded Cobb a trophy for being the champion batsman of the world. Also of note, Evans had previously hired an athlete to perform with his troupe, former heavyweight

Jim Corbett and "Honey Boy" Evans in Ty Cobb's Motor Car.

from left to right in Augusta, Ga., after the 1910 season: Cobb and guests Corbett and Evans

boxing champion James "Jim" Corbett. In the theater season of 1910-11, Corbett was an interlocutor in the first part of his show. In a later segment, he told boxing stories. As of the fall of 1912, Corbett was unavailable to return, as he was recovering from appendicitis.

Reporting exists that supports the notion that Cobb's wife Charlie was weighing in on her husband's offseason plans, such as joining a minstrel troupe. In 1908, two months after their marriage, she was quoted on his abandoning a plan to go on a baseball barnstorming tour of Japan that winter. A report with a Columbus, Ga., dateline quoted her as saying that instead, "Ty will put in the winter hunting. You may say for me, and I speak for him." Two weeks later, another report from Columbus stated that he had signed to play winter baseball in New Orleans, after having "secured consent from Mrs. Cobb."

COBB AS MINSTREL MAN

"Ty" COBB

Tyrus Cobb has another chance to shine in the footlights glare, which he renounced forever last year. His latest offer is the job of interlocutor with George Evans' minstrels. Two year ago Evans had Jim Corbett in this position, and now hopes to land a diamond favorite.

Cobb lost weight as an actor last year, grew nervous, and was afraid the stage might hurt his invaluable batting eye. Therefore he quit and announced that he would stick to baseball. Besides Cobb, Evans is angling for Charley Dooin, Mike Donlin and Christy Mathewson.

Based on the absence of reporting to the contrary, Cobb presumably did not mind being associated with a report that he might appear with minstrels. That said, it is ambiguous whether he would have followed through anyway. When he performed on stage in the previous offseason, 1911-12, he stayed with that theater company into early 1912, even after declaring in December 1911, "I can't stand the strain. I haven't had a good night's sleep since we opened the show in Newark[, N.J.]. If I kept on until baseball training time, I would be totally unfit to join the Tigers," his major league team.

A third discovery, which an unheralded Web site found first – and which is also easier to quickly run through than support for institutional racism – is that Cobb played the popular racist carnival and amusement park game African Dodger. The game was also known as Hit the Nigger Baby or Hit the Coon.

Before detailing Cobb's playing of the game, here is some contemporaneous background. Also presented are his own figurative references to it.

Although the following event never transpired, the *Washington Post* reported on plans to hold it in 1913: "The St. Louis Press Club is hunting for several alert negroes to act as targets" for Washington and St. Louis pitchers as a side spectacle during an upcoming Washington series in St. Louis. The negroes "will compete in a 'soak-the-African-dodger' contest at a carnival Wednesday night at Delmar Garden[, a popular carnival location]. The event is being arranged by Col. Robert Lee Hedges, president of the Browns, who confesses a curiosity to see big league hurlers heave spheres at the elusive negroes who make a living by pitting their heads against hard baseballs." Days later, sports columnist Louis Lee Arms of the *St. Louis Star* interviewed someone who was willing to be an African dodger for that occasion. According to Arms, "George" the interviewee "doesn't read the sporting pages. That's why he doesn't know anything about Walter Johnson," Washington's great fastball pitcher.

a circa 1940s cartoon with All-American Comics character Popsicle Pete (the one above with the rolled-up sleeve); All-American Comics was a forerunner of what is now known as D.C. Comics

An update days later declared, "As a usual thing it is not difficult to secure the services of negroes in St. Louis when the pay is good and the exertion required not excessive, but a committee of the Press club, which is giving a carnival here, was unable for hours today to secure an 'African dodger' who would allow base balls to be thrown at his cranium at the usual rate of three for 5 cents [about $1.25 today]. The reason became known this afternoon when it was found that some joker had circulated the story that Walter Johnson, the speed ball artist of the Washington Americans[,] was to visit the carnival."

In 1960, the collaborator on Cobb's 1914 book, features syndicate owner John N. Wheeler, had lunch with Cobb in New York City. They got together days after Cobb received an award from the New York Chapter of the Baseball Writers' Association of America. Wheeler broached the subject of pitchers brushing him back during his career and conveyed his reply:

"'When I was young, I used to be an African dodger in a circus,' he answered with a grin. 'So I learned how to duck. As a matter of fact, the way I stood at the plate, I could move fast and get out of the way. No, I never had any trouble with bean balls.'"

Wheeler told his readers, "Of course he was kidding about having been in the circus."

On having been the target of bean balls, Cobb wrote the following in 1926: "In the old days the habit of 'dusting 'em off' was more common than now. The expression originated from a cry from the bench to a pitcher: 'Dust him off,' meaning come so close with the ball as to knock the dust out of his clothes." Against such dusters, "I fought back with my spikes." That last line, by the way, could be considered a self-inflicted wound by Cobb to his own reputation.

Apart from that last line, just one of the above thoughts is in a Cobb book or Cobb-written article to date. The exception is that in his 1961 biography with Stump, *My Life in Baseball: The True Record*, he was quoted as saying that he had been called "'an African dodger' at the plate, for I was rarely [actually around the major league average over his career] hit by a pitched ball."

In addition to Wheeler's 1960 article, I found a second loose match for that 1961 quote. Back in 1957, Newspaper Enterprise Association (NEA) sports editor Harry Grayson sat next to Cobb during a game at the Polo Grounds in New York. Asked by Grayson if he had ever worn anything in his cap to protect himself against beanballs, Cobb replied, "Not a thing, and I was the original African dodger." Cobb also had used the term "African dodger" in 1922. In that instance, wrote Frank G. Menke of King Features Syndicate, Cobb said that it is less dangerous to face a hard-throwing veteran pitcher such as Johnson or Grover Cleveland Alexander than it is to face a more inexperienced pitcher, "all due to control." When batting against a rookie, you must "be prepared to do an African dodger act on a half second's notice."

Had Cobb been racially negative in his 1961 book, by stating that he had actually played African Dodger at a segregated amusement park with a black person willing to be paid to be potentially beaned, he would have been correct. That is because in 1911, Bob Thayer of the old *Washington Times* saw him at the Glen Echo one in Maryland just outside of the District of Columbia, while Detroit was in town for a series. Thayer wrote, "I was amused at Glen Echo last night to see Ty Cobb give a real demonstration of his ability to throw straight balls. Accompanied by a couple of members of the Detroit club, Cobb arrived at the amusement resort and the first thing he did was to look up the African dodger booth. No one there seemed to

HELP WANTED—MALE

YOUNG man for small hotel office; room and board; very small salary. Box 193, this office. 25

YOUNG MAN to learn the drug business. Apply to Flemer's Drug Store, 7th st. and Md. ave. ne. 27

YOUNG man, with experience, on soda fountain. Simons' Pharmacy, 14th st. and N. Y. ave. 27

YOUNG colored man, with experience, as coon dodger, for park work. Apply Gayety Poolroom, bet. 10 and 11. 27

from the Washington Post of May 25, 1911 (the ad ran the next two days too)

recognize the great ball player, and he took three balls. These went true to the mark, and he repeated seven times in succession before every one became nervous and inquired who the man was. When it was discovered that it was the

LATEST NEWS If You See It In The Defender It's So

Chicago Defender

HOME EDITION

VOL. IX., NO. 25. SATURDAY CHICAGO, JUNE 20, 1914 SATURDAY PRICE 5 CENTS

DRIVE OUT DISGRACEFUL AFRICAN DODGER

one and only Cobb[,] quite a crowd gathered. Cobb was offered ten cigars, which he did not smoke, but moved away and soon returned to the city."

According to baseball racial historian Sarah Trembanis, African Dodger "involved an African American man placing his head in an opening, while white fairgoers threw baseballs at his head. The black man would try to duck 'or dodge' to avoid being hit by the onslaught of baseballs." A similar version of the

AFRICAN DODGER AT SUMMER PARKS SHAMEFUL DISGRACE

Degraded Men Posing as Targets at Amusement Places Should Be Condemned by all Self-Respecting People—Ought Not to Be Identified as Human—Eastern Newspaper Joins Defender Fight.

MEN WHO SEEK THIS WORK ARE CRIMINALS AGAINST THE RACE.

the subheadlines are also from the *Chicago Defender* of June 20, 1914 game was the fifth-most profitable exhibit at the 1933 World's Fair in Chicago, she later noted. The fair's version "featured a sideshow game called 'African Dips.'" In that case, if the contestant hit a target, a black man would fall into a tank of water. According to 1974 Babe Ruth biographer Kal Wagenheim, Ruth "loved to dunk the African Dodger" in that version of the game.

Trembanis cited, as an analogy to African Dodger, an audio interview comment made by early black National League star Roy Campanella to Stephen Banker, in his 1978 cassette interviews, "Black Diamonds: An Oral History of Negro Baseball." She paraphrased Campanella as saying, "hostile white pitchers would at times intentionally throw at the head of an opposing black batter."

Unlike the institutional racism and minstrelsy reports, which I found in newspaper databases, I first saw the African Dodger detail on a Web site devoted to amusement parks. Wheeler's lunch interview inspired me to poke around.

Focusing on just Cobb's playing of African Dodger, anyone willing to potentially hit a black person in an amusement park game (even if the balls, presumably tennis ones, "are soft and cannot do serious injury," as a feature story stated that year, although "other missiles are sometimes worked in") arguably was not better than most Southerners of his day on race to shower with brownie points. But a prize-winning-for-its-great-research (and by implication analysis) book by Simon & Schuster in 2015 missed that. It also missed Cobb's being open to minstrelsy and his reported opposition to the presence of blacks in major league baseball up to at least the early 1940s.

That personal opposition to integration of baseball had dried up by 1952, when he was asked twice how he felt; one response is paraphrased in the first of the "Potpourri of Quotes" that starts this book. Assuming that, indeed, no Cobb views survive on the subject from 1947 to 1952, arguably the next-best thing is the mixed reaction to integration by a 1924-25 and 1950 Cobb serial writer, longtime *Detroit News* sports editor Harry G. Salsinger. Warm Cobb letters to him survive from the 1950s. While Salsinger in 1947 backed Jackie Robinson's entry into the majors and said still-minor leaguer Campanella might be the best catcher in all of baseball, he criticized the play of fellow blacks Larry Doby, Hank Thompson and Willard Brown, saying they are "not representatives of top Negro talent."

In 1952, a hot issue at the time that Cobb was interviewed was whether the minor Texas League should now be integrating. While the major leagues had started to integrate in 1947, and its teams had done so to varying degrees as of 1952, a few lower minor leagues in the Deep South began having black players only in 1951.

Coincidentally or not, Cobb had played in an old-timers' game at a Texas League ballpark in 1950 that inaugurated that league's season. In the minors nearly a half-century earlier, he had played in the South Atlantic (Sally) League, which also as of January 1952 had yet to integrate. The Texas League did integrate in 1952 and the Sally League followed in 1953.

The two integration interviews with Cobb, both in January 1952 at his home in California, resulted in articles by West Coast writers for the Associated Press and the *Sporting News*.

Russ Newland circa 1950

The first of the two focused on the Texas League and was by longtime San Francisco AP sports reporter Russ Newland. Newland had done a range of features on Cobb. One was the AP's interview with him in San Francisco upon his return from a baseball tour of Japan after the 1928 season. Another was Cobb's revealing personal remarks, at a 1934 banquet to be noted later. One other overlap is that Cobb was a Shriner and Newland a Mason.

On top of that, Cobb was an avid golfer in California and Newland was both the longtime president of the California Golf Writers Association, from the early 1930s into the 1950s, and the first president of the national Golf Writers Association of America, starting in 1946. Finally, Newland is one of just two reporters who I found mentioning his dog Chudley by name; he did so in 1951 when the AP also ran a picture of Cobb with his pooch.

with dog Chudley in Atherton in 1953. The photographer was a teenager who Cobb taught in 1952 at a camp in the Ozarks.

Before 1952, one sign that Cobb moderated on racial equality is that in 1945, he announced plans to contribute toward the construction of a new hospital in the town where he lived in his teens, Royston, Ga. His contribution of $100,000, about $1 million in today's dollars, would end up helping persons of all races. (Dr. Stewart D. Brown, Sr., his longtime close friend and former Royston teammate, told sports editor Furman Bisher of the *Atlanta Constitution* in 1950, "Ty brought his wife here [to Royston, long after he had moved to Augusta, Ga.,] and I operated on her in 1929. I guess you'd say that's when the idea for this hospital was born. Ty's boy, Ty, Jr., doctor down at Dublin[, Ga.] now, came here and practiced some with me.")

Media Blinders

The writer of the two 1946 *Boston Herald* columns that point to Cobb's support of institutional racism, Bill Cunningham, was a native of Texas. In the latter of them, he told of having overheard Cobb a few years earlier explaining what native Southerners such as Cobb would willingly do together with blacks. After detailing activities that he would personally engage in, Cobb said, "But I won't play games with him. Neither will any other southern white man. When you do that, you accept him on your own social level, and social equality is the one place where the southerner always will draw the line."

Cobb biographers going back to the first passably comprehensive one in 1984 had not located as authoritative a report – let alone two at the level of the 1946 ones – on Cobb acting in a racist way or espousing racism. Besides Cunningham's high standing in the journalism profession, his reporting is enhanced by the fact that in 1948, Cobb wrote a lengthy letter to him on a different subject, which Cunningham cited at length and will be featured later. Had Cobb written to Cunningham to challenge the racism content of his 1946 columns, it stands to reason that Cunningham would have been similarly open to presenting Cobb's differing take.

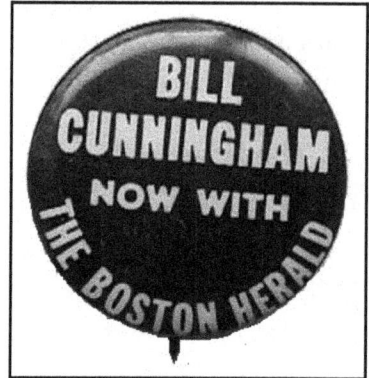

Cunningham's 1946 columns – which will be analyzed later – provide a huge helping hand to elevate some perfectly logical, critical-of-Cobb lines of analysis about his racism. Those lines of analysis did not appear in or were largely discounted by the 2015 Simon & Schuster biography while appearing in a 2015 Sports Publishing one released at about the same time. Sports Publishing is a fairly large publisher and with a good reputation.

Relative to the Sports Publishing book, the Simon & Schuster one, Charles Leerhsen's *Ty Cobb: A Terrible Beauty*, is more argumentative. The greatest stress in it that garnered coverage was on how weak the case is against Cobb as a racist, especially a violent one. But articles or book reviews that cited the

Simon & Schuster book for that analysis did not mention that its arguably two most important new details, relating to his not being a violent racist, were also in the Sports Publishing one, Tim Hornbaker's *War on the Basepaths: The Definitive Biography of Ty Cobb*. Those details are corrections to two major errors that had stood unrefuted for 31 years. They had originated in the first passably comprehensive Cobb biography, professor Charles C. Alexander's 1984 *Ty Cobb* for Oxford University Press.

As a result of their discoveries, the two 2015 books point to there being more balance in the number of Cobb's known off-the-field fights or other types of physical incidents with whites and blacks. That, as was especially argued in the Simon & Schuster book, disposes of any case that Cobb was a violent racist. For those who might want to argue the point, my book does offer up the possibility of still calling him one – for having no qualms about throwing a baseball at a black man's head, provided that the black man was willing, for money, to take the risk of being hit. It also could be argued that Cobb is a special case, entitled to leeway, because he had to cope with the worst possible violence: When he was 18 years old, his mom killed his dad. In other words, he was, through no fault of his own, desensitized to violence.

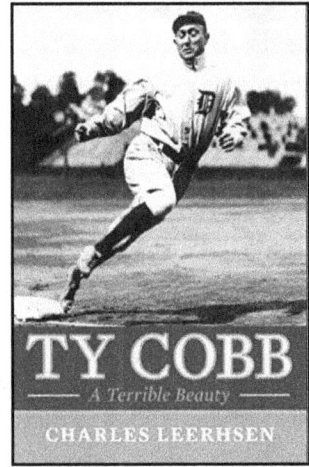

As the 2015 books discuss at length, his mom reportedly mistook his dad for an intruder in the family home and shot him fatally.

Cobb himself was called violent by Grantland "Granny" Rice, an Atlanta sportswriter into the first years of Cobb's big-league career who, later in syndication, became well known nationally. Perhaps referring to no later than 1907, his final year with the *Atlanta Journal*, Rice wrote, "During those early years, I found Cobb to be an extremely peculiar soul – brooding and bubbling with violence, combative all the way, a streak, incidentally, he never lost."

The Simon & Schuster book's liberal altering of original quotes, without alerting the reader, will be featured at greater length later. The quote above is from Rice's 1954 book *The Tumult and the Shouting: My Life in Sport*. In this case, the Simon & Schuster book changed the beginning from "During those early years" to the more narrow "When I first met Cobb."

In its racism argumentation, the Simon & Schuster book rightfully poked holes in some contemporaneous racial reporting on Cobb. But in a few instances, it did so by using argumentation that you might not think of unless you were a defense attorney, and at times hoping that the prosecuting attorneys had dozed off. One way it did so was by not acknowledging the existence or potential reliability of some sources that are building blocks to a solid case that Cobb was against social equality for blacks for much of his life. At the same time, it was overly generous in casting plusses on the other side of the ledger.

Of the two 2015 books, the Simon & Schuster one is more entertaining, with a catch: stressed is its discoveries, even if not new or provably wrong. If all authors wrote that way, award judges would go bananas. Sucked in was *Kirkus Reviews*, which gives free review consideration to books from mainstream publishers. It does allow other publishers to pay for a guaranteed but thus tainted review, $425 for 250 words, or $575 for 500 words. Apparently among all of its reviews since 2001, the full-text searchability span of its morgue, it has praised only Simon & Schuster's Cobb author for having "read all" newspaper clippings that are relevant to the author's subject. (By a landslide, the Sports Publishing book cites more clippings.) Then, at the end of 2015, *Kirkus Reviews* deemed Simon & Schuster's book one of the year's 16 "best" biographies.

One of that book's feats was making the *New York Times* Sports and Fitness bestseller list in May right after its release. The book came in ninth place on the list, possibly with help from the first of two *Times* articles, a book review posted online on May 26, although not printed until May 31, that omitted the Sports Publishing book. Simon & Schuster, a major *Times* book review section advertiser, later stamped "New York Times Bestseller" on the paperback edition in 2016. But consumers who see "New York Times Bestseller" are probably not thinking of a feat on a so-called "niche book list" of sports and fitness books.

I made the niche list discovery in 2017 after noticing that the *Wall Street Journal* had assigned Leigh Montville to review Marty Appel's new Doubleday biography of Casey Stengel. Appel has been a publicist for two of Montville's baseball books this century, and Montville was a 2017 Doubleday author, both blatant conflicts of interest. But I quickly found Appel linking to his own award-worthy article of 2016 that shows that, for the first time in 16 years, no baseball books (such as Simon & Schuster's Cobb one) were in any weekly traditional top 15 on the *Times* true bestseller list, its general one, in 2015.

Baseball blogger-author Ron Kaplan found this deception: "Leerhsen cherry-picked the [May 10] Boston Globe review by Allen Barra, selecting this quote for his Facebook page: 'Not only the best work ever written on this American sports legend: It's a major reconsideration of a reputation unfairly maligned for decades.'" I can add that on the back cover of the 2016 paperback edition, the first blurb is, "The best work ever written on this American sports legend."

What Barra had actually written in his review was conditional; namely, that if Leerhsen is correct in his take on Cobb, then it would constitute such a book.

By contrast, in several newspapers in 2008, Barra had been unconditional in calling Don Rhodes's newly released *Ty Cobb: Safe at Home* "the best book to date about baseball's strangest and most extreme personality."

Given the above, a rich line in Leerhsen's book is his referring to the modern-day Cobb as "a Wikipedia entry that can be edited at anyone's discretion."

Other Cobb Books, Plus a Housekeeping Note

There are earlier Cobb biographies, most notably Cobb's 1961 one with Stump and two by John D. "Johnny" McCallum. McCallum's first was his 1956 *The Tiger Wore Spikes: An Informal Biography of Ty Cobb*. That book included McCallum's personal observations of Cobb; Cobb provided some access to him before cutting it off, as Cobb explained in a letter that I add to the record later. McCallum's 1975 *Ty Cobb* is far more revelatory. Alexander's book, but not Leerhsen's or Hornbaker's, made wide use of McCallum's first-hand observations of Cobb. Leerhsen said McCallum's 1956 book is "not always trustworthy." Well, the same can be said about Leerhsen's, and especially, as will be noted later, wording within quotation marks from a newspaper and running two or more sentences. I cite some of McCallum's observations that Alexander omitted and which fit in with my topics or themes.

Along the lines of that last comment, I can now present a short housekeeping note. My content allows a reader of either of the 2015 Cobb biographies, or of only Alexander's 1984 one, to see how they can be reconciled, especially on Cobb's racism, while being fed fresh detail with an off-the-field emphasis. Presumably, the genre of full-blown Cobb biography has been exhausted. By the way, when I refer to the three biographies of Cobb later on, I am always referring to those by Alexander, Leerhsen and Hornbaker.

So as not to overlap with prior efforts, areas in which I cede large swaths include his childhood, the roots of his super-competitiveness, his physical fights, the ups and downs in his playing and managing career, his children and the negativity in a 1961 article by Stump several months after Cobb's death.

Much of this book is a chronology mainly of his post-career. That period was shortchanged in the two 2015 books, apart from mentions of his family life and medical problems. One of the better encapsulations of that later state of play was upon his death, by sports editor Art Rosenbaum of the *San Francisco Chronicle*: "Though inured to deprecating remarks about his fierce temper, his mean disposition and his many lawsuits [mostly tax disputes, mainly with California government authorities], he wanted desperately in his later years to leave a respectable picture of himself. Perhaps he succeeded through his charities, though his good side had been shielded too long from the public."

My emphasis in the chronology is in presenting the following:

(1) mainly in print media, the various ways in which Cobb promoted or had opportunities to talk about himself or his baseball views, in his post-career.

(2) the breadth of what was said by or about him in his post-career in print, including by baseball writers and contemporaries, while he was still alive.

Also, in light of the Leerhsen and Hornbaker books having "talked past each other" on race and there being so many discrepancies among Cobb biographers, I make it clear throughout my book which Cobb author said what, if notable, on a subject that I raise. More broadly, I readily name other authors within my text, as opposed to relegating them to endnotes or not mentioning them at all.

Because of its accessibility and clarity, the 1966 book *The Glory of Their Times: The Story of the Early Days of Baseball Told by the Men Who Played It* has been the go-to source for comments about Cobb by contemporaries. My book, I hope, will be the go-to resource for ones conveyed by journalists.

Cobb biographers have accurately portrayed him as a prolific writer of letters starting at a young age. He sent anonymous ones to Rice at the *Atlanta Journal* that declared how great a player he was. But the biographers minimally accounted for Cobb's correspondence in his post-career, when he was engaging with reporters and sports editors. Others who he engaged with privately included newspaper features syndicate owner Walter "Christy" Walsh.

Scholars of Cobb know just how extraordinary the 1961 Stump article was, in negatively casting Cobb's reputation after his death. But neither 2015 book cited enough sources to give a sense of how etched his reputation was during his post-career, among contemporaries or sports journalists who wrote about him nonstatistically. Also, neither did justice to how active Cobb was in writing letters, including to reporters after they wrote negative things about him. Cobb could be the biggest retired baseball star who weighed in on his life and legacy in interesting ways in wide-ranging letters that have been preserved. In one stretch of 1959, he sent more than 75, "many at unusual lengths,"

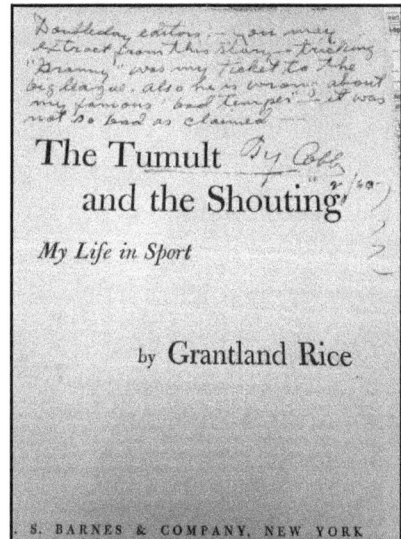

one of Al Stump's many forged "instructions" from Cobb

he wrote to his longtime financial advisor, Joseph "Joe" Hauck, in 1959.

My approach also touches on subjects that are often overlooked when it comes to book publishing: "best practices" issues for both publishers and book review outlets. One is: how could it be that Leerhsen's one received, exclusively, the overwhelming majority of the credit for making two huge racial corrections to Alexander's 1984 book that were corrected by Hornbaker's book too? One plausible reason is that Hornbaker downplayed one of those corrections, by relegating it to his endnotes. Another is a "what should be done now, if anything?" question. That question is based on the possibility that Leerhsen's book could have received a poor grade from some journalism professors. They could have cited him for implicitly taking credit at times for the research of others. His formula in those instances was: make a hullabaloo about a detail or observation while making it seem as if no one had beaten him to the punch. Journalism professors also could have cited his many transcription errors.

One can speculate at what point the *Times* would have felt compelled to mention the Sports Publishing book. My book does criticize the Sports Publishing book at times relative to the Simon & Schuster one. If I were scoring a boxing match, the Simon & Schuster one would both decisively win a few rounds and in a later round be disqualified for repeated hits below the belt.

Some reviewers could try to explain how they approach dueling books published in the same year. If they review one, do they entirely ignore the other? A solution would be to include a throwaway line letting readers know the name of the one that is not being reviewed. How much valuable space would that consume, and how would that not benefit the public?

Although it by no means excuses its being overlooked, since Hornbaker's tone on Cobb's racism is clearly more accurate, the Sports Publishing book tends to go light in trying to affirm or refute myths. An example is on the subject of whether Cobb was a deliberate spiker. The upshot is that writing in such a subdued style can give "looking for a hook" news practitioners an excuse to ignore one's entire book. Dull although valid lines that most jumped out at me in Hornbaker's book are ones where he wanted to leave open the possibility that Cobb was a racist.

WAR ON THE BASEPATHS
THE DEFINITIVE BIOGRAPHY OF TY COBB

TIM HORNBAKER

With my vouching for the greater accuracy of Hornbaker's book, a subject to explore is: What should Leerhsen be getting special credit for? Would it be fair to say that he provided greater context and analysis, but that in light of how much I cite from it relative to Hornbaker's, his book's new research is overrated?

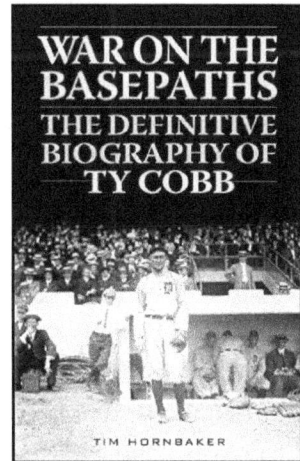

In the spring of 2017, a review of a non-Cobb book in the *Historian* said that Leerhsen "reexamined Cobb's reputation as a [violent] racist in order to prod readers to recognize the influence of public memory on the formation of such legends." I added the word "violent" in brackets to the review, by Paul Ringel, history professor at High Point University, because that is where Leerhsen deserves clear credit. On the other hand, Leerhsen deserves criticism for failing to show that Cobb was indeed a racist, although one with a mixed record.

Possibly the first formal scholarly review of his book appeared in November 2016 in *Sport History Review,* by history professor Kevin B. Witherspoon of Lander University in South Carolina. Witherspoon implied that Leerhsen deserves credit for pointing out both Cobb's far-from-hillbilly upbringing and relative tolerant views of blacks held by his father, William Herschel Cobb, who was a county superintendent of schools and a state senator. Leerhsen does deserve credit for being the first formal article or book writer to provide examples of his father's tolerant views. Aficionados did already know that Ty was instilled with the importance of becoming well educated. (Although I do not mention so elsewhere, my book fills a huge hole in prior Cobb ones: showing Ty's intellectual interests in exhaustive detail.) In 1984, Alexander wrote, "W. H. Cobb [Cobb's father] kept after his children to get as much as they could from the schooling available at Royston and then look forward to college."

On Leerhsen's racial findings, Witherspoon wrote, "In truth, Cobb had black fans and black friends." On Witherspoon's first point, there is a difference between appreciating an art form and personally liking an artist. On his second point, Cobb apparently had no black friends into the 1950s, beyond ones who he was in or had had a transactional relationship with, as I note later. By 1952, he had lifted his support of institutional racism in baseball, making him racially palatable. As Hornbaker found, Cobb put his arms around black Olympic gold track medalist Jesse Owens in 1959 and patted him on the back. I can add that they parted "with another arm-around-the-shoulder hug from Cobb."

Both the worthiest and least deserved praise that Witherspoon's review confers is that Leerhsen's "review of the previous Cobb literature, while primarily focused on overturning or correcting errors, is also thorough and laudable." Leerhsen did account well for relatively recent magazine articles and books. But he missed so much prior to his bogeyman, Stump's 1961 article, racially and otherwise. Had Witherspoon so chosen, he could have cited important detail from Hornbaker's book that Leerhsen did not find. One such omission is an admission by Cobb, in a 1954 letter to Dr. Daniel C. Elkin of Emory University Hospital, his scholarship fund chairman, that he was drinking too much and "very prone to depressionist feelings." The other omission is a 24-page "bill of particulars" that second wife Frances Fairbairn Cass filed in 1955. Hornbaker stated in his endnotes the unrelated court case, also in 1955, from which he obtained it. I was thus able to obtain it too and can add that Cass had it stricken from the divorce case. In a series of detailed vignettes, the document described his drinking and verbal abuse. Perhaps Stump saw it in Cobb's files and decided that his own chain of negative experiences with him sounded too disjointed, like Frances's, to string into a purely factual magazine article.

Witherspoon did not cite Leerhsen's at times ambiguous-at-best crediting of previous Cobb authors. Evaluating that kind of thing can be considered beyond the time constraints in writing a review. But Witherspoon still managed to criticize the book for being "smattered with first-person intrusions, reminding the reader that it is Leerhsen who is spearheading this process of discovery." My book has many first-person intrusions too, but as part of a scheme to not relegate the first modern-day author to discover something. As I note later on, if I do not attribute something to another modern-day author, I am claiming to be the first to be highlighting it. In a few such cases, a detail has appeared in a non-Cobb book such as a Tigers one, but by relying on an inaccurate source.

Witherspoon also panned Leerhsen "for returning again and again to pummel this straw man," 1961 book collaborator Stump, for his subsequent sensationalist article and 1994 book. Witherspoon stated that Leerhsen's writing "feels at times like a personal vendetta against Stump rather than an objective history."

I saw his review after having nearly finished my research. I feature a cross-selection of Stump's writing on Cobb, mainly having to do with Cobb's post-career. My stress is on colorful stories and anecdotes, and I rehabilitate Stump to a moderate degree. Hornbaker steered clear of trying to rehabilitate, with one huge exception: he deemed Stump's 1961 book collaboration with Cobb credible enough to cite. I agree with Hornbaker's use of the book, especially because it often seems to accurately reflect Cobb's point of view.

The Simon & Schuster book likened Alexander to Stump, in the following respect. Alexander, in his 1984 book, and Stump, in his 1994 *Cobb: The Life and Times of the Meanest Man Who Ever Played Baseball: A Biography*, "tend to depict their subject as a crabbed, sad soul." Regardless, Alexander was a lot nicer to Cobb and wrote in his introduction, "My efforts to explain Cobb's life have relied on common sense, logic, a broader awareness of the history of his times, and, I would hope, an adequate measure of sympathy and compassion."

To show how easy it is to deflate the Simon & Schuster book for one of its own excesses, boastfulness, consider how I can annotate the sentence after its "crabbed, sad soul" one:

It said that if one "steers wide of" Alexander and Stump, the reasons for

Cobb's attendance-drawing power can be gleaned from "letters by and to Cobb [about 1.5 percent of the Simon & Schuster book], the testimony of eyewitnesses [a tiny percentage too, and even if referring to mere after-the-fact recollections told to reporters; plus, as will be noted later, I refute the accuracy of one of its few eyewitnesses related to Cobb and Stump and counter some of its other criticism of Stump], and contemporary newspaper accounts [while overgeneralizing at some crucial points about them]."

Worth a brief mention is the "definitive" claim in Hornbaker's book title. (Simon & Schuster has pitched its book as "authoritative.") Putting aside that Hornbaker's racial hedges, but not Leerhsen's, hold up exceptionally well based on my research, Hornbaker's strength is referencing a far greater amount of sources on Cobb, especially newspaper prose. But, like Leerhsen, he missed so much key prose from 1929 to 1961. His book more lightly tries to refute (or create) myths than Leerhsen's and lacks Leerhsen's big highs and huge lows.

A publishing "best practices" issue that I feature, which supports the case that publishers can have huge blind spots when it comes to fact-checking their authors' work, makes its first appearance in the subhead that follows.

Introduction to Quotes, Schmotes

The Society for American Baseball Research awarded a pre-publication version of the Simon & Schuster book one of its three annual Baseball Research Awards. In the next cycle, its Deadball Era Research Committee honored it alone with its 2015 Larry Ritter Book Award. Although in comparing books for a research-heavy prize, basic accuracy should be a consideration, in the several two-sentence-or-longer newspaper quotations that I looked at in both 2015 books, I found a sizeable number of errors in the Simon & Schuster one. I found far fewer in the Sports Publishing one. The errors that I noticed in the Simon & Schuster one are mainly transcription ones. Authors or publishers are rarely called out for that, when done in great volume, for lack of a compelling reason by a third party to match up text. For example, once their publication runs a review, book review editors will rarely amend it later on to note categories of excessive flaws that would have been hard for a lowly reviewer to spot.

For lining up text, I did not pick just any quotations: only the ones that I thought were important – or where I thought I had come across interesting detail that neither author, and no prior Cobb biographer or article writer, had found. Only after deciding on that methodology did I find a 1912 interview with Cobb's mom Amanda that I thought no prior Cobb author had quoted. When I saw that the Simon & Schuster book had quoted two sentences from it, I analyzed the quotes and found four errors in two sentences.

Leerhsen wrote in his book that the person who was most useful in his research was Ty Cobb Museum (in Royston) historian Wesley Fricks. In a 2008 article on BleacherReport.com, Fricks said he had "over 40,000 newspapers articles" related to Cobb. Leerhsen did not explain any connection between the 40,000 articles and his own research. Regardless, the lack of time investment to quote articles accurately should be enough to banish Leerhsen's multiple-sentence quotations from being quoted as is. Errors of one major type or another appear in 100 percent of the multi-sentence newspaper quotes that I double-checked.

As will be noted later, in one of two cases where I found an admirable transcription, Leerhsen placed the quote into the forum of a public rally. In reality in that case, it had been uttered apparently in the Cobb home by Cobb's wife, possibly via telephone, based on a similar version I found reported by the United Press. In the other case, Leerhsen cited an apparent erroneous condensation of a multi-sentence quote.

In broadcast journalism, I know about the practice to splice quotes together that were not said consecutively and without clueing in the listener or viewer. I readily notice when that happens on TV; one can look for the slight "jumps" from one clip to another of the same person talking. It also strikes me as wrong that in a non-celebrity, nonfiction book from a major publisher, that extended newspaper quotations can be redone in a consistently fonder-sounding direction without disclosing that practice. There is apparently on the order of just six uses of "[sic]" in Leerhsen's book, to indicate that the spelling or syntax is correct.

Maybe times have changed. For one thing, many book publishers have apparently thrown in the towel in some aspects of quality control. One is in not leaning hard on their authors to fact-check their books better. But they could at least tell their authors that words within a previously published quotation cannot be unilaterally changed by substituting in words that sound better.

My impression from reading Leerhsen's book is that Leerhsen writes like an entertainer, based on experiences in proximity to the entertainment industry. While that style can have plusses, a minus of it can be likened to the tactic that TV entertainment-focused news shows use to generate person-on-the-street comments. To obtain the best-sounding comments, instead of just asking people what they think, the shows will set up a video station so that people will have their memory refreshed. Re-rendering so many words within quotation marks – all in a direction of making them "ring truer" to the ear of a 2015 reader – sounds sneaky to me too. After all, Simon & Schuster is one of the most famous publishers in the world. Surely most savvy readers of its books take it as a given that it would not knowingly allow the wording of quotations to be altered, except by use of brackets or accidentally.

Readers are more likely to be drawn to a book such as the Simon & Schuster one because the prose is engaging. To those who care more about facts than presentation, a danger of being engaging – to the extreme of trying so hard to strike just the right emotional chord with every word in a newspaper quotation – is being too sharply opinionated and turning out to be spectacularly wrong.

Cobb's Drive

An English professor who writes short but analytical baseball book reviews, Timothy R. Morris, said that compared to Alexander, Leerhsen presents Cobb as a fuller person, although Cobb still comes across as "unusually taken up with himself, even for a major sports celebrity." Morris also concluded, "Alexander drew Cobb as haunted; Leerhsen shows him more as driven. The results are the same, whatever the hidden motivations." Finally, of interest here, Alexander "revise[d] the popular conception (largely Stump's creation, and peculiarly viral) that Cobb was a sociopath, but retain[ed] the idea that Cobb was bitterly racist." So, loosely speaking, Alexander helped tone down Stump's characterizations. That said, he bought into dubious items from Stump's flawed 1961 article and introduced two key errors on Cobb's racism. The errors enabled others, including Stump in his 1994 book, to cast Cobb as a worse racist than he was.

After seeing Morris's review, I came across a newspaper article by a longtime Cobb friend, Augusta journalist Earl L. Bell. Cobb biographers have overlooked Bell, except for one with a Georgia focus, Rhodes's 2008 *Ty Cobb: Safe at Home*. Rhodes mentioned Bell four times in his book, but not for the following. Upon Cobb's death in 1961, Bell, then an editorial writer for both Augusta newspapers, wrote, "Cobb was roundly and roughly criticized for his belligerency on the bases and his reluctance to accept defeat gracefully. It is true that he seemed to believe that the bases belonged to him, and in his will to win was hot-headed, over-aggressive and even ruthless, if you please. But these traits were an ineradicable part of him – and without them it is probable that the sports world never would have heard of Tyrus Raymond Cobb."

That point had been touched on in Cobb's second offseason, 1906-07, by the *Detroit News*: "Those who are inclined to criticize Ty Cobb because of his 'freshness' at times must admit that he would never be the ball player he is if it was not for the very 'nerve' that is so galling upon some of his older associates."

In a serial he composed with Cobb's active help in 1924, *Detroit News* sports

editor Harry G. Salsinger wrote, "Cobb could never have plunged ahead, jumping into plays and into situations, had he lacked temperament. It was the fiery, unquenchable temperament that gave him the drive."

In 1945, former teammate Ossie Vitt, who was with him for three weeks that summer at his home in Nevada, told sportswriter Emmons Byrne of the *Oakland Tribune*, "Ty has mellowed with age and he often tells me he regrets some of the things he did when he was playing ball. But hell, that was what made Cobb great. If you got in his way he'd cut you down."

Alexander and a 1994 and 2005 biographer of Cobb, Richard Bak, both printed part of the following. In 1950, former Royston teammate Joe T. Cunningham told *Atlanta Constitution* sports editor Furman Bisher, "He was always driving and pushing." The next part of Cunningham's quote is not ", even in grade school," as Alexander wrote in his book and Bak in his 1994 and 2005 ones, but "Ty went with a girl whose daddy didn't approve of him

from left to right in 1946: Cobb and childhood friends and baseball teammates J. Frank Lee, Joe T. Cunningham and Stewart D. Brown, Sr.

because he was a baseball player. Ball players in those days were looked at as roughnecks. I always figured Tyrus drove hard to prove to everybody that baseball players were all right." Alexander credited the above to McCallum's 1975 book, whose likely source was the *Constitution*'s report in 1950. Bak seemingly piggybacked off either McCallum or Alexander.

Upon Cobb's death, former teammate Davy Jones told the *Boston Globe*, "Ty didn't have too many close friends among the ball players." He added, "I guess he was just too high-spirited and aggressive – and that had a lot to do with making him the player that he was." In its obituary, the *New York Times* said "he played every game as if it were the deciding contest in the world series."

In analyzing Cobb in 1952, early 20th-century *Detroit News* baseball reporter and later managing editor Malcolm W. Bingay wrote, "America's success was not created by men who waited for someone else to tell them what to do."

In a syndicated column marking Cobb's death, former *Constitution* executive editor Ralph McGill, who won the 1959 Pulitzer Prize for editorial writing, wrote, "All his life Tyrus Raymond Cobb was in competition with life, but chiefly with himself." McGill invoked another Georgian, Robert Winship "Bob" Woodruff. "Cobb and Robert W. Woodruff, with a competitive spirit to match, were friends when both were clawing their way up. It was advice from Woodruff, then a truck salesman but later Coca-Cola's chief executive [to buy its stock early in its history], which early made Cobb financially independent. It was Woodruff, too, who mellowed his latter years." I have no idea what that means beyond "financially eased." (Cobb, in Eugene, Ore., in 1951, would say that he was "forced" to buy that stock.)

McGill continued, "People liked Cobb [presumably for his feats]. He knew it. But he could not escape from his shell save on rare, wonderful occasions." The bulk of the rest of the column, "Old Man Makes Last Run of Great Career," will be featured later. Although only around 800 words, sports columnist Jim McKone of the *San Bernardino Sun-Telegram* in California deemed it the best Cobb obituary.

Cobb and Robert W. Woodruff in a reverse negative in the library archives of Emory University

He made the following odd choice of wording in the last sentence of his syndicated column: "And people will remember him for his gentleness, his charity, and the records in the book." Associating "gentleness" with Cobb seems bizarre, unless referring to some of his interactions with children; sentimental would seem more apt, as lifelong friend Ernest Tomlinson described him to *Constitution* sports editor Jesse Outlar in 1963. In a long *Sporting News* profile of Cobb in 1957, a veteran reporter who had moved to California to retire, Harry T. Brundidge, wrote that "underneath the thick crust of toughness, he has always been a very sentimental man."

Harry T. Brundidge visiting Cobb at his home in Atherton in 1957

McGill described his syndicated version as follows: "Others are writing about the records. They will endure. When he retired after the 1928 season he had a share in, or owned outright, 90 major league records. It is the man who interests us most. The fires which had flamed in him for most of his life had been slowly banked in the years of his retirement."

An *Atlanta Constitution* version of his remembrance reads more like a sermon, with a profound theme largely absent from his syndicated one: how much Cobb was affected by the apparent accidental killing of his dad by his mom in 1905. "The words 'my father' came often to Ty Cobb's lips when he let himself go in those rare times when he would talk in small gatherings of friends." Cobb, "who popularly was regarded as being hard as flint, remorseless and ruthless, could weep in recalling his father and his own boyhood days. In his latter years he paid more attention to poor boys and girls. He wanted some of his money to help the needy to be educated – as his father had wanted him to be."

The major leaguer who plausibly knew Cobb the best, former Augusta teammate Nap Rucker, said the following in 1952 to Willard Neal of the *Constitution*. "At heart Ty has always been a good guy. He likes to kid as well as anybody, and he often tried. But he nearly always wound up getting mad.

"I have a theory about Ty's terrible temper, too. I believe his flare-ups were deliberate. I don't know what doctors found out about adrenalin[e], that

Nap Rucker and Cobb in 1912

powerful fluid that your glands shoot into your blood stream when you get mad or scared. But Ty discovered that he had superhuman strength during and just after a fit of temper. He could throw himself into a rage at any time he needed an extra burst of power."

Rucker is one of three ex-big leaguers who would attend his funeral. A second is former catcher Ray Schalk, who would tell columnist David Condon of the *Chicago Tribune* of having become "close friends" with Cobb. Schalk went to visit him in Georgia in February 1961 when Cobb was very ill, four months before his death.

According to Schalk, the people who Cobb liked to talk about included Fred Haney, a 1950s manager who, as of 1961, was general manager of the new Los Angeles Angels franchise. Haney had begun his big-league career under Cobb in the 1920s, and Cobb's last trip would be to attend the opening home game of the Angels franchise that spring. Also according to Schalk, Cobb liked to talk about tough-to-hit White Sox pitcher Doc White. There was also White Sox manager Kid Gleason, who Schalk said was also a close friend of Cobb; Gleason died in 1933 and was a coach on the 1927 and 1928 Athletics, when Cobb was on the team.

Finally, as players Cobb liked to talk about, there were Hall of Fame pitcher Johnson and White Sox third baseman Buck Weaver. That said, Cobb "didn't talk about many players," Schalk told Condon. "It was the other way around. We all talked about him."

Cobb was "the fightin'est ball player of his or any other era," the *Boston Globe* said upon his death. It added, "Always a poor

Kid Gleason and Cobb in 1927

loser – every game was a life-and-death struggle to him – Cobb had a flaming temper and little patience with the faults of others. He could not stand defeat. His biting remarks on the bench and in the clubhouse brought on many pitched [verbal] battles with his teammates on the field and in hotel rooms."

Scary Monsters

Early on in his book, Leerhsen cited a 2004 one that cast Cobb as a "monster," *American Monsters: 44 Rats, Blackhats, and Plutocrats*. Near the end of his book, Leerhsen said he no longer thinks of him as one. Unmentioned is Mike Shannon's 1989 *Diamond Classics: Essays on 100 of the Best Baseball Books Ever Published*. Alexander's book "reminds us that Cobb was not a monster," Shannon wrote, immediately before quoting the following sentence from Alexander's book: "Actually, Ty Cobb was capable of warmth, compassion, kindness, and substantial generosity." Also unmentioned is Jim Stinson's long anti-Stump screed in *Sports Collectors Digest* in 2007, "Cobb Not the Monster He's Portrayed to Be."

I was drawn to Cobb from being the expert, especially racially, on another disliked, although much lesser-known racist Hall of Famer, Adrian "Cap" Anson.

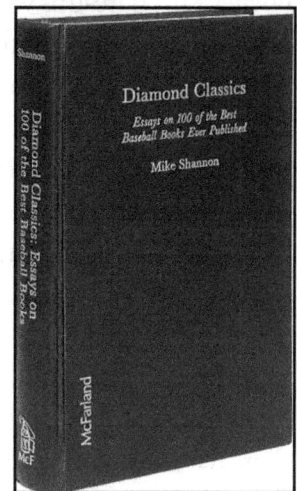

Anson played in the 19th century, mainly in Chicago. His racism, at least during his playing career, is not in dispute. What strongly is is what can be said of his role in something far bigger than Cobb: the drawing of the sport's "color line" in the 1880s, which led to the disappearance of blacks from organized baseball, with rare exception, until Jackie Robinson in 1946.

In June 2016, on the long-form Web site the Atavist, I wrote a 12,000-word essay that was devoted mostly to the color line issue. A column in December 2015 by the *Washington Post*'s Kevin B. Blackistone had focused on it. However, Blackistone, also a professor of journalism at the University of Maryland, did something that is bad form journalistically: quoting the words of a single source, and an Internet one at that. His only other cited one was a book written in 1983 by noted baseball historian Jules Tygiel, way before the proliferation of full-text databases. Blackistone's column hinges on analyzing the confluence of two baseball events on a July day in 1887. My essay pointed out that writers need to be differentiating, for their readers, between fact and speculation.

In observing that distinction, the Simon & Schuster book did so fairly well. Its great excess was being consistently pro-Cobb in analyzing Cobb's racism while wrongly conveying that it had adequately accounted for the key sources on that subject. On Cobb's racism, at least, for providing a hard-to-dissect line between the findings of former Ty Cobb Museum historian Fricks and Leerhsen, the book provides a spooky parallel to Cobb and Stump's collaboration.

Fricks has been pro-Cobb on matters of race. For example, in a 2011 article on BleacherReport.com, referring to 1994/2005 Cobb biographer Bak and 1961 collaborator and 1994 biographer Stump, Fricks wrote, "Richard Bak, of Detroit, shadowed Stump and Alexander stating that Cobb was a 'Mean S.O.B.' and Bak tried earnestly to settle his personal fight with the north and south through his book on Ty Cobb."

Possibly having drawn Fricks's ire, and rightfully, was this line in Bak's 2005 *Peach: Ty Cobb in his Time and Ours*: "Throughout his life Ty was an unrepentant bigot, casually sprinkling his conversation with pejoratives as 'coon,' 'Sambo,' and 'shine' and 'nigger.'" It happens to be true that Cobb can be found in a few contemporaneous newspaper reports either using the N-word or being alleged to have done so. I did not find him using the other terms. Bak's likely source for that is Stump's use-only-with-care 1994

book, in which he wrote, "Speaking to friends in private, he [Cobb] regularly dropped 'coon,' 'smoke,' 'Sambo,' and 'shine' into his discourse."

In an interview with the *Augusta Chronicle* in 2004, Bak had said that Cobb "deserves to be maligned for being a bigot, but no more than anybody else. If they were (condemning bigots), they'd have to clear out half the Hall of Fame."

The word "bigot," at least in Cobb's pro-institutional racism days, is too sweeping to apply to him, since racism is merely one form of bigotry. The only other type of bigotry of his that I found, anti-Semitism in the 1950s, dissipated fast, as will be noted later, about avoiding high-placed Jews in movie studios or book publishing outfits. As it turns out, after two such comments that I came across and, perhaps timewise as well, a similar one found by Bak, I found Cobb consulting with noted movie producer Leonard Goldstein, a Jew, in 1953.

Bak seems on the ball in stating that the vast number of future Hall of Famers who were his contemporaries were racist, which would minimally mean being supporters of institutional racism. Coincidentally, Bak may very well be the lone Cobb article or book writer before me to have used the phrase "institutional racism," albeit in an indirect way. "At the [20th] century's turn, North and South were bound together by more than institutional racism," he wrote.

He has also written or been quoted in articles that note how inaccurate the 1994 movie "Cobb" was on Cobb, on matters other than race; in it, the actor Tommy Lee Jones had the starring role. For example, in a different *Free Press* article in 2005, Bak wrote that a scene in which Cobb murders a mugger in an alley "has been satisfactorily debunked by baseball historians."

Finally, he can be cited positively, for having come the closest, among Cobb authors before me, to hitting on the distinction that Cunningham quoted Cobb as making on his racial philosophy. That quotation will be featured in full on the next page. Technically speaking, Bak hit on it in one of his 2005 articles. In it, he referred to Cobb's time in Nevada during his post-career. One of Cobb's homes was near Lake Tahoe, and the sports editor of the *Nevada State Journal* in Reno while Cobb had a home there was himself a Tyrus Richard "Ty R." Cobb; he had been so christened in 1915. The Reno Ty Cobb knew Cobb very well, as will be noted later. For his 2005 book, Bak spoke to Tyrus William Cobb, son of the now-deceased Reno Ty R. Cobb. As quoted in the article, the son recalled that the baseball Ty Cobb regularly bragged about the hospital that he was helping to fund back in Royston, Ga., for its black nurses, "though, of course, he could never bring himself to associate socially with blacks."

2. *Institutional Racism*

The fuller of Cunningham's two reports about Cobb, as a Southerner, being against integrating organized baseball was printed on September 28, 1946, as Robinson's first season in it was ending in the International League. Cunningham's column was then distributed by E. W. Scripps's United Feature Syndicate. In the *Herald*, Cunningham told of having heard Cobb "holding forth on this subject one time, and the time was only a few years ago. 'This is the southern viewpoint,' said the fiery and still belligerent baseball immortal who was known, in his day as 'The Georgia Peach,' 'and you can take it or leave it. So far as the Negro goes, I'll work with him, and I have. If he's helping me build a house, or dig a ditch, or load a truck, I'll work shoulder to shoulder with him, shed sweat with him, swap smokes with him, share my lunch or his own with him. I'll sit on the same seat with him, lie down in the shade to rest beside him, pass tools to him, even follow his orders, if I think he knows more than I do.'"

Those Cobb quotes, the racially positive side of what Cunningham heard Cobb say, comport well with Leerhsen's citing of some of Cobb's pro-integration quotes from 1952 and his adding in Cobb's later praise of early black National

Bill Cunningham of The Boston Post

has no peer among American newspaper columnists. His fan mail from readers is staggering. For years his daily feature stories have been one of the many reasons why *The Boston Post* is read in many thousands more homes than any other New England daily newspaper.

Cunningham was with the *Boston Post* for most of the 1920s and 1930s

League stars Campanella and Willie Mays. Leerhsen then asked, "Did Cobb, then on the verge of his dotage and embracing religion, brim with the convert's zeal, as some insist who can't get over the fact that he was, for Chrissakes, born in Georgia, in 1886, and therefore must at some point have been severely prejudiced? It will always be impossible to say, but it is not difficult to find stories of him in the 1920s and 1930s treating Negro League players and black trainers with the decency they deserved."

With regard to that last point, while Leerhsen cited a decades-later story from former Negro League player William "Bobby" Robinson, he cited none from any trainer. The favorable-to-Cobb racial stories from casual acquaintances or social friends are in short supply, despite Leerhsen's implying that stories of his engaging positively with blacks are "not difficult to find." That said, it is fair to assume, based now also on Cunningham's first-hand quoting of him, that Cobb was usually courteous to blacks who he casually met and to those who performed a business service for him. My larger point here is to make readers aware of the slippery style of argumentation that Leerhsen uses at times.

Another example of that slipperiness is that Leerhsen said it was "race relations" comments from Cobb that are hard to find. The term was not in vogue during much of Cobb's life. So, requiring that prose exist on that explicit subject instead of "racial attitudes" imposes a high threshold for allowing a case to be made that Cobb was still clearly a racist. Leerhsen does deserve the highest praise for conceding that the word "racist" was not in fashion when Cobb was a player. For example, black weeklies that were critical of Cobb used other words to criticize him. In 1927, when Cobb was under investigation for throwing a game in 1919, W. Rollo Wilson of the black weekly the *Pittsburgh Courier* referred to his alleged 1919 violent incident with a black chambermaid, Ada Morris, and wrote, "I would not put anything down as being too low for him to do."

After writing that, Wilson mentioned a not-in-dispute 1924 fight in which Cobb "tried to lick a colored employe[e]" at a ballpark for not discontinuing a phone call "so that he, the mighty Cobb, could use the instrument? That's how I feel about Master Cobb." Hornbaker found Wilson's 1927 comment. I found this similar one by Wilson after the 1924 fight: "This is not the first time Cobb has assaulted colored persons in the North, but one of these days he will get the surprise of his life. Perhaps our readers may recall that he beat up [allegedly kicked down a staircase] a chambermaid in a hotel some years ago. Such is the Georgia Peach, the Southern gentleman."

There are positives on the other side of the ledger. Hornbaker located a pair of blacks who Cobb knew from Augusta, one a tailor and the other someone whose college expenses he helped to pay. In newspaper databases regarding the tailor and Cobb, I found a compelling source that Hornbaker did not provide in his endnotes. In the *Pittsburgh Courier* in 1927, there is a short feature on Mable Ridley, a black singer and pianist. Her father Charles, in Augusta, owned a tailor shop there for decades, which Mable's brother was now running. Cobb had moved to Augusta in 1913. The elder Ridley "is a personal friend of Ty Cobb of the Detroit Tigers, and does most of the tailoring for the Detroit club through Mr. Cobb," the *Courier* said. (That use of a black tailor through Cobb squares with Cobb's statement in Cunningham's presence that he is open to relying on a black person to perform work for him if he thinks he can do it; that said, there is no basis to project that Cobb socialized with Ridley outside a business setting.) Hornbaker did provide a citation to the *Courier* for Cobb's having helped put through college a veteran black actor as of 1954, Arthur Lee Simpkins. One can speculate whether providing such help inspired Cobb in 1953 to establish his college scholarship fund.

In re-evaluating the intensity of Cobb's racism, a key issue is whether he was equally bothered by – and expressed disgust at – perceived slights, regardless of the race of the offender. An inherently racist view that he almost certainly held is that blacks had to respect him according to a white Southerner's warped standard for racial interaction. Far more open to speculation is whether any violation of that norm contributed greatly to his friction with them. Readily available now to tip the balance on that point is his being in favor of institutional racism, being open to minstrelsy and playing African Dodger.

Immediately after his long quote from Cobb, in which Cobb said he had no trouble working off the field with blacks, Cunningham inserted Cobb's thought on social equality: "But I won't play games with him. Neither will any other southern white man. 'When you do that, you accept him on your own social level, and social equality is the one place where the southerner always will draw the line.'"

At that point of the second of his two columns on the subject, Cunningham told his readers, "Maybe the solution lies in selling the South the idea that professional baseball is nothing but work. To hear some of the brethren in the industry moan, that shouldn't be very hard."

Five months earlier, in the first of his two racial columns mentioning Cobb, Cunningham had written, "The South considers 'the Negro problem' it's [sic] own business. It professes to be making steady progress. It resents dictation, which it considers interference, and the hard facts of the matter [are] that it will not consider what it calls 'social equality' now, and true southerners probably never will. That means living with, eating with, [and] sharing life with a Negro. I'm not saying that's right. I'm merely reporting how it is."

Cunningham added, "This gives baseball a tough one because it is heavily populated with deep southerners who will talk with, work with and walk with a Negro, but who will not play games with him because, as none less than Ty Cobb once explained it to the writer, 'that is social equality.' The magnates are afraid of what might happen if a white pitcher, especially a southerner, started to dust off a Negro batter, or maybe beaned him accidentally. They shudder to think of a Negro blocking a base on a southerner, or maybe slicing him with spikes. They're thinking not only about the player fights. They worry about riots in the stands." A few sentences later, he wrote, "Perhaps the war [World War II] has changed all that. If [Jackie] Robinson sticks we'll have a chance to see. That's the plain talk of the matter."

While softening the intensity of Cobb's racism, especially based on correcting 1984 author Alexander, the two 2015 biographies diverge greatly in tone. An example is in their assessment of Cobb's pro-integration statements in 1952. Hornbaker said those statements and what can be extrapolated as positive from his interactions with some blacks are not enough to "explain away the question [of his having been a racist] in any shape or form." That said, Hornbaker wrote that to "casually define him 'racist' is far too simplistic, and like everything else about him, certain events in his life have to be thoroughly explained in context. One thing can be said for sure, no one can honestly say what beliefs were in his heart one way or another. The facts can be studied, but the absolute truth will never be known." Although the thrust of his conclusion about Cobb racially seems to generally hold – thanks to not being so categorically dismissive of Alexander as Leerhsen was – Hornbaker also left the impression that he had accounted for the surviving record of Cobb's views on the subject.

A slew of books and articles have been written about Cobb, with a special emphasis being on his level of racism. A 2016 Rowman & Littlefield self-described "social and cultural history" of Cobb, Steven Elliott Tripp's *Ty Cobb, Baseball, and American Manhood: A Red-Blooded Sport for Red-Blooded Men*, endeavored at times to "set his behavior within the wider context of White Southern racism." I can set it within a popular pair of racial terms, individual racism and institutional (sometimes called systemic) racism. The voluminous

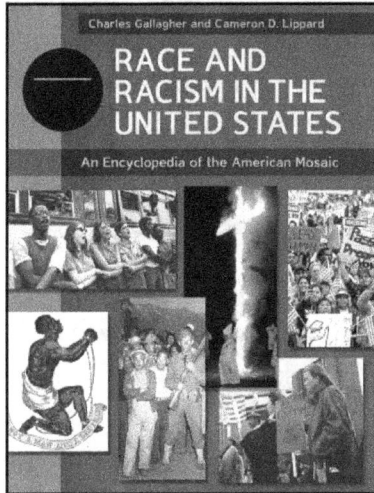

Race and Racism in the United States: An Encyclopedia of the American Mosaic states that individual racism "tends to be the type of racism that most people first think of and is typified by derogatory labels such as 'nigger,' 'wetback,' or 'chink,' and by racist beliefs such as 'All Latinos are illegal aliens stealing American jobs' or 'All black people are lazy, have too many kids and take advantage of welfare.' Institutional racism is discrimination that operates via the institutions of society such as government, schools and universities/colleges, the criminal system, and the media."

Assessing Cobb's degree of personal racism beyond his support for institutional racism (institutional racism can be considered a type of personal racism), being open to minstrelsy and playing African Dodger is complicated by there being few reliable, airtight primary and secondary sources to assess him. A second complication is that in his pro-institutional racism days, Cobb had positive interactions with some blacks he knew well, thus negating the case that he was a severe (Leerhsen's word for what his book swats down) racist.

I can offer the following far-fetched-sounding explanation for some of Cobb's business associations with blacks. Because he could be such a penny pincher, maybe he instinctively preferred blacks in some cases because he figured he could pay them less.

So, even my arguably most pro-Cobb finding on race, which follows, could be discounted if his ulterior motive was monetary. That finding is his statement in Cunningham's presence, "So far as the Negro goes, I'll work with him, and I have. If he's helping me build a house, or dig a ditch, or load a truck, I'll work shoulder to shoulder with him, shed sweat with him, swap smokes with him, share my lunch or his own with him. I'll sit on the same seat with him, lie down in the shade to rest beside him, pass tools to him, even follow his orders, if I think he knows more than I do."

A distant second to that in my pro-Cobb racial findings is that the Cobbs had a long-term relationship to a black cook, who moved with the family to California in the early 1930s and died soon after. Apparently no prior Cobb book or modern-day article states that the Cobbs had one. I found detail in the *Greenville News* in South Carolina, to appear later, in connection with Cobb's search in 1936 for a new one who knows southern cooking. That newspaper's sports editor, who knew Cobb personally, told of Cobb's "old negro mammy cook" in an anecdote about Cobb and cooking.

According to the 1920 Census, the Cobbs had a servant named Emerline Cosey, age 24. Cosey may not have necessarily been the cook who moved to California with the Cobbs. A detail that I can claim to be the finder of is that in 1926, the Associated Press reported from Augusta that a Negro woman and her husband had been arrested and jailed on charges of

HOUSEHOLD	ROLE	GENDER	AGE	BIRTHPLACE
Tyrus R Cobb	Head	M	33	Georgia
Charlie M Cobb	Wife	F	30	Georgia
Tyrus R Cobb Jr.	Son	M	9	Georgia
Shirley M Cobb	Daughter	F	8	Michigan
Roswell H Cobb	Son	M	3	Georgia
Beverly Cobb	Son	M	0	Georgia
Emerline Cosey	Servant	F	24	Georgia

larceny from Cobb's house. One of those was a former servant of his, and Cobb and a police officer searched the servant's residence "Saturday night and early Sunday morning for a set of valuable cuff links which had been stolen from the baseball [player-]manager [of Detroit] and the search revealed practically $150 worth of articles [about $2,000 in today's dollars] which have disappeared from the Cobb home, the thefts covering a period of five years."

Census records for 1890 no longer exist for much of Georgia. For 1900, 1910, 1930 and, with an asterisk, 1940, records show no one unusual living in the Cobb household except for, in 1900, the younger sister of Cobb's mom,

Eunice Chitwood, who was three years older than Ty. Fricks mentioned Cosey in an article in 2008 on BleacherReport.com, presumably based on having seen the 1920 Census. The asterisk for 1940 is because Cobb had apparently declared as his main residence his secondary home, at Cave Rock, Nev., on the eastern shore of Lake Tahoe, and was the only person listed there. Incidentally, the AP reported in 1952 that the California Franchise Tax Board was trying to determine if Cobb was a legal resident of Nevada or California. "Nevada has no income tax, California has," the AP said. The subject will be revisited on pages 150-51. In testifying before a U.S. House committee in 1951 looking into baseball's anti-trust exemption, he declared himself "Tyrus Raymond Cobb, Glenbrook, Nev., and Menlo Park, Calif." Despite living in Cave Rock and Atherton, he had his mail delivered to Glenbrook and Menlo Park, respectively.

Cobb's home in Cave Rock, circa 1954

Racist or Not

Leerhsen, reflecting Fricks's tone, avoided proclaiming Cobb a racist, based on sources that he consulted and his balancing of Cobb's positives and negatives. In some cases, Leerhsen's finding was easy, because he cited the ultimate in low-hanging fruit, portrayals by entertainment media. (Bak, in 2005 in the *Detroit Free Press*, wrote that "since his death from cancer in 1961, the pop-culture custodians of his complicated fame have had a field day with his image.")

On "closer calls," and presumably unaware of Cobb's support of institutional racism as of the early 1940s, Leerhsen did not readily concede much; the nearest he apparently came was saying that baseball "was just as racist as the rest of society." Not only that, but in the place in his book he wrote that, he had just misread an up-close 1909 editorial in the *Charlotte Observer*. A Cobb visit to Charlotte had been anything but routine. He was there with his wife after the 1909 season, in a Chalmers model car that had been lent to him as part of a national campaign to promote improved roads; it had been driven by other noted people on different routes earlier in the year. "Cobb is driving a car which is scarcely less known than himself," the *Charlotte News* said.

Leerhsen tried to make the following point: "In later years – probably to burnish his image as a hero and a spokesman for his sport – he and his boosters went out of their way to note that his early encounters with the Negro race were either inconsequential or benign." He quoted from the *Observer*'s editorial as follows: "Cobb, born with the prominence that is universal among white persons in Georgia, sought no further prominence by buckshotting his compatriots. So far as is known, he never attended a lynching." To that, Leerhsen added, "Faint praise indeed, but baseball was just as racist as the rest of society."

There are typos in the transcription, and a key omission. The actual verbiage was, "Colonel Cobb, born with that prominence which is universal among white persons in Georgia, sought no farther prominence by buckshotting his compatriots. So far as known, he never even attended a lynching." Besides omitting the crucial first word, the five flat-out errors that Leerhsen rendered, along with the corrections are: the/that, that/which, farther/further, (word missing)/is, (word missing)/even.

The key missing first word "Colonel" might have tipped off the reader to there being something else at play. A device that newspaper writers occasionally employed, based on my close reading of 19th-century baseball coverage, was to poke fun at how excitable the public could be over baseball. In the recently ended Victorian Era, excitability was a great journalistic pretext for poking fun. In this case, that is exactly what the *Observer* was doing; it was not trying to literally weigh in as a defender of Cobb on racial matters. To me, its giveaway sentence was one that Leerhsen omitted: "Colonel Cobb now stands on fortune's crowning slope, the pillar of a city's hope, etc., etc." The "etc., etc." could easily have been "blah, blah." Another giveaway is in the second paragraph of the editorial when it called him "Hon Tyrus Cobb."

After Hon Tyrus Cobb, it invoked Scottish philosopher and satirical writer Thomas Carlyle. Next came Achilles, followed by a Casey of "Casey at the Bat" fame. So the *Observer*, by calling him "Colonel" Cobb, was artificially elevating him as a

---

ON HAND, COBB AND ALL.

The Observer gives The Atlanta Journal-New York Herald automobiliste a glad welcome and hopes that they will carry away pleasant memories of Charlotte, Mecklenburg county's good roads should be to them pure joy. The automobile having succeeded the bicycle as a good roads propagandist, they are conspicuous representatives of a worthy cause

It is, naturally, the Hon Tyrus Cobb whom we welcome with most enthusiasm Admiration runs riot at sight of this great Georgian He would have inspired Carlyle had Chelsea's surly sage, living in twentieth century America, written of the hero as baseball artist along with the hero as warrior, prophet and poet He is an Achilles unstained by blood, a Casey who never strikes out. Magnetic in personality, wonderful in achievement—when has there been an American like Cobb*

Perhaps a glance at Colonel Cobb's early life may be edifying and instructive Such particulars as our knowledge does not cover our hero-worshiping imagination can readily supply, Colonel Cobb, born with that prominence which is universal among white persons in Georgia, sought no further prominence by buckshotting his compatriots. So far as known, he never even attended a lynching He thus lived, evidently, very much to himself It was not that his energies were sapped by bookworm, but that he was unhappy Pellagra passed by harmless The future artist simply needed to discover himself, to revel in the exercise of his special powers Though he got a rudimentary education, nothing gave him less pleasure than books Often the mere sight of them brought tears But a great day came at last, when young Cobb left off moping to take part in the school baseball games His genius flamed out. Five times up, he never hit for less than two bags and from right field he nelled three men dead at first Material for a marvelous right fielder stood revealed The school teacher, beside himself with joy and pride, embraced this gifted youth. A major league career was predicted by the whole township Ugly duckling had turned out to be swan Later on the county court, where ten prominent citizens were in due process of acquittal for homicide, adjourned that all might see Cobb play It was not long, of course, before Tyrus Cobb, with spirit high and eyes alight, left his father's farm for the career which has become history

Colonel Cobb now stands on fortune's crowning slope, the pillar of a city's hope, etc, etc Largely through his mighty deeds, Detroit won the American League championship and then, in an inter-league series with the National League champions, gave Pittsburg a close shave The Tigers believe that with him they can lick the earth next year We wish them well.

The Journal-Herald automobilists, Colonel Cobb, of course foremost, are cordially invited to make a return visit to Charlotte at their earliest opportunity.

TYRUS COBB A SENSATION

ROYALLY ENTERTAINED HERE

Mr. P. M. Cave, President of the Local Baseball Association, Host at a Charming Dinner in Honor of the Hero at the Selwyn Last Night Which Was Attended by Several Loyal Fans—Cobb Much Sought During the Evening and Had to Run Away From the Crowd Several Times—Men, Women and Children Look For Him With the Same Eagerness That One Would Want to Look Upon the President—Great Genius, This Cobb.

Ty Cobb, the blizzard of the baseball atmosphere, the demon of the diamond, and all those other things can be properly alliterated of any human genius, is furnishing just ninety-nine per cent of the sensation of the reliability automobile tour, the contestants in which reached here yesterday and who are Sundaying in the Queen City. Ty Cobb was showered with ovations during the afternoon and night and the dreams of many a small boy were realized when they scrambled upon some high pinnacle and looked down upon the hero. He had few spare moments last night, the most elaborate reception which was given him being a swell dinner at the Selwyn at 10 o'clock at which he was the guest of Mr. P. M. Cave, the president of the Charlotte Baseball Club, and several of the more loyal patrons of the game here. This closed his engagements for the night and what's before him today can only be touched upon in high places for the multitude will violate almost anything to get in touch with that elusive citizen of Georgia.

COBB DROVE IN FIRST.

Tyrus was at the steering department of the first automobile of the contest that reached the city. Men, women and children lined the streets to watch the procession, but mostly to see the greatest baseball player of the era. He tooted his whistle several times as he touched Charlotte bitulithic and on every side hands were clapping and shouts were being raised over his approach. He held no regard at all for the local speed laws, being somewhat of antagonist to all sorts of slowness and when he turned at the square, he chucked up a little more power and blistered down West Trade street until he stopped in front of the Selwyn. "Is that Ty Cobb?" It was asked of every man within a range of 100 feet and most of that territory was covered with humanity before you could catch a breath.

"Take off your hood, Ty," several shouted, and as the famous genius lifted his headgear, he smiled knowingly and the crowd yelled. The hero then removed himself from his car and rushed into the hotel. It was as bad as on Taft day, that crowd was. It was a hard matter for him to squeeze in the door of the hotel, so vast was the admiring multitude. Men and boys and some women "tromped" on each other's toes just to catch a vision of the boy. Very much abashed in appearance by this sort of an ovation, Cobb wiggled his way into the hotel and went to his room to wash and clothe himself in new apparel. When he came down at length to shake hands with Miss Lucy Oates, America's first feminine fan. In the genuineness of her enthusiasm, he was again surrounded by the curious and after being introduced to the ladies in Miss Oates' car, he darted back into the hotel to elude the mass. Again a demonstration resulted when he came down to supper and the hotel lobby was almost constantly crowded during the early evening with all sorts of people, all bent on getting a glimpse of the renowned baseball player.

COBB EXTREMEL CLEVER.

As a conversationalist and companion, Cobb is extremely clever. He is nothing but a boy, but with marked experiences. Thousands upon thousands of eyes have looked down from exalted seats upon his will-o'-the-wisp of the baseball field and thousands upon thousands of hands have applauded his marvelous prowess. It is a safe bet that his name is mentioned twice every time that of President Taft's is spoken, this because baseball is the greatest cosmopolitan game ever produced and Cobb the most versatile player ever developed. Transported from a little country town in Georgia where he was known as no more than an ordinary kid to the baseball centers of the world where he became the despair of every player in the business and the chosen hero of almost every game in which he played, and transported with a suddenness that would lift a susceptible human to colossal bigotry, this boy has not been disturbed by the ovations he has received, has not been exalted in his own estimation to that despicable point where he is above everybody else. He lies praise—name him who doesn't! It is manifest that his spirits are buoyed by the avalanche of fine things that are said of him—who would not be? But Cobb can shake hands with the greatest of his admirers and then take on the most natural air in the world. He wears a smile mostly. He's a happy citizen, with a fine disposition, a spirit of good cheer that is charming, a hero who is almost abashed under the laurel wreaths that cover his young brow. Oh, but this Cobb is a great fellow!

a news column in the 1909 *Charlotte Observer*, the same day as its Cobb editorial southern equal to those literary or mythological greats. After resorting to many more sentences of prose that had its witty moments, the editorial concluded, "The [Atlanta] Journal-[New York] Herald ['Good Roads' tour sponsor] automobilists, Colonel Cobb, of course, foremost, are cordially invited to make a return visit to Charlotte at their earliest opportunity."

Unwritten was a plausible next line: "So that we editorial writers can get another crack at making fun of such spectacle."

In his racial defense of Cobb, Leerhsen did not mention a key comment from Cobb that Hornbaker apparently is the first Cobb expert to have located. It is a "Course being from Georgia" line from Cobb that can be found in

Cobb and Atlanta Mayor Robert F. Maddox during the Good Roads tour. The 1909 *Charlotte Observer* editorial is on page 31.

the *Free Press*'s coverage of Cobb's 1908 fight with a black asphalt worker, Fred E. Collins. Collins had alerted passersby to not step in a particular area, because the asphalt was wet. Cobb, apparently thinking that the warning was addressed to him, started a physical fight that went on for some time.

DETROIT FREE PRESS: SUNDAY, JUNE 7, 1908.

TYRUS COBB INCREASES HIS BATTING AVERAGE BY BATTERING UP A NEGRO WEARING SPECTACLES

Detroit's Admired Slugger and Fielder Nearly Comes to Grief As the Result of a Fight With a Colored Man, an Asphalt Worker.

Tyrus Raymond Cobb, world's star baseball batsman, went to the asphalt with Fred Collins, a negro laborer wearing spectacles,' and barely escaped fatal injury at the hands of half a dozen other negro employes of the D. U. R., at 1:30 o'clock yesterday afternoon in a short, but fierce fight in front of the Hotel Pontchartrain. Two hundred people witnessed the fracas.

The negro, who was operating an asphalt ironer in the track construction work at the corner, raised his hand to head off an approaching auto, which would have cut into the newly laid asphalt, just as Cobb and Claude Rossman, first baseman of the Detroit team, passed, after leaving their hotel.

"You can't cross here," the negro told the chauffeur.

Cobb evidently thought that Collins spoke to him, and turned sharply on the negro, demanding:

SCENES OF THE COBB-COLLINS MELEE.

The asphalt worker pressed charges for assault and battery, and Cobb settled the case by paying a fine. The following is a correct version of a quote from Cobb as printed in several newspapers, including the *Chicago Tribune*:

"I settled not because I thought I was the offending party, but because I did not want to be inconvenienced later on." He added, "I would act again in a similar manner under the same conditions. When a man is insulted it is worth $75 [about $2,000 in today's dollars] to get satisfaction."

Leerhsen both made a pro-Cobb alteration to the most important part of Cobb's thought above and then italicized that alteration; he did let the reader know about his italicization, as a matter of emphasis, but not about his alteration. Instead of "I would act again in a similar manner under the same conditions," he wrote, "*I would have done the same thing to any man.*"

I did find Cobb saying something to that effect 11 days earlier: the asphalt worker "insulted me, and I wouldn't stand that from any man."

Leerhsen wrote that the fact that Cobb overreacted "seems beyond question." Also, he criticized the *Free Press*'s coverage for the stereotypical graphic on the previous page that accompanied the fight, which appears herein for the first time in a Cobb book or article. Leerhsen also pointed out, rightfully, that it is not clear today that Cobb had a racial motive; for example, I found the *Flint Journal* declaring the following in its coverage of some of the court proceedings: "Ty is a Georgian and isn't particularly impressed with a negro's rights."

The alluded-to key comment from Cobb that Leerhsen omitted was printed in part by both Hornbaker and by Tripp, the author of the 2016 "social and cultural history" of Cobb. Both Hornbaker and Tripp, however, omitted the second, third and fourth sentences below, making the first and the fifth ones consecutive. Also, Tripp omitted all the sentences starting with the sixth one, "I don't say my opinion is worth a---anything." Hornbaker did include the sixth one and ended the quotation with that. Here is the fullest version of the original quote that I found in a newspaper, eight sentences in all:

"Up here [in Detroit], they don't understand me – see? It's bad not to be understood, specially when you're sensitive and care. Yes, I've got to admit I do care a whole lot about what people think about [']em. I hate rows and fusses worse than anything. Course being from Georgia, I think different about negroes from what they do up here [in the North]. I don't say my opinion is worth a—anything. I haven't got the swelled head or anything like that, like some people think I have. I'm mighty sorry if I appear like that, but I know my opinion ain't much."

The "Course being from Georgia" line, the fifth, is the key line in that quotation. It will be placed, on page 148, in conjunction with an expression of the day, about Southerners being superior to Northerners in knowing "the ways of the negro perfectly." (A less formal version of that is, "We know our N-words better than them Yankees.") The presentation will be made as part of a discussion of supporting statements that at least plausibly support the case that Cobb was a racist, beyond being open to minstrelsy and playing African Dodger.

As noted earlier, a key in re-evaluating Cobb's racism is whether his known occasional rage toward blacks was motivated or fueled by racial bias. Leerhsen steered clear of calling Cobb a racist, such as by opting in his index for the headings of "rage of" and "and race." Hornbaker's book has no index. Tripp opted for "race" and "racial attitudes and behavior influenced by (honor)."

One racial subject that Leerhsen can be credited for touching on, which Alexander and Hornbaker overlooked, was raised in a 1912 article in *Baseball Magazine*, as follows: "When his animal spirits rose to concert pitch and he was too thoughtful of the Caucasian race to pummel the countenance of a white boy, he used to vent his spleen on the ebony 'pickaninnies' of the surrounding plantations. More than one incident is told of how Ty avenged a stolen watermelon or a missing chicken; and some would have us believe that this same fighting blood is not yet entirely absent from the veins of the Detroit 'Tyger.'" On the other hand, without providing a source, Leerhsen wrote in parentheses the following right after that in his text, presumably as an undeclared literary device: "'Just made up,' the elderly Cobb would say about such yarns. 'Just. Made. Up.'"

Even if he is figuratively right, Leerhsen did not alert the reader to his reworking of the underlying quote as well. First of all, he reworked it in a way that made it sound stupid. Secondly, he omitted the watermelon and chicken examples. Thirdly, he inverted the parts he did use. In addition, he attributed what he used to *Baseball Digest*, which would not come into existence until 1942, as follows: Cobb, he quoted the magazine as literally having written, "used to vent his spleen on ebony 'pickaninnies' when he was too thoughtful of the Caucasian race to pummel the countenance of a white boy."

Tripp also weighed in on the *Baseball Magazine* piece, without touching on Leerhsen's undeclared pro-Cobb alterations. Tripp said its author, Howell Foreman, had demonstrated a rhetorical style that "suggests he may have been more interested in mythmaking and playing off regional stereotypes than relating actual events." At the same time, Tripp stated that "other sources confirm that Ty enjoyed the primitive thrill of physical combat."

On safer ground, Leerhsen challenged the credibility of two contemporaneous reports of Cobb's use of the "N-word." However, he omitted, without explanation, this third reported use found by Alexander: In 1909, the

St. Louis Post-Dispatch had reported that Cobb and his business partners had built housing for black renters. Alexander paraphrased the report as follows: "As Cobb had sketched the plan the previous spring to a St. Louis sportswriter, 'this nigger property down home,' dubbed 'Booker T. Washington Heights,' consisted of a dozen houses constructed at a cost of $200 each and renting for $2 to $3.50 a week."

Leerhsen should have acknowledged that report. Hornbaker did, albeit without challenging its accuracy. The article was written by a *Post-Dispatch* cartoonist, S. Carlisle Martin, and the graphic depicting blacks on the next page contains stereotypes. The N-word appears twice in two sentences, and the word Negro does too, at least in the first reference to blacks themselves.

Cobb did invest in the construction of such housing. In his 2008 article on BleacherReport.com, Fricks mentioned the Booker T. Washington Heights subdivision in Toccoa, Ga., and said the neighborhood that the housing served in Cobb's day was predominantly black. The quote that Martin attributed to Cobb is that the building lots "are located at Toccoa, Ga., and we call this nigger property down home, for nothing but negroes live in it; and say, there's money in it. I mean in the niggers." By the way, that latter use of the N-word could be plural slang for the property and not literally a synonym for the Negroes.

Hornbaker wrote as if Cobb had actually spoken that, observing that the words sounded more like lingo than "textbook vernacular," formal writing in print. I can claim expertise on the wording of 19th-century baseball prose, from having glanced through close to the entire surviving newspaper record, on microfilm or in original bound volumes, from big-league cities for my four 19th-century-centered and quotes-galore books. There are levels of plausibility in quotes. The level in this feature is low, as if the cartoonist was reinterpreting Cobb for dramatic effect. A few 19th-century baseball writers had a liberal rewording reputation among their colleagues and were so noted by them for particular rewrites. The *Atlanta Constitution* did run a big chunk of the *Post-Dispatch* article that focused on Cobb as a player. It omitted the racial prose and possibly took a subtle dig at the strange writing style, speaking of "some of the remarks credited to the star member of the Tigers."

Regardless, besides it seeming improbable that Cobb refrained from using the N-word, at least unless especially angry, it turns out that he was likely one of the most quoted or paraphrased current or former 20th-century players on racial attitudes, without having to reach for decades-later stories. The mere fact that his attitude toward blacks in major league baseball as of the early 1940s was credibly conveyed elevates him, say, relative to the vast number of players whose racial views are lost to history. More broadly, it is apparently

A newspaper clipping from the *ST. LOUIS POST-DISPATCH*, ST. LOUIS, SUNDAY MORNING, MAY 9, 1909, with the headline "Ty Cobb Says He Has No Friends When Game Is On, but That He Is 'No Rowdy Like George Stone'"

hard to find more than a few major league players recorded for making multiple deep racial observations in the first half of the 20th century before 1947.

It could be said to be unfair to single Cobb out for supporting institutional racism as of the early 1940s, since the attitude was likely widely held among Southerners. It is also true that people can be judged for their own behavior and attitudes. Accordingly, Cobb could be evaluated from the standpoint of having been one of the most intellectual of players prior to baseball's integration.

With some early 20th-century players, where the paper trail on their racial views is thin, a flimsy substitute is trying to glean significance from the player's alleged use of the N-word. Cobb's use of it, which the 2015 books analyzed a bit, now can be cast as of marginal significance in the scheme of things.

To show how rich the record on Cobb is, relative to other players of his era, here is a relatively marginal report that shows awareness of racial differences; as with nearly everything "Cobb" that I have not attributed to others and that extends beyond the basic facts of his biography, I am claiming to be its first discloser of, in a modern-day article or Cobb book. In 1909, Harry G. Salsinger of the *Detroit News* spoke with him about Cuban baseball league players; teammates of Cobb were scheduled to play against some in Cuba in the coming offseason. Cobb would go to Cuba in the offseason of 1910-11. About the race of the Cuban players, many "claim they are blacks, but Ty Cobb says he knows an educated Spaniard who has been down in Cuba and met the players. This educated Spaniard declares they are all Spanish, but the question still remains:

"Why don't they use them in the big leagues?"

Cobb also answers that question.

"'There might be a lot of dispute about it,' says the Georgian, 'and many may maintain that the Spaniards are Negroes. They speak a foreign tongue, and their total ignorance might make them objectionable on any of the big league clubs.'"

(Although the following is not tied to baseball, in 1923, Cobb answered a letter from a D. Peirson Ricks about bringing about world peace. Cobb responded that "there should be some sort of an international understanding between the nations. Of course, different races have different ideas and interests; some are very selfish. Consequently, rules or laws governing such understanding between the nations would be a most important proposition to frame." In 1931, when asked by syndicated columnist Robert W. Edgren about the possibility of going on a tiger hunt in India, Cobb replied that he likes his tigers not "too wild. But I understand India is a civilized country. I wouldn't like to go hunting down in the middle of Africa."

Also, in 1915 after Jewish Georgian Leo Frank was lynched after the governor commuted to a life sentence his death penalty conviction, Cobb said, "It's a terrible thing for Georgia. Our state [image-wise] never suffered a heavier blow than when that mob stole Leo Frank from the prison guards and lynched him." That said, "I really have not been sufficiently in touch with the facts of this particular case to be justified in expressing even an opinion regarding Frank's guilt or innocence. If he were guilty, of course I should favor the utmost penalty. But that is not the question at issue. Georgia has courts, and they are fully capable of administering justice and punishment.")

3. *Argumentation on Race*

Alinchpin of Leerhsen's book is two 1952 Cobb interviews supportive of integration in baseball; the first was with the Associated Press, and the second appeared a week later in the *Sporting News*. Fricks reprinted the AP one in 2008 on BleacherReport.com. Bak had cited the AP one in 2005, in the *Detroit Free Press*.

Even though the 1952 interviews contain the lone known positive Cobb comments about whether segregated parts of organized baseball should integrate, Leerhsen

MLB

Ty Cobb Was Not A Racist

By Wesley Fricks, Analyst   Aug 2, 2008

referred to the *Sporting News* one as "one of the many occasions he spoke out on what was in some quarters still a controversial subject." He seems to have added to his count the occasions on which Cobb praised the talent of black players. If he was going to be expansive in that respect, he could have done the same by dishing out credit to an earlier source that cited or reprinted the AP article, perhaps Fricks in 2008 or Bak in 2005.

As I annotate below, relatively minor corrections can be made of Hornbaker for one of his racial hedges. He wrote, "The overall sum of evidence paints Cobb to be the kind of man who refused to take anything less than perfect etiquette [stemming, in at least some cases, from a white Southerner's warped standard for racial interaction] from people of color [those he did not have an ongoing positive relationship with; after all, he had the same black cook for many years, whose etiquette presumably was not always perfect]. However, he certainly coexisted [interacted] with African Americans his entire life, and was influenced by several blacks in his [adopted] hometown[, starting in his teens,] of Royston[, Ga.,] growing up."

Hornbaker's words are a mild softening of one of Alexander's key thoughts. Alexander had written, "Cobb's racial feelings appear to have been quite strong indeed. He had pleasant recollections of a black maid [a mammy different from the longtime cook that moved with the family to California] who had looked after the Cobb children at their home in Royston, and he was capable of acts of kindness toward particular black persons. But he had no patience whatever with blacks who were insolent, fractious, unsubmissive –– in a word, 'uppity.'" Hornbaker's prose is also a mild softening of the following line of Alexander's: "Cobb also remained quick tempered with people off the field who crossed him, especially if they happened to be black."

Still speculative is to what degree Cobb's negative reactions stemmed from

such differing expectations and thus made them racist. Leerhsen put the countervailing case on the table, that Cobb potentially was so progressive on race for a Southerner as to be colorblind in his expectations of others.

Worth taking into account is that anything could "set him off" at any time, regardless of the race of who he was engaging with. Furman Bisher wrote about Cobb in the *Saturday Evening Post* in 1958. In 1994, after the movie "Cobb" premiered – it was based on a discredited 1961 article by Stump months after publication of his book with Cobb – Bisher gave this recollection of the three days he spent with Cobb in 1958: "He could be kind and nice," he told the *Dallas Morning News*. "If you drank with him, you'd really be a pal. But anything might trigger a reaction, and he'd blow in any direction." Then, in early 1995, Bisher wrote, "The truth is, Cobb was no racist [at least as of 1958]. He had a very even temper – he could be just as cruel to one race as another. His own family was proof of that. His first wife finally had to take her leave after years of abuse [apparently both verbal and physical]. His second wife, with no children involved, ended her career as Mrs. Cobb after seven years."

A less direct argument along Bisher's lines was made by Claude "Blinkey" Horn, longtime sports editor of the *Nashville Tennessean*, in 1936. Horn observed that eccentric St. Louis pitcher Dizzy Dean was making public challenges "to whip" general manager Branch Rickey; manager Frankie Frisch; and his catcher, Virgil Davis. The challenges reminded Horn of "the many mixups in which Tyrus Raymond Cobb was involved when he made a million mortal enemies with his flying feet and flying fists. There were no newspaper challenges in Ty's fisticuffs. He hurled no long distance challenges. He fought on impulse, for the No. 1 man of baseball, filled with determination, would let nothing black, white or creole stand in his path once he had fixed his mind to reach a given destination."

Earl L. Bell

Also previously uncited is the following from Earl L. Bell, the longtime friend and journalist. In "Ty Cobb: A Personal Memoir" in the *Augusta Chronicle* in 1964, he wrote, "Ty Cobb was a man of incredible contradictions. Despite his inordinate bellicosity on the field, he had many warm and enduring friends [but not that many close ones, by Cobb's own admission] and in turn was deeply loyal to them. But there were no 'in-betweens' – he either liked you or he didn't. He was very appreciative, though, and fair to those who were fair to him."

Bell's "no 'in-betweens,' he either liked you or he didn't" can literally mean that Cobb was indeed colorblind in his personal relations. On the other hand, there is now clearly no compelling basis for speculating that he was colorblind, at least until late in life, about racial equality in social settings. In addition, he was open to doing minstrelsy and played African Dodger, which of course stereotype or treat blacks in substandard ways.

Leerhsen did not touch on the possibility that Cobb had different expectations on how each race should treat him. Having such differing expectations would naturally support any case that Cobb was a racist. He did write, "As a Southern gentleman," – as opposed to merely being a Southerner – Cobb "had always drawn a line in the sand that marked the leading edge of his honor." At another point, he wrote that Cobb was "ultrasensitive to any slight." After acknowledging that ultrasensitivity, Leerhsen singled out an extreme result of ultrasensitivity, physical fight. He wrote that the "sheer oddness of Cobb's alleged behavior – if he attacked people simply for being black he would not have had time to eat, sleep, or play baseball, and he no doubt would have met his match somewhere along the line, quite a few times – never sparked further investigation."

Leerhsen's emphasis was to show that Cobb was not a severe racist because he did not take every slight to the extreme of fighting. Still, if racism was a key component in his taking offense in slights from blacks – and the slights occurred often enough – that would help show that in social situations he was potentially more racist than other Southerners of his day. That said, there is no compelling body of evidence for reaching that conclusion.

Leerhsen also wrote that one reason why "we can't make assumptions about Cobb's attitude about race based simply on the year and location of his birth" is in light of members of his immediate family, going back a few generations, having been "rife with exceptions to the rule about Southern attitudes." That subject will be treated late in chapter 10. But as reflected by Cunningham's reporting, Cobb lumped himself as among Southerners in baseball, apparently as of the early 1940s, in stating that he stood with those currently in the sport in being opposed to racial equality in it.

As will also be noted later, Leerhsen made an unacknowledged assumption about Cobb's Southernness as being superior to that of two active players as of 1947 who reacted against Jackie Robinson's entry into the National League, Dixie Walker and Enos Slaughter. As it turns out, based on my research, Leerhsen's Cobb-was-superior-to-Walker-and-Slaughter argumentation is "in the soup." That is because it is at least plausible that Cobb felt the same way as Walker and Slaughter at the start of 1947, even if he did not express himself publicly at that time.

Also, calling Cobb a "Southern gentleman" rather than a "Southerner" is hard to defend, because his personality could be so sour. In defense of his being one, I can cite a long feature at the end of his career. In 1928, Carl Warton of the *Boston Herald* stated, "The Georgian's fiery temperament has been responsible for more fracases [with players, not umpires] on the diamond than you can shake a stick at." He added, "but he is a typical southerner, a gentleman by instinct, and has always regretted these unpleasant episodes." In 1927, after Cobb was implicated in a baseball betting scandal, one of his hunting mates in Ontario, Dr. R. D. Sloane, called him "one of the most honorable players of all time, a southern gentleman and the prince of sportsmen."

Whether Cobb was even a "Southern gentleman" or a "Southerner" was put in doubt in 1911, when an unnamed writer compared him to fellow baseball star "Shoeless" Joe Jackson, a South Carolina native. "Jackson and Cobb are temperamental opposites. Jackson is easy-going. Cobb is all nerves. Jackson is a typical southerner, with the southern love for rest and quiet. Cobb doesn't even talk like a southerner and has none of the southern love of rest."

Leerhsen used the term "Southern gentleman" twice in his book and without defining it. In the second instance, he said Cobb "often felt ashamed of his angry outbursts; he was, after all, "a true *personage* who played poker and sipped bootleg whiskey with the president of the United States, Warren Harding, [Cobb's 1961 book mentions the poker, but not any whiskey] at a private all men's club outside Augusta, not to mention a Southern gentleman."

In 1908, the *St. Louis Post-Dispatch* followed up a reader's comment that it had published by declaring, "Southern gentlemen, and women, too, disagree as to what constitutes a Southern gentleman." It quoted a female as having written in, in response to the comment, "For definition of gentleman read Psalm 15. It gave me satisfaction after months of search down South."

The *Post-Dispatch* then cited four paragraphs from the Psalm, including, "He that walketh uprightly and worketh righteousness, and speaketh the truth in his heart." Also, "He that backbiteth not with his tongue, nor doeth evil to his neighbor, nor taketh up a reproach against his neighbor."

The newspaper also informed its readers that a male who had sparked the issue in the newspaper "now says that a gentleman, according to the standard of civilized countries, 'is one who will not allow anyone to be more polite than he, be it in a public conveyance, theater, street or at a public function.'"

"Another writer says that a 'Southern gentleman is just as good and just as bad as any other kind of a gentleman.'"

I can suggest that future writers who want to call Cobb a Southern gentleman instead call him "a Southern gentleman with a lightning temper."

After all, Grantland Rice, in a column in 1912, said, "His one drawback is a lightning temper. In other respects he is clean cut in deportment and bearing both on and off the field of play." Also, "No man in the game plays harder to win – first, last, and in the middle." In 1915, Rice wrote that rival infielder Johnny Evers and Cobb, "high-strung, nervous, inclined to be excitable at any moment, are exceptions to the rule of sporting success. [Christy] Mathewson, [Walter] Johnson, [Grover Cleveland] Alexander, [Honus] Wagner, [Napoleon] Lajoie, [Tris] Speaker, Jackson, [Sam] Crawford – are all athletes of even nervous balance" who are "easy-going, rarely ruffled or rarely upset."

Cobb and Grantland Rice in 1930, in Augusta, Ga.

In 1922, Rice would write, "Ty Cobb has a world of nervous energy, or nerve energy, yet he isn't nervous in the accepted meaning of the word. The same applies to [former heavyweight boxing champion] Jack Dempsey, who can't keep still five minutes at a time. Yet neither Cobb nor Dempsey wears away his nerve reserve by fretting or fuming or throwing any act of fluttering duck fits in advance." In 1936, Rice again grouped Cobb with Dempsey, and added golfer Bobby Jones as "types who are naturally nervous." Black boxer Joe Louis "is a leading example on the other side of the wall. The Louis nerves are caked in ice."

Cobb, in his own newspaper serial in 1925, referred to his "rather stormy" baseball career, which he attributed to "my high[-]strung nature and rather fiery temper." Several sentences later, he wrote that the necessity of self-restraint "applies to other professions, but in baseball there is much more opportunity for flying off the handle and engaging in physical combat."

Jekyll & Hyde

Cobb and Jack Dempsey in 1931, in Reno, Nev.

Rhodes is the lone prior Cobb author to have pursued the theme of Cobb as a Jekyll & Hyde, although Bak delved more specifically into whether Cobb suffered from a mental disease. (My one fresh angle on that is Nap Rucker's speculation, on page 21, about Cobb and adrenaline.) Rhodes used the term "Jekyll & Hyde" in an interview with Cobb's daughter Shirley. She liked it and told Rhodes, "How could he have been so sweet to other people and not to his own family?" Explicit users of that characterization include a former utility teammate in 1921, Sammy Barnes, who said of him in 1973, "when he put on that uniform it was a case of Dr. Jekyll and Mr. Hyde – two completely different personalities." Some Web sites also have that quote. Barnes had witnessed his 1921 fight with umpire Billy Evans. This fuller explanation by Barnes is not online: "I remember talking to [Cobb] on the train one day and he told me that he had never played a game, exhibition or otherwise, that he did not try his level best." A bottom line seems to be that Cobb was as extreme as possible in his intensity during games and clearly less so otherwise.

In 1926, umpire Evans wrote, "His impulsive temperament and aggressive spirit kept him from attaining the popularity [personality-wise] achieved by some of the other outstanding stars. However, the fighter is bound to make enemies and Cobb has always been the fighter. He never admitted defeat. Off the field, after the battle was over, Cobb was quite a different fellow from the fiery Georgian who gave no ground or asked no quarter in the heat of the battle. He has been more or less the Dr. Jekyll and Mr. Hyde of baseball." (In his 1961 book with Stump, Cobb said this about his fight with Evans: "I'm the ballplayer who 'hated' an umpire so much that I fist-whipped and tromped Billy Evans under the stands until little of poor Evans was left to carry away. Or so grandfathers read forty-seven [should be 40] years back. And so [they] passed on to their sons, and they to the generation of the sixties [1960s].")

In 1931, Gabby Street, about to lead the Cardinals team he was managing to a World Series triumph, told sports editor Alan Gould of the AP, "Ball players and fans never really understood Cobb. He was a Jekyll and Hyde personality. Some days he was a great guy, easy to get along with. Others, you couldn't go near him. He was high-strung and, as I say, always thinking about two jumps ahead of everybody else on the field. Guess that's why he found it tough trying to succeed as a manager," from 1921 to 1926. (In 1950, former Royston teammate Joe T. Cunningham would tell Bisher, "Ty was awful hard to get along with, arrogant, almost. But we were friends, even after I became the only man who ever beat him out of his position [as shortstop on the team].")

Digressing to a short interlude of Cobb and Street, a native of Alabama:

In 1930, Malcolm Bingay wrote in the *Detroit Free Press*, "Now Gabby Street is hailed as the wizard of the Ozarks. And he says that, next to himself, [mediocre] Charlie Schmidt of Detroit was the greatest catcher of all time! How [fellow Cobb-Schmidt teammate] Bill Donovan would have laughed at that one. Gabby is all that his name implies. He was never even a smart catcher.

"Ty Cobb always played him for a sucker off the field – as he usually did anybody else he could. Whenever Detroit played Washington[, Street's team from 1908 to 1911], Ty would casually meet Gabby just before the series at the hotel or elsewhere and trade 'secrets.' He would tell Gabby [that Detroit star] Sam Crawford had a sore arm and couldn't throw for the time being or that [Detroit's] Germany Schaefer had a 'Charlie horse' and couldn't run the bases. He would just fill Gabby with feed box [miscellaneous] information. In exchange for which Gabby would give him the low down on all the ailments of the Washington players.

"Gabby, when play started, would tell his teammates to run wild on the bases whenever Crawford had to make the throw [from the outfield] as 'Sam's arm was lame.' They would take the tip as genuine and start running wild. Sam would throw them out by a mile. His arm was never better, they learned to their sorrow. And instead of a 'Charley horse,' Schaefer turned out on a streak of lightning.

Cobb (in a Cleveland uniform) and Gabby Street at a 1911 benefit game

"But on the other hand, the reports of injuries as detailed by Gabby were always accurate and were used by the Tigers to glorious advantage – when Cobb told them.

"It took [Washington manager Clark] Griffith a long time to tumble to how the Tigers were getting the low down on his gang and

Cobb and Street in 1934

he was getting a lot of misinformation about the Detroit team. He threatened to fine, or kill Gabby if he ever caught him even saying 'hullo' to Cobb after that.

"Managerial brains? Horsefeathers!"

Street would be manager of the San Francisco Mission Reds in the Pacific

Coast League in 1934 and 1935. Cobb's youngest son Jim, born in 1921, disputed the notion that his dad was morose and without friends. "He was nice to people and he had a good sense of humor," he told Newspaper Enterprise Association (NEA) sports editor Ira Berkow in 1969. Presumably referring to 1934 and 1935, Jim said, "I remember Gabby Street coming to the house often and he and dad reminiscing and sometimes I'd be awakened at three in the morning by their laughter."

In the offseason of 1910-11, Street, upon returning home to Pennsylvania from a hunting trip, had noticed an odd-looking express mail package. When he opened it, he found a Louisville Slugger bat and a worn Detroit uniform. After thinking it was a joke, he found a "neatly written note" in the uniform, "pinned to the back pocket of the baseball pants, and signed by Ty Cobb." About Street's having received his favorite style of bat, the *Washington Herald* also reported, "Street and Cobb have been fast friends" for years. "Street claims the worst spiking he ever got was at the hands of Cobb, and that the famous ball player would rather have sacrificed the game than to have had it occur."

Cobb and Street later were World War I veterans; Street was awarded the Purple Heart at the Battle of the Argonne. Cobb was not in any combat.

Street appears a grand total of one time in the three Cobb biographies, and only for being ejected from a game. A humorous quirk is that at the 1934 banquet to be noted later for Cobb's revealing comments, Street was the guest of honor. For "one solid hour" at the start of the evening, wrote Newland of the AP, Street's guests "engaged in animated conversation. Then someone discovered that 'Gabby' wasn't present. They had forgotten to tell the guest of honor where the banquet was to be held."

One final Jekyll and Hyde quote is from three decades after Cobb's death, from a retired journalist who knew him well, Jack McDonald. McDonald wrote, "The Ty Cobb I knew was a Jekyll and Hyde. He was a complex man who was very controversial on and off the field. He was a dynamic, sometimes ruthless, surly, flaming-tempered and a restless soul. But beneath a rough and sometimes selfish nature beat a human and compassionate heart."

Selective Argumentation

On page 131 of his book, Leerhsen wrote, "let the record show that this inconsequential little blurb [in the *Detroit Free Press* in 1906] is the only example of Cobb even *purportedly* talking about race relations until the 1950s, when he hailed the advent of Jackie Robinson."

Leerhsen's stringency toward others and leniency toward himself and ally Fricks, on the quality of their respective research, produced such an excess of spin that it reminded me of a let's-see-what-sticks debate class that I took at Cornell University in the mid-1980s. The rules of debate followed that of so-called forensics clubs nationwide. One could possibly win an argument by, in the time one had to speak, speaking so fast as to bombard the other side with arguments. If the other side did not keep track of all the arguments and address each even by saying, "that's a far-fetched point," a fast-speaking arguer could easily win in the eyes of the judge. That is because the judge would write down every line of argument and check to see if there had been a rebuttal to each.

A Simon & Schuster marketing pitch for Leerhsen's book states, "An authoritative, reliable and compelling biography of perhaps the most significant and controversial player in baseball history." It is definitely more compelling – engaging – than most baseball biographies, especially other Cobb ones, and, at least factually, more accurate too. It also managed to do what Cobb biographers have been doing for decades: missing or muffing a whole lot on its most critical issue, the extent of how racist Cobb definitely or plausibly was.

An Interlude: Writing Styles

I can be considered a research-first writer. In researching my prior books, all focused on the 19th century, I came close to exhausting the surviving record that relate to my subjects, from 1871 to 1900. Having a sense of how wide-ranging newspaper reporting on baseball can be made me ideal to try to upstage the Cobb biographers. Early on I discovered Cunningham's reporting. That led me to conclude that anyone making strong revisionist claims on 20th-century subjects without having done or commissioned comprehensive research is asking for trouble.

That is because newspapers that covered 20th-century baseball are continually becoming available to search in full-text databases. Timing may be everything, as to whether a particular newspaper is searchable when an author is finishing up his or her research. While use of such databases was a tiny proportion of my overall research effort in my prior books, for this one, I made maximal use of them. But even such shortcuts only go so far. For this book, having ready access to the Library of Congress, for being the top holder of U.S. newspaper microfilm (such as the only full *Detroit News* run outside of Michigan), and for the breadth of its books and magazines, was essential too.

While the quality of a book is determined by a range of factors, such as on the readability side too, I have rarely come across a review that noted the Library of Congress as a research-intensive author's base library.

Putting aside how the non-Michigander 2015 authors performed or obtained their research, there are other ways to compare them. Leerhsen is a think-of-the-casual-reader-first type of writer, as if having a conversation with one in the present day; hence, his 38 uses of the expression "in those days" and around 30 "we's" to Hornbaker's 0 of each. Also, Leerhsen does not mind making references to more modern times (author Stephen Hawking, ESPN, "The Beverly Hillbillies" TV show, retired boxing promoter Don King). Hornbaker's possibly lone modern-day reference was less jarring: "Interestingly, had Cobb performed in the television age, his amazing deeds and dynamic style would have fostered an even greater sensation. He was a must-see performer, and the marketability of Cobb as a mainstream TV celebrity would have been huge.")

Using the unscientific method of a Google Books words search, I initially thought that Leerhsen was by a landslide more opinionated. But if you add up all the uses of certainly, definitely, obvious/obviously or, a Leerhsen landslide favorite, "no doubt," the total is 53 for Leerhsen and 54 for Hornbaker. That said, at least on racial matters, Leerhsen is the more argumentative of the two.

Both Hornbaker and Leerhsen provide a lot of analysis and so much of it is valid. Where they diverge, as so many pairs of authors do, is where they generalize or where they stress disconnects on particular subjects, in this case racism.

To me, argumentation can be said to fall on two extremes: generalizing and poking holes in generalizations. I can provide a contrast between Hornbaker and Leerhsen by showing how Anson's racism can be written about differently, depending on the author's emphasis.

A 2008 book, *Northsiders: Essays on the History and Culture of the Chicago Cubs*, contains an essay by professor Steve Andrews that touches on Anson's racism. David L. Fleitz, the one other book-length biographer of Anson, wrote that growing up in Iowa in the 1850s, it "appears that Adrian [Cap's given first name] developed many of his attitudes toward minorities during his childhood through his contacts with the Indians." Andrews quoted that comment in noting that Fleitz "traces Anson's racism to boyhood encounters with local 'Pottawattamie' Indians invariably described as 'friendly' or 'peaceful,' in which 'teasing'

a photo with a possible connection to Cobb's competing in California Indians golf tournaments in the 1930s. He won its 1937 one on the Del Monte golf course at Monterey.

became a favorite pastime." Fleitz, Andrews wrote, does not literally detail an episode from Anson's ghostwritten autobiography published in the year 1900 that touches on such encounters, "while the more skeptical Rosenberg does. Rosenberg casts doubt on the impact of such encounters, since it is 'unlikely that Ady [Anson's boyhood first name] met many Indians growing up.'" I had also written, "That is because by 1846, when Iowa became a state, it had been rid of the vast majority of them, with the Sioux staying until 1851."

On this particular topic, Fleitz was looking to connect the dots on Anson racially, and wisely used the word "appears" as a hedge. Although I did not say so in my 2006 biography, the episode struck me as yet another overblown story of adventure from a male who grew up in the United States. I found the point about Iowa and its emptied-out-as-of-1852 Indian population in the 1940 book *Iowa Through the Years* published by the State Historical Society of Iowa.

A larger point is: Just as journalists, generally speaking, are trained not to rely on a single source, book writers and book reviewers (and even readers, if they are that curious about someone) should not look at just a single book-length biography of a baseball player for anything that might be controversial. That is because authors can vary so greatly, by attaching significance to, downplaying, or failing to note a detail. In trying to change conventional wisdom on Cobb's racism, Leerhsen used all three of the above tactics.

Tripp, by the way, prominently featured some of Cobb's overblown retellings of myths about his childhood – and claimed that they had something to do with his being "a product of the late nineteenth-century rural South." In his next sentence, he wrote, "Like most Southern men, he grew up believing that a statement was not really a lie unless someone else dared to challenge it." One was by perpetuating his father's "false impression that he was part of the prestigious Georgia Cobb clan [a different ancestral line from his]."

For comparison's sake, as both Anson book-length biographers have noted, Anson's claim to have descended from William Anson, an eminent English barrister at the time of King James I, is bunk. Counter evidence by Anson genealogist Shirley Anson shows that as of 1647, the last name of Cap's ancestors was Austin, not Anson. Cobb, by the way, was of Scotch-English descent, according to 1956 biographer McCallum.

Anson's ghostwritten autobiography in 1900 contains embellished stories about his youth. But I did not give any thought to blaming that on his having grown up in Iowa or in a frontier culture. A merit of books that do not try to wrap long-ago history into bows – a style sometimes dubbed "antiquarian" by scholars who favor "deeper meaning" over "no notable meaning" – is that detail can be interesting for its own sake. Also, a seemingly lowly detail may mean nothing to one person but something to another. On-the-hunt-for-meaning Tripp was so obsessed with the roots of Cobb's manhood – a subject that qualifies as serious enough for academics to tackle – that he made the argument that there was something inherently Southern about Cobb's bends of the truth.

Not only that, Tripp used that as a springboard to criticize Cobb for telling conflicting versions of some of his stories. Tripp then declared, "Lies, whether willfully fashioned or not, enabled Cobb to assert power over others."

One of Tripp's examples of conflicting versions was in the pair of articles that Cobb wrote in *Life* magazine in 1952; the better known is the first, "They Don't Play Baseball Any More." Unfortunately, Tripp did not realize that while the two articles have Cobb's byline, that a savvy ghostwriter on the magazine's staff, Ernest C. Havemann, allegedly made editorial changes on his own. So, unlike standard procedure in academia, Cobb had seemingly lost editorial control. Examples of how that played out will be noted later. As will be repeated and expounded on, sports editor Bob Cooke of the *New York Herald Tribune* disclosed that at the Alexandra Restaurant in New York City, "we learned that Cobb didn't write the stories at all. They were done by Ernie [Ernest C.] Havemann, whose name appears inconspicuously among the staff writers listed on the magazine's masthead. But who cares whether Havemann says they don't play baseball any more?"

St. Petersburg Times sports editor Bill Beck wrote that if Cobb's claim were true, he "has been victim of a grave injustice and one that occurs with alarming frequency in the world of highly competitive metropolitan 'big time' journalism. The tendency of over-enthusiastic rewrite artists to twist a given set of facts until they take on a reader-catching air of sensationalism is to be deplored."

Another Tripp trip-up, to be noted later, is where he seems to conflate Cobb's changing lists of who he deliberately spiked with whom he deliberately collided.

In the fall of 2017, the *Journal of Sport History*, the best-known U.S.-oriented scholarly sports journal, ran a joint review of the Leerhsen and Tripp books. Hornbaker's book was not mentioned even in passing, which is a colossal omission. That is because Hornbaker is the best hedger of the three authors, and a book's accuracy – on as complicated a subject as Cobb – is probably more important to many scholarly readers than innovations in argumentation. On presenting insight into Leerhsen's book, the review, by University of Central Arkansas history professor David Welky, is a weak sister to Witherspoon's 2016 one in *Sport History Review*. While lulled, as Witherspoon was, into stating that the book is "exhaustively" or "thoroughly" researched, Welky did not find fault, as Witherspoon did, with Leerhsen's fact-finder tone. As I noted earlier, journalism professors could have graded Leerhsen poorly for implicitly taking credit at times for the research of others and for his many transcription errors.

The other half of the Welky review is significant in a positive way: in having been the first professorial one of Tripp's in a non-Southern history journal. Welky's shrewdest point, a criticism of Tripp, boosts my case for Hornbaker's book as the best of the three – for those who want authors, at minimum, to be excellent hedgers. Of the three authors, only Hornbaker's writing technically resembles that of top print journalists: liberally presenting multiple sides of disputes and exuding comfort when not conferring validity on any one of them.

Welky's shrewdest criticism, more specifically, is that Tripp "sometimes allows his arguments to overwhelm his subject." Independent of seeing Welky's review, I had settled on the point on page 49 that includes ascribing the "On-the-hunt-for-meaning Tripp" moniker.

Meanwhile, although Hornbaker may not have submitted a copy to the *Journal of Sport History* or was given a chance to nix any unfavorable review, other books reviewed in the same 2017 issue as the Cobb ones include: *Baseball in Territorial Arizona: A History, 1863–1912, Happy Felsch: Banished Black Sox Center Fielder* and *Ralph Kiner: A Baseball Biography*. Also by contrast, a decade ago, it did not even send out my exhaustively endnoted Anson series for review. Besides tricky and dirty play from 1871 to 1900, the books are definitive on Anson and Mike "King" Kelly, the lone early players who rise to the significance of Cobb and Babe Ruth in drawing big newspaper coverage.

In his Cobb fibbing section, the most space that Tripp allocated was to a trick that Cobb claimed to have pulled on "Shoeless" Joe Jackson during their playing days. Tripp admirably noted there being different numerical detail in Cobb's 1952 retelling of it in *Life* and in Cobb's previous ones. (Elsewhere, I show Cobb garbling the names of authors in making requests for books to his apparent long-distance bookseller of choice, Helene Champlain of the bookstore at the Waldorf Astoria Hotel.) I can add that Cobb's 1961 book with Stump has different detail on the trick against Jackson than is in the *Life* article in 1952 and in previous retellings. In Cobb's defense, before the personal computer and the Internet, it was much harder to organize and double-check factual detail.

On a separate score, as every baseball fan should know, Jackson is the greatest star in baseball history who was banished from the sport during his career. That happened after Commissioner Kenesaw Mountain Landis declared that he had conspired to throw the 1919 World Series. Distinct from Cobb's differing

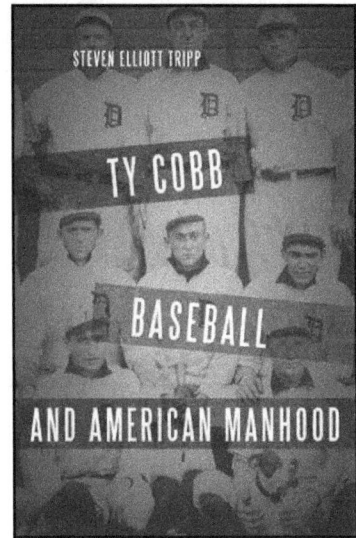

versions of his trick on Jackson is there being differing versions of a possible Grantland Rice yarn about Jackson acting sheepish. On that occasion, supposedly, Cobb and Rice visited Jackson at his store in South Carolina in the 1940s. I will note those versions later.

If forced to play the analysis game too, I can hypothesize that something unrelated to the South explains why Cobb and Rice each came up with flawed stories about Jackson. The theory is: Jackson had been so unique that Cobb and Rice had an unstated desire to "one-up" each other. A Trippian Southern hypothesis could be that since Rice was born in Tennessee, and Cobb in Georgia, that noted Southerners tied to baseball who knew Jackson well gravitated more than persons born elsewhere toward telling mythical stories about him.

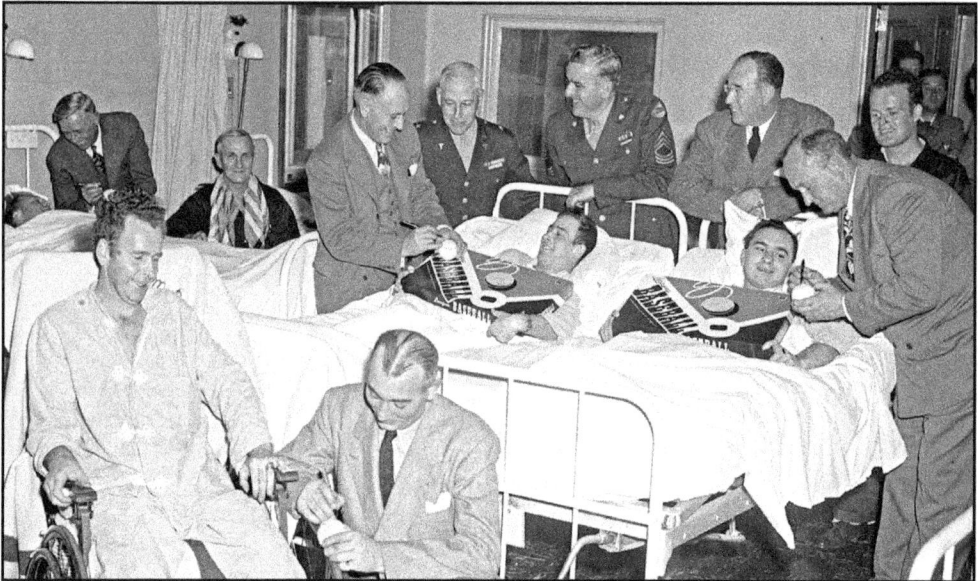

(a late addition) at Letterman General Hospital in San Francisco in January 1945: former major leaguers among the patients are Tony Lazzeri (low in front), Ossie Vitt (talking to the veteran in the bed in the back on the left), Walter Mails (an active sergeant in the state guard, with his back to the door), Lefty O'Doul (to Mails's right) and Cobb (leaning over on the right side). Sportswriter Alan Ward of the *Oakland Tribune* was on hand and said Vitt (also to the left), using various props, gave a witty demonstration of Cobb's infamous 1909 spiking of Philadelphia's Frank Baker; the spiking will be noted a few times later. Reporting on a dinner in Oakland in 1933, the *Tribune* conveyed part of Mails's remarks, as follows: "He said Ty Cobb drove him out of the majors by telling fans he had 'rabbit ears,' and told how he returned to make good by kidding Cobb and other stars whenever he fooled them at the plate."

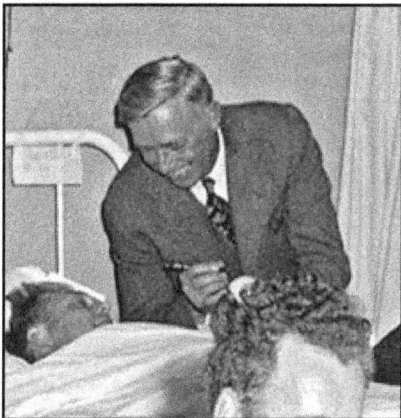

4. *Myths Versus Facts*

With apparently one exception, Leerhsen shied away from crediting prior Cobb authors for their particular refutations or their having made strides to refute key aspects of some of the more negative myths about Cobb. In one of his wrap-up chapters, he told the reader that he had engaged in a process of discovery: "When I started researching this book I believed, like a lot of people, that Ty Cobb was a wonderful ballplayer but a maniac, meaning a racist [he was a racist] and a mean, spikes-sharpening [he was] son of a bitch [mean is better; second cousin Harrison Gailey, his closest regular family companion late in life, told Harry Atkins of the AP in 1985 that even at that stage, Cobb 'was mean' at times]. This was not a professional opinion based on knowledge; it was an assumption based on stories I'd been hearing all my life." Shortly thereafter, he wrote of "investigating the matter myself."

Here is the only place where I found Leerhsen crediting a prior writer for debunking or making strides to debunk what he cast as a Cobb myth:

Regarding an unsubstantiated claim in Stump's 1994 book that Cobb had killed somebody in 1912, Leerhsen cited a legal expert's 1996 article in the *National Pastime*. The expert found no corroborating news report or processing of a corpse by the relevant authority, Wayne County, Mich. The expert, Doug Roberts, had been a prosecutor with expertise in crime investigations.

While Leerhsen admirably gave prominent general kudos to debunker William R. (Ron) Cobb, he was no more specific than in the following reference. In referring to behavior by Stump, he wrote, "The Jo Mosher [Stump's second wife] quote about Stump getting people to 'act up' (p. 386) appeared in William R. (Ron) Cobb's article 'The Georgia Peach: Stumped by the Storyteller,' which ran in the summer 2010 edition of *The National Pastime*, published by the Society for American Baseball Research; it has since been republished as a small book." As I detail further in an appendix, Leerhsen should have stated that the article is a searing indictment of Stump whose contours he followed.

To reflect how the discrediting of Stump had progressed before him, Leerhsen could have compared Bak's 1994 *Ty Cobb: His Tumultuous Life and Times* and his 2005 *Peach: Ty Cobb in his Time and Ours*; the 2005 one also is the lone and original source for highly incisive Mosher quotes about Stump. She died on March 18, 2017, at 97. Bak mentioned Stump in only favorable ways in his 1994 book; for example, the 1961 book and Stump's article later that year "reveal both sides of what Stump called a 'badly disturbed personality.'"

In a far more expansive treatment in his 2005 book, Bak referred to as "specious" a Stump explanation for why he went ahead with the 1961 article.

In addition, Bak referred to Stump's "penchant for consistently delivering wildly colorful anecdotes in his profiles of sports figures." In interviewing Mosher for his 2005 book, Bak quoted her as saying, "Al was not a character himself. He was quiet. But he loved oddballs. He'd encourage them to act up, to really be bad. He'd get good stories like that." Bak added to that, "One has to wonder if that methodology was in play during any of Stump's private moments with the ailing, unstable, and frequently disoriented Cobb."

Also in his 2005 book, Bak questioned some of Stump's details and cited criticism by Ted Williams about Stump's accuracy. Then Bak, presumably rehashing the following from Alexander's introduction to the 1993 University of Nebraska Press reprint of Cobb and Stump's 1961 book, wrote, "Stump disingenuously told his readers in his *True[: The Man's Magazine]* piece in 1961, 'During the final 10 months of his life I was his [Cobb's] constant companion.'"

Leerhsen implicitly conferred to himself too much credit for correcting the record on Cobb. At times as a result, he likely fooled most of his readers, by showing a disregard for the spirit of a rule of plagiarism. As explained by Purdue University's online writing lab, it is, "Give credit to previous researchers BUT Make your own significant contribution." One form of it is not explicitly crediting fellow authors, including when they clearly made strides on the author's themes. Noted only once by Leerhsen, for a quote about Cobb's youth, is Bak's 1994 one. And yet, the timing of Bak's book had allowed Bak to play the future Leerhsen: to refute aspects of the 1994 movie "Cobb." On top of that, playing that role likely led Bak to be critical of Stump in his 2005 book.

In examining Hornbaker's book, I did find a place where Hornbaker should have given credit. I was awed for months, thinking that he had unearthed Cobb's letters to the FBI in 1942 in which Cobb offered help with snuffing out espionage during World War II. Then I realized that 2008 Cobb Georgia-focused author Don Rhodes had extensively written on the same subject. Not only that, Rhodes was transparent as can be in writing, "These letters can be accessed through the Federal Bureau of Investigation's Web site, fbi.gov, using the Freedom of Information Privacy Act link on the home page that offers several letters of public officials and celebrities in the FBI's files."

Leerhsen's understated crediting of other authors smacks of being a hyper-competitive, Cobb-like trait. The following example struck me as audacious:

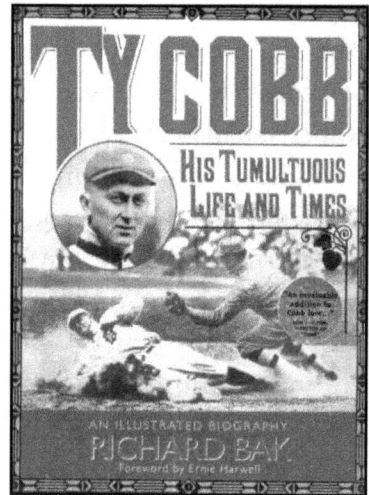

While his endnotes credited Fricks for obtaining the coroner's report on the death of Ty's father, dated August 9, 1905, that was where his praise ended. In William R. Cobb's 2010 article, one can find Cobb, after crediting Fricks, writing that "the arrest warrant for Amanda Cobb [Ty's mother], states clearly and unequivocally that a pistol was used by Amanda Cobb and that the death of W. H. Cobb [Ty's father] resulted from a pistol bullet."

Possibly looking for a way to get in on the action, Leerhsen tossed writer Cobb aside and took center stage by writing, "And how come, as the coroner's report showed, he had a pistol and a rock in the pockets of his suit jacket?"

Cobb had written in his article, "Having proved the shotgun story false, my investigation turned to an interesting and obvious question: what is the origin of this sensational and widely believed story that Ty Cobb's mother killed his father with a shotgun? I completed a thorough review of the biographical literature on Ty Cobb, in a search for the answer." Cobb proceeded to trace the tale through a range of books and articles.

Considering the impressiveness of Cobb's article, Leerhsen should have written something like the following, albeit in shorter sentences. In a 2011 dissertation that can be found online, University of Illinois graduate student Travis Wayne Stern wrote, "Evidence has recently been presented by William R. Cobb's article, 'The Georgia Peach: Stumped by the Storyteller' that investigation into Al Stump's famous article 'Ty Cobb's Wild, 10-Month Fight to Live' printed in *True: The Man's Magazine* in 1961, as well as the expansion of that article into Stump's subsequent *Cobb: A Biography* (1994) [the 1996 version of the book had that title], has shown that some information cannot be corroborated, and that Stump may have embellished or even fabricated several stories in order to sell memorabilia. As a result information that seems to have originated solely from Stump's work has been largely omitted here unless it could be verified with other sources."

in a 1985 magazine-length article of his in the *Los Angeles Times*, "The Last Days of Ty Cobb," Stump said that the 1961 article won the AP best sports story of the year award. The claim also appeared in an advertisement in the *Times* that teased the *Times* article. Director of AP Corporate Archives Valerie Komor, when asked to track down the claim, informed me that she found no evidence that the AP bestowed such an award on Stump. A plausible explanation is that Stump made the AP award reference in place of a different superlative: the 1961 article's having been included in the anthology *Best Sports Stories 1962* published by E. P. Dutton. Meanwhile, an error in the anthology as late as 1959, that Stump graduated from the University of Washington, was corrected in the 1960 edition to read that he "got his education" there.

In his main text, Hornbaker wrote, "In 2010, William R. Cobb (no relation to Ty) [sic] [actually he is a distant cousin] presented a separate dissection of Stump in his article, 'The Georgia Peach: Stumped by the Storyteller,' featured in the 2010 edition of *The National Pastime*. He too called attention to unverifiable statements in the *True* magazine story, and questioned the validity of a shotgun Stump said was used in the murder of Ty's father by his mother in 1905. In his thorough evaluation of the facts, Cobb outlined a number of instances in which memorabilia Stump tried to sell was proven forged, including numerous letters and signed baseballs. There was a Cobb diary as well and, after FBI analysis, was deemed a fake."

Also, Leerhsen, without giving credit to author Cobb, repeated details or followed up ones from his article in a sleuth-like tone. The effect was to make it possible for a casual reader to think that Leerhsen did all of the legwork on the following: analyzing Stump's handling of memorabilia; locating a favorable-to-Ty-Cobb eyewitness who Leigh Montville of *Sports Illustrated* interviewed in 1992; engaging memorabilia expert Ronald B. Keurajian; and extracting detail from public remarks uttered by the 1994 director of "Cobb," Ron Shelton.

Illustrating my point is a 2016 review on HaveChanged.blogspot.com. A reviewer wrote, "Leerhsen interviews someone who was a medical student at the time of Cobb's last hospitalization at Emory [University] Hospital in Atlanta." It was Montville who had conducted the groundbreaking interview with the medical student, Rex Teeslink.

Not only that, but I can challenge, in every respect, the way that Leerhsen presented his addition to Montville's 1992 interview. Leerhsen did quote Teeslink's statement to Montville that he had spent 24 hours a day with him from May 18 to July 17, 1961, the date of Cobb's death. Teeslink was with Cobb in his home and during hospital stays. But May 18 is an error because on May 22, Cobb dictated a letter to Teeslink in response to one of his; it was also on May 22 that, while hospitalized, Cobb signed his will.

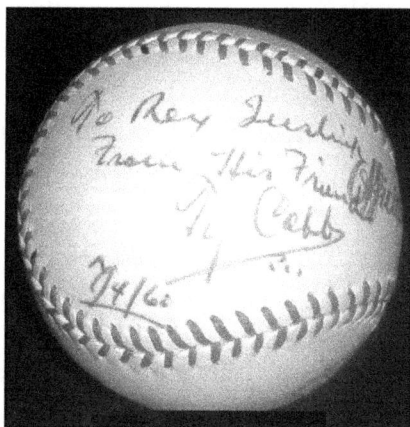

Without giving Montville credit for extracting the following points from Teeslink, Leerhsen wrote, "'He [Cobb] was a real redhead with a hair-trigger temper,' Teeslink told me when I interviewed him in 2012. It's not that Cobb was mean, exactly, he said; he just couldn't tolerate incompetence, or as Teeslink called it, 'the lack of that drive for excellence that was so much a part of the

Cobb philosophy. He was an unusual man with a keen mind and yet he could never put up with people who didn't, like him, strive to excel.'"

Teeslink had told Montville that Cobb "had zero patience and hair-trigger temper. He always set a high standard for himself, and when he felt someone else wasn't measuring up, there was trouble." Teeslink also had told Montville that he had met Cobb previously and that he was apparently among several nurses who Cobb tried and let go. As a reason for why they clicked, Teeslink said it could have been, "I liked baseball a lot and I respected him. He had [in their previous stint together] asked me to help him answer some mail, but now he asked me to stay with him for the summer."

Montville also wrote that at one point, Cobb asked Teeslink to drive him about 20 miles to Royston, his adopted hometown. During the trip, on back roads, Cobb pointed out sights along the way, including "the gas station that now occupied the spot where his boyhood home had been. But none of this was the reason for the trip. The ultimate destination was the [family] mausoleum" at Rose Hill Cemetery in Royston. Cobb showed Teeslink where his mom, dad and sister were buried. Cobb also told him that after he died, Teeslink should signal his visits by knocking six times.

Leerhsen conveyed some of the above detail, with special emphasis on the knocking six times – immediately after a paragraph in which he had quoted his own interview with Teeslink on a different manner. He never returned to mentioning Montville. To those who lack a handy copy of the *Sports Illustrated* of October 27, 1992, Leerhsen again can be construed as soaking up Montville's credit. The knock-six-times paragraph was not just any paragraph in Leerhsen's book: with it, the main text concluded. The book's epilogue followed.

Some crumbs of Montville's interview that Leerhsen did not cite or borrow in any manner are pretty good too. Here goes:

"Cobb asked one night if Teeslink thought he was addicted to the pain medications the doctors were giving him. Teeslink said no, knowing that Cobb was the type who would never let himself become dependent on anyone or anything. Cobb said there should be a test. Full of pain, he refused the narcotics for 36 hours. Was that proof? Would an addicted man be able to stay away from his drug for a day and a half? No, sir."

Secondly, in his own words, Montville wrote, "Cobb would sleep only three hours a night" in the last two months of his life, thus "wringing out the maximum waking time from each day. Teeslink was with him. They talked endlessly." (As a player, Cobb had averaged eight to nine hours of sleep as of 1915. Undoubtedly in the last months of his life, Cobb would have preferred to have slept a lot more, since he would not have been in so much pain. In a 1924 feature in *Liberty* magazine, he said he was getting at least eight hours a night and, during the day, lying down between a half-hour and more than an hour.)

Thirdly, Cobb did not want Teeslink to convey his thoughts to reporters. Teeslink told Montville that he now felt it was important to help set the record straight in light of untrue portrayals. One can speculate why Montville's eliciting of that did not make the cut for appearance in Leerhsen's book.

Hornbaker mentioned Montville's 1992 interview briefly, in a quickly hedged manner, as follows: After noting Teeslink's observation of Cobb's having had a "hair-trigger temper," Hornbaker quoted Teeslink's wanting to let the public know that Cobb "was a fair and meaningful guy."

As noted above, Montville deserves credit for the last paragraph in Leerhsen's main text. Leerhsen's next-to-last paragraph was fine in stating that Cobb "could be a difficult patient, but he wasn't a psychiatric patient [as implied by Stump]." But in his next sentence, Leerhsen left out credit to a similar 2010 refutation by William R. Cobb in asserting, "He didn't have a gun in his hospital room or a fortune in cash and securities on his nightstand, as Stump would say [claim] in his *True* article a few months hence. 'Those things are just lies,' Teeslink told me. 'I was there, Stump wasn't. He wanted to portray Ty in a certain way, and so that's what he did. It wasn't about the truth; it was about Stump.'"

Much later in this book, San Diego will figure in the flukiest important story that mine brings to light; it has something to do with Cobb's racism. In the mythical category for a new award I can suggest, titled "The Pro-Stump, Eat-Crow Leerhsen Whammy," San Diego figures once again. The person for whom San Diego's baseball stadium is named, when he was sports editor of the *San Diego Union*, wrote the following upon Cobb's death:

"Yesterday came word that Tyrus Raymond Cobb, the incomparable ballplayer, had succumbed to cancer at Emory [University] Hospital in Atlanta. Cobb was 74 and he had retired as a player in the distant year of 1928; yet the memory of this remarkable man was as vivid as the sun dappling the water of San Diego Bay.

"I learned of Cobb's death while attending a small, informal luncheon honoring [John George] J. G. Taylor Spink, publisher of the baseball trade paper, 'The Sporting News.' Several of those at the table, including Spink, had known Cobb as a friend [and a great one at that] and one, Hollis ['Sloppy'] Thurston, had played against him."

The sports editor, Jack Murphy, then printed five

Jack Murphy

paragraphs that featured Thurston's recollections of pitching against Cobb, especially in 1927. For example, "'Nobody ever threw at Cobb,' said Thurston, 'they didn't dare.'" Fortunately, Murphy quoted Spink as well, and left the final paragraph to him.

"'He was the damndest fellow,' said Spink. 'A week ago he was lying in that hospital – waiting to die and knowing it was coming – and he had a million dollars worth of securities beside his bed. On top of the piles of securities was a pistol. I don't know how he got that stuff into the hospital, but he did.'"

Along the same lines, in 1965, Knight Newspapers Washington bureau chief Edwin A. Lahey, in predicting a future book-length biography of President Lyndon B. Johnson, would write that Johnson "has probably never really belonged to anybody in his life. You meet lots of people like this as you go through life, people who live and die in secret. You recall the piteous deathbed story from Atlanta about Ty Cobb, one of the all-time greats of organized baseball. When Ty Cobb's number finally went up, he put all his stocks and bonds on his bedside table in the hospital. Then he placed a revolver on top of the pile of securities. And with this sense of 'security,' the man died."

Lahey added, "It may be stretching things to equate President Johnson's 'aloneness' with Ty Cobb's deathbed scene, but the threat in both instances comes from the dreadfully cynical attitude of the world's loners – 'who needs people?'"

On this matter, independent sources on the same day in 1961 counter Leerhsen: Spink and, to be noted later, former *Atlanta Constitution* executive editor Ralph McGill. Stump's 1994 book echoes some of McGill's reporting on securities and a gun, although, unlike McGill, Stump did not explicitly explain the gun's fate. Stump wrote, "The black gun made his nurses nervous, and Dr. [Hugh] Wood [of Emory University Hospital] persuaded him to store the documents [Stump did not say anything about the gun] in a hospital safe."

In addition to Spink and McGill, close Cobb friend Dr. Brown wrote to Spink in 1961, "Without a doubt, the fact that Mr. Cobb displayed this gun his last few months was a result of a complication of his cancerous condition."

Another dear friend of Cobb's, George H. Maines, will be featured later. Alexander made great use of a 1961 letter that Maines wrote three weeks after Cobb's death. Maines and his wife spent a week with Cobb at his Nevada home in late 1959. Alexander did omit these two Maines observations from that visit: "I noticed he had a loaded pistol on a stand at the head of his bed. Later I learned that he had thousands of dollars in dividend checks, and some valuable stock certificates in the stand." Citing Stump, Alexander wrote that Cobb had a gun and securities in the hospital. Hornbaker avoided the subject.

Reassessing Leerhsen

If Stump is Cobb's worst dream, Leerhsen is Cobb's best one. The truth is no doubt closer to Leerhsen, but Leerhsen assumed too much on the pro-Cobb side of some key issues. Overall, Leerhsen was too negatively one-sided on Stump and positively one-sided on Cobb. On racism, Hornbaker out-researched Leerhsen (and Fricks) in several respects.

In examining a wide range of reviews of Leerhsen's book, I found critics taking issue with his argumentation, but fewer, such as Allen Barra, reserving judgment about his level of research. For example, none challenged his statement, "Cobb himself left very little evidence of his feelings on the issue [of race] prior to the advent of Jackie Robinson." More understandably, none was presumably aware of Leerhsen's rewording of so many quotations.

Leerhsen coupled a defense lawyer style at times with not being transparent about the extent of his research relative to Fricks's 40,000 articles, and his analysis relative to Fricks, who he said "vetted" his manuscript. In the following respect, Leerhsen was transparent about his relationship with Fricks – when it advanced his theme of casting himself as a dexterous, all-around rebutter of Cobb myths. Here is how he achieved that. Instead of merely stating that he approached Fricks, who he acknowledged as a great collector of Cobb articles and documents, and that he impressed Fricks with the seriousness of his interest, Leerhsen said he impressed Fricks by being "open to questioning the myths." On page 103, I quote a 2008 Fricks article in which Fricks stated that he had already figured out that each of Cobb's altercations with possible racial overtones can be chalked up to a reason unrelated to racism. Leerhsen's book challenged each such altercation as unprovable in some way. In none of the instances did Leerhsen give credit to Fricks, nor did he give Fricks general credit on that subject.

Leerhsen's book can now be used to treat the public to a civics lesson – possibly by avid public speaker Leerhsen himself – that a book taking the reader on a valid journey can also be a runaway train.

Hidden Treasures of the Spink

As it also turns out, several of Cobb's letters to Spink were specially preserved by the *Sporting News*. Both Leerhsen and Hornbaker missed them in reasonably plain sight. While some of Cobb's other letters to Spink were indeed printed in the magazine, for example, a 1950 one about the state of current play, the specially preserved ones may have been hardly quoted even in part. One that has is by a biographer of fellow Hall of Famer Frank Baker. I learned about Cobb's personal letters to Spink from a major baseball research source: *Baseball:*

A Comprehensive Bibliography: Supplement 2 (1992 Through 1997) by Myron J. Smith in 1998. Entry 3521 is "Selection of Letters Between Ty Cobb and Taylor Spink, 1941-1958." The entry contains a link on the *Sporting News's* Web site, http://www.thesportingnews.com/archives/ty. The link is now dead.

J. G. Taylor Spink

But one can plug it into the Internet Archive's Wayback Machine Web site and see at least transcriptions of the letters, plus an original copy of one of the originals.

As a taste of the high regard with which Cobb held Spink, Cobb wrote in a 1953 letter to Harry G. Salsinger of the *Detroit News*, "there is nothing I would not do for this guy." The context for that was Spink's suggestion, which did not come to fruition if Cobb pursued it, that Salsinger and he collaborate on a book-length biography about him. Salsinger was then 68 years old.

As a second taste of the high regard with which Cobb held Spink, Maines wrote the following in his 1961 letter: As of the end of 1959, "it was not generally known that Cobb was real sick. We had kept Taylor Spink of The Sporting News informed, but didn't want it generally known, fearing the truth about his condition might leak out."

Cobb and one of his bird dogs on a quail hunt in 1929 at Louisville, Ga.

Cobb, widow Eleanor Gehrig and Paul Gallico in August 1941, at the DiMaggio family restaurant, Joe DiMaggio's Grotto, to mark the upcoming movie "The Pride of the Yankees," based on Gallico's 1941 biography of the late Lou Gehrig. On the phone is either DiMaggio or Yankee manager Joe McCarthy. Newspaper syndicate owner Christy Walsh, in later putting Cobb on the line, said he was introducing McCarthy to a "Peninsula [Atherton being on the San Francisco peninsula] golfer." According to the *San Francisco Chronicle*, McCarthy didn't get the humor and said, "Who is this? Cobb? Oh, TY Cobb. Well, why didn't they say so? How're you, you old boy!" In 1948, Salsinger of the *Detroit News* would report one of the "most embarrassing moments in McCarthy's life." At the 1947 World Series, "McCarthy shook hand[s] with Ty Cobb in the Yankee office. Ty's face was somewhat familiar but Joe could not place him. Cobb let him fidget uncomfortably for a minute or so, then said: 'I remember YOUR name Mr. McCarthy.'"

5. *Back From Cobb's Last Years*

In weighing in on the reliability of the Stump-Cobb 1961 book, University of Illinois graduate student Stern was more accurate than Society for American Baseball Research award winner Leerhsen. Even though his dissertation had little to do with Cobb, Stern wrote that the book is indeed useful factually, but mainly for what can be corroborated from it. Based on my analysis of how Hornbaker used it, it is pro-Cobb and thus, as Alexander wrote, it is "self-serving and self-justifying." The one genre of erroneous story that I have noticed in it is stories from prior authors that Stump may have blended in. Later on, I analyze such a story, whose originator may be Grantland Rice.

Leerhsen dismissed the 1961 book as "highly fictionalized" and a work of "hackwork and half-truths. The only things coauthor Al Stump explored deeply were Cobb's reserves of Scotch and bourbon."

Leerhsen deemed it flawed for some of its wording. So, one workaround is not to quote it directly, which was generally Hornbaker's practice. Another, which Hornbaker tended also to do, is to use it where the detail either does not undermine the contemporaneous record or gives a sense of Cobb's point of view. About the book, Alexander had observed, "Factual mistakes abounded, as did distortions and half-truths." Still, overall, Alexander wrote, "The basic Ty Cobb – sensitive, distrustful, courageous, often arrogant, and sometimes mean – came through clearly." In a review in the *Boston Globe*, sportswriter Harold Kaese described errors in Cobb's recollection of some baseball incidents.

Leerhsen's singling out of Stump as mucking up the book seems trumped up, given that Cobb wrote to longtime financial advisor Hauck in 1957, "My memory as you know faulty," and since Leerhsen himself observed that the book contains "no dirt in it, no bombshells." As an example of its treading lightly, I note 14 pages from now its treatment of nemesis Horace Fogel. Also, as Hornbaker conveyed, close Cobb friend Dr. Brown wrote to Spink that Cobb's "multiple diseases were making him lose his finer grades of discrimination, memory, concentration, insight, equilibrium and such." But of all the stories that can be told about the 1961 book, I surely found the hands-down best:

Maury Wills, whose 104 thefts broke Cobb's single-season steals record of 96, told Ira Berkow of the NEA that a sportswriter gave him Cobb's book in 1962, the year he broke the record. "I still read it for inspiration," Wills said. He had it with him in spring training in 1969 when he told Berkow, "Cobb and I were alike in many ways. Funny thing, his theories on basestealing are exactly like mine. And I arrived at them independently, before having read the book. Another funny thing, it was the first book I think I ever read through."

So, Cobb can be said to have done his part, with his 1961 book, to advance black literacy, even if whites like Leerhsen have no use for it.

In his negative assessment, Leerhsen may have been influenced by being told of two letters of complaint that Cobb (allegedly) dictated or asked to be written on his behalf to Doubleday. Despite having a lot of unused white space in his endnotes, he did not state how he learned of those (alleged) letters, which he wrote were written by Cobb relative Theresa Gailey. Leerhsen's lack of clarity on such a thinly documented, anti-Stump point should have raised red flags with whoever edited his book, because of Leerhsen's visceral hate for Stump. On the pro-Stump side, Cobb wrote to financial advisor Hauck on January 26, 1961, "<u>Book</u> <u>coming</u> <u>great</u>[;] only 2 chapters to go – I like it also others" [presumably meaning others like it too][.]

Another example of Leerhsen's lack of credibility on this subject is that he states, "The fact that Al Stump, his ghostwriter, featured the period [of hazing by teammates] prominently (and inaccurately) in chapter one of his autobiography is a key reason Cobb was preparing to sue to stop publication of the book when he died in July of 1961." Other than pointing out some odd word choice, Leerhsen did not touch on what was erroneous in the hazing verbiage of the book or manuscript, and how he learned or gleaned that.

I can make additions here to the chronology of the evolution of Cobb and Stump's book; other additions, including some more notable, will appear later.

In 1955, when syndicated columnist Leonard Lyons asked if he planned to write a book that would become a movie, he said, "No movie." He added, "A book? Maybe. Just to correct some errors, some misconceptions. I was hurt, often, but nobody knew it. The trouble is, if I wrote it that way, people might say I was trying to alibi." He said that he had no alibis and that "I was in a competitive sport, and I played it to win." (After telling a Cobb story in 1960, 1924-to-1926 teammate Frank O'Rourke added, "There was one thing Cobb wouldn't stand for, though" when things went wrong. "That was an alibi.")

In 1956, Jim Scott of the *Los Angeles Times* wrote, "A. S. Barnes was about to come out with Ty Cobb's autobiography when the old Peach changed his mind. Said he'd sue if the book were issued. So Ty's ghost (Johnny McCallum) came to life to redo the tome in the third person, and come out it will as Ty's biography." Barnes indeed later that year released McCallum's *The Tiger Wore Spikes: An Informal Biography of Ty Cobb*.

Scott's summary does not square with a page of a Cobb letter that I saw from apparently 1956. On the page,

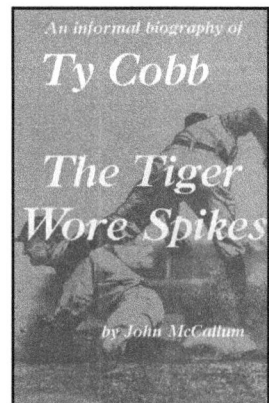

with reference to McCallum's planned book, Cobb wrote, "this book has not my cooperation nor my OK. As a real correcting of the record as to facts & truth, this man McCallum came out here for A. S. Barnes & Co.[,] wanted to do a book[,] etc.[,] was here for several days, I refused to enter any contract, but in his trying to sell me an idea, talks, fawning etc.[,] he secured from me some material, I would not consent, he went back with what he learned also all talks was [sic] confidential and off the record, he went into files and plagiarized, and they brought out a book, these people use very bad tactics as you know, on the cover, 'An Informed Biography of Ty Cobb, The Tiger wore spikes, By John McCallum,['] the two letter word, by, makes it impossible for me to proceed against them, I think this book firm had some trouble with Jack Dempsey also Ben Hogan (golf). Any fee I received would have gone to a Charity Educational Fund I has [sic], and has been that for all fees for 5 years, I receive nothing."

In a 1972 feature, sports columnist Don Duncan of the *Seattle Times* paraphrased McCallum as having told him that Cobb, after reading proofs, had threatened a million-dollar lawsuit. Duncan also stated, without giving the contexts, that "Cobb threw knives at McCallum" and that Cobb "threatened to shoot him with a German Luger he always carried."

By the way, the Cobb letter above marginally improves Stump's credibility: Cobb is confirming in it that he refers to his baseball material as "files." Stump would use that term, by my count, twice in his 1994 book.

Also incidentally, while professing to avoid Stump's 1994 book, Leerhsen, in

at Toots Shor's in 1951: Cobb chum, fellow golfing aficionado and former teammate Mickey Cochrane is having the best time. Cobb is in the front left in the picture at the bottom.

stringing together Joe DiMaggio stories, unwittingly relied on it for the following one. According to Stump's book, journalist-popular author Damon Runyon, Sr., in an excerpt from his memoir in the *New York American* (then the *New York Journal-American*) told of a night at Toots Shor's, a popular-with-athletes restaurant in New York City. One night, Cobb showed up at the same time as about a dozen other Hall of Famers, and "what does Joe DiMaggio softly say but, 'Here comes God.' And everybody there nods his head."

Leerhsen wrote the following in his book: DiMaggio "revered Cobb, both as a great hitter and, like him, [was] an artist of aloofness. [More about Cobb's informal advice to the San Francisco native will appear much later.] One night in the 1950s, when Cobb strolled into Toots Shor's, Joe, at the bar, turned to his drinking buddies and said, with no sarcasm, 'Here comes God.'"

One problem is that Runyon died in 1946. Another is that Runyon never wrote book memoirs. His journalist son, Damon Runyon, Jr., did write memoirs for Random House in 1953, but that book hardly mentioned baseball.

Although it may not rise to the severity of the Cobb-as-victimized-by-Stump theme, a Leerhsen favorite, I can claim to be the first Cobb author to be airing a young Prentice-Hall editor-as-allegedly victimized-by-Cobb one. Here goes:

Robert Edward Auctions, a premier U.S. sports auction house, wrote up the following still-Internet accessible description of one of its sale items in 2012:

"In 1959, Ty Cobb, who was in failing health and dealing with the ever-pressing issue of his own mortality, decided that the time was right to finally tell his side of the story regarding his life in baseball. With that goal in mind, he began negotiating with two publishing houses for the rights to his autobiography. In typical Cobb fashion, however, he kept his negotiations with each of the two publishing houses secret, never letting either of them know that they were in competition. This archive of letters and correspondence chronicles the negotiations between Cobb and one of his literary suitors, John Evangelist Walsh, an editor with New York publisher Prentice-Hall. When Walsh originally sold this collection of material, he included a one-page signed letter to help put the archive in its proper historical context, and also to offer his own personal assessment of Cobb's underhanded dealings throughout the entire process. In part[, he wrote]:

"When Ty Cobb died in the summer of 1961 he took with him my blessing. I say this even though the year before he died I became probably the last victim of his old-time slashing tactics. Publishers for years had been trying to sign Cobb for his autobiography but without success. The personal story of his twenty-three [24] years in [major league] baseball was certain to be a big seller. The trouble was that during his thirty-two [31] years of retirement he had refused all offers. When, late in 1959 as a young editor with a New York publisher (Prentice-Hall), I was given the chance to discuss it with him, [by] drinking with him, listening to his endless talk on every conceivable subject, and following him to his hospital bed in Georgia, the withered old Peach neatly spiked me and sent me bloody from the field while he romped on toward home. It turned out I was not the only editor he was talking with about his autobiography.

"Also active in the negotiations was an editor from Doubleday, though neither of us knew about the other's involvement. Cobb saw to that. . . Late in the afternoon, believing I was at last to get the great Cobb's signature, I was taken back to his hospital room. His advisors standing round, he sat up in bed and in a quiet but strangely belligerent tone informed me that he was refusing my offer. 'I'm not going to sign with you,' he announced with a touch of triumph in his eyes that puzzled me. He didn't say much more, didn't explain, and refused further discussion. I departed within a few minutes feeling crushed. It was weeks later that I first heard about the Doubleday offer. . . My Life in Baseball – The True Story, written with leading sportswriter Al Stump, and with a foreword by Gen. Douglas MacArthur, appeared some ten months [actually two months] after Cobb's death. It was a good book, and I felt glad that fate had allowed Cobb to complete it. But for the young and hopeful editor that I was then, the whole incident stayed with me for a long time as a rather brutal experience."

marking the publication of John Evangelist Walsh's Random House book *The Shroud* in 1963 (from left to right in the Waldorf Astoria Hotel): senior editor Paul K. Lapolla (partially showing); Walsh (autographing); Holy Shroud Guild co-founder the Rev. Adam J. Otterbein; Umberto II, briefly the last King of Italy (his father was 1900-to-1946 King Victor Emmanuel III); Holy Shroud Guild co-founder the Rev. Peter M. Rinaldi; and Random House publisher and co-founder Bennett Cerf. Doubleday, the publisher of Cobb and Stump's 1961 book, was and still is a sister imprint of Random House under the same publishing company.

When Walsh died in 2015 at age 87, Sam Roberts of the *New York Times* stated that he had written more than two dozen books, "on subjects as diverse as Abraham Lincoln's first girlfriend, the Shroud of Turin and Piltdown Man, as well as literary biographies of John Keats, Edgar Allan Poe and Robert Frost."

Roberts added soon after, "But his most widely read book was undoubtedly the Reader's Digest Bible," a condensation of the original.

In assessing the resulting Doubleday book, Leerhsen gave examples of some of its errors. He cited ones in proper names and players' fielder positions, and in Cobb's baseball wisdom.

Leerhsen also pointed out a strange phrase in the book, about not having held a grudge against fellow players "except when they decided to play beanbag with my slender 168-pound body." Slender, by the way, as a self-descriptor appeared in a gag quote attributed to him in 1911, to be noted on page 166.

In two instances, Leerhsen did accept Stump's 1961 book with Cobb as accurate, and without explaining why he was doing so (on his pages 39 and 45). Sandwiched between them, on his page 41, Leerhsen termed the 1961 book "only slightly reliable." He was more consistent on not using the 1994 book, by making just one declared exception to not borrowing from it. Although he could not confirm that particular story, Leerhsen in printing it observed that "it was indeed the *kind* of thing the young Cobb might do to amuse himself and onlookers." (The flawed Cobb-DiMaggio story noted earlier is a second story that he used from the 1994 book, but in that case presumably unwittingly.)

Hornbaker, by contrast, used the 1961 book 66 times by my count. About one-third of Hornbaker's uses were for stories prior to Cobb's big-league career. Of that roughly one-third, at least several had been previously told with variations by Cobb or sportswriters. The remaining two-thirds of the references relate to activity during his major league career, including the state of his health. Of the 66 references, 14 involve controversy in his relations with other people. Hornbaker did not place greater credibility on the 1961 book's explanations relative to what was reported contemporaneously; he mainly used such explanations to fill in gaps.

The only use that Hornbaker made of the 1961 book that I found hard to defend — and it is minor — is his repeating the term "black-hater" from it. It was in reference to what one of Cobb's black combatants accused him of being in 1908. Hornbaker inserted the term into his in the context of Cobb having disavowed having been one. A better use would be to have paraphrased that in the main text and included, for the record, "black-hater" in the endnotes. At the time of the 1908 incident, Cobb had been quoted as saying, "I'm going to go to court about that negro affair." In a 1916 letter to hunting dog breeder Fred Hall, Cobb wrote, "Negro claims he can show 50 coveys of birds on big place." As I cite elsewhere, Cobb also used the word "colored."

The Cobb-Stump book seems to have been, in the instances that Hornbaker cited it, an accurate-sounding reflection of how Cobb recalled or felt about his life close to the time of his death. If anything, the book comes across, overall, as only mildly contradicting his prior writings and quoted thoughts.

Razor Sharpness

Other than weakening the case that Cobb was a violent racist (while missing his playing of African Dodger), Leerhsen did not do much myth-correcting of note. While making valid points about assumptions parading as facts that Cobb was a racist, he assumed too much about Fricks's and his accounting of the record. If you add in the book's technical flaws, it may be the most overrated baseball book proximate to the current golden age of "fake news." Add to that the widespread snubbing of Hornbaker's better-hedged one.

A myth that Leerhsen detailed as if he had refuted it, but with some key argumentation that tracks prior refutations made by Alexander and Bak, is that Cobb filed his spikes. "Cobb didn't sharpen his spikes," Leerhsen wrote. For his part, Hornbaker cited just one source, to undermine the "rotten tales" about Cobb's sharpening of his spikes "to achieve better results in slashing rivals on the basepaths." *Times* senior staff editor John Williams, in reviewing Leerhsen's book, said Leerhsen's "correctives are convincing," particularly "against two of the more serious and persistent criticisms of Cobb." One of the two was on Cobb's racism; at least that one, as I show, merely has major holes. The other, Williams claimed, was about Cobb having "purposely endangered opponents by filing his shoe's spikes to an extra-fine point before flying around the bases."

One of seven sources that I unearthed on his sharpening of spikes is Detroit native-turned-big leaguer and later Dodgers coach Greg Mulleavy. In 1960, Mulleavy told sports reporter Frank Finch of the *Los Angeles Times*, "As a high school boy [in the early 1920s], I was asked to work out with the Tigers one day, and I actually saw Cobb sharpening his spikes before the game. At [Detroit's] Navin Field, the visiting players had to come through the Tiger dugout to get onto the field, and Ty sat there at the head of the stairs and filed his spikes while they walked by. It must have been pretty terrifying for those guys."

The second source is Charles "Charley" Gehringer, a brief 1924-25 and full 1926 teammate and future Hall of Famer. In 1985, Gehringer told sports reporter Mark Kram of the *Detroit Free Press*, "Cobb put the fear of God in you." Immediately after that, Kram paraphrased him as saying "it was really true that Cobb sharpened his spikes with a file." In Bak's one-on-one interview book, the 1991 *Cobb Would Have Caught It: The Golden Age of Baseball in Detroit*, Gehringer closely tracked what Mulleavy had said in 1960. When passing Cobb while he was sharpening, the eyes of rookies on other teams "would bulge out a little." Despite playing fewer games, a reference to 1926, "he'd still cut you to pieces if you got in his way, and they all realized that." Stump in his book quoted Gehringer to a similar effect, but to presumably add drama referred to a 1946 article, as follows. When asked what he should do with it, Stump said Cobb told him, "Flush it down the crapper!"

Meanwhile, in his own 1994 book, Bak did not account for his Gehringer interview in his 1991 one and instead generalized about "the spike filing fiction."

The third source is 1912-18 teammate Ossie Vitt, a later-in-life chatty chum of his. Vitt, as manager of the Newark Bears of the International League in 1936, had just seen his first big-league game in 15 years. He told the AP that his impression was that the players "don't fight so hard" as they did in his day. "When I played, the pitchers used to dust off every hitter. We used to threaten every enemy batter from the field and every player from the bench. I'll never forget how Ty Cobb used to sit on the bench, file his spikes,

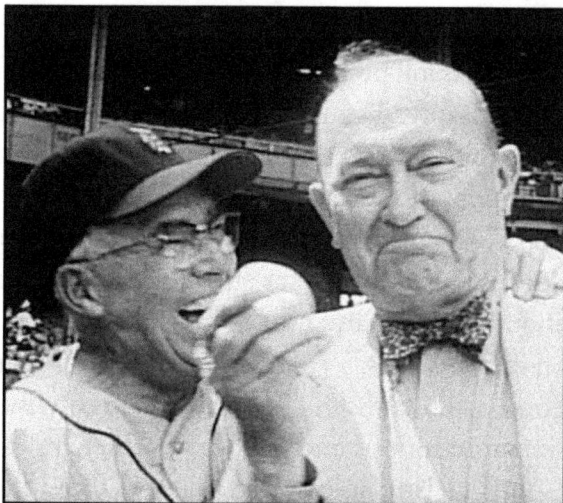

Ossie Vitt and Cobb at Yankee Stadium in 1957

and shout: 'I'll get you in the third inning!' to some infielder."

The fourth source is Red Ormsby, an American League umpire in Cobb's last six seasons. In Salina, Kan., in 1954, at a banquet of the city's Knife and Fork Club, Ormsby reportedly kept the audience interested and laughing for well over an hour. He called Cobb a "rough and tough man, the greatest player ever to live." He also declared that Cobb "did file his spikes."

The fifth source, 1919-22 Detroit batboy Eddie Forester and half-century Tigers employee, did not clarify the location of Cobb's spike sharpening. In a 1990 interview with ESPN, as paraphrased by Michael Betzold of the *Detroit Free Press* in his 1991 obituary of him, "Mr. Forester said Cobb sharpened his spikes every day on a wheel used by the [presumably Navin Field] ground crew."

The sixth source is Joe Judge, a regular American League first baseman in Cobb's final 13 seasons. In 1947, at the University Club in Washington, D.C., as conveyed by sports reporter Burton Hawkins of the *Washington Star*, he called Cobb "the meanest man who ever pulled on [sic] a baseball uniform." Judge explained, "We hadn't spoken for 25 years" until recently, when Cobb made up with him. "It all came about over a rather small thing. Cobb loved to pass our [the Washington] dugout, show his spikes and say, 'They're sharp today, boys, so look out.' Well, one day he was sharpening his spikes near our dugout and I got sore and said, 'Who are you trying to scare?' That's all, but that was it.

"From then on he tried to kill me but, of course, he tried to cut everybody who ever played against him. He'd slide a yard inside of first base to try to spike me deliberately, but when Cobb was sliding Mr. Judge was taking those throws on the far side of the bag. He never nicked me."

The seventh source is ex-big leaguer Walter H. Nagle, who was both a half-century-long friend of his and a longtime county clerk of Sonoma County, Calif. Upon Cobb's death, he told the *Press Democrat* in Santa Rosa, Calif, "I asked him once, 'Do you really sharpen your spikes?' and he said, 'I sure as hell do. They can say I'm dirty, but I'm entitled to the baseline.'"

I also found Cobb telling the NEA in 1952 that it was "partly" true that he sat in the Detroit dugout and sharpened his spikes: "It started as a gag against the Yankees. We figured it might intimidate some of the younger players."

Leerhsen wrote of Cobb's "profound sadness" at falsehoods about him that had gained currency; for example, "his sharpening his spikes and insanely sliding into rival infielders." Leerhsen did tell about a play in which Cobb was ejected for spiking Washington rookie third baseman Ossie Bluege; his source was Bluege's comments in Donald Honig's 1977 *The Man in the Dugout*. Those comments closely track a 1943 Bluege interview with Tommy Devine of the United Press. Leerhsen added the caveat, "Cobb's spikings almost always came in the course of a larger and more philosophical dispute over right-of-way."

In 1951, sports columnist Will Connolly of the *San Francisco Chronicle* was at a luncheon where player-turned-longtime-umpire Babe Pinelli engaged Cobb on the subject. Pinelli, a 1920 teammate, plus a lifelong Californian and an amateur golfing rival, listened as Cobb groused about a new rule that prohibits a base runner from coming in "high" to break up a possible double play.

"'In my day, we didn't need any laws to protect the infielders. They took care of that little matter themselves. If a runner came in high[,] the first time, he was warned. If he did it the second time[,] he got the ball right here.' And Ty pointed to a spot between his eyes."

Babe Pinelli (gesticulating)
to Cobb in 1951.
Columnist Will Connolly is
directly behind them.

Pinelli responded by observing "that as he remembered, Ty used to come in with his spikes flying." As paraphrased by Connolly, Cobb replied, "Yes, but he didn't chase the SS or 2B all over the lot" and that he observed the base line. Then Connolly quoted Cobb as saying, "I deliberately spiked only two men in my career and they had it coming. The other cuttings were accidental. Everyone got spiked now and then when I was active. I took a lot myself."

On the other hand, 1919-28 Washington second baseman Bucky Harris recalled the Bluege play in a gory way in 1956, in the *Saturday Evening Post*. A throw to third base by outfielder Sam Rice had Cobb "dead to rights [sic] by ten feet" and Bluege "went down the line to take the ball. Cobb leaped at Bluege with his spikes and slashed him down both thighs. It was the most sickening sight I ever saw."

"'That'll teach you to go off the bag to tag me,' Cobb snarled."

Harris added, "I know of at least one player whose career was ended by Cobb in his first big-league game. Jesse Baker, a kid shortstop with the Senators, was spiked so badly by Cobb that he never came back." (A story about Harris's inability to hit Cobb's head on a throw is on page 223.)

Pro-Cobb writing on this subject that I can bring to light is by sportswriter William "Bill" Veeck, Sr., who wrote trailblazing spiking prose in 1909 that will be quoted later. In 1938, he declared, "Many stories have been told about Ty Cobb, one of them about filing his spikes on his shoes so he could slash basemen who got in his way. They never have been able to prove that Cobb did this and few ball players ever believed it." But Veeck did not touch on the possibility that Cobb sharpened his spikes openly at least to intimidate.

In a pro-Cobb feature in 1949, James P. Sinnott of the *Newark Star-Ledger* dismissed base-running criticism by longtime player, manager and coach Jimmy Dykes as coming from "baseball's 'All-American pop-off [blowhard].'" In 1950, in the presence of dear Cobb friends Connie Mack and Mickey Cochrane, Dykes said that as a young second baseman, around 1920, "I was tired of dodging off the base to avoid his spikes and so I got me a pair of shoes with leather tops laced halfway up to my knees. When Cobb spotted those leggings just before the game, he said he'd cut the laces. And I'll be darned if he didn't rip the laces off one of those shoes with his spikes the first time he slid into second base," conveyed Cullen Cain of the *Miami Daily News*, an ex-National League publicist.

As for whether Cobb tried spiking anyone on purpose, Leerhsen and Hornbaker differ in subtle ways. Unlike their poor spikes-sharpening analyses, each of their spiking ones at least has minimal credibility, by conceding confusion.

Without adding a value judgment, Leerhsen noted how Cobb's list changed with every recitation. With that comment, he ended one of his chapters – and his kicker was that Frank Baker, who will be featured in a bit as the most publicized alleged deliberate Cobb spikee, never appeared on it.

In his book, Tripp fleshed out some of the inconsistencies. "At the start of the 1909 season, Cobb answered critics by claiming that he had 'cut down' only a 'few' players, naming catcher Bill Sullivan and infielder Frank Isbell of the White Sox and third baseman Bill Bradley of the Cleveland Naps [then named for captain-manager Napoleon Lajoie] as his victims. In his [Cobb's] 1925 autobiography [which was derived from a newspaper serial of his], he put the number at four ['whom I have gone at with the deliberate intention of knocking them out,' which seems to mean colliding with, not necessarily spiking]. While it is understandable that the list would have grown since 1909, what is less clear is why none of the people he mentioned in 1909 made his 1925 list; the new list included infielder Hobe Ferris and pitchers Dutch Leonard and Cy Morgan of Boston and St. Louis catcher Lou Criger." (Criger and Leonard would be singled out by Cobb in a 1950 interview with Furman Bisher. He would tell Bisher, "I can honestly say that I only tried to spike two men in my whole life.")

Tripp continued, "In later years, he became somewhat more circumspect when he offered names. For a *Life* magazine piece he wrote in 1952, he listed just two people, Leonard, who made the 1925 list, and a new name, Cleveland catcher Harry Bemis. Four years later, Cobb gave two answers when John McCallum interviewed him for his biography *The Tiger Wore Spikes*. In the flyleaf of *The Tiger*, McCallum quotes an emphatic Cobb proclaiming: 'I never deliberately spiked a player in my life!' Yet in the body of the biography, he admitted to spiking Bemis and Leonard intentionally." Tripp went on to observe which names showed up in his 1961 biography with Stump and questioned the absence of three other players from any of the lists who Cobb "admitted to going after in other contexts." Tripp then observed, "Clearly Cobb hoped to minimize the damage to his reputation that his confession might create; this seems to have been especially true after he ended his career."

I can add some more detail to this discussion:

In a syndicated feature in 1925, Cobb told veteran sports editor Ed Hughes, "Some people called me an unscrupulous base runner in my prime, but let me tell you something. There are at least twenty-five players using the straight slide in, feet first, who spiked more players than I ever did. I never wil[l]fully spiked a player in my life." In 1943, Cobb was more expansive when NEA sports editor Grayson interviewed him as part of a full-blown feature: "I never deliberately cut a fellow except to protect myself."

A juicy quote that I found, to show that at least in key game situations, Cobb may have been an occasional spiker or encouraged or condoned rougher play by teammates, is from the baseball figure who admired him the most, new Browns manager and former teammate Haney in 1938. Haney told Grayson about a play in a close game where, as a runner, Haney was heading for home at top speed from second base on a wild pitch. "The Yankee pitcher, a good friend of mine, covered the plate while the catcher ran to retrieve the ball. Instead of upsetting the pitcher, I slid around him" and scored feeling "happy."

"Cobb was waiting for me as I neared the dugout. 'Why didn't you cut down that pitcher at the plate?' he roared. 'You could have cut his leg off, and we'd have an easier time winning.'" (Hornbaker wrote that in 1923, ex-Tiger pitcher Howard Ehmke claimed that when he played under Cobb, Cobb tried to order him to "dust off" or hit batters. I can add that in 1941, Joe Williams of the *New York World-Telegram* wrote of having broached the subject of beanballs recently with Cobb. "We remembered one of his Detroit pitchers telling us that Cobb had given direct orders to bean dangerous hitters and the penalty for failure was a stiff fine." In reply, Cobb volunteered Ehmke's name and said that he did not tell his pitchers to aim for the head. "To throw a fright into" batters, the pitcher "can do that just as well by throwing the ball at his knees. Or even behind him." In 1952, Ehmke told Cain of the *Miami Daily News* that at worst, he hit batters unintentionally but that he, Ehmke, still "got a bad name on that [Cobb's] account.")

As I note later, my research shows that the 1890s Baltimore Orioles were a "flying mouths" team and not notably a "flying spikes" one. To that, I can add that Cobb's loosely parallel "flying mouths" characteristic was his sour, hypercompetitive persona. I have no solid basis for opining on the extent of his deliberate spiking, since I did not track his playing career.

On that subject, close friend Maines said the following in a long interview in 1967 with the *Arizona Republic*: "Ty told me he never purposely spiked anyone." And yet, as Hornbaker wrote, and as I quoted Tripp above, in 1952 Cobb "admitted in *Life* magazine that there were two instances in his career that he actually did try spiking someone, and Harry Bemis and Dutch Leonard were the intended victims." Also, Cain interviewed Maines in 1954 and wrote, "Of course Maines had no excuse for Cobb's violent treatment of players on opposing teams, especially on the baselines." By the way, the *Arizona Republic* called Maines "a self-appointed biographer" of Cobb who "delights in furnishing 'truthful versions' of several popularized tales of Cobb's antics."

Digressing to more about Maines and Cobb:

In 1921, he had chaired a huge banquet to mark Cobb's naming as manager. In 1951, as a minor league club president, he suggested having a commissioner of minor league baseball and said that Cobb had shown interest in serving as one. Feats of his outside baseball are having been a founder of the American Legion in 1919, which Cobb joined early on, and father of the military mothers' group Blue Star Mothers of America. He was also a publicist for a half-century, with comedian Jimmy Durante as one of his last clients. During a Maines visit to Cobb in Cave Rock, Cobb spoke with Durante on the phone.

Maines was not mentioned by Leerhsen and Hornbaker even though Alexander had featured him as a witness to Cobb's deteriorating health. Although Alexander did not state the following, the Maines letter that he cited was to Rowan D. Spraker, Sr., who had been mayor of Cooperstown when the Hall of Fame was dedicated in 1939. Maines wrote it three weeks after Cobb's death and began it this way: "This is a testament recording the events in the life of our friend, the late Ty Cobb, which led to his decision to have a complete medical and physical examination in late 1959 to try to determine the cause of his physical incapacity which overcame him while on a hunting trip earlier that year near his Lake Tahoe home."

The significance of the Maines letter extends to a symbolic moment in Cobb's life. Referring to the 1939 dedication, Alexander wrote that Cobb arrived late "to avoid having to be photographed with Commissioner [Kenesaw Mountain] Landis." He prefaced that by writing, "Twenty years later he admitted that he had purposely missed the noontime ceremony."

For Cobb's Landis story, Alexander omitted a citation to his almost certain source for that, Maines's letter. On page 3 of that letter, Maines wrote, "He [Cobb] said the reason he wasn't in the first picture taken with the group that attended the original dedication ceremonies was because of his dislike for Judge Landis, the Baseball Commissioner." On that point, Leerhsen wrote, without accounting for

Captain Maines (center) in 1924, with a pushball (a scheme of his to promote the Citizens' Military Training Camp movement) that was literally pushed, especially by Boy Scouts, from Chicago to Boston

Maines's paraphrase of Cobb, "Some said he was late because he wanted to avoid having his picture taken with Commissioner Landis."

Hornbaker instead cited three reasons that had been reported at the time, only one of which Alexander and Leerhsen mentioned, for Cobb possibly encountering delays: problems related to travel. While Maines is very likely the original and conceivably the lone existing first-hand source for Cobb's alleged intentional avoidance of Landis, the fact that Alexander did not make that clear likely led Hornbaker to stress reports that he could account for. Leerhsen's different decision, to loosely rehash Alexander's point, may be a sign that Leerhsen has a softer spot for colorful detail on Cobb on select topics.

Bell and Maines

Bell, the longtime Augusta friend and journalist, wrote in 1964 that Cobb was "my good friend all the many years he lived in Augusta and up to the day of his death." Bell first got to know Cobb around 1920, when he was a young sportswriter for the *Augusta Herald*. Cobb, after returning from Europe after the Great War, World War I, "graciously enabled me to score a nationwide 'scoop' – by revealing to me exclusively his long-delayed decision to return to baseball." In later years, "I was, to some extent, his confidant. The last letter I had from [Cobb] came about three months before his death from cancer. He told of some of his other troubles, but did not mention his painful illness."

Bell and Maines gave a contrasting analysis of Cobb. Bell said nothing negative about their interactions and explained away the negative aspects of his hypercompetitiveness. Arguably the most important item in Maines's letter is something that Alexander omitted. Still, it is possible that Maines's most important observation led Alexander to, in his own words, observe that Cobb's friends over the decades "were mostly non-baseball people [which presumably includes persons associated with the sport who had not been big leaguers] and they had to be willing to take him on his own terms."

To set the context, Maines wrote that in one late night talk, "We sat up past midnight, and discussed many things. One was the actual state of his health and where he ought to spend his remaining days." Then Maines said, "To get along good with Ty I had learned through the years to let him have his own way, and let him do the talking, and the guidance [sic]." The last three words seem out of place. The previous ones, though, may provide the most compelling explanation available for why Cobb did not have many friends.

Bell said "the ugliest charge against him – that of sharpening his spikes with a file – was never proved, and Ty himself denied it." He wrote that after stating that Cobb "doubtless was the keenest-minded – and most hated – man in baseball throughout his 24 years in the American League."

"And to my way of thinking," Bell wrote after commenting on Cobb's spiking, "one thing is for sure: His spikes were never as sharp as his mind. The 'Georgia Peach' was perhaps the game's master psychologist. He studied and knew the strengths of every opposing player and used his knowledge to confuse and out-fox them."

Bell alluded to Cobb's various fights and called Cobb both hot-headed and hot-blooded. Then he added, "Not commonly known, however, is the fact that he had a dash of Cherokee Indian blood which might have sparked his truculence." Actually, the Cherokee tie of Cobb's is that his father had been born in Cherokee County, N.C.

In his 1961 letter, Maines quoted Cobb as telling him during one of his 1959 visits, "I never started a fight, but if another got after me, I'd get even."

Regarding his most controversial spiking, of Philadelphia's Frank Baker in 1909, in an important time in the pennant race, Cobb told Kaese of the *Boston Globe* in 1948, "I was trying to get away from Baker, and I have a picture to prove it. I just nicked him on the forearm, and he did not miss a game." When Detroit and Philadelphia next played in Philadelphia, Kaese wrote, "250 special police protected him against the crowd in Shibe Park. There was no violence, although in the second game Cobb spiked Jack Barry and the A's shortstop could play no more in that series."

(The three biographies mention the writer whose coverage of the Baker incident especially irked Cobb, Horace Fogel of the *Evening Telegraph* in Philadelphia. In his 1961 book with Stump, without mentioning Fogel by name, Cobb alluded to Fogel as "the author of a barefaced fraud that set a local mob – and a good part of the nation – against me fifty-two years ago." As a taste of how the 1961 book can be considered toned down, and thus more harmless than distortive, Cobb wrote the following in 1947 to a Joe Fisher:

"It was Horace Fogel[,] long since dead, a Philadelphia writer [sports editor of the *Evening Telegraph*] (also this happened in Detroit) who wrote a most lurid & inflammatory story about it, he was half drunk most of the time and had a poisonous spirit, had the play happened in Philadelphia nothing would have developed as it did for they there could have seen the play.")

Cobb told Kaese, "You hear about me spiking infielders, but you never hear about these," and he pulled up his pajama legs to show many white scars on his thighs, knees and shins. "[This is] Where fielders jumping for throws would land on me when I slid under them," he said, before adding, "Accidentally, of course." In the presence of sports columnist Arthur Daley of the *New York Times* in 1945, Cobb had pulled up his trouser legs and, in Daley's words, "displayed the most amazing collection of scars ever seen outside of a dissecting room. 'Of course, I never before admitted to any of these,' he said. 'There never was any sense in tipping off the opposition on how black and blue or damaged I was.'"

In 1955, he told Carl Lundquist of the United Press, "I never tried to hurt anybody in 24 years of baseball and I got hurt a lot more often than anybody knows." Talking as if he was still an active player, he said, "I'm not a spiker. I run the bases hard. But those base lines belong to me – the runner. It was up to the baseman to protect himself when I would slide. I can get hurt too, you know. When that guy goes up in the air to get the ball he's got to come down and he can come down right on top of me. Look at those spike scars on my legs." Cobb pointed to a long one near his knee.

"Joe Sewell [a star opposing shortstop in Cobb's final nine seasons] gave me that one. Took four stitches to close it up. But nobody ever remembers about the times old Ty got spiked. Only about the guys who got hurt because I ran into 'em."

Cobb, who while saying that was wearing a bright red bathrobe in a New York City hotel, recalled an incident from several years earlier that "hurt me right in here" – and he tapped his heart. "I had an old friend and he wanted me to meet his son." When introductions were made, "the son said – 'Oh yes, I remember you, you were known as the Spiker.' Somehow I don't want to go down in people's memories like that."

Made public in 2013 was a Cobb interview with Bob Wolff, a longtime broadcaster who had interviewed him in Washington, D.C., around 1950. The *New York Times* was given access to recordings that Wolff had donated to the Library of Congress and were being digitized. *Times* sports reporter Tyler Kepner listened to the Cobb one and said at one point, "Wolff flatters Cobb, calling him the game's greatest player, but also asserts that Cobb was 'a pretty mean man on the bases,' a characterization Cobb disputes. As much as he hears about his aggressive style, Cobb grumbles, plenty of fielders spiked his ankles and knees by jumping for throws and landing on him."

Also, "Wolff goes on to ask Cobb about his technique on the bases, how he read pitchers and got jumps.

"Cobb plays along for a while, but he is still agitated." Except for my adding an "s" to "runner," the following is a play-by-play from Kepner's article, starting with Wolff:

"Getting back to this spiking business," he says, "you know, the baseline belongs to the runners!"

Wolff hangs in, like a fearless second baseman with Cobb barreling down.

"And you played up to the rules all the time, I'm sure of that," Wolff says.

At this point, Cobb lets up.

"Well," he concedes, after a pause [Cobb used the word 'uh'], "a lot of the times."

Digressing to observations about the terrible sight of Cobb's legs:

After the 1907 season, Bingay, then of the *Detroit News*, stated, "Half the time during the season his sides were bruised and raw from sliding. The writer was in the club house one day when he was taking off his uniform. The new skin that had just formed over an ugly red spot on his thigh had been torn open and blood trickled from the sore. He had no sliding pads on.

"'Why don't you wear pads?' was asked in amazement.

"'I do, once in a while,' he said, his face twisted in pain, 'but the blame things retard my speed.'"

Also, Bingay reportedly recalled a game in Washington where Cobb was in such pain that he had to withdraw after collapsing on the way to the plate. "The Dixie Demon sat there throwing dust for awhile, then managed to get up." Earlier on that trip around the bases, he had stolen second base "and st[ru]ggled to his feet holding his side. [Detroit manager Hughie]

Malcolm Bingay

Jennings yelled to him to leave the game, but he growled and shook his head; then [he] stole third. To do so he had to slide and he again came up slowly as though the task were almost too much for him."

(In a long interview in 1925 with sports editor Hughes, Cobb said, "In all my base running I never suffered an injury [actually, he tore three ligaments in his right knee while sliding in 1920]. Perhaps you have noticed my base running form some time. The left leg is drawn under the right knee, making a sort of shock absorbing frame for the weight of the body. I always relaxed my muscles as I hit the dirt. I fell in a limp mass, which helped prevent injuries.")

In 1909, soon after the spiking of Baker, Cobb was giving an exhibition of his own leg injuries. In Charlotte at the time, he said, "Many a time have I been spiked, but I didn't say anything about it. I would keep it to myself if a fellow accidentally cut me and many a time have I been cut pretty badly." The *Charlotte News* added, "And here Mr. Cobb revealed his ankles on both legs.

They were covered with scars where his opponents cut him, but he did not squeal but stood the pain manfully."

In 1914, New York sports columnist Herbert "Hype" Igoe recalled Cobb sitting on a billiards hall table in New York City and pulling up both trouser legs to the knees. "Each leg was cut from ankle to knee in a frightful way. Hardly an inch of whole skin remained uncut or bruised." Cobb told him that he had cried often after games when his deep spike cuts were cauterized.

In 1932, sports editor Paul Gallico of the *New York Daily News* sat with him, only wearing towels, in the locker room of a golf club, and reported on his scars. "One on his left knee runs a good six inches. The scars on his right knee are crossed and double crossed and look like the set-up for a game of tic-tac-toe. I count four long scars on one knee and three smaller ones on the leg." In reply, besides sarcastically saying that they were not spike scars, Cobb told him, "Look at that one. Isn't that a beauty? That one was right down to the bone."

In 1939, Cobb told Bob Considine of the International News Service, "I got spiked more than I spiked. Take a look at these." At that point, Cobb "pulled up his grey trousers to show us deep white scars from knee to ankle."

In 1943, the AP mildly reworded part of a 1942 *Sporting News* interview with famed athletic surgeon Robert F. Hyland, who had told of treating Cobb at the height of his career. Hornbaker featured part of Hyland's comments in his book, but not this part about the extent of his leg wounds: "You never see anything like that today. Occasional 'sliders' [slide burns] and 'strawberries,' but nothing even faintly resembling the contusions and generally cut-up condition of Cobb." In *Life* in 1952, Cobb said he "often played with spike wounds, a knee swollen up like a cantaloupe or a slide burn that had barely healed over with a scab that was sure to rub off the next time I hit the dirt."

Another Hyland, sports columnist Dick Hyland of the *Los Angeles Times*, wrote in 1951, "I remember dressing with Ty Cobb at a [Bing] Crosby Golf Tournament at Del Mar [a beach city in San Diego County]. Undressed, Ty's legs showed a mass of white and red scars from ankles to hips." Also in 1951, at the point where I left off in Cobb's chat with Pinelli about spiking, the next detail is that they each rolled up their trouser legs and compared their wounds.

Also on spiking, a 1955 letter to Spink entirely had to do with Baker. Cobb wrote of having received a letter from Spink and presumed that Spink had received Cobb's "offering re this." Two weeks earlier, the Hall of Fame veterans' committee, headed by Spink, had elected Baker and Ray Schalk to the Hall.

In his letter, Cobb stated that he was approving something that Spink had asked of him with regard to Baker. Cobb said he "appreciated what Baker said," apparently referring to a just-published *Sporting News* article that featured

Baker, "but the Perry part I did not." Bill Perry, sports editor of the *Easton Star-Democrat* in Maryland, had written an "as told to" article. What may have bothered Cobb was a photo caption that he may have presumed Perry had written. It read, "Ty streaked in with spikes high and inflicted a deep gash in Baker's right arm." (In the *Star-Democrat* two months

from left to right in 1959 at Cooperstown: Frank Baker, Cobb, Zack Wheat, Frankie Frisch, Joe McCarthy, George Sisler and Pie Traynor

earlier, Perry had written that Baker "nearly caused a riot in Philadelphia the day Ty Cobb deliberately slashed his arm with his razor sharp spikes.")

Cobb continued as follows, in his letter to Spink: "If I am allowed to state Baker's spike wound was in no way intentional and was unavoidable, per picture, also he did not lose an inning's pay and think records will show he played in all games for rest of season, that I have always resented the unfair and untrue account of this matter, I will give you anything else you want me to say in Baker's behalf, mind you I do not & would not say Baker was responsible for the charge of untruth in papers, etc."

Contacted by the *Boston Globe* upon Cobb's death, Baker repeated the news as a question and added, "why, I just sent him a telegram this morning." He added, "I was looking forward to seeing him at Cooperstown this Sunday as I have in the past." Baker also said, "On the field he was a fighter but off the field he always showed me the greatest consideration."

In the *Manchester Guardian*'s obituary, Alistair Cooke wrote, "The most typical of all the uplifting stories told about him is that of Cobb in retirement being reminded, by chuckling cronies, of the innumerable times he had put opponents in hospital [sic, British usage] or in temporary retirement, by stabbing them with the spikes of his shoes as he slid on his back into a stolen base."

"A Law Unto Himself"

At the time he spiked Baker, the *Chicago Tribune* called Cobb "a law unto himself" in a regular news pages editorial. It declared, "Every one likes a winner, but there are ethics to be considered besides mere victory, and no action on the ball field is more contemptible than the willingness to injure an opponent." Before that, it stated that Cobb "will make few friends outside of Detroit by his definition of his rights as a base runner." After calling him "a law unto himself," it said "he bears a bad reputation along the whole league circuit for his 'ready feet.' Lee Tannehill of the [White] Sox, who knows what spiking means, wears a special protection beneath his socks with Cobb especially in view."

A week later, Bingay used "a law unto himself" construct in declaring that Cobb has never spiked anyone intentionally. "Anyone who has played with the team knows that he has not. He has made many rival players his enemies because he broke in as a 'kid' and did things that made them look sick while they were still laughing at him as 'fresh.' They don't laugh any more, they can't, so they think up mean things to say.

"Tyrus is a law unto himself on the ball field. He is like a piece of India rubber. Famous sprinters have said that Cobb would have set all sprinting records down [sic] if he had gone into that game instead of baseball. But fast as he is, his mind seems to move faster than his body, for while his rivals are momentarily dazzled by his desperate, devil-may-care play, he has conceived something else and is off again before they can recover from their first shock."

The Two Texans

The most racially controversial star player of the first half of the 20th century was Cobb, who played from 1905 to 1928. He was the all-time hit leader before Pete Rose eclipsed him in 1985. Besides Cobb, two other Hall of Famers of that period who are alleged racists are Texans, Tris Speaker and Rogers Hornsby. According to early 20th-century reporter Fred Lieb, writing in his 1977 *Baseball As I Have Known It*, both Texans told him that they had been members of the Ku Klux Klan. Alexander, a Klan expert and biographer of Speaker and Hornsby, as well as Cobb, has written, "If Speaker or Hornsby had ever belonged to the Klan [in the 1920s], by 1925 they would also have been part of the mass exodus from the movement" when its popularity notably declined. A widely reported contemporaneous report of Hornsby having been rumored to be in the Klan appeared in 1929; the rumor was cited by a boxing manager during a hearing of the Boston Finance Commission. (Gabby Street is among the few other rumored KKK members, by name, in baseball history.)

Rogers Hornsby

In 1938, *Sporting News* columnist Dan Daniel called Hornsby "the writers' pal. In fact, the Rajah talked too much for his own good. He never hid anything, always called a spade a spade, refused to put the brakes on criticism, had the impatience of genius with the fuddling of the inept, and undoubtedly was staggered when he read what he had told you – and told you without reservations." Hornbaker quoted a different part of Daniel's column that day: Cobb "was not hard to talk to – if he liked you. If he didn't, you knew it. He was caustic. Very shrewd in his observations, but the most sarcastic hombre baseball has seen – or heard." A later Daniel twist, in one of three Cobb obituary articles of his in 1961 in the *New York World-Telegram and Sun*, would be, "Cobb had the memory of an elephant. He never forgot a friendly action, and he never forgave anything unfriendly."

Satchel Paige

In contrast to Cobb, Hornsby managed and coached in the major leagues after they became integrated. Also, although being in need of money to pay off debts may have been his main motivation for doing so, he played in a series against Negro League stars in 1935. That helps to balance out the KKK rumor. A colorful Hornsby-racial story is from 1952, when he was managing the St. Louis Browns. Satchel Paige, the quotable Negro League pitcher who was now in the majors at the estimated age of 45, was with the team. Right after Hornsby was fired that June, Milton Gross of the *New York Post* conveyed that three weeks earlier, Paige had asked general manager William "Bill" Veeck, Jr. for his release, to allow him to return to the Negro Leagues. "'The manager and me,' said Paige, 'we don't hit it off.'" To that, Veeck responded, "I don't think race means anything to Hornsby." And, "I don't think he treats you any differently than he does the other players."

"'He don't, Mr. Veeck,' Paige replied. 'He treats [white Browns players Ned] Garver and [Dick] Kryhoski worse than he does me.'" Hornsby biographer Jonathan D'Amore cited part of that article, which had been preserved in the Hornsby file at the now-defunct St. Louis headquarters of the *Sporting News*.

As far as Speaker, no report has been found of his playing in exhibition games against teams with black players. The following positive detail on Speaker and race was cited by Speaker biographer Timothy M. Gay. In 1936, the city of Cleveland held a victory parade to celebrate native son Jesse Owens's triumphs in the Summer Olympics in Germany. In the convertible with the city's mayor and Mr. and Mrs. Owens was Speaker. Jumping to 1947, while a coach for the Cleveland Indians, Speaker was assigned to Larry Doby, who broke the color line that year in the American League. Speaker also was assigned to Doby in 1948, when Doby was its Rookie of the Year. As a taste of Speaker's relative geniality, in 1924, Detroit players were polled anonymously to choose an all-American baseball team. Speaker was their top choice for manager. "He scored on personality, baseball ability and knowledge of the game," according to a report that ran in multiple newspapers. Interestingly, the genial Connie Mack received just one vote, and yet that "was one more than the Detroit athletes slipped the fiery manager of the Tigers." Cobb was player-manager of that latter team from 1921 to 1926.

If trying to weed through reporting to figure out how racist they were, the amount to pore through on Speaker cannot hold a candle to Cobb, and Hornsby probably cannot either. Among major leaguers, at least Hall of Famers, Cobb was in an unmatched number of contemporaneously reported fights or violent incidents with black (and white) civilians during his playing career. Lieb, in his 1977 book, wrote, "I do not know whether Cobb was a Klansman, but I suspect he was." There is nothing in Stump's 1961 article that supports the baseless claim – although Stump's "anything goes" writing at times could have emboldened Lieb. (Another suspect 1970s Lieb story, which Bak twice, Alexander, Stump, Rhodes and the 2015 authors did not mention, relates to Babe Ruth's so-called "nigger lips" complexion: "Once when Ruth and Cobb were fellow guests at Dover Hall, a big league hunting lodge near Brunswick, Georgia, both stars were assigned sleeping space in the same cottage. Cobb would not permit his luggage to be brought to the cottage, saying, 'I never have slept under the same roof with a nigger, and I'm not going to start here in my own native state of Georgia.'") In his 1994 biography of him, Stump said Cobb used the N-word throughout his life and that, "By inheritance, communality [presumably having to do with his preferred social circle], and disposition, Cobb was a fixed racial bigot."

Tiger Bullies

Leerhsen and Hornbaker wrote books of similar length, if one accounts for the many more words on the pages of Hornbaker's. The

GIANTS vs. WASHINGTON-WORLD SERIES 1924

LIEB ALTROCK COBB RUTH McGRAW JOHNSON SISLER WALSH

amount of detail or analysis that is exclusive to one of the two books, and that had not previously appeared in one, seems quite large.

One subject that I did not research is the extent to which Cobb was in fights growing up or was bullied in his first big-league seasons. Leerhsen focused a bit more deeply on the fighting and Hornbaker on the bullying or hazing. For example, Leerhsen quoted from a 1914 article in which Cobb told of having had a bad temper in his younger days that got him into a lot of trouble. Leerhsen added, "There is no denying that Cobb was a born battler, just as some people seem to come into the world as jokesters, wimps, loners, or bores." He also quoted from a book about manhood in the South from 1865 to 1920 in which author Ted Ownby stated that Southern men "have always felt a need to exert their will over any enemy as directly and immediately as possible." (In his book, Ownby had used the word "wills," not "will.")

In his next sentence, Leerhsen quoted Ownby as also stating, "The driving influence is not primarily a taste for blood but rather a consistent readiness for confrontation. Southerners have long been quick to take offense, quick to go to war, and, when at war, quick to mount a direct assault." (The first sentence has three errors and the second has none. In his book, Ownby wrote, "The driving impulse was not primarily a taste for blood but rather a constant readiness for confrontation. Southerners have long been quick to take offense, quick to go to war, and, when at war, quick to mount a direct assault.")

I can add that in 1945, Cobb told columnist Daley of the *New York Times* that the hazing was "a better system than the gentlemanly treatment the rookies get these days. If I became a snarling wildcat, they [my teammates] made me one." Also of relevance, in a special remembrance for the *Free Press* upon his death, 1907-to-1917 *Free Press* baseball reporter and sports editor E. A. "Eddie" Batchelor, Sr. wrote, "The mere fact that he had come from a higher social plane than that which had spawned the Tiger bullies made them all the more determined to drive him off the squad."

The quote sounded familiar to me, but it took extra work to determine if it was in a Cobb biography. The reason? I could not match up words easily in a full-text search. I will number the errors as they appear in Leerhsen's book:

Leerhsen wrote that Batchelor said – and Leerhsen enveloped all of the following in quotation marks, with the following exact start and end points – "that Ty came (#1 change of tense) from a higher social plane than had (#2 wrong word, #3 word missing) spawned the (#4 word missing) bullies made them all the more determined to drive him off the squad."

I found Cobb talking in 1924 about rookie hazing as a thing of the past. Salsinger, in covering the team's spring training that year, wrote, "Today, the recruit finds it [spring training] a parlor game. As soon as he appears in training camp he is placed on a rating equal to the veterans. The object is to make him feel at home, to remove all embarrassment, all obstacles. He is told to go ahead and show his stuff. Everybody is out to help him. If he fails to make good it won't be the fault of anyone but himself."

Then Salsinger told of a recent chat between Cobb and fellow future Hall of Famer Fred Clarke. "They were mourning the departure of the red corpuscles from the body of base ball." Salsinger added, "They were sad about it."

Salsinger continued by quoting Cobb as saying, "Look at these boys out here trying to break in. Everybody nice to them, everybody helping them, doing everything possible to push them along." Clarke then told a story about breaking into the National League in 1894 and how "I brought my own bat along. It was a little bat and they all made fun of it. They said it showed what kind of a brain I had

from left to right in 1951: Fred Clarke, Charley Gehringer,
Cobb and Rogers Hornsby

and they made a lot of other snappy cracks like that. I didn't get any batting practice because every time I tried to take my turn at bat some big bruiser pushed me out of the way." Clarke said a lot more that Salsinger related, before Clarke and Cobb agreed that "those were the days."

Presumably because Cobb had recalled his hazing story in 1945, that helped it make the cut for a 1952 AP feature on how "green" players have been treated in baseball history; Cobb served as the finale to Joe Reichler's article. For example, in referring to a week early in his career, he told Reichler, "That week[,] I had five fights in the Detroit dressing room." In a 1961 NEA feature on 1908-to-1921 teammate Donie Bush, two months before Cobb's death, Bush seemingly cast Cobb's personal unpopularity with teammates as extending well into Cobb's career. Cobb "liked to shoot dice, but he didn't get invited very often" by his teammates to do it with them. A second Cobb-was-no-fun-to-roll-the-dice-with story will appear later, from rival contemporary Luke Sewell.

6. *Cobb v. Cunningham (and Leerhsen v. Hornbaker)*

In a 1948 letter to Cunningham of the *Boston Herald*, Cobb wrote, "I will make a little confession to you." He wrote that after reading over one of Cunningham's recent columns about him several times. The letter and Cunningham's prose will be featured at length much later. "Up to the time I came into the American league [sic], I happened to be a [Baptist] church boy, Sunday School, prayer meeting and Sunday Services. I did not take God's name in vain, but I met some pretty hard old-time ball players. I was heckled plenty and put through the paces. They taught me I'd better look out for my own interests. It probably made me a more effective ball player."

In his newspaper serial in 1926, he had made a similar point: "I sincerely believe I was a much better ball player for all those hard knocks." Also in the serial, Cobb said that before starting out with Detroit, "I had never understood rough kidding, had never heard some of the language used on a big league bench. At first it actually shocked me. It was unbelievable to me that men could take some

BILL CUNNINGHAM
Boston Herald

of the epithets and be manly. I didn't understand that these things were not meant as insults." Back in 1911, in a long interview with Bozeman Bulger of the *New York Evening World*, he had said pretty much the same thing.

(In searching to see if any of the other biographers had used a "hard knocks" quote from Cobb to free me up to use it, I found Leerhsen using one in a much different context, and not being true to either the newspaper version or a Dover reprint called *My Twenty Years in Baseball*. In both the newspaper and book versions, Cobb referred to his semi-pro manager in Anniston, Ala., as follows: "In fact, a life of hard knocks and experience had given him a broad understanding of human nature in general." Leerhsen's version features a subset of that quote, with the words "and experience" dropped out from the middle of it. His resulting quotation reads that "a life of hard knocks had given him a broad understanding of human nature," with an acceptable comma at the end to switch to a different thought.)

Also in the serial, Cobb wrote, "I do not propose to defend myself against the charge of being a belligerent, nagging ball player. I simply nagged back when they nagged me. My own belligerency was merely a defense against belligerency. I never did and never do intend to take the worst of it in open

competition unless I have to." Cobb addressed those points with different emphasis in his 1911 interview with Bulger: "The reason I had so many fights at the start was because I did not understand what was meant by 'kidding.' I took it as an insult until I learned better."

In his 1945 interview with Daley of the *New York Times*, Cobb said that after newspapers "started to put my picture in the papers and give me some publicity," veterans on the team "began to work on me." (In his 1911 interview with Bulger, he had said that teammates "thought I was swell-headed" because "I didn't understand human nature and my success came too quickly.") He singled out fellow future Hall of Famer Crawford, who was at the time

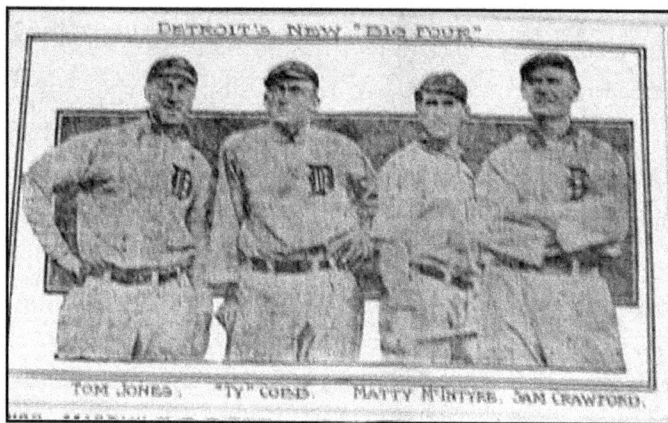

DETROIT'S NEW "BIG FOUR"

TOM JONES.   "TY" COBB.   MATTY M'INTYRE.   SAM CRAWFORD.

"the big dog in the meat-house and I was just a brash kid."

Digressing to more about the falling out and an eventual reconciliation between Cobb and Crawford:

In 1939, former teammate Davy Jones told sportswriter Bob Murphy of the *Detroit Times*, "It's one of those feuds that will live forever." He recalled a time when Crawford came to the defense of teammate Donie Bush, who Cobb was in a "red-hot" argument with and had thrown a bat at. Crawford "grabbed Cobb, shook him viciously, and tossed him into the dust." Then "Cobb, the fighter, got up and skidded away. It was the smartest diamond trick Cobb ever pulled. Crawford would have killed him. I know that Crawford and Ty have never forgotten. Neither have they ever forgiven."

In 1943, future Hall of Famer and Cobb contemporary Eddie Collins claimed that Cobb and Crawford "hardly were on speaking terms, all because Sam, up right after Ty [in the lineup], wouldn't lay off some pitches on which Ty had got a great start for the base ahead." (Stump's 1994 book claims that in a letter to Spink that Cobb kept a copy of, Cobb complained about having run hundreds of miles going back to first on balls that Crawford fouled off.)

In 1951, Cobb and Crawford reconciled at a reunion in Detroit to mark its 50th anniversary as a major league team. The morning of their reunion, former teammate Harry Heilmann died; Cobb had visited him that very morning. "I'm too old to hold grudges," Crawford said, when a photographer suggested that he pose with Cobb. Crawford then went to Cobb's hotel room and stayed for more than an hour. Later that day, Cobb and Crawford visited former teammate Bobby Lowe in a nursing home.

In 1957, *Pittsburgh Press* sports editor Chester L. Smith said that one explanation for Cobb and Crawford not getting along was "that their temperaments were so different – Cobb a fireball, Crawford a stolid sort. But there's another story that recalls that Sam, who hit behind Ty in the lineup, grounded into four double plays in one day, all with Cobb on first, and the Georgian merely needed a few seasons to quiet down."

Upon Cobb's death, Jack McDonald, veteran sports editor of the *San Francisco Call-Bulletin*, said Crawford and Cobb would not speak to each other for years, but that later Cobb worked behind the scenes to get him elected to the Hall of Fame. Besides providing lots of detail about Cobb's effort, saying Cobb had agreed he could do so upon his death, McDonald also wrote that Cobb refused to discuss their feud, including off the record. The AP reprinted McDonald's report in its entirety after adding a short introduction, including by using the word "secretly" to describe Cobb's effort.

The secret had drawn a 1955 headline in the *Detroit Times*, "Cobb Goes to Bat for Wahoo Sam: Wants His Old Foe Named to Hall." When the news came in 1957 of his election, Crawford told sports

Jack McDonald

reporter Finch of the *Los Angeles Times*, "And listen, young fellow, if you don't write anything else, please thank Cobb and [veterans' committee chairman] Taylor Spink and all the other men who fought to win me this wonderful honor." What Cobb had done that McDonald disclosed in 1961 was having written to "hundreds of influential baseball people" on Crawford's behalf. (Seemingly more accurate on that latter point is Maines's 1961 letter; Cobb told Maines that he wrote dozens on that subject and had enlisted others to write some.)

Of the three biographers, Hornbaker did the closest tracking of the Cobb-Crawford relationship. His spin, though, was too positive, by not stressing their decades-long falling out, as previewed by Crawford in a 1918 interview, to be featured later, and not locating their reconciliation in 1951. Having found that sports editor George S. Alderton of the *Lansing State Journal* in Michigan was clued into Cobb going back to the 1920s, I looked for any other reportage by him of note before Cobb's death. I did find one thing related to Crawford. In 1954, Alderton wrote, "Somebody on the Pacific coast surprised me by telling me that Ty Cobb and Sam Crawford, great oldie Detroit Tiger stars, had great respect for each other as ball players but no regard at all for each other as people, and refused to speak for years."

Leerhsen, in telling about Crawford and Cobb, said that Crawford "was never able to get beyond the resentment he felt about the relatively huge salary" of Cobb and "special treatment Cobb received." One of the examples that he cited was Cobb's having been able "to travel during the season without a roommate (as Cobb did from 1912 onward)." I found some roommates during that span and run through them much later.

On a different subject, Hornbaker delved into whether Cobb's having a limited a sense of humor may have encouraged more bullying. In 1918, Cobb told former heavyweight boxing champion/former minstrel troupe interlocutor/occasional article writer James "Jim" Corbett, "I have been accused frequently of keeping off by myself and not mixing very much with my teammates. People have construed that to mean that I have been quite up-stage [haughtily aloof]; that I have felt that I am a whole lot better than my teammates. But they have misjudged me, Jim. I have always been a poor mixer, not because I wanted to be a poor mixer, but simply because nature intended me that way." Hornbaker said Cobb's rigidity toward the humor of those around him "hampered his development as both a player and as an adult." I actually have nothing to add to what Hornbaker wrote in this instance, other than to re-insert Corbett's first name and words, including the slangy "up-stage," that he bracketed out.

Leerhsen v. Hornbaker

Even though there is so much exclusive detail or analysis in either of the 2015 books, both authors missed major detail about Cobb's racism and about his life off the field. As far as what they wrote about his playing career, with few exceptions did I read original coverage closely enough to weigh in.

Hornbaker's writing style is straightforward, but according to one reviewer, to a fault. A 2015 reviewer for *School Library Journal*, Mark Flowers, described Hornbaker's Cobb biography as "dry as dust." In defense of Hornbaker, he is adept at paraphrasing news reports, for those who dislike reading quotations, and the breadth of his sources is greater than Leerhsen's. That said, I think that Hornbaker eerily mimicked Cobb himself in hardly finding humor in anything.

Another criticism by Flowers of Hornbaker is both well-taken and maddening. Flowers observed, "Those who have not read Leerhsen may never realize what evidence Hornbaker is relying on, and his pronouncements come across as holy writ rather than well-reasoned arguments."

The one place where I found Hornbaker not making clear what his originating source was, was in the softenings that he did to Alexander's racism generalizations about Cobb. For example, as I noted on page 39, Hornbaker wrote, "The overall sum of evidence paints Cobb to be the kind of man who refused to take anything less than perfect etiquette from people of color." I then added a caveat that began, "presumably meaning those he did not have some existing positive relationship with." I explained that that would have solved his problem because I discovered that the Cobbs had the same black cook for apparently well beyond a decade.

But Flowers's criticism about Hornbaker having trouble making well-reasoned arguments hardly holds up to scrutiny, beyond some minor flaws in his racial prose. Even though Leerhsen may have made what *sound* like well-reasoned arguments, my negative findings, by default, elevate Hornbaker as the more accurate racial Cobb historian.

While one can quibble about Hornbaker's racial nuances, Leerhsen's writing on Cobb and social equality in baseball before 1952 is now unsubstantiated. Some of my positive racial findings on Cobb could help Leerhsen formulate a new ultra-favorable case. But he should not be let off the hook too easily; a first step at redemption would be his declaring that *Ty Cobb: A Terrible Beauty* demonstrably suffers from a similar problem that afflicted Stump's 1961 article and 1994 book: shouting too loudly for media attention in their respective media ages, by straying from the journalistic and academic norms of a book.

A taste of what Leerhsen wrought appears right after Flowers's argumentation critique above, as follows: "On top of that, Hornbaker skips a some [sic] essential details that Leerhsen includes – from small points such as Cobb's obsessive reading habit to huge points in Cobb's defense, including his vociferous defense of Jackie Robinson and the integration of baseball – which made this reader wonder how much independent research Hornbaker had done."

On those points, Flowers is entirely off base. If anything, based on the breadth of his stated sources, Hornbaker comes across as having done vastly more research on his own in comparison to Leerhsen. After all, Leerhsen had in his corner some portion of the pot of Fricks's 40,000 articles. On areas of his own emphasis, such as Cobb's racism and Stump's credibility, Leerhsen generalized too strongly in a pro-Cobb direction. In addition, he juiced his book with confidence in a way that likely fooled many prospective readers, book reviewers and, assuming Hornbaker entered its two relevant competitions, the award-bestowing baseball research society. Leerhsen also likely deluded many readers and evaluators by not delineating where his research, themes and analysis began on some impressive subjects and where the work of prior authors ended.

Flowers conceded that Hornbaker's book gives "a real picture of Cobb. But teens should read Leerhsen's book because it is a veritable master class on how to write a biography. Rather than simply pronouncing the facts from on high, Leerhsen collects all the evidence he can find about each controversial issue and presents it to the readers. To be sure, he makes a strong and persuasive case for his opinion about each issue, but by grappling with the evidence in print, and by wearing his prejudices on his sleeve, he gives readers – especially adolescent readers – a rare glimpse into how history is created."

Flowers is right that Leerhsen is a masterful writer in the sense of writing with verve. But such praise has to be tempered since he demonstrably fell far short in collecting the key evidence, especially on racism, his book's key subject. As a result, his is the rare book worth favorable examination by creative writing students and, as a case study in going off the deep end, by journalism ones.

Continuing with Flowers's take: "History – and biography – are not simply a regurgitation of known facts about a subject, but a careful balancing of facts, opinions, and questionable sources – and at best an approximation of what could have, might have, or probably did happen. And that is critical knowledge for teens, who are too often required to memorize names and names by rote without critically engaging with the practice of history."

While high-minded in thinking of teenagers, I think Flowers is again off base. It is true that Leerhsen's book is more engaging and, at times, shows how one cannot connect the dots negatively on Cobb. On every other measure, Hornbaker's book is better, including in following the norms of an academic book. Mainstream publishers are sometimes lax about those standards, since their chief aim in history books is to make it "come alive" to a wider audience.

Such standards include: reasonable accuracy in transcribing prose, accuracy in hedging and not stepping on the significant contributions of others. The one place where Leerhsen's book is vastly superior, technically, is in its index. The accuracy of its index also is in stark contrast to its transcriptions from newspapers. Hornbaker instead has endnotes, and those are highly accurate and vastly more extensive than Leerhsen's; Leerhsen followed the less useful, less transparent method of citing sources for select material only. I recommend that Simon & Schuster and other publishers insist on printing full endnotes from future authors who want to write revisionist nonfiction.

Given that Hornbaker's book has greater breadth but no index, a workaround is to do full-text searches in its eBook format. The word "definitive" in Hornbaker's subtitle does still hold true, at least in comparison to all other cradle-to-grave Cobb biographies to date.

A hint at what may have inspired Leerhsen's writing style is in his background. Besides having been executive editor of *Sports Illustrated*, he has been an editor at *People* and *Us Weekly*. As of a few years ago he was teaching feature writing as an adjunct faculty member of the Graduate School of Journalism at the City University of New York. He has collaborated on books with the first pilot confirmed to have surpassed the speed of sound, Chuck Yeager, and Donald J. Trump, on his *Trump: Surviving at the Top*. I think it goes without saying that Leerhsen has mastered the art of trying to appeal to a mass audience.

In a 2016 speech at Hillsdale College in Michigan, Leerhsen stated, "I knew going into this project – having been at one time an editor at *People* magazine – that human beings take delight in the fact that the rich and famous are often worse and more miserable than they are. What I didn't understand before was the power of repetition to bend the truth. In Ty Cobb's case, the repetition has not only destroyed a man's reputation, it has obliterated a real story that is more interesting than the myth. Is it too late to turn things around? John the Evangelist[, as opposed to John Evangelist Walsh, the Prentice-Hall editor,] said, 'The truth will set you free.' But against that there is the Stockholm syndrome, whereby hostages cling avidly to what holds them in bondage. I guess it's me versus Al Stump. Who knows who will win?" Perhaps Leerhsen now has a new contestant.

Leerhsen rightfully criticized Stump for his flawed 1961 article, which was the basis for the 1994 film "Cobb," and for the many errors in Stump's 1994 book. But, as already noted, he overreached in maligning the general usefulness of Cobb's book with Stump. On biographical detail or to show Cobb's opinion on events of his life, it seems or sounds accurate enough. Also, even Stump's 1994 book has redeeming qualities.

Blurbs

Because I tend to overlook Cobb's youth and playing career, which consume huge chunks of Stump's book, I did not find much in it to try to follow up on. Hands down, it was the blurbs at the start of Stump's book that excited me. I succeeded in tracing down three: from President Dwight D. Eisenhower and two that will appear later, from writers Ernest Hemingway and Harry Golden.

Neither Leerhsen nor Hornbaker tried to dignify or refute a blurb at the start of it allegedly from Eisenhower and dated to 1964: "Once, on a golf course, I was about to putt on the fifth green when I heard a voice yelling, 'Get out of my way, I'm coming through!' Then came the demand again. So I made way and Ty Cobb played right through me without apology. I guess nobody but the great Cobb would dare to do that to a president."

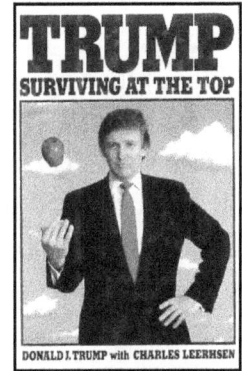

Stump had written a Cobb-focused golf article in 1990 in *Golf* magazine entitled, "Bobby & Ty." Its subtitle was, "From One Legend to Another: Bobby Jones Introduced Ty Cobb to Golf, But for the Georgia Peach, It Was the Pits." In it, Stump said this about Cobb and Eisenhower: "According to a published story, Cobb once shouted from Augusta Country Club's fourth fairway to a group ahead, which included President Dwight Eisenhower, that he was playing

President Eisenhower on the USS Canberra in 1957 en route to Bermuda

through. Ike, reportedly, reacted with shock when Cobb went ahead and did it, without apology or permission."

Stump added, "Asked years later by a sportswriter if the story was true, the Peach [sic] grunted, 'I don't remember.'"

The original source for the story is almost certainly John McCallum, in the first paragraphs on page 1 of his 1975 *Ty Cobb*. McCallum spoke to Eisenhower in connection with a 1960 book that he was researching on the six Eisenhower brothers who lived to adulthood: *Six Roads from Abilene: Some Personal Recollections of Edgar Eisenhower.* The book featured the perspective of Edgar the eldest, who is credited as its main author.

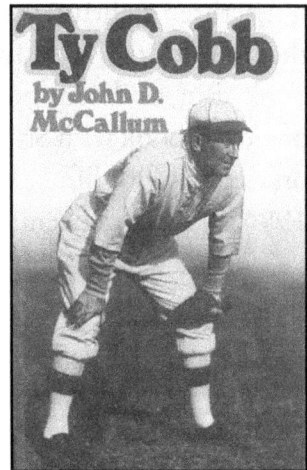

The wording of McCallum's quotes from Eisenhower and those in Stump's book match up reasonably well, although the golf location was the fifth green in the original, not the fourth fairway. Also, Stump dated the Eisenhower anecdote to 1964. Cobb had died in 1961 and the Eisenhower-McCallum book was published in 1960.

President Eisenhower told McCallum that the incident occurred during his presidency and that "I guess nobody but the great Cobb would have dared drive through the President of the United States." The only problem is that Cobb was down to an occasional round of golf as of 1948, and then had cut back under doctor's orders as of 1952. I did come across a December 1949 interview with Cobb in the *Sporting News* in which *San Francisco Call-Bulletin* sportswriter Jim McGee wrote that he "rises early every morning for a walk before the dew is off the grass and is returning to the golf links." To his Idaho doctor in 1953, Gordon Oldham, he wrote, "have played not less than two rounds per week since returning home [to Atherton]." In April 1957, in a feature in the *Sporting News*, veteran journalist Brundidge told of Cobb's return from a four-mile hike.

Also in his 1990 article, Stump quoted lifelong San Franciscan and ex-big leaguer Lefty O'Doul as saying, "On California courses, Ty raised hell. He'd yell, 'I'm coming through!' when the foursome ahead was slow. He'd charge right on past without even tipping his hat. It got so that members at Del Monte [in Monterey], Olympic [in San Francisco] and Pebble wouldn't play with him." (Sports editor Paul Gallico of the *New York Daily News*, after golfing with Cobb in 1932, wrote, "My ball had a handicap stroke on the last hole of a nip and tuck [close] match. He beefed all the way up the eighteenth fairway.")

'The Old Fire Eater'

The last notable Cunningham column on Cobb that I tracked down touched on Cobb's golfing persona. Cobb ended up responding at length; both the column, from 1948, and Cobb's response will be featured later. One chunk was noted earlier, for the part of Cobb's response that Cobb called a "little confession." The confession touched on how his church-going upbringing had clashed with being a new player in the American League.

In his initial golf analysis column, Cunningham recalled covering a Dartmouth football game at Stanford, while humbly omitting that he had been a second-team All-America center at Dartmouth in 1920. Presumably referring to a November 1938 Dartmouth game at Stanford, Cunningham recalled that Cobb at the time was a member of an exclusive golf club. About Cobb and the club, he wrote that Cobb "haunted the place and wanted to play every day, but his fellow members dived into holes when they saw him coming. He seemed to want to play mostly for the purposes of arguing. He liked to make a lot of small bets 'just to make it interesting.' Then he questioned every shot, every score and played every blow himself as if a World Series depended upon it. Very few of the brethren could take it. Golf wasn't fun the way he played it."

"'If a ball player of mine did something corresponding to that in a tight place, I'd fine him,' the former Detroit manager declared."

In his follow-up column after receiving Cobb's letter, Cunningham paraphrased Cobb as denying that he was "an antagonistic sort of golfer." Cunningham immediately added, "As I recall it, that ranking encyclopedia upon [sic] golf, golfers and golfing lore, Mr. Fred Corcoran [who became known in the sport as 'Mr. Golf'], was my authority for that bit years ago" about Cobb's golfing behavior. Corcoran arranged a three-part charity golf match between Cobb and Babe Ruth in 1941 that has been treated at length elsewhere.

The last great commentator on Cobb who I learned of is Dan Parker, sports editor of the *New York Mirror*. Parker was Cobb's type of columnist: pro-Cobb, as will be explained later. And yet, in 1939, he wrote, "Ty Cobb is just as hot-headed on the links when he dubs one [hits a bad shot] as he used to be on the diamond." Cunningham himself wrote in 1941 that Cobb "says these golfers miss the whole idea of competitive sport by chumming around together, eating together and even sympathizing with each other away from the course." Cobb instead thinks that they ought to get mad at each other "and pour it on each other."

DAN PARKER

"'Why, if I were competing in one of these things,' the old fire eater blazed, 'do you think I'd even eat in the same dining room with the guy I was going to play? I wouldn't even speak to him. I'd give him the absent treatment, even on the course, until I ran him nuts. That's the way to beat somebody, get his goat!'" That reporting by Cunningham plausibly led to the 1941 charity match between Cobb and Ruth, because in the column, Cobb made the following offer: "I'll meet him anywhere for any charity and I'll pin his ears back." Cunningham added, "In fact, Mr. Corcoran and I have wired Mr. Ruth just to obtain his reactions if any. Cobb says he'll gladly come to Boston for the duel."

Although Cobb uttered the following in 1957 in the context of how he had not lost his fierce competitive instinct if he were to golf again, he did tell sports editor Rosenbaum of the *San Francisco Chronicle*, "I sure love to give the boys hell on the golf course."

In one of his two long columns upon Cobb's death, Rosenbaum wrote that he played golf "almost as though the sticks were swords, to be thrust through an opponent if necessary." He continued, "One day Cobb was surveying a 12-foot putt at the Olympic [San Francisco-based private social and athletic] Club here. A biplane [a classic primitive-looking aircraft, with wings stacked one above the other] sailed noisily overhead and Cobb missed the putt. He was enraged. 'You yellow blank swearword,' he shouted into the skies. 'If you had any guts you'd come down and fight like a man.' Then he threw his putter high in the direction of the departing pilot. He also missed that shot."

Rosenbaum also told the following Cobb golfing story from the late Frank J. Corr, an Olympic Club member. They played for $5, on the scale of around $100 in today's dollars. "I won our match on the eighteenth green of the Lake course [of the Olympic Club] and the so-and-so threw the money down on the grass. A little wind came up and blew it into a sand trap. I took my time and walked after the swirling bill and finally picked it up, wiped off the sand, and placed it neatly into my wallet. All the time Ty was burning inside. I didn't mind a bit stooping to pick up his money. The only satisfaction he would have gotten was if I had refused to bend down, or had fought with him about it."

Speaker, in a 1939 interview that Hornbaker located and quoted for an entirely different reason, to be noted later, recalled golfing with Cobb during the baseball season. "I used to go out with him now and

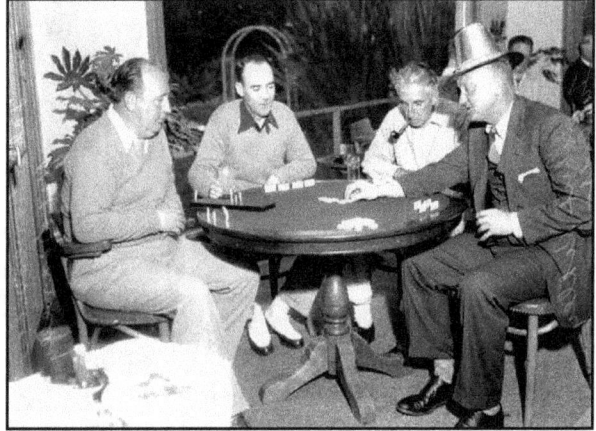

Cobb (in St. Patrick's Day hat) playing dominoes at the Olympic Club in 1938

then – and beat the pants off him – and the poor guy would be speechless if he dubbed a couple [missed some shots]. Finally, he gave it up and came out with the story that it was bad for ball players."

Digressing to how friendly Cobb was with golf critics Parker and Corcoran:

In 1951, when Cobb was pushing for dying former teammate Heilmann to be elected to the Hall of Fame, he said the following to former teammate Haney, in the presence of sports reporter Frank Finch of the *Los Angeles Times*: "Tell you what I'm going to do, Fred. I'm going to write some of my old friends like H. G. Salsinger, Arthur Daley [of the *New York Times*], Dan Parker and J. G. Taylor Spink and see if we can't get the ball rolling." (Daley, two weeks earlier, had written a Cobb-Ted Williams feature, "The Persuasive Ty Cobb"; it included a mention of Cobb's new "Science of Batting" booklet that Cobb had sent Williams.) That said, Parker did write whoppers on Cobb, while compensating for them by sharing Cobb's old-time baseball outlook.

As for Corcoran – who also was Williams's agent – he told the AP in 1938, "It isn't lack of courage that makes a golfer miss a three-foot putt at a crucial moment." He then cited Cobb and added, "He was as fearless as they come on the diamond. Yet, when he steps up to a six-foot putt he says his knees shake."

As of 1942, Cobb had told his training theories to Corcoran, wrote Whitney Martin of AP's Wide World news service. Martin also wrote, "Corcoran arranges the tournament tour [also dubbed by the AP as the 'cash and carry caravan'] for the P. G. A. [Professional Golfers' Association of America], but is a baseball nut on the side. Cobb's fame is associated with baseball, but he is a golf nut on the side, so when the two get together there is an amazing confusion of mashie shots over the left fielder's head and three-baggers to the 16th green." Martin continued, "Cobb pointed out that golfers, like baseball players, must keep in shape 12 months of the year, and he said the secret of whatever success he enjoyed (a mere trifle, naturally) was the fact he always was pointing toward the next season as soon as he completed the last game in the fall."

In 1951, when Corcoran was running a women's tournament at Pebble Beach, Corcoran and Cobb met up. The AP reported on their chat and thereby updated two of its recent Cobb-Williams swinging advice stories:

"Having more than a rooting interest in Williams, Corcoran was ready to listen to any remarks Cobb had to make concerning Ted's batting talents. Cobb even demonstrated, with the aid of a pillow serving as home plate, how simple it was for Ted to hit to left field consistently. Cobb suggested that Williams draw back his left foot slightly with the pitch and meet the ball with his normal swing. On the same occasion, Corcoran had Cobb autograph several of his booklets containing hints on batting. These he dispatched to Williams when the Red Sox took off on a swing around the Western loop. Ted found one of these booklets awaiting him at each

Fred Corcoran and Cobb

hotel." (The booklet, "Science of Batting," had been recently printed. It was based on prose by Cobb that first appeared in *Famous Slugger Year Book 1944*. The booklet prose was revived in *Famous Slugger Year Book 1950*, which, like the 1944 edition, was published by Hillerich & Bradsby Co., maker of the Louisville Slugger bat. When the 1944 yearbook was published, sports editor Howard V. Millard of the *Decatur Herald and Review* in Illinois wrote that in it, Cobb advises against trying to imitate any particular big-league batting star. According to Millard, "Each had his own way up at the plate and as Cobb puts it, it's each to his own taste and if you don't [are not able to] hit[,] you are simply no hitter." Leerhsen was too sweeping in writing that Cobb "wasn't big on dispensing [hitting] advice," although he said that held especially true during Cobb's playing days. From 1944 on, Cobb readily dispensed hitting advice.)

On the Stump

I can add another boost to Stump's accuracy about Cobb on the golf course. In searching for an antecedent to his 1990 Cobb-Eisenhower golfing story, before noticing it in McCallum's 1975 book, I stumbled across the following AP one. In 1930, Atlanta native Bobby Jones would have one of the great years in the sport's history, by winning a combination of major amateur and pro tournaments. One day that April, Cobb was attending the Southeastern Open being held at the Augusta Country Club and, fortunately for posterity, hanging around the 16th hole.

you can see this photograph of Bobby Jones and Cobb from 1930 in this book's frontispiece, on a wall of Cobb's home in California

Ahead of Jones were two groups of players "and the Jones party was forced to wait a good twenty minutes before it could continue. Up to this point Jones was five under par and had only to negotiate the last three holes in standard figures for a new course record of 66. Bobby was tired and lay down on the grass. When the way was cleared, Jones drove, hooking his iron shot on the short par three sixteenth into the woods. The ball lay behind trees, making it impossible for Bobby to play for the pin. He landed in a trap, chipped out, overran the cup and needed three putts to go down in six and ruin a great round score.

"'Did you see what that boy did?' Cobb exclaimed. 'He lay down on the grass, right when he was hot and keyed up. Why do they warm up a horse before they put him over the jumps? Why does a pitcher put on a sweater between innings? How can a man expect to hold his poise and his fitness when he lies down on the ground and rests 20 minutes?' he asked."

Stump's 1990 version is similar to the AP's 1930 one. His cites Grantland Rice as the eyewitness and contains florid dialogue between Cobb and Jones.

By the way, one non-golf but intriguing aspect to Martin's 1942 AP article on Corcoran and Cobb is related to Cobb's racism. In it, Martin wrote that reigning heavyweight boxing champion Joe Louis "might be exhibit 'A' for Cobb. Joe was in training practically the year 'round last year, and the oftener he fought the better he got, reaching a climax in a superb performance in his recent [1941] hurried meeting [boxing match] with Buddy Baer." Cobb was no doubt very much aware of Louis's conditioning; he had been avidly following boxing around Oakland in 1935 by virtue of often being in the company of

Oakland boxing commissioner and state athletic commission member Claire Goodwin. Besides being together at ringside, Cobb and Goodwin, a former minor leaguer, were "deadly golfing rivals," the *Oakland Tribune* said. The following year, Goodwin would institute a semi-annual Ty Cobb invitational golf tournament "of Cobb's sidekickers" [sic] that was still being held as of 1941.

Cobb and Louis were at a testimonial for Goodwin in Oakland in 1935. Earlier during his visit, Louis drew a crowd of 1,000 people to see him spar.

The only comment I found Cobb making about black athletes outside of baseball was in 1937. That June, *Oakland Tribune* sports editor Art Cohn was with him at the University of California's track and field venue, Edwards Field, on the eve of an NCAA track meet to begin nearby. They were standing in the middle of it, and Cobb said, "No wonder the Negroes mop up all the first places in these track meets. They were born with rhythm in their souls." University of Oregon track and field coach Bill Hayward was with them and replied, "Yes, that's it, Ty; without rhythm no one can excel in sport. It doesn't take much imagination to see the legs of [then-Jesse Owens rival] Eulace Peacock churning to the age-old beat of the tom-toms in the African jungle."

Cap Anson Books

Relative to Cobb, Anson's reputation is arguably in much better shape. One reason is that his name is far less recognizable today, at least for his negatives. His personality was more of a traditional fit: being his team's leader on the field, when the captain could also be a team's manager. He did that for 19 seasons. Nearly all of the bad reputation that Anson has, in a mass sense today, is for a tiny slice of his 27-year career: being the 19th-century player most often associated with the drawing and implementing of the sport's "color line" against blacks. The contemporaneous record, if fully utilized, shows the case against Anson as being mostly speculative, except for his reinforcing the National League's unstated policy of not having black players. Simply put, years- and decades-later stories that single out Anson do not add up and are contradicted in key ways by the contemporaneous record. My June 2016 essay on the Atavist Web site went beyond my previous writings by closely critiquing additional "color line" analyzers, in favorable and critical ways. The analyzers include two notable ones who are now deceased, Jerry Malloy on the favorable-to-Anson side and Jules Tygiel on the critical one.

I first became conscious of Leerhsen's book in 2016, while researching my essay. In a Google search, one of my four showed up in his bibliography. I did notice a typo in his rendition of it, changing "Muggsy" to "Mugsy" in the title, *Cap Anson 3: Muggsy John McGraw and the Tricksters: Baseball's Fun Age of Rule*

Bending. I did not realize until after starting to research Cobb that there is also a *Cap Anson 3* mention in his endnotes. One of his synopses of the 1890s Baltimore Orioles references it along with a Simon & Schuster book by Burt Solomon, which both feature McGraw's career with the team. The thrust of my research was to quantify Baltimore's tricky and dirty play, including by comparing it to Anson's Chicago team that decade, and show flaws in some years-later stories. Seemingly not aware that *Cap Anson 3* was revisionist, Leerhsen, in his prose on the 1890s Orioles and on a notable tricky Hall of Famer of that era that I am also the definitive biographer of, Mike "King" Kelly, gave credence to sensationalist years-later stories of the type that I poked holes in in *Cap Anson 3*. *Cap Anson 3* has a long Kelly trickery section beyond my main biography of Kelly, *Cap Anson 2* for short.

A finding in *Cap Anson 3* is that the 1890s Orioles rarely spiked opponents on purpose. I can add here that, perhaps surprisingly, the tale of Orioles sharpening their spikes within view of opposing players may have been first told only after the Cobb version was told in 1908. In *Cap Anson 3*, the earliest mention of an 1890s Orioles spikes-sharpening story like that is from 1909, from an interview by 1890s Oriole-turned-longtime-Cobb-manager Hughie Jennings. I found it in microfilm of the *Chicago American* in the Chicago Public Library while tracking Anson in the 20th century.

Jennings declared in that 1909 interview, "We had a bunch of files at the clubhouse. When the visitors came our way the gang would have their files out

Bill Veeck, Sr. circa 1910

sawing away at the spikes." New big leaguers on opposing teams were the targets. "As the recruit came up[,] McGraw or some of the other fellows would casually remark to another: 'I've got a razor edge on mine, and I'm going to get that fellow. If I get a good chance I'll drive these spikes into him for an inch at any rate.' You may be sure that the recruit if he was an infielder took no liberties with us." Jennings said that to Bill Veeck, Sr., who would become president of the Chicago Cubs in 1919. *Cap Anson 3* stressed that the 20th century contains the most embellished stories about the 1890s Orioles, several of which appear in a chapter titled "The Wild Twentieth Century."

With regard to the 1890s Orioles and Kelly, years- and decades-later prose tend to introduce big errors by overstating their amount of tricky or dirty play, or by embellishing particular examples that they cite. A major finding of mine is that the Orioles were marginally a "flying spikes"-type team but rather a "flying mouths" one.

Hornbaker innocuously referred to the 1890s Orioles for being a three-time National League champion. About Kelly, he wrote imprecisely, although merely in an endnote, that Kelly "was said to be an 'earlier edition' of Cobb for his 'color [personality, on an extreme: Kelly was about as personally popular as Cobb was unpopular] and the audacity of his baserunning.'" That said, "audacity" seems like a good word choice. In 1908, Jennings said that Kelly and Cobb were about as equally tricky on the basepaths. Of the two, he declared Cobb the overall better runner because he was speedier.

In 1912, retired future Hall of Famer Billy Hamilton, who is third on the all-time stolen base list (Cobb is fourth) and was then a scout, said the following about Cobb and Kelly on the narrow subject of their base-running. Cobb "is not the speediest runner," but "a very lively man and one of the hardest to get [out]." Kelly "was not a speedy man, but made a great reputation by his ability to get away quickly and by his wonderful ability in sliding." So, the consensus of Jennings and Hamilton is that Cobb was the speedier runner. Where Kelly stands out is on sliding ability, at least according to Hamilton, and as memorialized in the popular song crafted in the late 1880s, "Slide, Kelly, Slide." In their fielding, neither were standouts, but Kelly's fielding percentages as an outfielder or catcher were among some of the worst of all-time: .873 as an outfielder and .912 as a catcher. That is awful even relative to contemporaries who were also playing with flimsier, or in the outfield, no gloves.

(Cobb touched on his own sliding ability in the 1925 syndicated feature cited earlier with sports editor Ed Hughes. When sliding to second base, "several things guided my flight to the bag. For one thing I used to watch the eyes of the shortstop and the baseman. By then I could tell whether the throw was high or low, wide or straight. My 'fall away' slide was the product of a little thought on the thought [sic] of base running. When I first broke into the game the long 'take off' was very much in favor. Players often slid many feet in a

Ed Hughes in 1927

line, feet foremost. I noticed, however, that many of them lost momentum just when it was most needed – near the bag. Some with too long a slide, [sic] even failed to make the sack. I figured that running almost to it and then falling away abruptly to the side was a better plan. It was naturally harder for the baseman to make the touch, for it drew him out of range.")

Fight Night

By my count, Cobb was in five fights or violent incidents with whites (1907, 1909, 1912, 1913 and 1914), plus four with blacks (1907 (borderline), 1908, 1919 and 1924), with a big caveat: I am omitting those with teammates or players on other teams, since the pool of potential combatants was nearly all white. In two of his four fights or violent incidents with blacks, Cobb was quoted as using the N-word: one was with the asphalt worker and the other was when he allegedly pushed chambermaid Ada Morris down a staircase.

Leerhsen questioned the accuracy of reporting surrounding his fight with a half-drunk black friend of black groundskeeper Henry Cummings in 1907. There are indeed discrepancies in the stories between the *Detroit Free Press* and the *Detroit News*. But the *Detroit News* version, the one more favorable to Cobb for not stating that he threw a punch (Hornbaker accepts the *Free Press*'s version that Cobb punched Cummings in the face), lends support to the speculative case of his having a shorter fuse with blacks, for not meeting his standards for social interaction. The *Detroit News* version will be noted later.

Leerhsen also challenged the veracity of chambermaid Morris's story in 1919. Apparently casting aside the 1907 altercation and the out-of-public-view chambermaid one, a run of Leerhsen's prose, along with my annotations, reads as follows: "Two of the many men with whom he engaged in physical combat were black [an asphalt worker and a ballpark attendant], it is true, but in his lifetime Cobb was not known as a bigot (few people not dressed in bedsheets were). He had black friends [but conceivably only rarely socialized with them, including in public] and fans [presumably for his athleticism, not for his having a likable personality], and on at least one occasion [apparently just one occasion] threw out the first ball of the season at a Negro League park [in 1930]."

An uncredited myth-buster and plausible inspiration for Leerhsen's fighting argumentation is Fricks. In his 2008 article, Fricks wrote the following: "Ty Cobb did have an altercation with at least four African-Americans during his lifetime, but I have all the documents from these incidents, and in every case, the problem can be traced back to an action, unrelated to racism, that was committed by Cobb himself, the black person, or a third party, which caused the issue to escalate into an altercation."

Arguably the biggest shock in the 2015 books is that they both contradicted Alexander's for stating that Cobb's 1909 and 1914 combatants, George Stanfield and Howard Harding, respectively, were black. They did so by using census records or analyzing contemporaneous reporting. Leerhsen contacted Alexander to try to learn his sources for those errors, and Alexander could not provide one. One possibility I can raise is that Alexander saw Cobb's use of the word "workman" in his 1961 book with Stump, in referring to the asphalt worker combatant in his 1908 fight, and mixed up the "workman" in 1908 with the "watchman" in 1909. In newspaper descriptions of the fight in 1909, the word "watchman" can be found.

The Leerhsen and Hornbaker books also help take the negative edge off some prior writings on Cobb's racism. For example, 2007 Cobb-Ruth golf-themed biographer Tom Stanton wrote that "Cobb had more than his share of fights with both blacks and whites, but those with a racial tinge were often the most brutal and indiscriminate."

Hornbaker, and not Leerhsen, retained a taste of that argumentation, and could be what reviewer Flowers meant in labeling Hornbaker's writing as in the form of "holy writ rather than well-reasoned arguments." Hornbaker wrote that Cobb "had expectations from African Americans to respect and adhere to a subservient doctrine he accepted as normal. He didn't automatically hate on first sight, but presumed all blacks would conform to the tenets he grew up on. He gave respect where he felt it was deserved, but the moment anyone talked back to him, regardless of their color, he was fuming with wrath. The several moments of physicality against African Americans during his life cannot plausibly be explained other than conceding that he let his madness rage out of hand. They weren't targeted events, but played out in impulsive fashion, leaving behind an embarrassing stigma that haunts his legacy to this day."

Hornbaker could have jazzed that up by adding in a main generalization of Bak's, as follows: "As Cobb biographer Richard Bak wrote in an article in 2005, 'Deference, not chumminess, was what kept the social order to Cobb's liking.'" (That would have aptly matched a point made by Leerhsen, who, in trying to bail Cobb out on a different front, conceded, "Cobb, it must be remembered, was extremely sensitive to anything that might contravene the social order.") On top of that, although it would have required more definitive research, Hornbaker could have tried spinning a line about there being no evidence of Cobb having purely black friends, as opposed to blacks with whom he had or had had a transactional relationship. One such person who I note a little later, for having a reunion with Cobb in 1924, is Robert L. Wynn. As an employee of Cobb's father, Wynn had taught Ty how to swim.

Moore is Less

Although it does not rise to the level of a fight or violent incident, both Leerhsen and shunner-of-years-later-stories Hornbaker omitted one from brief 1925 teammate Bill Moore, who also spent the 1924 spring training with Detroit when he was with its top farm team. Leerhsen, but not Hornbaker, told any kind of story from Moore. Leerhsen's stated source for his was Bak's 1991 interview book. Two pages later in Bak's book, subsequent to the Moore story that Leerhsen used from it, is the following:

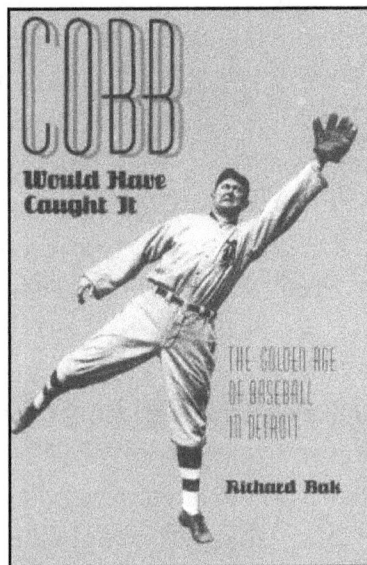

"Cobb hated a colored person worse than anything," Moore said. He told of being in a restaurant in a small Georgia town after a game "when Cobb asked this black waiter something. I don't know what was said, but he said, 'No.' God almighty, you would've thought a bomb exploded in there! Cobb jumped out of his chair and grabbed that waiter by the lapels and told him, 'You so-and-so [N-word], it's "No, sir" and "Yes, sir" when you talk to a white man!' And then he went on a tirade about the blacks."

Bak had visited Moore at his home in upstate New York in 1982. "Cobb didn't like me for some reason or the other," he told Bak. After retiring from baseball, Moore worked mainly as a police officer.

Without acknowledging doing so, Hornbaker generally stayed away from years-later stories from books, regardless of their bent. A great example already cited was his not noting the decades-later story about Cobb's having deliberately showed up late to Cooperstown at 1939 in order to avoid being pictured with Commissioner Landis. Hornbaker's weighing of sources is so good that I would speculate that since he could not easily figure out Alexander's source on that point, that he cast Alexander's writing aside.

Hornbaker did make a major exception in using years-later stories that originated in books: he used the Cobb-Stump 1961 one at least 66 times. As noted earlier, the book seems to be a largely accurate reflection of how Cobb recalled or felt about his life close to the time of his death.

Leerhsen may have done his cause a disservice by considering as reliable-enough-to-mention some favorable-to-Cobb decades-later ones from persons other than Cobb. That makes it harder for him to be so skeptical or avoiding of negative-to-Cobb ones. In my research on Anson and Kelly, I came across nothing of a decades-later nature that was as potentially significant from a former teammate of theirs as what Bak obtained from Moore.

I had written all of the "Moore is Less" prose exactly as it appears in each paragraph above, before discovering the following on Thanksgiving Eve 2017:

From San Antonio in March 1909, Paul H. Bruske of the *Detroit Times* began an article with this: "Tyrus Cobb came very near adding to his remarkable record one more episode arising out of the race question when, at dinner, he took exception to the actions and words of a Negro waiter and chased him into the kitchen in an attempt to administer a more effective form of rebuke. To the fact that the waiter lost no time in putting a considerable distance between himself and the Menger hotel was the one consideration which averted what might have been more serious trouble.

"The Negro, known to the ball players as 'New York,' brought [Tiger player] Eddie Summers a slice of meat looking remarkably like roast pork.

COBB FRIGHTENS NEGRO WAITER OUT OF HOTEL

GEORGIA PEACH RESENTS BEING REFUSED COLD ROAST PORK AND REBUKES ATTEMPT TO ARGUE THE MATTER.

By PAUL H. BRUSKE.
SAN ANTONIO, Tex., March 30.—

Cobb ordered roast pork included in his order, too. The waiter alleged that there was no roast pork; what Summers had[,] he declared was veal. The argument continued and the waiter forgot two or three other things, included on the bill of fare, which Cobb had also ordered. When called down by the base ball star he accused the latter of trying to rattle him.

"Cobb retorted with some heat and the waiter left for the kitchen, ostensibly to rectify the mistake.

"Cobb kept his eye on the glass doors which connect the dining room with the kitchen. He saw 'New York' peer out of one of these, call another waiter and point Cobb out to the latter. The Georgian's blood boiled. He pushed back his chair, rose, and charged down on the kitchen door with blood in his eye.

Paul H. Bruske
circa 1910

"'New York' saw Cobb coming and decamped in a hurry. When Cobb arrived, he was nowhere in sight. The house detective, head waiter and two or three other waiters followed Cobb into the kitchen, but took no action in the matter."

One of the players said, "If you'd started anything in there, you'd have been killed, Ty. Somebody'd have hit you over the bean with a cleaver or something about as heavy."

Cobb retorted, "I'll stand for his forgetting stuff I order, but I'll not stand for his pointing me out through that door."

Bruske ended his story with, "Another waiter served Cobb and the other players through the rest of the meal."

At a point in his book, Leerhsen invoked the alleged violent incident with chambermaid Morris in 1919 in which, according to the *Chicago Defender*, he used the N-word. Upon Cobb's death in 1961, Leerhsen said "the *Defender* eulogized him as 'the greatest,' called him 'a daring and impulsive base runner,' and, just as significantly in a paper that viewed the world through the prism of race and wasn't too polite to point a finger, even in an obituary, had nothing to say about alleged character flaws." Leerhsen also wrote, "The *Defender* started the same year Cobb came to the majors, 1905. A graph depicting its coverage of him over the decades would show a single angry spike in the spring of 1919, set off by peaceful prairies of positive prose."

Leerhsen is wrong. Racial criticism of Cobb – and even an explanation for its absence – was published in the *Defender* in 1938. It also printed criticism in 1949, after the major leagues had begun admitting black players.

I searched through the *Defender* for anything notable related to Cobb and discovered the following; it can be found, at least in part, in Roger Bruns's 2012 *Negro Leagues Baseball*. In 1938, Al Monroe of the *Defender* wrote, "Old timers will remember the much-talked-of case of Ty Cobb, greatest player the game has known, who is charged with having kicked a Race [black] girl who was serving as maid in the ball club's hotel in Philly. This case did not attract the national attention that is following in the wake of the [Jake] Powell slur [against blacks by a then-current big leaguer], mainly because of lack of circulation. In those days there were no Race [black] papers to fight the battles of their people. Thus when the daily scribes decided to end the discussion the Cobb episode died of its own lack of noise."

Hornbaker referred to the 1949 report. Although he did not fully attribute the following in his main text, merely saying it was written by Lucius Harper, the source is the *Defender* of October 15, 1949. In his "Dustin' Off the News" column that day, Harper wrote, "(P. S. – Wonder what Ty Cobb – who was Commissioner [Albert 'Happy'] Chandler's guest at the [World] Series – thought when he saw [Brooklyn Dodger black players] Campanella, [Don] Newcombe and Robinson, three Negroes, trot out on the diamond to participate in the game? If our guess is correct, it certainly must have galled him. Cobb, a rabid race-baiter, with very pronounced prejudices against Negroes, never would play against them even on barnstorming tours. What Negro talent this great national sport has lost through the decades by such narrowness and nonsense, plus downright racial prejudice, cannot be estimated[)]." Hornbaker printed a snippet from all of the above, the words "a rabid race-baiter, with very pronounced prejudices against Negroes."

I can put a mixed spin on Cobb at the 1949 World Series, on a story that both Hornbaker and Leerhsen missed. (That said, it was an easy year to have overlooked, because Cobb did little of interest in the public realm, presumably being occupied with courting his future second wife; they would marry in September.) It is possible that Cobb still personally was opposed to integration as of 1949, as far as picturing himself appearing in such a game. On the positive side, photographs of Newcombe and Cobb shaking hands exist from the first game of the series, a week after his second marriage.

throwing out the first ball at the 1951 All-Star Game; Commissioner Chandler is to Cobb's right

'A Chastened and Changed Man'

In early 1952, Cobb spoke in favor of how the sport had become integrated over the previous few years, although minor leagues in the South were lagging badly. At a time when the Texas League had yet to integrate, he told the *Sporting News* that blacks in baseball should be accepted "not grudgingly but wholeheartedly." Leerhsen printed a long excerpt from Cobb to that effect. Leerhsen then made his one explicit comparison of Cobb to other Southern-born players. Cobb's comment, he wrote, "set himself apart from fellow Southerners [in the sport] like Dixie Walker and Enos Slaughter, who had nothing good to say about the black men in their game, and openly resented their arrival."

Cobb and Don Newcombe at the 1949 World Series

As noted earlier, Cunningham's reporting makes it possible to argue that Cobb felt the same way as Walker and Slaughter at the time of integration. That said, Walker is on record as having mellowed on Robinson by the end of the 1947 season, although not explicitly on race. In September 1947, Spink wrote the *Sporting News* article to mark its naming of Robinson as the major leagues' Rookie of the Year in 1947. "He's 'Ebony Ty Cobb' on Base Paths" was the main subheadline. On the one hand, Spink wrote that the barriers that Robinson broke down "did not enter into the decision." On the other, Spink may have been deliberate in who he chose to quote first:

"Dixie Walker summed it up in a few words the other day when he said: 'No other ball player on this [Brooklyn] club, with the possible exception of Bruce Edwards, has done more to put the Dodgers up in the race than Robinson has. He is everything that Branch Rickey said he was when he came up from Montreal [in the International League].'"

Slaughter, by the way, as of 1952 was in the 12th of his 13 seasons with the Cardinals. For Robinson, St. Louis happened to be the last major league city in which he was still not staying in the same hotel as his white teammates. A day before the Paige-Hornsby article quoted earlier in the *New York Post*, the *Post* covered a Brooklyn series at St. Louis. One day starting in the seventh inning, according to Robinson, Brooklyn pitcher Joe Black and he were the subject of "racial slurs" from the St. Louis bench. In a later game of the series, Robinson heard, "You black" N-word coming from the bench. Asked about Robinson's latter claim, the *Post* quoted St. Louis manager Eddie Stanky as saying, "All I heard was 'porter' and 'shoeshine boy.'"

from left to right: Enos Slaughter, Cobb and Stan Musial during Cobb's 1952 visit to St. Louis

Besides the possibility of grouping Cobb with Walker and Slaughter, a within-his-generation comparison of Cobb could be made to purported one-time Klan members Speaker and Hornsby. As noted earlier, Speaker was on the Indians' coaching staff as of 1947 and assigned to Doby. Hornsby in October 1951 had made his return to the majors as manager of the Browns. That preceded by three months Cobb's apparent first comments in favor of integration.

After seeing some of Cobb's comments in 1952, Gordon Blaine Hancock of the Associated Negro Press wrote, "Cobb is today a chastened and changed man." Hancock, a Baptist minister and economics professor who was serving as dean of the seminary at Virginia Union University, added, "This writer has always known and has always expressed that Negroes have no stauncher friends than converted white Southerners. I have great respect for our Northern friends of the white race, but a Southerner is something different. One thing about a Southerner, he will fight for his beliefs, and once he is converted he becomes an evangel of his faith. Ty Cobb by his latest deliverance becomes one of the great benefactors of the Negro race, in that he is willing in this day of the Ku Klux Klan and Florida bombings to stand up and be counted."

Right before calling him a chastened man, Hancock wrongly recalled Cobb's fight in 1912 in the stands with a fan, by saying the fan was black. "Be that as it might, Cobb was fresh from Georgia and had the 'Georgia feeling' about Negroes."

Gordon Blaine Hancock

Leerhsen, but not Hornbaker, quoted from Cobb's pro-integration interview with Russ Newland of the AP. With regard to his own experience with blacks, Cobb told Newland, "I like them personally. When I was little I had a colored mammy. I played with colored children." Leerhsen prefaced that by writing, "Cobb's own statements about black people can by today's standards sound cliché or politically incorrect."

I can put on the table, "Cobb's own statements about black people, by 1952 standards, sounded bad. In the *Charleston Daily Mail* in West Virginia, on February 3 of that year, the following letter to the editor appeared:"

To the Editor of the Daily Mail:

This concerns the attitude of Ty Cobb, as expressed in Tuesday's paper and shared by a great many others.

The time-worn statement that 'I like colored people because I had a colored Mammy and played with colored children,' is one of the most insulting and unconvincing that could be made.

If he is really 'for' Negroes why can't he find something more substantial and authoritative to say?

I, too, played with the opposite race when I was a child; but to use such a meager experience as a basis for adult likes or dislikes, would be totally unjustified and immature.

I agree with Mr. Cobb when he says that Negroes should play in the Texas league [sic]. I go further and say that Negroes should do and be everything that ability permits, without racial restrictions.

Not because some bighearted (?) [sic] person like his colored 'Mammy', but because it is our right, God-given, when He created all people of one blood and in His own image.

Mrs. William Christian
Charleston, Jan. 28, 1952

In Cobb's defense, there is more to the story. But first, I can provide the lone clue that I discovered of how Cobb and his mammy interacted. In one of Cobb's first autobiographical articles, in 1908, he told of some of his superstitions. One is that even though umpires like to keep their broom for cleaning home plate on the left side of the plate, he likes for it to be on the right. If he sees the broom on the left side when he comes to bat, he always will "hoist it over to the right." Then he continued, as follows:

"You see I am a left[-]handed batter, and I hate to have that broom staring me in the face when I'm trying to solve the pitcher's delivery. I never did take kindly to brooms, anyway. When I was quite a kid I used to have a burly negress for a nurse [mammy], and she used to scare me half to death by threatening to sweep me off the earth if I didn't behave myself. Then she used to tell me about a 'passel [large group] o' [sic] witches' that rode about on dark nights on brooms, and I guess these things prejudiced me against brooms. Funny, isn't it?"

More to the point in Cobb's defense:

A black man briefly mentioned earlier, Robert L. Wynn, had taught him how to swim. The detail was revealed in 1924 when Cobb and Wynn had a reunion in Greensboro, N.C. Salsinger was presumably the first to report on it. I learned of his reporting because the *Greensboro News* had cited it when Salsinger was covering the Detroit team's week-long spring training trip to North Carolina. Salsinger also reported that Wynn had previously served as the first black president of the Head Waiters' Association of the United States and Canada. The Greensboro paper added the following detail: While Cobb went on to pursue a baseball career, Wynn served in the British army in India and Egypt for eight years. As of 1924, he was the head waiter at the O.Henry Hotel in Greensboro.

O. Henry [sic], by the way, was the pen name of William Sydney Porter, who was born in Greensboro. Wynn knew Porter before he knew Cobb, Salsinger wrote. Also, Salsinger referred to O. Henry as "America's greatest short story writer. He was the only writer in English who ever achieved literary pre-eminence through the sole channel of the short story." Leerhsen, presumably not aware of Salsinger's initial report, instead referenced a subsequent serial in which Salsinger omitted Wynn's name.

William Sydney Porter
(aka O. Henry)

Salsinger also wrote in his spring training story, "Wynn is a Negro and today he is a white-haired man, but years ago, when Cobb was very small, Wynn used to take care of him. Wynn taught Cobb how to swim. He used to have Cobb put his arms around his neck. Wynn would then swim out. After swimming around for a while he would release the boy's grip and push him free. The boy would have to swim or sink. He always managed to get back to shore without Wynn's assistance."

Wynn's name or how Cobb learned how to swim do not appear in his 1961 book with Stump. One can find in it that Cobb worked under the supervision of a black man, who he dubbed Uncle Ezra, on the family farm in Royston of, apparently, between 50 and 100 acres. Also in that book, after recounting the black asphalt worker's claim after their 1908 fight that he was a "black-hater," Cobb stated, "My true feeling was that of anyone who'd had a Negro 'mammy' as a child, which I did, and who had lived most peaceably with colored folk for years."

Leerhsen positively spun Cobb's having had such experiences. He stressed that Cobb worked "not as the owner's son, he swore, but as just another laborer" under Uncle Ezra's supervision, who taught him how to use a plowshare. Hornbaker also was positive, with a bit more restraint. He said that the swimming and farm experiences showed that Cobb "was influenced by several African Americans." Without knowing about her, Tripp was closer to Mrs. Christian, writing that Cobb's recollection of his interactions perhaps "followed the uniquely Southern pattern of selective intimacy with African Americans – an intimacy orchestrated wholly by whites. Whites, including Cobb, used terms like 'Mammy' and 'Uncle' with considerable condescension, implying a familial bond of affection that the recipients of these salutations may not have shared."

7. Food, Glorious Food

We know food down there [in the South] and we know how to relax. – Cobb to Harry G. Salsinger, sports editor of the *Detroit News*, in a serial on Cobb in 1925

I can be titled the gourmet expert on Cobb. I found that the *Greenville News* in South Carolina exclusively covered some Cobb food topics. One of its reports became a national story. The *Greenville News* has not been quoted by a Cobb article or book writer before me. Next to the *Boston Herald*, another exclusive discovery, it should endure as the newspaper with the most interesting exclusives on his retirement. One way it achieved that was by quoting from a highlighted commodity in Leerhsen's book, letters from Cobb.

Leerhsen wrote, "Looking back at the way Cobb lived out his retirement years, it's hard to guess what he thought he was up to. In hindsight he looks very much like a man without a plan." That is a fine observation, which, I can add, Cobb tackled in a *Parade* newspaper-insert magazine feature in 1958 about living long: "Live a God-fearing life, take care of your health through life and do all you can to help others. After you've been active and competitive, cut down on activities and learn to take things easy." I sensed early on that Cobb remained interested in all things baseball, including down to its amateur spirit – as evidenced by the fan mail that he routinely answered. However, he did not attend more than a few dozen big-league games and, as will be noted later, apparently went to high school ones near him in California only on special occasions. He did relish hunting, golf, reading and being a lifelong Shriner. In interviewing him in 1946 in Detroit, the AP stated that fishing, hunting and golf "occupy most of his active time." It also said he keeps track of baseball through "what he terms 'an intense reading interest.'" Reported detail about Cobb's Shriner activity is relatively hard to find.

About Cobb's roughly quarter-century around San Francisco, Hornbaker wrote, "The sizeable San Francisco sporting community, plus the vast surrounding area, was never at a loss for social events,

and Cobb was busy attending dinners, on the golf course, and hosting friends at his Atherton home." Besides noting his long stretches of being on travel, Hornbaker said Cobb had a lifetime pass to go to any big-league game. All that said, considering he had so few close friends by his own admission, food plausibly was a great comfort to him. Being wealthy, he had the

Cobb in Trenton in 1955, flanked by Imperial Council member George E. Stringfellow (left) and illustrious potentate Walter S. Gibbs (right)

money to pay for good food, including by having a regular cook, provided he found one who suited him.

Before getting to his mid-1930s search for a new cook, there is one other food story worth noting:

Cobb hosted a dinner party in 1935. On hand was boxing writer Alan Ward of the *Oakland Tribune*, Oakland police chief Bodie A. Wallman, city

Cobb feeding Bobby Jones at Waynesboro, Ga., the bird-dog capital of the world, in 1927

manager John F. Hassler and others. Writing about it days later, Ward said, "The other night he [Cobb] came up with a platter in his hand and said: 'C'mon now, have some moah of this nice ham.'"

In a letter in 1936, he was seeking a black cook from the South to relocate to him. To hunting chum John L. Bussey of Greenville, Cobb wrote that the

Cobb family is "in a bad fix at home." The black cook who had been in the Cobb household since his playing days had died. "I'll have to try to dig up another one from the South," he wrote. "Don't suppose you would know of a good one around 40 or 45 years old, who would want to come out, all expenses paid, naturally, to live on the place. I'll pay any reasonable amount." Cobb also wrote that all of the cooks where he was were either Chinese or Fillipino and added, "I can't use them. We want somebody that can cook country-fried chicken, grits and gravy and other southern dishes." J. Carter "Scoop" Latimer, the sports editor of the *Greenville News*, reprinted parts of the letter.

That December, Latimer updated the story. "Several weeks ago Ty was in a dilemma. His old negro mammy cook he had taken west with him from his Augusta, Ga., home died out in California. Chinese and Fillipino chefs simply couldn't satisfy the Georgia Peach who wanted his chicken dumplings, apple tarts, fluffy biscuits and other dishes for which the South is noted in the epicurean arts. So Ty wrote his friend and, asking John if he knew where he could get a Southern 'darky' for a cook. Bussey turned over the letter to this department and, for the news features in it, and through our old friendship for Ty, we printed it. The Associated Press picked up the yarn and soon the world knew of Cobb's plight. But in the light [sic] of recent developments that plight has been transformed into a gastronomic delight for the former major league star.

"But let Ty tell it. The following is an excerpt from a lengthy letter Cobb wrote Bussey under the date of November 28:"

"I have you and Scoop Latimer to thank in helping me secure a cook. I had between 200 and 250 communications from prospective cooks. As you know the Associated Press picked up Scoop's story and it went all over the country. I had all kinds of answers. I selected one from an Army captain at Fort Scott, Omaha, who had been ordered to Honolulu and had to give up his cook that he thought enough of to want to see her get placed with someone who would appreciate a good Southern cook. He sent me her picture. It seemed [s]he was interested, and his [her] communication appeared to have merit. It

J. Carter "Scoop" Latimer
circa 1940

is the only one of many that I answered. I got in touch with her, sent her a ticket. She is here now and believe me she is a good one. I am much pleased. She is originally from Mississippi. So I thank you and Scoop for helping me out." The AP then distributed Latimer's updated story on its wire. The story produced mostly mild headlines like, "TY COBB YEARNS FOR DIXIE

DISHES," in the *Spokane Daily Chronicle* in Washington. The *Bee* in Danville, Virginia, titled its story with a possible typo in place of "cook": "Ty Cobb Sends Out Call for Southern Coon"

Possibly not coincidentally, syndicated columnist Hugh Bradley was reporting around that time, "Ty Cobb, once blessed with a sylphlike [thin] figure, now has trouble keeping down to a mere 206."

In a letter in 1938 to an Idaho biologist who had founded one of the country's commercial trout operations, Jack W. Tingey, Cobb first thanked him for arranging his recent pheasant hunt. He also ordered a shipment of 20 pounds of trout around a particular date and in a certain proportion of large and small.

Cobb feeding himself at Waynesboro in 1927

In 1939 to longtime friend Hayward "Tom" Binney, he wrote, "I am sending you a case of sardines of all things but these are different a new process and as an Hors d'Oeuvre[,] they I think fit in nicely, serve in platter juice and all, plenty (word illegible) sour salt and with crackers, hope you find them o.k. Sent them to 277 Park Ave."

In 1940, Cobb wrote to Latimer in search of 30 pounds of good old country sausage. "I am very fond of hams, sausage and other products of our South," he wrote. "I boast of them, that is the quality. I have things shipped out. I enjoy them but I get greater joy from showing these [West] 'Coasters' what our South has, etc." Bussey was reportedly going to fill Cobb's request.

Latimer wrote, "What a treat is in store for Ty's friends – the big names of Hollywood, the industrial giants of the West and the sports celebrities of the nation. For, if they've never tasted hog and hominy they have been merely subsisting on so[-]called victuals of high-sounding French and Italian en brochette [cooking on a skewer]."

"If I can accomplish this I will be ever grateful," Cobb's letter stated in conclusion. "I know it sounds silly but I must have the sausage."

In 1942, when general assignment reporter Ward Morehouse of the *New*

York Sun interviewed him at his home in California, Cobb made him a sardine sandwich for lunch and poured him some bourbon; Alexander mentioned both the food and drink, and not the part about Cobb doing the pouring. Morehouse, a native of Savannah, Ga., who, like Grantland Rice, had written for the *Atlanta Journal*, said that Cobb was employing a "Filipino houseboy" named Juan. When two other visitors were hungry, Juan "appeared with more sardines," which had come from a sardine cannery in Monterey, Calif.

Also in 1942, Cobb mailed Latimer a sack of yellow grits, "ground exceedingly fine by an old-fashioned water mill." Latimer added, "We were breakfasting together recently when white hominy was served at a hotel, and Ty was surprised that we'd never seen the yellow kind, not even at [Greenville's well-known] Scooperoo ranch." Latimer said Cobb's grits were delicious. Right before Christmas, Cobb sent him a so-called Christmas folder, likely a card plus several photographs, and wrote, "Scoop – Hope to see you on my next trip South. Looks bad for the grand old game at least for awhile. Every good wish – Ty."

As noted earlier, in 1945, former teammate Ossie Vitt spent three weeks with him in Nevada, at Cave Rock. After returning to Oakland, he told Byrne of the *Oakland Tribune*, "The first morning Ty called me out into the kitchen. 'We've got to start the day right, Os,' he said, and put a couple of big glasses on the table and brought out a bottle of rare old bourbon. 'Not me,' I says. 'Nobody likes a snort in the cool of the evening better than me, but in the morning it's too tough.' Cobb didn't pay any attention. Just filled the glasses up with honey and hot water and handed one to me. 'Southern hospitality, Os,' he said. 'That's what we call this drink down in Georgia. Southern hospitality.'"

While having dinner in 1949 with Morehouse and their new respective wives at the Stork Club in New York City, Cobb at one point "jabbed a fork into an unresisting oyster."

In Georgia a few years before 1950, former Royston teammate Joe T. Cunningham went out to dinner with Cobb. "We had butterbeans and sliced tomatoes and buttermilk, nothing fancy." Similarly, a nurse near the end of his life, Betty Jo Parsons, said in 1962 that when out to dinner with her and her husband, Cobb preferred turnip greens and buttermilk to steak and caviar. (In 1959, a California state board would take into account "dairy [milk] deliveries" to his Atherton home in ruling that he was a resident of California.)

As of late 1948, he was again searching for a cook. He disclosed that in a letter to Helene Champlain, a friend as far back as the early 1920s who was now managing the bookstore at the Waldorf Astoria Hotel in New York City. In the interim, she became a book dealer and was a reporter for the *Washington Post* in the mid-1940s. In the letter, he wrote of a quirky acquaintance, Tom

McClure. "When I first met Tom I figured him out right as has been proven. I needed a housekeeper, knowing I was getting rid of her, Tom was told this, he has reversed charges on phone to me[,] was getting someone etc., fine cook, turned out to be just a lumber camp cook, and a drunk."

In 1951, Latimer reported that Greenville coffee seller and Georgia native D. Paul Simpson had mailed Cobb several packages of his home-roasted coffee. Cobb thought Latimer had done so and wrote to him, "It was fine of you to remember us with some coffee that arrived O. K. and now being consumed. We appreciate your thought very much and thank you." Latimer explained to his readers, "I once got an old-fashioned colored mammy cook for Ty, at his request, and guess he thinks the coffee was a postscript to that job."

By the way, also in that letter to Latimer, Cobb wrote, "Well, Clemson won [the most recent Orange Bowl game] and I was glad to see that; also, every team I pulled for won except West vs. East, the Shrine game here in San Francisco. Scoop, these California people are so one-sided that even if I live here I cannot help but pull hard against them."

In 1953, in a letter to Kahn's, the still well-known meat processing and distribution company, he wrote the following, as reported by the *Cincinnati Enquirer*:

Sirs:

No doubt this is no unusual request.

Recently, on the George Washington train from Richmond, Va., to Lexington, Ky., I had some real ham on the diner.

I asked 'whose product?' and so forth and was given the above name (Kahn's) and also was told that it was 'American Beauty' brand.

Would like to know if you have a dealer here in California so I could find some retailer who handles your line. Needless to add, I recognized what I thought was very fine ham.

Thanking you, I am,

Sincerely,
Ty Cobb

The *Enquirer* added, "Needless to say, Kahn's sent one of its hams to the Georgia Peach in California."

In 1954, in a letter to a former student at a baseball camp he helped instruct at, in 1952 in the Ozarks in Missouri, Cobb thanked him for the "very fine

Canadian bacon you sent me some time ago. It arrived in good condition. By the way how did you happen to know I was fond of it?"

In a 1955 letter to Salsinger, he recalled going to the Hotel Pontchartrain bar in Detroit after games, and "all I would take was a 'sherry flip' egg," a drink featuring sherry, egg and simple syrup. In 1958, the former head waiter at Clarke's Hotel in Boston, Peter Salerno, told columnist Ted Ashby of the *Boston Globe* what Cobb most often ordered in his playing days while dining there: lamb chops or roast lamb.

In 1957, while being interviewed at his home by the *Sporting News*, Cobb was served coffee by his cook, Ruth, and sipped fruit juice.

Upon his death, sportswriter Jerry Magee of the *San Diego Union* would recall Cobb's menu selections at a La Jolla, Calif., restaurant while going to visit a nearby doctor: green salad, lamb chops and peas. Plus, he ordered a bottle of beer. "The waiter brought the beer. Cobb sipped it, set it down and reached for it to sip again. He knocked over the glass." Magee added, "The hands which once swung the surest bat in baseball history shook perceptibly." Magee said Cobb reacted by saying, "Now look what I've done, just look what I've done."

In 1985, the Tyrus Richard Cobb who was sports editor of the *Nevada State Journal* in the 1940s and 1950s wrote that ex-ballplayer Cobb "had us [my family] over for southern meals."

The next subhead will feature quotes from Cobb's first wife and his mom that, except where noted, are apparently not in any other Cobb biographies or articles. One is inserted here from his wife because she discussed Ty's eating habits in a poignant way. In 1909, she said, "Oh, it is just dreadful when Ty isn't up to the top notch in the game." He becomes "so downhearted he won't talk, and, would you believe it, he won't even eat.

"'Oh, don't bother about the dinner tonight,' he'll say when the game has gone wrong. 'I don't care what I have to eat.' And then he'll take the [news]paper and sit down, and won't even talk."

(In a 1922 letter to female acquaintance Champlain, who will be featured later, he wrote, "Well, we lost a very bad game today, thanks to a couple of umpires. It is really too nasty to talk about.")

"But I tell you it is different when the game goes right. Then I say to my sister-in-law, who lives with us, 'We must hurry home now, Florence, for there won't be stuff enough in the house to feed Ty tonight.' And how changed everything is then! We are all happy, for we worry over the game just as much as he does. In fact, I made myself ill last fall over those [World Series] championship games in Chicago."

She continued, "Ty is never cross. He is just discouraged and he can't shake it off for one minute. He just broods and broods over his bad luck and looks glum and sorrowful. Then I tease him and tell him that is what comes of loafing, that he gets to thinking the game is too easy and grows careless. But this he will never admit, no, indeed, he will never give in that the Detroit team does any loafing; it is just a bit of bad luck."

The following story at least in spirit captures the above; it was told by the *Boston Globe* upon his death: "His wife once said that she could tell whether his team had won or lost by the sound of his footsteps on the porch." In his 1924 serial, Salsinger of the *Detroit News* wrote, "Nothing so hurt him as to lose and he has sat in his room after a losing game and literally wept." His daughter Shirley told sportswriter Skip Bayless of the *Los Angeles Times* in 1977, "When you have a genius and a man as devoted to one thing as Mr. Cobb was, you certainly don't think he could come home and forget it, do you?"

In his book, Leerhsen did not broach how she handled Ty at home during his playing career. Without having come across her interview above, Hornbaker still made the seemingly spot-on observation that "she was patient with him" and "allowed him to rule according to his own sensibilities."

Hornbaker listed as Mrs. Cobb's baseball-related worries those of "death threats, riotous masses, and fisticuffs involving her husband."

Off the subject of food but in the same interview in 1909, Cobb's wife touched on another major point that Leerhsen and Hornbaker never did. She spoke of being worried about his injuring himself "seriously on the diamond. He is perfectly reckless, and I am in constant dread all the time. Day after day I make him promise that he will be more careful, but it is no use; when he gets to playing he forgets everything but the game. He will never admit that he suffers, though, no difference how much he may be hurt." She told of a recent injury, possibly referring to being spiked in an exhibition game, that he considers "a mere scratch." (In a 1951 interview in Eugene, Ore., Cobb said at the end of his career, "I was mighty tired the last five seasons and I didn't want to finish with less than a .300 batting average, and I was afraid that I might get hit or injured with my reactions slowed down – and that's why I quit." He pointed out that it was his legs, not his hitting eye, that were the first to go.)

Still in the same interview, the reporter said that Ty was learning how to drive his new car and that he would in turn teach Mrs. Cobb, "so that she may enjoy the summer in Detroit while the team is away. Mrs. Cobb found traveling with the team too strenuous last year, and she will remain in Detroit this season." She said that in the coming offseason, they would be taking "an auto trip to our homes [sic] in Georgia. We will go leisurely and stop at some hotel every night.

What I should like to do is to take a tent and live real gypsy fashion, but Ty won't hear to that. He thinks I would not stand the outdoor life at that time of year. But I love life in the open."

In their books, Leerhsen's generalizations about Ty are easier to counter than those of Hornbaker. Hornbaker did make an error about Mrs. Cobb, on a subject Leerhsen did not address. Hornbaker wrote that she "was a lot less adventurous than he was." The previous paragraph has to be one of the few in baseball history showing the wife of an early baseball Hall of Famer – for which newspaper coverage is the near-exclusive source for such detail – as, in a way, surpassing her husband in adventurousness.

wife Charlie in one of Ty's scrapbooks

In 1931, the AP did a retirement story on Ty. A highlight was his saying that he "thinks the American people as a whole eat too much. For a day's food he is satisfied with a light breakfast and dinner at 6 p. m. [sic]." Leerhsen made three comments in his book about Ty and food. The first was that he ate only two meals a day. The second was that his ideal baseball weight was 190 pounds. The third was that he avoided coffee, milk and chewing gum.

An early Cobb food story, from his 1904 and 1905 seasons with a minor league team in Augusta and a semi-pro one in Anniston, Ala., provides me a chance to digress. Of the three books, Hornbaker's has the most detail on those two seasons. To find something that the three biographers did not touch on, I had to reach to the name William J. Croke. Croke was a part-owner or business manager of the Augusta team in those years who was telling Cobb stories as late as 1939. Hornbaker found a story from that year, as told to NEA sports editor Grayson. Without mentioning Croke as the source, Hornbaker described how Cobb's personality meshed with the team. A leftover quote from Croke tied that meshing to the subject of food; the ellipsis in it is true to the original:

"The hot-headed Cobb liked his own way from the outset . . . would fight for it. On the road, I had to feed the rest of the players before Cobb and [teammate and future big leaguer Nap] Rucker got into the dining room. If I hadn't the others would have gone hungry." I found Cobb mentioning Croke one time: In Augusta in 1957, he said that when he started his career, "The owner was a fellow named Bill Croke and the manager was Con Strouthers." Strouthers's name rightfully is featured in the three books and Cobb's 1961 one for his negative interactions with Cobb. Croke made an appearance in McCallum's 1956 book, perhaps only because McCallum presumably came across the same 1939 clipping. Accordingly, the 1956 book contains Croke's story about Cobb and Rucker as dining room eaters.

Charles D. Carr was the main owner when Cobb was sold, but it was reportedly Croke who earlier cancelled a hasty, bargain basement sale of Cobb to a rival Sally League team in Charleston, S.C. Less clear is whether Croke was the one who, as Grayson wrote, "peddled the greatest ball player of all time" to Detroit. As Croke told Grayson, Detroit manager Bill Armour had seen Cobb the year before and thought favorably of him. Croke said that the sale was wise for his team because otherwise, a rival Sally League one would have been able to draft Cobb for half the price that Detroit paid. Newland of the AP, in 1954 on the 50th anniversary of his signing with Augusta, rehashed Croke's nixing of the bargain sale. Carr, at a barbeque in 1923 with the Detroit and Augusta teams, told the *Detroit News* that the money he got from Detroit was one-third more than what any big league team could have drafted him for five days later.

An early turning point of Cobb that McCallum stressed was causing his Augusta team to lose a game because he was more preoccupied with his peanut taffy (popcorn is in some other versions) than catching a fly ball. Hornbaker cited a 1911 version of that story, and Leerhsen a similar later one. The episode led to his being benched. McCallum and the three biographers also noted that a veteran on the Augusta team, George Leidy, had a huge impact on him in improving his play and his game-day preparation. McCallum, apparently stemming from having interviewed Cobb, made the most use of the taffy (or popcorn) to make a larger point:

"Cobb says that in a way it was that sack of popcorn that started him thinking seriously about professional baseball. He learned from that embarrassing experience that baseball is worth a player's full-time attention – and all the practice he can get – if he is going to play it at all. Ty was only seventeen years old and playing mostly for the laughs [enjoyment seems literally more accurate, since he hardly comes across as a laugher], without any real thought of someday going to the big league. He liked to run the bases and take his turn at bat, but he couldn't be bothered with the finer points of the game."

In a 1925 serial, referring to his early Augusta playing days, he had said, "I had my lesson right at the start, and it was a valuable one. I have never been so evenly balanced that I could concentrate on my work one minute and see the funny side of it the next. I don't know if I am lacking in a sense of humor, but I have never been able to see the comical side of baseball until it was pointed out to me by someone else."

Weighty Matters

In his second offseason with Detroit, 1906-07, Cobb wrote to Frank Dean, operator of the Hammond Building cigar stand, that his weight was 186 pounds. "I try myself out once in a while to see if I am getting too big to get up speed and, so far as I can see, the new weight is all beef and carries itself."

Soon after the 1909 season, he was at 174. In an April 1916 interview with *Baseball Magazine*, he said, "I am a little heavy now – weigh 192 – but I don't take on weight very much." Magazine editor Ferdinand Cole "F. C." Lane stated that Cobb "carries the summer habit of two meals a day right through the winter as well." In an article in 1913, Cobb had said that during the season, he skips lunch to feel lighter and more active. Also in the article, he criticized coffee because it is very hard on the eyes. He was also against sweet milk because it makes the eyes smoky or hazy. Buttermilk he endorsed because it seems to clear one's eyes or is useful when eating a big breakfast and dinner and one wants to avoid overeating. As a general beverage to combat staleness, he recommended ale, an alcoholic brew, in large amounts.

In *Liberty* magazine in 1924, writer Hugh Fullerton, Sr. revisited much of the above in interviewing him. At multiple times, though, he stressed Cobb's view that drinking ale or beer should not be a habit, but done just as needed, and with no consumption of hard liquor. As far as coffee, Cobb said he drank it daily, but no more than one-and-a-half cups.

He was at 185 a month before spring training in 1922 and hoping to lose 5 pounds, to get down to 180. In spring training in 1925, he was at 195, hoping to get down to 185. A reporter who provided the 1925 detail said Cobb had weighed 155 in his big-league debut. During spring training in 1925, Cobb said, "Ball players eat too much, except when they are working under me. Two meals is enough for any man in active training." In his final spring training in 1928, he began at 191 pounds.

His putting on weight in his later seasons will be alluded to much later by Steve O'Neill, who was a catcher in the American League in 17 of Cobb's 24 seasons. O'Neill would assess how the gain affected Cobb's batting.

In 1961, when he was at 186 pounds, he told now-syndicated writer Morehouse, "My playing weight in my prime was between 178 and 188. I retired as a player in 1928 weighing 192."

On the subject of conditioning:

In offseasons, Cobb kept in shape by hunting. Former big leaguer Doc Johnston told Jack Troy of the *Atlanta Constitution* in 1940, "He always stayed in shape following his bird dogs in the wintertime." As a result, Johnston said, combined with having a natural batting eye, Cobb would need a week or less of spring training to be ready for the new season. A few weeks after Johnston said that, sports columnist Connolly of the *San Francisco Chronicle* wrote, "Ty, an extreme individualist, conditioned himself privately by walking his native Georgia hills in heavy boots on hunting exhibitions. He always reported late to camp but always in the pink of fine fettle."

(In his 1949 book *The Golf Clinic*, famed golfer Gene Sarazen wrote, "One day I was talking to Ty Cobb and asked him how he trained for running bases. He told me that he had a pair of shoes with lead in the soles and he used those to run around the bases in practice. Then when the game started, he would slip into his regular shoes and would feel considerably lighter on his feet."

Sarazen told of being inspired by Cobb to devise a golf club with extra weight, to strengthen the hands.

On a different front, in the *Saturday Evening Post* in 1941, Sarazen said Cobb had made the following point to him recently in Augusta: "Slumps in both sports are born of the same thing – too much tension. And the only way to get out of them is to relax and forget about it." In 1944, as accurately recalled in 1946 by syndicated columnist Tommy Hart, then-top golfer Byron Nelson had

Grantland Rice and Byron Nelson in 1939

credited Cobb with providing him the following tip. "The Georgia Peach once told Lord Byron he shook off batting slumps by bunting." Hart added, "Now when Nelson starts slicing, or hooking, he shortens his backswing.")

In 1948, Red Sox player-manager and future Hall of Famer Joe Cronin said, "I'll never forget talking with Ty Cobb and [current Red Sox general manager] Eddie Collins at the last world series time [sic] and hearing them tell about how they usually found it possible to duck several weeks of the training season, which in other years was much more brief than it now is."

In his 1951 interview in Eugene, Ore., Cobb said, "I did lots of fishing, hunting and running during the off season and kept in good condition. Others who allowed themselves to grow fat, [sic] need the spring workouts."

On his family's move to California for weather reasons:

In 1934, at the headquarters of San Francisco's other Pacific Coast League team, the Seals, he said, "Since coming to live in California I have had but one cold and that came right after my arrival. If I had it to do over again I would play out here, and I know it would have prolonged my baseball career many years and I would have felt better for it." He recalled "those cold-one-day and warm-the-next spring days" in the East, followed by hot summers. "You rush onto trains from one city to another and the temperature varies from 20 to 30 degrees. I was continually troubled with colds and fevers."

While in Cooperstown in 1939, Cobb reportedly said that "the Summers are intolerable down in Georgia," wrote *Oakland Tribune* sports editor Cohn, who conveyed an unnamed Eastern newspaper report second-hand. "We spent three months in 1930 in Atlanta and it was unbearably hot. Whew, we had to run electric fans in every room for 53 consecutive nights!" Hornbaker found the *Atlanta Constitution*'s take on those comments; as a reason for the move, Cobb had also cited the state's quality of education at that stage of the depression.

While visiting Augusta in 1944, Cobb wrote to Hauck, "Boy, it is hot, would not live here again for a salary and it[']s not June yet much less July & August."

Youngest son Jimmy told Bayless of the *Los Angeles Times* in 1977 that his dad had sprinkled ice water on the kids' bedsheets at night in Georgia, and had tired of doing so and preferred the weather and air on the peninsula below San Francisco. The earliest mention I found of a possible move is in a 1928 letter to Maines. A note that Maines typed onto it reads as follows: "Ty had told us he planned to move to California."

Returning to his weight variations and conditioning, throwing in drinking along with eating, and adding in his eventual health problems:

In Detroit in 1934, he said, "I keep in good shape golfing and riding."

In 1936, passing through Jackson, Miss., en route to his mother's funeral in Georgia, Cobb said his current weight was around 205, compared to 195 at the end of his career. Cobb recalled weighing 172 early in his career, "but I was not through growing then," he said with a grin while wiping coffee from his lips. In Amarillo, Tex., two days before arriving in Jackson, the *Amarillo Globe-Times* said he was bronzed and fit from, as Cobb put it, "rounds of golf and hunting trips." Cobb spoke to the reporter "of everything from cabbages to kings over coffee in the airport grill."

In New York City in 1939 after the Hall of Fame dedication, Cobb told Jesse Abramson of the *New York Herald Tribune*, "I've picked up about eighteen pounds since I quit the game when I weighed 192. I play a lot of golf, and keep active that way. A man has to taper off after a long athletic career."

Back in 1929, as conveyed in an article by a then-U.S. senator who was also a doctor, Royal S. Copeland, Cobb had boasted to him that he had not eaten even 150 midday meals in the past 22 years. "And at that the evening meal may consist of nothing more than several juicy apples," Copeland wrote. "The trouble with us is that we eat with our eyes," Cobb told him. "We sit down at the table and look over the attractive things displayed there. Then we decide we will have a little of this and quite a lot of that."

In 1941, on the eve of the first leg of his charity golf match with Ruth, Cobb was with Corcoran, its organizer, in the popular players' hangout Toots Shor's in New York City. Recalling that occasion in his 1965 memoirs *Unplayable Lies*, Corcoran wrote, "Toots put us at a remote table to keep the tourists from bothering Ty, and then kept pouring tankards of beer into Cobb who was a pretty good suds man for his age."

In 1942, Cobb referred to himself as "a little fat now, a little too fat." His weight later "zoomed" to 230 pounds, the

TY COBB reports
"My guests like the chance to say 'make mine Wine'"

an advertisement for a California association, circa 1941. Perhaps in gratitude, a winery sent Cobb bottles with a special Cobb label. Al Horwits, a Philadelphia reporter as of 1927-28, said that on a 1940s visit to San Francisco, Cobb gave him such a bottle. After visiting in 1940, sportswriter James C. Isaminger of the *Philadelphia Inquirer* wrote, "His wine cellar is a revelation. To favored guests he serves 44-year-old bourbon. He has a heavy stock of French vintages, still and sparkling."

AP said. Alexander attributed some of the weight gain to his drinking, while the AP said Cobb traced the problem to a goat-hunting trip. "He and his guide were forced to sleep out in the rain for several nights and, as a result of the exposure, he came down with bursitis[, a painful joint condition]. He was unable to continue his active outdoor life, which included a daily round of golf." In a 1941 letter to friend Hayward "Tom" Binney, Cobb wrote, "I had a set back last October as I developed a bursitis of right shoulder from a fall while on a goat hunting trip and could not play [golf] for 5 months." In 1944, he reportedly had a bad case of poison ivy.

In 1945, he told the *Detroit News* that he was at 214 and fishing, boating and running, and had cut down on golfing due to gas and rubber rationing. He was back to golfing three or four times a week as of late 1946.

While in Detroit in 1946, he contracted acute tracheal bronchitis.

As Hornbaker found, he was diagnosed with a faulty gallbladder and enlarged liver, and early jaundice in 1947. He was put on a strict carbohydrate diet. I can add that he named to Hauck about three dozen foods that he could no longer have or only in moderation. Also, "am not allowed to exercise because of the very low calorie diet, less than 1[,]500 per day." Three months later, he had lost 28 pounds and visited noted Boston doctor Frank H. Lahey in 1948.

In January 1949, he wrote to Helene Champlain about a recent "severe" gallbladder attack. "I was in worse shape than I thought, was intending to plane to Georgia for holidays, Doctor would not stay on case should I attempt it, later told me he did not think I would arrive there alive etc. my nails were white, lips blue and sweating & head swimming, took me to hospital and first thing one quart of dextrose and some other medicine in vein, also shots, next morning nails pink." The doctor said "reducing diet was simply dynamite for persons [in] my case & condition" and he restored presumably some foods; the copy of the letter that I saw was missing the next page. Connolly of the *San Francisco Chronicle* wrote a feature story two days later, including on his diet.

Two weeks later, he wrote to Salsinger of the *Detroit News*, "While it is true that I have tried to discipline myself in pursuit of good health I have discovered that at my age 62 that one must exercise more precaution along the lines of food indulgences also rest is important and moderation in exercise, in other words, slow up the old tempo." In March 1949, in advance of a visit to Greenville, Latimer said that Cobb was now reportedly at 185. "He's frisky and full of pep," Latimer wrote. He conveyed that from a friend of Cobb's who had recently seen Cobb, A. C. "Gus" Skelton of Hartwell, Ga.

He was back up to 195 pounds in 1952 when he boasted in the presence of Detroit close friend Dr. Charles S. Kennedy and *Free Press* sports editor Lyall Smith, "That's only five more than I weighed when I quit playing in 1928." In saying that, which he prefaced with a "Look, I'm fit," he "stood up, flipped open his double-breasted coat and patted his stomach."

In 1955, when Frances was seeking a divorce, her bill of particulars stated that he will sometimes drink a quart of wine before 8 a.m. "and then start in on whisky and milk." It also stated that in 1952, after a liver doctor told him he would not last long if he kept at it, he went almost five months without drinking (in a presumed letter that year to Hauck, Cobb wrote "no 'spirits' for some time"), but then resumed daily drinking. The *Reno Evening Gazette* referenced something from a pending case against Cobb by Elbert D. Felts, to be noted more fully later. When Cobb's lawyer asked Cobb if he had poured himself a five-ounce shot of whiskey at Felts's home, Cobb replied, "That was impossible, sir. I was a guest in the house, and a guest never pours." Cobb was found not guilty, and the *Corpus Christi Times* headlined as follows an AP story that repeated that exchange: "DIDN'T POUR: Model Guest Ty Cobb Wins Suit"

In New York in the summer of 1955, Cobb told syndicated columnist Leonard Lyons the following while sipping beer at Toots Shor's: "In my day, ball players drank beer and chewed tobacco. Now, they smoke and drink hard liquor. We ball players were taught that hard liquor was the road to hell."

In 1957, Cobb was at 200 pounds as of April, the *Sporting News* reported. Two weeks later, 1914 book collaborator Wheeler recalled Cobb's playing career and being with him off the field. "I have watched him fill up on frogs' legs and champagne and get to bed at 3 a.m. Then the next day he would go out to the park and make three hits out of four and steal a couple of bases. 'It loosens me up,' he would explain. 'But I only do it once in awhile.'" In a 1952 version, Wheeler mentioned "assorted cocktails" in place of frogs' legs.

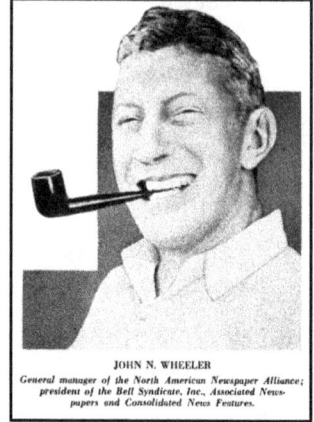

JOHN N. WHEELER

General manager of the North American Newspaper Alliance; president of the Bell Syndicate, Inc., Associated Newspapers and Consolidated News Features.

circa 1936

In 1960, when Wheeler and Cobb had lunch together in New York City, Cobb replied to a question about earlier players "drinking and raising hell" by saying that some of them did. "Once in a while when I began to feel tense and stale in the middle of the season, I might drink some champagne." Wheeler also recited to his readers the frogs' legs and champagne story. (In a 1973 book by Jerome Holtzman, then-long-ago reporter Al Horwits said Cobb drank only wine, presumably as of 1927-28, and kept his hotel bathtub filled with ice and champagne.)

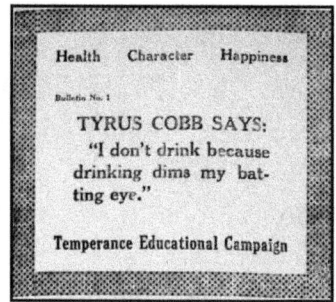

Health   Character   Happiness

Bulletin No. 1

TYRUS COBB SAYS:
"I don't drink because drinking dims my batting eye."

Temperance Educational Campaign

A month later in Scottsdale, Ariz., during spring training, Cobb drank a glass of milk in the press room of the Red Sox. Sportswriter John Gillooly of the *Boston Daily Record* added that "since his career ended, he has been known to partake of some Scotch. 'I never drank during my playing days,' said Cobb, 'but now it helps me, never hurts me.'"

Back in 1916, Cobb had been widely featured in a campaign that would lead to

Champions of All Kinds Strong Against Liquor

Jess Willard:—"The best thing that ever happened to Kansas was when it went dry."

John L. Sullivan:—"Leave liquor alone. It leads to disease and destroys the home and the nation."

Ty Cobb: "No nips for me; they dim my batting eye."

Eddie Collins:—"Tell me that a youngster drinks, and I'll assure you he will be a failure in this game."

Connie Mack:—"I never fool with a youngster who drinks; alcohol slows a man down."

"Joe Stecher never touched liquor in his life."—The Butte Miner.

Robert E. Peary:—"If I had depended upon booze I would never have gained the pole. I never touch it."

national Prohibition from 1920 to 1933. As reported in the *New York Sun*, "A chart showing the deadly effects of alcohol was the centre [sic] of attraction today at the exhibit of the Society for Organizing Charities" in Philadelphia. "On this chart, after numerous German, French, English and American scientists had been quoted on the deadly effects of liquor, there appears at the very end the following, attributed to Ty Cobb of the Detroit American team: 'No nip for me; it affects my batting eye.'"

A year earlier, Cobb had told John M. Austin of the *Boston Post* that "if I were called upon to lay down a sort of 10 commandments for the education of youth, that [the first is that] men should leave liquor absolutely alone."

In 1917, right after a local Prohibition-type law went into effect in the District of Columbia, Robert Hill of the *Washington Post* wrote of a change downtown. For the "wets" of the city, "Washington as a center of social intercourse was dead and could bury itself." The wets "sulked in their tents and would not come forth to play." On the other hand, Hill wrote, "The 'drys,' after years of weary waiting at last were having their innings." Hill told of learning that a prominent dry organization would be holding "a session of thanksgiving over the arrival of the saloonless era. Now at first blush this did not sound exciting. The meeting was to be held in a church.

"The writer, in the course of his wanderings, drifted over to the building where the meeting of rejoicing was to be held, took one long slant at the church door – and staggered feebly against a protecting tree box. On the outside of the sacred edifice was a large lithograph of the immortal Tyrus Raymond Cobb, which led to a mild wonder whether Tyrus Raymond had ever been nearer to a church than this [he had very much been, especially before his baseball career]. Under the inspiring picture was this legend:

"Ty Cobb says: 'No nip for me – they dim my batting eye.'"

Beyond not heeding his own advice on eating and drinking, he was a mixed bag on smoking. In 1914, in a short anti-smoking book by automaker Henry Ford, Cobb wrote the following about cigarette smoking: "It stupifies the brain, saps vitality, undermines one's health, and lessens the moral fiber of the man. No boy who hopes to be successful in any line can afford to contract a habit that is so detrimental to his physical and moral development." Back in 1912, Cobb had addressed an association for needy children in Detroit. According to the *Detroit Times*, he "told the boys that the way to grow up worthy citizens, is to take the best possible care of health, be diligent in school, respectful and obedient to parents and elders, to 'cut out' tobacco and to save the pennies."

In 1915, he told Austin of the *Boston Post* that he never smokes cigarettes "because I have never acquired a taste for them. I smoke cigars, a few a day, but I never inhale the smoke." The cigar habit was detailed by Fullerton in the *Chicago Examiner* in the spring of 1910. One day, when Cobb was discouraged about his batting average, teammate Wild Bill Donovan "informed him gravely that what he needed was to smoke in order to improve his batting eye. Bill produced a cigar warranted to kill or maim at forty yards and Cobb lighted it.

He smoked that cigar, survived, and the next day he got three hits. That settled it. Within a month Cobb was getting his two and three a day and smoking cigars as fast as he could consume them." As of September 1910, on the advice of his doctor, he had eliminated his daily habit of smoking them.

For a 1924 Fullerton article in *Liberty*, Cobb would tell him, "I always smoke cigars – two a day – and play with cigarets[, presumably meaning he rolls them]. I don't really smoke cigarets, just puff at them and never inhale, and I put a limit on smoking because I find that more than two cigars makes me nervous and cuts my breath." In 1952, at the *San Francisco Examiner*'s seventh annual baseball school, he would tell hundreds of kids, "Don't smoke until you're 21. It will make you better ball players." That said, he made advertisements with his image, in 1928 for Old Gold and in 1953 for Lucky Strike. In an interview feature in 1941, sportswriter John Walter of the *Detroit News* wrote that Cobb "is rolling his own cigarets these days. He used to be a cigar smoker, burning up four or five a day. That's why he took up cigarets – to break up his cigar habit. 'And when you roll your own you don't smoke so many,' said Cobb."

In 1961, he would light a cigarette in his hospital room in the presence of Ward Morehouse – and presumably was not inhaling. A picture survives of Cobb with a cigarette in his mouth, in his hospital room in 1960. (In Google, if you search for "Royston, Georgia, January 20, 1960", you will be able to see at least one image of Cobb on that date. If you click on Cobb's name in the hyperlink in the subject field, you will see a range of Cobb images, including ten others from that date. One of the ten similar ones shows him seemingly lighting up, presumably as a stunt.)

I have one loose end involving food and the *Greenville News*; it relates to Cobb's 1952 statements in support of integrating the Texas League and, by implication, the other remaining all-white minor leagues.

After reprinting some of those statements, Latimer ended with Cobb's saying, "When I was little I had a Colored mammy. I played with Colored children." Latimer told his readers that Cobb "was thinking back, back to the time when he was a towsie-headed [light-blond-to-whitish] chap in the village of Royston, Ga." Then, without missing a beat, Latimer wrote the following, including with an ellipsis:

"When Cobb moved from Augusta to Menlo Park, he carried with him his old Negro mammy cook. She died and the Georgia Peach then tried out a Filipino chef. Ty missed the old cooking, and several years ago he appealed to me to get him a Colored cook of the old school. He wanted his fried chicken, grits and gravy, Southern country style. . . Pretty soon an old mammy was on her way, and Ty was happy again."

8. *Amanda and Charlie (Quotes, Schmotes II)*

In Cobb biographies, there are few quotes from Cobb's mom Amanda and his first wife Charlie. Two do stand out. One is from 1926, a brief quote from Charlie about game-fixing allegations against her husband. The second is a long interview from 1919 in which Amanda speaks of her son's youth and baseball success. Quotes from the 1919 interview appear at length in Don Rhodes's Georgia-focused 2008 biography. One line from the 1926 quote is probably the most quoted one in Cobb books from either of the women; it is in the Alexander, Rhodes and Leerhsen ones.

The full version of Charlie's brief but notable quote in 1926, as reported by the Associated Press, was, "He may have his faults, but dishonesty is not one of them." Also, "I believe that Mr. Cobb has completely answered the accusations, and I wish only to add that I know the charges are untrue in every detail. I know him better than anyone else. He has lived clean and played the game clean. His case is safe in his friends' hands."

Without labeling it as such, Leerhsen found a special-to-the-*Atlanta Constitution* variation of that. His transcription is close to what I found actually ran in that newspaper, which is: "'Above all persons, I should know that Ty Cobb is absolutely fair and square,' she declared. 'We have been married 19 years and have five children. My husband may have his faults, but dishonesty is not one of them.'" The dishonesty sentence is the one that the above Cobb biographers have extracted from that.

I can claim to be bringing to light the United Press variation: "'My husband has his faults, goodness knows,' Mrs. Cobb said over the 'phone [sic]. 'But I'll tell you one thing – dishonesty is not one of them.'" As proof that no one else has cited that version, no one has quoted the next line of the United Press report, a seeming gem: "Ty, Junior [one of their sons], has a chip on his shoulder. 'Just let anyone say anything about my dad.'"

The only problem with this rare commendable multi-sentence transcription that I found Leerhsen making is: He placed it in his narrative as if Mrs. Cobb had uttered it at a rally in Augusta, days later. He wrote, "At a rally for Cobb in Augusta, his wife, Charlie, told a crowd of about 500 people standing beneath a banner ('TY IS STILL OUR IDOL, AND THE IDOL OF AMERICA') on Broad Street, 'above all persons I should know that Ty Cobb is absolutely fair and square. We have been married 19 years and have five children. My husband may have his faults, but dishonesty is not one of them.'"

Here are some other quotes from Charlie that I seem to be the first to be publishing. They are from when Charlie, while in Georgia and he was on a trip to California, first filed for divorce. Ty was there, he told the Associated Press, "to attend the opening of the San Francisco baseball club's new Seal Stadium and to seek a home with a view toward living in this state."

According to the AP, she "refused to be advised of [Ty] Cobb's statement made in Monterey, Calif., saying 'I do not believe you have a statement from Mr. Cobb' and 'I've tried to keep this matter very quiet. I am very sorry the newspapers had to get anything about it. I flatly refuse to make a statement.'" The AP added, "With this Mrs. Cobb said 'good bye' and hung up the telephone."

Cobb at the Augusta rally

While those quotes may not be notable in and of themselves, I also glanced at what Ty had said. Alexander related the following: Speaking from California, "Cobb told newsmen that he was shocked, didn't know what to say 'except that I have always loved my wife, my children and my home.'"

If you look at Leerhsen's book, you will find the following quotes from Ty: Cobb was "surprised and shocked." Also, "I have always loved my wife, my children and my home." After printing that latter quote, Leerhsen wrote that that "was about all he could muster for newsmen who came looking for a response to her divorce filing."

Leerhsen was presumably fooled by Alexander's "don't know what to say except" characterization of Cobb's reaction and did not look at Rhodes's book for the following, which appears after the full sentence that Leerhsen cited. I have made minor corrections to Rhodes's transcription:

"I am sorry such apparently hasty action as this was taken in my absence from home and without having first consulted me in the matter. A family is an institution where the children's interest should come first, and even now I say that Mrs. Cobb and I should think of our children and not bring them into any court procedure."

Switching focus, I can bring to light an undated letter from Ty to Charlie in which he blames her for their problems; it could have been sent anytime between

1931 and 1947, the year that their divorce became final. In the letter, one reference is to documents he supposedly is to sign, and he makes reference to a will. The transcriptions are from Profiles in History, an auction house that sold the letter in 2013. The full version ran more than 1,700 words.

Ty's first criticism was, "It is very clear to me now, how wretched and poisonous you can be. You have gone on & on, developing & showing what[']s really inside you. No one of those closest to you, your own family, has done as much for you and shown the fairness to you, tried to tell & help you in your own affairs, even after & when you flaunted any decent position of a wife to a husband in asking advice & direction. Your crude and pointed arrogance & ignorance in not asking & presenting the problem which you knew nothing about as proof your asking a minor child, [their son] Herschel."

He continued, "No you showed your stripe there and where you stood. No fairness or decency of womanhood was present. You have done those things to me which clearly showed what was in you, so don[']t mention to me as you did in last note, 'I shall always be available, also if I (you) have thought unfairly of you (me).' If I were you I would be ashamed to utter such hypocritical words."

The letter then has a large section that either sounds repetitive in tone or focuses on issues referring to their children; one admission in that part is, "Yes I drink, why should I not have, to try and get my worries & mind off the sad mistake I made." After that section, it continues as follows:

"You can[']t be my boss. You are trying to put me under your thumb. I was trying to have an honorable and decent home, no tragedies, no lies, few failures, no courts, no penitentiaries, no debtors courts, no trades people criticizing, and no ostracism, children going to college and having & holding the regard & respect of the instructors, making & holding fellow students friendship and loyalty, coming away from schools with the desire of fellow students to keep in touch to correspond . . . Oh! Yes we have had hell I will admit. It[']s a wonder there were no tragedy. Yes I have done things in resentment & for cause that I never dreamed would happen to me, but when I married you I never dreamed a person could be so much against truth & right, how they could ever be so in opposition to those principles. Most of the very many of these wrongs could have been amended for and a desire for forgiveness and desire to correct. Of course you were different. You would not, and it was these things of wrong that was done and stood for by you, that infected the children and that is what really drove me wild, and proof, pray remember & think, from Ty [Jr.] on down each one has followed and done the things of wrong, right in some pattern, the same things, you did and to this day so strange, all have refused as you keep getting advice and poisons from your oldest boy or someone."

Daughter Shirley told Rhodes that her father "blamed my mother for the attitude of the children, but I also blame Mr. Cobb. There's an attitude that develops when you are raised in an atmosphere of fear." She gave examples of her mom at times being dishonest to him, and that she was now finding comfort in sweet letters he sent her mom during his playing days. I can quote from a 1955 one from him to stepdaughter Geraldine Cass Sutton, the daughter of his second wife Frances; they would divorce the following year: "So again I say I have and do yet really love your mother and I hasten to say one with such love, never, never, never can in any way mistreat or be rough with the one they love, every desire or wish is a pleasure to grant, and I say and she will tell and assure you personally if she has not already and at all times told you this for it is the truth." In his 2017 Simon & Schuster book on Joe DiMaggio with a 1990s focus, the author, foot and ankle doctor Rock G. Positano, wrote that DiMaggio once told him, "Ty Cobb beat up his wife." Positano did not indicate which one, but he plausibly hit both.

from left to right in Casper, Wyo., in 1954: Frances, Ty and Madge Mapel (sister-in-law of ex-big leaguer Rolla Mapel)

As far as Charlie, neither 2015 book cites Rhodes's one in its main text, which states, based on speaking with Shirley, "Cobb would hit his wife and kids." A direct quote from Shirley is, "He beat everybody, and we weren't bad children." Hornbaker alluded to that broad claim and cited Rhodes's book in his endnotes. On family members who got hit, Leerhsen did not repeat Shirley's claim and implicitly narrowed it, by stating that Ty probably struck Ty Jr.

As far as Frances, the bill of particulars that she filed in 1955 states that in August 1952 at Cave Rock, Cobb was "very drunk and very abusive" one day. While Frances was talking to a visiting female friend of hers in the living room, Cobb "drew his knee up and caught her [Frances] in the groin." Hornbaker deserves kudos for being the first Cobb author to have obtained the document. But he omitted her groin-strike claim. Instead, he stressed, as did the AP and United Press, his alleged frequent excessive drinking and profanity. Hornbaker was more explicit than the wire services in conveying that the profanity stemmed from the drinking. He did not repeat, as the AP and UP did, her saying that Cobb had engaged in frequent "violent behavior." The worst that Hornbaker described was, in his words, Cobb's having made "horrid threats" to her.

In conveying the following three acts, the document in only the first case indicated that he was drunk at the time. When she did not want to go to Cooperstown with him in 1954, "He picked up a potted plant from a table and threw it against the front door." Also that year, out of the blue, he "stated to the plaintiff that he would have shot his ex-wife if he could get away with it." At a dinner at home in 1955, he vowed to, in her words, "break up the place. He shoved a table over and broke all the glasses and chinaware."

As noted earlier, Rhodes found the 1919 long interview with mom Amanda. I found a 1909 one, plus a 1912 one in Denver after the wedding in Lincoln, Neb., of son Paul, a right fielder for the Western League team there. In 1909, she said, "When Tyrus was a boy I encouraged him in all outdoor recreation, and when the time came that he was called away from home in order to pursue his vocation as a professional ball player, I prayed that he might become an honor to his profession. He has more than realized expectations, and it makes me infinitely happy every time I see his name or his picture in print."

The 1919 interview featured the following subjects: A story from when Ty was age five, watching Ty play, his personality, her views and those of her husband on his originally becoming a player, and Ty's baseball talent. Quotes that stand out from her 1912 interview, with the *Rocky Mountain News*, are:

"I am not so proud of Ty for the name he has made for himself as I am that he grew up, left home and met hundreds of new friends and always remembered me." She added, "Every opportunity that he gets he sends me some little greeting and he likes to run home whenever he gets a vacation."

In a reference to his earliest baseball league play, she said, "When everybody about home began to talk about Ty making good, as they called it, I was unable to follow his movements, as my husband was ill. He died soon after that."

The reporter commented, "Mrs. Cobb objects to the stares of the curious who gaze upon her as the mother of the world's greatest ball player. To her Ty Cobb is no more of a hero than Paul Cobb. With the usual pride of a mother she announced that he would have had the same success in anything he took up, but his favorite pastime was baseball."

The *Denver Post* interviewed Mrs. Cobb three days later and ran the family graphic that appears on the following page. Its article pointed out how young Mrs. Cobb still was – she was 15 years old when she gave birth to Ty in 1886. Hornbaker found the *Denver Post* article and singled out, for quotation, "When Ty was 'making good' I couldn't appreciate it much, because Mr. Cobb died then and I was so grief stricken Ty's success was secondary."

Here is a point of emphasis in the *Rocky Mountain News* that is a bit different from the one that Hornbaker featured from the *Denver Post*: "When everybody about home began to talk about Ty making good, as they called it, I was unable to follow his movements, as my husband was ill. He died soon after that." So, it sounds like Mrs. Cobb was preoccupied both before and after her husband's death.

In his book at that point, Hornbaker, in his own words, said that Mrs. Cobb doted on her grandchildren. Something I had inserted from the *Denver Post* interview, before seeing his book, makes that point more vividly, plus sheds light on her personality. She told the newspaper, "Ty is married, and has a sweet, good little wife, and the whole of my heart is wrapped around little Ty Jr., who is 2 years old now. He is the cutest, brightest youngster! He has his little bat and ball already and plays with them in the back yard."

After writing the above prose, I saw that Leerhsen cited part of Amanda's 1912 interview, the one with the *Rocky Mountain News*. It is another quotation adventure. Also, he cited the *Los Angeles Times* and wrote as if she had spoken to it. She had actually spoken to the *Rocky Mountain News* in Denver an entire month earlier. The *Los Angeles Times* had removed outdated detail from the story that was specific to Denver.

As far as what Leerhsen quoted, the Los Angeles and Denver newspapers have virtually identical prose; the only difference is one comma. Ignoring the comma discrepancy, Leerhsen introduced the following errors:

Error #1
"I am not so proud of Ty for the name he has made for himself

Leerhsen transcribed that as:
"I am not so proud of Ty for the name he made for himself

Error #2
as I am that he grew up, left home and met hundreds of new friends and always remembered me."

Fay King Interviewing Members of Ty Cobb's Family.

Leerhsen transcribed that as:
as I am that he grew up, left home, made hundreds of new friends and always remembered me."

Errors #3 and #4
"Every opportunity that he gets he sends me some little greeting and he likes to run home whenever he gets a vacation."

Leerhsen transcribed that as:
"Every opportunity he gets he likes to send me some little greeting and he likes to run home whenever he gets a vacation."

Another of his sources is a 1920s interview with Amanda by the *Springfield Sunday Union and Republican*, based in Massachusetts. I looked for it only after seeing it in his book. The interview contains a 21-sentence uninterrupted quotation, and Leerhsen featured parts of it. Here is what he selected:

"'He was always thinking up ways of earning money to buy baseball supplies,' she would tell a writer for the *Springfield* (Massachusetts) *Sunday Union and Republican* in 1928. 'He was always playing when he was a child. In fact, we had a hard time getting him to go to school. I remember that the first money he earned he spent for a mitt. He couldn't have been more than six years old when a neighbor asked him to take his cow to the pasture and gave Ty some change for doing it. Ty didn't buy candy or ice cream. He knew what he wanted, and he got it – a baseball glove.

"'He must have been thinking baseball all the time,' she went on, 'because when he wasn't actually playing, he was swinging his arms about as he threw or caught an imaginary baseball. I can remember seeing him on the way home from school, fanning the air the whole way. He played on all the school teams, whether he was asked to or not.'"

In this case, Leerhsen aced the quotation – in the sense of the words themselves of what he quoted – except for the most minor of things, adding an extra comma. Leerhsen did take the following liberties, however, all without telling the reader: He made sentence 15 of the quote into sentence 1. Then, after running with sentences 2 and 3 of the quote, he dropped sentences 4 and 5, thus jumping to sentences 6, 7, 8 and 9. That last change would have been perfectly fine – had he used an ellipsis.

The missing sentences 4 and 5 of the original are, "In fact, we had a hard time getting him to go to school. He wanted to play baseball all the time."

On top of that, a perfectly understandable error, because dates are mind-numbing to ace, is that Leerhsen said the interview was in 1928. It was in 1926.

Also in his book, Leerhsen cited a reporter's write-up of a visit to the Cobb home in 1921, which included a quote from Charlie. His stated source for the quote is page one of the *Milwaukee Journal* of October 28, 1921. I found it on microfilm on the last page of the day before, October 27. With that in hand, I compared Leerhsen's transcription to what the newspaper said.

Leerhsen quoted her as telling the *Journal* the following; I have made one minor fix so that there is no interruption in her remarks: "Yes, we're all fans in this house, and in between times I suppose I'm the biggest fan of all!"

The *Journal*'s quote is: "Yes, we're all fans in this house, and in between times, I suppose, I'm the greatest fan of all."

In case you missed it, "biggest" is in Leerhsen's quote and "greatest" is in the other. In addition, Leerhsen added an exclamation point.

I can bring to light that the *Detroit News* had a female reporter interview Charlie in 1921. Charlie told her, "Of course, it is nice to have my husband honored and I am interested in his base ball career, but the fact that he is a good husband and a home-loving man means more to me than all the pennants in the world."

I can also note the following that Leerhsen passed on from the 1928 (really 1926) article in the Springfield, Mass., newspaper. Besides interviewing Amanda, the reporter interviewed Charlie. The reporter paraphrased her as saying that she hoped, but was not optimistic, that Ty would quit baseball after having just resigned as Detroit's manager. Then the reporter quoted her as follows:

from left to right in St. Augustine, Fla., in 1927: (adults) mother Amanda, brother Paul, Paul's second wife Ella, sister Florence, Charlie and Ty; (children) nephew John Paul Jr. and son Jimmy

"'Ty has been under a severe physical and nervous strain for something like 22 years,' said Mrs. Cobb. 'He has been away from his home and his family and we certainly are glad to have him back. I just hope he rests up and doesn't play baseball again for a long time. Whether he can settle down to ordinary business after all the excitement of managing a big league baseball club is a problem.'"

9. Cobb and Negro Leaguers

The three Cobb biographies can be revisited for their analysis of a series of exhibition games that Cobb and Detroit teammates played in Cuba in 1910. The opponents were local players, plus a few U.S. blacks who played on one of two opposing Cuban teams. A black catcher, Bruce Petway, threw out Cobb twice one day, first on a bunt and later on a try to steal second base. Leerhsen wrote, "Petway's superb defensive feats led to stories about Cobb angrily vowing that he would never play against black players again, but those are unsupported by any contemporary news accounts and clash tonally with Cobb's other quotes from the time, which, while not particularly diplomatic, praised the local weather and extolled his teammates for demonstrating the superiority of American baseball." Leerhsen is right that there was no angry vowing, but hold the thought, along with whether there was tonal clash.

In searching through the *Macon Telegraph* online, I found the likely Cobb quotes that Leerhsen was referring to. Macon is the closest large city in Georgia to where Cobb grew up, and the *Telegraph*, apparently relying on a "letter from Havana" it received, got a rise out of Cobb by its characterization of the Tigers' play on the island. "Tigers Show Weakness at Bat in Their Cuba Games," its offending headline proclaimed. In its third paragraph, it said, "the thermometer has hovered around the ninety mark" and that the climate "simply makes the players languid, and try as they might they are unable to show the aggressiveness that characterizes the play of all American teams." Also, for the Cubans, a "two-hour workout or an extra inning scarcely gets up a perspiration, while the Americans are in lather [sic] before the preliminary practice is over."

The *Telegraph* said the Tiger pitchers seem to tire after six or seven innings, thereafter relying on their "gray matter to carry them through the later part of the game." Also, it singled out seven of the Tiger hitters by name and "the rest" as "not breaking any fences" in Cuba.

Two days later, the *Augusta Chronicle* ran an article with the following headline: "TY. COBB LAUGHED HEARTILY OVER THE MACON TELEGRAPH'S STORY ON THE CUBA GAMES"

"I wonder where they got their dope on the Detroit team," Cobb told the

Chronicle. Also, "It's hard to see how they could write such dope and overloo[k] Detroit's record where we won seven games, tied one and lost four. The stick work was just the opposite to the Telegraph's talk."

After providing a few paragraphs of detail, he said, "The Cuban teams are about on a par with the fourth leaguers [possibly meaning 4-A high school players] in America when it comes to baseball and the reason they can put up a good game against the winning American teams is because they are always in form, having a year[-]round season, and because the American clubs have not played ball in two and one-half months."

Although Cobb was not explicit in saying that Petway threw him out because of the following reason, he called the Cuban field "sandy, and that makes play slow, whereas the American clubs have been used to grass diamonds and fast play. The Cubans could not beat our fourth league [worst] teams in this country in mid season when they are in practice, and we didn't have any trouble copping [winning] the series under adverse circumstances."

Cobb also praised the Cuban climate as "delightful. A stiff breeze is blowing all the time and that makes playing pleasant. Wake up Telegraph: Detroit played rings around the Cubans and would have circled more but for their lack of condition."

BASEBALL

AMERICAN GIANTS
OF CHICAGO
RUBE FOSTER'S Great Aggregation of NEGRO BALL
PLAYERS, CHAMPIONS OF THE WORLD
V S.

ALL STAR TEAMS
OF THE CAPITAL CITY LEAGUE

Athletic Park
Monday, Tuesday, Wednesday
SEPT. 15, 16, 17

SEE THESE GAMES
ADMISSION **25c** TO EVERYBODY
GAME CALLED---3:00 P. M.

BRUCE PETWAY
a Nashville boy is the leading catcher for the American Giants. He stopped Ty Cobb from stealing bases. See him in action.

a longshot is that Cobb learned of the advertisement from 1913 and vowed no longer to play against blacks. (I did not find the ad in a prior modern-day article or book.)

While there is no evidence of Cobb angrily vowing and there is "tonal clash," Cobb apparently did not play in exhibition games after that with blacks on the field at the same time as him. Alexander wrote that "according to various accounts, Cobb vowed never again to take the field against blacks. At any rate, he never did." The closest he came after that was in 1916, according to Hornbaker. In an exhibition game at Putnam, Conn., Cobb played first base for an independent New Haven team for five innings. Hornbaker paraphrased the following: Cobb "by previous agreement stopped playing when it [the game] was half over when Cannonball Redding the great colored pitcher went in to work for Putnam." For his appearance, Cobb reportedly received $500, about $11,500 in today's dollars. Redding happens to have been a native of

Atlanta. Herein is the first Cobb book- or article-related reproduction of an advertisement for the game. Redding's name appears too, in smaller type.

A line of argument that plausibly relates to Cobb's decision not to face Redding was propounded decades later, without reference to that incident,

Baseball Fans, Attention
"TY" COBB
Detroit American League Star
WILL POSITIVELY APPEAR AT
PUTNAM, SUNDAY, OCTOBER 8
PLAYING WITH THE
COLONIALS, New Haven v. PUTNAM
CANNONBALL REDDING, THE COLORED WONDER, AND
JIMMY CLINTON, THE MILLION DOLLAR KID,
PITCHING FOR PUTNAM.
GAME AT THE FAIR GROUNDS, 3 P. M. SHARP.
Special Trolleys North and South.

by noted mid-century sports columnist Tommy Holmes of the *Brooklyn Eagle*. The Brooklyn-born Holmes responded to Cobb's early 1952 pro-integration comments and wrote, "Sign that the world does make progress is Ty Cobb's indorsement [sic] of Negroes in organized ball. Back in the days Cobb played, such a statement would have resulted in the ostracism of the old Georgia Peach by the home folk."

Putting aside how Cobb personally felt, at minimum he may have felt under social pressure not to face Atlanta native Redding, to avoid blowback from whites back in Georgia.

Beyond the 1916 game, Cunningham's quotes from Cobb make it possible to speculate whether Cobb was already feeling differently about exhibition games thereafter, against teams that were partly or entirely composed of blacks. Detroit teammates played in exhibition games against black players in just one later year of his long career with the team, 1923. Those exhibition games took place after the season, and the opposing players were all black. As located by Hornbaker, Alfred J. Roy of the *Chicago Defender* wrote in 1936, referring back to the 1923 series, "Ty Cobb, Georgia peach, would not play of course, but the rest of the players were glad to mix with their darker brothers." (Hornbaker erroneously capitalized "peach.")

I came across one other source that professes to have some knowledge of Cobb's attitude toward such games. But the source's comments, made by Ted "Double Duty" Radcliffe, a longtime Negro Leaguer who died in 2005 at age 103, are so muddled as to be impossible to accept at face

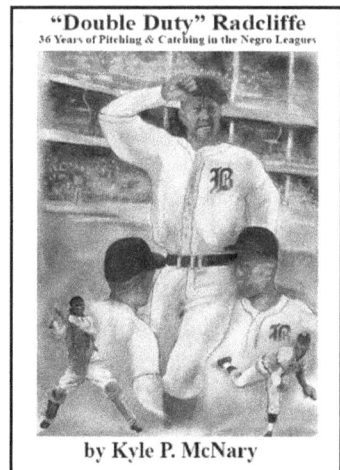

"Double Duty" Radcliffe
36 Years of Pitching & Catching in the Negro Leagues

by Kyle P. McNary

value. Radcliffe, in his own 1994 book-length biography, told author Kyle McNary that he personally played against Cobb but that Cobb "didn't play but two games against us because he was a racist." It seems highly unlikely that Radcliffe ever played against Cobb, because Radcliffe was too young to have appeared in the last apparent offseason that Cobb did some barnstorming to make extra money, 1916-17.

Bak, expounding on a point from his 1994 book, referred to Radcliffe's comment above as "uncontested nonsense," in one of his 2005 articles in the *Detroit Free Press*. Also in that article, Bak echoed his 2005 book in writing that Cobb's being "thrown out even once attempting to steal and struck out against men of color was more than his injured pride could take."

A still-problematic source but better one than Radcliffe is Redding, since at least he has some known overlap with Cobb. In a 1932 interview with the *Defender*, Redding referred to Cobb's games in Cuba in 1910 – without clearly noting that he had nothing to do with them. About that series, Redding said, "What we used to do to Ty Cobb in those games was a-plenty. We just kept him off the bases to make him sore. And you haven't seen a man sore until you see Ty Cobb raving mad because he couldn't hit the ball safely. Incidentally, they were world's champions at the time." Actually, they were not, although they had won the American League pennant from 1907 to 1909.

Also, Radcliffe made the same mistake as Hancock of the Associated Negro Press in 1952: stating that the fan who Cobb fought with in the stands in 1912 was black. In addition, Radcliffe changed the fan's gender to female.

For the record, I found one additional series of quotes by Radcliffe relating to having played against Cobb. In a 2001 interview with the *Chicago Tribune*, he spoke of having played against Ruth, DiMaggio and Cobb, "and we whipped all of their asses."

The *Tribune* continued, "Of Cobb, whose prejudices are well documented, he says: 'He was a racist but at least he was up front about it. There was some others like him too. They didn't like me but they had to respect me 'cause I could do something on the field. They had to respect me.'"

Richard "Cannonball" Redding
as of 1912

10. *Racism or Not?*

> I have over 40,000 newspapers articles, and NOT one article makes any correlation to Ty Cobb being a racist. – Wesley Fricks, "Ty Was Not a Racist," BleacherReport.com, August 2, 2008

Cunningham's two columns containing Cobb's racial views on baseball are supporting statement number one that Cobb was a racist. Support of institutional racism constitutes racism, even if there are worse forms of it.

Although the following falls short of being a supporting statement, Dodgers general manager Branch Rickey singled out Cobb in a racial analysis quote in 1950. Rickey was the baseball executive who most closely guided Robinson's entry into organized baseball. Rickey made his comment at a press gathering that January, three months after Cobb shook Newcombe's hand before game one of the World Series. The press assembled to learn about Robinson's new contract. I did not find the following in books or any historical article, other than in its original source, a column by veteran sportswriter Harold C. Burr of the *Brooklyn Eagle*:

"'When [Jackie] Robinson first came to the Dodgers,' he said, 'our colleagues all wanted to play us, but they couldn't get the use of the parks. Today that's all changed and we have no trouble booking Robinson. But we must still go ahead slowly. Some day there may be an incident. Ty Cobb used to get into trouble at least once a year. When the time comes that a Negro is involved I trust that too much significance isn't attached to it. But it's a matter of concern. The problem of the Negro in baseball hasn't been solved.'"

SALUTE

It would be absolutely impossible for me to salute all the writers across the country who supported the campaign in behalf of Negro baseball players. I would, however, like to acknowledge the efforts of Al Laney, N. Y. *Herald Tribune*; Dink Carroll, Montreal *Gazette*; Harold Atkins, Toronto *Star*; Frank Young, Chicago *Defender*; Will Connolly, San Francisco *Chronicle*; Bob Hursted, Dayton *Herald*; Dan Burley, *Amsterdam News*; Harry Keck, Pittsburgh *Sun-Telegraph*; Lem Graves, Rick Roberts, Herman Hill, Rollo Wilson, and Billy Rowe, Pittsburgh *Courier*; Roger Treat, Chicago *Herald American*; Joe Cummiskey, N. Y. PM; Joe Williams N. Y. *World-Telegram*; Sam Lacy, Baltimore *Afro-American*; Bill Cunningham, Boston *Herald*; Vincent X. Flaherty, Los Angeles *Examiner*; Ric Hurt, N. Y. *People's Voice*; John Carmichael, Chicago Daily News; Lanse McCurley, Philadelphia *Daily News*; Jack Carberry, Denver *Post*; and Lee Dunbar, Oakland *Tribune*.

I am particularly indebted to the following writers assigned to cover the Dodgers. Roscoe McGowen, N. Y. *Times*; Mike Gavan, N. Y. *Journal American*; Arch Murray, N. Y. *Post*; Harold Burr, Brooklyn *Eagle*; Gus Steiger, N. Y. *Daily Mirror*; Dick Young, N. Y. *Daily News*; Bill Roeder, N. Y. *World-Telegram*; Bob Cook, N. Y. *Herald Tribune*; and Herb Goren, N. Y. *Sun*.

from the inside of Robinson's book; Cunningham's name is on the 12th line

A speculative interpretation is that Rickey was thinking of a combination of Cobb's rage and a Southerner's brand of racism stemming from challenges to his honor. Rickey was exceptionally knowledgeable of Cobb; he had been a major leaguer in mainly two seasons – two early ones in Cobb's career: 1906 and 1907 on the St. Louis American League team. Then, from 1913 to 1914, he managed the Browns, well before becoming manager and longtime general manager of the St. Louis Cardinals in the National League. In addition, Rickey and Cobb were among the few players who were soldiers in Europe who served in the Chemical Warfare Service during the Great War. More on that overlap will appear in an appendix.

Five days before the press gathering, Rickey had been the principal speaker at the second annual awards dinner of *Sport* magazine. He spoke about equality for blacks. Robinson was honored at the event, at the Hotel Astor in New York City, and gave brief remarks to the more than 1,000 attendees. The many guests included Doby, Newcombe, Speaker and Cobb. I first learned of the dinner because Cunningham covered it and, in passing, mentioned Cobb's attendance. Of Rickey's 10-minute address, he wrote, "Mr. Rickey was in full voice and splendid vocabulary, but he got off the game of baseball onto the history of human slavery and, between quoting some Columbia professor, and getting mixed up with the 18th Amendment [which ended Prohibition], orally, of course, he seemed to go drifting off into space completely away from the central theme of the occasion." Cunningham said that afterward in the lobby of the hotel, Rickey was reportedly punched on the chest for his views on racial equality.

In his speech, Rickey had declared, "And yet it is not so long ago in this country that the Negro was a slave." Holmes of the *Brooklyn Eagle*

Chemical Warfare Service veterans Cobb and Branch Rickey in 1960, at their final meeting, at a sportswriters' dinner. A candidate for the top "what was one of the parties really thinking" baseball photograph. Cobb's thought could have been, "I made far more of my playing career, but Rickey's post-career, thanks to his superior ability to get along with others, ran circles around mine." Also worth noting: Besides moving in Rickey's direction on integration in baseball, Cobb toward the end of his life increasingly invoked religion, and Rickey was devout.

reported that and all of the following. "The institution of slavery had a logic all its own and worked its way in spite of law, custom, tradition or belief." Rickey also spoke of a "vertical mobility of society" and a number of times quoted the Columbia University professor. He cited four factors that slowly are moving the country in the direction of achieving a solution to social and racial problems. The third of those is "the growth of a middle group, rich in experience and equipment, between the upper and lower classes."

One of Rickey's stranger stories was flying over Manchuria, a region that includes China and Russia, and looking down below to scout for baseball players and finding one, but not caring about "his background or his antecedents." Holmes reported that and the following after Rickey's speech by noted journalist Quentin Reynolds: "If [incumbent Harry] Truman could make a speech like that he'd be regarded by everyone as a great President." Other attendees, Holmes added, "obviously got lost trying to follow the Rickey rhetoric. Then there were those who took him too literally and wondered whether he actually has sent his scouts into Manchuria."

The dinner could have been the first occasion in which a black person was formally honored in Cobb's presence. Although it would seem likely that Cobb previously heard someone else deliver a pro-equality speech, odds are he had not heard one by an important person in the world of baseball. Also in a likely first, Cobb got to hear his name mentioned when a major league black player was receiving an award. *Sport* managing editor Albert R. Perkins, in introducing Robinson for his, called him "the most electrifying base runner since Ty Cobb."

Rickey does not appear in Leerhsen's book and is in Hornbaker's only in a passing reference for his similar service in the Great War. When, as noted earlier, Rickey spoke to the press five days later and singled out Cobb, it is possible that Cobb was on his mind from having just seen him at the dinner.

A second statement supporting the case against Cobb was dismissed by Leerhsen as at best an exaggeration and given credence by Hornbaker and Tripp.

In his 1906 paraphrase to end all paraphrases, which is shown in full on the next page, Joe S. Jackson of the *Detroit Free Press* wrote that Cobb "knows the ways of the negro perfectly, and is ever ready to prove that the colored man more readily responds to the requests or demands of those of the South...."

Leerhsen dismissed it on the basis that the comment was a paraphrase made in a rambling way (the "run-on nature of the writing suggests that Jackson is bluffing his way through a few column inches on a day when the Tigers didn't play") and that Jackson "often liked to portray him as a backwoods exotic, the classic rube (à la Gomer Pyle or Jethro from *The Beverly Hillbillies*) who often spouts wisdom or folksy humor."

At the time he wrote that, Leerhsen gave no indication whether he was aware of Cobb's likely related-to-knowing-the-ways-of-the-Negro-perfectly "Course being from Georgia" comment in 1908 to the *Free Press*, which Hornbaker found. Leerhsen wisely did write, in prefacing his book's main analysis of Jackson's writing on Cobb, that Cobb's "colorful style and obvious intelligence" was a "blessing to a baseball writer" and "he received not just attention but also sympathy from Joe S. Jackson, the most influential scribe in Detroit."

I can add support to Leerhsen's case that Jackson was at times a florid writer. Two weeks before his key prose on Cobb's alleged racial views, he had written the following; in reprinting it, the *Augusta Chronicle* proclaimed it "another Cobblet from Mr. Joe Jackson." Jackson wrote, in part, "Ty Cobb, the 'Georgia Peach,' or the 'Georgia Cracker,' is the only one [on the team] who has the whole town [his fans from back home] with him. If Tyrus had fewer friends it would save the newspaper men many steps. We know the red hot fanatics of the town – the present writer got a line on them a year ago – and when one is seen approaching in the offing, apparently with much time to spare, we desert the main street for the alley route to the hotel."

On the other hand, Jackson showed a deep interest in Cobb's doings in Georgia. In 1909, when Cobb was having houses built near the city of Brunswick,

> **The Loyal Southerners.**
>
> One section of the Southern population always has its welcome warm for the baseballist. The colored odd jobs man is there strong with the City-of-Welcome stuff on all occasions. Ever our Afro-African friend has his eye out for the visitor from the North, who tips more often and more strongly than his Southern cousin, and who doesn't get one-half as efficient service as the latter, as has been well brought out on divers occasions by Tyrus Cobb. The latter, born and bred in the South, knows the ways of the negro perfectly, and is ever ready to prove that the colored man more readily responds to the requests or demands of those of the South, who maintain the old relation of master and man between the races, than to those of the Northerner, who proceeds on lines that indicate that he believes that the fourteenth amendment means just what it says.

the Fourteenth Amendment reference, at the tail end of the above paragraph, is likely a reference to its "equal protection" clause, meaning that blacks should be treated as equals to whites. As of 1906, Cobb's support for institutional racism was a widely held view in the North too. It is for his espousal of institutional racism circa 1940 that one can criticize Cobb relatively harder.

Joe S. Jackson circa 1910

he wrote, "No one ever doubted that Ty believed in the south, and in Georgia.

Now he is giving practical proof of his belief in the future of his native state. When the money panic was on, in the early winter of 1907, Ty had a chance to help out some friends, and at the same time to make what he considered a good investment for himself, by purchasing about 100 acres of land at Hazelhurst, Ga. He completed the deal and secured title to the property, and then let it lie untouched for a time. This land is just outside the timber country of Georgia, and, according to its owner, in fine farming country. Cotton, corn and even a peach crop, [sic] can be raised. At the present time the tide of home seekers in Georgia is all towards the southern part of the state, in which Cobb's property lies. From north Georgia, in which his [adopted] home town, Royston, is located, he says that hundreds of families will go to the country around Brunswick in the next two or three years." Jackson continued on that subject in a favorable-to-Cobb way for five more sentences, including one that ran 67 words. I can offer this corollary to Leerhsen's criticism of Jackson's 1906 paraphrase of Cobb: the run-on nature of Jackson's writing merely suggests that Jackson liked to write run-on sentences.

Also on the other hand, one of the most serious subjects in Leerhsen's book was the killing of Cobb's dad by his mom in 1905. There was a court trial, and, as Leerhsen did not note, the *Free Press* printed news of her acquittal the same day that it ran what

COLD SHOULDER FOR TIGER BRIGADE

Weather Man Refused Our Boys Farewell Augusta Game—Detroiters Bid Good-Bye to Training Camp Today—Visit Has Been Fairly Satisfactory—Players All in Pretty Fair Condition — Cobb's Mother Acquitted of Murder.

BY JOE S. JACKSON.
Augusta, Ga., March 31.—(Special.)—

AFTER TIGER SCALP

CLEVELAND PLAYERS TO BACK BLUES AGAINST DETROIT.

WILL POOL $2,000 ON CHANCES AGAINST OUR BOYS.

May Be Something Doing if Ban Doesn't Object.

Cleveland, O., March 31.—(Special.)—Manager Lajoie and his men have

Leerhsen suggests constitutes Jackson's "bluffing." Not only did it run a report about the acquittal, but Jackson also was the reporter who wrote it. To accuse Jackson of bluffing the same day as his acquittal story on Cobb would seem to be the equivalent of accusing Jackson of being inconsiderate. But that is what some of Leerhsen's argumentation seems to boil down to – when one looks at the broad record.

Hornbaker and Tripp noted the knows-the-ways-of-the-negro paraphrase and cited the "Course being from Georgia" quote. However, they did so with intervening pages (21 and 6, respectively) that dilute any impact. I can add that knowing "the ways of the negro perfectly" was an expression of the day.

In 1909, black writer I. M. Robbins wrote the following in the U.S. Socialist

Party journal *International Socialist Review*: "For over forty years the south has insisted that to understand the real negro it is necessary to live very close to him; that for that reason the south knew and understood the negro perfectly, but the north not at all, and that therefore the north was altogether incompetent to form an independent opinion; furthermore that for this reason the south and only the south was fit to solve the negro question, and that the north had better keep its hands off." Tripp touched on Robbins's point anyway. After repeating "the negro perfectly" phrase, Tripp wrote, as his next sentence, with my annotation for clarity, "Northerners [supposedly] lacked this sort of insight."

To support a case that on Cobb's rhetoric, Leerhsen is too sympathetic, he omitted a credible source, which Hornbaker and Tripp also missed, in which Cobb expressed a racial thought that sounds negative. The source is a Cobb-inscribed copy of the classic pro-slavery book *Eneas Africanus* by Harry Stillwell Edwards, a native of Macon. In a 1940 Grosset & Dunlap edition of it, Cobb wrote, "Mr. Holden: – Note author[']s preface, remember the southerner likes a negro, not the negro. Hope you enjoy this book, Ty Cobb."

That detail is a matter of public record. Hunt Auctions offered the book in a 2011 auction, and its auction site as of this writing still has both an image of the inscription and full-text searchable detail. James Spence Authentication authenticated both Cobb's inscription and his signature. I could mention Cobb's inscription in other places of this book. Because Leerhsen parsed Jackson, I am doing so here – and nowhere else.

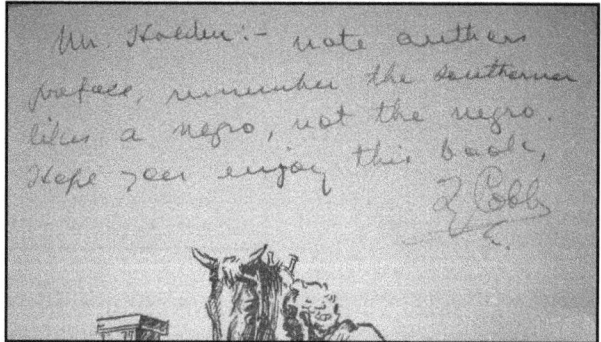

A third supporting statement was made by an unnamed *Free Press* writer in 1907. It had to do with Cobb's verbal, at least, altercation, at Augusta before a Detroit exhibition game, with the half-drunk black friend of the local black groundskeeper. "Presuming on an acquaintanceship that began when Cobb was with the Augusta[, Ga.,] club, the negro stepped up to the Georgia boy, held out his hand, and said: 'Hello, Ty, old boy.'"

The *Free Press* reporter then wrote, "Being a southerner, Cobb considered the action of the negro in putting himself on an equal footing with a white man, an insult. He drew back the hand that the negro had reached for and, instead of extending it for a handshake, drove it forward, hitting the man a hard blow. He chased the negro off the playing lot and into the club house."

Hornbaker and Tripp mentioned the fight, plus the reported "equal footing" part. Leerhsen mentioned the fight but not the "equal footing" part, possibly to win his bigger perceived fish: his Cobb-did-not-disproportionately-fight-for-racial-reasons case against a *Free Press* reporter who was separately fingering Cobb on social inequality grounds.

Leerhsen should have acknowledged the "equal footing" part and then panned it, if he wanted to, as, say, a reporter's editorializing. Instead, at the same time that he was omitting the "equal footing" part, Leerhsen advanced his viewpoint by remarking how in "modern retellings of the story, people often ascribe Cobb's actions to racism."

Future *Detroit News* managing editor Malcolm W. Bingay was its reporter that day in Augusta. Bingay wrote that "Cobb resented the familiarity and went into the [groundskeeper's] cabin inside the [ball] park. The Negroes [the groundskeeper and his half-drunk friend] answered him when he spoke and he [Cobb] lost his head, he began to raise a rough house and in a few minutes the players and fans in the stand watching the practice, were startled by screams. They saw Cobb standing in the cabin with the ground keeper's wife crying so that she could be heard all over the park, a big ax lay nearby on the table and the trouble might have been serious." Also, "Cobb could be heard calling the Negroes names and vowing dire vengeance for their familiarities in addressing him."

Without explicitly writing that he was citing Bingay, Leerhsen alluded to him by stating that it is unclear if there was a physical contact of the fighting kind involving Cobb and one of the blacks. Also, Leerhsen opined on the lack of a clear racial motive. While Hornbaker and he touched on issues relating to the fight or questions about its having taken place, I relish Bingay's coverage. My reason? It may be the best surviving reporting on what Cobb sounded like when very angry at blacks: calling them names and "vowing dire vengeance."

Cobb's extensive profanity while drunk was alleged in second wife Frances's bill of particulars in 1955. Hornbaker briefly touched on the following episode of his profanity in public. The setting was a radio station in Dallas in 1950 before a live audience of 150 people. As reported by the AP, when Cobb said he was about to tell the funniest story of his career, station owner Gordon McClendon "reminded Cobb that he was on the air. Cobb had begun to relate a story in which Dav[y] Jones of Detroit was a central character, but Mr. McClendon has [sic] sensed that it might not be the proper one to go out on radio. Cobb backed off. 'Well,' he said, 'I'll have to retreat from this one.' So he told the other, but in his enthusiasm to emphasize the point blurted out two well-known words that would appear in print only as blanks."

"McClendon then arose and grinned: 'Well, we've been on the air two years; I guess that's long enough anyway.' The crowd of 150 roared."

A fourth possible supporting statement was made in 1990 by Jack McDonald. McDonald conducted the 1952 Cobb pro-integration interview for the *Sporting News*, and Leerhsen's paraphrase from it appeared at the start of my book. In his, Leerhsen gave no indication that he was aware that it was McDonald who had been the interviewer. As of 1952, McDonald was about halfway through a 12-year run as sports editor of the *San Francisco Call-Bulletin*.

Diverting a bit before getting to McDonald's statement in 1990:

Leerhsen told some positive McDonald stories about Cobb and misspelled his name as MacDonald, including in making the following argument regarding the aftermath of Stump's 1961 article in *True*: "Clearly, it was Cobb's misfortune to have been known and liked by people who as columnists and beat writers had access to acres of newspaper space, but who were better at describing a baseball game than repairing a person's reputation."

Leerhsen cast McDonald differently, as among the journalists who "had a more intimate knowledge of Cobb" and who contended "that the monster stumbling through Stump's article bore no resemblance to their departed friend." He stated that McDonald "visited Cobb in his [Lake] Tahoe home [in Nevada] during the period when Stump was supposedly doing his court-plaster impersonation [of having been spending time with Cobb], yet he found no evidence of the writer, nor heard any reference to him by their genial and generous host, who served the MacDonalds [Helen and Mr.] breakfast in bed."

Leerhsen's book is missing the following from Frances's 1955 document. On a double date in May 1955 with the McDonalds, Mr. Geniality "was just plain drunk. He was disgusting at the table" at San Francisco's Poodle Dog restaurant.

Relating to Nevada, I can take a whack at Stump's article too. While some of his supposed trips with Cobb were interstate, the wildest adventures were in Nevada. "California had turned him down at his last [driver's license] test; he hadn't bothered to apply in Nevada." Contradicting Stump is Cobb's legal team. In January 1959, when Cobb was set to appear before a California state board to argue Nevada as his state of residency, the *Reno Evening Gazette*, citing his lawyers, said he has "Nevada license plates on his car and a Nevada driver's license." Cobb did tell UPI in 1958, "I haven't had a California driver's license."

Otherwise on the wider messy subject, the California State Board of Equalization made a final ruling that ordered him to pay $41,054, about $350,000 in today's dollars, in back taxes for the years 1949 to 1957. Incidentally, as stated by the AP, reasons for its ruling included, "He had and extensively used his telephone service at Atherton; he didn't even have a telephone at Glenbrook until 1953. He had a post office box in Atherton but none in Glenbrook. He used a California resident hunting license [he had been arrested for illegally using one in 1951, based on his legal residency in Nevada, and then forfeited bail]. And he couldn't spend extended periods in high-altitude Glenbrook because of a heart condition."

Around New Year's Day in 1952, Cobb told the *San Mateo Times*, "Most of my time is spent at Glenbrook, Nev., but during the severe winter months, I am here in Atherton." However, in its ruling in 1959, the California state board tallied that in 1951-52 he had definitely spent 393 days in California and 18 in Nevada. In 1958, he told UPI that the state of California "gave me a complete clearance in 1947, but when they heard [in 1957] I was going to move [back] to Georgia, this thing came up." In the same article, Cobb's lawyer, George H. Koster, said, "In 1950 the state investigated Cobb's status, sent him a letter saying he was a legal resident of Nevada and cleared him through 1947. This [latest] action was a complete reversal and an arbitrary assessment. Naturally he did not file returns after the state said he did not need to." In UPI's next article, Cobb gave as proof that he resided in Nevada that he had his bank account and did his voting there; he had been voting in Nevada since 1939, he told the *Times*. The *Times* also reported, "The [California] state office announced that if anybody in the state has anything other than a temporary or transitory residence, he is a resident of California."

Leerhsen told of running into, on the New York City subway, an actor who, around 2000, played Cobb in the play "Cobb." They then realized each other's tie to Cobb. After the play debuted in 1989, Frank Rich of the *New York Times* reviewed its appearance in New Haven, Conn.

I can add a McDonald story about the play; he was born in 1899 and lived until 1997:

The tour in 1990 included the Old Globe Theatre in San Diego, where McDonald had moved in the late 1970s. McDonald not only saw it, but wrote about it that year for the *Los Angeles Times*. His 1,800 words included telling of his "35 years of close association" with Cobb.

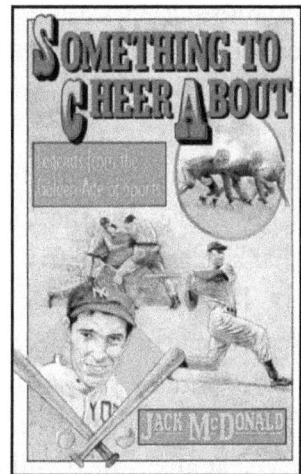

a 1986 book by Jack McDonald with some Cobb stories

McDonald found that some of the play "contained half-truths, with little regard for the facts." Also, it "greatly overemphasizes the racist angle as it had to do with Ty's life. He was a racist, but 99 out of 100 white Georgians were racists in Cobb's day. It was the curse of his era. But in his will, Cobb made sure that black students got their share of the scholarships" to a college fund that he endowed in 1953, which is administered by Emory University Hospital. His point is that only late in life can Cobb be seen in a favorable light racially.

A fifth supporting statement, a Leerhsen omission, is from the *Free Press's* coverage of a home game in 1910. Alexander and Hornbaker both noted the following, concerning a black fan who was among several fans one day who chewed Cobb out from the stands. Toward the end of the game, a detective and police officers

McDonald circa 1952

"separated the Georgian and the negro who had aroused his wrath, and Cobb went back to his place in the field. After the game, he attempted to find his tormentors, but they had fled. The Georgian was feeling low-spirited as a result of his [recent] argument with [teammate Davy] Jones, resulting in Ty's absence from the line-up for two days. He was in no mood to be criticized, especially in the vein adopted by the men who aroused his wrath. The offense was magnified in Cobb's eyes by the fact that a negro was party to

COBB ATTEMPTS TO MAUL NEGRO WHO INSULTS HIM

Fan Addresses Abusive Remarks to Georgian and Ty Enters Stand to Take Vengeance—Boston Offers Two Stars for the Peach.

the *Detroit Free Press's* headline from the game

it. Ty is a southerner born and bred, and naturally holds ideas of his own regarding the right of a colored man to abuse him in public."

Beyond the supporting statements above:

As for Leerhsen's contention that Cobb cannot be said to have been a severe racist at any time, I will leave it to others to weigh in on whether his playing of African Dodger is significant enough to cast his racism as "severe" as of 1911. A pro-Cobb spin would be that Cobb saw African Dodger as a game of skill posing a physical challenge and that he is drawn to challenges. Another spin in his favor is that one cannot assume that he would have refrained from playing a white version of African Dodger, had one existed.

To argue that Cobb might not even have been a racist, Leerhsen cited a different source: references to Cobb's great-grandfather, William Alfred Cobb. Leerhsen obtained the references from various sources, including his likely key one, Fricks. Hornbaker did not mention William Alfred. In previous modern-day accounts of Ty, William Alfred was mainly noted for having been a Methodist minister in North Carolina. Leerhsen wrote that William Alfred "tested the patience of parishioners by preaching to Indians and whites alike, then pushed the congregation around the bend by preaching against slavery. In 1848 he and his family were run out of Haywood County for their abolitionist beliefs; they resettled in Union County[, N.C.], a more mountainous region where slaves, being less vital to the economy, were not such a hot-button issue." As Fricks did in his article, Leerhsen detailed the tolerant political views of Cobb's father; Hornbaker did so too.

I found generic prose that reflected Ty's having some unusual roots. In 1953, the *Anniston Star* in Alabama recalled Cobb's 1904 brief career in that Alabama town and his now-recent philanthropy. It said, "For all his brawling reputation as a ball player, Cobb came into the game with a better family background than most of his contemporaries. His father, who bitterly [at least strongly, at first] opposed Ty's entrance into baseball, was a State Senator in Georgia and later county superintendent of schools."

Leerhsen deserves kudos for bringing the great-grandfather's background to light in a Cobb book or article. In addition, his crediting of his findings is impressive. He cited "Wesley Fricks, Ancestry.com, Genealogy.com, the *Pittsburgh Press*, Dec. 10, 1911, and the *Atlanta Constitution*, Feb. 27, 1921."

Even with such an impressive attribution, I came across a 2013 blog post that contains the contours of the finding about Cobb's great-grandfather. In an entry dated February 23, 2013, Civil War Bummer referred to Cobb's great-grandfather as having been "a Methodist Minister, who could not abide slavery." The entry is titled "Confederate Racial Heritage or Baseball's Georgia Peach."

The blogger told me that he came across that in a Civil War-related source. As of this writing, if you Google the above seven-word string, Civil War Bummer's entry will readily appear. He did not want to be identified by his

non-Civil War moniker when I spoke to him in March 2017.

One of Leerhsen's speculations that I liked is wondering about influences on Ty from his family tree. He said one possibility is that he resented and rebelled against his father, who "brought at least a measure of disapproval on the family for his softhearted views on Negroes." Ty's fighting nature, he speculated, may have been reduced had he had a more "'normal' and less Negro-friendly father."

In reviewing Leerhsen's and Hornbaker's books on the sports Internet site Deadspin, Jacob McArthur Mooney added the following, after a range of reader comments: "even liberal Southerners (and even abolitionists!) fought for more freedom or rights for African-Americans while simultaneously looking down on them; they thought they should be treated better, but did not necessarily believe in equality or that they should be considered equal. Cobb's racism shouldn't be seen as a divergence from his father's non-racist treatment of black people, but as an evolution of the patronizing racism of many Southern whites – like his father. That patronizing racism can easily breed contempt because it is still built on a chassis of racist perceptions."

Points that Leerhsen made and that Hornbaker omitted are that Ty's grandfather, John Franklin Cobb, had been an "antislavery Republican" and that William Herschel Cobb, Ty's father, "out of necessity" became a Democrat. Leerhsen said William Herschel became one because he wanted to go into politics in the Democrat-dominated South. Ty, in his 1961 book with Stump, did not ascribe a motive. William Herschel and his three brothers, Ty stated, all went to college and returned to their father's "Republican stronghold as Democrats. The arguments! The boys had book-learning to back their political beliefs, but Grandpa, without formal schooling, destroyed them with his logic."

Hornbaker should have printed the above from the book. If he doubted its accuracy, he could have tried doing genealogy research on great-grandfather William Alfred. Even Bak, the Cobb author who Fricks chewed out presumably for calling Cobb a bigot, mentioned in his 1994 and 2005 books that Grandpa had been an anti-slavery Republican.

Meanwhile, Leerhsen could have disclosed that page 34 of the, to him, not "useful" and "highly fictionalized" 1961 book had described Grandpa as "an anti-slavery Republican."

The strongest genealogy-based analysis that Hornbaker mustered is that while William Herschel was "liberal," he "didn't altogether sway his son toward free thinking in racial subject matter." Indeed, thanks to reporting on Cobb's views on social equality for blacks in baseball, on playing African Dodger and openness toward minstrelsy, we know of Cobb's negative racial record as of the early 1910s and the early 1940s. So, even where Leerhsen presented better research, Hornbaker was still spot-on in generalizing negatively about Cobb racially.

11. 'Not a Very Controversial Figure'

Whereas Fricks wrote in his 2008 article that Cobb's "racist reputation came only after he had died in 1961," Leerhsen wrote, "At the time of his death, Cobb was not a very controversial figure."

Leerhsen's characterization could be the worst media analysis of the main subject of one's book, as of the time of the subject's death, by any prize-winning U.S. author this century. With that characterization, Leerhsen then piled up the blame on Stump for ruining Cobb's legacy.

It is true, for example, that Hornsby, in a radio interview in Chicago immediately upon his death, called Cobb the greatest player he ever saw. With that, sportswriter Arthur Siegel of the *Boston Globe* began his remembrance feature. But right after that, Siegel wrote of Cobb, "Once on the field, the opposing team became a hated enemy and the umpires were just as bad. He slid into bases with spikes high and he'd come off the ground with fists flying."

It is also true that a death remembrance in the Associated Negro Press noted his later support for "racial freedom in baseball." But compare that to an AP one that began, "Ty Cobb probably was the most disliked baseball player the game has known. He was a 'loner' who preferred his own company on and off the field. His quick temper led him into fights with players, fans and even his teammates." In its obituary, UPI said he had been the "most hated player of his time" and had mellowed in his later years. Also, "Ty had a razor-edged temper with spikes to match that made him perhaps the greatest – and most feared – player in baseball history."

New York Post columnist Gross said cancer "is a terrible way to go out of the world, but this is also the man whose spikes were sharpened with a file and who bullied his way through baseball as much as he batted his way through it." Gross added later that "in my personal relations with Cobb I never heard him do anything else but protest how much baseball history had maligned him." Near the end of his column, he wrote, "the literature of his life cannot be altered now that he is dead."

In a Western U.S.-focused obituary, UPI's longtime West Coast sports editor, Hal Wood, who was based in San Francisco, recalled Cobb as an "embattled 'native' Westerner," who made impressions on the residents he encountered in his three homes there, in Atherton, Calif.; Cave Rock, Nev.; and Twin Falls, Idaho. "Cobb gave no quarter in baseball – and was the same in the social world. He would fight at the drop of a speck of dust. And his foes included public utilities [at least as late as June 1960], his wife, neighbors, the state government or anyone else he figured had crossed him."

Wood recalled spending time with Cobb and Cobb's late son Herschel in Idaho, when Herschel was a district distributor for Coca-Cola. "We sat in a room in the old Riverside hotel there in a bull session with Al Schacht, the famous baseball clown[, a major leaguer from 1919 to 1921], that lasted until daylight. During the six or eight hours, Schacht applied the 'needle' so deeply that by the morning Cobb was ready to battle the world. And that he did for the next quarter of a century. His fiery disposition never changed."

(In a 1955 interview with Gayle Talbot of the AP, Schacht had responded as follows to Talbot's characterization that he loved Cobb: "Love him? I hated him the way everybody else in the game did. Cobb was the meanest man who ever wore a uniform. But that has nothing to do with the fact he was so much the greatest player who ever lived it's not even close." Schacht thereby counters an argument made by a 2017 scholarly reviewer of Leerhsen's book, Robert G. Smith, professor of security and global studies at the online American Military University in Charles Town, W.V. Smith wrote, "But the facts do not hold up to the legend. If Ty Cobb was so hated, why did he rate first among the initial inductees for the Baseball Hall of Fame, to include more votes than Babe Ruth?")

Al Schacht and (pictured on pages 84 and 369) Nick Altrock were players-turned-Washington coaches who amused fans at each World Series from 1921 to 1933. Possibly only Schacht's 1955 book, until this one, notes that Maines persuaded Yankees co-owner Jacob Ruppert in 1921 to let the two entertain at the entirely played-at-the-Polo Grounds series. Maines was then the secretary of the philanthropic All-Star Service League of America, which had signed up the two to appear in film comedy roles, the proceeds from which were to be used to buy athletic gear for poor children. For detail on Cobb and 1924 article writer Fowler, see page 279.

Wood also wrote, "There's a story that he left some canned dog food for his hunting dogs with a caretaker a few years ago. Orders were to feed them only so much per day. When Cobb returned from a trip just about all the dog food was gone – when there should have been several cans still there. The millionaire [Cobb] then accused the caretaker of gypping him by eating some of the dog food." Wood preceded that part by writing, "Generous in philanthropies, the idea of anyone getting something for nothing galled him."

He also noted Cobb's great wealth and opined, "If Cobb had come west with the '49ers [in the days of the California gold rush], it is possible that he would have ended up owning most of the west – or with a bullet hole in his head. But he would have loved every minute of the battle."

Only somewhat less luridly upon Cobb's death, Emil Tagliabue of the *Corpus Christi Times* wrote of his exemplifying a "win at all costs" temperament. "They say today that [pitcher] Early Wynn would knock down his mother with a pitch if it would help him win a game. Cobb would probably have spiked Mom if it had helped achieve another win."

In its lead editorial upon his death, the *Louisville Courier-Journal* included a sketch of a ballplayer with the letter D on the front of his uniform sliding on the clouds, as if in heaven. Titled "The Georgia Peach Liked to Win Games," it began this way: "TYRUS RAYMOND COBB was the greatest baseball player of his time, which we think of as the golden age of the sport. He was a ruthless competitor, hot tempered and never a good loser. It is no wonder that he was treated ruthlessly by the fans of opposing teams and once in a while even by his own teammates."

In 1960, a new biography of former heavyweight boxing champion Dempsey was published in which Dempsey said, "Ty Cobb was the roughest, toughest, meanest ballplayer I ever saw. [The late] Ty Cobb, Jr., turned out to be a nice tennis player." Popular columnist Westbrook Pegler reprinted that in 1961, several weeks after Cobb's death.

The title of the 1960 Dempsey biography is *Dempsey by the Man Himself as Told to Bob Considine and Bill Slocum*. The publisher? Simon & Schuster.

Cobb himself was likened to Dempsey upon his death, by *Philadelphia Daily News* sports editor Larry Merchant, the future boxing analyst. "Arrogant, aloof, taunting, vicious, Cobb was common enemy No. 1. Those who would douse his fire with theirs, according to the code of that day, were burned. It was like slugging with Dempsey; only finesse could lick him." Merchant may have been emboldened to write that in part because, in another fluke, one of the oldest still-active figures in baseball as of 1961 was Hans Lobert, a Philadelphia-based scout who had played in the National League from 1905 to 1917. "Many of the players Cobb spiked deserved it," Lobert, with a grin, told Merchant. "I ought to know. I was one of them."

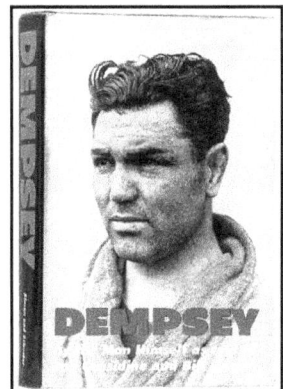

Lobert told of an exhibition game in Cincinnati in which his teammates decided never to try to pick Cobb off by throwing to a base that he was at.

That strategy was in effect when Cobb, as a runner, trotted to second on a single "and then turned it on about three steps before he got to the bag. We were ready for him. The throw to third had him beat by 40 feet. But instead of waiting for him like I should, letting him tag himself out, I went up the line to meet him. He flew at me and spiked me in the thigh. It was my fault."

Presumably without knowing about Considine's Dempsey book, Leerhsen mentioned Considine in a mixed way in his. After stating that Considine is the author of both *Thirty Seconds over Tokyo* "and a bad book about Babe Ruth," he said that Considine declared Stump's 1961 article "perhaps the best sports piece I have ever read."

I can bring to light the following detail from Considine – his own negative Cobb story. He included it in a column that also praised Stump's article. Considine wrote that Cobb, in his last years, visited now-New York restauranteur Lawton Carver, the former sports editor of the International News Service. Presumably that was at Camillo's, which Carver co-owned from 1951 to 1957.

"After a couple of drinks he became bluer than blue. 'I haven't got a friend in baseball,' he said, as the tears began to come. 'And you know why, Lawton, I cut 'em whenever they got in my way, I kicked them, I gouged them, I did everything to them – to win those ball games. Now look at me, friendless, absolutely friendless.'"

Considine added, "Carver let him weep for a time, then said, 'Ty, if you had your life to live over again would you do all those things?'"

"Cobb stopped the tears, blew his nose, glared at Lawton like an eagle and swore: 'You're dam' [sic] right I would!'"

On the pro-Cobb side of the ledger, back in 1947, Considine had devoted part of a column to players' sharp tongues during games, especially as directed at the opposition. He wrote, "The good jock picks his spots. Ty Cobb was one, and got by great without profanity."

from the 1929 Hillerich & Bradsby publication *Famous Sluggers of 1929: With Tips on Batting*, which featured the recently retired Cobb

12. *Odds and Ends*

When I started researching Cobb's racism, I began accumulating material that I did not find in any prior book or article on him. Except as where otherwise noted, everything in this chapter seems to be making its first modern-day article or book appearance here.

Graphically, because of my post-career emphasis, my book hardly overlaps with those of McCallum (1975), Alexander, Stump, Bak, Leerhsen and Hornbaker. Of McCallum's 27 graphics, 1 is a near match, of Cobb and Roger Maris. Of Alexander's 28 graphics, there are 0 matches. Of Stump's 19 graphics, 1 is a match, Cobb and Christy Mathewson in 1918, and 1 is a near-match, Cobb and Ruth in 1944. Of Leerhsen's 18, there are 2 matches, Cobb in 1921; and in the mid-1910s with a black personal aide, Alexander George Washington "Alex" Rivers. A third is a near-match, of Cobb in 1924 receiving books from members of Congress. Of Hornbaker's 29, there are 0 matches.

Of the 109 graphics in Bak's 2005 book, there are 3 matches: the black personal aide; Cobb with two Reno, Nev.-based Tyrus Cobbs in 1950; and Stump in the 1950s. There is 1 near-match, a variation of Cobb and Ruth in 1944. Of the 309 in Bak's 1994 book, without counting some generic Coca-Cola ones, there are 2 matches: again the black batboy/personal aide and a 1911 image at the Indianapolis Speedway. There are 3 near-matches: the 1944 Cobb-Ruth image, a 1911 zoomed-in one of Cobb with Gabby Street and a 1929 one of Cobb with naturalist Jack Miner. My book has 388 graphics. None of the counts include images appearing only on a cover or dustjacket.

Also worth noting is Marc Okkonen's 2001 *The Ty Cobb Scrapbook*. It is loaded graphically and, in scrapbook style, is devoted to his playing days.

In 1904:

After finishing up a stint with the semi-pro team in Anniston, Ala., Cobb wrote of having "2 or 3 boils coming on me and I pick them and stop them from coming but others come and they won't quit until I have let 3 or 4 come to a head and then lance them. So I don't want to lay on the beach and be an expense to the club. So I have decided I will come home and get well." Cobb included all of the above in a letter to former Royston teammate Erwin Manley.

In 1907:

He wrote to Frank Dean, operator of the Hammond Building cigar stand, "to the effect that a letter of his recently published to the effect that he would not act like a 'kid' any more was misunderstood," the *Detroit News* said. "What the star batter really meant to say was that when [teammate Matty] McIntyre and he met[,] 'Matty' would have to understand that he was not running across some 'kid' who would stand for any abuse. His letter goes on to say that he stood for a whole lot last year, purposely, because he did not want them [his teammates] to think he had a 'swelled head.'"

In 1908:

He explored doing offseason coaching at the University of Georgia. In a letter to George Craig, house electrician at the Detroit Opera House, he wrote, "Let me tell you George right now I can make 4 or 5 hundred dollars more this season [as much as about $12,000 today] coaching that team and playing outlaw ball [for teams outside organized baseball that sometimes are located close to organized baseball ones] than Detroit offered me which was $3,000 [about $75,000 today]. I would be a chump to play with them at that figure."

A Cobb nemesis, White Sox pitcher Doc White, managed "a triple whiffing of Tyrus Raymond Cobb," the *Chicago Inter Ocean* said in a recap. "Yes, sah, Mistah Cobb done struck out on three separate and distinct occasions. Glory! How mad dat boy did get!"

"The dentist [White had a professional dentist degree] had a high inside ball that came in dangerously close to Ty's wishbone, and had him bluffed to death. Ty struck at the ball so hard and so often he resembled a whirling dervish." The only time he reached first base that day was when White hit him with a pitch.

In a different letter to friend Craig, Cobb wrote, "Say I heard Sam Crawford lost his diamonds by robbery hard luck if it is so."

The *Boston Globe* noted that former Boston player-turned-sportswriter Tim Murnane had explained how the term "south paw" came into baseball. Then the *Globe* asked, "now will someone explain who let Ty Cobb in?"

James Crusinberry circa 1910. In 1960, three months before his death at 80, he would suggest that Cobb and Mays pose for a photograph at a preseason game at Scottsdale, Ariz. Crusinberry was a huge admirer of both players, wrote Jack Hanley of the *Press Democrat* of Santa Rosa, Calif., upon Cobb's death. The image is on the AP Images Web site, and Hornbaker reprinted it. According to Hanley, Cobb replied to Crusinberry's request as follows: "Jim, it would be my honor. Do you think he will pose with me?"

After the season, James Crusinberry of the *St. Louis Post-Dispatch* wrote that second baseman Hobe Ferris of his city's American League team sat out a series at the end of the season, "but very few knew that the spiking was the result of a little personal affair between Hobe and Ty Cobb. Hobe had 'kidded' Cobb in the previous series when Detroit was playing in St. Louis. Cobb is a hot-blooded Southerner and every remark is serious with him. Hobe meant nothing in his remarks except to get the young speed marvel rattled so he wouldn't play his best game. Cobb looked at it differently and threatened revenge."

In October at the Georgia State Fair, "he sustained painful injuries as a result of a wet plank and tumble" while visiting its midway. He was being followed by large crowds throughout his visit. "As he was picking out footing he slipped when trying to avoid a mud hole. He missed his usual spiked shoes or might have avoided the tumble, which caused him to hunt [for] a physician, suffering great pain. His throwing arm and hand were injured."

In 1909:

Even though the Cobbs had married the prior summer, a letter from her from early 1908 finally reached him when Detroit was in spring training in San Antonio. The future Mrs. Cobb had written "Hotel Pontchartrain" on the envelope, the place in Detroit where Ty stayed during the season. But she forgot to write "Detroit" on it too. The *Atlanta Constitution* ran a report from San Antonio that began, "It took Uncle Sam just a whole year to locate the whereabouts of his [sic] most famous athlete, and this in spite of the fact that the public prints [newspapers] of every city in the broad land were proclaiming daily the deeds of this same young man and his daily whereabouts."

In a feature, Bingay of the *Detroit News* said he is always quiet, well-mannered, "nattily dressed" and "a bundle of nerves." In addition, Cobb "is always seeking knowledge" and "can ask more questions to the minute when something interests him that he is not familiar with than any youth of his age." The "always seeking knowledge" description provides a boost to *Free Press* reporter Jackson's 1906 report on Cobb's racial views – since Cobb seems plausibly so intelligent at that time for Jackson to have tried to comment on them.

Bingay also wrote, "In action Ty Cobb comes closer to the athletic ideal than any other man in base ball. Built like a greyhound, his wonderful lithe body is always a study. His slight waist, his magnificently formed shoulders, his wiry limbs with slight ankles and wrists, and his well-poised head make one think of the idealized Grecian youth who lives now only in the marble of the museums and art schools."

In Pittsburgh with his team for the World Series, Cobb was sitting in the lobby of the Colonial-Annex Hotel waiting for the dinner hour to approach, the *Pittsburgh Post-Gazette* reported. At one point, "a boy with an armful of roses came through the lobby" offering sweet Maréchal Niel buds to those who might want to buy them.

"Cobb saw him and called him over. The boy told his price per bud, but that didn't suit the famous heavy hitter of the American champions; he wanted more than a bud or two. How much for the bunch was the query the youth had to answer. He looked over the lot and figured that about $2 [about $50 today] would do. Cobb took them all and gave the lad a dollar extra for good measure.

"'I want to take them up to my wife and my mother,' he explained; 'they're both here with me.'"

While in North Carolina that offseason, soon after his fight with the white watchman, he told the *Charlotte News*, "Of course I appreciate all the good things the people and the papers have been saying about me and I keep a big scrap book to save the clippings of the papers. I don't want to appear in the light of one seeking notoriety, but when one says a good thing or does me a kindness I appreciate it. Everything I do now is magnified so many times, I have to be careful for I have enemies as well as friends. My ambition is to make friends as a man as well as a baseball player. I love to have friends."

He continued, "When a fellow works himself up in the baseball world he has a chance of meeting some of the best people in the entire country. I have met many big people and have the friendship of many of them. Those fellows in Detroit seem to like a Southerner and have been particularly nice to me. You know when you have friends like that they are always ready to back you with any amount of money you want and they have begged me to stay there and go in [sic] business." On the prospect of his fight resulting in a court trial, he said, "I have lots of friends who have offered to help me by putting up my bond and so forth and I appreciate all that, but I hate to see so much made of it."

Cobb and his wife were traveling through North Carolina in his new Chalmers racing car. At a hotel in Winston-Salem, wrote F. Ed Spooner of the *Winston-Salem Journal*, a crowd of "small boys and girls and grown up boys and girls" insisted upon gazing at him. "'If I get away and go up stairs,' said Cobb, 'they will think me a prig [a person with a superiority complex]. If I stay they will make me feel like thirty cents.' And just then a man brought up a dozen ladies and insisted upon introducing Ty to all of them.

"The next time I tour it will be 'incog,' said Ty."

In 1910:

In April, the *Cheboygan Democrat* in Michigan stated, "Ty Cobb is threatened with malaria. Ty is undoubtedly a stinker, and has shown it many times in rows and fights. If he don't make good very soon, the fans will do things to him."

After criticism of him appeared, Cobb wrote the following in an open letter: "Much has already been said about me and my connection with the Detroit ball club. I realize I am not above making mistakes. As yet, however, I have not burned any orphan asylums or robbed a blind man. Critics say I am getting a fabulous salary. Whatever that salary is, I feel that my employer, Mr. [Detroit owner Frank] Navin, believes I am earning it to the best of my ability. I have always given the public the best I have in me. If some of my critics who have been roasting me in the papers would work as hard and honestly, they would find out the real facts connected with recent trouble on the team and would not be misguiding their public."

Leerhsen quoted part of Cobb's letter and began doing so as follows: "I realize I am not above making mistakes. If some of my critics who have been roasting me in the paper would work as hard and honestly as I do they would find out the real facts connected with recent trouble on the team and would not be misguiding the public."

I found a match for Leerhsen's version of the quote in a full-text database. The apparent true correct version has the four intervening sentences in the version that appears above his.

Nap Rucker in his racing car in Atlanta, prior to the Cobb race being called off

In 1911:

Hornbaker mentioned that Cobb did some speed laps at the Indianapolis Speedway. I can add that racetrack authorities gave him special permission to drive. In one of his laps, he went 2.5 miles in 2 minutes and 20 seconds, a feat that "shows that he was hitting it up some, although, as he expressed it, 'It was fun – not half so hard as judging a long fly,'" the *Brooklyn Eagle* reported. The *Eagle* was presumably following developments because Brooklyn pitcher (and fellow Georgian) Nap Rucker was an aspiring racer as well. In December 1910, *Sporting Life*'s Detroit correspondent, Paul H. Bruske, wrote that a planned race between Cobb and Rucker "had to be called off on account of the lack of suitable inducements." In explaining the cancellation, Hornbaker cited Bruske's reason and that Detroit owner Navin, for safety reasons after the death of a driver at the planned venue, had sent a telegram to Cobb instructing him not to race. In its report in 1911, the *Eagle* said Detroit's and Brooklyn's management had told Cobb and Rucker, respectively, not to do so.

Also in his Indianapolis Speedway appearance, Cobb drove with various riders, including a Detroit newspaper reporter, and Brick Owens, an American Association umpire at the time. At the track, the *Eagle* said, "Owens, with his usual good-natured funmaking, kept joking the diamond star on all occasions. But at first he did not evince any desire to ride."

After driving on the track in a particular type of car, Cobb showed interest in trying out a test car. Then, after doing a lap in one, "Cobb halted in front of the grandstand" and "Owens agreed to trust his life with Cobb if the latter would agree to 'let her out,' [drive at a fast speed] as Owens expressed it." On the backstretch, to show "that he was a real 'speed maniac' Cobb let the motor out enough to rip the tread of[f] the right rear tire."

Cobb and Brick Owens at the Indianapolis Speedway

Owens would later umpire in the American League, starting in 1916 and well past the end of Cobb's career in 1928. He would recall that experience in 1941, in an article under his byline. "I once received a personal demonstration of Cobb's daring," he would write. A few sentences later, he would add, "Cobb drove a mile in 45 seconds, which was high speed in those days, when you remember that [auto racing legend] Barney Oldfield's record run over the same distance under far more favorable circumstances was 36:63." I found one additional Cobb racing story of some note:

While the called-off Rucker-Cobb race in 1910 was in Atlanta, the one that was floated for 1911 was in Savannah. To drive a racing car in the so-called Vanderbilt and Savannah trophy races, Cobb was offered $1,000, about $24,000 today. "In a workout over the seventeen-mile course, Cobb was clocked in seventeen seconds flat, the best time yet made in practice," stated a report from Savannah. The manager of the racing team, J. Alex Sloan, "was so

enthusiastic over Cobb's ability as a driver that he made him the offer." The only overlooked racing story after that that I found was in 1913. At that year's Georgia-Carolina state fair, he was the official starter at its auto races.

Barney Oldfield, Who Will Race at the State Fair

BENZ 200 H.P.

BARNEY OLDFIELD AND HIS MONSTER
ILLINOIS STATE FAIR, OCT 1-7, 1910.

LIST OF ACCIDENTS IN WHICH BARNEY HAS "PARTICIPATED."

1902, Detroit—Turned around on Grosse Point track while driving the "999" a mile a minute. Thrown from car and badly bruised. 1904, St. Louis—Blinded by cloud of dust, ran through fence with Green Dragon racer. Killed two spectators. Oldfield's leg broken, head badly cut, chest crushed, and otherwise hurt. In hospital three months. 1904, San Bernardino—Ran off track. Car smashed and Oldfield's arm cut and head struck by flying fence rail. 1905, Detroit— Cut off by a competitor at Grosse Point track. Went through inner fence with Green Dragon. Shoulder broken, arm smashed and face cut. 1905, Ormond Beach, Fla.—Tire exploded and Green Dragon ran into ocean. Oldfield thrown out in water and nearly drowned. 1905, Chicago—Crashed through fence with Green Dragon at Harlem. Side hurt and hip dislocated. 1907, Lowell, Mass.—Driving Stearns racer on road race course, struck tree at junction of roads. Badly hurt about head and ankle broken. 1908, Ascot Park, Los Angeles—Ran into the rear of competing car, which skidded and cut about the arms. 1909, Indianapolis—Arms paralyzed while driving Benz on speedway. Thrown from seat and badly bruised. Mechanic grabbed steering gear wheel and prevented car from capsizing. 1910, Indianapolis—Steering knuckle of car broke while it was going 100 miles an hour on speedway. Car struck protection wall and was thrown back onto track. Oldfield was cut about the legs.

In 1957, 1914 book collaborator Wheeler provided perspective that apparently is in reference to that last detail. Referring to time spent in Georgia with Cobb in preparing the book, Wheeler wrote that there were a "series of auto races at an old dirt track, and Cobb was selected as referee. He had a Chalmers car, which I believe he had won for leading the league in batting. He asked me to get in and, to familiarize himself with the conditions, he drove around the course at 85 miles an hour. We made it, but on a couple of the turns we skidded so, [sic] I thought we were sliding into second base. That is the way he did everything."

Returning to the chronology:

In June, Ring Lardner, Sr. of the *Boston American* wrote, "The general impression prevails that Cobb is not popular with his teammates and that he has hardly any friends on rival teams. Nothing could be farther from the truth. Ty has an argument with one of the other Tigers almost every time the Detroit club engages in a close game. Other great ball players have their 'spats' under similar conditions, but that does not mean that they are disliked. Cobb quarrels more often with his mates simply because victory means more to him than it does to the majority of athletes. He is crazy to win, and he sometimes forgets his manners in the heat of battle." Later that season, Cobb would have an alleged physical fight with teammate George Moriarty, which will be featured later.

Syndicated sports columnist Tip Wright called Cobb the John Pierpont "J. P." Morgan of the national game. "He wins fame and filthy lucre on the diamond like Morgan does in [sic] Wall Street – by going out and getting it with a club. Cobb uses every drop of his energy to win games and keep himself ahead."

A few weeks later, Cobb was arrested in Highland Park, Mich., for violating by 10 miles the speed limit of 15 miles an hour. The arrest came when "a figure in khaki, astride a motorcycle, loomed up beside his car and announced that he was 'pinched.'" The marshal at the courthouse in Highland Park said, "We don't care who they are, Ty Cobb, King George or anybody else. If they speed we get them. That's all."

Ring Lardner, Sr.
circa 1910

In December, Salsinger wrote in the *Detroit News*, "Ty Cobb will have a merry yuletide if he reads an interview published in a Detroit paper and which makes Cobb say: 'I slide into a base because it is less of a strain on my ankles. I have very slender ankles.'" Salsinger opined, "Tyrus should have made the joke complete by adding that the reason he runs when trying to steal is to save his feet, as they are very tender and it hurts him to walk."

The *St. Louis Post-Dispatch* reprinted Salsinger's quip under a short subhead, "Detroit Dopester is a Joker." Days later, sports columnist John E. "Ed" Wray of the *Post-Dispatch* reprinted Cobb's comment too and added, "The interviewer might have added that the reason Cobb spikes basemen, when sliding, is in order to have his feet come to a full stop against something soft and bone-saving."

TY IS THE J. PIERP. OF THE NA-
TIONAL GAME.

The supposed quote from Cobb, which many newspapers printed unconditionally, went on further, as follows:

After he noted that he weighed 178 or 180 pounds, he said, "I would soon weaken them [my ankles] if I went into the bags standing. There are many ball players who would make their running and their playing more effective if they would slide into the sacks. The strain on the cords about the ankles is minimized, and really the chances of landing in safe are much enhanced. I tear

J. Edward Wray
circa 1910

into a bag with all my force, and I keep going until I feel my toe touch it, then a twist about stops the speed."

In 1912:

He sailed on an iceboat in February on the Detroit River. After misconstruing a sudden order from the captain, "having something to do with the mysterious bit of rigging known as the 'sheet' – Cobb said he saw a sail but not sheet – [he] caused the craft to capsize while going at the rate of about sixty miles an hour. A fifty-foot slide along the ice, which was covered with an inch or two of slush, resulted." Days later, a writer said, "We hear almost every day about Ty Cobb, Ty Cobb and Ty Cobb. When news is scarce and there is nothing to write about, we again hear about Ty Cobb. The way people eat up Ty Cobb sayings and stories about Ty Cobb pretty soon there won't be much left but the Cobb."

A report from Detroit stated, "Ty Cobb holds another record. Through his lightning speed the Tiger star recently appeared twice in the same photograph – and the picture wasn't spoiled either. Neither was it a fake. The team was lined up in the new ball lot before a panorama camera[.] Cobb was fourth [actually third] from the left end [look for the white arrow on the next page]. The camera used exposed only a small part of the film at a time the lens [was] traveling in an arc. As soon as the lens passed[,] Cobb raced to the other end of the line and took a position [at the very end] alongside Manager Jennings[,] thus appearing twice in the same picture."

Popular Mechanics printed it and ran a similar explanation to the above. It added, "Some of the baseball fans surmise that he did not like the serious expression of [sic] his face when the camera first caught him and sprinted around to the other end to get his smile into the picture. Others remark that he is most of the team anyway and in full justice [his image] might have been taken four or five times instead of only once."

WHO'S TY COBB--AND WHY?

Tyrus Raymond Cobb is 25 years old.

He was born in Royston, Ga.

Detroit secured him from the South Atlantic league for $700.

He was 17 years of age when he broke into the major league.

His first league game was played in 1904 at Augusta, Ga.

His family opposed his playing ball, thinking his life would be a failure.

He weighs 176 pounds and is 5 feet 11 inches tall.

He bats left-handed, but throws with his right.

He's an all-wool Democrat and can argue free trade all night.

He's a crack rifle shot.

His big regret is that he never took up football.

His father was principal of a preparatory school.

He's got a temper like a stick of dynamite, but behind it there is a wealth of common sense.

His father was a rifle shot, horseman and athlete.

His mother has said of him: "When Ty was a child I used to worry about him, because he was so impulsive and strong willed, but his father, whenever I spoke of it, would always say, 'Never mind that boy; he'll get along all right. He's a law unto himself and even though he is impulsive he's got good common sense to rally under the bumps he's bound to get.'"

an item printed in many newspapers in 1912

Copyright, 1912, Daines & Co., Detroit

A Unique Photograph of the Detroit Baseball Team

After Cobb mauled an abusive fan and his Detroit teammates went on strike when he was suspended, Cobb said, "Players are subjected to abuse each afternoon. I do not object to being 'kidded' or 'ragged,' but I do not want to be cursed at." He said that in road games, if he makes a good play that "knocks the hopes of the home team – I have sometimes grinned at the fans, but I have never cursed or lost my temper."

American League President Ban Johnson imposed the suspension, for jumping in the stands in New York and assaulting the abusive fan, Claude Lucker. Cobb then received political support from the entire Georgia delegation in Congress, all Democrats, including Senator M. Hoke Smith. "We congratulate you as a leader and a fighter in your profession," their collective telegram to Cobb read in part. In an editorial on its regular news pages, the *New York Sun* observed, "His team mates mutiny in [sic] his behalf. Georgia rallies to his defence [sic] as one man. The

Senator M. Hoke Smith as of 1912

Presidential ambitions of [House Majority Leader and 1912 presidential candidate] OSCAR W. UNDERWOOD are seriously imperilled. Is MR. COBB a Hokesmither? If so, HOKE is safe. If not he should be on the lookout for another job when his term in the Senate expires.

"Michigan and Georgia join hands in defense of the mighty wielder of the wagon tongue [bat]. As many thousands of ball players as there are rise to honor him. Distracted Republicans see in his nomination their only hope of victory at the polls. He is threatened with reduction from his high place on the diamond to a mere Presidency, possibly a Governorship. We warn him to exercise great care and not to associate with Republican scouts unless he is accompanied by a strong guard.

"Meanwhile we are somewhat puzzled by the fine distinction on which the Georgia Congressmen insist in their message of support to TYRUS. They 'as Georgians commend his action in resenting an uncalled for insult.' Exactly what, in the minds of these eminent statesmen, is a 'called for' insult?"

Two days later in a briefer editorial, the *Sun* said, "The only drop of bitter in the national thanksgiving over the settlement over the momentous Ty Cobb question is the fact that, something of justice being granted to TYRUS, the Hon. HOKE SMITH refuses to leave the Union."

The *Macon Telegraph* saw the first *Sun* editorial and said, "In its usual merry fashion, the New York Sun turns to political account the trouble in the baseball world brought about by Ty Cobb." Then the *Telegraph* reprinted much of it, stopping right before the start of the "Meanwhile we are somewhat puzzled" paragraph. It opined:

"To our view Ty Cobb thrashing an insulting spectator is a less unwelcome spectacle than an ex-[Republican] President [Theodore Roosevelt] hurling 'liar' at a [incumbent Republican] President [William Howard Taft] daily from the stump, and 'distracted Republicans' may well see in the champion batter's nomination 'their only hope of victory at the polls.'

Character Sketches in Five Words of Ten Ball Players

McGraw—Quick, Decisive, Business-like, Aggressive, Domineering.
Daubert—Kindly, Sincere, Conscientious, Hard-working, Capable.
Griffith—Shrewd, Keen, Stubborn. Crafty, Persevering.
Cobb—Impulsive, Impetuous, Open. Fair, Daring.
Mack—Quiet, Cautious, Reserved, Farseeing, Sagacious.

Collins—Blunt, Impulsive, Outspoken, Dashing, Spectacular.
Jackson—Proud, High-spirited, Ambitious, Hot-blooded, Impetuous.
Lajoie—Cool, Unemotional, Reserved, Graceful, Steady.
Wagner—Active, Awkward, Comic. Serious, Silent.
Evers—Nervous, Quick-witted, Earnest, Keen, Brainy.

descriptions from 1912 of John McGraw, Jake Daubert, Clark Griffith, Cobb, Connie Mack, Eddie Collins, "Shoeless" Joe Jackson, Napoleon Lajoie, Honus Wagner and Johnny Evers

Ty would impart more dignity than Teddy to the chariot of the G. O. P., but distracted Republicans may tear their hair and beat their breasts in vain. Fame and fortune have not made Ty any the less a true Georgian boy, and we may rest assured that no amount of persuasion can induce him to ride the elephant [of the Republican Party] Washingtonward."

That August, a Methodist pastor in St. Louis, Louis Scott de Burgh, delivered his promised sermon after attending a Sunday baseball game.

"How pleasant it would be if Ty Cobb could bat the head off the Devil," he said. "And how much better it would be if we had a Bishop [Giants manager John] McGraw with $20,000 a year [about $475,000 today] to preach the word of Christ in a baseball park.

"What a beautiful sight it would be to see Hans Wagner catch some weary soul and point him to Christ, or a Connie Mack sitting on the stand of some Christian orchestra and giving the secret sign to play 'Rock of Ages.'" That report, by the United Press, ended with, "Rev. de Burgh reiterated his assertion that baseball was wrecking the nerves of the nation."

In 1913:

In April, famous tenor Enrico Caruso and Cobb visited a prison in Atlanta. Leerhsen mentioned that visit quickly before moving on. I can add that around 900 inmates were there, many of whom were of

Enrico Caruso

Italian descent. "All the prisoners were allowed to hear the noted singer and many were moved to tears when he sang the 'Sob Song' from Pagl[i]acci." That was his last aria that day for the prisoners, and Caruso cried along with them. "'I can't help it,' he said. 'When I think of these 900 men shut away from life [sic]. I would rather give them a moment's pleasure than sing before kings.'" Cobb made "a brief sympathetic talk" after that.

Cobb muffed a fly ball at New York that led to the winning runs. The ball "filtered through his hands like light through a window," the *New York Times* said. After cracking his bat in the next inning, he returned to the bench and smashed it "to bits in a cute little outburst of temper. Ty is temperamental, like an opera singer."

In September, the *Tampa Tribune* said he was doing some "grand" base-running "just now. The Georgia Peach is showing his Southern raisin'. Who but a Black Mammy every [ever] taught a person that 'It sho' ain[']t no disgrace to run when yo' ahm scaird.'"

In 1914:

Grantland Rice criticized Cobb for exploiting his fame as a condition for playing in an exhibition game fund-raiser. Fellow big leaguer and Georgian Rucker, by contrast, had offered to play unconditionally for Augusta's team, without demanding a cut of the gate receipts. Rice wrote, "Cobb is not a native of Augusta, but has his home here and should have been willing to help out, as the team is backed by local business men purely out of public spirit, and none of them expect to get back what they put in. Ty did a trick like that last year when he was managing a semi-pro club and sought Nap to pitch for him to make an extra attraction. Ty wanted all the money and Nap was to get nothing. That was a commercial game in which the Augusta people had no interest except to give up their coin at the gate. This latest case is entirely different, and even the ball players do not sympathize with Cobb."

About a week later, in Jackson, Miss., Cobb addressed the lower house of the legislature. "The solons are not given to light and frivolous things like baseball and they would not carry on like this for anybody but Ty Cobb, 'than whom in the diadem of Dixie shines no brighter jewel, suh [sir],'" wrote Batchelor of the *Free Press*. Batchelor "reported" the following resolution from the local board of trade: "Whereas Ty Cobb hadn't been born at the time of the Misunderstanding of 1861-65 and the north got all the better of the umpiring the south was slightly outpointed. But whereas, if Cobb had been old enough to fight, there would have been another story, be it resolved that Jackson turn herself loose in honoring him."

Upon the team's arrival in Jackson at a very early hour of the morning, more than 60 men and boys were there to see them. "Rapture, reverence and enthusiasm were blended upon the countenances of those who for the first time beheld this man who means so much to every southerner," Batchelor also wrote. "All day a crowd has followed the peach just as though he were a popular murderer or something of that sort."

Nap Rucker

The *Shreveport Times* in Louisiana noted the honor that was accorded to Cobb and opined, "Perhaps the day is not far distant when flags will be placed at half mast throughout the country if Tyrus Cobb should develop a 'charley horse' or if Christopher Mathewson should sprain his pitching arm."

After he pulled a gun on a white employee at a butcher shop in Detroit, the *Macon Telegraph* said, "We do not mind Tyrus whipping an insolent 'yank' every now and then, but he ought to leave his gun at home. He does not need it. Take a baseball bat hereafter." Days later, under the headline, "Cobb Should Play the Man," it said Cobb is "a man of sufficient importance to be urged to play a man's part in future [sic]. He is not an ordinary citizen, though his fame

TYRUS RAYMOND COBB, THE "T. R." OF THE SPORT PAGE, DOES NOT REQUIRE A BATTING AVERAGE TO BE IN THE PUBLIC EYE

Ty Cobb, the Tiger star, need not depend on his speed on the bases or his deftness with the bat to bring him public notice. Ty has a faculty for engaging in fisticuffs and angry disputes that gets his name in the paper with unfailing regularity. His latest rumpus was with a butcher, so it is seen that Tyrus isn't afraid of anybody.

does not consist so much in his intellectual attainments as it does in the physical and psychic. Still, on account of his prowess in his line, he has been lionized by old and young. He has received honors from the President and other high officials." It also cited his contract renewals in 1913 as having led some members of Congress to show interest in revoking baseball's anti-trust exemption. In urging him to "play the part of a man," the *Telegraph* said, "He ought to be worthy of the admiration which Young America, especially, has of him."

Leerhsen trumped Hornbaker in level of detail on an August fight at Washington between Cobb and local pitcher Joe Engel. It took place after a game, and Engel needed five stitches. Leerhsen presumed correctly that

TYRUS RAYMOND COBB GETS HELP FROM CONGRESSMAN IN FIGHT WITH ORGANIZED BALL

it had to do with an occurrence that day. In 1951, a former teammate of Engel, Cobb chum Clyde Milan, was present with Engel in Orlando, Fla., for Washington's spring training. Milan recalled that one day, "Cobb thought Joe was being wild on purpose, firing at his head. After Engel knocked him down twice, Ty stormed out to the mound and asked, 'You throwing at me?'"

Milan said Engel replied, "Yeah, and I'm gonna do it again just because you asked." Engel interrupted Milan and stated, "I knocked him down again, but it was costly. Cobb caught up with me later and beat the daylights out of me."

In 1915:

An unattributed, widely published feature declared, "Ty Cobb makes a great fuss before going to the plate, and generally creates a great fuss after reaching it. Ty swings an armful of bats for a long time before he stalks to the plate, but he only uses one, although many pitchers imagine he still has the armful by the manner in which he lambasts the ball. Cobb has some stunts that are annoying to the pitcher that he pulls off in between balls and strikes, whichever the case might be. He will pose as if ready for the onslaught, then suddenly stoop down and grab a handful of dirt just as the pitcher is about to pitch. Ty does not seem to worry whether the ball goes over the plate or not, for Cobb takes a strike about as meekly as any man in the league – but he can afford to."

In *Baseball Magazine*, Georgia state trapshooting champion James M. Barrett wrote that Cobb "loves shooting. He will get up and meet you at 5 A. M. [sic] to go hunting. I know this, as he has sounded his Claxon [car horn] at my door many mornings at 5 A. M." Later that year, the *Augusta Chronicle* would describe Cobb and Barrett as "almost inseparable while Cobb is in Augusta." In a feature under his byline in *Sporting Life*, Barrett would profess that Cobb "has a wonderful personality and a genial hospitality that makes him an ideal companion on a hunting trip. With this [sic] personality, his shooting skill, and his wonderful dogs, Cobb is sought throughout the South" for hunting trips.

While hunting, Cobb "gets entirely away from the diamond, and makes everybody in the party feel the same. He is then a hunter first, last and all the time, and talks game and dogs and guns, thinks them and dreams them." They had gone on about 20 quail hunts during the prior offseason. On one of them, Cobb killed 45 birds. (In the following offseason,

Cobb and James M. Barrett circa 1915

Barrett and Cobb would go on a two-day duck hunt on the South Carolina side of the Savannah River. In a late 1923 letter to Salsinger, Cobb wrote of his intention to go on duck-hunting expeditions that offseason. In a 1925 hunting article in the *Atlanta Constitution*, photographer-reporter Tracy Mathewson would say that on hunts, there is a way to get him to talk baseball: by starting an argument on the subject.)

On a spring training visit to New Orleans, manager Jennings wrote an extraordinary article in the *New Orleans Item*. It was titled, "'Ty' Cobb Gives His Views on Suffrage" and subtitled, "World's Best Baseball Player Also Discusses [sic] Tango and Modern Dres." [sic]

The article begins with Jennings's byline, and with Jennings declaring, "The city editor of The Item said to me: 'Hughie, I want you to interview Tyrus Raymond Cobb for The Item.'"

Jennings continued as follows:

So, I found Tyrus in the dining-room of the St. Charles Hotel and asked him the question that I understand is always asked first in every interview:

"Do you believe in woman suffrage?["] Tyrus blushed.

"What right have I got to talk about that?" he wanted to know. "What are you trying to do? Get me in bad with the women?"

But I explained to him that everybody who was really interviewed these days had to talk about votes-for-women and the tango and the latest styles in women's dress.

Tyrus squirmed and dug a spoon deep into a baked apple and blushed some more. But he was game.

"Votes for women," he said finally, "let me see. There are arguments on both sides. Yes, it's a question."

"That's right, I encouraged him. That's the way to begin."

"The convict and the lunatic can't vote and it seems like putting women in the same class to keep them from voting," Tyrus said, taking heart. "That doesn't seem right, now, does it."

There was a period of thought, while he ate another spoonful of apple.

"On the other hand," he went on, "we put woman [sic] on a pedestal; if you let her mix in politics and mingle with the sort of men who go there, wouldn't that tend to remove some of the delicacy of the position that we have given her?

["]Wouldn't that cause us men to lose something of the chivalry with which we now invest our attitude towards women?

"Mrs. Cobb is not a suffragist; she is not an anti-suffragist. She finds her interest in other problems."

"That's fine," I said, and took a lot of notes. "Now, talk about woman's dress.["]

I sort of hoped that he'd say that woman's dress was showing a tendency toward the improper. Almost everybody now days [sic] says that in an interview. But somehow I couldn't trap him into saying anything of the sort. He just blushed a little deeper.

"Hughey," he pleaded, "you know that I never made a study of this sort of thing. Ask me something else."

But I was obdurate, because I knew my duty as a reporter. At least I made him say:

"Woman's dress – why – er – woman's dress should be – should be created so as to allow freedom of movement. Woman's dress

THE NEW ORLEANS ITEM

SUNDAY MORNINNG, MARCH 28, 1915

THESE remarkable photographs, posed and given especially to The Item, are of the world's greatest baseball player, Tyras Raymond Cobb, his family, Mrs. Cobb, Ty Cobb, Jr., and little Miss Shirley Marion Cobb and Hughey Jennings, manager of the Detroit baseball team. Mr. Cobb is known all over the civilized world for his athletic prowess on the ball field. To his friends he is also known as a high-class gentleman, a splendid husband and father. Mr. Cobb comes from a distinguished Georgia family and takes his profession seriously. In a baseball game he is a hard player and a hard fighter. Off the field, he is a quiet, dignified and charming gentleman. The photograph of Mr. Cobb and Mr. Jennings is perhaps the only one they ever had taken together in street attire. The public is familiar with their appearance in baseball togs.

COOK WHOSE CAKES HAVE TICKLED KINGS TO BE HERE

Grace, Land Registrar, Out for Re-election

"Ty" Cobb Gives His Views on Suffrage

that is well, I'll tell you, I believe that woman's dress should be utilitarian instead of ornamental. A woman should attract because of herself; not her dress."

It was here that I thought of something clever.

"How about the poor woman who can't attract because of herself?" I shot at him.

"She should try to improve her mind," Tyrus answered.

After I had written that down, I was ready for him to discuss the tango.

"You've got to do it," I commanded. ["]There's no way out, Tyrus."

He looked at me pitifully but I was firm – as all interviewers should be – so he sighed, turned a shade redder and stammered out:

"The tango – I guess it's all right. I never saw anything improper on a dance floor. But then, you know, I don't dance much. [In 1907, around the time that he was dating his future wife, he was said to be spending 'a great deal of his spare time in learning new fancy steps.' A short feature in which that was reported had, as its punch line, teammate Crawford telling Cobb that he would be a swell dancer but for two things: his feet.] I wouldn't say that it ought to be dispensed with. I believe, though, that most of the trouble with dancing comes from lack of proper chaperonage for the girls who attend. I guess parents are growing too confident. They don't give enough consideration to the character and personality of the men with whom they allow their daughters to associate. It looks to me as though the country is growing so prosperous that it is growing careless. Take the case of the Roman empire. It was all right as long as its people were poor and hard-working but as soon as they began to acquire wealth, degeneration set in and by and by the Roman empire became dissolute and fell."

But what is an interview without the personal touch.

"You are a busy man are you not?" I asked him.

I knew that he was, but I had to ask him to get in the record.

"Why, –O, I guess so," he said. "You're trying to jolly me, are you?"

"How about the life of the ball player. Say something about that and I guess that'll be all."

"Well – the life of the ball player – why – I've been playing professional ball for ten years, now, and I've seen a lot of improvement in the class of men who are being recruited into the profession. The big trouble about the personal side of playing ball is that if you are a married man you've got to spend a mighty lot of time away from home."

I don't mind breaking up this interview right here to remark that Tyrus is proud of his home and his wife and his two babies. I took the pictures of the three of them away from him. If the city editor prints them along with this interview, you can see that Shirley Marion Cobb is growing up on the athletic plan. She is three and one-half years old now and – just look at the way she doubles up that arm. And as for Tyrus Raymond Cobb Jr. – he is 5 years old and the most important gentleman whose photograph ever adorned a ball player[']s suitcase.

I guess I s[h]ould have made him talk about something else but I never saw an interviewer that needed anything except talks about suffrage, dress and tango, so I folded up my notes and Tyrus sighed in vast relief.

"I didn't know I had it in me," I said when I left him. "Tyrus, this is some interview. I'm proud of myself."

Leerhsen cited from a highlights-type condensation of the above and took credit for having found the original version. He stated that the *Times-Picayune* in New Orleans had "the doubly odd notion of having Hughie Jennings interview Cobb on a number of nonbaseball topics." He then reprinted quotes that were not true to the original, because the condensed version had altered it. The condensation did run in some newspapers, but not the *Times-Picayune*.

In Jackson, Miss., days after the *Item*'s feature, Cobb was presented with a bouquet of carnations by Mrs. Annie Kincaid Dent, president of the Mississippi Woman Suffrage Association. He stated, "I'm not strong on political economy [the interrelationship between government policies and economics and their societal effects], but it's been my observation that when women want anything they always get it. Since it is evident that the women want to vote we may as well give them the franchise without any more fussing about it."

A week later, when the team was in Cincinnati, Cobb "declared himself in favor of woman's suffrage." He consented to having his views published, according to a news report, "with the understanding that certain restrictions as to his belief in woman's suffrage must also be included."

"'I think women are capable of voting,' said Cobb. 'They could do a whole lot of things for the government that would help living conditions considerably, but I hate to see them mixing with some of the men who are now in politics. I am in favor of equal suffrage. But I have such a high ideal of womanhood that I hate to see good women become contaminated by the things they would necessarily have to come in touch with if they were voters.'" Hornbaker cited something different from the Cincinnati interview for having a tie-in to Ty Jr.

Cobb's views on giving women the right to vote reflect well on him on a major rights issue, by showing that he could be ahead of his times. His analysis shows that he had given much thought to the issue. Next to civil rights, women's rights and immigration could be among the next-most significant subjects on which to know how a racist felt as of the 1910s.

Stepping further outside the chronology to present his political views and interactions with politicians:

While living in the South, he always preferred the Democrats, who were by far the more popular party there among whites. At the national level, he apparently was open to supporting Republicans, including William Howard Taft. Taft, in 1908, had defeated an economically radical Democrat, William Jennings Bryan, who was hugely popular in Georgia. Because of Bryan's extremism, Cobb presumably preferred Taft at the national level.

At the Augusta Country Club in 1909, Taft played a round of golf and, as Hornbaker noted, then was introduced to Cobb by a White House aide of his, Augusta native Capt. Archibald "Archie" Butt.

I can add that a few weeks after that, Taft was honored at a banquet in

Savannah. "Taft scored a hit with the banqueters when he praised Ty Cobb, the baseball player recently indicted in Cleveland for stabbing a hotel watchman," a reporter related. (As the 2015 biographies relate in slightly different ways, he had been in his fight with a white watchman. It included, according to Cobb's account, raking the watchman mildly with a penknife; at the time, it was reported as a stabbing.) Taft told the banqueters, "The gentleman who figures more largely in Georgia than the president is our friend the hero, Ty Cobb. I saw a public statement that he is being made the victim of a damnable conspiracy. I haven't seen the result but I hope the Georgian bar will rush to his defense and by a writ of habeas corpus if no other means are available, restore him to the people whom he loves and which love him."

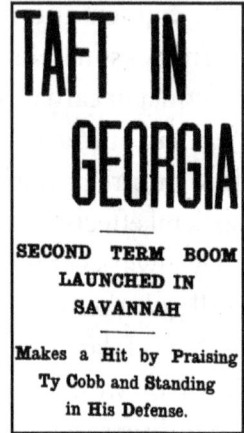

TAFT IN GEORGIA

SECOND TERM BOOM LAUNCHED IN SAVANNAH

Makes a Hit by Praising Ty Cobb and Standing in His Defense.

In 1910, Taft and Vice President James S. Sherman watched a Detroit game at Washington. Reportedly, Taft went mainly to see Cobb, and Butt was among his aides who joined him. For his part, Cobb visited the U.S. Capitol building that day. In both the House and Senate cloakrooms "he was introduced to many of the lawmakers. He and Vice President Sherman, who is a 'dyed-in-the-wool' fan and rarely misses a game, talked baseball for a long while."

In 1911, Cobb and teammate Jack Lively visited Taft in the White House. In a letter to his own sister-in-law, Butt wrote, "Ty says Lively was caught in a trap twenty miles from any railroad, at a place called Hopla in Alabama. As he is a Southern boy, Ty has taken him under his wing, and for the same reason I have introduced him to the President and saw that he went everywhere he could around the White House."

from left to right: Vice President James S. Sherman, Archibald "Archie" Butt, Bureau of Indian Affairs Chief Clarence R. Edwards and President Taft

In 1912, he was a supporter of New Jersey Governor and Democrat Woodrow Wilson for President. As a boy, Wilson had lived in Augusta and later practiced law there. Cobb also supported him in 1916, and conferred briefly with him that year at the White House. On that visit, Cobb pledged his support despite a recent picture of him with his

Republican opponent, Charles Evans Hughes. It was taken in Detroit about ten days earlier. Cobb had presented Hughes with a baseball "bearing the autographs of Colonel [Theodore] Roosevelt, Christy Mathewson, [pitcher] Chief Bender and of Cobb himself."

In 1912, Cobb had been named a vice president of Detroit's newly formed Woodrow Wilson Club. Late in the 1916 campaign, he said, "Next to Hughie Jennings, manager of the Detroit team, I consider Woodrow Wilson the greatest American." Also, "My first ambition, of course, is to have the Tigers win the pennant, but next to that my most earnest desire is to see President Wilson reelected." Indeed, Wilson would be.

Stepping back to 1914:

That Cobb, a Southerner, was still friendly with Taft as of that year was noted in a letter printed in a daily newspaper in Norwich, Conn. The writer, Dr. Frank C. Atchison,

Cobb and Charles Evans Hughes
in 1916

said that the Republican Party would not make a comeback at the national level until it named a popular ballplayer for president. "We must have a man of sporting blood, preferably a Southerner[,] Ty Cobb, for instance – who, being from 'good old Georgia,' would split the Solid South and get 90 per cent of the 'fan' vote, too. I don't know Mr. Cobb's politics, but he might be induced to try the party of William Howard Taft, who once, down in Augusta, patted him on the back and told him he was the most popular man in Georgia."

In 1920, as Leerhsen noted, he was a supporter of the Democratic ticket, James M. Cox for president and Franklin D. Roosevelt for vice president.

In August of that year, a general columnist for the *Sacramento Union*, Lambert St. Clair, told of an idea from Senator Pat Harrison of Mississippi. In New York days earlier, Harrison had announced a proposal to take Cobb with him on a campaign tour in support of Cox and Roosevelt, to be a "spell binder" over audiences, as a reporter conveyed in the slang of the day. Harrison had led the pro-Cox floor fight at the party's recent convention in San Francisco. Days later, St. Clair wrote, "One proposal that Pat has made to leading Democrats is that they conduct the picture side of the national election something after the fashion in which the liberty loan campaigns [to finance the costs of the Great War] were run. He desired, for instance, to get Ty Cobb, who is a lifelong Democrat, to take the stump for Cox. It may be, Pat says, now that Ty is faltering as a baseball player, that he can be gotten before the season is over, and if he can[,] Pat is for putting him at work immediately."

St. Clair added, "Such a plan, Pat thinks, is the finest sort of an antidote for the Republican plan to run an advertising campaign for its candidate. Live persons of wide renown, the senator says, will offset page ads any time.

Senator Pat Harrison umpiring a game on Capitol Hill

Republicans respond, however, that they are well satisfied with their proposed newspaper advertising campaign. It will be in keeping with the general dignified tone of their drive, they insist. It has Senator [and Republican nominee] Harding's unqualified approval."

Although I did not come across any formal stumping, Jennings and Cobb did meet a month later with Harrison and Democratic National Committee Chairman George White in New York City. Cobb would golf in tandem with still-Senator Harrison on a 1939 visit to the Washington, D.C., area, and they would lose to Merle Thorpe, editor of *Nation's Business*, and Rodger H. Pippen, sports editor of the *Baltimore News*. Upon Harrison's death in 1941, Cobb would send a small arrangement of peach gladioli that would adorn his casket.

In 1924, a dinner was held in Cobb's honor at the Hotel Roosevelt in Washington, D.C. Its organizer was Robert H. "Bob" Clancy, a U.S. House member from Detroit. A Democrat, Clancy had been the president of the Woodrow Wilson Club in Detroit when Cobb was a vice president. Cobb's final visit to Detroit would be in 1959, and he would tell the *Detroit News* that seeing Clancy was his main purpose.

At the dinner, Harrison was the toastmaster and a range of House and Senate members attended, including Representative Nicholas Longworth III of Ohio, the then-Republican Majority Leader. Baseball attendees included star teammate Harry Heilmann, and Washington owner Clark Griffith and star pitcher Walter Johnson. As reported by the *Washington Star*, "While the affair was planned as a tribute to Cobb and the game he pursues, it almost developed into a love feast with Cobb and Johnson exchanging verbal bouquets. Cobb averred that 'no greater pitcher nor better sportsman ever graced baseball than Walter Johnson,' while the National moundsman was equally emphatic in naming Ty as 'the most remarkable player ever in the game.' President Griffith, too, accorded to the Detroit manager the premier position in base ball.

"In speaking of his team, Cobb said that 'no rules are needed on the club; the men know how to conduct themselves. The present day base ball is played by a high type of man. I could offer no better example than Harry Heilmann, whom I consider as fine a fellow as ever stepped upon the diamond. He is two-thirds of my team, not alone for his excellent hitting and fielding, but for the splendid influence he has upon the club.'"

Robert H. "Bob" Clancy circa 1917

Clancy as of 1923 was a first-term Democratic House member. He lost his re-election bid, switched parties and was elected as a Republican House member for three terms starting in 1927. Except for an endnote, Clancy does not appear in any of the Cobb biographies. And yet, he was one of his two great Detroit friends at the end of his life; the other was Dr. Charles S. Kennedy, a board member in his scholarship fund. As evidence of the latter, Kennedy visited Cobb over the weekend before his death on a Monday and told sports editor Smith of the *Free Press*, "He had been dying for two-three years and he knew it. He had a combination of ailments – including diabetes and cancer – tough ones to beat."

Clancy could have had impact on Cobb's transition to supporting Republicans. He was prominently named in 1920s celebrations in Cobb's honor in Detroit, while Cobb prominently appeared in an advertisement in 1924 endorsing his re-election with the words, "I have known Bob Clancy intimately for 12 years. He knows the ropes in Washington and can do much for you. We all know he is absolutely unselfish."

Politically, Clancy was a moderate. He spoke unsuccessfully on the House floor against the Immigration

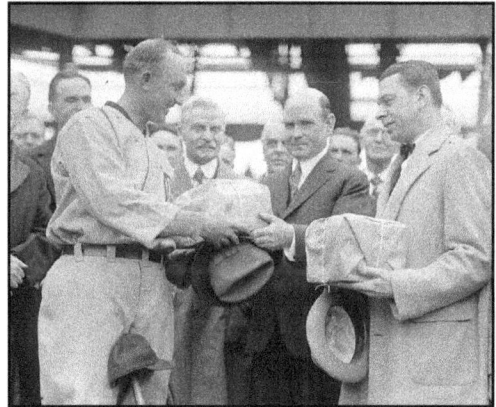

from left to right in Washington, D.C.: Senator William J. Harris (D-Ga.) (to the back right of Cobb), Rep. Clarence J. McLeod (R-Mich.) and Sen. Thomas J. Walsh (D-Neb.). Clancy conceived having lawmakers, prior to a game, present Cobb with classic books to mark his 20 years in professional baseball. Harry G. Salsinger wrote that Clancy "thought he had been in baseball 21 years and so he secured 21 books." Cobb's assertion to Clancy that he had been playing (presumably meaning completed) 20 "cost him one book." Included were works on Socrates, Plato, Jesus and P. T. Barnum.

Act of 1924, which ended up strengthening the quota system in the landmark 1917 act based on national origin.

In 1934, after having moved to California, Cobb expounded as follows on his support for Republican Frank F. Merriam over muckraking writer Upton Sinclair, who won the Democratic nomination: "In my home state of Georgia I always voted Democratic, the party of my forefathers for generations past; and although I will always remain a Democrat, I will cast my vote for [then-interim] Governor Merriam; and propose working diligently from now to November 6 to help bring about his election." Merriam would prevail.

A California district attorney as of 1934 was Republican Earl Warren, the future governor and U.S. Chief Justice. That year, to mark the opening of a minor league season in Oakland, Cobb took a swipe at the honorary first pitch, with Warren serving as the catcher. In 1950, a committee of 500 California sports figures, including famed retired boxers Jack Dempsey and Gene Tunney, and Cobb too, was organized to support the re-election of Warren as governor. In 1952, he backed the re-election of GOP U.S. Senator William F. Knowland.

Cobb also supported a former Republican mayor of Detroit, John W. Smith, in a comeback campaign for his office in 1929. In a letter of endorsement that was printed in the *Free Press*, Cobb wrote, "For real constructive guidance, your fairness and democratic manner at all times and desire to govern for the people, is just what this throbbing and thriving city of Detroit needs." In 1936, petitions were reportedly being prepared to nominate Cobb as a candidate for supervisor of San Mateo County in California.

In 1952, humorist Ollie Crawford of the *Philadelphia Inquirer* said that Dempsey, Tunney and fellow famed retired boxer James Jeffries were all on an "Athletes for Eisenhower" committee. Then, recycling a 1917 quip by to-be-featured-later humorist Arthur "Bugs" Baer, Crawford said that Cobb was on it too, "in charge of spiking rumors." Indeed, the National Baseball Hall of Fame Library has a certificate to Cobb attesting to his being on the committee that year. Presumably, Cobb supported Dwight D. Eisenhower for re-election in 1956. In 1960, he was on the so-called Dick Nixon Sports Committee seeking to elevate Eisenhower's vice president, Richard Nixon, to be his successor. The committee had around 50 founding members including Cobb; Ted Williams; and golfers Bobby Jones, Sam Snead and Byron Nelson. Two others were football running back Jim Brown and Olympic gold medalist Jesse Owens.

On a different matter, McCallum wrote in his 1975 book that Cobb kept what "he called his private sonofabitch list." On it was Eleanor Roosevelt for what McCallum alluded to were "purely personal reasons." Also on it were "the Democrats."

Returning to the chronology of 1915:

An early colorful quote about Cobb appeared in the children's magazine *St. Nicholas,* in an article by umpire Billy Evans. Evans attributed it to Philadelphia manager Mack, in reference to a close game in which Mack wanted his catcher to be alert to Cobb should he get on base: "Keep a tight hold on that glove of yours, or he will be stealing it before you get out of the park!"

After Canada's entry into the Great War, as part of the British Empire, the Toronto City Council

Vice President Richard M. Nixon and Cobb at Candlestick Park in 1960. In 1962, *San Francisco Chronicle* columnist Charles McCabe would quote an unnamed *Chronicle* staff member as having overheard Nixon introduce himself by saying, "I remember you, Mr. Cobb, you always came in with your spikes up."

sent a large shipment of baseball supplies to France. The shipment included 3 bats and 15 balls donated and autographed by Cobb.

He was the defendant in a suit for $2,432, about $50,000 today, relating to a loss on cotton futures. It occurred when the brokerage firm he was using went into bankruptcy. Wheeler wrote in 1952 that for some time on visits to New York, Cobb would invite him to invest with a cotton broker friend that he, Cobb, met up with. "When he was a big leaguer, Cobb was interested in money and romance in the order named," he also wrote. Cobb's cotton expertise was such that when he was without a baseball contract after the 1912 season, a cotton broker reportedly offered him a longtime huge contract to work as one.

The reporter of the latter detail added, "It is a fact that no man knows cotton better than Cobb. He was born and raised in the heart of the Georgia cotton belt. Since becoming a major league ball player he has added to his income each year by successful deals in cotton."

In an early Cobb autobiographical article from 1908, there is this gem about his becoming so knowledgeable about cotton:

"The first thing that I can remember of my early life is that I picked cotton along with a lot of other kids. Most of the other kids were 'shady' characters, and their mammies carried baskets filled with cotton on their heads. Not on the kids' head, but on their own, the mammies' heads.

"Fooling with the cotton balls and fighting pitched battles with them got me into the habit of handling the sphere, and this early education stood me in good stead when, many years later, I broke into baseball."

He also knew plants. In a 1948 letter to Helene Champlain after she visited him, he wrote, "In the patio it was not wisteria [a climbing shrub] – it is a trumpet vine, rather than an unusual growth. You can look it up." A former big leaguer who interacted with him in Twin Falls in 1948 and 1949 was Charlie Metro. In his 2002 book, Metro recalled that on a Cobb visit to his home, Cobb "got down on his knees and told my wife how to plant nasturtiums [a type of fully edible flower], how to weed them and everything else."

Returning to 1915:

Humor columnist George Fitch wrote, "He can run faster than a darky chased by a graveyard and has a way of lying down when approaching second and feeling for the base with his versatile and prehensile feet[,] which is very corrosive on the nerves of the opposing catcher and baseman. Cobb steals twice as many bases as any other man in the business. This is because, like every other Georgian, he is passionately fond of home and begins suffering from nostalgia whenever he gets on first base."

While sightseeing on an off day in Richmond, Va., he talked about alfalfa, the *Richmond Times-Dispatch* said. One of his tour guides, Hunter McGuire Cardoza, was an agent for a Midwest milling company. Cardoza told Cobb that chemists had recently discovered that alfalfa may be used as human food and not just to feed animals. He said that Cobb should be growing some on his farm and "that the latter was letting his Georgia farm go to the demnition bowwows [dogs] if he was neglecting to put a very large acreage of it in alfalfa, because wheat and flour prices would be soaring in the next year or so and the demand for alfalfa flour from Europe would be something tremendous.

"Cobb said he would communicate with the manager of his farm immediately and inquire about that alfalfa thing."

As noted by Hornbaker, he became part-owner of a hunting preserve on the Savannah River. Others included John Philip Sousa Jr., son of the composer-conductor. I can add that for hunts on the grounds, "Cobb has been assigned the job of training dogs." Also, "Only he and his partners in the ownership of the preserve will be allowed to hunt on it." By having private grounds, Cobb, according to the *Detroit Times*, will avoid a repeat of a recent experience near Augusta: being sidetracked on his hunts by parties that sprout up in his honor.

(A 1916 story noted by Alexander is worth inserting here: Cobb that year added to his kennels a puppy that was the son of the national pointer champion. The puppy was not Cobb's Hall, who will be featured later. To Alexander's writing I can add, "The pup will be given his initial field test on George Stallings' plantation at Haddocks, Ga." In mentioning the plantation, Alexander made a pro-Cobb correction that is worth rehashing: "Stallings's place was what northern writers often mistakenly termed the Cobb farm at Royston: an authentic plantation, a 4000-acre domain on which as many as fifty black people produced cotton.")

In 1916:

In transcribing two long sentences from Detroit manager Jennings, Hornbaker aced more than 50 words in a row. However, he eliminated three long sentences sandwiched between them without using an ellipsis, resulting in an exceptionally crisp quote. I looked it up because I found both a limerick and a quip that dovetailed on the following part of Jennings's quote: that every time in road games when Cobb "fails in an attempt to make a brilliant play, he is hooted and abused just as though he had committed some frightful crime."

Cobb and George Stallings in San Antonio in 1921

The context for the Jennings quote, whose wording is not significant enough to reprint, was that League President Johnson had suspended Cobb for throwing his bat into the stands at Comiskey Park in Chicago, with Jennings coming to Cobb's defense. Alexander and Hornbaker briefly mentioned the episode.

The limerick, by the *St. Louis Star*, was:

> Ty.
> There is young swatter named Cobb
> Whose temper is sure on the hob
> With a twist of his hand
> He threw his bat in the stand
> And the ump shooed him hence off the job.

The following day, that newspaper came up with a sequel, referring to Detroit by one of its nicknames:

In Jungletown.

In Jungletown there is no joy, for Ty has been suspended.

His temper for a week or so is not to be commended.

Hugh Jennings rants and tears his hair, for he has lost the swatter

That made Dame Victory come so near she was just like a daughter.

The saddest bit of all this tale, so bitter and so tearful,

Is that beneath the jungle boys the cellar looms up faithful.

And now for the quip. It was by a sports columnist for the *El Paso Herald*:

"Hugh Jennings is out with an alibi for Ty Cobb's temper. Hugh says that the fans look for Ty to make a hit every time he comes to bat and when he strikes out they jeer him. According to Jenning[s], this would jar any player's temper. But we can't figure out whether Hugh thinks that the opposing pitchers should be real kind to Tyrus, pet of Detroit, and slip him an easy one so that he can get a hit every time up! Some one has greased the skids for Cobb[,] and Tyrus don't fancy the toboggan."

Some additional context is that days before that in St. Louis, a fan had uttered a slur from behind the Detroit bench and Cobb had to be restrained by teammates and police. In response, Cobb told sports editor

TY COBB WILL APPEAL TO MAGNATES TO CURB ROWDY BASEBALL FANS

"I'm a Gentleman and a Ball Player," Declares T. Raymond, "but I Will Not Put Up With the Hoots and Abusive Language From the Rooters Any More—If the Owners Want Clean Baseball From the Athletes Then We'll Have to Get It From the Grand Stand and the Bleachers"—Says He'd Rather Quit the Game Than Continue to Accept the Vulgar Howls From the Rooters.

By SID C. KEENER,
Sporting Editor St. Louis Times.

the headlines on Keener's 1916 article

Sid C. Keener of the *St. Louis Times*, "I'm a gentleman and a ball player. Yes I am, and I don't propose to put up with this stuff any longer. The magnates want clean baseball from us. Now what are they going to do with the rowdy fan? They'll have to stop him, that's all."

(Upon Cobb's death, Keener would tell sports editor Paul Pinckney of the *Rochester Democrat and Chronicle* of a time where he wrote something negative about Cobb, after Cobb had been "discourteous, pushed somebody around, or something like that. Anyway, I printed the incident and pointed out that he was wrong. I made the mistake of going into the Detroit clubhouse the next day. Actually, I wanted to talk to Harry Heilmann. But Ty spotted me first. 'There you are, you little so-and-so,' he shouted. Well, I started running. I ran as fast as I could, Cobb only a few feet behind me. Into the grandstand I went. I found an exit and got away. Boy, was I scared! My phone rang that night at home. It was Ty. Never so apologetic," and inviting Keener to breakfast the following morning at Cobb's hotel.)

In July, the *Detroit News* possibly was the original source for the following: "Ty Cobb asserted himself recently in an unusual way. The action throws an interesting sidelight on his personality. He directed a personal letter to each and every college ball player taken on by the big leagues after June graduations, inviting them, one and all, to take the professional [sic] somewhat seriously. He told them that base ball is a great and growing career. He reminded them of the importance of taking care of themselves, not for six months only, but all the year around [sic]. He gave them his best wishes for success.

"This letter must have given [m]any of the light-hearted young collegians a new point of view. On those who regarded the breaking into base ball in merely a spirit of adventure, Cobb's letter must have had a sobering effect. We should also like to make the comment that Cobb is a far-sighted individual. Some day the game is going out of merely commercial hands into the active direction of practical base ball men. That day will come as soon as baseball players are intelligent enough to voice a collective demand. And in that way, we fancy, T. R. Cobb will be one of the leaders."

That offseason, a writer predicted, he would try his hand at quail hunting with fellow Augustan Stallings, manager of the Boston Braves. The writer added, "Ty has done some trapshooting [at live birds], and we are told he will likely go in for the inanimate 'bird' sport after he has killed off most of the quail south of the Mason and Dixon line." In a column in 1951, Wheeler recalled hunting quail on the Stallings

John N. Wheeler
circa 1910

plantation with Cobb and others. In 1955, Wheeler devoted a column to a story that Cobb had recently recalled at Augusta. Stallings "was the darndest practical joker I ever knew," Cobb said. "Sometimes he would need a week to build up a good one. We used to go down to his place quail shooting every winter." Some of their companions included the writer Damon Runyon, Sr. and player-turned-manager Wilbert Robinson. At lunch one day, somebody asked for honey. In response, Stallings told of there being good wild honey on a tree on a neighbor's property.

In his paraphrase of Cobb's recollection, Wheeler wrote, "It seems there was a good deal of talk about the virtues of wild honey, both as a medicine and a tasty trimming. Also Stallings continued to emphasize the risks involved in

trying to get it from the tree[,] which seemed to be practically the only known source of supply for miles.

"A few nights later a possum hunt was organized which is regarded by some to be first-class sport. As for this writer, I would rather be home in bed. You stumble around in the dark, trip over roots, and eventually the dogs tree the poor animal. Finally, some intrepid soul either shakes him out or shoots him. The Stallings safari got one possum. Then old George said in a whisper, 'We're not far from that wild honey tree. Let's try to sneak over there. It's a black night.'

"The boys reached their destination all right, and one of the guides had started to climb up, when there was a holler from behind a nearby bush. 'Get out of here,' shouted the man, 'before I shoot.'

"Apparently being trigger happy, he let go with both barrels. Flames squirted out of the end of the gun. Everybody scrambled. Runyon fell backward into a ditch, picked himself up, and ran panting to the house. The fellow dropped out of the tree, writhing and groaning, and holding his stomach.

"'I'm shot,' he shouted. Nobody paid any attention to him. 'It's a wonder somebody didn't really get hurt the way they scattered in the dark,' went on Cobb. 'Of course, I was onto it all the time. We finally all got back or we thought we had until we found [hunting chum] Bill Mac[b]eth was missing.'

"'Maybe he got shot, too,' said Stallings gloomily. 'We'd better go look for him. It's our duty.'

"Everybody started out again, some a little reluctantly, when we met four men carrying Bill on an old door like a stretcher. His pants were pretty nearly torn off, and there was blood all over his legs. He was moaning.

"'Well, to make a long story longer,' concluded Ty, 'of course, George Stallings had staged the whole show. The shotgun was loaded with blanks and newspapers stuffed down the barrels to make the flames shoot out. The blood on Mac[b]eth's legs came from the possum.'

"'I don't think it was very funny,' I remarked. 'He might have been a great manager, but he was no [vaudeville entrepreneur] Flo Ziegfield when it came to showmanship.'

"'I don't think now it was very funny either,' agreed Cobb. 'But as I look back, it seemed to me to be a hell of a joke at the time.'"

Another tale of Cobb as the key accessory to a Stallings hunting calamity prank appeared in the inaugural issue of *American Shooter* in January 1916.

"One night, when it was dark as pitch on the island and one needed a lantern to find his way among the trees and to escape the marshes, Stallings and Cobb decided to put across their favorite practical joke. Accordingly, laying particular stress upon the darkness of the night, Stallings began to tell his guests [fellow players, and journalists and cartoonists from New York, Boston and other large Eastern cities] about the alligator holes which were everywhere on the island."

In the next issue, editor George "Stoney" McLinn told of having spent a day shooting birds in South Carolina with him and golfing 36 holes in Augusta the following one. The day of the hunt, Cobb woke McLinn up at 3 a.m. by yanking the blankets from his bed and whipping him with a towel soaked in ice-cold water. "'Come on, come out of it, you lazy, good-for-nothin' Yankee; reckon you think we sleep 'till noon and then go hunting in the South,' were the words that brought me back to life." At the end of the visit, Cobb wrote, "Thirty miles on horseback, bird hunting. He did it, much to my surprise."

In 1917:

Cobb and Stallings, "farmers, who indulge in baseball as a side line, have been attending livestock sales in central Illinois," a reporter declared from Bloomington, Ill. "They came to invest in thoroughbred cattle for their farms near Macon, Ga. To see Cobb sitting upon a fence and appraising a herd of cattle, nobody would suspect that he is regarded by many as the world's greatest ball player." Stallings "with a wisp of straw in his mouth, a slouch hat upon his head and a shrewd grin upon his face, would never be accused of being the 'miracle' [1914 World Series-winning] manager of the national game."

Eugene Ruppert "Jack" Veiock, sports editor of the International News Service, wrote the following poem, "Baseball Up To Date:"

In days of old, so I am told, a baseball star was far from meek;
He used to drive a bunch of five, against a rival player's beak.
He used to fuss and rave and cuss, he was a bear in every fight,
But he was there, and on the square – he only used his left and right.

Today the mob hails Tyrus Cobb, a prima donna of the game;
'The only Ty,' we hear 'em cry, 'A model in the Hall of Fame.'
Ty hates the rough and tumble stuff, all rowdyism he dislikes;
So in a jam he takes a slam, at rival players with his spikes.

Veteran St. Louis writer John B. Sheridan interviewed Cobb and wrote that off the field, he is "a very modest young man. He moves about the hotel corridors very quietly, always making way for others. He smiles gently and speaks with a low voice. His accent is Southern, but not markedly so. He does not slur his r's or say 'you all.'" A main subject of the interview was Cobb's support for the U.S. entry into the Great War. "I'd like to do my bit," he said. "I would like to do it without any noise or advertising. I admire the man who keeps his mouth shut, smiles, gets into no arguments and fights like fifty. If I go through this war I'd like to go through without saying a word. The silent man who does not boost his friends nor abuse his foes, but who knows why and what he is fighting for and fights is my idea of a good soldier."

Cobb commented to Sheridan about his recent fight off the field with a rival player, Buck Herzog of the New York Giants. A confrontation during a game had sparked it. Skipping over some quotations that sound like hokey rewrites, Cobb told Sheridan that "no man, large or small [Herzog was smaller than him], can apply abusive and degrading epithets to me with impunity. I would not mind it if done in anger or in the heat of a game. But this was done in cold blood and with a cheap purpose. I could not forgive that."

He would refer to that fight in 1921 in a long statement in response to an article after his naming as Detroit's manager. The very end of that statement touches on his fighting career in baseball: "A pet subject for writers has been to elaborate on my ability to get into fisticuffs with other ballplayers, it having been intimated that I would get into a fight with every member of the team. I have had only two fights with members of the Detroit club in 15 years, and I

Nig Clarke and his mother
as of 1919

wish to say that when I broke into big league ball Detroit didn't have exactly a Sunday school team." Besides the two Detroit players, Herzog was the only other big leaguer he fought with, he wrote.

In 1918:

In January, former catcher-turned-U.S. Marine Nig Clarke visited Cobb in Augusta. In a letter to someone, Clarke wrote that Cobb would soon enlist in the U.S. military. "Ty drove me out to Camp Hancock [near Augusta], where 43,000 men are in training, and introduced me to several of his friends at the camp. It was funny to hear Ty introduce the marine to the army officers. He said: 'Lieut. So-and-So, I want to introduce you to a real soldier from one of Uncle Sam's training camps.' Cobb is coming over to Par[r]is Island[, S.C.] to see me next week. He is just itching to get into harness with a gun and bayonet or cheese knife and get at the Germans. He kept me busy showing him all the bayonet exercises and manual of arms, always watching me like a hawk."

In 1919:

Regarding his alleged violent incident with chambermaid Morris, the *Evening Review* of East Liverpool, Ohio, said she "alleges that the Georgia Peach so far forgot himself as to kick her in a spat she had with him on April 23. A Southern gentlem[a]n should be able to handle a wench without using the boot on her."

from left to right: Roscoe "Fatty" Arbuckle, Cobb and Buster Keaton

In 1920:

At a press luncheon in San Francisco, Cobb "expressed his thanks to the newspaper men of the country for what they have done for him and declared that if he was half the ball player his friends said he was it was due to the newspaper critics who have spurred him on to better results." Days later in Los Angeles, he visited actors Buster Keaton and Roscoe "Fatty" Arbuckle in their respective film studios and "went elsewhere to witness the blowing up of a castle. It was necessary for him to stick around until almost nightfall to be an eyewitness of this outrage," the *Los Angeles Times* said.

Ty Cobb, Roscoe Arbuckle and two of the Cobb children. The photograph was taken in California in November, just before Mr. Arbuckle left for a vacation in Europe

Nothing textually of note stood out to me from 1921, Cobb's first of six years as Detroit's manager. Graphically, something does: pictures of the team's spring training in San Antonio. If you Google "Ty Cobb and the Detroit Tigers riding donkeys," you can find a 17-second clip at the video Web site of Getty Images that was likely shot by a Georgia-based all-around film-and-print journalist, Tracy Mathewson. (If you Google "Ty Cobb videos and b-roll footage," you can find and watch Getty Images's other Cobb-related videos.)

from left to right: Doc Ayers, Clarence Huber, Dan Howley, Bernie Boland, Larry Woodall, Paddy Livington, Red Olham and Lu Blue

In 1922:

The AP interviewed him and said, "Of all that has gone from the game Ty regrets most keenly the fighting spirit of the old teams; the combative mood of men like himself who came into the profession when loyalty to his club was demanded and who fought as defenders and conquerors, not as interesting entertainers drawing great salaries for cold skill. 'The "old home town" has gone,' he said."

Cobb in San Antonio

In 1923:

He responded to a proposal by the *Brooklyn Eagle*'s Thomas S. Rice that numbers be added to uniforms.

Dear Mr. Rice:

Your clipping of recent date received, and in regard to my opinion of your idea of numbering ball players, will say that I feel a hesitancy in expressing myself upon this subject, for I am really just a

Tracy Mathewson as of 1921. Images from his film footage also appear on pages 114, 116, 132, 231 and 443.

player and hardly know just how to express myself.

There is a certain feeling of not wanting to be numbered – well, you have seen horses numbered at a sale, numerals stamped on their backs. A number, if such procedures were in vogue, should be placed on one's back. Well, all that I can say is: Just to think of it makes me feel uncomfortable.

Now, if it were decreed that we ball players should be numbered, naturally I would consent and wear my number. I will do anything

Cobb and retired pitcher Ed Walsh, a fellow future Hall of Famer, at the December 1922 baseball winter meetings. It is apparently the last notable graphic of Cobb before December 31, 1922, the end of unrestricted use of images under current U.S. copyright law.

within reason for the betterment of the game if the powers that be should say the word. I do not wish to add my say, either pro or con.

I wish to say to you that your suggestions, of course, sound good – you have many good ideas encompassed within your story. For one argument I could advance against such a scheme, you have many for it.

I believe there would be lots of disgruntled ball players over the numbering system. Some ball players get disgruntled easily, and if it were not the numbering system it might just as well be something else. But, I reiterate, there would be lots of growling about the numbering system.

I hope you will understand my position. Looks as if we were going to have a good season.

With every good wish, I am, very truly

TY COBB

In 1924:

On opening day in Cleveland, one of the two bands that was participating in the ceremonies "has a leader who cannot regard himself as a friend of Ty Cobb," the *Free Press* said. "When the Tigers appeared on the field for preliminary unlimbering[,] the group of musicians, under instructions, dashed off a couple of stanzas of

'Marching Through Georgia.' Cobb bit his lips in resentment and muttered something that wasn't complimentary."

In a newspaper serial, Salsinger, sports editor of the *Detroit News*, wrote that Cobb "had a violent temper when he broke into the game, a temper that he has learned to control to some extent since his debut. He has become involved in many misunderstandings, disputes, arguments and fights." (In the *New York Tribune* in 1920, reporter William J. "Bill" Macbeth had described Cobb in those early years as someone who, on the one hand, was temperamental and "ready to resent the slightest disposition at hazing." [sic] On the other hand, Cobb "was a very observing young man and always kept his eyes open.")

In a different part of the serial, Salsinger made a similar point. In his long career "his disposition has always been of a truculent nature. He never was able to stand reverses in good grace. He often expressed a selfish nature and too frequently lacked sympathy." Salsinger began that piece by saying that at times, he has "the polish, the gloss, the culture, the bearing and supreme suavity of George Bryan (Beau) Brummel[, the well-known arbiter of that era of classy taste] and, at other times, when he loses his temper and lashes into a wild fury, he resembles the Bill Sykes, of Charles Dickens' 'Oliver Twist.' His composition is of Jekyll and Hyde construction."

The McFarland Historical Baseball Library (12)

Ty Cobb *Two Biographies*

"Our Ty: Ty Cobb's Life Story" (1924) and "Which Was Greatest: Ty Cobb or Babe Ruth?" (1951)

H.G. SALSINGER Edited by William R. Cobb
SERIES EDITORS Gary Mitchem and Mark Durr

Later in that piece, he wrote, "Cobb has always been a student. His mind is one of the keenest in his native land. He was quick to grasp, to understand any subject. He has an inquiring mind, a thirst for knowledge of all kinds." Subjects he knows "a great deal about" are finance and business. One level down, he knows "much" about manufacture. Below that, he knows "a good deal" about literature and music.

Salsinger told of Cobb sitting one evening in a famous restaurant, with an orchestra playing classical selections. "During the intermission the conductor came to Cobb's table and was introduced. Cobb invited him to sit down. The composer asked Cobb how he liked the orchestra, and Cobb criticized certain phases of the rendition. The orchestra leader, a really gifted musician," including being a noted violinist, "immediately tried to corner Cobb in a technical discussion." Cobb then analyzed the violin. "A stranger hearing the conversation, [sic] would have experienced difficulty in choosing the musician if told that one man was a musician and the other was not."

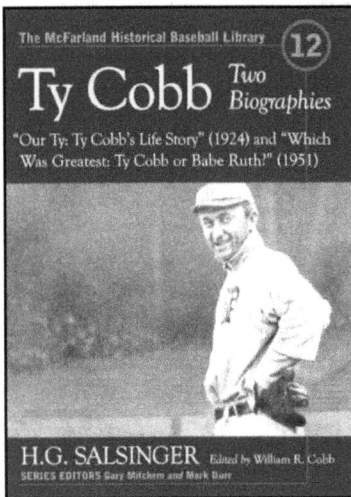

Digressing to two stories about Cobb's love of music:

The following one from 1939 refers back to 1927. A one-time Cleveland-based friend of his from Georgia, Kenneth Stambaugh, would recall being in a Cleveland Heights home with Cobb on the night of a heavyweight fight between Dempsey and Jack Sharkey. Many guests had gathered and champagne was flowing freely, Stambaugh wrote in a letter to the *Atlanta Constitution.* "But where was Ty? In a musical library at an expensive electric player piano, playing with great feeling, the classics. He would move the loud, medium and soft levers with the real touch of a master."

Back in 1916, in *Baseball Magazine,* Cobb had said that while he had often wished he could have been a composer, that he did not think he had the talent to become one. Leerhsen quoted the 1916 article without mentioning Salsinger's take on Cobb's musical talent. I can add that as a backup to baseball, a music-related career was far from Cobb's mind in 1912, when he bought a share of a Detroit sporting goods chain. Back then he had declared, "I desire to have a good business position awaiting me when I get through with baseball."

In his serial, Salsinger also made these observations on subjects on which Cobb is knowledgeable.

In sculpture, the "ruggedness, virility, power and force" of 19th-century French sculptor Auguste Rodin "appeals to

Cobb at a banquet celebrating the 75th anniversary of the National League in 1951

Cobb more than that of any other man who works in stone, wax, clay or bronze."

Of precious stones, besides knowing the history of many, he is a "judge of diamonds and the nativity of the different diamonds, their cut, their value." Cobb also knows rugs, and Salsinger listed about a dozen types. Cobb's expertise on rugs had been featured in 1914. His hobby was revealed after two days of rain in spring training, in Jackson, Miss. The Detroit players "were ranged around the hotel veranda in chairs discussing and cussing the weather, when a vendor of rugs came in, more to get out of the rain than anything else.

"Then it was that the immortal gardner [sic] sprung his hobby – RUGS. For just as soon as the merchant stepped upon the gallery, Cobb cheered up and astounded his companions by chatting with the vendor about the beauties in the most mysterious and technical terms. Not of the common kind did he speak, but of the Oriental kinds, and [of such] frequently mentioned names as Kirman, Tabriz, Razac, Soumak and others.

"'It just so happens that I have made a study of rugs for years,' said the Georgia Peach when the man had again gone forth into the rain. 'Let me warn you, though, that a little piece of tapestry the size of a napkin can run up a cash account as fast as anything I know.

"Rugs, like diamonds, increase in value as they grow older. I like to study them, for it takes one back into other centuries and the study is exceedingly attractive. I suppose that I have the 'rug bug.'"

Prior biographers and modern-day article writers have overlooked the extent of Cobb's specialized knowledge. Alexander has detailed it the most. One taste of his doing so is having quoted the last three words of the following from 1914 Cobb book collaborator Wheeler. Wheeler declared in that book, "He can absorb information rapidly and set down his impressions easily and graphically. He is an intellectual blotter." Alexander gave some other examples, one of which I was able to confirm: that he especially enjoyed reading about Napoleon. Alexander implied that Cobb would have identified with Napoleon for being an indomitable figure who imposed his will on the events of his times.

On his interest in books, especially history ones, the AP quoted him as follows in 1930: "'I'd recommend reading history to anybody,' said Ty in a burst of enthusiasm. 'I'd rather read it than any other literature. I've learned a lot since I left school and a lot since I left baseball.'" *Atlanta Constitution* photographer-reporter Mathewson in 1925 said Cobb has lots of books, mostly history ones.

Upon his death, sportswriter John Gillooly of the *Boston Daily Record* would state, "For a man with little formal education, Cobb was a tremendously smart man. A voluminous reader, he was an authority on the Civil, Revolutionary Wars [sic]." Also, "He enjoyed playing a war-quiz game. He'd say: 'Too bad General Johnson was killed by Union soldiers at Chickamauga.' If you were hep, you'd correct him and say, Ty, it was Stonewall Jackson and he was accidentally fatally wounded by his own troops. Then Cobb would grin that parchment grin and aver, suh, [sic] that you knew your Civil War."

Leerhsen, to give a sense of Cobb's intellect, printed a quote from intellectual 20th-century catcher Moe Berg. Berg, in talking to biographer McCallum, called Cobb an "intellectual giant." Berg's point absolutely rings true, since it matches Wheeler's in 1914. Also on this subject:

Earl L. Bell, the longtime Augusta friend and journalist, wrote in 1964 that Cobb "could converse knowledgeably on almost any topic. His private library was an enviable one." At the start of Cobb's retirement in 1929, an item in many newspapers was, "Now it's out: Ty Cobb reads Shakespeare, according to a reporter who was a guest at Cobb's home in Augusta."

Upon Cobb's death, sports editor Smith of the *Free Press* would quote Cobb as having told him, "I studied baseball like a lawyer studied his law books, like a doctor studied anatomy. If I was anything at all, I was an educated baseball player."

The following 1941 comment of Berg's was made in conversation with Ted Williams, in the presence of Edwin M. Rumill of the *Christian Science Monitor*. Berg said of Cobb, "He had a brain – probably the keenest baseball has seen. He'd outthink you if he thought he couldn't beat you any other way." By the way, the 1941 feature in which Berg was quoted ended with the following quotes from him: "Can you blame me for praising the old Georgia Peach? He got into town this morning and the first thing he did was call me up on the telephone." (In an hour-long interview in 2007, longtime Cobb friend Jimmy Lanier told Jewish Atlanta lawyer/newsletter editor Abe J. Schear that Berg had been a guest at Cobb's hunting preserve and lodge.)

Digressing to one of the more unusual coincidences I came across, and involving Berg:

When the Red Sox released Berg as one of its coaches in 1942, one of Cobb's older good friends, former Detroit catcher Larry Woodall, replaced him. Woodall would work for the Red Sox for the rest of Cobb's life and likely supplied Harold Kaese of the *Boston Globe*, a prolific book writer, with stories about him. Kaese told one such story in the newspaper in 1946. In turn, upon Woodall's death in 1963, Kaese made one of the most insightful observations about the type of personality that could get along with Cobb, over the long term.

HAROLD KAESE
Boston Globe

Woodall had been a catcher in all six of Cobb's years as a player-manager. Kaese wrote, "They were temperamental opposites who got along well, Cobb being highstrung and irascible, Woodall even-tempered and good natured."

"'You got to say one thing for old Ty. He sure wanted to win,' Woodall would drawl." Also in his remembrance of Woodall, Kaese recalled Cobb's last visit to Boston and Cobb's having noted that Woodall had a fine arm before his throws began to sink. Woodall said Cobb was right. Cobb then uttered some additional critical analysis. Kaese added that Woodall was "not the least perturbed because his old manager was second-guessing his throwing 33 years later. That was Cobb, and that was also Woodall."

Returning to Cobb's intellect:

Cobb, in his own newspaper serial in 1925, said that baseball has "taught me the necessity of concentration and application. I have learned the difference between a real idea and one that merely bobs up in conversation only to be forgotten. In baseball a player has a chance every day to find out where he is wrong. An idea that doesn't stand this daily test is no idea at all."

In the next installment of his own serial, Salsinger told of some of the findings in a U.S. Army psychological examination of Cobb: "Cobb has genius without the usual neurotic trend." Also, "Cobb never was, is not now, and never can be an egotist. True, the ego, or the psychological equivalent for soul, is highly developed, but the soul of Cobb is never expressed through the medium of egotism. One single trait in his character proves, beyond the possibility of doubt, that egotism can no more be expressed by Cobb than the Iliad of Homer by the Wild Man of Borneo. That single trait is bashfulness."

Salsinger himself observed, "Cobb has never been an egotist. He has a bashfulness unusual in men. Until a few years ago it was impossible for him to talk in public. He would stutter and stammer. Only when among a few that he knew well was he at ease."

On an entirely different subject in Salsinger's serial, Cobb talked about life in the South. "'Down South we knew how to live,' he would say. 'Down South there is not the hustle, the bustle, the tear and wear that you find in the North. We get something out of life down there. We know what home is and where: in the North, most people believe that an apartment of a few rooms is sufficient; we could never think of such a thing down South. We know food down there and we know how to relax. There is not the battle and strife for the dollar that you find in the North. Tell me, what do they get out of life – these people that are fighting for fortunes that few of them ever get?'" Also, "By the time they accumulate their fortunes they don't know how to enjoy the money."

In 1925:

George Chadwick in the *Charlotte Observer* wrote, "It will soon be time for Ty Cobb to tell the world that his legs feel all right. That will be a sure sign that the great Georgian is looking forward to another wonderful season." Chadwick continued, "Cobb believes the secret of his success as a ball player is in the care he has taken with his feet and legs. During the playing season he will sit patiently on a rough stool in the clubhouse putting on his stockings and shoes to suit him. Sometimes he will pull a stocking off a half dozen times to get it to 'feel' right to the bottom of his foot. Ty will put [sic] off his shoes and tie the strings.

"Then he will stamp his feet and if the feeling is not to his liking, he will sit down and take off his shoes and put them on again. He will repeat the performance until he can stand on the shoes and feel that they respond to ev[e]ry pressure of his body. Not until then will he walk out of the clubhouse to play ball."

a studio portrait that Cobb inscribed to Robert W. Woodruff

Julian Griffin of the *Atlanta Constitution* wrote a hunting feature on Cobb, including by noting a recent hunt with Coca-Cola head Woodruff. *Constitution* photographer-reporter Mathewson told Griffin that Cobb "is never in too big a hurry to speak to the people" he encounters while hunting "and take up time with them, young and old alike." Mathewson told of having hunted with Cobb "many a time, and I've never seen him miss a bird."

Griffin wrote, "He loves dogs and children and knows and understands both, an indication of the human qualities of the man." Griffin ended his piece by quoting Mathewson as follows:

"I know only one other man in all the world with the same quick mind, charm and delightful personality as Cobb, and that is the Prince of Wales [Edward VIII]. They are of absolutely differen[t] types, but the quick mind and charming personality and knowledge of the beautiful in art, etc., and love for animals, are strikingly similar."

About Woodruff's hunting forays with Cobb, Ralph McGill, executive editor of the *Constitution*, wrote the following in the *Saturday Evening Post* in 1951:

"The bird-dog fraternity still recalls an episode of those early days when the star[-]struck salesman and the great Detroit outfielder put their favorite dogs down with sizeable bets on their covey-finding abilities. At the end of the first day, Woodruff's Lloyd George was ahead of Cobb's Connie Mack by two coveys. 'Hold the covey count, double the bets and we'll hunt again tomorrow!' stormed the angry Cobb. When the soft, smoky haze of a deep-South autumn twilight fell through the pines and fields on the following Saturday to close out six consecutive days of hard hunting, Lloyd George was still ahead. The hard-losing Cobb looked blackly at his dog and walked off. 'That damned dog of Woodruff's has got his nose for prospects,' he said, in deep disgust, and refused even to speak to his friend for the next six or seven months."

A 1979 biography of Woodruff recalled Cobb for having been a regular shooting partner of Woodruff's over a long period. "He and Woodruff were imbued with the same kind of competitive drive," wrote biographer Charles Newton Elliott. "When they hunted together, they usually made a bet on the number of birds each was able to bring in during the course of a hunting day. Woodruff frequently beat him, and this made Ty so mad that sometimes he wouldn't speak to his host for the remainder of the trip."

Returning to the chronology:

In *Hearst's International*, noted novelist and interview journalist Theodore Dreiser visited the Cobb home and got Cobb to observe, "As a matter of fact when all the fame and applause is all in and you get to figuring on real values the financial end of it is probably the only real thing left. That sounds pretty practical, but I've been disillusioned and I'm calloused. If you have money you can take care of your wife and children and that's all a man has after all is said and done. They are the only ones you can turn to if you are in trouble or if you stand in need of sympathy and understanding."

On less lofty matters, in a railroad terminal in Augusta, Cobb disputed his check. On what then ensued, Cobb denied

Cobb quail hunting with friend Forest H. Willis and one of their bird dogs in Louisville, Ga., in 1929

being hit on the head with a glass by the wife of the restaurant's manager. The Cobb biographies have various twists on what transpired. Sports columnist William Peet of the *Pittsburgh Post* wrote that with his arrest on a charge of disorderly conduct, "the newspapers of the Michigan metropolis quickly printed Cobb's pugilistic record, which is an interesting one, and sets off that fiery disposition of his. Like [now-manager] John McGraw of the [New York] Giants, it seems Cobb has lost most of his battles off the field."

A week later, Cobb typed a letter to syndicate owner Christy Walsh. The lone subject was coverage of the incident in the *Detroit News* and the *Detroit Times*; a front-page *News* story was headlined, "JUDGE BLAMES COBB IN FIGHT: Thinks if Ty Gets off Merely by Forfeiting Bond He's Lucky." The *Times* ran this headline over a two-paragraph story: "Ty Cobb Arrested in Atlanta After Food Price Argument."

Cobb told Walsh, "I have been through lots of things but this is the most uncalled for punishment that I have ever taken and everything surrounding the entire proposition is absolutely rotten. I have been up against lots of things but this incident which gave the News the opening is the worst that I have ever experienced – so you see I have been punished from two directions. Have lots to tell you when I see you concerning their efforts to injure me." Cobb said he "is absolutely sure" that the reason he has "gotten in very bad with the Detroit News" is either having signed with Walsh (a Cobb serial would appear in the *Detroit Times* via Walsh in the next offseason) or having signed a letter, which the *Times* printed, in which Cobb noted having an arrangement with the *Times*.

(Cobb had been cool to the idea of signing with Walsh in late 1923. In a letter that year to Salsinger, he expressed a willingness to cooperate on Salsinger's serial. He wrote, "I must shake this fellow Walsh some way. He has certainly been after me of late, and I am, in a way, duty bound to get rid of him in a nice way and I can do so by waiting until the beginning of the year," 1924. Salsinger wrote his serial for the syndicate of 1914 Cobb collaborator Wheeler, the North American Newspaper Alliance.)

At the start of July, writing in his home newspaper, the *New York Telegram*, sports editor Ed Hughes declared, "Cobb is getting 100 per cent work out of his men for the first time since he took over the management of the Tigers. Formerly Ty, the temperamental, did not have the full good will of his mates, owing to the severity of his discipline. This year it is entirely different. Cobb, getting along in years, is becoming more tolerant of mistakes and shortcomings. He realizes that all cannot be endowed with such diamond gifts as he possessed, and still possesses."

In late August, he was honored at a banquet by the city of Detroit. All three biographers mentioned it, but not his remarks. After receiving an expensive grandfather's clock that the city of Detroit paid for and a huge check from Detroit owner Navin, money that Cobb later said he was owed anyway, Cobb said, according to the AP, "Now I see how selfish I have been. My career has been selfish – nothing else. I have done no great good that you should so signally honor me. Oh, why didn't I try to do more? Much of what success I may have had has been due in large measure to the help of others, especially the owners of the Detroit club and the Detroit public."

According to a version in the *Detroit News*, he said, "I have been rewarded. I have been inspired. I have the most wonder[ful] set of fans in the world. I am sorry that I have not been worthy of all the fine things done for me tonight. I have been selfish. Everything I have done has been selfish. In the future, I will try to be worthy of all of the fine things said and done for me tonight. I will try to be an inspiration to our youth, in everything I do or say. I have been selfish and I am sorry." In a general editorial, the *Macon Telegraph* reprinted the AP's quotes from Cobb, although stopping with the line, "Oh, why didn't I try to do more?" and said, "It is a lament that many make as years grow upon them. A distinguished Georgia man, a few months before his death some years ago, told a young reporter, who had always stood in awe of his austerity and his 'offishness [aloofness],' 'Son, make friends. I am a man who has a certain number of admirers, but very few friends. If I had my life to live over, I should devote an appreciable part of it to making friends. Any man worth while must have enemies, but have friends also.'"

The *Telegraph* continued, "Ty Cobb is a man who has always captivated the admiration of a tremendous number of people, particularly those who have followed baseball, but he has devoted little of his time to making friends. By one stroke – his frank confession of selfishness – he has made friends of men who were simply his admirers."

That offseason, hunting expert Morris Ackerman penned a roundup on offseason trips by players. "Ty Cobb is moose hunting in the province of Ontario. Ty, one of the best wing shots in the south, is a strong devotee of big game hunting. He has hunted moose, deer, caribou and bear in Canada. In the winter he hunts quail in his native state. He raises blooded bird dogs." Cobb and Speaker were already reportedly

from left to right in Wyoming in 1927: Garland "Gob" Buckeye, Speaker, Cobb and guide Max Wilde

planning to go to Jackson Hole, Wyo., next fall "in quest of elk, moose, grizzlies and sheep. Wyoming is the only state in the Union where moose hunting is now permitted." Ackerman added, "Nearly all the players in both major leagues are hunters. They claim hunting trips keep them in top condition between seasons." (In September 1930, Ackerman would write a feature on Jackson Hole. Now both retired, Cobb and Speaker had recently hunted there, and Ackerman reported, "The fighting Georgian and the smiling Texan brought down their quota of each variety of the Hole's game. Mrs. Speaker also landed trophies of elk and moose." A third former big leaguer and footballer as well, Garland "Gob" Buckeye, "bagged everything except the elusive big-horn.")

Cobb near Jackson Hole in August 1930

In 1926:

In a March letter to Walsh, in addition to touching on some minor baseball subjects, he expressed condolences on the death of Walsh's father. "You know Christy we have no control over these matters – the schedule is prepared by someone higher up." Cobb had recently published a newspaper serial about his life through Walsh's syndicate.

In August, H. F. Manchester of the *Boston Herald* wrote a remarkable story. Without knowing that Cobb was about to finish up his 22-year Detroit career, he wrote probably the most descriptive account of him in a public situation. At a restaurant or hotel grill, Cobb was with former big leaguer Nig Clarke, who was now in the minors. After Cobb waived to a waiter, the waiter brought them menus, "and there was a moment of silent study, while the waiter stood by nervously and with glances of covert curiosity at the Georgian's neck. Cobb lowered the [menu] card slightly and raised his left eyebrow. The waiter swallowed, shifted to a position at right angles to the ball player's vision and leaned over solicitously."

"'You may bring me – ' the waiter's pencil hand paused in suspended animation – 'some sliced peaches.' The tension was broken, the boy walked away with alacrity, and the sun ventured to illuminate a larger portion of the table cloth. Cobb took a sip of water, softly unfolded his napkin, and looked idly about him, as if in lazy, cynical, and somewhat amused contemplation of the prospects of another day. Then that restless, mobile eyebrow returned to its original position."

Then the reporter wrote of engaging Cobb on his playing career now winding down. As Cobb was making a point, the waiter "approached discreetly with Cobb's 'two eggs fried in butter.' The plate was set before him. Cobb picked up the cover, holding it poised aloft to be taken. The waiter did not take it. Cobb's left eyebrow went up another quarter-inch as though he would hold it there all day if he had to. Then the boy perceived the warning signal, and advanced to the rescue. For a moment there was deep silence. Cobb inspected his eggs from all angles, and gave one a contemptuous prod. Clark[e] looked at his eggs, looked at Cobb's, then the two looked at each other. The waiter stood stock still as one being silently crucified."

After the boy at the next table glanced over, Cobb said, "I hate to look at these eggs askance, but I asked for two eggs fried in butter and this — "

The waiter attested to their being fried in butter, to which Cobb replied, "Possibly, possibly, but the main point is, how long were they fried? There were on the fire too long — ."

"Right, Ty," Clarke agreed, "they're just fit for sandwiches."

"And I know what I am talking about when I speak of eggs. I've cooked 'em for 20 years. When I go out on a hunting trip, sometimes we all take turns at cooking, and I have a picture in my mind's eye of what two eggs fried in butter ought to look like. Now, my boy, will you take these eggs away, and bring me back some scrambled eggs – and don't cook them too long."

After Cobb stepped away to take a long-distance telephone call, Clarke and Manchester spoke about mutual friends in the U.S. Marine Corps. Cobb heard Clarke say the following about his own service in the Corps during the Great War.

"When I came out I was in great shape, and have been ever since – just as good as I ever was."

"No, you're not, Nig!"

"Yes," Nig insisted. "I feel just as good — ."

"Now, look here, Nig, you know better than that, and I hate to hear you say that when it isn't so."

Clarke turned to Manchester, a little aggrieved, and said, "He's always pickin' on me like that."

"Now get me right, Nig. I know you're in mighty good shape for you[r] age and the amount of baseball you've played. That much is true. But when you say you're as good as ever, it just makes me sore. Not that it's you, but just in the interests of truth, I don't like it. We've all got to take our beating sooner or later, and when we begin to slip, why not admit it, and guide ourselves accordingly?

"And that is in line with what I'm telling you about getting out of the game. Too many of the athletes who retire don't realize that they have reached the age where they can't do just anything they want to. You've got to take care of yourself in this life – you've got to fight your own battles and look after your own interests. If you don't, no one will do it for you, no matter how many friends you have. Now, my plan of retiring is right in line with my policy of baseball efficiency – that of playing the game to the limit, and watching for all the breaks. We have only one life to live, and we should live that as efficiently as possible. We should watch for efficiency leaks in our living just as we do in our ball playing."

A few sentences later, he said, "Now I am going to stretch out my actual retirement from vigorous physical work over a period of years. I like golf, but I haven't played it for over eight years. I am going to take it up again. Then I like to hunt quail in Georgia, ducks in South Carolina, and larger game in

Canada. So I will probably do more hunting in the next few years, to partially compensate for any cutting down on the baseball."

Just then the waiter came back with the scrambled eggs "and an anxious smile." Then he suddenly disappeared "kitchenward. Meanwhile there was a resumption of the council of war. The waiter had forgotten that 'Nig's' water glass was empty, and had to come back. He was caught."

"Now about these eggs —," Cobb said, and the waiter "gave a good imitation of the boy standing on the burning deck, whence all but him had fled."

Cobb asked, "Did the cook break two fresh eggs into the pan, or did he dip some yolks out of a big bowl, after the pastry cook had skimmed off the whites?"

The waiter did not know, but said he was sure that they had been prepared properly.

"Well, you can see for yourself there isn't much white in that. It seems to contain the yolks of about four eggs, with no whites. Now you know for yourself that the owner of this place would never let you use four eggs for one order. That being the case, the question is, what became of the whites?"

The waiter had no answer.

Then Cobb said, "Did you ever hear of Chinese eggs?"

The waiter had not, "but strove desperately to look interested."

"These are not Chinese eggs, but I am going to tell you about them, so when I get through with you, you'll know something about eggs, and why it is so hard for travelers to get good ones. In China, you know, they are very fond of chicken, and have large flocks of poultry, but they don't eat eggs. They consider them offal – waste [parts of an animal]. But enterprising foreigners buy them up in large quantities. The whites and yolks are separated, and then dried and packed in bulk and shipped to this country and others, where they are used in making pastry, custard, etc. The scrambled eggs we used to get in the service [in the Great War] were often made of them. So when I speak of eggs, I am not talking through my hat – I know 'em."

The waiter again went on his way, and Cobb repeated for Manchester some of his eating habits. Also, Cobb told him about players sometimes eating themselves out of baseball by chowing down too much hotel food.

Asked by Manchester about his investments, he said, "My big rule is never to buy anything that seeks me. I always decide first exactly what I want to put my money in, and then go and look it up." He spoke of how easy it is for players who make a lot of money to become victims of con artists.

After a friend of Cobb's joined the discussion, there was a discussion of jinxes and good luck signs. Cobb said, "It's all a mental thing, a psychological phase. The feeling that a certain thing will help is bound to bob up, but it is by no means always harmful. The wise manager is the one who can control the jinxes for his own benefit, rather than have them control him. The main thing is to drive out fear from the gang, to make them unified in thinking of winning. There are several things that will do this. You get a man good and mad, and that is one of them." He also spoke of the need to have "a fresh angle on things." He told of a time when a stray dog came to him in Detroit's ballpark "and sniffed at my hand and wagged his tail. Then I got a hunch. I adopted that pup and took him back to the boys. I told them this dog was a good luck sign" and that with it the team was going to break a slump. The team named the dog "Victory" and proceeded to win its next two home games. So, the dog went with them on their next road trip. With that story, the article ended.

Later in the month, Cobb tried to get even with Washington owner Griffith for having complained to American League President Johnson about him. Griffith's complaint concerned Cobb's dilatory tactics during a series in Washington. Johnson then instructed umpires to pay closer attention to Cobb. During Detroit's next series in Washington, two weeks after the previous series there, Cobb sent a long letter to Griffith and leaked it to the *Baltimore News*, which printed it in full. Some of its more loaded thoughts appear below:

He began, "Dear Sir – On our last trip to Washington it fell to my lot to experience one of your many outbursts, in which you enlisted the aid of some of your local papers in broadcasting the fact that I should be curbed."

Much later, he wrote, "Now, Mr. Griffith, you are very inconsistent. You have been very proud of having the reputation of being the slowest and most aggravating pitcher ever in the game. In fact, I have heard you discuss this subject in a very pleased manner."

Griffith's reputation for fooling around during a game was touched on at length in *Cap Anson 3*:

In 1899, Brooklyn outfielder Joe Kelley said Chicago pitcher Griffith had the following practices: "He not only hits the ball against his heel plate [before pitching it], but also smooths the dirt around the pitcher's box before and after each inning." After seeing Griffith pitch in 1899 and 1900, Walter Barnes, Jr. of the *Boston Journal* alluded to his having a practice of pounding new balls against his spikes.

In 1895, the *Washington Post* had printed a generalization about Chicago pitchers stepping on balls with their spikes. Presumably, Griffith was who was meant. In 1896, the *Chicago Tribune* said Griffith "annoys opposing nines by knocking the dirt from the heel spikes of his shoes with the ball. The cry is made that he spikes the ball and twenty times in a game he is called on to give the ball to the umpire for inspection. It is examined and invariably found unscratched, to the surprise of the annoyed ballplayers and the amusement of the crowd."

In 1898 at Cleveland, Griffith used the ball to jar dirt from his spikes. After players on the home team complained, umpire Hank O'Day deemed the ball to be fine. Cleveland captain-manager Patsy Tebeau "imitated the trick once or twice in passing the ball back from the bleachers. Pat's 'kidding' was good-natured, and he kept the crowd amused." In the ninth inning of a later game, Griffith placed the ball under his foot and O'Day put in a new one.

In 1899, in a scoreless game with Chicago in the second inning, Boston's Hugh Duffy took the ball from his pitcher, Kid Nichols, and stomped on it with his feet. "It was meant as disapproval as well as an imitation of Griffith's habit of hitting the ball against the heel of his shoe," a Chicago writer said. Griffith was the opposing pitcher. A month later, umpire Tom Lynch removed two balls from a game "because it looked as though Griffith had tapped them on his spikes too hard. Lynch gave him [a] warning once."

Ten days later, umpire O'Day twice removed the game ball, once after Baltimore accused Griffith of cutting it, and another time after it accused infielder Gene DeMontreville of doing so. A month later, umpire Ed Swartwood twice asked to see the ball after St. Louis players complained that Griffith was knocking it against his heel. When Swartwood said the balls were fine, Griffith "smiled defiantly and gave his shoe a few extra raps."

Returning to Cobb's letter:

"Is it not a fact, Mr. Griffith, that you trained small Joe Doyle, who used to be with the New York Yankees when you were manager, and did you not have something to do with the Cuban pitcher [José] Acosta's slow work [in 1920 and 1921 for the Senators]? Now, Mr. Griffith, how about [1921-to-1925 Washington] Pitcher [George] Mogridge, and [1919-to-1925 Washington] Pitcher [Tom] Zachary? Did you ever rave about the slow manner in which they worked? Truly, Mr. Griffith, you are most inconsistent. Another thing is your many outbursts and the fact that your feuds are many."

Cobb then referred to criticism by Griffith of Connie Mack, Griffith's "feud" with Baltimore manager Jack Dunn, Griffith's jumping on comments by Yankee manager Miller Huggins concerning waivers, Griffith's being "inconsistent" for holding Cobb and the umpires responsible for the alleged dilatory incidents, and Griffith's supposed criticism of League President Johnson related to a recent World Series. After giving all that detail, Cobb wrote, "In fact, Mr. Griffith, you seem to be a very vicious gentleman."

Cobb continued by noting that Griffith's own manager, Bucky Harris, had just been suspended by Johnson and added, "I wish to acquaint you with the fact that I have not been suspended this season." After one intervening sentence, Cobb concluded by writing, "It is needless for me to add, since [publication of] your criticism through your press in Washington, that I have lost respect for you and if you will go over my letter carefully you will realize that you are guilty of prevarication."

As quoted by the *Washington Times*, Griffith responded by saying, "I shall take the proper steps to settle with Cobb through the regular channels of the league. That's all I have to say. I am not entering into any argument with him through the newspapers."

Alexander, in summarizing the incident including by providing brief snippets from the letter, concluded that Griffith "let Cobb's blast go unanswered." That would be wrong, assuming that Griffith did follow through via league channels. Leerhsen briefly noted the incident without mentioning Cobb's letter. As for Hornbaker, he found a *Sporting News* article quoting the *Baltimore News* sports editor, Rodger H. Pippen – two weeks before Cobb's letter. Pippen had come to Cobb's defense. Perhaps the support from Pippen emboldened Cobb to write the long letter, knowing that he could leak it to him.

Rodger Pippen

Pippen would be in Chicago and then Buffalo with Cobb in 1949 and breaking the story of his second marriage-to-be: "I have been Cobb's close friend for 35 years. He wanted me to be the first of his friends to meet Mrs. Cass, and I made a special trip here for that purpose," he wrote in the *Baltimore News-Post*. Cobb had been his guest earlier in the decade. In 1955, the *Detroit Times* (a fellow Hearst newspaper) ran a "Cobb wants Crawford in the Hall of Fame" headline over a Cobb letter to Pippen. When Ruth died in 1948, he wrote, "I was the first reporter the Home-Run King ever knew. I played in the first ball game down in Fayetteville, N. C., in which he participated as an Oriole [minor league] rookie [in 1914]. I measured the first home run he hit as a pro. I roomed with him for three weeks on the first Northern trip of the Orioles that spring. I wrote his first love letter to the first of his thousand and one sweethearts." In a Pippen feature in 1963, four years after his death, sports editor Ed Brandt of the *Virginian-Pilot* in Norfolk said Pippen had been "a first-rate hockey player, and continued to perform in the local semi-pro hockey league until he was 45. He finally quit, not because he was too old, but because the fans simply booed him off the ice. They criticized him for what they called dirty playing and said he was too rough on the younger players."

Cobb, Speaker and Buckeye went in October to Wyoming. They were there, a reporter stressed, "miles from telegraph or telephone communication." Not to be denied daily reports of the World Series, "Cobb today exhibited a radio set, which, he said, would be taken along to snatch details of the big baseball conflict out of the ether."

The AP did a feature in December that coincided with his birthday. "In all his long and colorful career, the 'Georgia Peach' has never been away from his family on his birthday. Ty spent most of the day on a train, speeding home from the North, and arriving in Augusta in time to take his place at the table tonight as the guest of honor at a little family birthday party.

"'The nearest I ever came to missing a birthday at home,' said Cobb tonight, 'was during the World War. On Dec. 10 [actually Dec. 9], 1918, I was in Brest, France – Just eight days before my birthday. I sailed on the Leviathan and landed in New York, Dec. 16. Coming by train I reached Augusta on my birthday.'"

Cobb, Buckeye and Speaker on their 1927 trip to Wyoming

But the big story that December, which is rightfully a feature of the three biographers, is that President Johnson had circumstantial evidence that pointed to Cobb and Speaker as having conspired to throw a game; it had been provided by then-pitcher Dutch Leonard. Speaker was then Cleveland's player-manager and a highly successful one that season. Despite leading Cleveland to a second-place finish, he resigned after Cobb had been forced out by owner Navin. Behind the scenes, Johnson and Navin had bought off Leonard's silence by paying him $20,000 for two relevant letters, about $250,000 in today's dollars.

The three biographers touched on all the salient points. That freed me up to look for color. Without much effort, I stumbled across possibly the most emotion that Cobb was reported as showing at any point during the scandal, and none of the three cited it. Initially, Johnson had announced that Cobb and Speaker had been "dropped from baseball." In Chicago at the time, where the American League had its headquarters, Cobb spoke to reporters at his hotel. "Tears dripped down his cheeks as he denied in a lengthy statement any wrongdoing," the United Press reported. "He denied ever having wagered on an American League ball game. He did offer the information that he had wagered on the White Sox in their first two games with the Cincinnati Reds during the well-remembered world series of 1919. Both of those bets the Georgian lost."

Cobb, the United Press also reported, "has nothing but kind words for Commissioner K. M. Landis, but he does feel as though Frank Navin, president of the Detroit club, deserted him in the 'pinch.' He believes himself an unfortunate victim of circumstances.

"I was tired of baseball and wanted to quit, but God knows I did not want to go out this way. It is too horrible to think about and to me it is a horrible nightmare. I have a clear conscience and, of course, that is going to help

A MILLIONAIRE—PENNY ANTE—MARKED CARDS!
Alleged Intrigue of Ty Cobb And Tris Speaker Has That Flavor

me a lot, but I never shall be satisfied until my name is cleared of this nasty charge." Cobb said that just before leaving for home. Commissioner Landis would reinstate Cobb and Speaker three weeks later, although, as Alexander wrote, Cobb never forgave Landis for not clearing his name fast enough.

I also can add to the record of Cobb's reaction his letter to big leaguer-turned-evangelist William "Billy" Sunday. He sent it during a letter writing spree around the time of a February 19, 1927, one to sports editor Alderton of the *Lansing State Journal*. In both his letters to Alderton and Sunday, Cobb made the point that, as he wrote to Sunday, "I know you think I am terribly lax in taking care of my correspondence but I received an awful lot of mail and did not care to answer any of it until certain matters had been taken care of."

One such consideration was waiting until after he had signed with his new team, Philadelphia. Replying to a Sunday letter of December 25, Cobb told of having had "a most terrible winter and it has certainly been hard on me to have to defend myself after 22 years of the kind of baseball that I have

Now that the baseball scandal is formally closed a check-up shows the following results.
Ty Cobb—One black eye.
Tris Speaker—One black eye.
Ban Johnson—One breakdown.
Judge Landis—One new contract.
The Game—One swift kick in the pants.
The Fans—One violent and lasting attack of nausea.

tried to play. I have been north nine times this winter – had gotten to the point where I was sour on the world for it looked as if a man couldn't get a square deal. The public reacted wonderfully and a lot of pressure was brought to bear as we were ready to go the limit. Finally everything came out alright. It only goes to show that right will 'out' and that one must have faith. The next time I see you I will tell you more of my angle." He also referred to having been "under the depressing influence of Navin."

Cobb and Billy Sunday in 1924

Sunday, in releasing Cobb's letter, said he "never believed him guilty of the devilish stuff told Landis by disgruntled outcasts." He praised Cobb as "one of the cleanest players in the business today."

Although I do not know how it panned out, I can also add to the record a July 4, 1927, letter from Cobb to Landis. Cobb wrote, on Philadelphia Athletics letterhead, "Dear Commissioner Landis; I have yet to be fully compensated for my contract dispute with the Detroit club, sometime ago. It has now been a full five years and no creditable progress has been made. Your office spoke to Mr. Navin on the 5th of April last year for a knowledgeable account of past events. Despite the fact I am of knowledge of this[,] there has been no notification by this office at any time of a feasible settlement conductive [sic] to both parties. I will wait a reasonable amount of time to [sic] an efficient and quick response, before I must employ outside legal counsel to settle this dispute, I look most forward to your cooperation. With much appreciation, Very truly yours, Tyrus Raymond Cobb"

To cover one loose end relating to Cobb and Navin:

A far-fetched story with a racism twist concerns the possibility that Detroit could have signed a Negro League catcher in 1925, Larry Brown. The *Pittsburgh Courier* told it in 1961 upon Cobb's death. The *Courier*'s source was a Pittsburgh-based former Negro Leaguer, Ted Page. Supposedly, Navin and two other team officials decided to propose that Brown go to Cuba for two years, learn Spanish and return to the United States as a Cuban. Brown himself was ahistorical in John Holway's 1975 book *Voices from the Great Black Baseball Leagues* in telling Holway that in 1926, he threw out Cobb five times in succession in Cuba. The kicker to the 1961 story is that Brown indeed went to Cuba and mastered Spanish, but then felt that he could not trust Cobb to have reacted well after he would have invariably learned of Brown's true race.

In 1927:

The *Macon Telegraph* printed the photograph on the left. In its caption, it declared that this was "one morning's bag" from his hunting for turkeys in the Georgia swamps; it was then printed in other newspapers. Several days later, it said that numerous citizens had forwarded the photo and caption to the state Fish and Game Commissioner, who, as a result, had opened an investigation and had summoned him. According to state law, one may kill no more than two wild turkeys in any hunting season. In an AP follow-up story, Cobb indicated that the birds shown in the picture were killed in South Carolina, not Georgia. "Friends of the ball player are laughing over the incident. Cobb, they said, did not kill any of the turkeys. Ty went hitless that day but the photos were taken with the bag of all the [hunting] party."

Early that season, Blinkey Horn, sports editor of the *Nashville Tennessean*, wrote, "Tyrus Raymond Cobb is trying to act very coltish. He is behaving far too frisky and too spryly. A gent of his advanced years should be too dignified to be stealing bases and stretching singles into doubles. That's for the young folk." What happened was that Cobb had fooled Yankees outfielder Earle Combs after hitting a single. Cobb paused at first base. Combs took his time throwing the ball back to second baseman Tony Lazzeri and Cobb "slid into the satchel safely a second before Mr. Lazzeri could swipe at him."

Upon Cobb's first visit to Detroit on a visiting team, the *Detroit News* did a feature on Alexander George Washington "Alex" Rivers, a longtime Cobb personal aide. Before citing it, I can note that Hornbaker mentioned Rivers in one neutral sentence. For his part, Leerhsen cited a 1996 online feature by *Detroit News* librarian Patricia Zacharias. In it, she cited a *News* article in which Rivers said he named his first son after Cobb. Fricks had quoted the *Detroit News* to that effect in a May 2004 letter in the *Augusta Chronicle*. The *New York Post*, in 2015, noted Leerhsen's firstborn-son detail.

Leerhsen also included prose from a 1928 feature in the *Chicago Tribune* in which Rivers professed his love for him; the occasion was Cobb's final career game at Detroit. Leerhsen included the comment in his brief survey of Rivers

Alex Rivers and Cobb
in the latter 1910s

and Cobb, which also has an unattributed reference to Rivers and Cobb sobbing during a brief reunion in the mid-1930s in California (a reunion that decade would have been more likely in Detroit). Then Leerhsen added, "Not that any of this was a consolation to [1919 incident chambermaid] Ada Morris, who in the 1930 federal census turns up as a domestic employed by a private family in Detroit, but whose full story we shall apparently never know."

Tripp, presumably thus tipped off to the 1928 column, quoted from it too, that Rivers was "as much a slave as Uncle Tom was." Leerhsen had printed the five words prior to those eight, in which columnist Westbrook Pegler had called Rivers a "niggerish blue gum colored boy."

I can add that Pegler, who Leerhsen called "a truly horrible fellow," awkwardly described recent interaction between Detroit owner Navin and Cobb: "They did not speak as they passed by, each one claiming he made the other rich and each calling the other an ingrate and all so heartily that you might believe both were right to a certain extent."

Rivers had been a personal aide in New Orleans prior to joining Cobb. Had he learned of the 1927 *Detroit News* feature, Leerhsen might have cited its declaration that Rivers "began yesterday his eighteenth season as personal mascot, bat burnisher, chauffeur and factotum [servant] for Tyrus Raymond Cobb." On the other hand, he might have criticized the broken English in which Rivers was quoted at length.

Cobb and Rivers in the mid-1920s

For his part, since Tripp wrote in his book, "So accustomed to the South's practices of racial deference, Rivers referred to Cobb as 'Mistah Cobb,'" I think he would have highlighted the following from the feature: When the Philadelphia team arrived in the city, Rivers "was one of the first to greet Cobb at the D. & C. [line] docks. Mr. Rivers drew himself up to his full 5 feet 2, yanked his hat off and bowed to the ball player."

"'Yes, suh,' he beamed, 'heah Ah is again Mistah Cobb.'"

Leerhsen and Tripp could have then debated whether the bowing was an act of racial deference, possibly based on accounting for whether white servants in that era bowed to their employers.

The article has other "Mistah Cobb" utterances, including when Rivers was in Cobb's hotel suite. "Yes, suh, Mistah Cobb an' mahself is defiliated fo' do eighteenth season. Ah gave up mah job washing D. S. R. [Department of Street Railways] buses yesterday in depreciation ob Mistah Cobb's detaining me again."

The *Detroit Times*, prior to a May 1928 Philadelphia visit, interviewed Rivers, who said, "Mistuh Cobb shore to[o] deep mighty pert fo' his age. Look how he am knockin' in a raft of runs for Mistuh Mack with dem Athaleticks." Asked if he personally liked Cobb, he replied, "Lak him. Do a hawg lak corn? Mistuh Cobb bin mighty good to ole Alex. He nevah cut me aroun', even when Ah am bad. Sometimes he do speak some POW'FUL TENDAH words to me, though. But evah time he scold me, Ah get even. Ah borrow money off him."

That June, a strange odor in a package being mailed to Cobb was inspected in Galveston, Tex. It contained 11 bottles of white table wine, 2 of which were broken. The shipment originated in San Francisco. From Galveston, it was supposed to go by water to New York. The AP reported that and then ran a separate story featuring Cobb's reaction in Philadelphia. "'I don't use it [such wine] you know. Fans all over the country have a habit of sending little tokens to me. But who in the world could be sending me such a gift?'"

He told about the last year of his playing career, 1928, in a 1959 interview with Kaese of the *Boston Globe*. He had worried during 1928 that he would not surpass .300, but did end up at .323. (Batting .300 that year is an overrated feat, as it was one of the top 20th-century seasons for batting averages, due to the lively "rabbit" ball. American League batters that season, including pitchers, averaged .281.) "I was under .300 for awhile and worried I wouldn't make it. I wanted to go out hitting .300. A fellow has his pride, you know." Kaese paraphrased him as saying that he quit because he was tired physically and had mentally "gone to the defensive."

"I always tried to think offensively," Cobb added. "I never let myself admit a pitcher had a lot of stuff. It was a state of mind, but it worked. But then I began to think of eventualities – of maybe getting a crack on the skull. I got apprehensive. That was bad." Also, "My legs lost their rubber; I was just being nipped on the bases. I rested all I could, staying in my hotel room when I wasn't playing. The schedule was a terrible grind."

Lou Gehrig of the Yankees wrote a newspaper serial, and Cobb consumes chapter 14 of it. After differentiating between Cobb as "a soft-spoken, good natured sort of fellow" off the field and a "fighter who doesn't give an inch" on it, Gehrig wrote, "Ty likes to ride young players. He got a lot of riding when he broke into the league and he figures everyone else should get it too. He was 'on me' as they call it from the moment I joined the club. Every time we met the Tigers I was Ty's own special property and the things he used to say to me out there on the diamond would have me boiling.

"The tamest thing he called me was a 'fresh busher' and from there he climbed upward. And he never quit." Some of his lines one day were, "You think you're a ball player" and, "All you can do is hit that ball." Supposedly also that day, he said, "If you're a ball player I'm the 'King of Siam'" and did so "in a nasty tone of voice."

Gehrig's backside and Cobb at first base in 1926

Also, at one point in 1925, Gehrig wrote of having asked manager Miller Huggins that he be sent to the minors where he could play regularly. Cobb apparently heard about it, Gehrig added, and told Gehrig that he would then claim him on waivers and send him to China "where it'll take the rest of your life to get back."

"The real laugh though," Gehrig continued, "happened at Detroit one day when I was on first. Cobb came rushing over swinging his arms and apparently calling me all sorts of names. The fans thought he was going to fight, and they began riding him all over the park. All the time Ty stood there with his jaw stuck out, his fist clenched and his arms swinging."

Gehrig then observed, "And what he was really saying all the time was this: 'Make 'em think you're sore, kid. They like it. Put on the old fighting attitude. Let 'em see you're interested in the ball game. The more fight you put into it, the better the fans like it. Double up your fists. Talk loud. Make 'em think you're going to sock somebody.'

"I've laughed about that a lot of times. And I laughed most when my mother got hold of the paper and read that Cobb and I had been near coming to blows. She saved the paper to show me when I came home, and like all mothers she wanted me to promise her that I wouldn't get into any fights."

On the other side of the ledger, Gehrig said Cobb was one of the first players to congratulate him when he became a regular. "And many times he has gone out of his way to show me little tricks in hitting and in baserunning – tricks that only Cobb can show." Gehrig added, "And if you want a real treat[,] get Cobb in a visiting [friendly] mood sometime and listen to his wonderful ideas on raising children. Or his opinions on books, art, the stock market or nearly any subject you choose. He gets terribly serious if you once get him started on one of his favorite subjects which by the way includes Ruth. It would be surprising to many people to hear the way Ty praises Babe's all[-]around work."

Gehrig concluded the piece by writing that right now he considers Cobb one of his best friends in baseball.

After finding the above article, I looked to see what the three biographers included about Cobb's relationship with Gehrig. Alexander told one story, of a game in 1923 in which Detroit ruined the Yankees' pennant chances. Cobb, in the third base coacher's box, taunted Yankee players in their dugout until two of them, Everett Scott and Gehrig, "just up from the Eastern League, charged out to confront him. Umpire Tommy Connolly threw both of them out, while Cobb stood by innocently."

Leerhsen overlooked the relationship between Gehrig and Cobb. Hornbaker did describe it, without mentioning the 1923 episode. Stump touched on the episode imprecisely in his 1994 book, claiming that "Cobb ducked and their punches [those of Gehrig and Scott] missed." What Hornbaker wrote generally about Cobb and Gehrig overlaps neatly in three respects with Gehrig's 1927 article, without his quoting from it: Cobb's riding of Gehrig, his congratulating of him upon becoming the regular first baseman and providing him with batting tips. Plus, Hornbaker mentioned a possible actual fight between Cobb and Gehrig in the prior season, 1926, for which there is some strong contemporaneous supporting evidence.

That fight took place after a game had ended, when Gehrig "accidentally hit his head on a [concrete] wall and was knocked unconscious," Hornbaker wrote, citing veteran New York writer Joe Vila. That said, Hornbaker found so many discrepancies in different versions of the story, including from 1931 and Cobb and Stump's 1961 book, that he concluded, "As with many things in baseball history, the truth and sensationalized legends often become entangled, and this story was no different." I would advise that if presenting juicy years-later stories, one should try to keep in mind the contemporaneous record. Some secondary sources, books, have already scrutinized it, if one would rather search books than newspapers.

In my four 19th-century baseball books, I found enough 19th-century prose that was interesting and easy enough to reconcile, that, with few exceptions, I shied away from reaching into the 20th century to cite "more interesting versions" or entirely new stories that had no contemporaneous basis. In general, wild stories should be discounted unless a named journalist is vouching for something or has interviewed a plausible observer to an event.

The following story from 1950 relates to this season, 1927. "Cobb had some peculiar notions of fun," former teammate George "Moose" Earnshaw told Spink of the *Sporting News*. "He would run up to [teammate] Joe Hauser while the first baseman was under the showers and pluck a couple of hairs off his chest. Painful experience. Joe used to plead with Ty to lay off him. Then one evening [teammate Bullet] Joe Bush jumped into the situation. He tore a handful of hair out of Cobb's sparse scalp, and Ty never bothered Hauser thereafter." That story has credibility because Spink was a pro-Cobb journalist.

(A similar-sounding undated Cobb prank story was told in 1934 by pitcher Fred "Firpo" Marberry, a rival pitcher of his from 1923 to 1928. Marberry's story is also especially credible because 1934 was his second year playing for Detroit, and he told it to the *Free Press*. The newspaper conveyed, "The Marberry-Cobb feud started in a funny way. Fred came into the league a great admirer of the fiery Georgian. Though Cobb 'rode' him when the Griffs [owner Clark Griffith's Washington team] played the Tigers, Fred took it philosophically, holding that Tyrus was trying to weaken his pitching poise by getting his 'goat.' He retained his admiration for Cobb.

"But one day Tyrus went to[o] far. Passing Fred when the teams were changing sides, he grabbed Fred's shirt and gave it a jerk, leaving Marberry standing before several thousand fans with his shirt tail out." The *Free Press* reporter telling that story added, "If there is one thing Marberry will not tolerate it is an affront to his dignity. He is an easy-going, likeable fellow, one of the finest characters in the game. But don't offend his dignity.")

1928: Whose Goat?

In the final season of Cobb's career, 1928, the story that has gotten the most legs is that young opposing player Leo Durocher got the better of him verbally on the field. Hornbaker wrote in his book that Cobb, figuratively, "ran into a cocky twenty-two-year-old in Leo Durocher, an infielder for the Yankees, who was verbally aggressive toward just about everyone, and showed no fear against Cobb. As legend has it [Hornbaker cited the *Sporting News* of April 16, 1947, for the following], Durocher told him, 'Don't flash your spikes at me or I'll show you how to really spike a guy.'"

Neither Alexander nor Leerhsen mentioned the story. McCallum did tell it in his 1975 book, but erroneously, about there having been a collision.

In the earliest detailed version that I found on my own, in 1938, Grantland Rice said second baseman Durocher had "given him the hip" as Cobb was trying to go from first to third, "thus throwing him out of his stride so that he was nailed at third." Then Cobb, "walking angrily to his post in the outfield, snarled at Durocher as they passed: 'The next time you try that I'll cut your legs off, you fresh busher!'" Rice did not include any quote from Durocher.

The earliest reference that I found on my own to there merely being something unusual between Cobb and Durocher was in 1930, when the *Boston Globe* said that Durocher had gained a "goat-getting" verdict over Cobb in 1928. That was Durocher's first year in the American League, and the *Globe* had a special reason to be tracking him: he was a native of Springfield, Mass.

Leo Durocher as of 1928

In a 1939 feature on Durocher in *Collier's*, associate editor Quentin Reynolds rehashed Rice's faulty version and made his own faulty addition. He claimed that Ruth had prepared Durocher <u>in advance</u> to call Cobb a penny pincher, if Cobb was fresh to him. Then, right after the incident, Durocher blurted out the line, Reynolds claimed.

An indication that Reynolds was wrong is that the kicker in two later versions of the hip story, both containing no collision and told in 1958 and 1975, had Ruth giving the name-calling advice <u>after</u> the non-collision. Durocher told the 1958 version to Lester J. Biederman of the *Pittsburgh Press*. The source for the 1975 version is Durocher's biography with Ed Linn, *Nice Guys Finish Last*.

In both the 1958 and 1975 versions, immediately after the incident, Ruth asked Durocher what Cobb had told him. Ruth then supposedly told Durocher that the next time Cobb comes to bat, that he should call him a penny pincher. It is not clear if Durocher used the line. Later, also in both versions, Cobb angrily approached Durocher after the game, and Ruth intervened in a way that allowed him to escape to the locker room. "Nothing happened, thanks to Babe," was Durocher's punchline on the 1958 story – although, if Reynolds were right, it could be that thanks to the Babe that something might have.

To mark Durocher's 66th birthday in 1972, columnist David Condon of the *Chicago Tribune* told a version with the whopper about there having been a collision. He also conveyed debatable detail about Durocher's mouth that day, that he "outroared the [Georgia] Peach."

Roaring detail can be found in sportswriter-screenwriter Jack Sher's unreliable 1948 *Sport* magazine profile of Cobb. Sher wrote, "The one player Cobb has never forgiven is Leo Durocher. It was a case of hate at first sight when rookie Durocher broke into the big leagues and began to play against Ty. The Lip [Durocher] was probably the only player who could dish it out, with his mouth, on a par with the jaw-wagging Cobb. Ty was getting on in years, while Leo was full of spunk and fight, bouncing players off the base-paths with a hip that swung like a barn door.

"Ty would get to first base and Leo would begin to yell.

"'Come on down, you old has-been! I'm waitin' for you. Come on, you're yellow!'

"Cobb would go crazy with anger, spluttering oaths at the rookie which could be heard by the people in the farthest bleacher seats. He threatened to murder him.

"'Aw, shut up!' Leo would scream back. 'You been [sic] terrorizing this league for years and now you're gonna get it back! You'd better stay there, you old goat!'

Durocher also in 1928

"On the next pitch, Cobb would take off like a comet for second base. What infuriated him more than anything else was that he could seldom hurt or annoy the Durocher kid. Leo was very cute around second base, almost as tricky and nasty as the old master himself. Even today, Cobb bridles whenever Durocher's name is mentioned. But there is little doubt that if Leo had tangled with Ty during the height of the Tiger's career, the Lip would have been chewed to pieces. When Cobb was mixing it up with Leo, he was crowding 40."

The following, unfortunately, turned out to be a red herring, although it adds to the biography of Cobb. I found a 1939 story in the *Springfield Republican* that I initially thought could have mixed up Durocher with a Springfield baseball personality as of that year, Spencer Abbott, the now-veteran manager of its Eastern League team. A writer for the *Republican* said that Cobb "once cut one of the shoes right off" Abbott. And the reason why Cobb did so is that Abbott had given Cobb "a piece of his lip." It was in an exhibition game at Evansville, Ind., presumably around 1908, and Cobb "sliced the leather

on one of my shoes" at first base, Abbott said. "I was burned up aplenty. I gave Cobb [a] kick in the pants as he lay on the ground. He got up swinging and I started to do some swinging of my own. 'Germany' Schae[f]er, coaching at first, and the late Hughey Jennings, Detroit manager, pried us apart."

I did all of the above research – but was mixed up on whether there was a collision – before seeing a review copy of Paul Dickson's 2017 *Leo Durocher: Baseball's Prodigal Son*. (Dickson's formally released book retained the review copy's presentation on this subject.) One of his themes is hate: Durocher was "one of the most hated men in the game," he wrote early on, and "Ty Cobb hated Leo because he constantly baited him with insults."

The working title for his book had been *Leo Durocher: The Man They Loved to Hate*. I found contemporaneous support for the being hated part. In a lengthy profile of Durocher in the *Saturday Evening Post* in 1939, sportswriter Arthur Mann wrote, "Only Ty Cobb, of the battering fights under the grandstands [sic], ever approached his record for causing player dislike. Only Cobb was more hated by his fellow players." For the record, Mann recalled a lot in his article about Durocher's 1928 season and wrote nothing about interactions that year between Cobb and Durocher.

Dickson did not cite a reliable source for Cobb feeling hate toward Durocher; as noted, Sher claimed "hate at first sight" in his 1948 article.

So what was Dickson's take on the 1928 incident?

He wrote, "Durocher himself never claimed the hip [part of the] story was true." Dickson chose well, going with the version from Durocher's 1975 book. In it, Durocher told of accidentally changing Cobb's running route from second base to third. Dickson added, "Whatever else was true or false about that first game [against Cobb], Durocher knew he was going to pay for riding Cobb and other opponents without mercy."

Not directly related to that incident, Dickson reprinted direct quotes from a Cobb-Durocher barbfest, from some other time in 1928, as conveyed in Frank Graham's 1943 *New York Yankees: An Informal History*. Here they are, as originating from Durocher to Cobb:

"Why don't you give yourself up?"

"What are waiting for them to do – cut your uniform off and burn it?"

"Go home, Grandpa."

"Get wise to yourself. If you keep on playing with us young fellows, you might get hurt."

Dickson also printed the one part of that exchange that Graham attributed to Cobb: "Cobb snarled threats at him, and he [Durocher] laughed."

In his book version, right after the direct quotes, Graham had transitioned to telling a whopper version of the incident, one containing a collision. Graham ended with, "Cobb could have killed him and looked as though he was going to try it when other players and the umpires got between the pair."

As it turns out, Dickson gave me a present, beyond helping me reorder my thoughts. For a Durocher quote, "Any time the great Ty pulls a crack, he's going to get one right back," he cited the *Springfield Republican* of May 29 and June 8, 1928. Not evident from Dickson's book is that the *Republican* article of June 8 had cited the *New York Sun* of June 7. When I looked at the *Sun* of June 7, which the Maryland-based Dickson could have looked at in the Library of Congress (he did cite the *Sun* of June 12), I found a roughly 1,600-word Graham feature on Durocher, with lots of quotes that Dickson could have made great use of. Here is just the Cobb part of that feature:

Durocher told Graham that the jousting with other players "started with Cobb on the opening day in New York. Long before I'd ever seen Cobb I had heard all about him – what a tough fellow he was coming into the bag and how he'd ride a young fellow out of the league if the young fellow would let him, and I made up my mind he wouldn't scare me or ride me out of the league either. In the opening game he came around second base and I made him make a wide turn, so that he was thrown out at third. Walking back – he was the last out in the inning – he said to me: 'If you don't get out of my way you little so-and-so I'll cut your legs off.'

"And I said to him:

"'You will like hell, you big so-and-so. You ain't going to cut me or do anything else to me, and if you think you are, come right ahead. I'll be right here waiting for you, you so-and-so.'

"Well, he didn't try to cut me but kept on riding me and [Philadelphia Cobb teammate Eddie] Rommel, and some of the other guys on the bench took it up and of course I hollered right back at them."

To weigh in on one loose end, the quotes that Dickson used from Graham in 1943 are reliable enough, based on the coverage by Graham that, thanks to Dickson's research, I found in 1928. The supposed Ruth follow-up with Durocher suggesting that he use the "penny pincher" line on him is significant because there is a scarcity of reliable Ruth barbs about Cobb. To all of this, I can add postscripts from various publications:

As will be noted later in passing, in one of his *Life* magazine articles in 1952, Cobb would name now-managers Casey Stengel, Durocher and Paul Richards as sharing some of the strategy acumen of his favorite manager of all-time, Connie Mack.

One of the more interesting comments by Cobb about his own playing style came perhaps as a result of a 1948 article by Durocher in *Cosmopolitan* titled, "Nice Guys Finish Last!" Just as it was appearing on the newsstands, somebody asked Cobb if it was true that Durocher once tagged him in the teeth at second base, with Cobb then threatening to get even on his next trip on base. "No," he replied, "had I been going to get Durocher, I wouldn't have told him first." NEA sports editor Grayson reported that.

Echoing that is Corcoran in his 1965 memoirs, to whom Cobb had mentioned the incident. Corcoran wrote that Cobb "was not one for giving advance warning. Anything Ty had in his mind, stayed there. He didn't speculate for the benefit of others. In his playing days he was a lone wolf who roomed alone off the field [apparently in several seasons, mainly his 1920s ones] and if he decided to use his spikes, the first you knew of it was when you got jabbed, maybe in the Adam's apple.

"'If you're going to hit somebody, you don't warn him first,' he said [to Corcoran] by way of refuting a famous story of the days [sic] when Leo Durocher was a rookie shortstop for the Yankees." In telling Corcoran that, and noting that many other stories about him were false, Cobb "pulled up a pant leg to his knees, displaying a lacework of old wounds. 'You don't warn a man and you don't complain,'" Corcoran recalled being told.

However, Dickson found a Durocher interview in August 1928 with Burr of the *Brooklyn Eagle*. In it, Durocher did not explain the basepath incident. Durocher did say, "He yelled out he'd cut me if I didn't get out of his way the next time he came into second." That could vitiate the quotes above from Cobb and Corcoran: if Cobb had followed through had Durocher gotten in his way again, then his remark would have to be considered advance warning.

Digressing to a different conflict-with-Cobb story that *Tribune* columnist Condon may have been the earliest or the only one to report:

At a 1956 baseball dinner in Milwaukee, he was present when Braves coach Charley Root recalled his debut year, 1923 with the St. Louis Browns. "We were playin' Detroit and I was sent in to relieve whoever'd been pitchin'. Well, guess who was at bat? It was Ty Cobb. So I tossed the first one right at his head and he went for the dirt." Cobb strode out menacingly toward Root and said, "You fresh busher, I ought to teach you a lesson." Then catcher Henry Severeid joined them and informed Cobb, "Listen, you so much as touch this young kid and I'll knock your brains out." Root's story ended with, "I dusted off Cobb again and went on to strike him out."

For this next retrospective, *Chicago Tribune* sports editor Arch Ward was on hand, in Cleveland in 1954. Stan Coveleski, a top pitcher during the second half of Cobb's career, said that Washington's Sam Rice was the batter who gave him the most trouble. Asked how he pitched to some of baseball's greats, Coveleski said, "Ty Cobb wanted outside pitches so he could punch the ball. My best throw against him was close at the belt. He'd take a lot of those pitches." Coveleski then described how he pitched to Ruth: "I'd pitch him high inside, then try to get him out with low outside stuff."

A related story had been told in 1952. On Cobb's first visit back to St. Louis since his playing days in 1928, at his hotel were three former rival catchers, Steve O'Neill, Benny Bengough and Cy Perkins; a Perkins story will appear later. Asked by Robert L. Burnes, sports editor of the *St. Louis Globe-Democrat*, how they had their pitchers pitch to Cobb, O'Neill said, "I had my pitchers throw everything inside to Cobb." He added, "You get the ball outside and he'd murder you. It helped a little bit in later years, Ty got a little paunch on him and couldn't get around on the ball quite as fast. It never hurt him much, though, I'll tell you that." Somewhat off that subject, the catchers then got into a discussion of Cobb's final two seasons, in which Perkins was a teammate, especially on how many bases he stole. Burnes told his readers that Cobb stole 22 in 1927 while batting .357 and 5 in 1928 while batting .323.

Two decade-or-later stories involving Cobb and middle infielders other than Durocher follow.

In a 1939 feature, Drew Middleton of the AP described a fanning bee in which was recalled the time that Yankees rookie second baseman Tony Lazzeri "bawled out Ty Cobb for running into him as he pivoted on a double play."

In his 1949 *Bill Stern's Favorite Baseball Stories*, mid-20th century sportscaster-author Stern said that when Bucky Harris was a rookie (in 1919 and 1920), "the mighty Ty Cobb, the most feared baserunner in the game, tore down on Bucky covering second. But the kid gave no ground to the mighty Cobb, and treated him none too gently.

"'Do that again and I'll cut you to ribbons!' snarled the pugnacious Cobb.

"'If you try it,' advised the rookie calmly, 'next time I tag you it'll be right between the eyes.'"

Stern concluded with, "Bucky Harris was never bothered again."

Harris attested to that story in his earlier quoted *Saturday Evening Post* article in 1956 with Stanley Frank. The 1956 version closely tracks Stern's one. Written in the first person, it ends with, "Mr. Cobb gave me no trouble thereafter."

In 1947, Hawkins of the *Washington Star* spoke to Harris, who "admits he never fulfilled an ambition – to slam Cobb between the eyes with a throw. 'I used to try it,' confesses Harris, 'when Ty was coming into second base on the first end of a double-play. I'd always draw a bead on his forehead, but he always ducked.'"

In a 1950 letter to Harry G. Salsinger, after Salsinger wrote a pro-Cobb article in the *Sporting News* that included challenging the accuracy of the colliding-with-Durocher tale, Cobb referred to "the Durocher thing where he shouldered me at short on my way to third on a potential three base hit, knocking me on my 'can' and I was thrown out. First by the time Durocher was in the league, I knew enough and big enough [sic] not to let such happen again[;] if true I would have been entitled to third for interference."

More broadly, in a 1953 letter to Salsinger that Bak cited in his 1994 book, Cobb said, "It always hurts me deep" to be portrayed as a dirty player. "It happens to be the real weak spot in whatever armor I have."

And yet, in 1961, Parker of the *New York Mirror*, who was very knowledgeable about Cobb and was on Cobb's short list of close media allies, wrote, "Durocher won attention as the freshest rookie who ever came up when he belligerently warned Ty Cobb what he'd do to him if he dared to come into second with his spikes high to break up double plays." Plus, as will be noted later, in 1951, Parker recalled "the good old days when Ty Cobb gave and took in the constant duel of spikes."

Returning to the chronology:

As Cobb's playing career was ending in 1928, the *Los Angeles Times* opined on its editorial page that "he wants to look around a bit and get acquainted with his family, and as he has saved some of his money he may do pretty much as he pleases. The foremost citizen of Georgia might even undertake to run for Congress and get away with it."

In 1929:

Likes To Loaf

COBB TELLS OF HIS DESIRE TO QUIT BASEBALL

Long Career Just One Fight After Another He Confides

LEAVING   FOR   EUROPE

By DAVIS J. WALSH

New York, June 15.—The old fire horse sniffs eagerly at the first wisp of smoke; the bus driver, of course, always enjoys his day off by riding over the route with his substitute. But Ty Cobb never was addicted to custom in habit-forming quantities and so today he finds himself with nothing to do for the first time in twenty-five years and is glad of it.

In April in Atlanta, he told Eddie Brietz of the AP that he had had enough of baseball. "If I ever come back it will be as an owner. I will never sign again as a player and I have no desire to manage another club."

He said he rejected an offer to manage in the National League that season and predicted that he would buy a team, probably one in the South.

In June, the day before leaving for Europe, he sent a typed letter to good friend Maines. Its key detail was, "As per our conversation[,] you make [sic] have the right to make the annual Ty Cobb Award to the boy in the Junior Baseball League whose batting average is highest."

Hours before Cobb set sail with his family, Davis J. Walsh of the International News Service interviewed him. He told of having no desire to return to baseball. "Don't misunderstand me. Baseball has given me everything and probably far more than I deserve. But I'd hate to live all over again some of the anguish I experienced during my twenty-three years in the majors."

While in Paris, Cobb over several weeks had not missed "a single night at the movies," the AP reported. "'You see for 24 years I did not dare to attend the movies for fear of injuring my batting eye,' Ty explained to some friends the other day. 'My family tells me that some of the films I have gone to see in Paris

clockwise on the eve of their trip to Europe: Ty, Charlie, Herschel, Shirley, Jimmy and Beverly

were thrown on the screen in America some years back but all are new to me.'" (In Jerome Holtzman's 1973 *No Cheering in the Press Box*, longtime including late 1920s Philadelphia reporter Al Horwits said on off-days, Cobb would call him and invite him to go to the movies. "He would see four or five in one day. I'd give up after the second. I had to go back to work." In May 1913, sports editor Ralph L. Yonker of the *Detroit Times* had reported, "Ty Cobb is wearing black spectacles now, trying to get his eyes in shape. He blames a night ride in an automobile from Ann Arbor to Detroit for his misfortune.")

An independent version of Cobb's 1929 explanation would be provided in 1961 upon Cobb's death. Sports editor Sec Taylor of the *Des Moines Register* had interviewed him in 1945 but had omitted the following from his write-up that year. Regarding his entertainment habits as of 1945, Cobb told Taylor that he was then enjoying stage shows the most, particularly dramas, and that he had not gone often to them during his playing career. The reason that he gave was that if he went, he would have the urge to go on subsequent nights. Cobb did admit to Taylor to doing the following after games in New York City:

attending shows and then, for relaxation, hiring a horse-drawn carriage and riding through Central Park.

Digressing some more:

At dinner in New York City in 1949 with Ward Morehouse and their new wives, Cobb fleshed out the above. After recalling the hotels that the Detroit team had stayed in, in New York – "the old Fifth Avenue Hotel and the Bretton Hall and the Ansonia and the [Hotel] Somerset" – he said, "I went to see a lot of Broadway shows – 'Madame X' [featuring a woman put in great distress by a jealous husband] was one of my favorites. I cried real tears at that one. Used to like to take a brougham [horse-drawn carriage] through Central Park on a hot night. Been here a lot of times, but I suppose the Big City still scares me. You mustn't forget that I'm only a country boy. I'll never forget it – never!" (In 1961, Cobb would tell Morehouse, "I never liked cities anyway.")

Returning to 1929:

In December, a few months after his trip, he said Italy had been his favorite country to see. "'Everybody is working in Italy,' says Cobb, 'because [Prime Minister Benito] Mussolini doesn't tolerate loafers and the country is making great strides industrially.'" Hornbaker passed up that while paraphrasing this: "I got a great kick out of walking on the Appian Way and recalling that the famous highway was used in the days of Caesar. I liked Rome and Venice better than any cities I visited while abroad. St. Mark's Square in Venice, about eight in the evening, is all too wonderful to describe. It was the big thrill of my trip." Hornbaker also passed up this: "London is a beautiful city and England a great country but industrial unrest appears everywhere in Great Britain. I never saw so many unemployed people. Like Italy, everything is all business in Germany."

Separately, in a syndicated sports column by Walter Trumbull, Cobb upon his return said that Andrea Del Sarto was his favorite painter. Hailing from Florence, Del Sarto painted, most notably, solemn religious scenes in the first three decades of the 1500s. In his 1975 biography, McCallum recalled driving Cobb to the Hall of Fame in 1955 and Cobb telling him that his father had always told him to live on the side of right. The way to solve problems, his father told him, was to imagine kneeling in front of God. His father also told him that sometimes Ty's resulting decision would be unpopular, but that Ty would have nothing to fear provided he knew that he was on God's side.

A contemporaneous, religious-sounding line of advice that his dad gave him can be found in a 1902 letter. Alexander and Leerhsen mentioned it without stressing the tie-in to religion. Leerhsen quoted the following sentence from it: "Be under the perpetual guidance of the better angel of your nature." One of those words resonated greatly with Cobb. Upon his death, sports editor Rosenbaum would write that in interviewing Cobb in 1957 at home, he referred to his scholarship fund, after his death, as having "perpetuity." Rosenbaum also recalled him saying, "Perpetuity. We Cobbs will have that."

Back to more earthly matters as of 1929:

How Cobb's setters were to be cared for while he was in Europe was discussed in an article by dog training expert Albert Frederick "A. F." Hochwalt. About the trip itself, Hochwalt wrote, "Of course the family will see all the sights, but Ty has arranged to enjoy a few weeks of grouse shooting on the moors of Scotland. He will not only gun [shoot] over dogs, but has a good prospect of being among a party of drive shooters up near Keith, Scotland on the opening day of the season, which is August 12."

Hochwalt said Cobb would not be taking any of his

Cobb, Forest H. Willis, their unnamed hunting aide and bird dogs on their 1929 quail hunt at Louisville, Ga.

dogs to Great Britain because they would first need to be held in quarantine for six months "and by that time the Cobb vacation would be over. He will not suffer for the want of dogs, however, for up at Keith, there are any number of good ones – pointers, setters, retrievers, Labradors." At Dildawn, Castle Douglas, in Scotland, Cobb "will be the guest of Charles A. Phillips, and shoot over his beautiful moorlands consisting of thousands of acres. Here the game includes not only grouse, but hares, rabbits, blackcock [male black grouse], duck and snipe; and they are to be found in plentiful numbers.

"At Di[l]dawn, however, Ty Cobb will do his shooting over spaniels instead of pointers or setters, for his host is the best known breeder of springers and cockers in Great Britain and he has a great string of well broken [sic] ones. The writer shot over these two varieties on these very same moors two years ago and knows at first hand [sic] just how much pleasure is in store for Ty Cobb during his stay in Scotland."

In 1930:

In January, a writer said, "Ty Cobb entertains guests at his home in Augusta[,] Ga., with movies of European scenes taken on a trip abroad." The writer did not mention if they included hunting ones.

In a boring video interview with sound recorded at Magruder, Ga., on February 28, one of the few highlights

Cobb and his unnamed interviewer at Magruder, Ga., in 1930

was his stating, "although I don't want to say that I will never play again, I will never, uh, I, I take that back, I, I, I never want to play again, but I might want to be connected in some capacity; for instance [his interviewer interjected "for instance" before Cobb repeated those words], the directorship of a club, the presidency of a club." (A more formal newsreel was made by MGM in October 1929 that contains a segment titled, "Home from European tour, Ty Cobb declares he will never return to baseball." The lone library copy of the reel is at UCLA. But on YouTube, if you search for "Coca-Cola", "Ty Cobb" and "1930", is a livelier six-minute radio interview with syndicated columnist Grantland Rice.)

Over the summer, Cobb told the AP that interest in baseball is declining. "People are not following the teams. Back in the old days a sixth-place club could pack the stands in late August. It's not the game it was 10 years ago. They are missing the finer points. The big punch is all that counts nowadays." As far as the possibility of his buying a team, "The franchise prices for most clubs are too high," he said. "I don't think it's a good business investment to purchase a club now."

On the way from Augusta to Detroit, he stopped off in Cincinnati to help dedicate a new amateur ball field. "Ty is living quietly and h[a]ppily with his family on his estate, playing plenty of golf and doing some hunting and fishing on his hunting preserve, which comprises 11,000 acres," wrote sportswriter Jack Ryder of the *Cincinnati Enquirer*.

A longtime Ontario, Canada, friend of Cobb's, waterfowl sanctuary founder Jack Miner, brought a wild goose to Georgia and freed it, after affixing a legband indicating that he, Miner, was freeing it. A party of hunters near Augusta shot the goose, and after reading the legband and knowing Miner was friendly with Cobb, presented the goose to Cobb. The AP reported all of that in December. Also, it said Miner was notified of what had transpired.

(Back in 1924 in Ontario, Cobb was with Miner after the season. A message from Cobb that the *Ottawa Journal* printed during his visit was: "It's great being lulled to sleep by the hoot of the owl and awakened in the morning by the howling of the wolves." In a 1925 dinner speech, Miner recalled that experience: "I wish every boy could sleep with 'Ty' Cobb for a week, as I did, for he would be a much better boy. 'Ty' left home when he was 17 to play ball, but was followed by his father's letters, to the advice in which he paid heed, so that he kept himself clean and straight. Oh, I know he has a temper. So did I when I was young and red-headed, and I would not give much for any man who hasn't a temper." Back in 1922, Cobb had given a taste of how much he enjoyed a recent trip to Canada. He had written to Orin Champlain, father of longtime acquaintance Helene, "I took a short hunt into Canada for fishing and Moose [sic]. It was successful in every way, you can guess the rest.")

Returning to 1930:

In December, the AP interviewed Cobb at his home on his 44th birthday. About baseball, he said, "To me, the game seems to lack a sort of spontaneity now. The close plays, base running and other interesting features have been lessened by the orgy of home run hitting." It was also two years into the Great Depression, and Cobb said, "Nowadays only the leaders and the first division clubs play to full stands. The others have meager attendance." Also around that time, he was named chairman of a central committee in Augusta to coordinate all of its winter sport activities, including golf, polo and tennis tournaments; horse racing meets; and baseball and football games.

Cobb and Jack Miner
in 1929

In 1931:

In February, besides noting his 11,000-acre hunting preserve, and that he spends a few days a week at his lodge there, the *Augusta Chronicle* reported on his recent local hunting trip. It did so in a feature on the hunting available at Rochester, Ga. The *Chronicle* spoke with Rochester resident and Cobb hunting companion Forest H. Willis. The two can be seen together in this book thanks to surviving film footage of them that can be made into still images. Willis said, "I have never hunted with a finer sportsman and one who had a keener eye for birds. Cobb loves the great outdoors and does not hunt chiefly to see how many birds he can bag, but is satisfied to bring down a few to test his skill and to see his dogs in action."

A week later, the city of Augusta was touting its campaign to be an ideal winter resort. "Two and a half months ago a fund of between $5,000 and $10,000 [up to around $150,000 today] was appropriated and contributed for the purpose of disseminating interesting information to newspapers and magazines through Lockhart In[te]rnational, Inc., a New York publicity organization, which has maintained a staff here since December 1 to gather and distribute news, features and pictures about Augusta to newspapers everywhere."

The *Chronicle* reported that, and it gave a number of examples. One was that "papers all over the country have carried stories and pictures of Ty Cobb and Dr. William Lyon Phelps playing golf by airplane; prominent society people and other notables hunting quail, 'possum and other game; Ty Cobb, [noted amateur golfer] Maureen Orcutt, [Great War Major] Gen. Peter E. Traub and Sir Derrick [Julius] Wernher[, 2nd Baronet,] playing bridge in a plane high over the city; Mrs. Orcutt working as a dress model, 'realizing her life's ambition,' and scores of others, including daily telegraph stories about sports in Augusta."

Without referring at all to the above campaign by the city of Augusta, syndicated columnist Grantland Rice, a former *Atlanta Journal* reporter, wrote the following:

"Ty Cobb has now added polo to his athletic menu at Augusta and he still keeps on the jump. He shows no other way. On a recent morning things were quiet at one of Augusta's polo fields so Ty picked out a single opponent and played a match, one of the few one-man polo teams on record. It was a wild gallop back and forth as both Ty and his competitor had to be a No. 1, 2, 3 and 4." Then Rice switched to discussing the state of Cobb's golf game.

In case aerial golf is unfamiliar, Cobb and a rival player had teammates who dropped balls from on high as close to the greens as possible, for Cobb and the rival player to play. According to the *Chronicle*, "The planes were flying at an altitude of 500 feet and every ball dropped fell within fifty feet of the greens. A gallery of 200 or more persons witnessed the unique contest."

In a retirement feature quoted earlier for Cobb's eating habits and views, the AP said, "Next to golf, Ty likes to fish and hunt. He prides himself on being able to take young fellows out and walk 'em down." Also, "He goes after birds on horseback and hunts fox at night. He has to exercise daily or he feels badly." Another hobby is riding "fine saddle horses," on which he is "a stickler for obedience." Another part of the feature will be noted shortly, related to his love of dogs.

In April, Cobb wrote apparently his first major post-career magazine article, for *American Legion Magazine*. He fleshed out themes from his December 1930 interview with the AP, relating to too much stress on hitting home runs and to attendance problems. He began with, "A lot of people say that baseball is sick. Maybe it is. At any rate, it's displaying symptoms of one sort or another, though whether they indicate a basic disorder or just a passing headache, I'm not going to guess."

He also said of night baseball, which had recently begun in some minor league ballparks, that "a better system of lighting the diamonds" is needed to make players as efficient as they are in daylight. On a different subject, his second-to-last paragraph began with, "The bench, you know, is the hotbed of team bolshevism. One or two misfortunes will start the warmers [sic] to second-guessing the manager, who, after all, knows his men best and must make all decisions in accord with his own seasoned judgment." After giving some detail, he added that when he was the Tigers' player-manager, he never had such trouble "in the open. Of course there was an undercurrent of unrest, much as with any other team (and particularly violent it gets with losing teams, too); but for the most part matters went smoothly. I had taken over a demoralized club."

Sportswriter Ryder of the *Cincinnati Enquirer* read the article and said Cobb "was the smartest and most interesting player of his day and generation, but he does not seem to be as keen an observer as he was a base-runner." Ryder contested the following comment of his: "And where, in 1907, even cellar teams would attract thousands, though at the very end of the season, today you'll find only two or three hundred spectators at the games they play."

Ryder continued, "Ty suffers from a narrow outlook, based entirely on his own personal experience. When he was a member of the Detroit Tigers in 1907 and many succeeding years, it is quite true that his team played to exceptionally large crowds, even though it might be in the second division. It is a matter of history that the Tigers, in more than one season, out-drew the Philadelphia Athletics, even though the Detroit team was a trailer, while the A.'s were consistent pennant-winners for many years. This was due entirely to the presence of Cobb himself, who was the greatest drawing card the game had ever known until the advent of Babe Ruth."

Several sentences later, Ryder wrote, "As to the remark that second division teams now play to two or three hundred fans, nothing could be farther from the truth. That may be the case in Augusta, Ga., but not in any of the big league cities." In the most recent season, the Reds were in either seventh or eighth place, in an eight-team league, and rarely played in front of fewer than two or three thousand spectators. "Ty should put on his glasses and take another look around," Ryder wrote in concluding his piece.

In April, after wife Charlie filed for divorce, including on cruelty grounds, a report from Augusta said that in February, brother Alfred Lombard had "stuck a gun in the ribs of the great outfielder, according to police, and announced he intended wiping out all the insults and abuse his sister had suffered, then and there." Patrolman W. T. McWatty, who had "separated the men and pleaded with Lombard to give up the weapon," said today that "he was firmly convinced Cobb had escaped being shot only by his intervention." The report also stated, "Another brother-in-law had announced his intention of visiting harm upon Cobb if he persisted in his cruelty, according to friends of the family."

In July, on a trip to California to make plans for his new home there, Cobb stopped for gas in Sallisaw, Okla. His reason for doing so was that his traveling companion, John Hampton of Memphis, was a friend of the editor of *Sallisaw's Democrat-American*. Hampton "quietly" presented Cobb to the editor, because, as the editor reported, Cobb "had previously indicated to his traveling companion that above all else he wished to avoid newspapermen."

In September, Cobb helped mark the annual track and field championship at the San Quentin Prison in California; Hornbaker's book tipped me off to it, in saying that Cobb "helped arrange a special track and field event, a vivid example of his commitment to the entire community. Cobb was always busy, lending his name to various causes, attending luncheons and dinners, and was more sociable than he'd ever been in his life. Reborn, in fact, and his new, outgoing attitude was not temporary."

Highlights that Hornbaker omitted were that the "kitchen crew scored 115 points for a smashing victory, while the shop team was second with 84 points." As also reported by the *Riverside Daily Press*, a robbery convict, Paul "Dutch" Kellner, "emerged as San Quentin's new distance runner." Of more relevance about two weeks later, Cobb told the International News Service, "One day each week, a group of schoolboys should be taken inside a prison. A glance at convicts serving their long sentences might be a good lesson. Also, it would be a good idea to take the young offenders and those serving short terms as spectators to each hanging."

The INS recalled that at San Quentin, "Cobb mingled with the convicts during the prison's annual track and field meet. He was given an ovation."

"'I'm happy to be here, boys,' Cobb told the prisoners, 'but only as a visitor!'"

The INS added, "A voice from the convict masses replied: 'If I could have run as fast as you did on the baseball diamond, I wouldn't be here either!'"

Soon after, the *St. Louis Post-Dispatch* weighed in editorially. Under the short headline "BY HORRIBLE EXAMPLE," it said, "Tyrus Raymond Cobb of baseball celebrity visited San Quentin prison the other day and got some ideas for impressing youth with the value of going straight. He thinks it would be a good plan to take boys of high school age on tours through penitentiaries to show them what crime leads to; he also suggests that first-term offenders be permitted to witness hangings, in the belief that the horror of such a fate would have a salutary influence. In batting, fielding, base running, together with diamond strategy and tactics, Mr. Cobb was a star of the first magnitude. As a penologist, he is still groping along the abandoned paths of terrorism."

(He would fill a more formal track and field role starting in 1939. For Pacific Association meets, he would be appointed a judge.)

After the season, the pennant-winning manager of the Pacific Coast League's San Francisco Seals, Nick Williams, either resigned or was fired. Bob Shand, sports editor of the *Oakland*

from left to right, in April 1931 (Cobb is in the rear, participating in the dedication of the Seals' new stadium, a week before the first report of a possible divorce from his wife Charlie): Seals manager Nick Williams; Billy Putnam, son of Seals' co-owner and Cobb chum George Putnam (whose family Ty was staying with, including later when the divorce story broke); and Portland manager Spencer Abbott. Abbott was the Springfield, Mass., red herring on page 219 related to Cobb and Leo Durocher.

Tribune, said Cobb had something to do with the decision. "Cobb, the old Georgia Peach himself, was induced to come west by George Putnam, one of the owners of the ball club[,] and Ty was a constant visitor at Seals' stadium[,] where he instructed the young players. Nick, as manager, thought the inspiration of the great Cobb would be a fine asset until the visits became too frequent. Then the novelty of having Cobb as a volunteer assistant palled on Williams and there was[, as coined by poet Alfred Lord Tennyson,] a rift in the lute."

In 1932:

In Chicago en route to California, he told the AP that he would be going to the spring training camp of the minor league San Francisco Seals to help coach but "principally to play golf" there. He added, "I haven't bunked in a baseball training camp for any length of time since my last year with the Athletics in 1928." Regarding the possibility that he might buy the Cincinnati Reds, he said, "Everything is too uncertain" in the baseball world, "and I've worked too hard for what money I've got to risk it in any baseball venture." As far as his holding positions in baseball, he said, "They'll never, never see me on the playing field as a manager. I'm sick of competition except in a business way." Also to the AP, he called himself "a funny golfer, I guess. Never want to shoot in the seventies. Why? If I start shooting in those figures I'll take the game seriously like I did baseball for 25 years. I'll start watching my diet and I'll get grumpy. No, thanks! When I start getting down in the seventies too consistently, I'll change styles or toss my clubs away. I'm an odd-80 shooter now and that suits me. Once I shot a 79 and started to dream about the game the next night!"

Days later in Chicago, the AP ran a new feature. Its opening quote was, "It's a funny thing, but I can't get a single kick out of the game [of baseball] now that I'm through as a player. Sure, I think baseball is a great game, the one and only national pastime, but when I watch it from the sidelines – well, frankly, I'm bored.

"Maybe it's because I played the game so hard when I was in it. Maybe it's because I have to have a bat in my hand or go charging down the base lines. Anyway, I usually go to twelve games or so a year and then find myself walking out about the fourth inning." Also, "When I try to reminisce [about baseball] I find myself thinking about golf."

A public policy observation that he made about baseball was, "Something must be done to make it the undisputed national pastime. Just take a look at our public playgrounds, for instance. Appropriations are made there for almost every sport except baseball."

(In 1934, in an interview to be featured later with David W. Hazen of the *Oregonian*, he would say, "Here [in San Francisco] the fans sit around and let the cities spend a lot of taxpayers' money building municipal tennis courts and putting out public golf links, but you don't hear of any municipal baseball fields being laid out for the kids to use. And here's where your fans are to blame. They are just sitting back and not putting up a fight for their favorite sport." In Georgia in 1950, he would say the following after meeting the ball-playing 16-year-old son of his fourth cousin Bob Cobb. "You know, these youngsters are getting the finest breaks imaginable today. When I went off to play ball the first time, I paid my own expenses. Now they've got [American] Legion programs, and this Little League program, and these sandlot programs. All a boy has to do is want to play." Furman Bisher reported those comments in the *Atlanta Constitution*. (In 1953, Cobb would tell the INS that the major leagues contribute to the baseball program of the American Legion but not to Little Leagues even though the latter "may prove to be the savior of baseball in years to come." McCallum, then an NEA reporter, countered his Little League claim, naming six teams that were contributing and said there were others.)

Cobb, though, was not the type of person to be seen at, say, high school baseball games in California, with the exception of being a celebrity judge at a top annual game, which he was multiple times. Upon Cobb's death, sports editor Rosenbaum of the *San Francisco Chronicle* would refer to a comment by a friend of Cobb's son Herschel, Pinky Garcia. Garcia and a friend, Bill Byrd, who were both on the team of Herschel's high school, made many visits to the Cobb home in Atherton. Both recalled to Rosenbaum that Cobb never went to the high school field to watch practices or games. "'I asked him about that,' said Garcia. 'He told me he was happy to teach us professional tricks and happy to have us in his home, but if he went to the field some people, and maybe the newspapers, might get the idea that he was hogging the spotlight.'")

Returning to 1932, only to jump to a multi-year run of stories about Cobb and bird dogs:

Future sports and executive editor McGill of the *Constitution* wrote on the occasion of the retirement of Woodruff's bird dog Lloyd George. His piece featured a picture of Cobb binding a wound on its leg that it suffered during a hunt. McGill wrote from the perspective of the dog. The dog was quoted as saying, among other things, "It was funny about Ty Cobb. All the colored boys called him Mister Ty-Cobb just as if it was all one name. I guess they thought so because everybody called him Ty Cobb and never Mr. Cobb."

The *Atlanta Georgian* had apparently printed a story in the 1920s on the death of one of Cobb's hunting dogs, also from the dog's perspective. In 1942,

Henry McLemore, a native of Macon, Ga., took credit for that and a horse interview and declared them "standard 'don't's' in every decent school of journalism in this country."

MAKES TYRUS COBB CHECK HIS BIRD DOG

Georgia Baggageman Doesn't Care if "Peach" Is Entire Team.

the headline is from the 1918 mild garbling of the 1913 original, which Hornbaker found. Cobb had confronted a train baggage handler in Athens, Ga., over the fee for transporting one of them.

A mini-burst of Cobb bird dog stories appeared in January 1940. Umpire Bill Klem was the source for one, with the highlight arguably being some dialogue that Klem attributed to a black boy attending to them on Cobb's behalf. About his wing shooting, the boy observed one day in Klem's presence that Cobb did not seem to be doing so well.

"What do you mean, not so good?" Klem replied. "Why, he hasn't missed a bird yet!"

The boy thought over his point for a minute. Then he replied mournfully, "Ah know. But he almost did."

In a retrospective a week later, Mathewson, a now-NEA reporter and photographer, wrote, "Tyrus Cobb gave full credit to Connie Mack and his other bird dogs for keeping his underpinning as hard as dogwood and as supple as a young muscadine [grape] vine in early spring." That Connie Mack was one of his treasured bird dogs. In 1957, he would write, "Connie had the happy faculty of putting on classic points in the most advantageous spots for picture-taking." Also, "Connie had to be fast to stay ahead of Cobb, the hardest hunter who ever blew a whistle over a pointing dog."

Digressing even further about Cobb and bird dogs, and comprehensively in various years:

McGill, despite being seemingly sympathetic enough to Cobb in his

from left to right: Ralph McGill, Bobby Jones, 1920 Democratic presidential nominee/Cox Enterprises newspaper chain founder James M. Cox (which acquired the *Atlanta Journal* in 1939 and the *Atlanta Constitution* in 1951) and Robert W. Woodruff

writings, did draw a barb in Cobb's 1961 book. That was for writing, apparently as a 1950 exclusive to the *Miami Daily News*, that Cobb "kicked" his bird dog after losing a six-day informal contest to Woodruff. Inexplicably, McGill omitted that detail from a similar version he related in the *Saturday Evening Post* in 1951 and which appears earlier on page 199. I found McGill standing by the detail in a syndicated column in 1966, as follows: "Once, I recall, I watched him handle his bird dog in a field trial. The dog broke a point, flushing up the birds [allowing them to turn in the wind] to give victory to the other dog. Cobb's impulsive anger was immediate. He kicked the dog. Hard. It was not good to see. But that was how he felt. The dog unpardonly [sic] had, for Cobb, failed."

Stump wrote in his 1994 book that McGill "allegedly never retracted the story, but stood by it."

Two notable bird dog stories are from 1923 and 1924. In 1923, the NEA wrote this short feature on Cobb from Augusta:

"'Every man, woman and boy should have a hobby. The country would be a heluva lot better if more people went to the dogs.'

"It is the voice of Tyrus Raymond Cobb speaking. He ought to know. He has a hobby and its dogs. Down the way the papers refer to him not as one of the greatest, if not the greatest, ball player ever, but as Cobb, the dog fancier. In this field he's a star, too.

"'Why, not,' he asks. 'Baseball is my profession and dogs my hobby. If I were a dog breeder by profession then I would play ball for the fun of it, as my hobby. Everybody should have a hobby – some recreation which is a complete change from his regular line of work.'"

The feature ended by stating that "Cobb's Hall, a fine setter, has won numerous championships, including the Georgia field trial title for two years and the Continental event as well." Hunting pictures dominated the walls of Cobb's home as of the early 1920s, relative to other subjects, with the featured picture being of Cobb's Hall.

In 1915, upon the then-puppy's arrival, Cobb wrote to its donor, Detroit breeder Fred Hall, "while I was away the pup came and I want to tell you he is the handsomest thing I ever saw and seems to have lots of sense and I only hope I will be lucky enough to raise him." The puppy arrived "in excellent shape but hungry." Later that year, Cobb provided Hall

with this update: "The pup is growing fast and certainly looks good. Of course I will have to name him after you if you don[']t seriously object."

Four years later, in his 1919 book *The Modern Setter*, Hochwalt added some sequels: "When Cobb went to France with the American Expeditionary Forces [in the Great War], he placed his dog, registered as Cobb's Hall, with Dr. E. M. Wilder of Augusta, who put him in the hands of Charley Babcock to fit [sic] for the Georgia Members' all-age stake of 1918. Dr. Wilder handled the dog himself and won first with him." After praising the dog's qualities, he wrote, "It is just possible that Ty Cobb will campaign this dog in the open stakes and Llewellin breeders will certainly hope that he does."

(Hochwalt, in an article under his byline in 1931, would write that Cobb personally offered a trophy for three years to the winner of the all-age stake in Georgia. It was known as the Ty Cobb Cup. In 1957, photographer-reporter Mathewson would write a magazine article about Cobb as a hunter and state the following about Cobb's Hall: "No matter how hot the weather, or how

Cobb, Willis, and their hunting aides and bird dogs on their 1929 quail hunt at Louisville

heavy the cover, Hall always kept bouncing. It was a toss-up between Hall and Cobb as to which of the two hated most to see the sun go down.")

In 1921, Cobb told syndicated columnist Robert W. Edgren, "I like to see a ball player always at ease, loose, not tense. He has a reserve of force to use in emergency [sic]. You take a good bird dog as an example of what I mean. A good bird dog will sleep and loaf, but put him in the field with a covey of quail and he's all action."

In 1924, he spoke at length on his love for dogs. Frank F. Dole, veteran kennel editor of the *New York Herald Tribune*, wrote that he broached the subject with Cobb after a particularly tough Detroit loss and that Cobb "seemed to find it pleasant to forget all about baseball and talk about dogs." While being interviewed in his hotel room, Cobb did not mention baseball. Dole, besides being a breeder on the side, had been the first head football coach at the University of Pennsylvania.

Cobb's love of dogs was natural, Dole explained: "One who is playing the game every day, where teamwork and sportsmanship play such a large part, is bound to find satisfaction in the comradeship of loyal and game dogs. His first words summed up his attitude toward dogs. He said: 'Why, dogs are the greatest things in this world outside a man's family. You can't tell me that dogs haven't souls, and consciences, too. They will stick to you more closely than human friends. And did you ever notice that the morals of dogs are much better than those of men?'"

He said dogs had taught him much more than he had taught them. "There is nothing I like better than a day in the fields with my dogs. They will help you hunt and will furnish entertainment. Then when they get home at night, thoroughly tired out, they are still ready to defend you and yours. They will lie at your feet, ready to obey any command, and they will look up into your eyes and seem to say, 'Well, we had a good day of it to-day, old pal, and to-morrow's [sic] coming.'"

"There is no gainsaying the intelligence of a dog. Turn one loose in a room full of fellows and he will pick out the real men without hesitating a bit. Dogs are better judges of people than people are judges of dogs. Those who say that they do not love dogs will bear watching." Also, "Give a boy a good dog for a companion and let him get back into the woods and fields and he will grow up into one of God's own people. God wouldn't have put the wonderful things there if he didn't want people to appreciate them."

In a feature in 1931, the AP said, "He loves dogs and often judges at field trials, but is losing interest in the competitions because he thinks trainers are going in more for speed than accuracy in developing the bird spotters." In 1924, he told Dole, "I don't know much about the [competitive] showing of dogs. I have wanted to spend all my spare time communing with nature. On that account I have had hunting dogs largely and have trained them for the working end of the game, letting them compete under hunting conditions in field trials rather than in bench shows. I am strong for this campaign against [canine] distemper[, a viral disease for which a vaccine had just been developed]. Those who have seen a dog suffer realize what it will mean to find a preventative for this disease, or some some [sic] manner of combating it successfully in its early stages. Once they have succeeded in finding out about the germ that causes the disease[,] scientists will be able to find an agent to destroy it."

Salsinger would devote a chapter of his 1924-25 serial to Cobb's love of dogs, with a lot of detail that is different from the above. Dole's interview is far more interesting, especially because so much more of it is in Cobb's voice.

Another sign that he loved dogs can be gleaned from a 1948 letter to Helene Champlain. In it, he wrote, "may I ask you to send any negatives of my dogs that you have. The picture you sent of them was one of the best ever taken."

The last bird-dog stories of any note that I found were in 1957. One is Cobb telling the *Sporting News* that one reason why he was looking to move back to Georgia was to "hunt birds." The other was Mathewson's capstone article on Cobb's hunting, which appeared in *Southern Outdoors* magazine. Mathewson, who died that year, wrote that Cobb treated his bird dogs "as if they were young children. When we stopped for lunch at some spring or well-house near the plantation or farm quarters, he unfailingly had a tid-bit for his dogs. Ty would reach inside his hunting coat pockets and pull out several baked sweet potatoes. He'd carefully pick the quail feathers off them and feed them to his dogs. He also carried several extra sandwiches for the dogs."

Returning to the regular chronology as of 1932:

That June, as noted by Hornbaker, Cobb accepted an offer from vaudeville comedian Clarence Kolb to join him and others on a fly fishing trip to Oregon, where Kolb had a cabin. I can add that upon arriving, he told a local reporter in Eugene, "I'm doing

COMEDIAN HOLDS PIN FOR GEORGIA PEACH!

—Carl Baker photo

Ty Cobb at bat, Clarence Kolb on deck and the ball in the hole! And did he miss it? The Georgia Peach never missed poling out a hit when a hit was needed and on this eighteenth hole at the Eugene Golf and Country club with plenty of—er—incentive to sink, Ty sank it. The picture was snapped as Cobb finished a round of golf at the club Friday afternoon with his fishing pal, Clarence Kolb, noted stage comedian, holding the pin for him. At the extreme left is Bill Hayward, host for the two noted sportsmen on their fishing trip here this year. Next is Billy Reinhart, Tod Gardner, club pro, and Earl Immel, other members of the foursome in the match. Cobb and Kolb left Saturday for California after week's fishing here.

those things I couldn't find time to do while I was in baseball. When I retired from the game in 1928, I resolved to make up for a lot of lost fun and I'm doing it now. Not, you understand, that my baseball career wasn't fun – it was a wonderful experience and I think every American youth should play as much baseball as possible, but it was hard work, too and now I'm fishing and traveling and growing young again." It was Cobb's first visit to the state.

In 1933:

Latimer of the *Greenville News* began keeping closer tabs on Cobb, and Cobb kept in regular touch with him. One extraordinary way Latimer did so this year was by being the rare journalist who repeated all of what Dan Parker wrote in the *New York Mirror* about the rocky relationship between Ty and Ty Jr. What Parker had written contained some interesting racial detail. I have inserted the *Mirror*'s original wording and punctuation:

Latimer began by writing, "Like father, like son, Ty Cobb, Jr., is made of the sterner stuff to battle his way through life. The [Civil] war's been over these 68 years, now, but the Cobbs are still rebels at heart, to put it in Dan Parker's crisp way. Ty the Elder fought umpires, players and anyone else who wanted to fight during the two decades he was the American League's leading firebrand. Now that he has no umps to fight with, Ty battles with Ty, Junior. Being a Cobb, Tyrus the Second fights right back. And that's why he has quit his studies at Yale [University] and launched out for himself, says Parker in the Daily Mirror. He'll show 'em he doesn't have to be wet-nursed through a career on the strength of the pater's [father's] reputation.

"Let Mr. Parker finish the story in his own inimitable way:

"When he had a falling out with the greatest umpire baiter of all time [actually, Cobb was far from the top in that respect], not long ago, over financial matters, Ty quit college and got himself a job with a coal and coke company in New Haven[, Conn.]. To test the stuff of which young Tyrus is made, the owner of the company[,] knowing young Ty is a hot-blooded Georgian, put him to work under a colored foreman, who had instructions to teach him plain and fancy shoveling. Young Ty was game. He was pronounced a talented shoveler by the colored gentleman when his apprenticeship on the business end of the spade had come to an end.

"Now Ty is soliciting orders, doing well at the job and saving his pennies to continue his education. He wants to be a surgeon and my guess is that that's exactly what he'll be – and a good one in the bargain."

(In 1935, Ty the father would write to Manley Miner, son of waterfowl preserve founder Jack Miner, regarding Ty Jr.'s recent visit to Jack and Manley in Ontario. Ty asked if Manley could confidentially take in the following detail, including by not mentioning it to Jack: "Ty has been a disappointment to me[,] he failed in prep school and utterly failed in college[,] would not apply himself[,] also ran up lots of bills which I paid up 6 different times and got to where I could not begin to control him and his promises were always broken so after he was 21, I put him on his own[,] thinking that would wake him up, he has made many bills & borrowed money, though happy to say he has not done anything else wrong, just uncontrolled spending & no respect for his obligations and he thinks he has been treated badly because I would no longer be accessory to it all & called a halt."

In a new paragraph, Ty began, "You see Manley I was away from the children so much when they were coming up and their mother indulged them & they developed wrong attitudes, she thought she was doing the right thing but it proved wrong.")

in a happier moment in 1933: Cobb with humorist Will Rogers (left) at a polo match in Santa Monica, Calif.

In 1934:

Don Rhodes quoted reminiscences from Cobb at a banquet in San Francisco, as conveyed in the *Augusta Chronicle*. Hornbaker used a different version with similar quotes. Key parts had Cobb saying, as reported by Newland of the AP, "If I had it to do over again, I wouldn't take baseball so seriously." Also, "I could have cemented some wonderful friendships in those days with fellows who would be real friends today. I believe I made a mistake there. Baseball is a great game but there is such a thing as taking it too seriously."

In 1951, Cunningham in the *Boston Herald* updated those remarks. Cunningham had spoken a week earlier in Sarasota, Fla., to clownish former big leaguer Al Schacht, to whom Cobb had said not long ago, "I wish I had the chance to do it again, and do it the other way. As a man grows older, he realizes that friends are worth a lot more than money."

Upon Cobb's death, the *New York Times* would echo the tone of Cobb's 1934 remarks, without citing them: "In a soft-spoken way he liked to make jokes about his days as a 'difficult player.'" A sentence earlier, the *Times* said,

"Where as a player he had battled with his own teammates as well as with opposing team members, and had only a few intimates, he seemed in his later years to want to atone for his long period of aggressiveness."

(In analyzing coverage of Cobb's death, Leerhsen printed some positive thoughts from the editorial page of the *Times* and then opined, "In this way, the *Times* spoke for the majority of journalists who preferred to say something polite and move on." Even if the *Times* editorial page was being polite, the *Times*'s sports page was not, as evidenced by the paragraph above that I took from it. Meanwhile, the AP and UPI, as noted earlier, went farther, calling Cobb arguably or definitely the most disliked or hated baseball player of his day or of all time. The *Times* also went negative on a different front, saying that "Cobb was noted for the deadly use of his spikes on the base paths.")

Returning to 1934:

Bill Dooley of the *Philadelphia Record* saw Cobb's banquet remarks and, writing in the *Sporting News*, said he had no one but himself to blame for not having any baseball friends. Hornbaker found that and a Cobb reply letter. Here is the best chunk of the letter that he did not quote directly:

"There always have been several things distasteful in my experience in baseball, matters which shadowed the pleasant angles of the game, the enjoyments and gratifications in one's work." Also, "Of course, the grind, the hard work, etc., were difficult, but the selfishness, bad language, backbiting, intolerance as to religion amongst the narrow and uneducated, the unfairness and crudeness and the cliques – these were the things I did not enjoy. I don't say a majority were this way. I say a percentage were; yes, just enough to make things unhappy. I was tolerant of this class, and this, with the twenty-five [24] years of hard work, travel and being away from home, caused me to welcome my retirement."

Hornbaker printed five sentences, one very long, from the letter and nearly aced the transcription, merely changing a "towards" to a "toward." But he spliced out, without an ellipsis, the following chunk of four full sentences and awkwardly part of a fifth, which follow: "I was always for the manager and the club's interest and was opposed to loafing and maligning. If I have failed to make friends with this class, I am not unhappy. In fact, it has been as I wished it. Now, I never have said at any time, or to any one, anything about not making friendships or lasting friendships. I said I was strong for the old type of player, but [Hornbaker capitalized the next word 'If' and resumed the quotation]."

I can bring to light a parsing of his banquet speech by sportswriter James C. Isaminger of the *Philadelphia Inquirer*; the effect is to make Cobb's letter prose seem less accurate. Isaminger wrote, "Players seemed to shrink from him, never knowing what tack the well[-]known Cobb temperament might take. This is not to imply he was never cordial or lacked politeness. He could be the most congenial and at a table of friends he would entertain friends for hours with stories. He made many friends among businessmen and 'big shots,' who were proud to be seen in company with the only Cobb, but he rather neglected his own profession.

"Now that he is retired, he probably meets players of his own day who have felt the sting of his tongue or perhaps the cut of his spikes and who are a bit icy when they come in contact with him. That's why he says today he regrets he did not cultivate more friendships among players and now wishes he had not taken baseball too seriously."

As noted earlier, possibly based on an observation by Maines, Alexander wrote that Cobb's friends over the decades "were mostly non-baseball people [which presumably includes persons associated with the sport who had not been big leaguers] and they had to be willing to take him on his own terms."

Returning briefly to the 1934 part of the chronology:

While sitting in the Olympic Club in San Francisco, Cobb told Hazen of the *Oregonian* that the new lively ball "has simply made caddies out of the outfielders – they just catch flies and chase long hits. Anyone can score from second now. The fielders lean up against the fence, and when a long fly comes their way they get it and throw it back to the pitcher. One-third of the team isn't in the play any more. The fine points of pitching are being neglected. Just any little, hinky-dinky batter can hit 'em over the fence."

Cobb had also made that point, albeit more diplomatically, back in 1925. He had said the following to *New York Telegram* sports editor Hughes:

"The lively ball is a menace all right [indeed] in many ways. In the first place it has practically withered up the once fine art of base running. In the days when there wasn't such wholesale hitting there was some percentage in stealing bases. In fact, it was a feat expected of a really smart ball player. But today, when an ordinary swipe at the ball makes it rebound like a rifle bullet, there is no percentage in taking chances with base stealing.

"At best a base runner's chances of succeeding are only about forty per cent. And what is the use in taking chances when hits are so plentiful? A chap nowadays gets on base and simply waits for the hit that will advance him. It is too bad, for it's hard on the pitchers, the fielders, and the fans who liked to see a display of individual initiative on the bases.

"'The lively ball,' continued Ty with a frown, 'has other drawbacks more perceptible to the manager than to the layman. It is ruining his pitcher, making it more difficult especially for rising young moundsmen to break into the majors.'" He explained that earlier in his career, in the days of the dead ball, "many a rookie [pitcher] in a tight place was salvaged by double plays on infield hits. These same wallops today too often rip through the infields, which decline to take chances of injuries."

Returning to 1934 and his interview with Hazen of the *Oregonian*:

Asked about the state of interest in the game among youngsters, he said "a majority are gravitating to other lines of sport. A few years ago the boys didn't have much else in the way of outdoor sport, but now there are other things. And the colleges are to blame for keeping a large number of good boys from taking up baseball. Did you ever hear of any college in the last 15 years offering scholarships to good baseball talent? No, not a damn one! The football coach gets all of them, or all that he needs.

"Then does the baseball coach get what's left? He does, in a pig's eye! The track coach takes the rest, if the school doesn't have a crew [a rowing team]. Where they go in for rowing the crew coach gets a whack at the scholarships, but the poor old baseball coach now gets the 'women and children,' so to speak. That's why the halls of higher learning are not sending forth Greek and Latin scholars to burn up the diamonds. You recall when they used to say [in a way that was hopeful of the sport's future]:

"'It is only a question of a short time when all the professional baseball players will be college graduates'? I think that baseball is still a wonderful game. It develops the initiative in a fellow; it develops him physically, and it don't beat hell [sic] out of him like some other games they are now boosting. Baseball doesn't take so much of life out of a young chap as many other games do." (Coincidentally, several weeks earlier to Burr of the *Brooklyn Eagle*, he said that other than being a surgeon, his career, if not baseball, "might have been football, golf or tennis. But there was no football, golf or tennis in the South when I was a youngster.")

In 1935:

In January, apparently at the first tee of the Los Angeles Country Club, he spoke about football and baseball to Brian Bell of the AP. About baseball, he said that players are not so polished as in his day. "Most of them can't use the hit and run, and it's surprising how few really know how to slide." He also spoke of Mack, his former manager, and Ruth. "'Mr. Mack is not only a great character,' said Cobb with a look of reverence in his eyes, 'but he is still as great a manager as we have. That old gentleman certainly knows just what it is all about out on that field.'"

Ex-minor leaguer-turned-actor-comedian and baseball fanatic Joe E. Brown wrote to Cobb, asking him to play a character in his forthcoming baseball film "Alibi Ike." Cobb reacted by telling the AP, "It sounds interesting. Money talks pretty freely these days. No, I never acted before but I think I could do pretty well as a player in a mob scene. Maybe I would be a 'bust' and then my friends would start calling me 'Ham' Cobb."

The movie was released later that year without Cobb appearing. Brown also wrote in vain to Ruth. (Brown was a huge sports memorabilia collector. As of 1946 and until his death in 1973, he owned a uniform from Cobb's last big-league season.)

One story from spring training came from former

from left to right in 1947: actor-singer Roy Rogers, Joe E. Brown and then-Hollywood Stars/Twinks radio broadcaster Fred Haney

Philadelphia teammate and future Hall of Famer Mickey Cochrane. He was in his second year as the Tigers' player-manager and is the last of three ex-players at his funeral to be quoted herein; Rucker and Schalk are the others. To sports editor Bud Shaver of the *Detroit Times*, Cochrane gave examples of Cobb's scientific mastery. For example, "Cobb even figured out the number of bounces he could hit a ball to the shortstop and beat it out."

"Cobb had an impetuous, disagreeable personality," Bingay wrote in the *Free Press*. "When he left the game he left few personal friendships behind him. The only one I can compare Cobb to is Wagner and I don't mean Honus. I mean Richard Wagner. As the Colossus of music recreated that art so did Cobb recreate baseball. Both were the master geniuses of their art – one deathless harmonies, the other baseball. Wagner, master of them all, was as personally unpopular as was Cobb in baseball. But genius transcends personality and Cobb was as great a genius in his art as was Wagner in his."

Two weeks later, Cobb told the AP that baseball has "gone softie." He said baseball had deteriorated lately because of the lively ball and the umpiring. "'The outfielders are too far away from the action,' is one complaint. 'The players all try for the home run these days. And that should not be. Baseball should be played on the grounds and not over the fence. The lively ball is hurting the game.'"

As for the umpiring, "Umpires have been given too much authority in ruling protesting players out of the game and levying fines. This practice has taken a great deal of the fight out of the players." Also, he predicted that more teams would be playing night baseball in the coming season and observed, "It's a funny thing, but under the arc lights the action of the players appears faster, and this probably is one reason the game is popular."

In 1936:

After it was announced that Cobb had gotten the most votes for entry into the sport's new Hall of Fame, Chief Meyers, a National League catcher from 1909 to 1917, said, "I can't stand for that." Speaking at the annual corned beef feed of the Professional Ball Players' Association of America, as reported on by Bob Ray of the *Los Angeles Times*, Meyers said, "Cobb was a wonderful hitter and a great base runner, but by no stretch of the imagination should he be number one in the baseball Hall of Fame. Ty was a poor outfielder and I can't ever remember of hearing anyone say he was what you'd call a team player.

Cobb and Honus Wagner in 1946: the players are authentic, the autographs are not

"Baseball's outstanding player, as far as I'm concerned, is Honus Wagner. I played against Wagner and I know he could do anything well. He was a wonderful fielder – big hands that scooped up ground balls like a steam shovel – and a great batter. Honus never had a weakness at the plate unless it was a base on balls. He hit the ball wherever it was pitched. And the old 'Flying Dutchman' could run those bases, too. The best thing I can say about Wagner is that we ball players regarded him as an artist on the diamond. We'd just sit back and admire him during batting and fielding practice, and cuss him during the game. Honus Wagner was a ball player's ball player and he's number one in my Baseball Hall of Fame." Days later, the report was shown to now-Red Sox general manager Eddie Collins, a Cobb friend, who responded, "Cobb was as good as anybody as an outfielder." Also, Collins told sports editor Burt

Whitman of the *Boston Herald*, "It is true that in the last years of his greatness he rather stressed the offensive rather than the defensive side of the game. I also believe that his arm suffered a bit by reason of his great ambition to become a pitcher. Yes, sir: Ty Cobb always wanted to be a great pitcher. I can recall him on countless occasions practi[c]ing pitching on the side lines before games. I actually believe that this had the tendency to hurt his arm.

"Yet he could cover the outfield with the best of them, and only a few outfielding geniuses like Speaker, [Happy] Felsch and [Johnny] Mostil, who had uncanny ability in defensive play, could be ranked above him as outfielders.

"So far as his team play went, let me merely say that he was a whole team in himself. So, please do not pay any attention to what some old National leaguer [sic] has to say about Ty Cobb's right to be hailed the top man of baseball."

Otherwise that year:

He was sued by a pedestrian, W. R. Turvey, who he had hit while driving in 1935 a bit south of San Jose. Turvey had been walking along a highway. "Cobb rushed Turvey to a hospital. Cobb was exonerated of blame for the accident," the *Oakland Tribune* reported. Turvey sued the following year for $50,000, about $1 million today, after claiming that he was suffering physically. The case was settled for an undisclosed sum. Later in 1936, Cobb received a speeding ticket in Oakland, for going 45 miles an hour in a 25-mile-an-hour zone.

He commented on whether he was worried that autograph hunters might try to slip him a blank check to sign. He said he always signs autographs as "Ty Cobb," but his bank checks as "T. R. Cobb."

A letter writer told of a problem relating to becoming part of a baseball team. In alluding to the issue, Cobb advised the writer, "don[']t be hot headed[.] baseball is more than fair to young men breaking in today and encourage[s] the youngsters far more than when I broke in[.] also remember you need them far more than they need you so cooperate and don[']t get your feelings hurt so easily[.] remember managers have far more weighty matters to attend [sic] than giving some individual lots of personal petting or attention." As a postscript, he wrote, "work hard and make them like you, don[']t find fault."

In 1937:

The World's Greatest Initials
T. R.
T. R. Cobb.

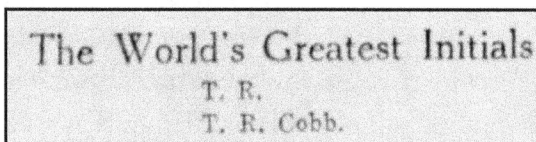

from a Grantland Rice column in 1917

In later years, especially in the 1950s, Cobb would get in hot water for praising only a few modern players for measuring up to old-time ones. In 1937, he told Harold Heroux of the

International News Service that Dizzy Dean, Lou Gehrig and DiMaggio "compare with the best players of my day."

"Dean certainly stacks up with Cy Young, Christy Mathewson and Walter Johnson – all really great chuckers."

In the interview, "Cobb didn't care to discuss 'the rise or decline of big league baseball' in recent years, except to say: 'Night baseball is just a commercial thing. It is not the same as daylight baseball, and I am sorry to see it come. Night ball is too much of a carnival, with all the lights and everything.'"

Heroux concluded by saying, "Cobb lives at his country estate here [in Atherton] – near the city of Palo Alto – but frequently drives into San Francisco. During the fall he may be seen in stadiums watching football games each Saturday. He admits he is quite a football fan."

(His interest in football was quite a change from 1915, when he said, "If football were a daily attraction it would last about a week." He spoke after seeing a North Carolina game at Georgia Tech. "Its brutality would kill it if nothing else. Several players were hurt Saturday and had to retire." In that era, football was indeed especially brutal, because of minimal protective equipment; things had improved considerably by 1937.)

The *Oregonian*'s Hazen wrote about the nine most enjoyable baseball player interviews he had done, and Cobb from 1934 was among them. "As outspoken as a blizzard [but hardly so before his retirement], he would have made the world's worst diplomat," Hazen wrote.

Brian Bell, the AP's San Francisco bureau chief, was in Portland weeks later to cover a golf tournament and conveyed the following in Hazen's presence: "Ty says the thing that is the matter with big league baseball today is there isn't enough big league ball players in it." Two weeks later, Brietz of the AP expounded on Bell's report: "Brian Bell, South Carolina's No. 1 story teller [Bell was a native of the state], now boss of the A. P. on the coast, played golf with Ty Cobb the other day and asked Ty: 'What's the matter with major league baseball these days?' Cobb "holed a six footer and came back: 'Only trouble is, there are not enough major league ball players.'"

Upon Bell's death in 1942, the AP would say that baseball men were among his closest friends, "ranging from magnates like Clark Griffith, president of the Washington club, to all-time playing greats like Ty Cobb. Bell and Cobb frequently played golf together when they were both on the West coast, and it was under Ty's tutelage that Brian Jr., [sic] developed talent like his father, as a first baseman."

Returning to the chronology:

Sports columnist Braven Dyer of the *Los Angeles Times* wrote the following, after seeing an interview that Cobb gave: "Glad to see Tyrus Raymond Cobb giving 'em the business because the art of base stealing has been lost. Cobb was the greatest of all time in this department. Never gave you more than the tip of his toe to tag with his fall-away slide. And if you tried to block him off the bag the next time he came flying along[,] you were in danger of having your throat slit or your ears cut off. Ty used to delight in sitting on the clubhouse steps as opposing ball players came on the field. He invariably had his baseball shoes between his legs, putting an edge on the spikes with a file."

at Oakland in 1938: Cobb greeting Georgia Tech football coach William A. Alexander, whose team was in town to face California. To Cobb's left is Georgia Tech alumnus Ed Hamm, who won a broad jump gold medal in the 1928 Summer Olympics.

(On a different point in Dyer's column, in 1950, Cobb would tell Bisher of the *Atlanta Constitution*, "Nobody can say that a man who uses the fall-away slide is deliberately trying to spike a player. The purpose of the slide is to fall away from the player, not toward him. You're making yourself an easy target if you go into a base with your spikes up.")

In the fall, a UP report from Bend, Ore., stated that Cobb had "failed to bag a deer on a recent trip here" and was back in the state to try his luck again.

Eddie Shore and Cobb at a B'nai B'rith dinner in Boston in 1959

After the season, an *Ottawa Journal* sportswriter with the byline of "Bradley" lumped Cobb with someone who Bradley said had been hockey's biggest villain, Eddie Shore of the Boston Bruins. Cobb was baseball's "most hated player. His deliberate surliness and sometimes ugliness gained him the admiration and hatred of fans and players alike in both major leagues. Despite the fact that they [Shore and Cobb] were hooted and jeered by onlookers, these athletes prospered, for, despite the fact that the fans sometimes hated them, they came to see them play."

In 1938:

E. B. Rea of the *New Journal and Guide*, a black weekly in Norfolk, Va., wrote, "The general trend of baseball is to recruit as many players out of white colleges and universities as possible. The old sandlot, rough and tumble players of the Ty Cobb class, like the American Indian, will soon be out of the picture and in his place a college[-]bred type capable of adjusting himself to any situation. The Negro must match this type."

The earliest report I found that cited Cobb conditioning tips to Joe DiMaggio, that DiMaggio was adopting, was in 1937, and will be noted later; it will be grouped with other tips that DiMaggio had adopted as of 1940, one year before the season of his 56-game hitting streak.

This year, 1938, featured the one contemporaneous report I found of Cobb being publicly alleged to have advised DiMaggio on his Yankee contract negotiations. Digressing to a long analysis of Cobb-DiMaggio stories on this topic, with Yankee business manager Edward "Ed" Barrow in a starring role:

The most often retold Cobb-DiMaggio-Barrow story in modern-day books was rehashed by Leerhsen. Leerhsen mentioned that when Cobb first learned of the Yankees' offer to him for his rookie season, in 1936, he invited DiMaggio to his home, where he dictated a letter for DiMaggio to send to Barrow asking for more money. After Cobb learned later of DiMaggio's having received a better offer,

TY COBB PERSUADED DIMAGGIO TO ACCEPT RUPPERT'S OFFER

Italian Player Uses Alias On Trip To New York City

IN POOR CONDITION

By HAROLD HEROUX

Aboard the Streamliner "City of San Francisco," en route East, April 21.—"L. Copolotti" hopped out of upper berth No. 9 in car 125 this morning, blinked his eyes and talked about confidence.

"If confidence means anything I'll hit .400 this season," he said.

"L. Copolotti" was none other than Joe DiMaggio, home run king and erstwhile New York Yankee holdout. DiMag used that alias when he secretly made reservations yesterday after conceding defeat to Col. Jacob Ruppert, Yankee owner, in their bitter salary battle.

"Why did you give in to Ruppert?" DiMag was asked.

"I figured I'd be the sport," was his answer.

One of DiMag's closest friends advised him in San Francisco that he would be a bigger man in the eyes of the fans, so far as sportsmanship was concerned, than Ruppert if he signed for $25,000 rather than the $40,000 he demanded.

This same adviser told him he shouldn't irk Ruppert because he had to live the rest of his baseball life—estimated at about 12 years—with the millionaire Yankee owner,

who announced he wouldn't sell Di-Mag for ten times the $150,000 offered by the St. Louis Browns.

"You'll make more than $25,000 this season," this adviser is said to have told DiMag. "With royalties and probably another cut in the world series will make your earnings over $35,000. And besides, Ruppert will have to give you plenty more room next season if you prove you're a sport this year."

DiMag claimed he had made up mind to surrender and that he had no advisors, but passengers aboard the train rapidly spread a rumor that he had accepted advice from Ty Cobb, the No. 1 figure of baseball's Hall of Fame, who now resides near San Francisco.

"I reached a decision yesterday and I called Ed Barrow, the Yankee business manager, and told him I'd accept their terms," said DiMag.

"I had been determined to hold out longer. But I couldn't—I couldn't for this reason: I was getting no rest. Every three or four minutes the phone would ring with somebody asking 'Joe are you going to sign' or 'have you signed?'

"I was being driven nuts—my whole family too!"

"Are you in shape to play?" he was asked.

"Nope. I haven't had a bat in my hands for more than a month. The last time I wore a uniform was with the San Francisco Seals at their training camp. But I've got plenty of confidence. I figure I'll be ready to play in about five days or a week after I reach New York."

from the *Evening News* in Wilkes-Barre, Pa.

$1,000 more, about $17,000 today, he dictated another letter the following week for DiMaggio to send. The next one produced a still-better offer, $2,000 more than the second offer. That latter letter indicated that it was the Yankees' final offer and that DiMaggio should tell Cobb to stop writing those letters.

The kicker would be wrong – if one believes what DiMaggio told Ernie Harwell of the *Detroit Free Press* in 1994 and not, as Leerhsen reflected above, what he had told Jim Murray of the *Los Angeles Times* months earlier. Perhaps DiMaggio rethought things through and corrected himself in speaking to Murray.

In his interview with Murray, DiMaggio provided this background before sailing into the contract negotiation part above: Cobb

"used to eat in our family restaurant at the wharf in San Francisco." In that version, DiMaggio said there were seven letters in all, presumably back and forth, including one in which Barrow told him to tell Cobb to stop writing letters. DiMaggio told Murray, "But I ended up with $8,500," about $150,000 today. "And Cobb ate for free in the restaurant."

Two months later, Joe told Harwell that it was his brother Tom, who ran the restaurant, who enlisted Cobb's help with the contract. "Cobb came into the restaurant often, and Tom either wouldn't charge him for his meal or he would let him have it at half-price. Of course, Ty was a millionaire several times over. But he still liked the idea of a free meal."

Joe said Tom accompanied him to Cobb's house on at least one of the occasions. Then Joe told of the sequence of letters to and from

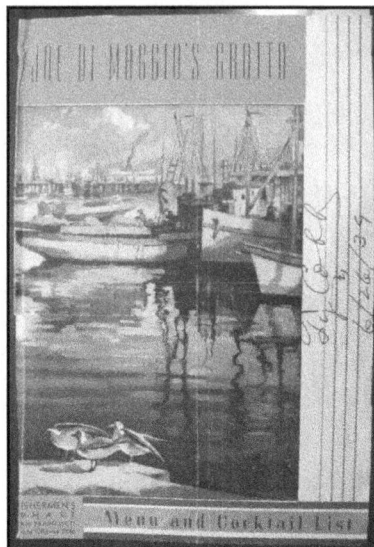

-:- Drink 'er Down! -:-

The scene isn't a barber shop, but the boys seem to be murdering that barber shop chord. They're Ty Cobb, left; Joe Di Maggio, and (at the piano) Buck Shaw, coach of the Santa Clara Broncos. The scene is the Elks' club at San Rafael, Cal.—Central Press.

from left to right in 1937 at the Elks lodge of San Rafael, Calif.: Cobb; DiMaggio; and Santa Clara University football coach Lawrence T. "Buck" Shaw, who had played under Knute Rockne at Notre Dame

Barrow. Joe also told Harwell, "Barrow never knew that Cobb was my unofficial adviser. He knew that my brother Tom was acting as my agent and thought that all the negotiating was done by Tom and me. Along with that final letter, Barrow got a little more generous and sent me a bonus. But the bonus wasn't for me. It was for my brother Tom – two new suits."

Harwell ended his column by writing, "And that's how two baseball greats hooked up to outsmart one of baseball's craftiest general managers."

Helping to break the standoff of whether Barrow knew earlier than the 1938 report of Cobb's involvement is John Tullius's 1986 *I'd Rather Be a Yankee: An Oral History of America's Most Loved and Most Hated Baseball Team.*

DiMaggio told of a series of five letters that Cobb helped him write that each resulted in a raise. Also, "Cobb dictated the letter for me to Barrow and in it I said, or rather Cobb said, 'I don't care if you trade me to the St. Louis Browns.'

Edward "Ed" Barrow

And I looked up at Cobb and said, 'I don't want to go to the Browns.' He said, 'Don't worry. This is just to get them to give you more money.'

"So I got a letter back that said, 'We're going to give you another five-hundred-dollar raise. And don't ever talk about where you want to be traded because when we want to trade you we'll tell you what club you're going to.'" DiMaggio added, "Oh, my goodness, that Barrow was tough." In Tullius's version, Cobb does not appear in Barrow's replies.

Barrow and Cobb did know each other well; along with Toronto International League manager Dan Howley in 1925, they had gone hunting together in Toronto. In 1938, in a 70th-birthday feature,

from left to right at Augusta in early 1927: Dan Howley, Cobb and Connie Mack

Barrow would say that in his career as a minor league manager, his biggest heartache was that he once had a chance to buy Cobb, but that his owner would not pay the necessary money.

Coincidental or not to his now definitely knowing of Cobb's advising of

DiMaggio, Barrow in 1939 would utter one of the more colorful criticisms of Cobb's playing ability. It helps balance out criticism dished out by Cobb of some fellow star players for not being so great in fielding.

Barrow weighed in after Tris Speaker was reported to have said that he could name 15 outfielders who were superior to DiMaggio.

at the *San Francisco Examiner*'s Christmas party in 1938

Barrow called the comment "foolish" and said that only Speaker was a better one than DiMaggio. Barrow also said, as reported by the AP, "What other outfielder does he think was better than Joe? He couldn't mean Ty Cobb. He never was more than a hitter." Speaker quickly denied stating the above claim.

One loose end on Cobb and DiMaggio fits here. Four months before Cobb's death, the AP would report from Florida DiMaggio's reply when someone asked him who taught him how to hit; he was now in his first year as a Yankees spring training instructor. "Nobody taught me. But Cobb showed me some tricks about contract signing." Hornbaker paraphrased that last sentence without putting it in a larger context; as will be noted soon, DiMaggio in 1940 would give Cobb credit on other fronts, especially for impressing on him not to tire himself out in pre-game warm-ups.

Also, in his 1946 autobiography *Lucky to Be a Yankee*, DiMaggio would single out four people for giving him advice about being confident at the plate: Cobb; his Seals manager, Lefty O'Doul; Joe Cronin; and Ruth. For his part, Leerhsen cited a source that Hornbaker did not, a 1968 interview in *Baseball Digest* in which DiMaggio gave Cobb the following credit. Speaking to Phil Elderkin of the *Christian Science Monitor*, who himself had exchanged letters with Cobb, to be noted later, DiMaggio said, "I can't ever remember telling anyone this before, but early in my career I got five or six letters from Ty Cobb. They dealt mostly with hitting and they gave me a lot of encouragement. I couldn't believe a man as great as Cobb would bother to take the time to write to me. I've still got those letters."

Returning to 1938:

Sports editor George S. Alderton of the *Lansing State Journal* in Michigan reminisced about a Tigers' batboy as of the early 1920s, Jerome Johnson, a Lansing resident. Johnson was 15 when he began spending "most of his spare time in and around Navin field at Detroit. He was ever alert to run an errand or do some odd-job that would earn him a pass to the ball game. One of his prized duties was the daily shining of Ty Cobb's car when the great Tyrus parked it at the field."

Cobb shot at clay pigeons, and despite a report to the contrary in 1917, claimed, "I never shot at the traps before. " Harry B. Smith of the *San Francisco Chronicle* quoted him after he shot at the Family, still a males-only private club in San Francisco, which at the time had its own camp about 40 miles south of the city. At its Family Club Farm, he strolled over to trapshooting grounds either in the camp or close to it. "The boys were shooting away at the clay pigeons thrown from the tower." Cobb borrowed a gun and scored very well.

A feature on Los Angeles osteopath Charles H. Spencer cited the many players who had been his patients, including Cobb. In the article, recalled was a Cobb suggestion that Spencer become a doctor of all big-league players, by signing a contract with each team. Spencer's response was to suggest a large amount that each team would pay, which Cobb considered steep. When Spencer then noted how highly he rates in his own league, medicine, Cobb supposedly agreed with his analysis.

Cobb ordered a set of left-handed golf clubs through a St. Louis golf professional, Benny Richter. In a reported two-page letter, Cobb described himself as a "nine-handicap golfer" and as owning five sets of clubs. The new clubs he felt would improve his "straying shots."

In September, he participated in a baseball game at the Family Club Farm, and the *San Francisco Chronicle* ran the following headline: "Two Greatest Outfielders in History of Game Seen in Action at the Family Club"

Lifelong San Franciscan Bill Lange, a top all-around outfielder of the 1890s who, had he not retired young (a decision unrelated to health), might have been a Hall of Famer, played on the other team. Lange had five putouts in left field, the last coming when Cobb came to bat with the bases loaded with two outs. Lange's team won, 6 to 4. A photo survives, in the holdings of the National Baseball Hall of Fame, of Al C. Joy, former sports editor of the *San Francisco Examiner*, calling Lange out on a tag by Cobb. The Hall of Fame obtained a customized signed copy of the photo that Lange sent to Clark Griffith, a Chicago teammate of his in the 1890s. The copyright status is unclear, so the Hall of Fame will not allow its use. If you Google "Ty Cobb playing with Al Joy and

Bill Lange photograph," you can see it. Lange and Griffith's Chicago team was led by Anson, and Lange and Anson were the ultimate of friends. Lange would have had many opportunities to tell him stories about Anson.

(As far as what Cobb thought about players of the 19th century, the best insight that I found was in a 1925 letter to Jim "Deacon" McGuire, a former player-turned-Detroit coach in four of Cobb's seasons. "You know Jim, such fellows as yourself came along at the wrong time, also I might say that the present ball player don't [sic] begin to realize what they owe to the ball players of 'yester-years'. They are enjoying the fruits of your labor. It was such ball players as yourself who really laid the foundation of baseball and helped to make it what it is today." The coming-along-at-the-wrong-time thought presumably is referring to the higher salaries of the 20th century.)

Cobb and Bill Lange, from the 1934 dinner for Gabby Street on page 46. Lange was at Cobb's house for the dinner party in 1935 noted much earlier. Each married into rich families.

The Olympic Club held its inaugural golf tournament. One finalist was Cobb. The other would go on to become a professional golfer and commentator: a then-12-year-old, Bob Rosburg.

Jumping to decades-later versions of what happened that day:

In a 1987 feature on

at a venison barbeque for Cobb near Millbrae, Calif., in 1931 on Lange's estate. On Lange's right is chef Bill Larue.

the club in the *San Francisco Chronicle*, sportswriter Art Spander wrote, "One year he [Cobb] ended up playing a junior member named Bob Rosburg in a

NOT FORGOTTEN.—At funeral services in Chicago for Adrian C. Anson, baseball's grand old man, oldtimers and present stars met to pay tribute to the famous star's memory. Left to right, Kid Gleason, James Callahan, Judge Landis, Ty Cobb.

round of the club championship; he lost and left the club for good. Rosburg, too, left eventually – to go on and become a pro and win the PGA Championship in 1959."

Stump ended his 1990 *Golf* magazine mention of the Cobb-Rosburg match by writing, "The members gave Cobb such a hard time [for losing to a 12-year-old] that he cleaned out his locker and never returned to the club."

In a video interview in 2007, Rosburg was asked about their pairing and said the following, with a few awkward transitions: "As I remember he was very nice to me. They said what a nasty man he was and everything like that, but he was fine to me. And I just annihilated him. I beat him 7 and 6 [by seven holes, with six remaining, thus ending the match]. Of course I couldn't go into the locker room. I was too young. They wouldn't let me in." Rosburg heard "they gave him such a bad time. All the other members, they thought that a 12-year-old kid beat a great legend like you – and they gave him such a bad time that he resigned from the club and didn't play as a member there any more. He came back a couple of times to play as member-guest but he went down to Menlo [Park] and finished out playing down there."

Asked about Cobb's golfing skill, Rosburg said, "Oh, he was a good player. Yeah, I would say, you know, he was an 8 or 9 handicap, something like that. Well I just had a good day and he had bad one."

Returning again to 1938:

In August, an article under DiMaggio's byline in *Liberty* stated that when DiMaggio was with the San Francisco Seals, Cobb "wised me up on the ways of the game and the habits of the fan. Cobb told me how he had had the wrong slant. In his big days with the Tigers, he was a snarly, resentful sort of fellow. He made few friends, even among the ballplayers. And for that he is very sorry. He wishes he could start all over again.

"Ty got in the habit of chasing hecklers into the stands [that seems way overstated]. And as he was hooted and booed all over the circuit, he had a very busy time of it practically every afternoon the Detroit club was on the road." Predictably, Cobb told him to ignore hecklers, and DiMaggio ended that subject by stating, "I realize what we call 'taking it' is a very important part of a player's daily life. I know that you can't expect a bed of roses all the time. When you sign your contract, you've got to accept the job for better or for worse."

In 1939:

Art Cohn was later a fine screenwriter. But in 1958, while writing a book about Elizabeth Taylor's third husband, producer Mike Todd, Cohn and Todd died in a small plane crash.

Sports editor Cohn of the *Oakland Tribune* told of there being a "yarn in a San Francisco gazette the other day [the *San Francisco Examiner*]." He then exaggerated its report. He wrote that "Mr. Cobb had begged Stanford [University] for the job of assistant baseball coach but had been turned down because Harry Wolter, the head coach, had threatened to quit if Mr. Cobb as much as stuck his nose on the campus." He added, "The picture of baseball's all-time hero, a gent with at least two million potatoes in the bin [about $34 million today], begging Stanford for an assistant coach's job is wacky, any way you look at it." In concluding his discourse on the subject, he wrote that "if I were the dope who wrote that phoney yarn about Mr. Cobb I would take the advice of that popular songwriter and – Get Out of Town!"

Two days later, Cohn dissected the yarn further, helped by having apparently spoken with Cobb. "Yes, there were a few inaccuracies in that San Francisco newspaper's story about me. 'Weary of idleness?' No, I love it. So much so that I rejected a tempting offer yesterday to appear on a coast-to-coast network at a fancy figure. 'Yearning for the game?' No, I turned down an offer to go back to Detroit, among several other baseball offers. 'Applied to Stanford for a job?' I most certainly did not. 'Stanford turned me down?' That is a lie. 'Is the story a fake?' Well, Art, I leave it to you." (In 1945, Salsinger would write of Cobb having turned down an offer to chair the California Athletic Commission.)

Collier's associate editor Quentin Reynolds interviewed him and noted that the Baseball Hall of Fame would be dedicated the following week. Reynolds said Cobb had been "the Beau Geste [adventure hero] of baseball – ruthless, colorful, asking no quarter and giving none. He'd fight at the drop of a bat

[sic] and he was a bad loser. Good losers are very common now in baseball. Players lose with a smile and a shrug of their shoulders; they get paid whether they win or lose. Cobb wasn't like that; he had to win. It is no wonder that in the balloting for places in the Hall of Fame the name of Ty Cobb led all the rest."

The article featured Cobb's opinions on the greatest players of all-time at the various positions. The paragraph in the piece that most jumped out at me seems out of whack to what is otherwise known about his early interest in baseball: namely, that there was no other profession that he strongly considered. Reynolds quoted him as being more serious in those early days about becoming a surgeon than I otherwise found:

"'Baseball has been good to me,' he said thoughtfully. 'Funny thing, you know I never intended to be a ballplayer. I wanted to be a surgeon. I went up [to Detroit] that first year hoping to make enough money to put me through medical school. I held out my second year and in those days owners were pretty strict about holdouts. I said to myself: 'I'll let this decide it. If the owner [Navin] gives in, it means I'm cut out to be a ballplayer from now on. If he doesn't it means that I'm cut out to be a surgeon and I'll quit baseball and go to medical school.' Well, he gave in and I was a ballplayer." While the interview is revealing, Cobb's surgeon scenario in his second season sounds far-fetched.

In June, he visited Detroit right before the dedication of the Hall of Fame. During a Tiger home game, manager Del Baker of the home team introduced him to one of his players, Buck Newsom. "How is the bird shooting down there now?" Cobb asked. Newsom, who was from South Carolina, assured him that it was very good. Cobb told of having gone hunting of late "all over Utah, Washington, California and down in Mexico."

The three biographers noted Cobb's late arrival for the dedication, with different emphases, as explored earlier. On a light note, George Kirksey of the United Press wrote, "Ty Cobb came across the continent to learn the truth of the old adage, 'Fame is fleeting.'" Late in the day, at the Hall of Fame game, "he spied Henry Fabian, groundskeeper at the Polo Grounds, lo [sic] these many years, and greeted him cordially. Fabian returned Cobb's greeting without enthusiasm and Ty realized he wasn't recognized.

"You don't know who I am, do you Henry?" Cobb asked.

"No, I don't," replied Fabian.

Moe Berg was watching, and turned to Ty's son Jimmy and said, "I'll bet that's the first time your dad ever had to introduce himself to anybody."

"No it isn't," Jimmy replied. "He had trouble convincing the gatekeeper who he was in order to get in to [sic] the game."

At the game, the NBC Blue radio network interviewed Cobb. Asked to assess the new "rabbit ball," he replied, "I'm not going to make any claims about the superiority of the player of yesteryear."

On the train down to New York City to attend the World's Fair, sports columnist Francis E. Stan of the *Washington Star* was with him as he was "holding forth during the night ride down through the big green hills of upstate New York as the greatest trainload of baseball heroes in history lounged in the club cars and swapped tales and replayed games of yesteryear." At a table in the dining car, Cobb and Walter Johnson "held the center of the stage. He was heavier, to be sure, and balder but the most remarkable part of Cobb always was the look in his eyes and now, at 53 [actually 52], he still has that quick, steely, eager look. It was as if he was sitting there and trying to find a way to steal a base or pull a squeeze play."

Berg joined them at one point and told of a game where Cobb had three or four hits and, in a later at-bat, complained to the umpire about a called strike. Berg recalled telling Cobb that he should not be serious, given all his hits in the game. Then, he recalled, Cobb suddenly looked at him and said something like, "Young fellow, this is how I hit .380." And on the next pitch, Cobb supposedly got a hit.

a scene change on a film with excerpts from the dedication of the National Baseball Hall of Fame

Cobb speaking at the dedication

A number of people came to Cobb to tell him a story with him in it. "Finally, Ty scratched his head. 'There are a lot of old stories,' he admitted, 'but, honestly, some of those about me are exaggerated to beat the band [they are extreme in their detail]. I hear about a time when I walked to first base, stole second while a pitcher held the ball, went to third when he threw it into center field and scored when I drop-kicked the outfielder's throw to the plate into a dugout. But doggone if I remember it.'"

Johnson interjected, "I'm not so sure" and pointed a finger at Cobb "with mock seriousness." Johnson then recalled a game in Washington "when you tried to score and we had you out by 30 feet. You were running toward the plate and Gabby Street, who was catching, had the ball in his glove and was walking up to meet you. Gabby figured you were going to give yourself up and the next thing the Ol' Sarge [Street] knew you had charged at him and kicked at the ball. The ball shot off in one direction and Gabby's glove in another and there he was, standing by himself and looking at his empty hands while you scored a run and beat us out of a ball game."

Johnson had told the story in 1931 in the presence of Street and Alan Gould, sports editor of the AP, at that year's World Series. In a hotel lobby on that occasion, the two former players "fell to reminiscing about Ty Cobb, a mutual rival in the old days, after they had agreed that the young Cardinal outfielder, Pepper Martin, displayed many of the fiery characteristics of the great Georgian. 'I never will forget that day Cobb tore into you coming home,' laughed Johnson. 'You had him out 20 feet, and there was a look of pained surprise when Ty lashed into you instead of taking the putout as most other base runners would have.'

from left to right in 1922: Cobb and Washington's Clyde Milan and Walter Johnson

"You said, 'Hey, what's the idea?' and Ty yelled back, 'What do you think? I'm trying to knock that ball out of your hands!'"

Digressing to more about Cobb and Street:

Upon Street's death in 1951, a former roommate of Street's and Tiger coach under Cobb, George McBride, told *Milwaukee Journal* sportswriter Sam Levy, "We called him Gabby because he was always jabbering on the ball field. He was a tough loser. One afternoon Ty Cobb told Street, whom he liked, 'Gabby, I'll get on base, and then I'll steal second, third and home.' He did."

Levy himself recalled hearing Street at the end of the 1949 season tell two Cobb stories. At the time, Street was a Cardinals radio announcer. Street told his listeners that he had an injured leg one day and that Cobb kept telling him that time was catching up with him. Street challenged Cobb to try to steal second, should he draw a walk. Street enlisted his pitcher's understanding and the pitcher agreed to throw a pitchout on the first ball. Both Cobb and the pitcher played along after a Cobb walk, and Street threw him out by 10 feet.

In the second story, Street told of a play where pitcher Bob Groom struck Cobb out, but Cobb still scored before the next pitch. The third strike was a spitball, and the ball rolled far enough away from Street for Cobb to reach first base. Then he tried to steal second, and the throw got away. Cobb kept running, and the second baseman threw wide to third, allowing Cobb to score.

Returning to coverage of the train ride from Cooperstown:

Also as reported by Stan, a reporter asked Cobb his biggest thrill, and he chose a game where teammate Claude Rossman, an excellent bunter, helped advance Cobb from first to third on a bunt. The game was in New York. After it was over, Cobb went over to the New York clubhouse to use the water keg and heard the voice of its manager, Clark Griffith. "He was bawling out his club and I could hear them mention my name. So I sneaked up and listened and they were saying they were going to get me the next day.

"Back at the hotel I got Rossman and we worked out a new sign. He was to give me the hit-and-run and, instead, he was to bunt again. Well, sure 'nuff, I got on first base again and Rossman flashed the sign and the same thing happened. We licked 'em another game on the play and when we left town Griff's face was purple."

Johnson said Cobb was "just too doggone smart for the rest of us fellows."

Cobb invited Johnson to recall a story of his own, and he told one too.

Arthur Sampson, sports reporter for the *Boston Herald*, also was in the dining car with Cobb, Johnson and Berg and described Cobb's "sharp blue eyes." He reported Cobb's got-the-better-of-Griffith story too, and closed it with Cobb saying "maybe Griff wasn't mad. It was things like that which gave me a big kick out of baseball."

Sampson also related a different recollection of Cobb's: a type of play while he was a base runner at third base. He accustomed rival first baseman Hal Chase, over several games, to watching him closely at that bag when Chase had the ball after a teammate of Cobb made an infield out. Cobb also got Chase used to his feinting as if inclined to make a dash to home plate. But Cobb always went back to third. Cobb said he waited for a truly key situation to finally head straight for home. Chase, accustomed to his returning to third,

ARTHUR SAMPSON
Boston Herald

threw to third, and Cobb easily scored the winning run standing up.

"Imagine waiting nearly a year to pull a play," Berg exclaimed. Then Berg told the story that ended with Cobb's line about hitting .380. (In 1941, Berg would repeat the Cobb-Chase story to the *Christian Science Monitor*.)

In New York City, Cobb told Jesse Abramson of the *New York Herald Tribune* that he decided to "go out at the top," not play in the minor leagues after his big-league days, "when I read that Cy Young, the great Young who had won 511 major league games, had been knocked out by a brewery team in St. Louis."

Pitchers in his day "were all out to get me out," he said as well. "A pitcher would dust you off. If you didn't get your hit that day they would say that's the way to get you out. You had to put the fear into them because they were trying to put the fear into you." Salsinger, echoing Cobb's 1926 "I fought back with my spikes" comment noted early in this book, wrote the following in 1935: "Ty Cobb had a way of taking care of the pitchers who dusted him off. He hit the ball to the right of the first baseman, making sure that he got it out far enough so that the pitcher would have to cover first base. Then Cobb went in, spikes riding high, and the pitcher was very careful not to dust off Cobb the next time he saw him." (In 1949, in evading a question posed at a Lions' Club luncheon in Elko, Nev., about his notoriety as a base runner, he said "some of the players [fielders] took more of the baseline than they were entitled to. If you put the fear of God in them, then you had no more trouble.")

A gentle relationship that Cobb had with a pitcher was with Johnson. A stock story of Cobb's, as told 12 years later to now-sports editor Dyer of the *Los Angeles Times*, was that Johnson "really was tenderhearted and wouldn't think of throwing at a batter. I knew this and took advantage of him by crowding the plate." A year after Dyer, Daley of the *New York Times* in 1952 would write that Cobb had confessed to him a few years earlier that he "took advantage of Walter's gentle nature. I knew he wouldn't bean me, and so I crowded the plate, forcing him to pitch where I wanted him to pitch. Soon I was hitting him as if I owned him."

Returning one more time to Abramson's interview with Cobb in 1939, but only to set off on a long diversion – the interview was that good:

Citing his "flaming truculence," Abramson wrote that Cobb "believes he was a product of his times, and that the ball player of today, mechanically every bit as good, is a product of the present-day farm system and paternal care he is given by coaches, managers and front-office guardians."

Cobb also told him, "The only regret of my baseball career, the only thing left incomplete is that I didn't get to play sooner for Connie Mack [his manager in Philadelphia in 1927 and 1928]. What fineness there is in that man," plus his baseball judgment was always right. In 1930, Mack reportedly told a radio audience that Cobb was the greatest player of all time. "Ty reciprocated by saying that Connie Mack is the world's peerless manager," said a writer, who added, "Usually such expressions of mutual admiration should be taken with a grain of salt, but in this case a majority of fans will probably agree with these distinguished knights of the diamond." In an exclusive to a Chicago reporter in 1954, Mack said, "He could field, run, bat – he could do everything best – he was a real competitor and he gave everything he had." The fielding praise seems overly generous.

Free Press columnist Bingay, in 1945, said Cobb and Mack make a strange pair. He referred to them as "Tyrus[, the] most fierce fighter baseball has ever known and Connie Mack, the saintly peaceful soul who is the closest thing to a Francis of Assisi that the national sport ever has known." Bingay explained Cobb's affection for Mack as follows: "When Ty joined Connie, he had already been so completely molded, Connie was too wise to make him over or to attempt same."

Many paragraphs later, Bingay recalled covering the 1907 season and Cobb asking him to ask then-manager Jennings why Jennings was not giving him any instruction; that happened during spring training, according to Bingay's version in 1933. The answer Jennings supposedly gave is that Cobb's baseball instincts were too good to risk potentially harming by making him play more mechanically. Bingay also wrote, "Hughie's biggest difficulty through that first famous pennant year [1907] was letting Cobb have his head [sic] without interference and at the same time not spoil him by telling him he was too great to need direction." In boldface right after that, he added, "All Jennings ever told him was to use his own judgment. And so it was that there were times when the tempestuous Cobb during play was actually running the ball club!"

Bingay then wrote that when other players protested about the freedom he had given to Cobb, Jennings's "stock answer" was that if they played as well as Cobb, they could be granted such freedom too.

In a long feature on the early Tigers in 1933, Bingay said that while Cobb's first manager in Detroit, Bill Armour, "found it impossible to handle the temperamental Ty Cobb," Jennings "had no trouble at all. He got along with him by letting him strictly alone."

Also in that feature, Bingay recalled the explanation that Jennings had given him – which Cobb had asked Bingay to obtain. An extended quote that Bingay printed from decades earlier is likely not literally accurate. The most interesting line in it to me was Jennings telling Bingay that Cobb "is a law unto himself." The second-most interesting one is that Cobb cannot be taught and needs "to work out his own salvation." Leerhsen captured the essence of the above, without naming Bingay, by noting that Cobb "asked one of the sportswriters to act as a go-between and ask Jennings if there was a problem." Also, Leerhsen, apparently relying on Alexander, cited a "salvation" line uttered by Cobb, as follows: Jennings "allowed me to seek my own salvation in my own way."

Alexander, presumably the original source, had written, "As Cobb phrased it a few years later, Jennings 'allowed [me] to seek my own salvation in my own way.'" Note that "me" is not part of what Cobb literally said. One of the two sources in Alexander's endnotes for that paragraph is a perfect match to the following original. In a long Cobb feature by Batchelor of the *Free Press* in 1912, Cobb said, "I have been treated with the utmost consideration and allowed to seek out my own salvation in my own way."

In conclusion, Bingay wrote that Cobb "blossomed because Jennings knew he was a genius and let him develop himself. Sometimes when he was in one of his temperamental outbursts Jennings handled him as a psychiatrist might a patient. Hughie's idea was always to win ball games, not arguments."

Alexander quoted from a 1955 letter from Cobb to Mack in which he said he was still bitter about Detroit owner Navin from his playing days and, as just noted, that his greatest regret was not playing earlier under Mack. Navin, in Cobb and Stump's book, would be the most criticized person. In reviewing it, Bob Broeg of the *St. Louis Post-Dispatch* would write, "Except for the contempt he felt for Navin, who frustrated Ty, too, by failure to buy players during the six tempestuous seasons Cobb managed the Tigers, the Georgia Peach appeared most eager to be remembered as a kindly old southern gentleman."

George S. Alderton

Alderton of the *Lansing State Journal* attested to Cobb's private criticism of Navin in a column more than a year after publication of the 1961 book. Alderton was cleaning up his house in preparation for a move and found a Cobb letter to him dated February 19, 1927. Cobb had ended his six years as player-manager in 1926. Cobb wrote the letter in response to an Alderton column after being let go as manager. Cobb recalled that prior to taking over, the Tigers had finished in seventh place in the eight-team league. "I finished in the money [fourth place or higher] four years out of the six I managed. Some 20-odd men developed under my management. Not a man was ever purchased who stood out in the league from which he came. [Heinie] Manush was the only outstanding player and we owned him two or three years before he came up. Two years ago I tried to get Mr. Navin to spend some money on some outstanding 4-A [high school] league pitchers, but he was not interested. I knew then I would never be allowed to win a pennant and since that time I have been very unhappy in the management of the club. I had nothing but a developing [rebuilding] job in Detroit. I hope that the team does well for the benefit of the Detroit fans, players, etc. but not for Navin."

In searching for an Alderton column that Cobb plausibly had responded to in the offseason of 1926-27, written days after he was let go, I came up empty. But while coming up short in that respect, I discovered Alderton reprinting some prose in November 1926 that ran in several newspapers in identical form around that time, from an unclear source. The prose referred imprecisely to an incident in the 1910s, when Cobb supposedly sent Navin an ultimatum that either then-captain George Moriarty or he leave the team. "Now after many years Moriarty comes back to take away Ty's job," was the kicker to the item; Moriarty had been named Detroit's new manager for the 1927 season.

Digressing further:

The Cobb biographies say little about Moriarty, who, except for managing the Tigers for 2 years, would be an American League umpire for 22 seasons, starting in 1917 and with a 2-year break in 1927 and 1928.

Leerhsen mentioned Moriarty once, and misspelled his last name as it appears on some cigarette cards as Moriarity. Alexander has a range of detail about Moriarty in colorful game situations and for the progression of his career with the team. Alexander's detail gives a useful sense of the Detroit team being bigger than Cobb. Hornbaker touched on Moriarty in a way that I can weigh in on.

George Moriarty

Moriarty was the team's regular third baseman from 1909 to 1914, except in 1913, when he mostly played first base. Moriarty was still on the roster as of early 1915 when Hornbaker observed that other than 10-plus-year veterans Cobb, Crawford and Moriarty, the team "mainly consisted of talented youngsters." At another point, Hornbaker wrote that beyond Cobb's known physical fights with a few players on his own team or others, "there were many close calls, perhaps a thrown punch here or there, and rumors of clashes with George Moriarty and even Sam Crawford, but nothing demonstrating the fiendish storybook warrior he was made out to be."

Cobb and Moriarty did figure in a "battle royal" late in the 1911 season, according to an unsubstantiated report that December. The result was that Cobb "issued his ultimatum which was that he would not play with the Tigers if Moriarty was on the team, unless Moriarty apologized to him. [Manager] Jennings put the proposition up to Moriarty and ordered the latter to make the apology. Moriarty refused and Jennings at once informed him that he would take steps to get another man in his place." A trade offer then made to Cleveland fell through; so stated the report, which had a Cleveland dateline. Moriarty would play for Detroit through 1914. The December 1911 report also stated, "Moriarty and Cobb started their argument upon the field at Detroit, and followed it up with an angry controversy [sic] at the club office. Finally, Cobb grabbed a bat and threatened to hit the big third baseman. The latter armed himself in a similar manner, and they started to beat each other up. But when about to inflict sundry bruises upon each other's anatomy, club officials and other players interfered and separated the belligerents."

About ten later, Cobb "spiked these rumors himself" while in Detroit with a theater company. He called the story "a fabrication. In the first place I had no grounds for such an action, and in the second place I wouldn't take such a step if I did have. I wouldn't put the Detroit club in a compromising position."

In 1932, umpire Moriarty and four White Sox players were in a fight after a game at Cleveland. Days later, Moriarty reportedly said, "Say anything else you like about me, but don't spread the report that Ty and I fought. We were room mates [sic], and while we may have disagreed we never came to blows." Sam Murphy of the *New York Sun* printed that and wrote unclearly on whether Murphy or someone else followed up Moriarty's comment by speaking to an unnamed "man who knew the circumstances" of their 1911 spat. Murphy conveyed the additional detail as follows:

"Cobb was rather cross one day after a tense ball game. A young clubhouse employee felt the venom of the Georgia Tornado until Moriarty stepped in and suggested to Ty that he might hurt the young man. All het up because his pal checked up on him, Cobb said he would not let any one [sic] from Chicago [a reference to Moriarty's hometown] tell him what to do and he offered to mix it [sic] with Moriarty." Moriarty supposedly responded by saying that Cobb could try to swing at him with four or five bats that were in a nearby locker, and that otherwise Cobb would be operating under a handicap. "Ty saw the situation and just laughed. That was as near as they came to a spat."

To contradict Leerhsen's statement that Cobb did not have roommates from 1912 on, along with any specifics that I found:

Moriarty was one for a time between 1909 and 1915, possibly after 1912.

Frank Walker played on Detroit for the entire 1918 season and briefly in 1917. Upon Cobb's death, Walker was quoted in an AP feature as having "roomed on road trips with Cobb from 1914-16." The years are obviously wrong, although the underlying detail may be true, as there is a second source for it. Walker had a long baseball association with Rocky Mount, N.C., and Negro League star Buck Leonard played for a semi-pro team there. In a 1970 article with black baseball author John Holway, Leonard said Walker had told him that he had roomed with Cobb in 1915 and 1916. Walker's big-league career did not begin until 1917.

A definite roommate was Del Baker. On a 1939 visit to Detroit, Cobb and Baker spoke about when "they played for Hugh Ambrose Jennings and roomed together on the road," conveyed sports reporter Sam Greene of the *Detroit News*. Baker played his entire major league career with the Tigers, from 1914 to 1916. Another roommate, to be featured later, is Harry Tuthill, the Detroit trainer from 1908 through 1919, who also gave Cobb boxing lessons. On a 1942 visit to Detroit, Cobb told sports columnist Charles P. Ward of the *Free Press*, "I made it a point to room with him when we were traveling and we passed our spare time in fighting wordy battles."

Cobb said he liked rooming with Tuthill "because I liked to get to bed early and keep in shape. He kept away people who might have kept me awake. But he was great company. He had trained several great fighters and the Army and [University of] Michigan football teams as well as the Tigers. And naturally he had a thousand stories to tell. He could tell them, too, and I loved to get him started, especially when I couldn't fall asleep. I'd let him talk me to sleep."

For example, he might ask Tuthill about a referee, Eddie Graney, who gave a Tuthill trainee, "Young" Corbett, of no relation to former heavyweight boxing champion James "Jim" Corbett, a raw deal in a fight. "That would start him off on a denunciation. I'd let him go until I was about to drop off to slumber. Then I'd yawn 'Harry, why don't you shut up?' Then I'd get it." [sic]

Cobb told Ward about another method of his to arouse Tuthill's ire. Ward related, "Early he discovered that while Tuthill was fond of a certain brand of little cigar, he could not tolerate cigaret [sic] smoke in the morning. So Cobb always kept a pack of cigarets on his person. When he arose before Tuthill, he would light a cigaret and then put it out. While it was still smoking he would put it in an ash tray [sic] and the tray under the trainer's bed."

"'In five minutes,' he laughed, 'I'd not only have Harry awake but also everybody else within a block of the hotel. Yes, Old Harry was a grand character.'"

Al Simmons was a roommate in Philadelphia, in 1927 and/or 1928.

One postscript about Tuthill is that the *Free Press* contacted him after Moriarty's fight in 1932 with White Sox players. After all, Tuthill had been the trainer during a big chunk of Moriarty's Detroit career. Tuthill was now the co-owner of an athletic club in Detroit. In the presence of a reporter, Tuthill was asked by co-owner Archie Sillman if "Mory" was really tough. He replied, "Well, he [Moriarty] was the only guy I ever knew that Ty Cobb wouldn't argue with. Ty argued with him once. He bawled him out. Said a lot of nasty things and Mory just sat in the clubhouse with his head in his hands until Ty got through. We all thought he was crying. But when Ty stopped for breath,

Mory looked up and said, 'Well, you so and so, are you all through talking?'"

Then Moriarty told Cobb to take off his coat and said he would beat the hell out of him. Cobb backed down, and Moriarty told him that instead he would do something to him with a knife and a gun. From then on, Cobb refrained from arguing with him. That was the end of Tuthill's story.

As far as Cobb's larger salary and the special treatment he received:

I found Crawford being interviewed about that in 1917, just as his own big-

from left to right in 1958 at Briggs Stadium in Detroit: Mickey Cochrane, Cobb, Steve O'Neill and former Cobb roommates George Moriarty and Del Baker. When O'Neill began his managerial career, in 1936 with Cleveland, Cobb wrote to him, in part, "I always felt closer to the player who fought and hustled and was free from petty disgruntled ways. Believe me, you were of my type. You will notice that such a player always receives his reward in time. Good luck, Steve. I'm pulling for you."

league career ended. Crawford was from Nebraska, and he told sports editor Sandy Griswold of the *Omaha-World Herald*, "I was in disfavor with Ty Cobb, the autocrat of the Detroit team, and that settled it. No player, not in this fellow's good graces, has a chance up there, and as great a player as he is, he is a hurtful and dangerous quantity to the game. But that is neither here nor there. Jennings thought that he would save the club one year of my salary by putting me on the bench – thought I'd get out, when I realized that I couldn't play, but I fooled him."

Besides Crawford and Moriarty, another relationship with a notable player that has been written widely about is the one with Charley Gehringer. Alexander's book cited Gehringer's recollection in Donald Honig's 1975 book *Baseball When the Grass Was Real*. A big chunk of Alexander's quotation from it was, "But he was tough to play for. Very demanding. He was so great himself that he couldn't understand why if he told players how to do certain things, they couldn't do it as well as he did." Leerhsen cited a different Gehringer interview, Bak's one in his 1991 book. I can add that in 1939, Alderton of the *Lansing State Journal* wrote, "There never was any love lost between Charley Gehringer and Ty Cobb. Both of them have admitted it." Also, in his 1985 interview with Kram of the *Detroit Free Press*, Gehringer said, "Cobb had a short fuse. Off the field he could be a gracious gentleman, but he had a hard edge. I guess he was typical in some respects of the player of that period. Players have changed."

from left to right in 1934: coach Cy Perkins (tells a Cobb story on pages 321-22), Cochrane, Cobb and Charley Gehringer

Finally returning to the chronology, which was in 1939:

After going to the dedication of the Hall of Fame, Cobb was in New York City for a few days to attend the World's Fair. As conveyed by the *Brooklyn Eagle*, he told a story "that dated back to his palmy days with the Tigers, when Hughey Jennings was managing the club."

Cobb began, "There was a young pitcher bothering Jennings for a tryout one Spring in the South, and the kid was very persistent. Trying to sell himself to Hughey, he kept saying: 'Why, Ty Cobb wouldn't get a foul off my stuff.'

"Finally, one day Jennings, out of pure exasperation, told the kid to put on a suit and warm up. I was about to hit in practice when Hughey put the youngster in the box. 'There's Cobb,' he shouted, 'see what you can do with him.'"

According to the *Eagle*, "The Georgia Peach went on, grinning, 'The kid wound up elaborately, the ball came up there as big as a grapefruit, and I smacked it over the fence. The next pitch came up the same way – he didn't have a thing on the ball – and I nearly tore his left ear off with a line drive.'

"After practice was over, Jennings walked up to the kid in the dressing-room. 'What have you got to say for yourself now? Still think Cobb can't hit you?'

"'Aw,' said the kid, 'I don't believe that was Cobb.'"

A postscript on 1938 and 1939 is that Cobb exchanged letters in those years with Hall of Fame museum planner Alexander Cleland, to coordinate its Cobb memorabilia holdings and plaque in his honor. Hall origins author James A. Vlasich summarized six letters, three each by Cobb and Cleland, plus a pair of letters exchanged by Cleland with ex-*Cleveland Plain Dealer* sports editor Henry

P. Edwards, manager of the American League Service Bureau, the press office of the American League. Vlasich did not include any direct quotes from Cobb. Fortunately, Sotheby's auctioned Cobb's three letters in 2007, and its synopsis, which I have in turn summarized, has quite a number of quotes:

In a 1938 letter, Cobb started out by stating that perhaps he owned "nothing that would be fitting to place in a museum." Then he complained that he had "never received an official and formal notification or been advised of a general plan of this museum." He went on to state, "I had hoped there would be an official opening so I could attend."

In his next letter to Cobb, Cleland sent him details in various formats, including a booklet, and Cobb mailed by parcel post "the best of what I have left of baseball mementos." They were: "something from my Detroit days, a sweater jacket shirt, and pants and stockings from the Philadelphia Athletics, and a pair of shoes, and sliding pads I used for many years."

Cobb then pointed out to Cleland two mistakes on the proposed plaque. One was that it listed his base hit total as being 4025 when it "should be 4191!" The other was its stating that his major league baseball career spanned 1904 to 1930; it had been 1905 to 1928. Cobb said "any one mistake rather discredits the proposition as a whole!" In a happier letter in 1939, a short one that I saw in full, Cobb said he had mailed a game-used bat.

Cobb's pair of shoes, spikes, were first displayed at the World's Fair, in its Academy of Sport exhibit. Cobb attended a private preview, with New York City Mayor James John "Jimmy" Walker serving as the master of ceremonies.

Christy Walsh, for whom Cobb had written his syndicated life story in the mid-1920s, was in charge of the sports exhibition at the fair. At the preview, Walsh "drew a broad smile from Cobb when he exhibited a pair of old baseball shoes with the explanation: – 'These are the ones Ty wore when he stole all those bases,'" wrote James A. Burchard in the *New York World-Telegram*.

from left to right at the 1939 World's Fair: Christy Walsh, Mayor Walker (holding Ruth's "King of Swat" crown), Ruth, Vera Stanwood (widow of boxer James "Jim" Corbett) and Cobb (holding his spikes)

Introductions were made from the speakers' rostrum. "Cobb, holding the cleated shoes in which he made his [all-time] stolen base record, first shook hands with Babe Ruth and then said he was proud to have been honored on the speakers' platform. Ruth brought along his silver baseball bat and silver 'best player' crown, as well as a few gracefully phrased remarks for the delectation of the visitors," wrote Fred Hawthorne of the *New York Herald Tribune*.

During the visit to New York, Cobb told Considine of the International News Service, "If I were playing today I wouldn't be stealing all those bases, and doing anything to get on base, or trying to punch a single through those infielders. I'd be out there like the rest of them – swinging for the fence." He recalled that with nine home runs, he led the American League in that category. That said, in the year that he did, 1909, all nine were inside-the-park ones.

Two weeks later, the NEA would quote Cobb as having said the following about why he would not be trying hard to steal bases today: "Why take the risk of stealing when any of the next four guys behind you is capable of hitting a homer?" (Upon Cobb's death, sports editor Gene Levy of the *Oneonta Star*, who had met him the prior summer in Cooperstown, would interview Sid C. Keener, a longtime sports editor who was now director of the Hall of Fame. Keener recalled Cobb on that final visit leaning against a case in which his old sliding pads were exhibited and saying, "They're a lot of sissies." That was in reference to current players, for seldom trying to steal a base.)

In 1940:

For the first round of the Bing Crosby Pro-Amateur, he was teamed with "Benny Hogan, the ex-Fort Worth, Tex., pro now from White Plains, N. Y." Coincidentally, Hogan, who turned pro in 1930, would win as an individual on the professional tour for the first time later in 1940 on the way to four wins that year. At the first tee on a practice round, veteran California tournament announcer D. Scott "Scotty" Chisolm declared, "And now I'd like to present America's baseball idol of all time – the one and only Tyrus Raymond Cobb –

come out, Ty." Cobb had been out of view, behind a post, and was "embarrassed as a kid with a patch in his pants." He "edged out by the kilt-costumed Scotty [Chisolm] as if it might be his first public appearance, bowed, chewed furiously on a long, unlighted cigar, and promptly faded back into the crowd."

Digressing to two postscripts related to Hogan and Cobb:

In a golf articles series in 1949, Hogan would quote Cobb as having said that in baseball, "One of the chief faults in hitting is over-eagerness or over-anxiety. This makes you throw your weight too soon. As you step into the ball your hands and body must be working together." Cobb, Hogan wrote, experiences the same thing on the golf course, and

at a baseball players' tournament in 1939 at Millbrae, Calif.

Cobb's knowledge of leverage and timing "makes him recognize the fault and correct it faster than an ordinary golfer would be able to do." Hogan garbled a different baseball point that Cobb had made, about having the manager or teammates keep tabs on your swing when you are hitting well. That way, when things go badly at the plate for you, others can help detect your problem.

In 1957, sports editor Al Warden of the *Ogden Standard-Examiner* in Utah would write that long ago, Cobb offered Hogan the following advice: "Take two scotch and waters before retiring [going to bed], and you'll never crack up."

Returning to 1940:

A movie short was filmed based on that tournament, Crosby's "Swing With Bing." The tournament took place at the Rancho Santa Fe course in Del Mar, and the short is accessible on YouTube. In the film, as can be seen on the next page, Cobb posed with Crosby, Chisolm and fiction writer Clarence Budington "Bud" Kelland before a new scene began. In that next scene, actor Andy Devine gave a baseball-like play-by-play of Cobb preparing to tee off at a hole and then doing so. Chisolm did his driving right after Cobb, with his ball hardly moving. As they walked off the tee, Cobb patted Chisolm on the back as if consoling him.

COBB TURNS TO GOLF ... Ty Cobb, greatest of baseball players, turns to competitive golf in Bing Crosby invitational tournament at Del Mar, Calif.

at the Bing Crosby Pro-Am

In a locker room interview in March in St. Petersburg, Fla., DiMaggio told Considine, "I see a lot of Ty in the off season.

He comes to my joint [family restaurant in San Francisco] and I just sit there and listen to him. What a man he is. I just keep my trap shut and listen. 'Anyway,' Joe said, finding his 'part' and slicking the hair back, 'Ty thinks I'll hit .400 this year. He lost a bet on me last year. He figured that last year would be the year I'd hit it, but I let him down at the end of the season. He gave me a talking-to about it, but he said that this would be the year.'"

DiMaggio also told Considine, "Ty's made it possible for me to take a lot of short cuts. Every time I see him I pick up something – something I might never have thought about. For instance this past winter he told me the way he used to break his batting slumps, and I'm going to try it this year, if I get in one." Cobb's idea was if in a slump, to have a batting practice pitcher throw to him from consecutively farther distances from the plate. To demonstrate Cobb's point, DiMaggio used his comb as a bat.

Also, "I'm doing more running this season than ever before, because Ty suggested it." According to Considine, while saying that, DiMaggio "went on, sitting down on the edge of one of the big Yankee uniform trunks and lighting a cigaret." [sic]

What's more, "I'm cutting down on my practicing before games, too. Cobb told me he never used to work out much before a game, and that's how he saved his strength for those tough days in the middle of summer. Golly, when I first came up [to the major leagues] I used to run myself ragged, shagging flies before the game. I asked [manager Joe] McCarthy if it would be all right with him, if I did like Ty used to, and he said okay."

(In 1937, DiMaggio had told Dan Daniel of the *New York World-Telegram*, "Cobb wised me up to another trick. He told me that after August 1 a good outfielder is crazy to spend fifteen minutes shagging flies. He said to me, 'Joe, the trick of conserving your energy and pacing yourself is one of the most important things a young fellow has to master. Don't spend your hitting energy chasing flies. Grab a few [meaning five minutes' worth, DiMaggio would tell Frank Reil of the *Brooklyn Eagle* two days later] and then sit down in a cool, shady spot. The flies you catch in practice never show in the records or the salary, because the fans don't pay to see that sort of thing.'" That and a second point in Daniel's article was alluded to by DiMaggio biographer Richard Ben Cramer and echoed by Leerhsen: DiMaggio had accepted Cobb's advice and was planning to use a lighter bat in the last months of the season.

The oldest Cobb-helping-DiMaggio report that I found is from 1935. *Chicago Tribune* sports editor Ward wrote that Cobb was credited with curing DiMaggio's injured knee.)

Returning again to 1940:

In *Look* magazine, Henry McLemore of the United Press did a pictorial feature, "Ty Cobb Picks Baseball's Fightin'est Team." A chunk of it, including the line, "We used to argue whether tobacco juice or raw whisky was better for a spike cut," appears in Cobb's 1961 book without reference to its origin in 1940. The article concludes with, "As for me, the way baseball is played today, I'll take fishing. A fish at least will always fight until you have landed him."

A few weeks later, then-gossip columnist and future well-known broadcast personality Ed Sullivan wrote that Cobb's "gruffness" was legendary at the peak of his playing career. He had been sent to interview Cobb at the Hotel Almanac in New York City and learned that he was having dinner. "Fearfully, I sent in a message to him explaining that the boss had given an assignment." He added, "Napkin in hand, Cobb came to the dining room entrance immediately and proved the most charming person and most helpful person I'd ever met." In

Collier's in 1956, Sullivan would write that on a particular occasion, Cobb "left a dinner table to chat with this unknown young writer. 'Incidentally, for your women readers, I'll give you a diet tip,' Cobb concluded. 'I use it all the time. Before dinner, tell them to drink a glass of buttermilk. It cuts down your appetite.'" As noted earlier, in a possibly ghostwritten article in 1913, he had endorsed buttermilk for ballplayers because it seems to clear one's eyes.

In July, Cobb wrote to Hyman Pearlstone, a huge baseball fan whom he had known for decades. Cobb told of having just returned from Twin Falls "where I had some wonderful trout

from left to right: Bob Hope, Yankees co-owner Delbert "Del" Webb and Ed Sullivan

fishing with my children." Also, "I have bought a Coca Cola plant and franchise at Twin Falls for my two sons." He alluded to the hot temperature on a recent visit to Los Angeles, where Pearlstone currently was, saying that he seldom goes there in the summer and does so in the winter.

Also that month, sports columnist J. Roy Stockton of the *St. Louis Post-Dispatch* wrote that DiMaggio, "taciturn and usually not inclined to look for or consider advice, is doing many of the things Cobb suggested to him during conversations on the [West] coast. Cobb was a great believer in the value of relaxing. He told DiMaggio not to hurry from the clubhouse after a game, to be the last one to leave. And DiMaggio follows the Cobb formula. He changes clothes leisurely, smokes a cigarette before his shower, [c]ools off slowly after the shower and then after quitting the clubhouse, he postpones dinner until he has had more time to relax."

Digressing to the play that DiMaggio's taking of Cobb's advice would get:

In a sidebar in his *Sporting News* serial on Cobb in 1950, Harry G. Salsinger would echo what Stockton wrote. That could have inspired the following dramatized rehash of how Cobb advised DiMaggio on the subject.

Writing in *Sport* magazine in 1951, Frank Graham of the *New York Journal-American* told of having spoken to Cobb in four different cities and once on a train ride from Cooperstown. Graham rehashed a few stories that Cobb had told him. Here is one with DiMaggio in its entirety:

Now it was in New York. A day at the Yankee Stadium in the Yankees' clubhouse a little while before game time. Another fellow listening. This one, Joe DiMaggio.

'What do you do right after a ball game, Joe?' Ty asked.

Joe looked at him, a little surprised.

'What else?' he said. 'Take a shower, get dressed, and go down to the hotel.'

Ty nodded.

'Like that,' he [Cobb] said. 'Take a shower, get dressed, and go down to the hotel.'

'Sure,' Joe said, laughing. 'Then I have dinner.'

'You should have said that in the first place,' Ty said. 'In other words, you run into the shower, run out, get dressed, run down to the hotel and have dinner. Is that right?'

from left to right: Frank Graham, Grantland Rice and, yet to appear in this book, Red Smith

'Yes,' Joe said. 'There's nothing going on around here after the ball game and I'm hungry. What's wrong with that?'

'This,' Ty said. 'A ballplayer is on the field only so many hours. Most of his time is spent away from the field. Those are hours in which he stays healthy – or doesn't. Don't get me wrong. I'm not preaching. I'm only telling you.'

Now he was talking to one of his all-time favorite guys, a guy who practically worships him, a guy who grew up wanting to be like him, a guy who, when he was younger and with the San Francisco Seals, had been grateful for Cobb's interest in him. A guy who always had listened to him attentively, and who, sitting on a rubbing table in the Yankees' clubhouse, was listening to him now.

'Joe,' Ty said, 'because you play ball every day, you don't realize the strain it puts on your nervous system. But it's there. It's in your head and in your stomach. If you don't check it, it can take years off your life as a big-league ballplayer. All the things I've ever told you – and what I'm telling you now – I had to learn the hard way. Such as what to do after a ball game.

'When you get in here after a game, you're all sweated up. Sit down – in your uniform. Sit down and smoke a cigarette if you want to. Have a cup of coffee if that's what you want. Let the other fellows run into the shower. Let them take as long as they please. No matter how long they take – and they won't take long – there'll always be soap and water left. When they're all through, you'll be dried out. Then you take your shower. After your shower, sit down or lie down and cool out. Then get dressed and go down to your hotel. But don't go to the dining room. Go to your own room. Read the papers or listen to the

radio or look out the window for an hour. By that time, your stomach is ready for food. Keep doing this and you won't suffer from colds or nervous indigestion.'

Well, there you are. Little pieces out of the making of a great career by a fellow who had too much spirit and too much guts to allow himself to be ordinary.

Returning a third time to 1940 and Stockton's column in the *Post-Dispatch*:

His column that day was devoted to Cobb in various respects: the St. Louis hook was that Browns manager Fred Haney had played under Cobb in the 1920s and was a huge admirer. In the offseason of 1938-39, after Haney had been named manager, Cobb mailed him advice on how to get along with his players and his superiors. In his column, Stockton wrote that in advance of a Browns home game and in the presence of some out-of-town reporters, Haney made Cobb-like observations, about players who hit singles to help win games. That reminded one of them of Cobb's formula for getting out of batting slumps. Stockton related this part of a reporters' fanning bee that ensued:

"Somebody remarked that they didn't know any other batter who held his bat exactly as Cobb did. There was a sizeable space between his hands as Ty gripped his bat and he explained that you could control a club better that way. He would ask you if you had a long pole in your hands, if you could control it better with hands close together, or farther apart."

One of the reporters, unnamed, said, "I'll never forget an exhibition he gave during batting practice while he was with the Athletics. Urban Shocker was with the Yankees then and he was riding Cobb good naturedly from the dugout. He yelled at Ty to hit one to right and Ty obliged with one down the foul line. Then he asked Cobb to hit to left and Ty complied. Ty hit one to center, too, on request and then Shocker called to him to hit one into the dugout. Cobb did exactly that, pulling the ball foul with the accuracy you'd expect from a man with a tennis racquet. And then, not on request, Cobb caromed a foul into the Yankee dugout and Shocker had to dodge to avoid being hit. Yes, Cobb could do more tricks with that bat than any other man I ever saw."

(An earlier story with a light, similar-sounding tone was told in 1925 by *Atlanta Constitution* photographer-reporter Mathewson. He recalled covering Detroit's spring training in San Antonio in 1921. After a game, Mathewson could not find Cobb and no one he asked knew where he was. "About 30 minutes later he was found back of the stands with a bunch of ragged urchins [boys], teaching them the correct way to handle a bat and throw a ball.")

In October, he began a five-week hunting trip in Idaho – which I gleaned from an autographed photo request letter from a Stanley Gray of Pasadena. Otherwise, Cobb replied with batting advice, as Gray had requested.

In 1941:

In January, McLemore of the United Press did a feature on his baseball views. To offset the lively ball, Cobb was now urging that home plate, and thus the strike zone, be widened a few inches. Bernie Boland, a 1915-to-1920 teammate, reacted by telling the INS about tricks that Cobb did in his playing days in the other direction. "'Cobb in his old age wants things the other way around,' began Boland. 'He was a great hitter and tough on pitchers, of course, but some of the things he did hurt his own pitchers.'" For example, Detroit's grounds had a flat pitching mound while "Cobb used to go out to the ball park in the morning with the ground keeper and they'd build up home plate." Also, "he'd be out to the park early and he'd soak the baseline 10 feet from home plate with water. The third baseman would have a devil of a time then trying to stand up on the slippery ground handling a bunt."

Gene Fowler as of 1949. Fowler was the 1924 *New York Mirror*'s inaugural sports editor, and a colleague of Maines in 1925-26 when Maines was the *Mirror*'s promotions/circulation manager. Fowler in 1957 sent Maines the autographed copy of his 1924 article that is shown on page 156. Cobb's daughter Shirley told author Rhodes that Fowler, a noted screenplay writer and book author in later decades, was someone who her dad had wanted to write his 1961 book, but that Fowler by that time was dying of cancer.

In April, Cobb, former teammate Ossie Vitt and DiMaggio were at a banquet in San Francisco. "After the banquet they got to chinning and Cobb grabbed a broom and started to show DiMaggio how to hit. 'I wasn't going to let Cobb get away with that,' Vitt said. 'So I took the broom and gave DiMaggio some tips. Imagine me with my [.]220 [lifetime batting average] stance! Naturally DiMaggio paid more attention to Cobb than me.'"

A couple of weeks earlier, syndicated columnist Leonard Lyons reported that former sports journalist-turned-screenplay writer Gene Fowler "has recovered from injuries he sustained when a car, driven by [Academy Award-winning director, for the 1937 'The Awful Truth' and winner-to-be in 1944 for 'Going My Way,'] Leo McCarey, cracked up in a collision. Fowler confesses that he has driven with what he regards [as] the three worst drivers in the world – Ty Cobb, Barney Oldfield and Leo McCarey."

"'Cobb's a bad driver,' Fowler explained, 'because he's always turning around to the man in the back seat, and telling just how he stole home, from second base. And Barney Oldfield's the only man I ever rode with who hit a plane flying overhead.'"

Auto racing legend Oldfield, as explained in a 1962 article, "was an extraordinarily bad driver in city traffic. One day in Los Angeles he hit an immense street-paving steamroller that was standing still." McCarey suffered extensive injuries in a car accident in 1939 and later was arrested for drunk driving, in 1945. Cobb himself had made drive safely remarks in 1923, at Detroit City Hall, on day six of Detroit's safety week. The one given the most prominence by the *Free Press* was: "Be as careful of your neighbors' children as you would want your neighbor to be of yours, when driving a car."

A suit for 15 cents, about $2.50 in today's dollars, was filed against him in Palo Alto, Calif. "Cobb contended the charge was unjustified and wouldn't pay it," the AP reported. "Arnold ['Parkey'] Sharkey, operator of the lot, had to pay $1.50 costs to file the suit. His point was that Cobb owed the 15 cents and he was going to force him to pay it. The argument started Friday night. Cobb parked his car while Sharkey was absent. When he returned for [sic] the machine, Sharkey requested payment. They couldn't agree, nor could a policeman who was called in as an arbitrator."

Cobb settled the case and paid Sharkey's filing fee. In a convoluted way, the AP paraphrased Cobb as saying that the dispute arose "because he didn't know a man who demanded the sum as a parking lot charge."

I found the article before noticing that Sharkey is in the Cobb-Stump book. Cobb and Stump are clearly right in calling him a "professional picket;" Rosenbaum of the *Chronicle* used "picketed" in a 1949 feature on him. A minor detail in the book that I could not confirm is whether, besides filing suit, Sharkey wrote a letter to newspapers to complain; as is noted below, he was a prolific letter writer.

In reporting Sharkey's funeral in 1969 in Redwood City, Calif., the AP would say, "Unsuccessful as a professional heavyweight boxer, he turned his experiences into a night club comedy act and later wrote two books [more like pamphlets]: 'Whiskey Road' and 'The Rape of California – Destroyed by Progress.'" The latter, actually titled "The Rape and Destruction of California by Progress," can be found in two University of California libraries, as well as in the Santa Clara County library system. Whiskey Road has showed up on eBay this decade; a *Los Angeles Times* local history blog called it a pamphlet and said much of it consists of Sharkey's letters to *Times* columnist and television commentator Paul V. Coates.

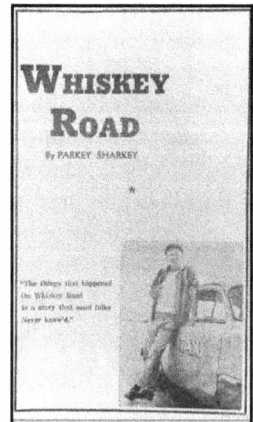

Incidentally, also in the funeral story is that actress Greer Garson once offered Sharkey a movie part, "but that career ended when he refused to memorize lines." In an epitath, the AP said, "He was a cab driver, author, boxer and would[-]be actor who once won a 15-cent court case from baseball's Ty Cobb."

That summer, as has even been the main subject of a book, the 2007 one alluded to earlier by Tom Stanton, Cobb beat Ruth in a three-city charity golf match. I can make three additions that relate to Cobb's preparation for it:

Considine told of a Cobb letter to someone in the East in which he asked "a dozen pertinent questions about Babe's game – his handicap, his condition, etc., etc., and insisted that a neutral course be chosen." Considine then observed, "Ty's old will-to-win flame never dies."

That someone may have been Brookline, Mass., friend Hayward "Tom" Binney. In a letter to Binney, Cobb wrote, "If any chance find out how Babe is playing now[,] get some official scores, think he belongs to Winged Foot [Golf Club in Mamaroneck, N.Y.,] also he lives at 173 Riverside Drive, N.Y.[,] let me know at once if you can get dope." Binney, a former semi-pro player, got to

know Ruth while hanging out in his teens at the Boston major league ballparks. In 1917, after Binney filled in one day at third base for batting practice, Ruth supposedly invited him to play in an exhibition game the next day, which he did.

In Boston, Sampson of the *Boston Herald* was with former Detroit teammate Joe Casey when they dropped in on Cobb at the Ritz-Carlton after a practice round. At one point,

Babe Ruth-Ty Cobb
CHARITY GOLF MATCH

Commonwealth Country Club
CHESTNUT HILL, MASSACHUSETTS
Wednesday, June 25 1941
2:30 p.m.

Match arranged by Bill Cunningham
and sponsored by
New England Association of
LEFT-HANDED GOLFERS
for benefit of
The Golden Rule Farm
New England's Boys' Town, Franklin, N.H.

Admission $1.00
Please observe all the obviously necessary grand rules.

Bill Cunningham is noted above for arranging the Boston leg

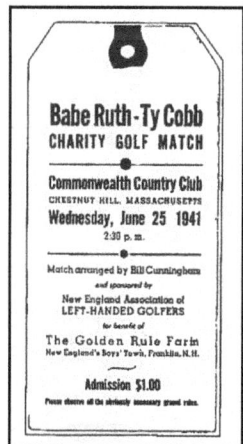

RUTH ON SPOT IN GOLF MEETING WITH TY COBB

Bambino Must Win or Admit His Rival is Better Man—Ty Says He Has Psychological Edge

Makes 4 Homers In Double-Header

Lenoir, N. C., June 27.—(AP)— Beattie Feathers, one time all-American football player at the University of Tennessee, hit four home runs as Lenoir while changing his clothes, Cobb dropped a piece of paper. In picking it up, he said, "I can't afford to mislay that. Those are some notes that I made during my practice round this afternoon. I've got to study them tonight." The notes, as far as Sampson could tell, related only to the course itself. It was presumably Sampson who then asked Cobb if he had any wisecracks prepared to try to unnerve Ruth. "I won't need any prepared list of ribs for a guy like Ruth," Cobb laughed. "I'll be able to think of plenty of things to burn him up by just looking at him."

One of charity match organizer Corcoran's stories from the eve of the match, Cobb imbibing lots of beer at Toots Shor's, was noted earlier. Another is from their train ride to Boston. "The train arrived in Boston at dawn, but it was customary to let the patrons of the sleeping cars snooze until seven A.M. when the porter made the rounds, routing people out. Cobb and I had opposite lower berths, and I was awakened by the most awful commotion in the aisle. I poked my head through the curtains to see Ty in his BVD's [underwear], his spike-scarred legs churning, as he chased the poor porter out of the car. He turned back, his face flushed and angry, and saw me. 'Nobody puts his hands on me,' he snorted."

Cobb, Ruth and Speaker at the Annual Amateur Day in Cleveland Stadium in July 1941

In late July, Cobb defeated Ruth in Detroit, to win the three-city match, two cities to one. The day of his win, Cobb told the *Free Press* that Palo Alto, close to his home, is delightful. "Best of hunting and fishing within a few minutes of my door. Fine golf courses. Five major football teams right around my place. Baseball in San Francisco. There's a town – an air conditioned town."

In predicting the Yankees' victory over Brooklyn in the World Series, Cobb said, "The Yankees will play level-headed baseball. Not the harem-scarem kind the Dodgers do. Why, that [Dodgers player-manager] Durocher is liable to blow his topper any moment. That will get you just nowhere in a world series."

In 1942:

He was fined $100, about $1,700 in today's dollars, for killing a deer in Idaho without a proper hunting license. To have been legal, he would have needed to establish voting residence first, the AP reported.

He became president of a new group, the Northern California Lefthanded Golfers Association. He

also in Cleveland in 1941

had played in 1941 in a lefties-only tournament in a neighborhood of Pasadena.

Jack Troy of the *Atlanta Constitution* wrote, "Just as [Giants general manager Bill] Terry enjoys unpopularity, so does Ty Cobb in popular opinion. He has been pictured as one of the meanest individuals who ever lived. Dickens' Scrooge appears as a benefactor of mankind beside him." Days later, *Omaha World-Herald* sports editor Frederick Ware called Cobb "one of the orneriest cusses ever to brandish a bat at a human skull, or flash his spikes at a baseman." He also noted that Cobb was named the greatest player of all-time in a recent *Sporting News* poll of 102 former players and past and present managers. Honus Wagner came in a distant second and Ruth

Cobb and Bill Terry, now a hugely successful car dealer, in 1957

was third. Ware added, "I'd have voted for Tyrus too. I'd have voted several times if I could have got [sic] away with it."

Syndicated columnist E.V. Durling likened Cobb to General Douglas MacArthur, who would write the foreword to the 1961 book. "Ty Cobb always had the opposition jittery. Even the most experienced men of the opposition. Why? Nobody ever knew what Ty was going to do next. General MacArthur fights the same way Cobb played ball. He has the Japs jittery. They don't know whether MacArthur is going to bomb Tokyo, attack Manila Bay or go after Singapore. MacArthur should be named commander of the entire United Nations war effort. That would make [Adolf] Hitler jittery. MacArthur is the only enemy general der fuehrer ever mentioned in a speech since the war began. 'Last Ditch Mac' is already under Adolf's skin a little."

Cobb was in Greenville, S.C., just as Durling was writing that. He had traveled there from Detroit, where the apparent one non-war story worth noting is that he gave batting lessons to two of DiMaggio's teammates, Charley Keller and Red Rolfe.

In Greenville, the World War I veteran said that while in Detroit he "wanted to inspect the new bomber plants and other war production factories." According to Latimer, Cobb "said it was a revelation defying all imagination, to see the stuff rolling out of some of the Detroit plants for the Allied effort to crush the Axis powers. 'And I begin to think we'll have the stuff with which we might end the war quickly,' he added. 'The most planes, informed observers said, Germany ever sent over Britain at one time numbered 500, and I rather believe when the Allies start sending 2,000 or more at a time over Germany the nazis [sic] will crack. The German army may not be thoroughly whipped until the people's morale in Germany cracks. I think a few raids by 2,000 planes daily will do the cracking.'"

Greenville was the longtime home of great hitter "Shoeless" Joe Jackson, who, as noted earlier, Commissioner Landis banned from baseball for allegedly conspiring to throw the 1919 World Series. Leerhsen became the latest author to recite the same years-later story from Grantland Rice. In it, Cobb and possibly Rice show up one day in Greenville at Jackson's small liquor store. When Cobb goes over to Jackson, Jackson sheepishly acts as if unsure whether Cobb wants to see him. Leerhsen's version, in wording and length, closely tracks the one in Rice's 1954 book *The Tumult and the Shouting*. It appears somewhat differently in Cobb's 1961 book, and I could not tell if Cobb wanted it added in.

A few dozen Stump forgeries of Cobb's handwriting survive. The writing is on images or copies of pages of other books where Cobb was supposedly guiding Stump on what to include in theirs. One of the forged signatures, which appears earlier on page 12, was written onto an inside title page of Rice's 1954 book urging that a different story be extracted from it. That story involved Cobb at a young age sending multiple anonymous letters to Rice at the *Atlanta Journal*, to drum up interest in himself. Nothing can be deduced from Stump's forgery of Cobb on a page of Rice's book, as far as the accuracy of the Jackson liquor store story. This just happens to be a convenient place to mention the forgeries.

According to Rice, the episode with Jackson and Cobb, with him as an observer, occurred in 1947. There is one tiny problem. Latimer was keeping tabs on Cobb's comings and goings from Greenville. In 1942, he wrote after one of Cobb's visits that "Jackson's is still a big-time name in baseball history and whenever an old player comes to Greenville he never fails to stop by for a friendly visit. . . [sic] Joe said Ty Cobb called on him the other day and they chatted for about a half hour."

One way to counter both Leerhsen and Rice – Alexander's book contains this tale as well – would be to figure out where Rice might have been leading up to Cobb's visit in 1942. Prior to it, his last non-New York byline was nearly a month earlier, when he covered the Preakness Stakes horse race in Baltimore.

In text that accompanies Latimer's long World War II piece above, Latimer stated that when Cobb goes back to California, he can often be found "on the Golden Gate golf courses with his old friend, Grantland Rice." I did find Rice and Cobb golfing together in California, at the Lakeside Golf Club in Los Angeles, where Rice was a member.

I also looked for a Rice column with the anecdote prior to his book and found one from 1952. Instead of Rice being present in Greenville with Cobb as witnesses, he wrote, "Ty Cobb one day told me a tragic story about Jackson."

Considering all of the ink that has been devoted to the tale, including book-length biographies of Jackson in 2001 and 2004, I did not have to work hard to counter it. Hornbaker briefly alluded to Jackson and Cobb meeting in a liquor store in Greenville, without biting on Rice's storyline.

Alexander and Leerhsen, but not Hornbaker, rehashed a second years-later Cobb story from Rice's book involving Cobb and an ex-catcher, Nig Clarke. It took place around 1935. Supposedly, Cobb got mad at Clarke in Rice's presence for claiming that some number of times, an umpire called Cobb out when Clarke faked out the umpire by applying a rapid tag and immediately throwing his glove aside. Leerhsen reprinted the dialogue while Alexander paraphrased it.

The Clarke story has far more credibility than the Jackson one. One reason is that Cunningham of the *Boston Herald* wrote in 1941 that he had just heard it the other day, while listening to "Grannie Rice and H. [G]. Salsinger swapping memories."

Rice, in a 1947 column, wrote the following: "On one occasion, long after

Cobb was through, Nig Clarke admitted he had missed Cobb at the plate at least a dozen times with a quick tag, where Cobb was called out. It took three of us to pull Cobb off Clarke." In 1939, he had written, "And one night, a year or so ago, I saw Ty Cobb fly into a rage at Nig Clarke because Clarke, telling what he regarded merely as a funny story, admitted that at least 20 times when Ty slid into the plate, he really didn't put the ball on him, but only stabbed at him and then tossed the ball away quickly, the speed and deftness with which he operated confusing the umpire. Ty didn't see anything funny in the story. His angle was that, by trickery, Nig had knocked 20 runs off his runs-scored record. Even 20 years after, that was a serious matter to him."

I think Rice made a poor word choice in stating, "It took three of us to pull Cobb off Clarke" part. The 1939 punch line, that "Ty didn't see anything funny in the story," is more credible and consistent with the way that Clarke and Cobb interacted at a restaurant or hotel grill in 1926, as featured earlier.

Leerhsen spoke of not trusting Cobb's biography with Stump, and he is right in the following respect: it contains a similar version of the Rice-Jackson-Cobb story. Leerhsen instead used the not-much-of-an-improvement version from Rice's 1954 one.

One of my favorite finds is on what Cobb thought of Rice's accuracy. In 1981, ostensibly to reprint a newly published account from a doctor who treated Cobb for prostate cancer in 1960, *New York Times* sports columnist Red Smith recalled some of his own interactions with Cobb. "He was through as a player before we ever met and our encounters were too few to influence to my personal view of him, though he did write [a letter] upbraiding me for using an anecdote I am confident was true because Grantland Rice had told it to me."

Cunningham of the *Boston Herald* wrote that often in sports, "There's such a thing as respecting the art while not caring for the artist." Seemingly parroting sports editor Ware of the *Omaha World-Herald*, he said that Cobb is "generally regarded as the greatest baseball player of them all, but the meanest, orneriest cuss to be around with [sic]." Cobb "just naturally loves to argue and to try to beat somebody doing something."

Back in the West weeks after his visit to Greenville, Cobb would be in Idaho, in a party of eight. Over a weekend, they caught 75 fish, mostly small trout.

In 1943:

In Philadelphia, former U.S. Olympic track and field coach Lawson N. Robertson was coaching at the University of Pennsylvania. When the Phillies named track coach Harold Anson Bruce to train their players, Robertson thought of Cobb. Paraphrasing Robertson, sportswriter Art Morrow of the *Philadelphia Inquirer* wrote, "It was Cobb's practice, before going to bat, to jog up and down in front of the dugout. Olympic Coach Robertson once asked him why." Cobb responded by saying that since he noticed runners always warming up before a race, that he figured doing the same would make him faster on the bases.

Sports editor Whitman of the *Boston Herald* noticed Robertson's remarks and checked with Cobb friend Eddie Collins, still the general manager of the Red Sox. "I do not recall Cobb ever limbering up that way," Collins told him. "When a man's in the game, and actively in it, his muscles are loose and free and it seems to me that he does not need any preliminary calisthenics to make his leg muscles react

from a benefit game in Dearborn, Mich., in 1943. Detroit Red Wings general manager Jack Adams and Speaker are to Cobb's left.

better." Collins conceded, however, that maybe Robertson was onto something about the merits of such activity.

A *Sporting News* staffer wrote to longtime baseball writer Sid C. Keener of the *St. Louis Star-Times* after he named some great outfielders and omitted Cobb. Keener had been covering baseball in St. Louis as far back as the 1910s, mainly as a sports editor. In a follow-up column, Keener responded, "On the basis of all-around ability, yes, Ty Cobb was in a class by himself. The original script on this 'Who's the best outfielder?' debate did not include batting, base running and daring individual play. Ty earned those medals."

Keener continued, "Cobb lacked the grace and ground-covering ability in the outfield compared with others. In going after a ball over his head, especially, Ty's Georgia temper whipped him on numerous occasions. He'd fight with himself whenever a drive cleared his outstretched hands. He was not eliminated [from superlative consideration] as an intentional slight by this observer."

International News Service humorist Arthur "Bugs" Baer quipped in one of his columns, "The right of eminent ankling domain was established by a lad

named Tyrus Cobb. He was the first runner to show the pedal hardware to basemen as he came tobogganing on his coat-tails with his choppers riding high and wide."

The following digression to Baer is one of the last major angles that I compiled. As noted earlier, *Cap Anson 3* contains definitive analysis of the myth of the 1890s Baltimore

from left to right in 1941: Damon Runyon, Sr. and Arthur "Bugs" Baer

Orioles as a spiking team in any notable volume.

In his 1961 book with Stump, Cobb would state, "It was Bugs Baer (among many writers) who convinced the country that I sat by the Detroit bench, whetting my spikes razor-sharp with a file, and then putting them to bloody use on the base paths." Earlier I showed that he did file his spikes openly; more debatable is how he used them.

In the 1910s, Baer was a sports reporter and cartoonist with the old *Washington Times* and branched out to write a syndicated column for decades.

Early in the 1916 season, he wrote, "The baseball season will not be really here until Ty Cobb misses Frank Baker's leg and spikes the bag." Late that year, he wrote, "If a player spikes himself with a knife while scoffing pie, should he

be remunerated as extensively as the player who gets spiked by Ty Cobb?" In 1917, he wrote, "Government should employ Ty Cobb to spike rumors." In 1930, he wrote, "Ty Cobb used to chop up second and third basemen during his famous spiking slides but Ty never sent them back to the kitchen to be heated up."

In 1933 for King Features Syndicate, he wrote of traveling in 1926 on the yacht of Christy Walsh: "It was just fifteen years after we wrote [in 1911] about Ty Cobb stopping at a barbershop to have his spikes

Bob Considine and Baer in 1949

honed that we met Ty in Christy's outboard lake greyhound [yacht]. Ty hadn't spoken to us [me] all that time. The motor wouldn't commence. Around midnight Ty and the Bug were each at an oar. At dawn Ty discovered he had been rowing around in a neat circle because the Bug had let his oar drift away and hadn't said a word about it."

In 1941, Baer recalled having written, presumably around 1911, "Before

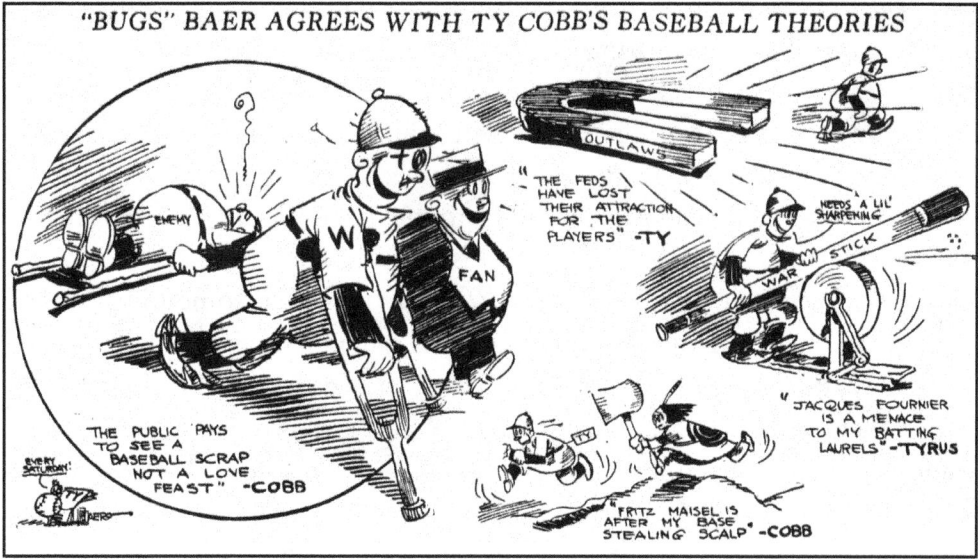

"BUGS" BAER AGREES WITH TY COBB'S BASEBALL THEORIES

Arthur "Bugs" Baer was also a cartoonist for the *Washington Times*

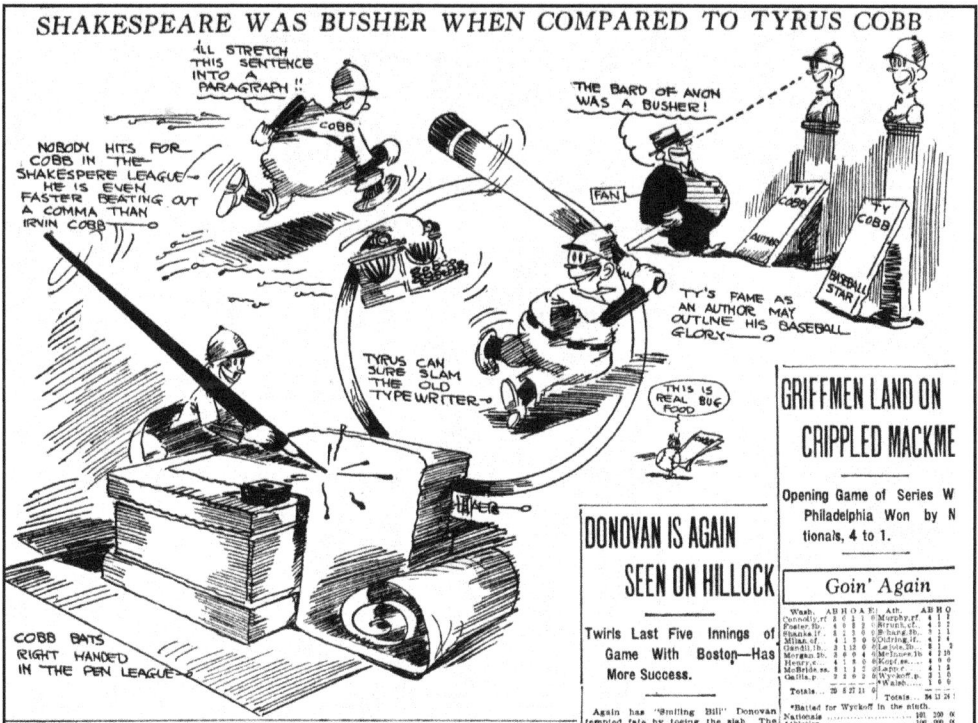

SHAKESPEARE WAS BUSHER WHEN COMPARED TO TYRUS COBB

going out to the ball park this afternoon Ty Cobb stopped at the barber shop to have his spikes honed." He added, "Well, Ty had a temper like a porcupine with ingrown quills and he declared war on me just short of cannibalism."

In 1942, Baer wrote of Cobb in a *Collier's* fictional feature, "But when he came up from Georgia to the Detroits he was gamer than a dentist pulling his own teeth and could take it like a carpet on the line [in the days when carpets were mainly cleaned by beating them while hung over a clothesline or railing]. But he was as touchy as fingerprint powder and would climb a mountain to take a punch at an echo. . . There's no living with Ty when he's in that mood, so when a grandstand manager in New York named Lucas or Lookis or something like that gives him the Bronx roll call from the dollar seats, Ty climbs into the stands and hands him a dry shave with his knuckles."

Sports editor Cohn of the *Oakland Tribune* reprinted something close to exactly the above and added, "And you bums call yourselves baseball writers."

In 1947, Baer re-ran a version of his barber shop quip and said Cobb and he "never met until years later when Christy Walsh got us together for a benefit game at Lake Oscawana [in upstate New York]. And those years hadn't cooled Ty off much. He still wouldn't take conversation for an answer. And it was there in the dressing room that I discovered the Georgia Slasher had a receipt for every strawberry he handed out. He was scarred from ankle to hip."

In 1948, Baer printed excerpts from a recent, second-ever Cobb letter to him. Then, in 1952, in light of Cobb's having "turned baseball upside down" with his *Life* articles, Baer printed it in its entirety. Cobb's 1961 book is very light on presenting letters that Cobb wrote – but it includes a less-than-half (but not noted as such) version of the circa 1948 one to Baer. A rough overlap is, as printed by Baer, "You mentioned sharpening spikes in a barbershop. No, Bugs. They have no equipment for that operation." Cobb also wrote that the sharpening story "was a prank hatched by the members of our team, Detroit." But, as detailed earlier, the story held true at various times. As conveyed by Baer, Cobb began the letter with, "Now that my face is toward the setting sun and approaching the evening of my life, I am at the letter writing stage."

In 1949, Considine wrote, "Ty Cobb once tried to get in the press box at Bugs, for writing that Ty had stopped on the way to the park to have his spikes honed. But Ty forgave Bugs when Bugs, writing of a rival base-stealer, said the man's heart was filled with larceny and his feet filled with lead."

About 10 days later, Baer wrote of having run into Cobb recently. Baer told his readers that 40 years had now passed since his barber shop line and 39 since his one about Cobb not being one to back up in a tunnel in the face of an oncoming freight train. I did not find either original quip.

The Baer-Cobb get-together was through the Banshees, a New York luncheon group of editors, artists and the like, with Cobb their guest of honor. "Just 20 years before that I had journeyed out to Detroit to speak at his dinner [a banquet in Cobb's honor in 1925]." At the luncheon, Baer said he asked Cobb about a recent key play in the pennant race on which Boston's Johnny Pesky somehow evaded a tag at home plate by Yankee catcher Ralph Houk. "To my surprise he [umpire Bill Grieve] declared against Pesky. He [Cobb] had been at the ball park that afternoon. And you all know that Ty uses built-in binoculars for eyes." Most of that column was deferential to Cobb, noting his great statistics and ending with he "still looks and handles himself like an athlete."

In 1952, Baer wrote that Cobb's first-ever letter had been 11 pages and arrived after he penned the barber shop line: "It was in agitated lead pencil and started, 'You snake in the grass.' It gathered speed with every line and tied off [sic] with a blast that shook the civilized world to its second mortgages."

In a column in 1955, Considine summarized the Baer-Cobb relationship. Finally, in 1966, just as Baer was about to turn 80, Considine wrote a feature that mentioned Baer's original column.

Baer appears sparingly in the three biographies. Leerhsen does mention Baer, for a different quip, which may be from McCallum's 1975 *Ty Cobb*: "Any ballplayer who could stop a grapefruit from rolling uphill or hit a bull in the pants with a bass fiddle was given a chance of going direct from the semipros to the Detroits and no questions asked." (Leerhsen changed that to "with no questions asked.") McCallum printed a long anecdote from Baer about having been a semi-pro player. One day, Baer was one of several emergency players for Detroit manager Jennings and was paid handsomely just to sit on the bench.

Returning to the chronology and a new year, 1944:

Sports columnist Ed McAuley of the *Cleveland News* was on hand in the Indians' training camp when longtime shortstop Roger Peckinpaugh, now the general manager, said the following about his 2,012 games in the American League during Cobb's career. Cobb "never so much as spiked me. On his slide to second, he'd usually throw his feet out toward center field, and try to grab the base with his hand. I'll never forget the feeling, though – just knowing that guy was taking that big lead off first and would be coming at me any second."

In June from a hotel in Augusta, Cobb wrote of the oppressive heat to broker Otto H. Sherlitz in Detroit and stated his hope to meet him in California. Cobb said he would be amenable to doing so in Menlo Park or Palo Alto, and greet him at the train station. "If you can, bring some food stamps or just meat stamps only in case we might need them but don't think so. Oh! yes steal some gas stamps this is important. I have really done some good here [in Augusta] in arranging some business matters, and feel have [sic] accomplished a lot."

In August, he placed an ad in a Nevada newspaper offering a reward for the return of his dog. Golfing acquaintance Charles "Tiv" Kreling, sergeant-at-arms for the San Francisco Board of Supervisors, was visiting Cobb in Nevada and conveyed that to the *San Francisco Chronicle*. Kreling explained, "I am here with Ty and he is very sad about the loss of his dog." Cobb placed the ad as well in the *Sacramento Bee*, as follows: "LOST – Gordon Setter, Black With Tan markings underneath. Untrained. Large for 8 months. Name Tex. Nevada side of Lake Tahoe. Reward $15 [about $200 today] for information of or recovery. Contact Ty Cobb, GLENBROOK, NEV." He increased the reward about three-fold a few weeks later in a classified ad in the *Reno Evening Gazette*.

The Ty R. Cobb who was sports editor of the *Nevada State Journal* in Reno from 1937 to 1958 lived from 1915 to 1997. In 1994 in *Nevada* magazine, he wrote, "Cobb had a habit of losing things and then putting ads in the paper asking for their return. He would tell the finders to bring the items to my house in Reno and get a reward. One day my wife opened the door and was startled to find a man who had two dogs, per Cobb's ad, and wanted a reward."

It sounds like what happened more often is that members of the public readily mixed up their addresses. "There was a great tangle concerning the Ty Cobb name," sports editor Cobb also wrote in that article. "Our mail, telegrams, and phone calls were frequently mixed up. Ty had a phone at Tahoe, but the number was unlisted. Therefore I got phone calls from Eastern writers and baseball figures," including Casey Stengel.

In 1951, Rosenbaum of the *San Francisco Chronicle* was sitting next to the sports editor at a hotel table when the sports editor stepped away to receive a phone call. It turned out to be for the baseball Cobb. The sports editor also told Rosenbaum, "Lots of times I get his dividend checks by mistake, and just as often he receives my department store bills by mistake. It's an even trade."

Their bank account problems was likely related to sharing the same middle initial, "R," since, as noted, the ballplayer signed his checks "T. R. Cobb." Beyond that, the sports editor told of receiving "tax bills for his boat, a beautiful Criss [Chris]-Craft that he kept in his somewhat dilapidated boathouse. One day my wife received *his* divorce papers in the mail, which was, to say the least, startling." (In a 1957 letter to Jack McGrath, advertising manager of the Hillerich & Bradsby Co., Ty said he had fishing boats and speedboats. The one newspaper report I found of Cobb using his motorboat was in 1945, after former teammate Vitt had spent three weeks with him in Cave Rock. "We caught nothing but fish – and all big ones," Vitt told the *Oakland Tribune*. Otherwise, in a 1958 hunting and fishing book, McCallum wrote that Cobb "dropped deer with his rifle from a moving speed boat.")

The Cobbs' earliest encounter was in 1940. In a column, sports editor Cobb wrote, "It was skiing, of all things, which brought us together." They met on

Mount Rose, which is close to Reno. Baseball Ty had recently bought a ski outfit and a new car, too, the sports editor wrote. When introduced by a mutual acquaintance with "Ty Cobb, meet Ty Cobb," baseball Ty responded with, "I'm honored, really." The sports editor conveyed to his readers that his namesake wears eyeglasses "and chaws a big cheroot," cigar.

In this next digression with the sports editor, Stump is in a supporting role:

The sports editor gives a boost to the accuracy of parts of Stump's 1961 article. Leerhsen omitted the sports editor by name in his one pertinent reference, which will be noted much later. In the article, Stump wrote of Cobb's being both a "scientific craps player" and inclined to argue in casinos, including by once being thrown out of one. "He liked to gamble and got into furious arguments with the casino dealers," the sports editor wrote. "Occasionally friends would tell me, 'I hear you made quite a fuss at the Mapes (or the Riverside, Harrah's, etc.) last night.'" Frances's 1955 bill of particulars states that he gambled at the Harold's Club casino in Reno one day in 1954.

The casino that Stump said Cobb was thrown out of was the Riverside, which closed in 1962. In a 1955 letter to McCallum, Cobb wrote, "Saw a fine show at Hotel Riverside Reno, last night, [comedian] Jimmy Durante and had [television personality] Dennis Day at our table last night." He had visited the Riverside in 1954 to see Day perform.

(Cobb conveyed knowledge of craps in a 1955 letter to Danny Goodman, advertising and promotions chief of the Hollywood Stars/Twinks. Goodman was about to visit Nevada, and Cobb wrote, "I should not tell you that you cannot beat the gaming tables[,] craps is lowest percentage for house but you

Tyrus R. Cobb of Reno, his son
Tyrus W. and baseballer Cobb

cannot beat them, even if you stay on back line play, which is lower percentage even than house gets with the player[,] (usual) back line you are playing with the house except only one number and that is a stand off. One can make winnings if he goes on back line and never double up, get ahead of house, then push your winnings (house money) on the come outs [rolls of 2, 3 or 12], strong, for you have 8 ways to seven and eleven and only 4 ways to crap out.")

On a different matter, the sports editor backs Stump's writing that despite his wealth, the ex-ballplayer could be tightfisted. According to the sports editor,

"He was notoriously slow to pay, and the *Nevada State Journal* dunned him to pay his subscription." More on that will appear later.

In a 1995 interview with the *Reno Gazette-Journal*, the sports editor criticized the movie "Cobb" for portraying the ex-player as a loudmouth who used foul language. "He was not at all like that [presumably he was not a loudmouth, although he no doubt cursed]. The Ty Cobb I knew never shouted that he was the greatest ballplayer of all time." He also criticized Stump for his treachery.

Parts of Stump's 1961 article are supported by the contemporaneous record.

In 1960, when they visited Cobb's home in Atherton, Stump said the "rich mansion had no lights, no heat, no hot water. It was in blackout." A front-page story in the *San Mateo Times* that June had detailed a decision by the Pacific Gas and Electric Company to shut off his services. A spokesman for the company said, "Cobb had his three strikes."

The *Times* also conveyed, "The Georgia Peach, ill in bed at his unlighted and unheated home, protested today that he was not concerned about the bill itself, which comes to something like $100 [about $800 in today's dollars]. 'It's the principle of the thing,' he asserted." (Leerhsen conceded Stump's accuracy on Cobb's having his power cut off.) A quip that ran in several newspapers stated, "Ty Cobb has sued a gas company over a bill for light in a house when he didn't occupy it. Does he claim he was victim [sic] of beanball or spiked shoes?"

To a *Times* reporter sent to the house, the bedridden Cobb said, "I'm rather under the weather and not able to be up much." Cobb told of having recently undergone an operation and having diabetes. Regarding his protest, he said he was not looking for publicity: "I don't want to be a monkey on a stick."

Hornbaker tracked down an original copy of Cobb's lawsuit for, as Hornbaker wrote, "inaccurate recording of his utilities." Stump said the error within the bill was $16, which is about $130 in today's dollars.

The situation allowed Stump to add detail that, in the scheme of things, is believable: "I arranged with Ty's gardener, Hank, to turn on the lawn sprinklers. In the outdoor sunshine, a cold-water shower was easier to take" than an inside one. "From then on, the backyard became my regular washroom." Stump continued, "The problem of lighting a desk, enabling us to work on the book, was solved by stringing two hundred feet of cord, plugged into an outlet of a neighboring house, through hedges and flower gardens and into the window of Cobb's study, where a single naked bulb hung over the chandelier provided illumination. The flickering shadows cast by the single light made the vast old house seem haunted. No 'ghost' writer ever had more ironical surroundings."

Possibly left out of the article for effect (although Stump noted the following to the *Los Angeles Times* in an interview prior to its publication) is that living in that neighboring house was Cobb's married daughter Beverly and her family.

Stump was also able to describe how, to reach their bedrooms, Cobb and he "groped our way down long, black corridors. Twice he fell in the dark, and finally he collapsed completely. He was so ill that he was forced to check in to Stanford Hospital in nearby Palo Alto."

There is a flattering detail about Cobb in Stump's article that Leerhsen and Hornbaker did not include – and which is true. In 1957, Goodman would tell sportswriter Jeane Hoffman of the *Los Angeles Times*, "I became great friends with Ty Cobb, and for years he used to send me checks through the mail to distribute to old-time players, because he didn't want them to know the dough was coming from him." Upon Cobb's death, he would say the sum was several thousand dollars, about eight times that today. Stump wrote in his 1961 article, "Regularly he mailed dozens of anonymous checks to indigent old ballplayers

from left to right at the Beverly Hills Hotel in 1958: Academy Award-winning director/notorious driver Leo McCarey; Frank Conniff, a 1956 co-Pulitzer Prize winner for international reporting; notorious driver Cobb (1935 hit a pedestrian, 1936 speeding ticket, 1947 and 1954 drunk driving arrests); Fred Haney; Toots Shor; Casey Stengel; and Danny Goodman. Haney and Stengel were former Pacific Coast League managers, Haney in Hollywood and Stengel in Oakland.

(relayed by a third party) – a rare act among retired tycoons in other lines of business." Alexander touched on this subject too, without citing Stump's prose.

I can add that a motive for anonymity may have been to avoid "bushels of mail." As will be noted later, Cobb used the phrase in criticizing friend Maines's successful planting of a Cobb-as-philanthropist newspaper story in late 1959.

Digressing to some of Cobb's surviving letters to Goodman:

In a 1955 one, Cobb was apparently referring to items that he had provided to Goodman, to either sell at Los Angeles Pacific Coast League games or give away at promotional events.

Referring to images of himself, Cobb wrote, "I have two or three large ones, maybe all in civilian clothes, which I like[,] also taken when I was younger, had more hair and less wrinkles. Will send them when you give the word." He also wrote, "I am your agent Danny without pay."

In April 1960, he wrote to Goodman after receiving in Cave Rock a package that Goodman had sent him that included a clock and a bridge set. Cobb told of his time in the East, which had just ended. It included having been "in 'hells hole' with pain and under sedative pain killers for a period of exploratory medicine to determine if drugs will handle my condition and of course to find out if operation not needed."

Referring in that letter to his January 1960 visit to New York, to be featured later, he said his back pain was so bad that he "had to resort to hotel doctor at night, shots in arm etc. just to hold out until return to Emory Clinic [University Hospital] & operation, it all worked out ok."

He also wrote, "Hope you got aboard of some Coca Cola stock per my telephone from Phoenix, if so you have your split also extra cash dividend and more good news to follow, per 'Cola.' market board wise at stand still, soon this summer Cola figures will be good, I do know, for instance, a weak & declining market, generally, this is merely a usual condition per season or months, Coke does not break below split price of $50.00 per share, the unusual record of financial position, absolute dominance of the soft drink industry, plus many millions of profit, in 80 odd countries of world, frozen, not reflected in Coke[']s annual statement, also no debt whatever, bonds, loans, even no preffered [sic] stock, all profits go to common stock holders, good dividends, has paid dividends since 1893, this stock is really fine, also now enjoying the best business in company history, all this Danny is inside information [from] my friend [Coca-Cola chief executive] Bob Woodruff, this is in confidence."

Back in 1955, Cobb had written to him, "Do you ever buy stocks if so write me for there is one stock that is in an unusual position and this stock has not had the usual advance that most stocks have had in the present market which has advanced for a couple of years, I have plenty of this stock myself also for my children, if you personally want the dope I will explain fully in answer also when I get the word which I am to get and if you want to buy some and promise not to do so until I give you the word, then I will lay the facts before you and you make the decision, this stock has paid their dividends since 1893 also now pays 5% or $5[.]00 at 100 dollars a share, no outstanding stock, preferred or otherwise, except common stock, will give you if interested to know, their financial status, surpluses etc. the present $5[.]00 a year dividend will carry interest charges on the full amount of cost of stock, any rise or split will benefit you without any investment of your personal money."

In April 1961, Goodman would write to Cobb, "I want you to know that I did very well with the Coca-Cola stock, and I am going to buy some Fairbanks-Whitney [manufacturing company stock], inasmuch as I am sold on Coca-Cola. I certainly want to go along with the winner." Days earlier, Cobb had written to him, "Did you cash in on Coke I contacted you about, I am no tout but I have 2[,]000 shares of Fairbanks-Whitney fine [something; word hard to read]."

I can digress to one other story about Cobb's generosity along the lines of what Goodman told the *Times*. In a long feature in 1959 to be detailed later, *Boston Daily Record* sports columnist Bill McSweeny described spending 48 hours with Cobb, including as a roommate, during Cobb's visit to Boston for a B'nai B'rith sports dinner. A former player who Cobb did not know visited their room, who "had a lot of personal stake" written in his face. Cobb waved him in and spoke with him for 20 minutes. "On his way out, Cobb stopped him in the hallway leading to the bedroom. 'Here, old friend,' he said. 'I've owed you this money since that card game years ago.'

"Cobb walked back into the room. He shook his head. 'It hurts to see them, living on dreams. These old ball players. They never had a pension plan, never made much money. All they have is memories.'"

In 1945:

In a smoke-filled hotel room in New York City, NEA sports editor Grayson was with a contemporary of Cobb, great fielding outfielder Duffy Lewis, who played mainly for the Red Sox. Others on hand included Bill Grimes of the *Boston American*. A subject up for discussion was: Was Cobb ever doubled off a base on a caught ball in the outfield? When someone answered in the affirmative, and that was met with skepticism, Lewis, now the Boston Braves' traveling secretary, said, "I threw him out."

Grimes seconded that and said, "I saw him [Lewis] do it and at the same time make the greatest throw I ever saw. It was on the Red Sox' first western swing of 1913. Cobb was on first base. He was either stealing or the hit-and-run was on. If it was the latter, it was either an outside pitch or a change of pace ball, for Sam Crawford belted it deep down the left field foul line of Detroit's Navin Field.

"Naturally Duffy was playing Wahoo Sam Crawford quite deep and the ball was curving away from him. Yet he got up to make a shoestring catch a good 20 feet beyond the foul line. Certain that it was a base hit, Cobb had rounded second base when Duffy made the catch, [and] turned back lickity-split when he saw the ball caught.

"But Duffy caught the ball and half spun and threw all in one motion and on a line – a perfect strike to Clyde Engle, who was filling in at first base for Jake Stahl. The Georgia Peach was out sliding in a photo finish. He was so mad he kicked Engle in the shins."

In Detroit in August, Cobb told sports editor Smith of the *Free Press* that the only reason why he stole so many bases was "that we had to do that to get in a spot from which we could score on a hit. That isn't necessary any more. And somehow I miss that part of the game today. There is nothing like a runner daring the catcher's arm. The sprint, the slide, the dust, the collision at the base. That sticks with me as the best part of the game. Somehow I miss that most of all."

His next notable stop was New York, where he managed the West team in the Esquire All American Boys game at the Polo Grounds; Ruth managed the East one. Grayson observed, "Cobb has repeatedly refused to participate in old timers' games. He declined to get in uniform and appear on the coaches' lines even in the All[-]American Boys' game."

Cobb told Grayson, "I want them to remember me as I was." Cobb would don a Tigers' uniform in 1947, for the first-ever old-timers' game at Yankee Stadium. He would also be in one and play at Corsicana, Tex., in 1950, to open that year's season in the then-still segregated Texas League. In 1954, *Boston American* sports columnist Austen Lake would write that Cobb "has the proper attitude toward these old-timers' follies. He refuses every invitation to make himself look ridiculous for the sake of scavenging a few polite plaudits. Some years ago when the VFW's [Veterans of Foreign Wars] of Boston put on a memorial game, Ty wrote that he wanted

the former players are real, the autographs are not

the fans to think of him as he was when he came skidding into home plate with his shoe-chisels flashing, or stretched bloopers into two-base hits, or beat out a drooling bunt. 'I do not want them to see what a pathetic shell I have become,' he said sadly but proudly." In 1955, Cobb told syndicated columnist Lyons, on the occasion of that year's old-timers' day at Yankee Stadium, "Call it pride, maybe, but I won't wear a uniform any more. I want people to remember me when I was slimmer."

from left to right in 1950: Dizzy Dean, Mickey Cochrane, Charley Gehringer, Tris Speaker, Cobb (in his last time in a uniform), Charlie Grimm, Duffy Lewis, Frank Baker and Travis Jackson

Returning to 1945:

That October, he would go to South Dakota for the opening of the pheasant hunting season. He would go back there perhaps twice, in 1953 and 1954. After the fact, he mentioned the latter trip in a letter. Also after the fact, in answering a letter in early 1946 from Manley Miner, son of recently deceased waterfowl sanctuary founder Jack Miner, Cobb wrote that he used a Belgian-made Browning Automatic, "a real shooting gun," on his most recent pheasant hunt.

In 1946:

His friend Hayward "Tom" Binney was profiled in the *Boston Traveler*. Not mentioned otherwise in this book are surviving Cobb letters to him that are loaded with stock tips. Contrary to auction house descriptions, Binney was not a stockbroker but a traveling salesman. The profile was the result of his having won the *Traveler*'s baseball "Play-R-Quiz," with the first prize being an all-expenses-paid trip to the World Series with, in his case, his wife. An estimated 50,000 people had entered the contest, in which the aim was to identify the picture of a baseball player printed each day and reply by providing background on the player. "It's almost incredible, but the report of Binney & Co. [an allusion to the research help provided by his wife Katherine] was the only one that identified all 40 players correctly. Moreover, not only did Mr. Binney give the complete playing records of all 40 players correctly, but he even added facts beyond the judges' master list that made the amazed judges append their master list."

Hayward "Tom" and Katherine Binney

Each contestant was also asked to write a brief letter that named the greatest player ever. The Binneys chose Cobb "and thus comes another startling development. Mr. Binney is a long-time personal friend of Cobb and back in 1928 [after that season] he made a barnstorming trip with Cobb to Japan."

Also, "His first boyhood hobby was a collection of pictures of baseball stars plastered over the walls and ceilings of his room." The pictures, which he still has, "fitted exactly to identify the Play-R-Quiz photos."

As noted earlier, Binney had played semi-pro baseball and had played in an exhibition game with Ruth in 1917. Binney first met Cobb in San Antonio in 1921. Cobb "just simply took a shine to me," he said. Binney estimated having shaken hands with 20 of the 40 players in the photos, and is able to identify 37 of the 40 "with an instant's observation." He supplemented his submissions with "what amounts to the complete life histories of each of the 40."

Over the summer, Cobb sent a private plane to Mt. Clemens, Mich., to bring friend Ernest "Ernie" Copeland to Cave Rock. Three of Copeland's Cobb stories, told in 1975, are Cobb's having anonymously clerked in his new hardware store for a few days in 1946, having played pinball for hours with him and his not having flashed his name when unrecognized at a Reno casino. Copeland, who may have met Cobb through Bob Clancy, also was quoted as saying, "It was said he had a terrible temper but it was brought on by others."

In 1947:

In a typed letter, Cobb wrote to Latimer, "Have read about your cold weather down South." He added, "Why not leave your fishing pole on the shelf and come out here, where it's nice and balmy, for a round of golf."

Cobb's hitting advice persona got a boost when sports columnist Wilbur Adams of the *Sacramento Bee* printed parts of a 1938 letter from him to now-veteran big leaguer Sam Chapman. Cobb had successfully tipped Connie Mack off to him that year, when he was a California collegian. When Chapman began his big-league career, he had trouble hitting a curve ball and decided to write to Cobb. "By return mail Chapman received a batting directive for his exclusive use," wrote sports columnist Bob Cooke of the *New York Herald Tribune* four months before Adams's column. "In his letter, Cobb discussed every possible mistake a batter can make and provided a formula for each."

Returning to the chronology:

At the end of the season, the Yankees held their first-ever old-timers' day that included a game. It would be Ruth's second-to-last attendance at one. He would be terribly ill, approaching death at the next one, which Cobb would not attend. This occasion was a relatively happy one, and Cobb also would stay for the start of the World Series days later at Yankee Stadium. Cobb arrived there by private jet from Phoenix. He traveled as a guest of Yankees co-owner Delbert "Del" Webb, whose construction business was based in Arizona.

A popular story from his visit names an erroneous catcher, Benny Bengough. The accurate, apparent original source, Lawton Carver, sports editor of the International News Service, was with Cobb multiple times during his stay:

"You heard about the gag he pulled on [Wally] Schang, who caught for the opposing team in that old-timers' game Cobb participated in last Sunday. [It concerns t]he way Cobb, on his first time at bat, asked Schang to back up a little, instead of positioning himself so close behind the plate. Cobb said he was afraid he might hit the catcher with his bat. Schang backed away a couple of feet and on the next pitch Cobb bunted and nearly beat it out."

After his return to Cave Rock, Cobb wrote to Hauck about the trip, "I was going to dodge it, as I knew what would happen in the way of food and celebrating, and had a telegram all written and declining, offering doctor[']s orders as my excuse. I went over to file the telegram and found telephone calls from their [Yankees] scout [Joe] Devine in San Francisco, also urgent telephone messages from Del Webb." Cobb then got in touch with Webb, who "offered to send [his] plane here to [San Francisco to] get me and take me to New York with him, that was too much for a 'country boy,' so I accepted." On the way, they played golf in Washington, D.C., with Postmaster General Robert "Bob" Hannegan. Also, Webb invited Cobb to send him the construction plans for the hospital he was funding in Royston, so that his staff could examine them.

Close to two months after the old-timers' game, Cobb wrote to Ruth to send him some signed documents as per his request. "I was much pleased to see you in New York and honored that Tris and I could pose with you. From papers I had gathered that you was [sic] not so well, well old boy you surprised me in how good you looked. Keep the old chin up boy."

Cobb went on to tell him "a little secret," that "I have always admired your ability because you were God[-]given great powers and were always a real great ball player, never made many mistakes, never many times threw to wrong spot, also fielded well, never caught making many mistakes on bases. Even if you were of unusual size and lacking in speed, your power at the plate also the mental hazard influencing the opposition, I need not even mention." (In the *Detroit News* two weeks before the old-timers' game, Salsinger had quoted Ruth as recently saying in Los Angeles, "Model yourself after Ty Cobb and not after me. He was the truly great

from left to right in Tucson, for spring training in 1947: Speaker, Bob Feller, Cobb and Hornsby. Columnist Pegler was with them and likened the three old-timers to "old generals, American, German, French and British, long after the wars when they do [write] their memory-books and tell when and how they sensed that a battle or a war was won or lost, how they knew they had hurt the enemy and felt him wince or sized up his tactics and laid for him to do the same thing again. They studied one another for unconscious characteristics, exploited them and kept their observations secret."

player of all time. He was the most scientific man who ever wore a base ball uniform.") In 1955, in the presence of syndicated columnist Lyons, Cobb would say, "I like guys with spirit. I loved Babe Ruth but nobody knew it."

In 1948:

Ernest Hemingway wrote a letter that Stump excerpted on an introductory page of his 1994 book. In writing to staff writer Lillian Ross of the *New Yorker*, the noted novelist and journalist stated, "The dirtiest and most hated guy in probably the baseball you have watched was Dick Bartell. He would give it to you and would cut you. Before him it was Cobb. The greatest of ball players and an absolute shit." Stump modified that slightly to make it read, "Ty Cobb, the greatest of all players – and an absolute shit."

Without giving any indication of being aware of the well-documented nature of what Hemingway thought of Cobb, Leerhsen wrote the following about Stump: "He wore a cardigan sweater, smoked a pipe, and in other ways tried to emulate Ernest Hemingway." Leerhsen did not touch on what the "other ways" were, but sharing a negative viewpoint on Cobb could be one. A second I can offer can be gleaned from William R. Cobb's article. Hemingway had died about two weeks before Cobb from an apparent accidental discharge of his gun. William R. Cobb speculated that some of the detail surrounding Hemingway's death has an eerie parallel to a story that Stump apparently concocted surrounding the death of Cobb's father in 1905. So, perhaps Hemingway's demise inspired some of Stump's dramatization of Ty's final years.

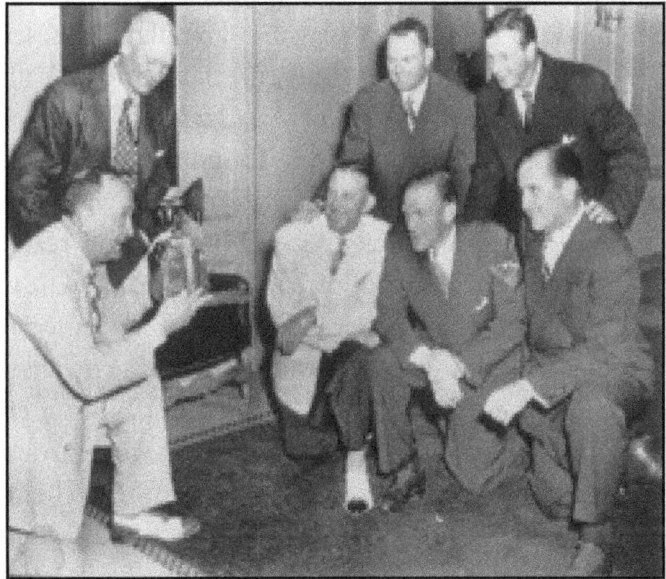

from left to right at the 1951 All-Star Game in Detroit: Cobb and Sam Crawford; top row: George Kell and Stan Musial; bottom row: Dick Bartell, Red Rolfe and Al Lopez

Since Hemingway is so famous, I can add one other tie-in to Ty. A 1981 book detailed the books in Hemingway's personal library. One of them was McCallum's 1956 biography.

Digressing to more about Ty and Bartell:

In 1937, sports editor Cohn of the *Oakland Tribune* wrote that Bartell "is the man Cobb was 20 years ago" as far as having a "fiery temperament. Dick, like Ty, would tackle a cage of wild tigers with his bare fists. Cobb did. They belong to the same school that hates to lose, whether it is a baseball game or a casino game. They admit they are tough losers. They don't smile when they don't win because they are that highest type of competitor, men who know no worse torture than defeat. Yet neither Ty nor Dick ever would make a good boxer." That is "because both always picked extemporaneous scraps just for the fun of it. With them, fighting is a pleasure, not a business."

Eddie Brietz of the AP wrote in January 1939, "Dick Bartell and old Ty Cobb are neighbors in California and go golfing almost daily." Also that month, Bartell had told NEA sports editor Grayson that his own legs were stronger now than they had been in the past four years: "I took a tip from Ty Cobb, who walked miles every winter day in heavy boots to keep his legs in condition."

(In his 1987 book *Rowdy Richard*, Bartell said that as a golfer, Cobb "couldn't stand to lose, even a dollar, no matter how much money he had. He'd cheat and chisel and do anything he could to gain an edge on you. But then he'd go into the pro shop and buy you a $50 sweater or anything you wanted.")

In February, Cobb told the annual dinner of the Elks of Alameda, Calif., "I am proud of being a ball player." The players present cheered and he added, "Yes, when I consider the fine genteel qualities of ball players today I am proud to be one of them." Ward of the *Oakland Tribune*, who reported that, noted that some of the old-time ones "found merriment" in his "genteel" line. Ward told his readers, "Cobb, in his playing days, was a hell-for-leather pirate who'd cut the legs from under a second baseman to reach the keystone sack; who would use every unorthodox trick in the book (if he thought he could get away with it) to win a ball game. Cobb was a fierce, uncompromising competitor to whom almost any ends achieved justified the means." That said, Ward opined that current baseball could benefit from having a few more players like Cobb "so long as their spikes weren't sharpened to a razor edge and horseshoe nails, fine weapons of defense, were taken from them before a game started."

In March, Cobb checked into a Boston hospital after being stricken on a train while en route to a routine checkup. He "appeared undisturbed about his hospitalization, other than to complain that he was refused permission to take an afternoon stroll about the institution's grounds," the AP reported. "I wanted to go out for an airing but a nurse came in and ordered me to take some medicine," he said. Dr. Frank Lahey "refused to comment about his patient's condition but Cobb insisted it was 'just something I ate on the train.'"

The next day, Harold Kaese of the *Boston Globe* went to visit him. "While the prestige and popularity of Babe Ruth mounts ever higher with each passing day he sacrifices himself unsparingly on the altar of consideration to kids, a greater player – and the only greater player – stirs restlessly in the comparative solitude of a sun-bathed room in the New England Baptist Hospital."

"Here is a man who wants company, and welcomes someone to talk to, but a man who still does not ask for sympathy, pity or quarter." 'No, the fans never scared me,' admitted Cobb yesterday. 'I never went into a city afraid to play. If anything, the riding of the fans made me play harder. I always wanted to fight them, show them, win them over, and sometimes I did.'"

Kaese also reported that "Cobb dislikes the modern lively ball game, and asks wistfully, 'Will they ever go back to the old game, when one run meant something?'" (Upon his death, Bob Addie of the *Washington Post* would write, "The baseball of Cobb's day had to be more interesting than the brand played today where one boom can destroy a suspenseful contest." Grantland Rice had made a different point in 1935: "Cobb was never the drawing card that Babe Ruth happened to be. The Babe's home-run bat made the brand of noise that crowds like. But, as an offensive machine, Cobb stands alone.")

Kaese added, "But when he lets a criticism slip, about midgets [in modern baseball] hitting homers, or [Ted] Williams sticking to one swing and one stance, or the commercialization of Spring training, he always adds, 'But who am I to be finding fault?'" The main headline on Kaese's article, after a tinier type introduction of "He Wears Battle Scars," was: "Ty Cobb, Who Reveled in Strife, Does Not Talk Baseball as He Played"

In its own story the day before, the AP quoted Cobb as now advising Williams, "Learn to hit to left field." Also, "You should be able to hit to all fields, regardless of how the defenses are stacked against you. Joe Jackson could hit them anywhere, regardless of how they shifted against him. And Babe Ruth could overcome defenses by choking up his bat and punching into left field."

Digressing to more about Cobb's interactions with Williams:

They first met at the 1947 World Series. At one point, wrote Whitney Martin of the AP, "Cobb rolled up a newspaper to use as a bat, and with the crowd jostling him, drew an imaginary line with his foot to indicate a home plate. 'If I were you I'd stand a little farther back of the plate, like this,' he explained. 'You get a better chance to see what's coming.'"

In 1951, Daley of the *New York Times* wrote, "Williams is as intense in his study of hitting as Cobb ever was and just as inquisitive." And Cobb "is anxiously counting the days until his next trip East because he wants to sit down for a couple of hours with Ted and exchange batting theories with him." Also in 1951, Williams credited Cobb with helping him end his worst slump ever. Agent Corcoran said that if over, "Ty Cobb rates an assist. Ty told me there were only two classic swings in his lifetime. One was Joe Jackson's; the other is Ted's. However, Cobb said: 'But I can't understand why he insists on trying to overpower the shift the other teams use when he's at bat. Instead of pulling the ball, he could raise his average 20 to 50 points by punching to left field.'"

Corcoran continued, "I asked Ty to put it in writing to Ted. About three days later, I noticed that Williams was hitting to left field. He was even bunting, when the third baseman moved to shortstop on the shift. Then I knew that Ted had heard from Ty."

As noted earlier, Corcoran that year sent Cobb's batting pamphlet to each out-of-town destination of the Red Sox, for Williams to review. Cobb had advised Williams "not to follow anything in the instructions except that having to do with the open and closed stance," wrote NEA sports editor Grayson. The instructions that he was told to follow were as follows, as conveyed by Grayson:

Ted Williams and Fred Corcoran

"Stand farther from the plate to hit to left field."

"Pick on the first ball that is over the plate."

"Do not take a strike with men on the bases. Get your three swings."

"A great hitter should be able to hit to all fields."

Hey Kids!—Even Ted Reads Batting Tips
Ty's Hints Give Williams Hits

a 1951 AP headline on a story quoting Corcoran on Cobb's tips to Williams; "Ted Takes Up Golf On Advice of Cobb" was the headline in a December one in the *Boston American*. In February 1952, Cullen Cain of the *Miami Daily News* stated that recently, Williams spoke to him more about the golfing of Cobb, Speaker and Ruth than about their baseball careers.

Williams would acknowledge the above in a 1954 article under his byline in the *Saturday Evening Post*. Williams by then had no longer kept Cobb's letter, but had seen a similar Cobb one to Corcoran. At the start of that letter, Cobb wrote, "I wrote 'Ted' a long letter two days before he broke loose. I hope the letter 'woke' him up, like to think it did. He has had four two-base hits to left field, also home runs, and failed to hit only two or three times since." Cobb had enclosed one of his new "Science of Batting" pamphlets.

(In his 1925 interview with Ed Hughes of the *New York Telegram*, Cobb had said, "When I first broke in left[-]hand pitchers bothered me considerable [sic]. From the position I took at the plate their curves broke almost in front of me. And I couldn't touch 'em. Then I began to figure out a way to mend my weakness. The solution was simple enough. I stood farther back, so that when I made my swipe the curve had begun to straighten out.")

In a 1950 letter cited in Corcoran's memoirs, Cobb had written to Corcoran, "Ted is like an outlaw horse who has certain fine ability, but rears and pitches in the harness of society and gets many burns and wounds. But that means nothing to him. He retires quickly to those who fawn upon him. Neither you nor I nor anyone else with the interest or desire to help Ted can ever accomplish one thing for him. . . so it's better to endure him and save one's self. . . "

By the way, Cobb's book mocks a whopper version of his help-to-Williams story: "With Williams, I'm supposed to have handed him some tips on how to hit to left field. The location varies – sometimes we're at Santa Anita race track [in California], in other versions at Boston, Yankee Stadium, and Chicago. The punch line, when I'm finished, is that Williams snorts, 'Oh, nuts,' and walks away." In his 1961 article, Stump told his own negative odds-on fable and claimed that his was based on having spoken to both Williams and Cobb. On the earlier whopper, Hornbaker found Williams saying in 1957 that such an incident never happened and that Cobb's advice had been sound. I can add that veteran reporter Harry T. Brundidge had analyzed the matter with Cobb and then Williams in interviews with them a week apart for the *Sporting News*.

Longtime Boston sportswriter Montville, in a 2002 book, told of meeting a friend of Williams, Joe Lindia. Lindia was at an hours-long argument between Williams and Cobb in a Scottsdale, Ariz., motel in 1959. The main topic was hitting, and there was shouting. *Boston American* columnist Lake, in Arizona around that occasion, wrote of Cobb watching Williams in an exhibition game one day. "I haven't seen much of this boy until this month," Cobb told Lake. "Hah! 'Boy' he calls Ted!" Lake interjected. "All I know is what I read. He's got great co-ordination [sic]. Watch the way he flicks those wrists. Look at the balance on his feet. Sees more of the ball than any man of his time, even Stan Musial." Lake continued, "Then Ty added a doubting corollary. 'BUT,' said he, 'Ted demands a perfect pitch.' That familiar refrain again! Like telling Richard Rodgers how to write a musical score or Henry Ford how to make autos. 'Takes too many bases on balls,' said Cobb. To which Ted answers, 'What's wrong with an honest base on balls? Good as a single, ain't?' Cobb's reply to THAT is, 'Not when other Red Sox are waiting on the bases.' [Cobb had uttered similar criticism after

Austen Lake in 1957. In his 1969 autobiography, Williams said Lake "was always trying to psychoanalyze me." About Cunningham, Williams said, "He was actually a pretty good writer, he had talent, but you've never seen such a swellheaded Irishman."

the Red Sox lost the 1946 World Series.] And yet even that argument begets a counter claim – that Williams, over his 20-year period, has knocked almost one[-]fifth of the Sox RBI total. That's f[a]r above his quota!" Lake also garnered a reaction to Cobb's statement, "All I needed to see was the last six feet of any pitch to hit it." Lake paraphrased Williams as insisting that, like Cobb, "he can, sometimes, see leather and wood meet."

In 1969, Williams told Daley that Cobb "used to argue with me about hitting to the opposite field." Williams also told Daley, "One thing about Cobb was that he got more out of what he had than anyone in the business. Of all the athletes I've met over the years two impressed me more than any others, Cobb and [retired boxer] Gene Tunney. Each got the absolute most out of his talents." In his 1970 book, Williams said Cobb "was more of a push hitter, a slap hitter."

Returning a second time to the chronology in 1948:

Future Dempsey co-biographer Considine wrote about how the first generation of blacks in the major leagues will be owed a debt by later black ones. At one point, he digressed to the dangers of violence that Jackie Robinson posed on the basepaths relative to those of Cobb. "Any man beyond 40 can recall the saga of Ty Cobb, his flashing spikes, his violent collisions and resultant fights with infielders – one of whom actually stabbed Cobb with a long nail one day as Ty plunged into third base.

"So it was into garish [violent] situations of this sort that Robinson soon found himself. Hairs would bristle on every slide he made, and rival runners who had to cross the base which Robinson himself guarded – first base – often found themselves colliding with him."

So, inadvertently in contrast to Stump, Robinson enabled others to promote a negative image of Cobb. Digressing to more about Robinson and Cobb:

Robinson was likened to Cobb in other ways. Noted black poet Sterling A. Brown did so in a book in 1951. He began by noting Robinson's greater freedom with the passing years to "argue with umpires and tangle with over-aggressive rivals as any other player can, and without its becoming a racial issue." A few sentences later,

Sterling A. Brown

he wrote, "The American public seems willing now to recognize that on the baseball diamond a Negro ballplayer may well be temperamentally closer to Ty Cobb than to [personable black botanist] George Washington Carver."

In 1957 at the end of Robinson's career, *Chicago Tribune* columnist Condon wrote, "Jackie Robinson was a turbulent, bellicose, and arrogant baseball player, and many criticized him as such, altho [sic] the motives of Jackie's most avowed detractors were always suspect, and you lamented the inconsistency of these detractors when they lauded the *great competitive spirit* of athletes whose behavior was identical to Jackie's but whose color happened to be different." A few sentences earlier, he quoted Robinson as having said, "If I'm a trouble maker, it's only because I can't stand losing." Condon followed that earlier quote by printing one from Cobb about not being able to tolerate being second best. In 1962, when Robinson was elected to the Hall of Fame, former Brooklyn general manager Rickey said, "He was Ty Cobb-ish in every way – perhaps not as fast – but nearly."

Returning a third time to the 1948 chronology:

In New York after his medical visit to Boston, Cobb said the main problem with the batters of today is that they are swing happy. "Too few study the pitchers," he said. As conveyed by NEA sports editor Grayson, Cobb "insists that even with the jackrabbit ball[,] there is still a place in the game for good place-hitters and baserunners. 'The running clubs win, don't they,' he points out, 'and the running clubs are the fastest ones.'" Cobb also told Grayson that if he had the batting eye of Ted Williams, he would now be hitting .450. "'Why of course, he should hit to left field,' he asserts. 'All he has to do is move his left foot back six inches or so with the pitch.'" With regard to pitching, "Cobb says the reason so many hurlers bob up with arm trouble is that they don't take care of their precious equipment. 'When I played,' recalls the greatest of ballplayers, 'pitchers wore woolen sleeves tied on under their arms in street clothes after working. Now they go around in sport shirts with no sleeves after pitching, ride in automobiles the same way, and left-handers drive cars with their arms hanging out.'"

In *Cosmopolitan* magazine, now-Brooklyn manager Durocher wrote that his general manager, Branch Rickey, "told me plenty about Cobb – the most feared man the game has ever known. 'When I was managing the Browns,' Branch said, 'Cobb walked one day with two out and nobody on, in the last of the eleventh. Before another ball was pitched, he had scored the winning run, even though he had to knock the third baseman and the catcher in different directions to do it as he made his own breaks and dashed around the bases. No, Ty never slid away from anybody, Leo. He was *not* a nice guy.'"

Rickey later told that story in 1952 at a banquet in North Carolina. On a pickoff play at first base, after the first baseman made a wild throw to second, he kicked the ball out of the third baseman's hands. Sportswriter Bill Hackney related, "Rickey said he [Rickey] stormed to the plate yelling 'interference, interference.' The plate umpire just took off his mask and calmly shut him up with these words. Give the boy credit, Mr. Rickey . . . he made his own breaks."

On a 1957 visit by Cobb to Kansas City, a reporter for the *Kansas City Star* mentioned Rickey's story to him. Cobb noted that he was familiar with it.

There is an inverse to Rickey's story. In his 1948 *Sport* magazine profile of Cobb, Jack Sher claimed, "The worst epithet you could hurl at Cobb was to call him 'lucky.' It would send him into a towering rage. 'I make my own luck!' he would shout back at rival players."

An early story along those lines is from 1913. The *El Paso Herald* printed this quip from Washington manager Clark Griffith: "Clark Griffith declared that Ty Cobb always gets the advantage on close decisions just because he is Ty Cobb. Griffith says that Cobb buffaloes the umpires into giving him the shade, as they know his ability, but it is unintentional."

Umpire Billy Evans, writing in a children's magazine in 1915, began with the quote, "He is the luckiest fellow that ever broke into the big league!" Evans explained, "That was what major league players in general thought about Ty Cobb after he had been in the American League for a few years. Little credit was given Cobb for his daring feats on the bases. He was simply classed as lucky." By contrast, such naysayers "are now willing to admit that brains and speed, not luck, made possible many of the tricks Cobb turned on the bases."

In 1933, Bingay of the *Free Press* devoted an entire column to luck, focusing on claims to that effect about now-President Roosevelt. Bingay contested the claim, noting that Roosevelt had been stricken with infantile paralysis. A few paragraphs later, he reprinted verses from the 1822 Sir Walter Scott novel *The Fortunes of Nigel* that I have modified to match up with an 1832 printing:

Chance will not do the work – Chance sends the breeze;
But if the pilot slumber at the helm,
The very wind that wafts us towards the port
May dash us on the shelves. – The steersman's part is vigilance,
Blow it rough or smooth.

In his next thought, Bingay wrote, "They once liked to call Henry Ford lucky." After a few observations about the automobile pioneer, he quoted Napoleon as having said, "I am the creator of my own luck." He added, "and by the same token he created his own Waterloo."

Bingay's next paragraph began, "Nothing made Ty Cobb wilder with anger in the days when he was recreating baseball than to be told that he was 'lucky.'

"'I deliberately create a situation,' he would scream, 'th[e]n take advantage of it – knowing what is going to happen – and they call it "luck." I could stand still on the bags like the rest of them and wait to be batted around to the home plate. If I did that they might be entitled to call it luck. But I don't. I create my chances.'"

Bingay told a long story of Cobb making a clever play, and said the next day, "the newspapers again proclaimed Cobb 'the luckiest ball player of all time.' And the strange genius [Cobb] went into a paroxysm of rage."

Then he remarked more on Roosevelt, before winding up, as follows:

"It took an Alexander [the Great] to cut the Gordian knot and it took a young Napoleon to shoot down the mobs of Paris [in the French Revolution]. 'There is a tide in the affairs of men,' said Shakespeare, 'which taken at the flood, leads on to fortune.' And in answer to this [19th-century poet and diplomat James Russell] Lowell wrote, "Truly there is a tide in the affairs of men; but there is no gulf stream setting forever in one direction."

A sympathetic Cobb-as-lucky take was offered up in 1908 by none other than teammate Charley Schmidt. Schmidt was the first of two big leaguers who Cobb was in a brief physical fight with; Schmidt apparently threw the only punch. The three biographies feature the fight, which was tied to Cobb's earlier noted altercation with a half-drunk black man in 1907. "Any man who can do what Cobb has done is not lucky," Schmidt said in 1908. "He's just a marvel. Of course, Ty did have luck. Any ball player who has a good year is lucky. But with his wonderful ability and his luck combined, Cobb last year was a player so great that his work can't be described; it's kind of beyond belief."

In 1926, veteran *Cleveland Plain Dealer* sports editor Henry P. Edwards wrote, "do you remember how they [fans] used to call Ty Cobb lucky when a series of errors would allow him to make the circuit of the bases? 'Lucky Ty,' they called him when it was Ty himself, by his daring that provoked the misplays." Cleveland's Lajoie, Edwards also recalled, would be called "Lucky Larry" when he hit a Texas leaguer, a fly that dropped between an infielder and outfielder. Fans "simply forgot that it was because of Lajoie's prowess at the bat that the outfielders played with their backs to the [outfield] wall and thus allowed the short blows to fall safely. Yes, I always noticed that it was the star ball player, the smart footballer and the best football elevens that got the breaks."

Returning a fourth time to the chronology of 1948:

In a general curiosity column, the *Tucson Daily Citizen* said, "The only man whose surname is Ruth in 'Who's Who in America' is Dr. Henry Swartley Ruth of Philadelphia, physician and anesthesiologist. There are 14 Cobbs in 'Who's Who,' but Tyrus Raymond Cobb is not one of them. There are no Durochers represented. But Branch Rickey is in there with a 14-line biography which states in part he was born in Stockdale, O. [Ohio], attended five colleges, has six children, and now lives in Brooklyn."

Next up is a meaty Cunningham *Boston Herald* column that I previewed twice earlier. One reason why Cunningham was so interested in Cobb is that personality-wise, Williams and Cobb were similar. As explained by sportswriter Stanley Frank in the *Saturday Evening Post* in 1950, players can be considered "loners" among their contemporaries. Frank added, "You could draw up a great all-time, all-star team of loners, including Ty Cobb, Rogers Hornsby, Grover Cleveland Alexander, Ted Williams, Joe DiMaggio, Lefty Grove and other aloof blokes too numerous to mention."

Cunningham wrote, "In reference to possible analogy [sic] between Tyrus and Theodore [Ted's given first name], however, Cobb has led a strange sort of life in his relations with his fellow man."

In his column that contained Cobb's response, Cunningham began with, "The greatest baseball player the world ever knew has written me a letter saying that, as a sports writer, I'm far from the likewise [sic]." Cobb had responded to a column of his from more than three months earlier that Cunningham reflected on as having been "intended to be complimentary." The headline of that original column was: "Ted and Cobb Good Fellas: 'Neath Rough Exteriors Pound Hearts of Gold"

Cobb's position "is that he never went after anything more than his rights on the base path, that he often deliberately refrained from piling into base guardians when he would have been within his rights to do so."

In his letter, Cobb wrote, "I do not know how far back you go, but you should know that [1906-18 American League shortstop]

NOW
Bill CUNNINGHAM
hangs his hat at the
BOSTON HERALD

I am looking forward, with keenest anticipation, to my new career as a member of the staff of The Boston Herald. To old friends, let me say nothing's changed but my base of operations. It's the same column, same guy, same policies, punditry and persiflage. I hope we'll still meet daily in the same old place and hold the same old town meeting upon whatever seems to be interesting at the moment in the same old way. To the Herald reader family, a polite How do you do. Ma'am. Sir, and those younger? The name, in case you didn't catch it, is Cunningham. C, as in catsup; U, as in usufruct; N, as in anyhow . . . and that's it. Anyhow and everyhow, a loyal and eager Heraldian, henceforth. I am.

Yours, in there pitchin',

Bill Cunningham

Heinie Wagner wore thick felt pads under his stockings and that he blocked off base runners, who were entitled to the base paths. You should know that [Bill] Carrigan[,] at the plate, dropped the mask and the bat in front of the plate to interfere with base runners trying to score."

(In 1960, Cobb would instead single out catcher Paul Krichell, from an incident in 1912. Speaking to columnist Joe Williams of the *New York World-Telegram and Sun*, he would say, "Just the other day a fellow wrote how I'd tear into home plate, with my spikes high, as if I intended to cut the catcher in half. What he didn't mention was that the catcher put his mask in front of the plate, and the bat, too, if he had time to reach for it. Paul Kri[c]hell of the Browns did that once too often." Asked by Williams what happened, Cobb replied, "I slid in high, scissored him between my legs, a bone snapped in his shoulder, and the guy never caught another ball game in his life." Williams then ended his column with sarcasm: "Disheartening thing about people is they don't recognize a Little Lord Fauntleroy [a rags-to-riches persona worthy of sentimental support] when they see one.")

In the next part of his 1948 column, Cunningham wrote that he did not understand the "and the bat" part. He then quoted this part of the letter: "Also that [Dutch] Leonard and [Carl] Mays and [the white Rube] Foster, possibly following their manager's instructions, did not hesitate to throw at the batter's head. I had two ribs broken by Foster, but this seemed to have been good procedure. . . anybody who retaliated suffered from the printed page. It might surprise you to see the spike marks I carry as scars. Oh, I know, an outfielder never gets spiked! Yet I probably have more scars on me than anybody can charge I ever inflicted. . .

"If you as a baseball writer analyze the way I made my slide, fallaway, fadeaway or whatnot, you'll realize that to spike anybody the spike would have had to be on the toe of my shoe. I am sending you an actual, on-the-spot photograph of my 'terrible, brutal spiking of Baker' that has been written so much about. You'll note that Baker is on the offensive and that I am clearly trying to evade him. Baker received a little cut on his forearm, and never lost an inning's play."

Cunningham's earlier column had said this of Cobb: "The fans of his long generation in baseball marveled [sic] at his feats and granted his kingship, but any use of the word 'love' in connection with him would have been like trying to apply it to a man-killing stallion with steel-trap teeth and razor-sharp heels. Ty played ball as if he resented the presence of everybody else, especially everybody else on the other team, the umpires and some members of the crowd, but he played ball." Then he cited Cobb's extraordinary statistics, including relative to Ruth. Later in that column, he wrote that Cobb played baseball "as if he were killing snakes."

(In a 1958 letter to a Mr. C. B. Hooton, Cobb would cover some similar ground to the above: "one in reading a story should remember, so many are bum raps and not true, I have never started anything but have retaliated if I had been inflicted, the individual cannot cry to the manager or [news]paper or umpire, he has to put the fear in the player who inflicts, I have dodged many balls at my head. I have never had a fight on the field." Also in that letter, he contrasted his fadeaway or fallaway slide to sliding styles of the 1950s, especially to break up a double play, that he implied were far more violent.)

Cobb also took issue with Cunningham's original article for mentioning his marital difficulties, saying that was out of bounds and that Cunningham had made up a story about Cobb's forgetting his wife's name. Cunningham countered that the story "was in all the nation's press, and the name anecdote [sic], true or false, in other print than this." Cunningham in his original column had transitioned to Cobb's divorce right after commenting on his arguing persona on the golf course, as follows: "Evidently he was something of the same way at home, for his family had moved out on him and, not so many months back, his long-time marriage was dissolved by divorce. The papers reported that he professed to be unable to remember Mrs. Cobb's first name. 'I'd hate to tell you,' responded Cobb."

(For the record, Cunningham's recollection was accurate, although it is possible that the underlying news report was faulty. In 1947, when the Cobbs were in their final divorce proceedings – they had been separated since 1939 – a California Superior Court judge signed an order that directed Cobb to appear for a deposition. The AP reported that "Mrs. Cobb's petition did not state her Christian name. When a newsman asked Mr. Cobb to supply it, he said he 'didn't know it.' She sometimes used 'C. M.,' sometimes just 'C.,' he said."

"'But what did you call her,' the questioner persisted."

"'I wouldn't like to say,' answered Mr. Cobb wryly.")

Cunningham continued and closed with the following thoughts:

Also, "Ty resents my having implied that he was powerfully lucky in having plucked practically all his early baseball salary into a little-known soft drink that turned out to be nothing less than Coca-Cola and which made him a millionaire. That particular bit was given me [sic] by a Coca-Cola official, but Ty says the timing is screwgee, that he broke into baseball in 1905, and bought his Coca-Cola stock in 1917 or 1918. He made other investments, he said, and has other investments now. The point of that, evidently, is that he wants full credit for being a smart financier, and not just a dumb bell [sic] player who chanced to hit it rich with one lucky buy.

"The old hero thus wants the record straightened to read that he was a generous adversary, a perfect gentleman, professionally and personally, and an astute business man who compiled a fortune with intelligent investments. That's O.K. here. That's what I thought I said the other time. Ty must be a little out of the swing of reading modern sports page journalese. Maybe we do occasionally make it too salty for an old-timer's sake. From here on, if ever again, I'll try to remember that the flavor is Peach."

One part of Cobb's dueling letter was quoted earlier, for Cobb's recalling that he had been a church boy and that being "put through the paces" by "some pretty hard old-time" players on Detroit "probably made me a more effective ball player."

In November, Cobb's old-baseball-was-superior take would get play in *Sport* magazine. A long feature combined his career and his modern-day views. Sports editor John M. Flynn of the *Berkshire Eagle* in Pittsfield, Mass., wrote, "The Sport article on Cobb points out that, though Cobb was the most hated and the most feared player of his or any other era, he played in more games, scored more runs, made more hits, stole more bases, [and] held more records than any other man in baseball history."

Flynn wrongly converted into a direct quote this paraphrase of Cobb by *Sport* article writer Jack Sher: "The 'live' ball has spoiled the game, [and] eliminated the speed and skill a player needed during the era of the squashy, slow apple."

Then Flynn correctly reprinted these direct quotes from Cobb: "Why, that rabbit-ball they use now has ruined the value of the one run and the double steal. Outfielders now are no more than caddies. They don't even attempt to cut loose with a throw to stop a run at the plate. Second base is no longer a place that puts a runner in scoring position."

Sports columnist Wray of the *St. Louis Post-Dispatch* featured excerpts too and added, "The old-timers merely built up the pitcher by using a mush ball" whereas today, "we build up the batters by putting jack-rabbit into the horsehide." The subtitle on Wray's column was: "Cobb's Remarks May Seem a Bit Corny"

In a letter from California to Helene Champlain, manager of the bookstore at the Waldorf Astoria Hotel, he wrote, "I found your gloves in front room here, asked the 'person' to wrap and address, I can never forgive or forget the actions[;] this was not only time, I am not in that sort of league, 'they' are leaving here within 3 days, fired, hope you understand can[']t write more now, will when in different mood and not in such a rush, party made themselves very important in service my home for work was fine, but liked to drink, very suspicious listening & snooping, talked seriously, tried to get too close, failed, that made it worse, hope you understand & can forget, am looking for someone to help me now."

(Cobb had written to Champlain at least as far back as 1922. Champlain's dad had recently been to a Detroit game that year, and Cobb quipped, "Tell your Dad, the next time he comes out to the Ball Park, to decorate himself with a few horse-shoes in advance, as I have discovered who was the jinx." In 1923, he wrote to her in advance of the season, "Yes, all of your favorites, or most of them will be back, [Bob] Jones, [Lu] Blue, [Bert] Cole, and others. When you get a little older I will select a nice one for you and try to make the match.")

A Literary Interlude

Possibly the greatest coincidence between a throwaway line in one of the Cobb biographies with something tangible to Cobb comes courtesy of Leerhsen. In his hazing discussion, he wrote that in the early 20th century, some people "were starting to see the stupidity in hazing, especially after a famous 1898 case in which a West Point Cadet Oscar Booze died after being held down and forced to drink Tabasco sauce. Yet most still believed, as Senator Albert [J.] Beveridge of Indiana did [in a 1905 book], that the practice had roots in healthy male aggression. 'A young man is like a male animal after all,' Beveridge said, 'and those who object to his rioting like a young bull are in perpetual quarrel with nature.'" (Leerhsen did relatively well in rendering this quote from the original, only changing one word, and only from uppercase to lowercase. But he added the word "like" in the fifth word of the quote. In the original, Beveridge wrote, "A young man is a male animal after all. . . ")

Beveridge was a progressive Republican senator from 1899 to 1911 and a future Pulitzer Prize-winning author. In a 1948 letter from California to Champlain, Cobb asked her to send him Beveridge's three-volume work on Thomas Jefferson. For what it is worth, in corresponding with Champlain, Cobb had some trouble with remembering names, a problem that would show up in his 1961 book. One problem is that he referred to Beveridge as having the first name "Alfred." Another is that Beveridge had not written about Jefferson; perhaps Cobb was referring to Henry S. Randall's trailblazing 1858 three-volume *The Life of Thomas Jefferson*.

In a 1949 letter to Champlain that I could not fully see, Cobb apparently asked her for a copy of one of any number of Jefferson books by Claude G. Bowers – who himself wrote a 1932 biography of Beveridge.

In a second letter back in 1948, he sought writings by Stoddard, presumably Lothrop Stoddard, a popular pro-white eugenics, geopolitical theorist between the world wars. A 1920 title of his was *The Rising Tide of Color: The Threat*

Against White World Supremacy. Also in that second letter, he requested Creel's "Patrick Henry, [Abraham] Lincoln, Andrew Jackson, and above all his [Confederate lieutenant general] Nathan [Bedford] For[r]est. His writings, I think for Collier[']s, I would be satisfied much, if I could receive these. If all his writings should be done in book form, including all, I would be happy if I could receive some, though if not, the ones I indicate would satisfy me."

The closest-matching Creel would be George Edward Creel, a well-known muckraking journalist and stalwart anti-German who led the Committee on Public Information, a propaganda arm of the Wilson Administration during the Great War. Creel wrote articles in the 1920s for *Collier's* that made the case for immigration restrictions.

Otherwise in the 1948 letter to Champlain, Cobb began by saying, "am here alone, housekeeper fired – been back to Detroit to get a Fleetwood model 60 cadillac, had a tough time through Nebraska in the snow." After mentioning the Jefferson volumes and before his closing sequence on his health and his conveyance of his best wishes, he wrote one other thing: "Enjoyed Farley[']s book."

No doubt he was referring to James A. Farley's 1948 *Jim Farley's Story: The Roosevelt Years.* Farley was a former chairman of the Democratic National Committee. With Franklin D. Roosevelt's election, Farley became the unofficial chief of patronage jobs in his presidency's first two terms and thus during much of the Great Depression, as Postmaster General when the postal service was still a government department.

Digressing to overlaps between Cobb and Farley, who would later become a Coca-Cola executive:

Farley was present at the opening of the Baseball Hall of Fame in 1939. As noted earlier, Cobb claimed to friend Maines that he was late for a picture-taking session so as to avoid appearing together with Commissioner Landis. Although, as Rita Reif of the *New York Times* said in 1996, "Cobb came too late to see Postmaster General James A. Farley hold up a sheet of freshly printed baseball stamps," Cobb and ten others "signed envelopes bearing the stamps that were

James A. Farley and the NEA's sports editor, Harry Grayson, in 1938

LUCKY

to

be

a

YANKEE

Joseph Paul
By (JOE) DI MAGGIO
(The Yankee Clipper)

Introduction by
JAMES A. FARLEY

Foreword by
GRANTLAND RICE

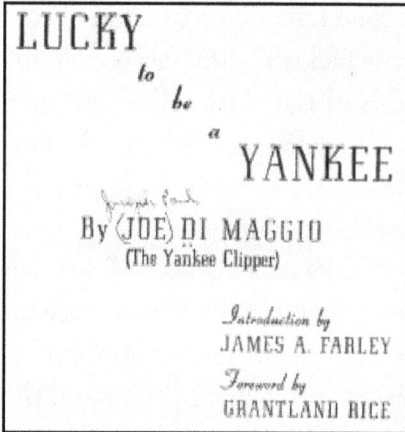

postmarked and cancelled that day at the Cooperstown Post Office."

After opposing Roosevelt in his 1940 re-election, Farley became chairman of the board of a chunk of Cobb's cash cow, the Coca-Cola Export Corporation. Farley was born in 1888 and lived to 1976. Baseball-wise, he was a huge New York Yankees fan with his own box seats along the first-base line in Yankee Stadium, Farley's Box. Based on a radio interview that he gave in 1973, he had seen Cobb play apparently over all segments of Cobb's career.

A big chunk of the 38-minute interview covers sports, especially baseball. When it turned to baseball, an elderly interviewer, George O'Brien, asked about Cobb's connection to the company. Farley replied, "Mr. Woodruff, who is now the chairman of the finance committee of Coca-Cola, he got Cobb interested in it and he bought stock in those days which was rather low-priced stock." Farley also said that he thought that Cobb had bought two bottling plants, in Twin Falls and California. Cobb did buy the Twin Falls one, while his son Herschel bought ones in Santa Maria, Calif., and Bend, Ore. Herschel died in 1951, and the Bend plant was sold by Herschel's widow in 1955. Then Farley said:

"Cobb was a mean fellow, you know, as a person he was as mean as he could be, mean on the ball field." After being briefly interrupted by O'Brien, he continued, "He got a lot of money, though, he made a lot of money in other stocks. I think Mr. Woodruff probably advised him. He left a lot of money."

(In possibly more than a coincidence, "mean" would be an adjective ascribed to

at the wedding of an unnamed couple: to the right of the couple are, respectively, Elizabeth and James A. Farley, and Nell and Robert W. Woodruff

Cobb by Woodruff biographer Charles Newton Elliott, in quoting the late Woodruff in his 1979 biography of him.

In it, as also related by Bak in his 1994 and 2005 books, Elliott wrote, "One of the incidents Woodruff tells happened after Ty Cobb's baseball playing days were over. He had ambitions to take over the Detroit Tigers, for whom he had played, as manager, and asked his hunting partner for advice."

"If you do," said Woodruff, "I'll have to lay odds that you wouldn't last out the season."

"Why do you say that?"

"You're too damn mean," Woodruff said.)

Returning to the interview of Farley:

Asked what Cobb would do if a catcher were blocking the plate today, Farley agreed with O'Brien that he would go in feet first: "Oh indeed he would, oh indeed he would. He was a mean ballplayer. He'd get on first base and he'd get the pitcher crazy. And then before you know it he'd be on second and before you know it he'd be [interrupts his own thought]. I saw him play against the Yankees many times. He was a great baserunner and a great, a great hitter. But he was a mean ballplayer. He didn't get along with the players, you know. He got in many fights." Farley referred to Cobb's fight with teammate Moriarty in 1911, which, as noted earlier, sounds more like a bad spat. In squaring off with combatants, Farley added, "he was beaten up by more than one." O'Brien mentioned the Buck Herzog fight in 1917 and Farley acknowledged having heard of that one.

For posterity, Cobb and Farley are also linked in a 1956 book. In humorist-smoker J. P. McEvoy's 1956 *Charlie Would Have Loved This*, McEvoy wrote, "Wasn't it Ty Cobb who said smoking stupifies the brain? I can't even remember that. Look at Jim Farley, he doesn't smoke and he remembers everybody and everything ever said to him."

In his recorded interview with Cobb circa 1950, broadcaster Bob Wolff had told him, "I understand you were a pretty mean man on the bases in your heyday." Cobb replied, "Well, I don't know about that being mean. I was sliding a lot but I did not slide like the boys slide today all up in the air and the boys tumbling around down second base but as far as the spiking business is concerned I could show you a lot of spike wounds on my ankles and my knees that was [sic] put there by basemen jumping up in the air after the ball and then coming down on my ankles and knees and so forth. But you never heard of me being spiked."

When Wolff asked, "And I wouldn't imagine that those fellows ever pulled that same trick twice, did they?" Cobb responded, "Oh no, most spike wounds are unintentional and absolutely the spike wounds that I received I considered absolutely unintentional."

Returning to the chronology and featuring a new year, 1949:

The year featured few waves by Cobb; the highlight was his marriage in October to his second wife. Over dinner later that month with Ward Morehouse and their new respective wives, Cobb said this about his own new marriage: "I had decided to go the rest of the way alone. Whenever I'd go to Georgia they'd introduce me to the eligibles – not that I was anything much – but I never got interested. In Frances I've found somebody who is wonderful. She will be the perfect companion for me. She likes golf, she likes to hunt. She's widely traveled. She's a wonderful cook. I guess I can teach her to like baseball." Two weeks earlier, Cobb had written to Hauck, "The photographers & paper boys sure has [sic] given us 'hell[,]' I mean being after us all the time."

Just one thing that year struck me as notable before his handshake with Don Newcombe at the World Series. He wrote an article for the International News Service, which the *Times-Picayune* in New Orleans titled, "Cobb Expert On Heckling."

Cobb began by saying that he did not want to comment on an incident between now-Giants manager Durocher and a fan that Commissioner Chandler was investigating. Then he told of some examples of heckling during his career and how he handled them. The article contains no revelations and has the tame ending, "The heckling isn't so bad if it's clean. It's hard to stand when the remarks go beyond the bounds of decency."

In Greenville after the World Series, he told sports editor Latimer, "The players of today are not clothed with the initiative they should have. In my time all great hitters [Honus] Wagner, [Eddie] Collins, Jackson, Speaker and others had certain freedom. By that, I mean they had liberties when up there at the plate when infielders rushed in on them, or at times of [sic] certain pitches. They seem to cramp present ball players."

In December, he said this about most valuable player awards, which were instituted in 1931: "I've always felt those awards were phonies." He explained, "As I see it, the trouble with the most valuable player award is that it always goes to a man on a first or second-place club. A player who does good work on a second-division club hasn't a chance."

In 1950:

A reporter for the *Arkansas Gazette* spent a working vacation in California, including an evening at Cobb's home. "While the beauteous Mrs. Cobb was busy knitting argyles, Ty knotted yarns from the memories of one of the greatest of all baseball careers." Cobb discussed his all-time all-star team. In explaining Buck Weaver as its third baseman, he said, "He was just coming to his peak when he [was forced to] quit the game [as part of the 1919 Black Sox scandal]."

At Toots Shor's in New York City after the *Sport* magazine awards dinner featured earlier for Rickey's keynote speech, Speaker asked Cobb to name the greatest ballplayer he had ever seen. DiMaggio was his reply, Ed Sullivan wrote at the time. Back in 1943, Rickey had told the AP that DiMaggio was the best player he had ever seen, "and that goes for Ty Cobb and all the other great ones."

After seeing Harry G. Salsinger's long positive analysis of his playing career in the *Sporting News*, Cobb wrote to thank "Sal" for "your appraisal and defense of me. As you see I am enclosing to you something, I want you to see which is relative to one person that has brought much into my 'late' life." Cobb was presumably referring to his new wife. "I feel too bad it was not of 25 years ago, every day I am forced to feel this, I never thought I would venture again, per past experience, this might sound like a cad [someone who behaves dishonorably] but I don[']t mean it that way, I have had disappointments in what I wanted to attain per ideals etc. but had no cooperation, our lives and reactions were so different, naturally I send this as I being proud of the one now, I knew before I went into it this last year, the enclosed [presumably photograph] is only of the mater [mother's] side, grand Father & Great Grandfather." Cobb also invited Salsinger to visit him in California and stay in his house as long as he wanted to.

To a boy, Art Bissell, Cobb provided a signed autograph as per the request, apparently for a photograph. But he refused to sign an enclosed book because he "did not feel alright" about doing so. In writing back, Cobb also explained, "there are things in book form[,] might say permanent[,] that simply is not true, there has been many thing [sic] untrue that[']s been printed, we call them rainy day stories where a writer has to manufacture it and as a rule it[']s to knock down some one that rates, if it was complimentary the story would not attract attention, many people read it and retail [likely should be retell] it, it gets to form a wrong makeup of a man in peoples mind, lots in this book is simply a rehash of some unreliable stories by some unreliable writers and the author of book has simply grouped them under his name."

For the NEA serial "My Biggest Boner," former catcher Cy Perkins described his as trying to block Cobb as a 19-year-old rookie in 1915. "My poor old ache will never forget it. I still ache and hurt all over when I think about it." On the play, Perkins had caught a throw from the outfield and started up the third base line instead of waiting at the plate. "Cobb was coming down the line like

[1919-20 dominant racehorse] Man o' War in a stampede, and I was on my way to meet him. I didn't have long to wait.

"Wham! Cobb hit me with everything he had – head, shoulders, torso, knees, feet and fists. Any medium old-timer will tell you how the greatest of all ball players did it. The baselines belonged to him, and he took full advantage of the right." Cobb ended up scoring the winning run. For his concluding paragraphs, Perkins wrote that that was the last time he strayed away from the plate to try to tag him and "quickly learned that a catcher met his slashing spikes soon enough."

In an article about stealing signs, Kaese cited

BRUSHING UP SPORTS ·· By Laufer

WHEN THE GREAT COBB KICKED ONE!

AS GEO. BURNS ROUNDED THIRD ON HIS LONG HIT TO THE OUTFIELD, THE EMOTIONAL TYRUS COBB FORGOT HIMSELF. HE LEFT HIS COACHING BOX WITH A SERIES OF WHOOPS AND BACKSLAPS AND ACCOMPANIED BURNS ACROSS THE PLATE. BUT FOXY OLD CLARK GRIFFITH KNEW HIS RULES, SO COBB JOINED THE "BONER CLUB."

COBB

BASEBALL'S **B**IGGEST **B**ONERS — EVEN THE GREAT TY COBB was guilty of a glaring mental blunder on the ball field. It happened in a game between Detroit and Washington. George Burns, Detroit first-baseman, hit a long liner to the deepest center field corner. Burns was rounding third before Clyde Milan, Washington outfielder, retrieved the ball. Cobb, coaching at third and seeing that a throw could not possibly catch Burns, accompanied the runner to the plate with a series of whoops and backslaps. Foxy Clark Griffith, Washington manager, contended that since the ball was still in play, Cobb had retired the runner by coacher's interference. Umpire Hildebrand upheld the contention and baseball's smartest player was that day crowned the goat.

a recent comment from a retired Cobb contemporary, Hall of Fame shortstop Joe Sewell: "The easiest way to get Cobb out was to keep giving signs and have the pitcher throw while Cobb was looking backward."

Sewell had played mainly for Cleveland, and Speaker, a longtime teammate, would say the following a year later, in a NEA feature on the heels of summer testimony by Cobb to Congress: "You know where he got most of his information about enemy pitchers? Why, from the pitchers. He would get friendly with a pitcher. He would brag about the pitcher's curve, get him so awed at praise from the great Cobb that he would show him the grip and the mechanics of delivery. Then the pitcher would wonder why he could not get Cobb out." As reported slightly ungrammatically, Speaker also said on that occasion, "No individual figure is more interested in the game. Who but Ty Cobb would go to the trouble to write to Ted Williams, pass along tips to help him break a slump?"

In 1951:

At a banquet to celebrate the 75th anniversary of the National League, Whitney Martin of the AP wrote, "There was the peerless Ty Cobb, the fire-breathing Georgian who asked no quarter and gave none, with tears welling in his eyes as old friends, and one-time enemies, surrounded him in a spirit of comradeship." The celebration took place at the Grand Central Hotel in New York City.

from left to right in March 1951 at a charity game of major league stars in Los Angeles to benefit the Kiwanis Crippled Children Foundation: Cobb, actor Paul Douglas, Fred Haney and George Sisler. Cobb and Sisler acted as rival managers, and Douglas presented awards to both.

Early in the season, star Stan Musial of the Cardinals was at Camillo's, the new New York City restaurant of Lawton Carver, the former sports editor of the International News Service. Considine of the INS was with Musial and noted when Carver handed him one of Cobb's new "Science of Batting" booklets. Musial then said, "He was the best. But I'll tell you this. Cobb wouldn't have played 24 years in these times, the way we have to keep on the go – with day games and night games and climbing in and out of sleepers [train sleeping cars] without enough rest." Musial added that he hoped that his words would not be viewed as criticizing Cobb. "Nobody was close to him," he then said, meaning in baseball feats, and he gave examples such as Cobb hitting .316 in his first regular season and .323 in his final one.

A week later, Cobb's theme of how current baseball was inferior to his day got a boost in *Sport* magazine. Sports editor Parker of the *New York Mirror* wrote a piece with the title, "Let's Stop Babying Our Ballplayers."

For example, Parker said that Williams had recently told sportswriters in Florida, "where he was enjoying his usual winter of fishing, that he hadn't made up his mind whether or not he would play in the exhibition games [for the upcoming season]. Any ballplayer from Ty Cobb down who dared tell his manager when he would or wouldn't play in the good old days would be fined and suspended so fast it would seem like an unassisted double play." Actually, Cobb received special permission in some seasons to show up late to spring training, by promising to train on his own.

Parker also wrote that "there's altogether too much fraternizing in modern baseball to keep alive the bitter rivalry that existed in the good old days when Ty Cobb gave and took in the constant duel of spikes." Parker, despite being

at Toots Shor's restaurant in New York City during the National League 75th anniversary celebration, all from left to right: (standing) Jimmie Foxx, Mel Ott, Mickey Cochrane, Ed Walsh, Toots Shor, Rogers Hornsby, Pie Traynor and Tris Speaker; (seated) Fred Clarke, Arlie Latham, Cy Young, George Sisler, Kid Nichols, Cobb and Charley Gehringer

below: (standing) Clarke, Cochrane and a Mystery Person; (seated) Nichols, Cobb, Gehringer and Ott

all-around athlete Jim Thorpe
and Cobb in 1951

pro-Cobb in philosophy, also bought into the image of Cobb as a spiker. (Another pro-Cobb writer was Daley of the *New York Times*, and yet Daley in a similar vein wrote in 1948, "The Old Catchers' Home is filled with chaps who were carved up by Cobb's spikes.") As a sign of where he stood overall, Parker also wrote the following in that article: "Ty Cobb, who had 'slumped' to .334 in 1920, jumped up to .389 the following season when the ball was enlivened for Babe Ruth's special benefit, and in 1922, Cobb reached the amazing figure of .401, as the death knell was sounded for freak deliveries such as the spitter."

Sports editor Lyall Smith of the *Free Press* saw Parker's article and seemingly was drawn to its

subhead, "Too many major-leaguers [sic] do their roadwork in shiny new cars given to them by hero-worshipping fans. Diathermy machines and whirlpool baths are now almost as essential baseball equipment as bats and gloves. What

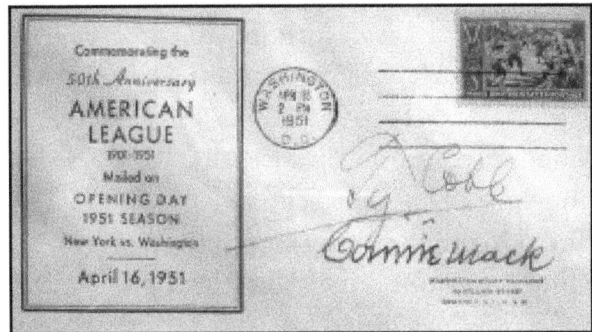

happened to the rugged old game played by Cobb, Wagner and Mathewson?"

Smith replied that Parker's article "pooh-poohs the fact that a trainer is attached to every modern[-]day club. It sneers at the use of such modern equipment as diathermy [body tissue heat-generating] machines and whirlpool baths. And it paints the oldtime ballplayer as a burly bruiser who laughed at such trifling injuries as a fractured skull, broken leg, or what-have-you."

Smith continued, "Such nostalgic cries of anguish must emanate from the same old codgers who would rather ride in a one-horse shay [carriage] than in a sleek '51 convertible. They'd prefer a leaky hot water

Lyall Smith

bottle to an electric pad, a pair of wrapped hot bricks to an electric blanket, and a hoot and a holler to the telephone.

"These are the same characters who insist that the modern game of baseball can't compare to the game of yesteryear. Why can't it? Simply because they remember one great player or one great play and compare every player and/or every play to that player and play."

Invoking Cobb later on, Smith wrote, "We have been told some stories about Cobb's daring base running and are expected to believe he could steal home in the ninth inning to win a ballgame [sic] anytime he felt like it. Of course, the fact that he was absolutely a flop in two [of his three] World Series[, batting a combined .217 in the two,] seldom is aired."

Returning a second time to the chronology of 1951:

In the summer, three weeks after throwing out the first pitch at the All-Star Game in Detroit, he delivered his testimony to Congress. He was the lead-off witness at a House Judiciary Committee hearing on baseball's anti-trust exemption. Alexander and Hornbaker summarized Cobb's serious views on the subject. Alexander examined videotape, noting that Cobb was wearing reading glasses "and frequently cupping his ear to hear questions." Despite watching Cobb on film, Alexander got carried away in saying that mostly "he entertained the congressmen with stories from his early baseball years." In asking about his early years, the subcommittee had him focus on details of his contract negotiations, some of which he could not recall.

at the 1951 All-Star Game, including with the American League's manager, Casey Stengel

Arthur L. Edson of the AP wrote that subcommittee members "seemed a little awed by the great man. Every question was respectfully phrased. The old needle, an instrument usually kept handy for investigations like this, was never once brought out."

The following is a slight substitute to Edson's reporting, to reflect the true hearing transcript and still reflect the humor that he was trying to point to. For example, the chairman, Representative Emanuel Celler of New York, asked Cobb to state when he was elected to the Hall of Fame.

"I couldn't say," Cobb replied.

Then Celler asked, "Was it recently?"

To that, Cobb replied, "It was when the Hall of Fame was inaugurated. I happened to have been the first elected."

The transcript indicates "[Laughter]."

Then Celler asked, "Did you say you just happened to be?"

"[Laughter]" appears at that point too. Cobb replied, "I felt honored to be."

Edson added later on in parentheses, "Too bad no one asked Cobb about the argument Cobb is reported to have had once with his roommate," Nap Rucker. The story was first reported by Daley in the *New York Times* in 1949 and told by Rucker in 1951 to Guy Tiller of the *Atlanta Constitution*. "It was on account of Rucker" having gotten to the bathtub first that the spat occurred, Edson added. According to Rucker, Cobb declared to him at the time, "I got to be first – all the time." The story will be presented later in fuller detail.

At the hearing, one of Cobb's more interesting lines off the main subject was being concerned about transferring big-league teams to cities such as Los Angeles, San Francisco or Milwaukee; they would all end up getting transferred ones. "In the first place, you have a travel danger. You would have to travel by plane. And if you owned a baseball franchise, you would not want to put all your players there in one ship and get it wrecked, maybe." When Representative Patrick J. Hillings of California said professional football teams do travel to California, Cobb replied, "The cost of travel is there, with the distance. And then how about those other teams in the Pacific Coast League? They do pretty well in Los Angeles and San Francisco. And what would happen in Sacramento? Where are they going to get their club to fill out their league? They haven't any other clubs there."

The AP ran a story on the Cobb-Hillings exchange. Its report ended by citing testimony from National League President Ford Frick. Frick said that if they so desire, Pacific Coast League and other cities will in the future be able to have a major league team.

A postscript to the hearings is that in conjunction with it, Cobb was named to a three-person panel to make recommendations about salaries in professional baseball. Cobb indeed participated in its set of hearings, which were chaired by a professor at the University of Maryland, Harry C. Byrd. While Cobb went along with the panel's findings, the panel itself was abolished in 1953 by President Eisenhower. In 2013, the University of Maryland Archives released a Cobb letter to Byrd in which Cobb apologized for not getting back for a long time to okay the report. The reason cited? He had been hunting in Idaho.

A second postscript is that two weeks after his testimony, he wrote to recently deposed baseball Commissioner Chandler, "I had no opportunity to say what I wanted about you, no questions were asked relative to commissioner[,] etc. I was ready." In apparently referring to Chandler's testimony, he wrote, "I enjoyed what I read of yours except you did not open up on the few that you could have. I traveled back there with [Yankees co-owner] Del Webb, but I think in his way is contrite, he asked me some questions, I told him the truth that you had never said anything derogatory to him, I did state I thought you had been treated badly and that you had been a fine commissioner and they had rocked the boat and stirred up a 'rat's nest' of their own making, he was very silent after that. Hope to see you sometime and tell you more, they have troubles." Webb had helped lead a successful effort to oust Chandler earlier in the year.

A prelude to the hearings relates to retired player Clyde Milan, who was a great base stealer in Cobb's day. As of 1951, he was a coach for Washington. After Cobb's first *Life* article in 1952, Milan would defend him in an interview.

Upon Milan's death in 1953, Hawkins of the *Washington Star* said that Milan had reminisced recently that Cobb had once told him not to try to steal so many bases, and that otherwise he would wear out his legs and shorten his career. "Ty just couldn't stand anybody being close to him in anything and he tried to talk me out of stealing so much so he wouldn't have any trouble leading the league."

Milan is the one semi-great player who Cobb sent letters to decades apart – and that have surfaced in auctions. He sent Milan a postcard in 1929 from Berlin, during his European vacation. "Saw Zeppelin [German-built hydrogen-filled commercial airship] start on trip around world – This is some speedy city." Then, in a 1951 letter right after his trip to testify, Cobb apologized to Milan by letter. During his trip to Washington, D.C., when they were both at a game at Griffith Stadium, Cobb had not stopped by the clubhouse to see him. He did note that he had the chance to "hail" Milan from a distance, from the personal box seats of Washington owner Griffith. He explained, "I had to go to press box, [to see Senators broadcaster] Arch McDonald, then to Griff[']s office to meet [Chief] Justice [Fred M. Vinson], so between Griff & [Yankee co-owner] Del [Webb] I had little to say." Cobb also wrote, "I would like to have been at least for a few minutes with you, one who I have always thought so much of."

Based on Cobb's comment about Vinson, and having seen a picture of Cobb and Vinson together from the game, I did a Google search and found a letter mentioning Cobb that Vinson sent days later to Sherman "Shay" Minton, an associate justice on the Supreme Court. It covered three distinct substantive topics. The first topic was Cobb, and Vinson wrote, "Old Ty Cobb certainly was well received at the ball park and before the Congressional Committee. His 'heads up' play on the

from left to right at Griffith Stadium in 1951: Cobb, Clark Griffith, Chief Justice Fred M. Vinson and Del Webb

diamond will never be forgotten by us old-timers, and the present-day sports writers do a very good job in keeping him at the top. I do not know what Congress will do in regard to the legislation before it affecting [sic] baseball. It would seem to me that they have gone afield in attempting to run the game from the committee room."

In Eugene, Ore., Cobb was honored at a game. "Cobb leaned over backwards in accommodating the fans – giving hundreds of autographs, picture posing, speech-making and handshaking. Despite a tedious trip from their summer home at Lake Tahoe, the Cobbs were extremely gracious." Ty "proved to be a genial

(Reg.-Guard photo. Wiltshire engraving)

THESE EUGENE KNOTHOLE BASEBALLERS are probably not lefthanded hitters, but they received expert instruction from the greatest of all Major League hitters at Bethel Park Tuesday night—the immortal Ty Cobb. The southpaw hitter, who had a lifetime average of .367, is demonstrating to these youngsters the grip he used through his 24 years of big league baseball. More than 2000 spectators were on hand to welcome baseball's first member of the "Hall of Fame."

guest – belying the reputation he acquired as a brusk [brusque] and unsociable man while fighting his way to the top of the 'National Pastime' with his hits, fists and wits during 24 years in the big leagues."

In an interview during his visit, when asked about the throwing of the World Series in 1919, he said baseball is the cleanest of sports. "There are too many people involved in baseball to fix the game." In 1919, "the White Sox had trouble throwing the World Series to Cincinnati by a 5-3 [5-games-to-3] margin," he said.

In October, Red Smith of the *New York Herald Tribune* reported that during a World Series game between the Yankees and the Giants, "Three thousand miles away in California, Ty Cobb watched by television and telephoned New York to suggest that Joe change his stance." Meanwhile, that very same day, Kaese of the *Boston Globe* wrote that DiMaggio "denied that a telephone tip from Ty Cobb, on the Pacific Coast, had straightened him out. He credited [fellow retired players] Lefty O'Doul and Lew Fonseca for suggesting changes in his stance, and a new 34-ounce Babe Ruth bat."

Digressing to more about O'Doul:

He was a disciple of Cobb who has the highest batting average for a non-Hall of Famer who is eligible for membership, .349; his Hall of Fame problem is that his career was too short, as he has just 1,140 lifetime hits. Cobb typically received special permission in the spring to train alone, in seasons other than the six that he was Detroit's player-manager. Cobb spent the early part of his final spring training, 1928, with the Giants in Augusta. One day during training, Rud Rennie of the *New York Herald Tribune* reported on an interaction between O'Doul, then a Giant, and Cobb:

"O'Doul also picked up a few tips from Cobb. He wanted to know how to hit to left field and Cobb told him how to do it by shifting his feet and stepping up to a curve ball thrown by a right-hander. Cobb also advised O'Doul to watch closely the movements of an opposing pitcher with men on bases and to look particularly for movements of the feet, head and hands, which might betray the pitcher's intentions as to whether he was going to throw to a base or the plate.

"Another secret imparted to O'Doul by the master of all base stealers was this: When

Lefty O'Doul and Cobb in 1933

running to a base, watch the eyes of the player who is in front of you receiving the ball. If he looks to his left you know the ball is coming in that direction, so slide to his right. If he looks to his right, slide the other way."

Russell P. "Red" Reeder, who played in spring training with the Giants in Augusta in 1928, touched on something else in a 1971 letter to former reporter Ken Smith; Smith had covered that spring training for the *New York Mirror* and was now director of the Hall of Fame. Reeder wrote, "Ty was concerned over Lefty O'Doul's grip; he was squeezing the sawdust out of the bat. This proved simple to correct, and O'Doul became the first of his pupils to react. He suddenly began to spray line drives."

from left to right in 1937 (at a Catholic Youth Organization benefit game): now-Yankee Joe DiMaggio, Cobb, and Seals outfielder Dom DiMaggio and manager Lefty O'Doul

Returning a third time to the chronology of 1951:

The baseball comedy movie "Angels in the Outfield" was released in October by Metro-Goldwyn-Mayer, and Cobb appeared as himself. DiMaggio made a vocal cameo appearance too, right before Cobb, in uniform and on the playing field. Then the scene shifted indoors, where Cobb was interviewed by a radio host. Asked what he thought, which was a reference to mystery angels that were helping the players, he said in a lively voice, "Well, all I can say is that this game of baseball has certainly changed."

In December 1951, after DiMaggio announced his retirement, Jack McDonald interviewed Cobb. Cobb told him that DiMaggio should stay completely away from the game for awhile and thus reject an offer to become a Yankees television broadcaster. "That's what I did. I got as far away from it as I could. I packed up and went to Europe, where I couldn't see a box score or hear a game broadcast."

Digressing to Cobb's advice to himself and to others about retiring:

He had spoken on this subject back in 1929, after spending the first summer of his post-career in Europe. At that time, he had told the Associated Press, "I have found that you cannot spend twenty-four years in baseball and then forget it, unless you do as I did and go a long way off." Also, "I have not felt a yearning for the game this Summer because I was in Europe and there was no baseball all about me as there would have been if I had stayed at home, but now that I am back it is different."

One other loose end is from 1960, when San Francisco native Jackie Jensen retired from the Boston Red Sox. Cobb wrote to him on his own initiative and told John Gillooly of the *Boston Daily Record*, "Now I am not a meddler. I don't want to stick my nose in anybody's business. [Red Sox owner] Tom Yawkey and I are friends but I didn't write to Jensen for his sake, although he's losing an important part of his machine when a 100-runs-batted-in player suddenly walks out on him. Jensen's a $300,000 asset [$2.4 million in today's dollars]."

He continued, "I wrote Joe DiMaggio an 8-10 page letter when he left the game. I told him he had a couple of years of good baseball left and that he owed it to the fans and his club to keep on playing." Cobb also told Gillooly that Jensen "couldn't afford to give up the salary he was getting to go into the restaurant business."

The Cobb-Jensen letter was auctioned by Christie's in 2006, and I saw its synopsis of it. Cobb advised that "the salary amount quoted is too much to toss aside. Your ability to earn now, also providing for your family's future is in the picture much. Remember you are not going to drop out of baseball for a year or two and come back in your present stride." He also advised Jensen, "Lay your true cards on the table. . . tell [owner] Yawkey you have stood for the second fiddle stuff long enough. . . tell Yawkey you will sign for as much as Ted or more. . . If it's your desire to quit Jackie that's your business, only but always remember this letter. Get the money sure."

The synopsis adds, "The real problem, it turns out, was Jensen's fear of flying! After quitting [prior to] the 1960 season he returned the following year, but so did his anxieties. When he refused to go on a road trip, Sox management docked him for the missed games. He quit altogether in August 1961."

Returning a fourth time to the chronology of 1951:

Starting in 1951, Cobb provided advice to a new Class C minor league team around his home in Twins Falls, Idaho, the Magic Valley Cowboys. He was also a stockholder in it. In 1952, the directors of the team elected Cobb its honorary president and presented him with a lifetime pass. Writing on the AP wire in late 1951, the sports editor of the *Times-News* in Twin Falls said representatives of the club went to a baseball meeting in Ohio "armed with letters and advance spadework by Cobb." Incidentally, that sports editor, Bob Gilliam, made an observation about Cobb that I did not come across otherwise: "Cobb was never a person for neat dressing and frequently appears with a day's growth of beard."

(One of his views as of 1953, as expressed to Nevada neighbor Frank H. Bartholomew of the United Press, was that minor league teams should have exclusive rights to all players developed within a 75-mile radius of their own ball parks. "It will help baseball attendance in the minors; everyone likes to see a home town kid making good. It will make for better baseball and give the minors something to build on other than the over-age players released by the big leagues." During the House Judiciary subcommittee hearing, retired big-league general manager Leland "Larry" MacPhail, Sr. had said, "I believe that Ty Cobb said to me at one time – he was a little critical of some aspects of baseball, and he said, 'It is losing its old home-town spirit.'")

In a letter to veteran hunting and general sportswriter George "Stoney" McLinn, who was preparing articles about him, Cobb said, "I have had many offers for story of life etc. also several for picture, (Hollywood), have turned them down because they would want to make me appear as an ogre and I won[']t subscribe to anything not true just to add something sensational & controversial for those jew [sic] picture guys." Also in the letter, Cobb wrote, "I am feeling fine but am a little heavy in weight and now on a reduction basis to take off 12 lbs."

In 1952:

After seeing Cobb's comments to the AP favoring integration of the Texas League, *Detroit Free Press* columnist Bingay wrote that Gustave Le Bon, "famed French psychologist and social historian, wrote a book some 60 years ago, 'The Crowd; a Study of the Popular Mind.' In it he said: 'Sudden political revolutions which strike the historian most forcibly are those of manners and thought. . . . The true revolutions which transform the destinies of a people are accompanied so slowly that the historians can hardly point to their beginnings. . . . Individuals and their methods, not regulations, make the value of a people. The test of democracy is the strength of its citizenship.'"

He added, "I looked that up after reading the statement of Ty Cobb that he was in favor of racial freedom in baseball." Bingay had notably covered Cobb's 1907 altercation with the black groundskeeper's half-drunk black friend.

Also in early 1952, weeks after Cobb's pro-integration interview with him in the *Sporting News*, McDonald devoted much of a *San Francisco Call-Bulletin* column to him. In the column, Cobb called himself a "big dumbbell" for misusing his throwing arm at a stage of his playing career, by trying to practice pitching. "I spoiled a very good arm by experimenting with knuckle balls and spitters when spring practice lagged. It was plain skylarking, that's all. I succeeded in almost ruining a good outfielder's arm by doing it."

Digressing to more about Cobb and his desire to pitch:

In 1918, syndicated sports columnist Paul Purman had written, "Ty Cobb always wanted to be a pitcher and several years ago would take his turn on the mound during batting practice. He stopped this when he found it was injuring his throwing arm."

While in New York City in 1960, Cobb told Williams of the *New York World-Telegram and Sun*, "I don't know whether I ever told anybody this before. I hurt my arm right here in this town. And guess what I was doing? Playing semi-pro ball with the [Brooklyn] Bushwicks."

Williams explained to his readers, "Before Sunday baseball was legalized in New York [in 1919], visiting stars, idling between games, made frequent appearances with the Bushwicks at fees ranging from $100 to $500 [as much as about $7,000 today], and presumably (we neglected to ask) that's how he happened to be over there."

Cobb had prefaced his remark to Williams by acknowledging that he had a weak arm during his career. "Actually, when I came up I had a strong arm. In the minors nobody ran on me, and for the first several years in the majors I also had the runners' respect." (In the 1928 *Babe Ruth's Own Book of Baseball*, then-ghostwriter Ford Frick had written the following about Cobb under Ruth's name: "He's one star who was hampered by a rather weak arm, and he had a weakness on ground balls too.")

Returning a second time to 1952:

clockwise from top right in 1938: George T. Bye, Eleanor's literary agent; First Lady Eleanor Roosevelt; Westbrook Pegler; and composer-music critic Deems Taylor

During the gap between his two pro-integration interviews, popular columnist Pegler analogized President Truman to Cobb in a potential re-election campaign. "Truman never tolerates political opponents. His opponents always are enemies. He is a free-style fighter on the order of Ty Cobb in his formidable prime." Pegler recalled in graphic detail a fight between Cobb and umpire Billy Evans. He ended with, "Ty fought for keeps and so does Truman, so, with Truman in it, this must be a dirty fight."

(In 1949, Pegler had recalled some of Cobb's fights and Cobb's having visited him in his Tucson, Arizona-area home some years earlier. When Cobb arrived on that visit, "I was a little uncertain whether to hide behind the door and pounce on him to get in first lick [sic] with a mesquite club [long bat] or take a chance." Then Pegler wrote of Cobb that day, "I have never met a milder man and I was specially impressed by his kind excuses for a young outfielder on the Giants club, who misjudged an easy fly the day before" and who injured himself badly on the play.)

A controversy ensued after Cobb's first of two 1952 articles in *Life* magazine, "They Don't Play Baseball Any More." The three biographers touched on them with brevity – a wise move because the subject is heavy on minutiae. Reaction to the articles, especially that first one, was varied. In the *New York Herald Tribune*, now-sports editor Cooke wrote, "As a hitter, he qualified for the Hall of Fame, but as a writer he should be admitted to the hall of shame."

Earlier, in New Orleans, Branch Rickey declared to sports editor William "Bill" Keefe of the *Times-Picayune* that Cobb was 100 percent right in most of what he said. His big disagreement was, "He's dead wrong in thinking most of the players of today should play as he played. And he also missed the fact that the system of baseball of today is far different from the game he knew."

In saying the above, Rickey digressed into perhaps his most extensive comments on him in print:

"I studied Cobb; had lots of opportunity to study him when I was with the Yankees [in 1907] and Browns [from 1913 to 1915]. I had to study men like Cobb. You never really learned them, but you learned a lot from watching them." Also in his remarks that day, Rickey said, "Cobb was a villainous, tricky, courageous and adventurous player. He wasn't satisfied with the commonplace. But then, most of the good players in those days accepted the responsibilities of doing everything in their power to win. They'd make enough runs with three or four hits [as opposed to hitting home runs] to win many a game.

"Cobb took advantage of every opportunity, and if one didn't arise he'd create it. He'd threaten, tirelessly, and when he caught a pitcher or a catcher or an infielder relaxed – flash! – he'd be in there [safely]. Do you think he'd go standing up back to first base when a pitcher tried to pick him off? No, sir! He'd have such a big lead that he'd have to slide back as if for his life. Many times they had him; many times I've seen a pitcher or catcher have him caught; but many times he'd slide in with such villainous, indomitable dash and such trickery he'd kick the ball out of the first baseman's hands, or upset him and cause him to drop the ball. Other times when his lead was very big, he'd dash to second when the throw was made to first."

Cobb had to play that way "because the manager of [sic] those days put responsibility on their players. The players wanted it that way. Why, Cobb would have laughed if a manager had told his team of that day that there would be a meeting in the dressing room before the game. Baseball wasn't such a complete bench game then."

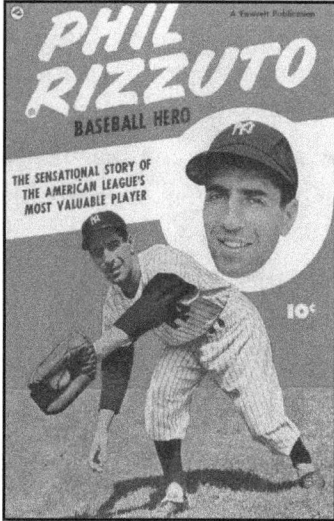

The AP's Jack Hand garnered reaction to Cobb's first article by interviewing members of the Yankees during their spring training in St. Petersburg, Fla. Manager Casey Stengel "was asked what he thought of Cobb's statement that Yankees shortstop Phil Rizzuto and Cardinal outfielder Musial are the only modern players who can stand comparison with the oldtimers.

"'I'm not going to comment on it,' said Stengel, [who] then commented for the next 30 minutes." Stengel, a National Leaguer from 1912 to 1925, praised Cobb in various ways. At one point, "Stengel spotted Rizzuto walking past the bench," and Rizzuto giving a big wink and raising his voice. 'I'm having a lot of trouble with Rizzuto since Cobb wrote that piece,' he said. 'Fighting with the other players, picking scraps. Thinks he's Cobb.'" By the way, in a separate Rizzuto story around that time, the AP said he is now known as "Little Ty, since Ty Cobb called him one of the great ball players of all time." For his part, Rizzuto told the AP reporter writing that story, "I'd like to go on an Italian diet with plenty of spaghetti to gain some weight, but I can't get the right ingredients."

Digressing to some of what Stengel generally thought of Cobb and Cobb of Stengel:

Back in 1949, Stengel had recalled his own first game in 1912 to Shirley Povich of the *Washington Post*. He had made four hits. "The baseball writers promptly decided they had seen the new Ty Cobb." Stengel added that it took him only a few days to rid them of that impression. In Hand's 1952 article noted above, Stengel said, "I can't say much wrong about the fellow. When I was breaking in with Brooklyn in Augusta [in spring training in 1913], he was home holding out. He'd come out to the park and tell me what I was doing wrong. In a way, the fellow helped me win my bread and butter."

In December 1952, Cobb sent Stengel a letter stating either or both that Stengel should be in the Hall of Fame and he is the top manager ever. Stengel told people about it but would not show it to Bob Myers of the AP. So Myers sent a note to Cobb and received the following back "in the fine Cobb scrawl:"

"In reply to your inquiry, I do not write things to anyone with the view of it finding public print, but you surely have my permission, for I do feel Case [Casey] rates any praise he should receive and as many as possible should also see it (naturally) [sic] in print." Cobb then praised Stengel's last three seasons – all as the World Series winner – despite not having a team of the caliber of some prior Yankee World Series-winning ones under managers Miller Huggins and Joe McCarthy.

Later in December 1952, Cobb sent the following in a typewritten note to Salsinger: "Sal, why don't you be the first to set a fire under the pot for Casey Stengel in the Hall of Fame. He is nothing to me but he surely has an enviable record and seems rightfully to belong there. He never had a club like Huggins[, who managed the Yankees to their first six pennants and three world championships,] and McCarthy[, who managed the Yankees to seven world championships]. Think of his terrific finishes the last three years, the men he lost, the unusual shifting of line-ups all this last year when reviewing back, any change that did not turn out well could have lost him the pennant. [Pitchers Ed] Lopat and [Vic] Raschi not near up to their form of the previous year, yet

Harry G. Salsinger and American League President William Harridge

Casey pulled them through. Even after they looked like they enjoyed coasting and it seemed two or three times that they were going to fall out of the race. He lost [infielders Bobby] Brown and [Jerry] Coleman and [outfielder] DiMaggio; had no real hitter on his ball club. Looks to me like Casey's record now is about the most unusual of any manager we have had in the past. He still may go further. I think he will win the coming season."

In a Cobb-focused feature in the *New York Times* in 1954, Stengel told Daley a range of stories about Cobb on the diamond. One was how well he did when caught in a rundown between second and third base. "I wish you could see Ty handle the trap, back and forth until you start to feel embarrassed

four Hall of Famers with future electee Stengel on his 65th birthday in 1955, at old-timers' day at Yankee Stadium. To the far left is Al Simmons, a 1927-28 Athletics teammate of Cobb. Atlanta native Bill Terry is to Stengel's immediate left. At the far right is pitcher Ed Walsh, a recipient of special praise from Cobb (as presented in the page 386 caption).

for the players which got him caught except that you know they ain't. And pretty soon Cobb is safe on third anyway." Stengel summed up his stories by saying, "Listen, you can't write too much about Ty Cobb. There never was nobody quite in his class." Upon Cobb's death, Stengel would praise him as the best player he ever saw, while noting, "He wrote me a number of letters, and I want to tell you it started you [sic] thinking from the shoulders up." One of those letters will be featured later.

Returning a third time to 1952:

Hand of the AP also spoke to a friend of Cobb, player-now-Washington coach Milan, who spoke of his competitiveness. "When he was fighting for the batting championship one year he made the groundskeeper let the grass grow down the third base line. Let it grow nice and high for about five days. Then he had it mowed down real close for about 10 days from third towards home. If the third baseman stayed back, he'd bunt in that high grass and leg it. If he charged in, Cobb could slap one past him where the grass was cut and it would roll into left field."

Syndicated columnist Robert C. Ruark devoted a column to Cobb's first *Life* article and said Cobb "just might be right about three-quarters of the time." He added, "The Georgia peach's tirade in Life suggests rather strongly that today's crop of major leaguers are a flock of bums, for the most part; that the hallowed game has lost its quaint purity, and that things just generally aren't what they used to be when he was a boy." The title of Cobb's article, Ruark concluded, rightly "refers to the game of his hey day. They don't box bare-knuckle any more, either, and you see so few horses used as common carriers. I also believe the bow-and-arrow is thought to be pass[é] as a method of warfare, but we still have wars, and they have become no less popular with the masses."

A week later, veteran sports editor Stanley Woodward, now with the *Miami Daily News*, was with Washington manager Bucky Harris in Lakeland, Fla. Harris had been a regular player in the 1920s in the American League. About Cobb's omission of DiMaggio, Harris said, "Cobb was a good offensive man but he wasn't in a class with DiMaggio as an outfielder. In fact, now that I think back, he wasn't so much of an outfielder in ordinary company [to have stood out]. He had a candy arm." When someone recalled seeing DiMaggio being thrown out when trying to take an extra base, Harris said he supposed that that happened every once in a while, "but I can't remember a particular instance. He was good at getting to a base he started for."

The *Akron Beacon Journal* in Ohio invoked Cobb in a regular editorial. Its main hook was to discredit retired General MacArthur, the future foreword writer to Cobb's 1961 book. "The party leaders who are planning the program for the Republican national convention could profit, we think, from an examination of the public's reaction to Ty Cobb's recently published memoir entitled 'They Don't Play Baseball Any More.' If they find that the reaction is almost universally anti-Cobb, they might be wise to reconsider their plan to invite General MacArthur to deliver an address at the national convention.

"Just as Cobb at 65 sees nothing worthy of praise in modern baseball, so does MacArthur at 72 see nothing

Giants manager Leo Durocher and retired General Douglas MacArthur at the Polo Grounds in 1951

that he can approve in the United States government today. And while criticism of the national administration is customary at conventions of the party which is out of power, General MacArthur is capable of overdoing it." The editorial went on for four more paragraphs and without mentioning Cobb again.

Digressing to MacArthur's familiarity with baseball and two of his baseball acquaintances, Hans Lobert and 1928 Giants training camp invitee Reeder:

After his big-league career, Lobert was the baseball coach at West Point from

1918 to 1925. From 1919 to 1922, MacArthur served as Superintendent of the U.S. Military Academy and every Monday, Lobert met in the general's office to discuss baseball. In 1942, Lobert told the United Press, "He liked to talk baseball and frequently our conference was nothing but a discussion of great ball players and stories about the diamond. The Giants and [Giant manager] John J. McGraw were the General's favorites, but he used to ask questions about all the players, among them Honus Wagner, Ty Cobb, Ed Delahanty, Amos Rusie, Larry [Napoleon] Lajoie and others. And mind you, while the General talked baseball with me there'd be a long line of people waiting outside to see him." In 1954, Considine quoted MacArthur as follows: "If [1910s-1920s star] George Sisler had had Ty Cobb's competitive fire he would have been far and away the greatest player of all time. He was, in my opinion, an even better young pitcher than Babe Ruth – and I've always considered Ruth the best young pitcher I ever saw."

The Hall of Fame library has a 1952 letter from Cobb to a former West Point player under Lobert, Reeder, who was mentioned a bit earlier for spending spring training with the Giants in Augusta in 1928. The 1952 letter includes these thoughts: "I think there is too much theory in correcting for good batting." In teaching batting on a given day, do not teach more than one or two things at a time, "for concentration will [be] affected."

As noted earlier, Cobb worked out for a time with the 1928

Durocher (far left) and MacArthur, throwing out the first ball, at the same game in New York, in 1951

Giants, mainly by using the practice field when the Giants had just finished up. That still provided opportunities for Giant players to get to know him. Alexander cited Reeder's 1971 letter for the following observations: he recalled Cobb as "a smart, crafty, dynamic and intense batting instructor." Also, "Ty Cobb absorbed you. You became *his* pupil. When he talked batting, if you were absorbing the instruction, his eyes glittered."

(What Alexander omitted between those two excerpts is pretty neat, because it may help explain how Cobb and Williams bonded so well. Reeder wrote, "I think he and Ted Williams knew the most about batting. I heard Ted lecture on hitting a dozen years ago in Baltimore, and he was excellent.")

In his 1966 memoirs *Born at Reveille*, Reeder wrote that Giants manager McGraw invited Cobb to work out with his more seasoned first team and that Cobb refused, because that would rob players of their time at bat. Instead, Cobb told McGraw that he would work out from about 5 p.m. until 6:30 p.m. Also, while Cobb said he would be glad to take batting practice from McGraw's pitchers, he also said he would hire boys to retrieve balls hit to the outfield.

swinging in Sarasota, Fla., in April 1927: Roger Bresnahan, Giants coach, is the catcher and John McGraw is to his left

Attendance at the ballpark in Augusta soared when it was announced that Cobb was working out with the team. "Because he was one of the best base runners of all time, I had visualized him as smaller. He was powerful, slightly over six feet, weight 185, as dynamic as McGraw and as smart," Reeder wrote.

The first day he came, about 15 Giants volunteered after practice to pitch to him. "The novelty wore off quickly." After the second day just five players remained, including Reeder. One of the other five was O'Doul, Cobb's future friend in California, and another was future Hall of Famer Mel Ott. "In appreciation, Cobb began to coach us in hitting. My batting average started to climb."

One day, Cobb "gave an exhibition in place hitting." He told Reeder to stand near the plate. Then, after each pitch, when the ball had left the pitcher's hand, Reeder was to shout "left," "center" or "right," meaning where Cobb should hit it. Cobb was able to do as told because his "reflexes let him wait until the last fraction of a second to swing."

Turning to other contemporaneous coverage of Cobb's 1928 training with the Giants:

Before mentioning Cobb in his story one day, Rud Rennie of the *New York Herald Tribune* mentioned other players including Reeder, "the dropkicker who spent six years on the 30-yard line for the West Point football team. The lieutenant is on a thirty days' leave" from Fort Benning, Ga., and "has a certain curiosity as to whether he has the making of a ball player." Reeder had played college football too at West Point and graduated in 1926.

During spring training one day, Rennie wrote, "Ty Cobb came to the park this afternoon to say hello to McGraw and with the Giants luck." Also, "McGraw offered the park to work out in, but Cobb thanked him and declined the offer. 'I'd only get sore twice,' he said, 'once here and again in Fort Myers.'" That was where the Athletics were in training, and Cobb would join them two weeks later. On a later day at Augusta, the AP said Cobb had "refused the privileges of the Giants field and clubhouse." That day, he "strolled onto the field" at the close of a practice game "and took his first warmup of the season. It wasn't much, just a few infield rollers and a jog around the bases." A week later, a coal miner from West Virginia who was there for a tryout, Andy Torkas, was told by the Giants' Freddie Lindstrom to bunt some balls to, in the AP's paraphrase, "that rookie over there."

"Torkas obediently ordered Ty afield. Ty went."

Returning to more of the aftermath of Cobb's first 1952 article in *Life*:

As did the *Akron Beacon Journal*, the *Washington Post* analyzed it in a regular editorial. The *Post* referred to parts of an article by Lester Rodney, sports editor of the Communist Party USA's the *Daily Worker*. In it, Rodney called Cobb a "65 year old millionaire" who "made his dough with early investments in Coca-Cola." The *Post* paraphrased Rodney by stating that Cobb had become "in Comrade Rodney's eyes the arrogant spokesman of a ruthless and decadent capitalism yearning nostalgically for" all of the following, which in the *Daily Worker's* original are the "'good old days' of low wages, no minimum [salaries], no medical care, solid jimcrow [sic] and Ty Cobb, Ty Cobb, Ty Cobb." Jim Crow is the catchall term for inferior treatment of blacks after the Civil War.

Rodney also wrote that one might have expected Cobb to say that baseball had advanced since his playing days "in that good ballplayers are not kept out because of the color of their skins [sic]. Oh no, not, 'the Georgia Peach.'"

Meanwhile, Irving Vaughan, longtime sportswriter for the *Chicago Tribune*, provoked a letter from Cobb for having written a column with the title, "COBB OFF BASE AS HE BELITTLES: Georgia Peach Sour in Berating Stars"

Vaughan, although he left open the possibility that Cobb was not aware of how his first article had been edited, said Cobb had been "an individualist on the ball field. He was strictly for Cobb." Also, "He ran wild by using his spikes on any guy who was in his path as an opponent."

Cobb's response, which I saw only excerpts from, stated that he was not paid for the article. He declared, "Irving, I don't think I deserve to be swiped at[,] by my receiving fees." Vaughan in his article had not referred to that. Cobb also mentioned the hospital that he was helping to establish back in Royston. On the playing of baseball in his day, Cobb reinforced to him, as follows, a point from his *Life* articles: "So the hit & run, the bunt, the sacrifice (or ability to execute as of years past) and the stolen base, the squeeze, when you take a lot of this play out of the game of baseball, it[']s not too good."

In Orlando for spring training, Washington owner Griffith called him "senile" for belittling modern players. Days later, Povich of the *Washington Post* reported that a contrite Griffith, for calling Cobb names, had sent "a note of apology, though not agreeing with him." A month later, on the public affairs television-radio show "The American Forum of the Air," Griffith said Cobb had nerve panning Williams for not hitting to left field: "Ty Cobb couldn't hit one to right field on a bet." As appears in a different context on page 356, Cobb retorted by citing a three-home run game of his, all to right field, in 1925.

(Despite Cobb's criticism of Williams on not hitting to left, the following from a Cobb letter from an unnamed friend of Williams – perhaps Corcoran – had been reported by Grayson of the NEA in 1951: "I did not say that Joe DiMaggio was a great hitter, or rank him ahead of Williams.")

On the show, interviewer Povich of the *Post* said he thought it was the first time anyone had leveled such a charge against Cobb. When pressed by Povich, Griffith added, "I will tell you why I raised it. I once said to Cobb, 'I bet you a dollar you can't hit a base hit to right field.' He would try to do it and pop up, and then go back to his old game of hitting to left. He was a late hitter. Why Cobb should criticize Williams for not being able to hit to left when he couldn't hit to right, I don't know."

I found the transcript while proofreading the show's title. It is a fitting near-finale because Griffith had played under Anson, a fellow contrarian, in much of his 19th-century career. Plus, Anson is the most documented bettor in big-league history (see the "Betting on Baseball" appendix of *Cap Anson 2*). If Griffith made the bet before Anson's death in 1922, odds are he would have mentioned it to him, plus 1890s mutual teammate Lange.

Cunningham responded to Cobb's *Life* articles by writing, "this is but [Cobb's] own opinion, and, although he's entitled to it, his sermon, however unorthodox, would be better if his pulpit didn't slant on one side. Cobb, who lives in California, doesn't figure to know much about the modern major league game. Barring an occasional World Series, he probably hasn't seen a half dozen games in 20 years."

The following could have been in the Cobb food section, but fits better here. In one of his *Life* articles, Cobb stated that slugging outfielders Gus Zernial and Ralph Kiner "are good examples of famous modern hitters whose fielding is not up to major league standards. He needn't even be in top physical condition, for hitting a baseball 350 feet is mostly a feat of sheer momentary strength like carrying a piano up a stairway. You don't have to be trained down fine to do it; some of our best piano movers have 46-inch waistlines and some of our long-ball hitters today will run them a good second."

Later that month, Biederman of the *Pittsburgh Press* asked Kiner from the Pirates' spring training site in Phoenix how he felt about being criticized. Biederman cited a different Cobb interview in the *San Francisco Call-Bulletin*. "'You saw Kiner the other day when he played here,' Cobb told the writer [McDonald of the *Call-Bulletin*]. 'Why he's got a bigger stomach than I have.

Ralph Kiner and Pirates part-owner Bing Crosby

I hope he hits 80 home runs and they pay him $100,000 [about $900,000 today] for doing it. But everything's ala [sic] carte in baseball today.'"

In reaction, Kiner "exploded, 'Why do these old time ball players always live in the past?' he asked. 'I have a size 32 waist right now and I defy any athlete in baseball my size to show me a smaller waist.'" Ten days earlier, Kiner had told Jack Hernon of the *Pittsburgh Post-Gazette*, "Anyone who doesn't think DiMaggio belongs on an all-star team needs his head examined." Also, "He said all I could do was hit the long ball, and there wasn't any extra work required to hit home runs. That's a lot of bunk and you know it. He says you don't have to be in top physical condition to hit home runs. I'd like to see anyone [do that] that isn't in top condition, who stays in the major leagues very long, regardless of what he does on the team."

Cobb also told McDonald that players in his day "didn't fill their bellies with rich foods and malted milks." Joe Molony of the *Florence Morning News* in South Carolina reprinted that and said, "Did he ever hear of the famous [Babe Ruth] 'stomach ache' which was brought on by a consumption of too many hot dogs and too much soda pop?" Molony also referred to the drinking done by noted earlier pitchers Rube Waddell and Grover Cleveland Alexander and added, "Nope, players in Cobb's day didn't fill up with rich food and milks – their diet had more kick to it."

On Ruth's eating, Cobb is quoted in his book with Stump as stating, "I've seen him at midnight, propped up in bed, order six club sandwiches and put them away, along with a platter of pigs' knuckles, and a pitcher of beer. He'd down all that while smoking a big black cigar. And all the time, he'd be smoking big, black cigars. Next day, he'd hit two or three homers and trot around the bases, complaining all the way about gas pains and a bellyache." Ruth biographer Robert Creamer, in reprinting the above quotation from Cobb but working before the personal computer age, garbled some of the wording, even while referring to Cobb as "no stickler for accuracy in his memoirs of baseball life." Creamer said that while Ruth had an enormous appetite, "accounts of it were often exaggerated."

Wheeler, Cobb's 1914 book collaborator, wrote in a syndicated column, "I am a little miffed he [Cobb] didn't ask me to be his spook [ghostwriter] for the Life articles." He also said that some of Cobb's remarks "surprised me. I gathered there were no dumb players in his era, and they all went to bed at 9 o'clock, never broke training, and did what teacher [sic] told them."

In his own piece, Grayson of the NEA wrote that "Cobb contends he was the victim of a foul ball in connection with his contemptuous pieces comparing the old baseball with the new. But what the Georgia Peach said still goes." He reprinted the following Cobb letter to Kiner, which was addressed "Dear Kiner:"

Menlo Park, Calif.

I read an article in the paper relative to you, and having been burned so many times in my baseball life unwarrantedly and by some obscure 'critic' of baseball writing, I decided to write you this letter. I don't blame you one bit for what you were supposed to have said about conditioning, etc., etc., etc.

I have been criticized much by such writings in the past but I have never made it a point to criticize my fellow ball players personally.

In my stories in Life, I was asked to make a comparison of the two eras in baseball, the modern vs. the time I played. This I did with no personal criticisms.

First, Kiner, I have not seen you since the Kiwanis charity game in Hollywood two years ago. So it's clear I could not have commented on your condition.

As to Life, naturally I had a collaborator [Ernest C. Havemann]. I furnished the subjects with explanations. He took those and composed the story. I had in my contract the right to correct and blue pencil, which I did. But back in New York, Life apparently missed several and published the story. So that's the story.

Now as to one era against the other, I mean the stand I took, Ralph. Just look at the records. That's all I have to say.

Much luck, boy, and I hope you understand, now.

I am, sincerely
TY COBB.

P.S. This explanation may not be necessary, but I wanted you to know the facts. – TRC.

Soon after, now-St. Louis Browns manager Hornsby wrote an article in *Look* magazine entitled, "It's Still Baseball, Cobb!" One point in it was, "Does Cobb honestly believe Jackie Robinson, of the Brooklyn Dodgers, with his speed, power and fire wouldn't have been a star in the old days? Robinson, [black Cuban] Minnie Minoso, of the White Sox, and [black] Sam Jethroe of the Boston Braves, says Cobb, wouldn't have been able to steal bases against the old pitchers and catchers." That last line has been cited by other authors, but not the following quip:

The *New York Amsterdam News*, a black weekly, featured that aspect of Hornsby's article under the following headlines: "WILL WONDERS NEVER CEASE? Hornsby, Cobb at Odds Over Merits of Robby"

Leerhsen, in reference to that controversy, called Hornsby someone with "a much worse reputation than Cobb for being an SOB." But Cobb no doubt had a much worse reputation than Hornsby for having been a mean player.

Right after Cobb's first article came out, Hornsby had been quoted as seconding Cobb's thoughts: "Cobb is right in everything he says. The players of today should be greater." In his second article in *Life*, Cobb called Hornsby the greatest right-handed hitter ever, "but you can't put him on the all-star team because his shortstop and first baseman used to have to go over to catch pop flies for him." Salsinger said Cobb was wrong not to include Hornsby for that reason, since "what player in the history of base ball was ever perfect? All had one or more faults." Salsinger also declared that Hornsby was wrong to get even in his article by picking "Shoeless" Joe Jackson over Cobb in his all-time outfield. Days after Salsinger wrote that, sportswriter Bill Leiser of the *San Francisco Chronicle* observed, "To get a barb to throw at Cobb, somebody [at *Look*] had Hornsby pick an all[-]time baseball team not mentioning Ty."

But for a Hornsby tie-in, it would not have interested me who Cobb considered the best second baseman ever. He consistently said Eddie Collins.

In the earlier cited 1942 interview with Ward Morehouse of the *New York Sun*, Cobb said Collins was his favorite. Napoleon Lajoie "was a great hitter,

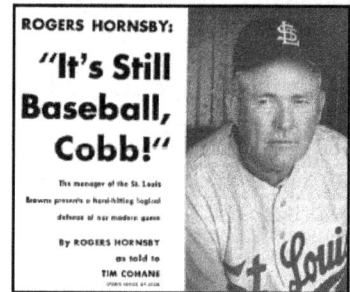

but he never could tag a runner and he couldn't go out for a Texas leaguer [a short pop fly into the outfield]. Neither could Hornsby." During the dinner with Morehouse and their wives in 1949, Cobb did criticize Collins: "Eddie Collins threw like a woman, but he was a marvel there at second base. He and Ray Schalk, when they were together on the White Sox, were the only players who ever made me feel defeated."

In 1944, he told Frank H. Bartholomew of the United Press that the "ballplayer's ballplayer" of all-time was still Collins. For a man "who could do anything – hit, field, run bases, and play real inside and brainy baseball – Eddie Collins stands in front." While they were chatting, they were in front of Cobb's "luxurious log home high up in the Sierra Nevadas," with Cobb looking "thoughtfully through the pines out over the sparkling waters of Lake Tahoe."

In 1945, he sent his all-time choices to Ernest J. Lanigan, historian of the Baseball Hall of Fame. He wrote most extensively about his choice for second base and made a presumed typo of Jimmy Collins, where he meant Eddie Collins, over Hornsby and Napoleon Lajoie. "To my way of thinking no contest at second base, Hornsby couldn't catch a pop fly, much less go in the outfield after them, could not come in on a close hit, Lajoie could not go out, nor come in, and did not cover too much ground to his right or left."

In 1953, Cobb told San Francisco writer Prescott Sullivan that Collins was greater than Hornsby and Lajoie. "I guess he was the smartest ball player of them all. That was his strength – headwork. Actually, he wasn't endowed with great natural ability. I mean he lacked the thing they call style. He had a peculiar loping gait as a runner and he threw the ball with a sort of pushing motion. In contrast to Lajoie, who was the picture of grace, Eddie was awkward and unorthodox." During the interview, Sullivan wrote, Cobb's "boxer dog [presumably Chudley] came along and licked at his hand. The one-time firebrand of the American League gave the pooch an affectionate pat in return."

(Believe it or not, in Stump's 1961 whopper on Cobb and Williams having had a falling out, a heated argument over whether Hornsby had been a good fielder was one of the cited reasons.)

Upon Cobb's death, Hornsby would call Cobb "the greatest ball player of all time." For one thing, "Ty would do anything to win a ball game but when he got off the field, he was a perfect gentleman."

By the way, Cobb did include Jimmy Collins, who played in the American League in four seasons into Cobb's career, on some of his all-time teams. In 1934, he named Collins at third base. In talking to a reporter in 1950, he mentioned Pie Traynor and Collins before settling on Buck Weaver.

Despite Cobb's public withholding of the highest of praise from Hornsby as a player, Cobb praised his managing privately in 1952 – in a letter that he sent after his *Life* articles appeared and before Hornsby's reaction piece ran in *Look*. Contents of the letter were made public either first by vaudeville historian Joe E. Laurie, Jr., or by Dan Parker, sports editor of the *New York Mirror*, who cited Laurie as the source. Cobb had sent the letter to a man named Rathbone who had received coaching from Cobb at a Detroit prep school. In turn, Rathbone apparently forwarded it directly or indirectly to Laurie.

In the letter, after criticizing the lack of stress as of 1952 on the fine parts of the game, such as the bunt, sacrifice, squeeze play, stolen base and hit and run, he wrote, "This type of baseball in a season wins many close games. The White Sox last year played the old game and were up there for quite a time. Watch Hornsby this year. He plays the right game." Hornsby, then managing the St. Louis Browns, would be fired by general manager Bill Veeck, Jr. in June. Parker stressed to his readers that Cobb wrote the letter before that happened and added that Hornsby "lost his job for not playing Bill Veeck's type of game."

In the interim between Cobb's articles and Hornsby's, Dick Young of the *New York Daily News* had asked Robinson about Cobb's take, including on base stealing. Robinson called Cobb "way off base" and also said, "I'm not looking for an argument with Ty Cobb, but I don't think Cobb is any smarter than I am." Young added, "It is Robinson's contention that modern ball players, generally speaking, know more about the game of baseball, and play a smarter brand of ball because they receive greater instructions in fundamentals."

An extended version of Young's column in the *Salt Lake Tribune* in Utah that is not in the microfilm-preserved version of the *Daily News* quoted Robinson as saying, "In Cobb's day, most of the players had to teach themselves. Few of them could [teach themselves]. That's why Cobb was such a stickout. He could think, and there wasn't much competition in that department. Now, the other players think right along with you. They've been taught what to look for, and they make it tougher for you." Another line of Cobb's that drew Robinson's reaction was, "Nor have today's pitchers and catchers ever learned how to stop a good base runner."

"I don't see how he can honestly say that," Robinson reacted. "Very frankly, I think the pitchers know more now about holding runners on. I don't know what he would expect me to do above what I've been doing. By that I mean I study the pitchers. That's how you steal – by getting that extra step on the pitcher. You watch him, and you look for one little thing he does that tips you off to whether he is going to throw to the plate or to first base." Robinson added, "During our games, there are 25 players sitting on the bench, all studying the opposing pitcher and looking for tell-tale moves. The coaches are doing the same thing every minute of the game, and so is the manager. We talk over things like that. As soon as one of the fellows thinks he has spotted something, he mentions it and we all look for it and decide whether it's a constant give away [sic]. The other teams do that, too. That's why you see good baseball – as good as anyt[h]ing they played in Cobb's day and maybe a bit better."

Also in the gap before Hornsby's article, Harvey Breitt of the *New York Times* had compared Cobb and Hornsby and wrote, "One cannot visualize Hornsby in any medium but baseball." By contrast, "one can visualize Cobb in another milieu, in another medium, functioning with equal brilliance." For Hornsby, there is "no drinking, no smoking, no movies, no television, no parties. Didn't Mr. Hornsby have friends, didn't he see people? 'I have a lot of friends,' he says. And then he takes it back. 'I'm not a very good mixer. I don't want to go to dinner or to the theater [he says thee-ay-ter] [sic]. Like I say, I am a peculiar fellow like that.'" He added soon after, "I don't like to be out on other affairs. I don't know about other things. It becomes, like I say, boresome. And I become boresome too."

Also in the gap, a Cobb letter to Spink had been printed in full in Spink's lead feature in the *Sporting News*, with the following headline: COBB TRIED TO HELP GAME, 'NOT BLAST IT'

Cobb wrote the letter possibly shortly after writing the Kiner one. Early on in his article, Spink wrote that Cobb "wants people to know he didn't intend to make personal comparisons" and especially "with a sting." For example, he quoted Cobb as saying, "I was not responsible for any captions on pictures nor many little barbs. I had the right to correct and did blue pencil some (statements) [sic], but with script here and Life man who phoned corrections back to Life in N. Y. they ignored and printed. Then what could I do?"

(Cobb made a similar point in a letter made public by Parker of the *New York Mirror* that I cited a little earlier for its praise of Hornsby's managing: "I enjoyed everything in the Life articles except some digs and barbs left in stories over my corrections and blue pencilling. They ignored my corrections and left in several sarcastic barbs which should not have been in the story. With my name at the head, I naturally got the 'credit.' I had never in my life criticized a fellow ball player in print." Presumably by that, Cobb meant that anything critical that he said or wrote should be viewed purely as observation. In his next sentences, Cobb built toward praise of the 1951 White Sox and 1952 Browns manager Hornsby, as follows: "There is no question on the records of the old era's superiority. The greatest pitching era in the game was from 1906 to 1928. Also, the hitting was superior, with men batting over .400, in the .390s and .380s against all the trick pitching and with a dead ball. A fine part of baseball, the bunt, the sacrifice, squeeze, stolen base and hit and run have been sadly overlooked.")

Cobb's letter to Spink contained a similar line to one he had sent Parker: "I have never in print criticized my fellow ball player." Also as reprinted by Spink, Cobb wrote that his references to Williams and DiMaggio were not a "blast. That's untrue. I have carefully read the story and my reference to them is in no way a blast. I acknowledged their ability 'potentially' and pointed out with a sense of regret what they failed to do." Three sentences later, Cobb wrote, "Had I wanted to do as some have painted me, I could have gone into it [detail on what they failed to do] and pointed out things but would not. For instance, doesn't it astound you to know that the four highest salaried players ever in baseball, stars like Williams, DiMaggio, Kiner and Musial[,] who should be leaders and developers, stole a total of only seven bases last year? Look that up."

In a sidebar box, Spink noted a second Cobb letter. That letter was in response to remarks in the *Sporting News* by 1930s-1940s star Billy Herman on his *Life* articles. Herman wrote that more recent players are better, including having better schooling in and being better versed in fundamentals. Cobb wrote to Spink about having looked up Herman in *Daguerreotypes of Great Stars of Baseball*, a book published by the *Sporting News*. He discovered that in his last season of 1928, Herman was just starting his career in Vicksburg in the Cotton States League. "How in h - - - did he see those of my era?" (In a time warp in the other direction, in 1984, pitcher Jack Morris would tell sportswriter Ross Newhan of the *Los Angeles Times*, "People have sympathy to the past. They talk about Babe Ruth as the greatest player ever, but could he hit the forkball? I saw Ty Cobb swing (on film). I know *he* couldn't.")

Sports editor Chauncey Durden of the *Richmond Times-Dispatch* in Virginia reacted to Cobb's first article by summarizing how Cobb had recently become semi-famous again. Durden tied the renewed fame to Cobb's managing in the Esquire All American Boys game in 1945 against Ruth. "Then it was that a newer crop of sports writers discovered Cobb the man. And found him a personable fellow – anything but the fire-eating, baseman-spiking terror they'd read and heard about. After that, Cobb made sporadic returns to major league parks, usually for some old-timers' day." Durden wrote that Cobb had been to no more than 20 or 30 big-league games in the last 20 years, and that at a number of them, reporters have "made live copy of him again. He has become someone approximating baseball's Elder Statesman. Cobb was the first witness called by a congressional committee investigating baseball. Whenever a baseball question of importance comes up, California reporters are dispatched with celerity to Cobb's home to get the word from the oracle himself."

On his modern-day roasts, the National Geographic Society said, "Obviously, Cobb hasn't analyzed all the ball players in the world." The most amazing ones, it said, are Fuzzy-Wuzzy tribesmen in Africa. "These Fuzzy-Wuzzies, who live on rocky desert near the Red Sea [in Sudan, Egypt and Eritrea], settle their minor squabbles by throwing rocks at each other. Everything goes – curves, sliders, fork balls, palm balls, fast balls," conveyed Herb Altschull of the AP.

In the *Detroit Free Press*, Bingay cheered Cobb on for his *Life* articles. "Most of all, his two articles warmed the cockles of this old heart by his fierce contempt for the modern master-minding of managers and the present vogue of platoons of batters by which good lefthand batters are jerked against lefthand pitchers and righthand batters are dropped for righthand pitchers. For years I have been protesting that this is the ultimate in nuttiness." After printing an excerpt from one of the articles on that point, Bingay added, "Ty could have elaborated on this for a whole chapter as a study of American initiative. To jerk a good batter – instead of teaching him how to bat against ALL pitchers – does, in my estimation, incalculable harm to the athlete."

(On platooning, Cobb had told Connolly of the *San Francisco Chronicle* in 1949, "There is too much masterminding by managers to no purpose. Managers juggle the lineup daily in order to display their authority and mystify the fans. It looks like they're thinking hard, to the stands. But actually they're outmaneuvering themselves. Baseball isn't that complicated.")

The controversy had the fluky benefit of leading to comments from Bingay about a hard-to-quantify side issue that is central to Cobb's baseball career: the extent to which he argued with umpires during games. Salsinger had weighed in in 1942 and 1947, and would again in 1955. About Cobb's playing career, Bingay recalled, "While his terrible temper flared off the field or after a game, his thinking apparatus was cooler than a deep freeze when the game was on. This was because he was a student of psychology. As all the old umpires now alive will testify, he did not badger the officials. He wanted any possible breaks on the next play. **Rarely was he ever sent to the showers.**"

In 1955, Salsinger would write that Cobb was the most aggressive player ever but during his pre-player-manager days, he argued with an umpire only once. "The argument was prompted by the loss of a base hit." Salsinger then recounted that supposed one argument, with umpire Tom "Tommy" Connolly. In 1924, in starting an installment of his serial, he had written, "Later in his career Ty Cobb changed his mind about the umpires, rather his attitude toward them. He became critical and soon was recognized by them as one of the worst kickers [arguers] in the league. Also he criticized them publicly; something he had never permitted himself to do when at the height of his career."

Upon his death, the *Boston Globe* would say that Cobb "didn't get tough with the umpires in his heyday, apparently figuring it was not good practice to antagonize those who decided the many close plays in which he figured."

Cobb biographer Dan Holmes has calculated in an article that he was ejected 20 times, including 5 as a player-manager. In 1960, Cobb told Willard Neal of the *Atlanta Constitution* that as a player, he would concede to umpires when he was out on a close play and wait a day to tell them when they were wrong.

Another of the few strong Cobb defenders was Parker of the *New York Mirror*. He wrote, "Did Ty Cobb have the audacity to say that Joe DiMaggio didn't spend his winters doing roadwork, exercising in gyms, and otherwise keeping in shape for next season? That's just what the horned toad said and all America is aroused – all of it, that is, except Joe himself. The fact that a retired player had expressed the opinion that the good old days were better than the present, [sic] whipped the nation into such a frenzy that it was ready to declare war on Georgia and the devil take the Russians and the North Koreans!"

A few sentences later, Parker wrote, "Meantime, Joe has received Ty's comments, [sic] with such nonchalance [Cobb did praise DiMaggio in the article as 'perhaps the greatest natural ballplayer who ever lived,'] that he'd be the greatest thing on TV next to [cool-headed telegenic] Bishop [Fulton] Sheen could he but translate some of it into his video personality." More on Cobb's take on DiMaggio's offseason lack of training and DiMaggio's commentary on the subject will appear later.

Parker, in an initial *Life* reaction piece a month earlier, had written of Cobb, "I don't think that he has done anything more than inspire a controversial article, which is giving Baseball [sic] millions of dollars worth of publicity gratis, and bringing new readers to the magazine." Rodney of the *Daily Worker* reprinted that and declared sarcastically, "This resounding statement of principle needs no comment."

Parker had also written the following in that earlier piece, titled "Baseball Intolerant of Cobb's Criticism":

"Cobb points out that the lively ball has robbed the game of much of its finesse, producing a race [sic] of players who can't bunt, steal bases or execute the hit-and-run play. All they try for is home runs. That's truer than all get-out [than can possibly be imagined]. But Baseball being more big business than sport, the answer to Ty's wail is that the magnates wanted it that way and that everyone, including the players, is getting much more money under the new arrangement. Call the magnates mercenary desecrators of a fine sport if you will[,] but you can hardly blame them for catering to public taste, since they are in the entertainment business. Certainly, the bigger attendance figures and higher admission scales that now prevail would seem to indicate that the public prefers the type of baseball Ty disparages."

Later in his column, Parker wrote, "Ty's fondness for the bygone days merely indicates that he has reached the stage of life where progress strikes him as a mistake." Parker concluded with, "The furors created by Cobb's two articles, in the second of which he picks Casey Stengel, Leo Durocher and Paul Richards as throwbacks to the days of Connie Mack, the master of them all in his book, makes one wonder if Baseball isn't a menace to good government in that it takes the average man's mind off what's going on in Washington, exclusive of [fans at] Griffith Stadium [in D.C.]. At any rate, if some way could be devised to make Baseball fans devote even half the time they spend arguing about foul balls, stolen bases and hit-and-run plays to dissecting some of the foul balls they have allowed to steal into office on hit-and-run plays at the polls, maybe the country wouldn't be as badly off as Cobb now seems to think Baseball is."

While the Cobb and Hornsby magazine pieces are well known among historians of that era, a third is not: one in *Pageant* magazine by Cooke of the *New York Herald Tribune*. As noted earlier, prior to his magazine piece, Cooke had disclosed in the *Herald Tribune* that at the Alexandra Restaurant in New York City, "we learned that Cobb didn't write the stories at all. They were done by Ernie Havemann, whose name appears inconspicuously among the staff writers listed on the magazine's masthead. But who cares whether Havemann says they don't play baseball any more?"

Ernest C. "Ernie" Havemann

Bob Cooke

Also in the *Herald Tribune*, he wrote, "In order to complete the series, Havemann spent two weeks with Cobb on the Coast. It is not known whether Cobb charged him for food and drink when Havemann visited him."

As for why Cobb chose *Life*, given that other magazines "have been after Ty for years in quest of his rancid beliefs," Cooke quoted a West Coast colleague as saying, "He wanted to be in 'Life' because the magazine did such a wonderful job on the memoirs of Winston Churchill and the Duke of Windsor [the former King Edward III, who had abdicated in 1936]."

Cooke ended his *Herald Tribune* screed by writing, "Ty is sixty-five now and it's more than likely that he's approaching senility. To test this theory we suggested it to an old acquaintance of Cobb the other day. 'Heck, Ty's not senile,' said our informant. 'He was like that even when he was young.'" Earlier on in his screed, as noted earlier, he had written, "As a hitter, he qualified for the Hall of Fame, but as a writer he should be admitted to the hall of shame."

In his *Pageant* article, "Ty Cobb Strikes Out," Cooke weighed in on the claim that players do not train nowadays. He wrote that if a player broke half of the training rules that Ruth did, he would be suspended, fined and possibly barred from the game. As evidence, he recalled that in the spring of 1952, the Phillies' Willie Jones had been fined $200, about $1,800 today, for a 15-minute violation of a midnight curfew.

On the claim that only Musial and Rizzuto measure up, Cooke quoted Stengel and Musial as uttering the highest praise of DiMaggio. In addition, he quoted Giants manager Durocher as saying, "Those old guys make me sick. They're always talking about how good it was in the old days. They played with a ball you couldn't hit across the room." On players not studying fundamentals, Cooke singled out Rickey's rookie training schools in his tenure with the Dodgers and now the Pirates. Also, he cited the Yankees for having three great coaches, Frank Crosetti, Bill Dickey and Jim Turner.

About Williams not hitting to left field, Cooke wrote that Boston reporters covering the Red Sox have computed "that Williams hit as many homers to left field as he did to right a year ago." About players of Cobb's day being more ambitious about and interested in the game in his day, Cooke quoted Cobb contemporary Bill McKechnie, now a Red Sox coach, as saying, "I never saw Cobb hanging around any lobbies. He was too busy doing a lot of other things to sit around and talk baseball." Cobb had told Hugh Fullerton, Sr. in *Liberty* magazine in 1924, "More ball players tire themselves out attending [sic] around hotel lobbies and lounging about hotels than are wrecked on ball fields."

Cooke concluded his *Pageant* article by quoting Washington manager Harris, who said, "I've often wondered whether some of those famous old-timers could have made the modern teams." A few sentences later, Harris said this about Cobb: "Having seen his swing and having heard old-timers describe it, I'm certain he'd be nothing more than a spray hitter today."

(I did not find Cobb responding to Cooke's writing. One taste of how he defended his *Life* articles, even while disassociating himself from them in some respects because some of the thoughts in them were supposedly not his, was in a 1953 letter to a Mr. Leroy Jacobsen. "I have received many 'brick bats' relative to the stories in Life magazine[,] but when you go to official records also how baseball is as of today I have no doubts as to my opinions as expressed.")

In July, on his first visit back to St. Louis since his playing days in 1928, he said, "I haven't meant to criticize because baseball was mighty good to me, and I've got a strong sentimental attachment for the game. I think it's a shame, though, that some of the finer plays have gone by the board." His interviewer, Bob Broeg of the *St. Louis Post-Dispatch*, wrote, "Cobb referred to the stolen base, the hit-and-run, the scheming and conniving to score a run, an art of offensive play that gradually has disappeared since Babe Ruth and a livelier ball put the emphasis on making the ball itself disappear out of the park."

Also, "Cobb considered it a 'crime' that 66 regular major leaguers didn't sacrifice once all last season, complained that 'you've got many stars getting big money who excite you only at the plate – not in the field or on the bases' and took a dig at an old rival, Rogers Hornsby.

"'Of course,' he said, 'we had men in our day who didn't run much either. Hornsby, for example, never stole more than 17 bases. Sam Crawford, a much bigger man, stole as many as 41.'"

He also declared that two of his contemporaries, Eddie Collins and Milan, could steal 100 or more bases in present-day baseball. "'A lot of people don't have to consult the records, past or present,' Cobb continued evenly. 'They jump at a man's statements and lash out without realizing what he's said.'"

Musial was sheepish about being praised by Cobb, including, by implication, over all other outfielders. In Cooke's article in *Pageant*, he said, "I couldn't carry DiMaggio's glove." In a letter to Musial in late April that apparently became public in 2013 in a collectibles auction, Cobb wrote:

Cobb and Stan Musial in 1952

Dear Musial:

Why in "hell" do you give me the "brush off" and at my expense and judgement [sic] of you and besides a compliment, just to be modest? I know the records and I don't spout off without being sure. Lots of people write stories, some of the 'new' sports writers <u>without</u> consulting the records, as they about me for instance.

Seriously, now, I know well that you averaged in 6 of your last 7 years .355

"does that give you a right be so darn modest,["] also you play a good first base, also did you see your [National] President [Warren] Giles statement, your grand average I could give you [that covers] all your St. Louis Years [sic] and that would also not be sneezed at.

So go out there now and lead the league again and if you don't lead both Major Leagues this year, you should be shot in the behind with mustard seed – Much Luck.

Cobb also wrote him a long postscript about avoiding or dealing with slumps. He recommended that he ask veterans on the team to watch when he is hitting well, and then ask those very players to analyze him when he is not. "No Charge Stan" for the advice was one of his final thoughts in the postscript.

Also on his July visit to St. Louis, Broeg asked Cobb how come he had recently singled out Musial and Rizzuto, but not Slaughter of the Cardinals. "'I must have missed him,' Ty said frankly, 'but do you know, I hadn't seen him play until this weekend series.'"

During Cobb's visit, Musial said, "I know he didn't mean that series [in *Life*] to be as strong as it sounded. I've known it all along. I'll tell you something else, too. I was quoted in an eastern paper at the time as saying Cobb was 'crazy' for overlooking Joe DiMaggio and Ted Williams. That was a lot different from what I really said, that I believe DiMag and Ted would have been outstanding at any time. And I was anxious that Cobb know that I hadn't been unappreciative of the honor he paid me."

Over the course of his weekend visit, Cobb was Spink's guest at the Cardinals' Sportsman Park. In Spink's presence, Cobb recalled a game there in 1925 when he set an American League record of 16 total bases in one game, including with three home runs into the right-field pavilion.

"Ty smiled when Spink brought up that memorable day, and then Cobb chuckled. 'Tell me, Taylor,' he said, 'whatever became of those guys who used to deliver their ice in the morning, come out in the bleachers in their blue work shirts in the afternoon here and spend their time giving Old Ty hell in left field?'" With that, Broeg ended his article.

During his visit, to sports editor Burnes of the *St. Louis Globe-Democrat*, Cobb said this about his *Life* articles: "If someone can explain to me why 66 major league ballplayers last year did not sacrifice even once and why another 60 sacrificed no more than once each, then I'll believe that I'm wrong. But it's there in the record." He also told Burnes, "I cannot accept the argument that a man is a great ballplayer because he has a good batting average." He added, "I want to know what that man did when he reached base, whether he stole occasionally. I want to know how many times he helped the ball club by sacrificing. I want to know how good a defensive ballplayer he is."

Good players should steal "often enough to be a threat to the opposing team. Then you've got the pitcher off balance. He's watching you concentrating on you more than he is the batter. He may throw the ball away or just get wild. And the second baseman and the shortstop will move up just a little closer to the base, giving the next batter more opportunity to hit."

Spink was listening in and said, "Fielder Jones once told me that his old Chicago [White Sox] ball club would go into huddles about stealing a base. Five or six players would study the pitcher, watch every move. They'd force a steal now and then just to see what the pitcher would do. Then they'd all get together and compare notes, to see if anyone had detected a weakness." Cobb singled out Eddie Collins and Milan as types who studied a pitcher's every move and said that is what made them great base stealers.

Cobb also explained his singling out of shortstop Rizzuto for praise in one of his *Life* articles. "In the last world series, he was in on almost every double play, eight of them, I think. They were key plays, cut off Giant rallies. Just a few days ago, he went to bat five times, walked twice, bunted safely twice and hit away safely the other time."

Finally of relevance to his earlier articles, he said, "Don't think I overlook the long ball. Hack Wilson's 190 runs batted in in one season is a tremendous record. Lou Gehrig with over 170 the same way [sic]. But I don't want somebody to tell me so-and-so is a great hitter because he drove in 50 runs with 25 homers. I want to know why he could only drive in another 25 runs in his other 175 times at bat that year. To me, that is not a great ball player."

throwing out the first ball at the new Little League ballpark in Palo Alto, in June 1952

After visiting St. Louis, Cobb did some instructing in the Ozarks in southern Missouri, at a baseball camp for 10- to 18-year-olds. In St. Louis, he had tried to dispel the notion that he had soured on baseball as a result of his *Life* articles. He spoke about 12-team Little League ball back in Palo Alto, where the kids wear "oxford tennis shoes with rubber spikes, just what they need to avoid injury." He said that a few years earlier, he had donated a trophy for the new Little League in Menlo Park. He also said he learned from the chief of police there that "after the first season of Little League ball there, do you know only two little guys were arrested by Menlo Park police for little acts for misbehavior and the police chief explained that both of those kids came from out of town – away from the Little League area."

A postscript on Cobb's 1952 articles is that he reportedly received a large sum, which he donated to charity. Hornbaker said it went to the Cobb Educational Fund; Broeg reported more generally that it had gone to charity. DiMaggio reportedly declined an offer to write a response article and to be paid double what Cobb received. The possible original source for the latter bit is syndicated columnist Walter Winchell.

On other fronts in 1952:

A letter in July to Christy Walsh contained some updates on his health. The main point of his writing was to explain why he was unable to attend a baseball luncheon. "I have had a fibrillation of the heart and followed with two different types of virus flu[,] was in hospital two weeks with heart thing and some 16 days with flu in bed at home. I now feel fine but if I increase pace at whatever I do which includes walking I have a shortness of breath, I am not allowed to play golf and of course think the doctor [presumably Dr. Hugh Wood of Emory University Hospital] is playing it too fine but he is the boss. My son Ty Jr. had a most serious brain operation in N.Y. [he would die in September]. I was not allowed to go, an aunt passed away in Georgia, not allowed to go, have a summer place on Lake Tahoe and just now given permission to go there, the elevation 6250 ft[.] at my place, the doctor may relent very soon but advises caution. I have reduced by dieting some 31 lbs[.] and really feel fine, but when the doctor states he will not take responsibility I heed."

I can add one detail about Ty Jr. and Cobb. While searching microfilm in vain for something by columnist Herb Caen in the *San Francisco Examiner*, I found Caen writing the following: "Dr. Ty Cobb, Jr., son of Atherton's immortal baseball hero (and a brilliant medico in Atlanta, Ga.) is now in P'Alto [sic], living with his mother; he's very ill – and in the constant care of a nurse."

A Russian magazine, *Smena*, tried to discredit U.S. baseball, including as a "beastly struggle, a blood fight with mayhem and murder." In one segment of its piece, as reported by the United Press, "Smena gave excerpts from the memoirs Ty Cobb wrote for Life Magazine, saying his body is covered with scars and adding that he, too, gave many damaging blows."

Back in the states, Cobb stalwart Parker wrote in the *New York Mirror*, "Ty Cobb prizes a color action photo of himself breaking through a panel on which has been listed every pitcher he batted against from 1905 through 1928."

Parker added that cartoonist Clement L. "Clem" Boddington gave it to Cobb. As will be noted later in this book, Boddington, who also did a lot of baseball reporting over several decades, was a near-miss major figure in the casting of Cobb's legacy. One other overlap that I came across between Boddington and Cobb is that Cobb wrote the foreword to a publication by Boddington to mark the National League's 75th anniversary.

Cobb and his second wife vacationed in Richmond, Va., where they visited colonial Williamsburg and he did some duck hunting. He told sportswriter Shelley Rolfe of the *Richmond Times-Dispatch* that he had watched the 1952 World Series on television. According to Rolfe, "he had liked it so much that now he doubted whether he'd ever come East to see another series." Cobb did offer the following solution for minor leagues "beset by the coaxial cable:"

"If they can show fights and operas and plays over a closed television circuit why can't the minor leaguers buy a circuit and pipe in the major league games at their parks. If I had a minor league team, I'd put three or four big screens in the grandstand roof. People could get a two in one bargain. They could watch a game on the field and ever [sic] so often look up and see a major league game." Rolfe said Cobb had yet to figure "what he'd do about the sore necks."

In a letter to veteran sportswriter-turned-radio editor and announcer McLinn, he wrote, "I know you think me a hell of a guy. I pleaded guilty on some counts. I should have written you long ago, but possibly the delay might help in negotiations, etc. I am truly sorry as I know what [it] means to wait and expect an answer, etc. But Stoney you know that I would let no one else other than you do a book and we will exact every recompense possible. . . Those jews [sic] are tough and develop some sensational angles to one's discredit. [That was probably not a reference to Jewish Cobb biographer Eugene R. "Gene" Schoor, who wrote the juvenile nonfiction 1952 book *The Story of Ty Cobb*.] The book I am in no way anxious but will do it. I would like it right and that would have to be our aim. I do feel there has been lots of garbled things not true that has been written, some down right rotten and damaging. . . I would like as I said to have something done that would clear up such as coming officially from me."

(That is two new anti-Semitic comments by Cobb, one about Jewish owners of Hollywood studios and the other about Jews in the book publishing industry. Bak is the apparent source of the lone previously noted such comment

Eugene R. "Gene"
Schoor

in a modern-day article or book, as follows. In a letter to Salsinger, Cobb wrote, in reference to either or both publishers or movie studio owners/ producers, "those Jewish boys promise but pay no attention" to the truth. Since he was chummy with Moe Berg and went to movie theaters with reporter Al Horwits, both Jews, he was at least not socially anti-Semitic. If the letter to Salsinger was prior to 1953, that would be good for Cobb's legacy. That is because early that year, sportswriter Al Wolf of the *Los Angeles Times* wrote, "Ty Cobb is working on 20th Century-Fox's production, 'Kid From Left Field,' which Leonard Goldstein supervises." A week after that, gossip columnist Erskine Johnson of the NEA wrote, "Ty Cobb and Producer Leonard Goldstein are huddling on a possible Cobb film biography." Incidentally, the writer of "The Kid From Left Field" was Jack Sher, who, like Goldstein, was Jewish. Sher had written the 1948 Cobb article in *Sport*. The earliest report that I found of a possible movie about Cobb was in 1950, when Catholic actor Eddie Bracken, upon buying a production company, said he was making plans for a film.)

In Georgetown, Ky., in a speech to the Georgetown Kiwanis Club, he said, "I am seriously considering moving to this area." A day earlier, he had come up short in an auction to buy a 632-acre farm near Lexington. The three next-highest bidders to the winner were Kentucky native Happy Chandler, the former governor and recently deposed baseball commissioner; University of Kentucky basketball coach Adolph Rupp; and Cobb. Cobb was on a visit and staying with Chandler.

When asked during the visit about his *Life* articles, he replied, "A lot of people apparently didn't like my opinions, but if you stop and think of all the major leaguers today, you couldn't name over [sic] two or three who would be ranked with some of the all-time greats. There would be Phil Rizzuto, Stan Musial and Pee Wee Reese [a Kentucky native whose name Cobb may have inserted in light of his audience]. That would be just about the extent of it." In that same interview, he singled out Kiner as not measuring up. "He is a great hitter, but what else can he do? They moved the fence in at Pittsburgh so he can pump that lousy ball over the fence into Greenberg Gardens," the part of the stadium named for retired Pittsburgh slugger Hank Greenberg.

Besides Richmond and Lexington, he also visited Detroit, but with an eye to not be noticed. That is because "when everyone knows I am there, so many feel I should see them or call on phone, if I do not they might feel I slighted them." One purpose of that trip was to commission well-known Detroit muralist and portrait painter Roy C. Gamble to paint portraits of his parents. Cobb brought with him pictures and biographical material, the *Free Press* said. His reported plan was to hang them in the hospital that he was helping to fund in Royston.

In 1953:

Cobb wrote to Brooklyn's Gil Hodges after having read something related to his having gone 0-for-21 at the plate in the 1952 World Series. The letter sold for $5,225 in 1990, about $10,000 today. Cobb wrote, "I think you can make all of them eat their words the coming season and this is not psychology, you have the power, nothing wrong with eyes, then it has to be wrong fundamentals, stance, body balance & position, stance as to plate position, grip on bat." Cobb invited Hodges to write to him for some tips, with "the only stipulation there is no publicity crediting me."

In advance of a Pacific Coast League awards dinner in Los Angeles, *Los Angeles Times* sports editor Dyer wrote, "If you haven't heard Ty talk you've missed a real treat. He gave a little spiel at one of our Times Sports Awards Dinners some years ago and stole the show from a star-studded cast. Cobb has a quaint sense of humor which flavors his authoritative discourses on baseball. When he talks about 'the good old days' he does so with becoming modesty if any yarn centers around himself."

Two days later, after the latest dinner, the main photo on the front page of the *Times* featured Cobb and DiMaggio on one flank with comedians Bud Abbott and Lou Costello on the other. Each was gripping part of a bat. Cobb and DiMaggio were smiling, and Costello's facial expression was moderately goofy, by Costello's standards. That is this book's cover graphic, as photographed at the dinner by the *Los Angeles Examiner*.

In a letter to Salsinger, Cobb wrote, "I have been like a 'shot cat' for some time also I do procrastinate, then I had some business affairs and illness, recurrence of trouble March a year ago which was corrected quickly, reason too much 'banquet league' appearances and so called talks, now since my second fibrillation of heart I have turned over a new leaf and put the eliminator on."

In a letter to Goodman, Cobb blamed a recurrence of fibrillation of the heart on "more or less too much stress & tension and trying to fulfill too many engagements for talks and appearances also meeting everyone and his cousin, coupled with light sleeping and too many hours without proper rest and at my age, it will not work, I now have to act my age and illuminate a lot of such."

A 1953 letter to a boy, Ronald, received iconic treatment from Iconic Auctions in 2016: "Feeling a tinge of guilt for misplacing a young boy[']s letter for some time and then discovering it, Cobb takes the time to answer the boy's letter and provide his insight into the fundamentals of how to successfully hit a baseball. Based on the content of the letter, the boy was in love with the long ball (as most kids were and still are today). Being a purist however, Cobb felt motivated to set the young man straight and impose upon him his great knowledge of the sport. Penned entirely in Cobb's trademark green fountain pen ink, this sensational letter reads in full:" Actually, only the postscript is noteworthy: "I like boys but don't sick others on me – my correspondence is really a task."

Newsday columnist Cannon began a column, "The tournament never ended for Ty Cobb. The competition is endless but he has no opponent but himself. The contenders are dead or have conceded or live out their last years amid the trophies of their youth. But Cobb still challenges inferior men, crankily denouncing a generation that has yet to produce his equal. He bickers with a grouchy sadness as though he were offended because baseball endured after his departure from the game." Cannon ascribed some of Cobb's attitude to jealousy of Ruth. "Ruth influenced the sport more than Cobb and this has always irritated him."

Cannon also cited a story that he, Cannon, was presumably told in 1952 by then-Reds manager Luke Sewell, and an unclearly sourced one involving former Yankee Joe Dugan and Cobb at Toots Shor's. In the story that Cannon was presumably told, Sewell recalled his Indians teammates playing craps on a rainy day and Cobb joining them. "Cobb took a lick at the dice and made some passes [bets on the shooter to win]. The amount he won wasn't important but it put him ahead. When he missed, he stood up and laughed and bragged he had won and quit the game. He had to beat you or he was miserable."

(In spring training in Tampa in 1952, Cannon had conveyed the following from Sewell, who had been an American League catcher in Cobb's final eight seasons. Sewell said that one rule bend that helped Cobb was during Detroit home games, in how portable bleachers were positioned in the Detroit outfield. "They'd move them around from right to left field, and stack them up so they would favor Cobb." (At a game at Yankee Stadium in 1955, Cobb sat with Sewell and "when a couple of sliced balls went into the stands, Ty moaned: 'Those are home runs?'"))

In 1950, Ralph McGill wrote, "He had to give up poker for the reason that none of his friends would play with him. One by one they dropped off because of the wild wrath of Cobb when others took the pot." A month earlier, a Cobb letter to Hauck had contained the following postscript: "I am taking Vitt at Gin Rummy and Mrs. C [sic] is taking him at cribbage. he don[']t like it."

The Toots episode supposedly took place after an old-timers' game a couple of years earlier. Dugan played in the American League in Cobb's final 12 seasons. He was standing at the bar when Cobb came in. Cobb said, "Have a drink," and Dugan replied, "You're twenty years too late" and turned away.

(One of Norman L. Macht's books on Connie Mack has the Dugan story plus two rarities in modern-day books and articles, without noting their apparent source: a Cannon column upon Cobb's death that, as of this writing, is not in a full-text database; I found it in microfilm of the *Las Vegas Sun*. Cannon quoted longtime player and manager Jimmy Dykes as saying, "When I broke in, I played second. Every time Cobb passed me on the field, he said the same thing. 'You stink.' He'd say it after every inning. He was trying to bull me." On another occasion, Cobb came into Dykes's Philadelphia dugout after Dykes yelled an insult. Cobb ignored Dykes and instead punched an unnamed pitcher.

Roy CAMPANELLA
catcher BROOKLYN DODGERS

The other Cobb story has him, after being tagged out in a Detroit exhibition game against Georgia Tech, throwing dirt in the second baseman's eyes. That is attributed to longtime Atlanta sports reporter and editor Ed Danforth in Cannon's column and appears in greater detail from Floridian Carey Parker in a 1952 Cullen Cain column in the *Miami Daily News*.)

In July, Cobb and his second wife visited Chicago after attending the annual Hall of Fame induction. After seeing Robinson play in Wrigley Field, Cobb said, "He's all right" and compared him to three Hall of Fame second basemen, including Hornsby. "Fellows like that, you know."

He also said that catcher Campanella reminded him some of Roger Bresnahan, a top catcher of his day. "The biggest thing they got to worry about in this fella's case is his weight," Cobb said of Campanella. "He has a tendency to take on pounds. If he gets too heavy, he won't be much good. A guy can't play ball if he's fat. He's gotta be careful what he does at the table. He can eat himself right out of baseball."

at Cooperstown from left to right in 1953: Cobb, former roommate Al Simmons, Dizzy Dean, Cy Young, Connie Mack, Ed Walsh and Rogers Hornsby

The AP and the *Pittsburgh Courier* reported parts of the above. The *Brooklyn Eagle* quoted Cobb as unwilling to compare Campanella to catchers of his day. "I don't like to make provocative statements," conveyed Dave Anderson of the *Eagle*, who added that he was "apparently forgetting his magazine essay in the Spring of 1952." Cobb told Anderson that he was not planning to write any more articles but if "they want one, I'll do it. And I'll say the same things." Anderson added, "Evidently, Cobb has not changed his mind because he mentioned, 'Just look at the records and you'll see that those players had it all over the players in the game today. Players hit .400 then. Pitchers won 40, 30, 25 games every year. Men knocked in 150 runs, stole 50 bases and with all those trick deliveries. There's just no comparison.'"

Much of the following is on baseballhistorydaily.com. In Chicago, Cobb told Wendell Smith of the *Pittsburgh Courier* that Robinson is "my kind of a ball player." Smith began that article as follows: "When Ty Cobb was the batting terror of the major leagues there were two things said about him that were, apparently, the gospel truth: (1) He could hit any living pitcher. (2) He would hit any living Negro." Smith said the second claim "is merely a matter of hearsay" – and then put some stock in its accuracy. "But he gives no indication today of intolerance. Perhaps he has mellowed with the years and wealth. He is now 66 years old and his investments have made him independently rich. Those two things, no doubt, have tempered his views, racially at least."

Poet, Novelist, Baseball Catcher

Leerhsen's narrative begins with blurbs from three sources: the poet William Butler Yeats, the Gothic novel pioneer Ann Radcliffe and the catcher Ray Schalk. The Schalk blurb is, "When Cobb is on first base and he breaks for second, the best thing you can do, really, is to throw to third."

Chicago Tribune sports editor Ward elicited a quote like that from Schalk, and it can be considered unusual: its origin was a telephone call that Ward was on in 1953 with Schalk and Schalk's wife

Ray Schalk and Cobb, probably in 1955, the year Schalk became a Hall of Famer

Lavinia. In referring to his original write-up of that chat, Ward wrote, "We have recounted here previously that a telephone caller once asked Mrs. Schalk if Ray ever had thrown out Ty Cobb three times in a game."

"Mrs. Schalk said if Cobb was thrown out three times in a game, Ray did it."

Ward told his readers that at the time of the chat his resulting article omitted this subsequent part of the conversation between Ray and Lavinia: Ray had told her, "Next time someone calls, tell him the truth. Tell them that when Cobb started to steal second I threw to third to head him off."

A variation that is consistent with Schalk's story above – and is instead attributed to fellow catcher Wally Schang – appeared in McCallum's 1956 book. McCallum prefaced it, and remarks that he attributed to Schalk, by writing, "Cobb gave catchers hallucinations. It was virtually mandatory for them to throw a base ahead of him to head him off."

Schalk had at least one other chance to tell his story. Upon Cobb's death, columnist Condon of the *Chicago Tribune* would speak immediately with him. Schalk recounted, "You ask about that old story about me throwing Ty out four times in a game? I can't remember it, and I'll repeat the answer I always give – when Cobb started to steal second, I'd throw to third to be certain to head him off. If Ty was stealing second and the ball was loose, he'd be up and off for third."

McCallum's book quoted Schalk as follows:

"On three different occasions during his career, he [Cobb] stole all the way from first to home. 'Cobb,' muttered Catcher Ray Schalk, 'would have stolen my mask if it hadn't been strapped on.'"

Right after that, McCallum printed the following:

"The Athletics were scheduled to play the Tigers one day and before the game Connie Mack called his players together for a skull session. 'Now, Wally,' he said, turning to Wally Schang, his spunky catcher, 'suppose Cobb were on second and you knew he was going to steal third. What would you do?'

"Schang evaluated the question for a flicker of a

Wally Schang

second, then blurted [sic], 'Why, Mr. Mack, I'd fake a throw to third, hold the ball, and tag the son o' gun as he slid into the plate.'"

McCallum's account is consistent with the 1928 *Babe Ruth's Own Book of Baseball*. In it, then-ghostwriter Frick wrote, "The Athletics were about to engage the Tigers in a crucial series and [Athletics manager] Connie Mack was holding a meeting to discuss the games. The boys went over all the Detroit hitters, one by one, and decided how they would pitch to each man. They discussed their own plays, and everything in the baseball category. Finally they came to the matter of stopping Cobb. Connie asked for suggestions[,] but no one came through. "Finally he turned to Schang, who had been with the club

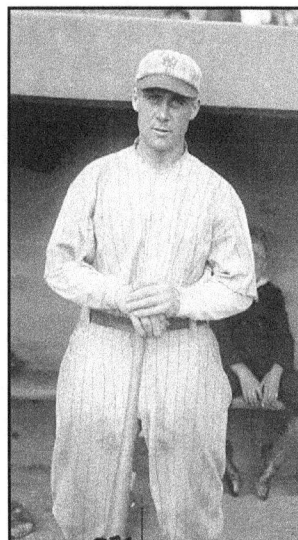

only a couple of seasons. 'Now Wallie,' Connie said, 'suppose the Tigers were one run behind, Cobb was on second base, and you knew he was going to steal. What would you do?' Schangie's answer was quick and to the point. 'I'd fake a throw to third[,] then hold the ball and tag him as he slid into the plate.'"

Subsequent versions in 1936 by syndicated Central Press columnist Walter Johns and McCallum in 1956 have Schang quotes that partially match up with each other and are similar to the above.

Without explicitly mentioning Schang, Grayson of the NEA broadened the anecdote in 1943, as follows: "Catchers actually threw a base ahead of him to head Cobb off." A few months later in 1943, AP Features sports editor Dillon Graham wrote, "Ty Cobb's favorite story is about a rookie outfielder. It was in the days when Cobb was the scourge of the basepaths and the unwritten baseball law was never to throw behind him. The Georgia Peach rammed a line drive out toward the youngster. Cobb turned first base as the rookie picked up the ball. Without a sign of hesitation, the green hand rifled the ball to the home plate. Ty Cobb was not going to outmaneuver him."

While it is hard to determine what came first, Cobb's reportedly favorite story or Schang's, the origin of Schang's can be speculated about. For that, thanks are due to an off-the-wall Schang-Cobb story that was told in 1914, Schang's second season in the big leagues, when he was with the Athletics. The story made the rounds of at least several newspapers into the following year. Supposedly, in March 1914 in East Aurora, N.Y., with his brother and their bowling team, Schang "caused a panic" in their hotel "by dreaming that he was playing base ball. He tagged Ty Cobb in his sleep, awakened everybody in the hotel, and nearly strangled his brother in an argument with the umpire."

"'He's out! He's out' cried Wally. 'I touched him when he was two feet off the bag!' It was all in the dream, but when the other members of the bowling team broke into the room occupied by the Schang brothers, Wally had the strangle hold [sic] on 'brother' Bob, and had nearly choked him black in the face. They had some trouble in waking him up, and making him understand that he was not playing the great national game, and that Brother Bob was not Ty Cobb, the player he was trying to put out at home plate.

"When Wally was thoroughly awake he laughed foolishly at his dream game of ball, and then explained: 'You see, it was like this. We were playing a close game with Detroit and Leslie Bush was pitching. There was a runner on first and Cobb was on third. I was afraid of the "double steal" and gave Bush the signal to look out for it. He threw to first trying to drive the runner back, but just as he raised his arm, Cobb started for the plate. The ball was returned to Bush from first and he whipped it home to me. I tagged Cobb fully two feet before he got home, but the umpire called him safe. I was crazy and I guess I'd have choked Bobby to death if you boys had not come into the room. It was one of the most real games I ever played.'"

I found two other tales along those lines, both from the perspective of a rookie pitcher. The first, notably, was told by Mack, his then-manager, in 1927, in Mack's "Laughs from Sports Arena" newspaper serial that year.

"Bryan (Slim) Harris, who chases rabbits down at Bangs, Texas, in the winter and hurls baseballs for us in the summer[,] dropped into Sweetwater to visit his brother. Once his identity became known, fans surrounded the pitcher and let down a barrage of queries about [Al] Simmons, Sisler, Ruth and other noted American leaguers [sic]. The amiable and modest Texan patiently answered every question until someone said:

"'Tell me exactly what you do when Ty Cobb faces you? What's his weakness and how do you pitch to him??'

"'Well, fellows, I'll tell you what I do,' replied Harris. 'I try to follow the advice of a rookie hurler we had a few years ago. Some one [sic] asked him how he pitched to Cobb and the kid promptly answered: 'I jes' tell the baseball, fool him, ball, fool him, I can't.'"

The second of the two rookie stories was told during a fanning bee in 1939. Ted Lyons of the White Sox, an active pitcher since 1923, supposedly said the following in the presence of teammates: "One story was about Cobb's speed on the bases. Some kid was going to pitch against the Tigers for the first time and his teammates were telling him how fast Ty was, and how he stretched hits for extra bases. The first time up that day Cobb laid down a bunt to the box and breezed over first base so fast[,] this kid didn't have a chance to make a play on him. When Cobb came up the second time he bunted again. This time the kid picked up the ball and threw it to second base.

"'What's the idea?' the second baseman wanted to know. 'The play's at first base, busher.'

"'Well, Ty Cobb ain't goin' to make any extra bases buntin' on me,' the rookie told him."

Upon Cobb's death, Schalk touched on various subjects with Condon of the *Tribune*; a chunk was presented near the start of this book. Schalk recycled for Condon a point he had also made in 1940 that conveyed Cobb's intensity: "Once Cobb spiked me when I was blocking home plate. He just continued on to the bench. Next day he put his arm around me and said, 'Remember I'm just as entitled to that plate as you are.' Never said he was sorry, tho [sic]."

Also, Schalk recalled a perfect game pitched by Charley Robertson of the White Sox against the Tigers in 1922. "The Tigers had a great batting order, but they couldn't come close to a hit. Cobb was fuming from about the fourth inning, running around looking at my glove, and at Robertson's glove, and at the ball. He was trying to get Robertson's goat. Cobb never got over that game." (Cobb had sent an eight-page protest letter, plus some allegedly tampered-with balls, to League President Johnson, who absolved Robertson.)

In apparently summing up that interview, Schalk said, "There are lots of things to remember about Cobb. The most vivid, however, is memory of his determination. He'd see a player who could do something great – and he'd say to himself '*I can do it better.*'"

One subject that Schalk apparently did not discuss was his own financial success in his post-career. It derived, thanks in part, to Cobb's advice to invest in Coca-Cola. Schalk's grandson James disclosed that to Schalk's book-length biographer, Brian E. Cooper, in 2008. Without alluding to Schalk or naming Coca-Cola in a 1939 interview to be featured later, Speaker said Cobb "had me buying it [stock] too, but I – well, that's another story."

Returning a second time to 1953:

Michigan bird expert Walter E. Hastings visited Cobb at his California home, apparently on short notice after calling him. Hastings reportedly said that Cobb could not have been more gracious. A sportswriter interrupted the visit by phoning to ask what Cobb thought of Pittsburgh's sale of Kiner to the Chicago Cubs. Cobb asked whether he meant who he thought was getting the better of the deal. Then Cobb said something like, "What do you think? Didn't [now-Pittsburgh general manager] Branch Rickey negotiate it?"

In a letter to Christy Walsh, Cobb wrote about some long-ago problem related to how a Ruth-focused serial crowded out his. Cobb had done his serial for Walsh's syndicate and, based on that experience, was now rejecting a new proposition from Walsh. Leerhsen reprinted a sentence that ended with Cobb telling Walsh how "New York scribes always play Ruth up." Leerhsen also quoted this sentence that appeared soon after: "Remember Christy I know who was voted in <u>first</u> to Baseball Hall of Fame (Cooperstown) [it was Cobb]."

I can add that the following appeared, respectively, after the above sentences: "I am not egotistic but I do know the score and what my position is as I left it with plenty of effort and deportment" and "and I know what the vote score was[,] you should so I won[']t quote it." In the letter, he also referred to a controversy involving presumably Salsinger's mid-1920s Cobb serial. "Salsinger received his orders, Bingay tried to hurt me and did, but later it burned his conscience & soul and made every possible amendments in a most contrite manner, poor fellow has passed on now."

On another matter, Cobb said he still wants to be Walsh's friend "but no more business relations." He referred to his own refusal "of this calendar thing. [Advertising company and then-major calendar printer] Brown & Bigelow are the finest people I have ever done business with, it[']s so refreshing, our contract limits might have expired don[']t know for sure, think it was only for a year that

from left to right at the 1931 World Series: Babe Ruth, Gabby Street, Christy Walsh, Connie Mack, Nick Altrock and John McGraw

I would not give anyone else permission etc. but with me it will be a long time before I give permission for anything that might conflict with Brown & Bigelows Calendars."

Walsh also had an association with the company; for example, it was behind his 1950 effort when he invited around 700 sportswriters to name a mythical top team of baseball stars who played from 1900 to 1950. Also in 1950, as described by a sportswriter in Waco, Tex., Walsh had added "a new twist to an old document – a calendar featuring incidents in sport history, from the day of your great-grandfather down to the current football season. Brown and Bigelow calls it 'An omnibus of sports information, divided into 365 single-sentence, pint-sized chapters.'"

Returning a third time to 1953:

In December, Cobb's

Cobb (second from left) around Lake Tahoe in 1953. Cobb gave the photograph to George H. Maines in 1959.

recent decision to endow an educational foundation to help Georgians pay for college drew an editorial in the *Cleveland Plain Dealer*. The beneficiaries would be persons of all races. "By coincidence, on the same day the Cobb announcement was made, Attorney General [Herbert] Brownell [Jr.] advised the United States Supreme Court it had full authority and the duty to outlaw racial segregation in the nation's public schools." In its concluding sentence, the *Plain Dealer* said, "Ty Cobb was right in assuming that nothing he could do with his money would be better than trying to elevate the level of education in his [home] state."

Digressing to Cobb's largesse:

In his 1994 article, the Ty R. Cobb who was sports editor of the *Nevada State Journal* in the 1940s and 1950s told of being one night at Cobb's home near Lake Tahoe when the ex-ballplayer "got out a big ledger. It contained the names of several young men. They were poor Southern youths, both white and black, whom he sponsored through college. He paid all their expenses."

Former *Atlanta Constitution* executive editor McGill, writing at the time of Cobb's death, recalled a hotel luncheon in Atlanta at which Cobb had announced the foundation. "The tall, graying man dabbed at his eyes with a napkin, pushing up his rimless glasses. He talked about his mountain forbears who, in by-gone years, never had much chance at education. He wanted his foundation to help needy boys and girls. But there was a typical Cobb touch. They had to have roughed it out one year on their own to prove they were eligible. Tears slid down his face. 'The Cobbs cry easy' he said, somewhat apologetically. And this was a strange thing, because Cobb and tears had never been associated. One wondered if this lonely and taciturn man, who could be so gentle and compassionate, and yet who could battle with his fists or at baseball with a ferocity which made men afraid, might not have wept many times in the secret hours of night."

Returning to the chronology and a new year, 1954:

In January, Burr of the *Brooklyn Eagle* wrote an interesting throw-in in a column focused on recently elected Hall of Famer Al Simmons, another great hitting outfielder: "Ty Cobb always played the outfield with the collar of his uniform shirt turned up – they were made with collars in those days – and would lift his hand along when running for a fly, like a football safety man signaling [sic] for a fair catch.

Harold Burr

Al Simmons frankly imitated the Great Ty's mannerisms."

A second story from January fits in with one about Cobb's relationship to

Hank Aaron, while one story not noted from 1953 involves a second Hall of Famer and a teammate of Aaron, Eddie Mathews. In 1953, Mathews ended his first season as a Milwaukee player, and Aaron began his big-league career in 1954 for the same team.

In a book-length biography in 1994, Mathews said that Cobb had sent him a letter near the end of the 1953 season. They had previously met one time in Atlanta, on "Ty Cobb Night" in 1950, when Mathews was on the Class AA Atlanta Crackers. In the letter, Cobb expressed the wish that it receive no publicity and Mathews in the book said that accordingly, he would not quote it. Mathews said he was never one to collect memorabilia or souvenirs, but that the Cobb letter is one of the relatively few that he still had as of the 1990s.

On the first page, Cobb said one reason for writing is that, referring to early in his career, "I was young and players then were calloused and tough, I never had anyone to tell me or help me." On the second, he wrote, "You have now proven you have every quality to be a real star, now remember this every day & night and in any situation, and it[']s all with and up to you, how far you go, discipline yourself at all times with rest (sleep) food and drink yes and smoking while you are a player, I say this Ed, remember it, and free from accidents (serious) you cannot miss."

Encouraging smoking but not advising Mathews not to inhale, as was Cobb's apparent custom, is only a mild surprise in Cobb's advice, since smoking was so prevalent in the 1950s. Cobb had previously advised DiMaggio to relax after a game in various ways, including by smoking. In the postscript, Cobb wrote as "my wish, no publicity as to this letter," and invited him to visit him in California if he ever is out there.

A widely credited-to-Cobb comment about Mathews is that he has seen only "three or four perfect swings in my time." The original source, as it appears in a 2005 Crackers book by Tim Darnell, may be Cobb as conveyed by big-time Crackers fan Zell Miller, who was later governor of Georgia and a U.S. Senator.

The author of a 2012 Milwaukee Braves book, John Klima, spoke with several former Braves and team officials and read through some old sources. One thing Klima learned is that in 1957, then-Milwaukee manager Haney invited

Cobb to speak with Mathews during the season. Klima wrote, "Eddie never hit left-handers very well, so Cobb suggested Mathews stand farther back in the [batter's] box to get a longer look at each pitch."

The *Milwaukee Journal* indeed reported something along those lines. In July of that year, Haney told sportswriter Bob Wolf that earlier in the season, Cobb had spoken to Mathews "for quite a while, and among other things he told him to move back in the batter's box when he faces a left[-]hander. Well, Eddie tried it the next time he faced a lefty and he popped one up. When he came back to the bench I heard him mutter to himself, 'That Cobb's all wet.'

"But you know, I've got a hunch he still remembers what Ty told him that day. Why, he may be following Ty's advice without realizing it."

Days later, Harry Grayson wrote that Mathews is a "left-hand pull hitter, especially when he faces a left-hand pitcher" and that the shortstop "plays well on the other side of second base." Cobb observed to Grayson that Mathews is unable to adjust his stance to hit to left field. "Against a left-hand pitcher, Mathews should close his stance, choke the bat a little and move a little farther away from the plate. Make that ball be right out there and just jab it into left field."

Klima's book, besides tipping me off to his tie-ins with Mathews, tipped me off to most of his ones with Aaron. Referring to spring training of 1954, Aaron's first season with Milwaukee, then-manager Charlie Grimm was reluctant to give Aaron a chance to displace recently acquired outfielder Bobby Thomson. On that decision, Cobb "chastised Grimm for being stupid," Klima wrote. According to Klima, Cobb had seen Aaron play against Macon in 1953 when

from left to right: Cobb, Charley Gehringer, Travis Jackson, Mickey Cochrane and Charlie Grimm

Aaron was with Jacksonville in the Sally League. I found a close match. In March 1954, a spring training report in the *Chicago Defender*, which Klima's

from left to right at the 1954 sportswriters' dinner in Philadelphia: (standing) Chuck Klein, Red Grange, Jack Kelly (Grace's father), Joe Louis, Jimmie Foxx, Frank Baker and Dave Bancroft; (seated) Mickey Cochrane, Speaker, Connie Mack, Cobb, Lefty Grove and billiardist Willie Hoppe

book reflects to a great degree, stated that Cobb had seen Aaron in action when Jacksonville visited Augusta.

Before spring training, Cobb and Grimm saw each other in Philadelphia, presumably at the pictured sportswriters' dinner that both were indeed at. When they met, "Cobb spent most of his time

Mack and Cobb in a different group photo at the dinner

[spent with Grimm] talking about Aaron," the *Defender* reported. The *Defender* also ran the following as a direct quote from Cobb, which sounds as if it could

Cobb during his 1957 visit to Milwaukee, to be featured later. The civilians, from left to right, are George McBride and Hall of Famer Ray Schalk. To the left of Hank Aaron is Chuck Tanner, and Bobby Thomson is behind them. To Thomson's right may be Johnny Logan and to Aaron's may be Joey Jay. McBride, a contemporary of Cobb, was a top fielding shortstop who has the lowest batting average for a player with at least 5,000 at-bats, .218. He coached under Cobb in 1925 and 1926 in Detroit. Schalk would be one of three former players at Cobb's funeral.

have been stated in a letter: "What I like about Aaron is his hitting and his mannerisms at the plate really impressed me."

(In 1974, Bisher, who had interviewed Cobb in 1958 on different matters, interviewed Aaron for the *Atlanta Constitution* around the time he was going to break the then-all-time home run record, Babe Ruth's 714. Bisher wrote, "Aaron and Cobb never met." That is wrong, based on the photograph above. A second confirming photograph, of the pair next to each other smiling, with Cobb doing the talking, ran in the *Manchester Union Leader* in New Hampshire in 1958 at the newspaper's 10th baseball dinner. At the dinner, wrote the newspaper's sports editor, Leo E. Cloutier, there was a "tremendous standing ovation" for Cobb "as he stood up to assume his position at the microphone. It lasted minutes and it touched Ty no little."

I was able to pose a question to Aaron through his personal assistant, Susan Bailey. Does Aaron recall ever receiving a letter from Cobb? The answer came back as, "Mr. Aaron does not recall getting a letter from Ty Cobb.")

Otherwise at that dinner, in January 1954:

Cobb gave a brief talk about his admiration for Connie Mack. Cobb had already posed for dozens of pictures when there was interest in having him join in another group one. Just then, "Ty was over in a corner, eye-deep in old ball players and particularly Chief Bender. Someone went over in the hope of moving the great Georgian in the direction of the camera.

"'– and Chief,' he was saying, 'he did it with the end of his bat. Yes, sir, with the end of his bat.'

"Cobb glanced then at the intruder who asked[,] 'Would you mind going over there for another picture?'

"'I'll go if you insist,' he said, smiling, 'but I'd rather stay right here and reminisce with this old dodger.' He was patting Bender on the knee," wrote sports editor Ed Pollock of the *Evening Bulletin* in Philadelphia.

In March, Cunningham recalled what Cobb and Speaker had told him about the legs of ballplayers. "They said the modern sort are no good – compared[,] that is[,] with the kind the old-time ball players had. They blamed it all on modern living and the style-change in general off-season recreation." Cobb recited his offseason physical activity to keep in shape, including hunting. By contrast, players like DiMaggio move into a city apartment and live like a banker or broker. Their longest walk is from the elevator to the curb when they catch a cab, and they drive to where they have to go. Instead of getting sleep, they hang out at clubs or restaurants. Cobb also told Cunningham that he was not criticizing such players, as it was none of his business, and just commenting. The legs are the one part of the body you cannot fool, he said: "Soft living will kill 'em and when they start to go[,] a ball player's through."

(In a 1922 interview with the AP, Cobb had said, "I'm slowing up. I tire more easily and I require more sleep – no more late nights for me." In a 1952 interview with Broeg of the *St. Louis Post-Dispatch*, he said that the last six years of his career, 1923 to 1928, "were torture. I'd play a game, go right to a hotel, take the newspapers and magazines to my room and eat both dinner and breakfast in the room, trying to conserve my strength for the next day. And I didn't have to go through this irregular day-night business.")

In April, Ted Williams began a three-part series in the *Saturday Evening Post*, "as told to Joe Reichler and Joe Trimble." In the second part's opening, Williams declared, "Ty Cobb was the greatest ballplayer of all time. But that's no reason why he should keep

Here, in his own words, Ted tells why he'll hang up his spikes this fall . . . a decision he made even before his recent injury. He reviews his own tempestuous career and he swings from the heels as he airs his pet gripes. He explains why he *still* dislikes most sports writers and some fans. He claims Ty Cobb is all wet about modern players and shows *why*. Here's the baseball story of the year! Get your copy of the Post and start it today!

the prose in a *Saturday Evening Post* advertisement in 1954 rapping the modern players. A couple of years ago the Georgia Peach said that only two men in the major leagues today – Stan Musial and Phil Rizzuto – could be mentioned in the same breath with the old-time stars. Recently he again put the blast on present-day ballplayers."

Also in his article, Williams said Cobb "has said some nice things about me, too, and I certainly appreciate them. Back in the spring of 1951, after a newspaper interview in which he was quoted as being very critical of my hitting, Ty wrote me a personal letter in which he tried to clarify his views. I no longer have that letter. However, Cobb later put much of the same thoughts in a letter to my friend and business manager, Fred Corcoran. Here are some excerpts from it:" The excerpts were featured much earlier.

Of the Cobb *Life* article headline "They Don't Play Baseball Any More," he wrote, "What bunk! I think we've got as many smart players today as there were in his day. You'd think the Lord stopped giving people brains." Williams named several and wondered if they would have been "dumbbells in his time?"

Williams also wrote, "It made me laugh when Cobb said that of all the present-day managers, only Casey Stengel could match wits with the managers of his time." For example, "Leo Durocher, of the Giants, has been called lots of things, but nobody has ever accused him of being dumb." Williams expressed agreement with Cobb on one point about players and their habits. "They could practice more," Williams wrote. "But they are no lazier than players of other days." As far as players and their weight, "it's only natural for ballplayers to put on weight as they get older. I'm forty pounds heavier than when I came into the big leagues. But [pitcher Bob] Feller, with those calisthenics he does! I asked him one day last season how much weight he'd put on since he started. The answer is that he's kept his weight the same."

Later in his article, Williams wrote, "I'll admit that one of the reasons you don't see any more .380 and .400 hitters is that everybody is swinging from the heels, trying to bash the ball out of the park. But the big reason, I believe, is that baseball is simply much tougher to play today than ever before. Look at those conditions we play under today. Today, we have night games followed by day double-headers followed by that stupid thing called a twi-night double-header. We have one-day hops and one-night stands. Sometimes we have to eat our meals on the run." Later, he wrote that "one of the things that have improved the quality of present-day baseball talent is the lowering of the bars against Negroes. This has brought in such outstanding new stars as Jackie Robinson, Roy Campanella, Larry Doby, Monty Irvin, Minnie Minoso, Don Newcombe, Luke Easter, Satchel Paige and others."

Williams gave Cobb's all-time team picks, as follows: Lou Gehrig/George

Sisler, Eddie Collins, Buck Weaver, Honus Wagner, Joe Jackson, Tris Speaker, Babe Ruth, Mickey Cochrane, plus three right-handed pitchers and two lefties: Walter Johnson/Christy Mathewson/Grover Cleveland Alexander and Eddie Plank/Rube Waddell.

Williams's were: Jimmie Foxx, Charley Gehringer/Bobby Doerr/Joe Gordon, George Kell/Al Rosen, Phil Rizzuto, Stan Musial, Joe DiMaggio, Hank Greenberg, Bill Dickey, plus a righty and two lefty pitchers, and a pinch hitter: Bob Feller, Hal Newhouser/Lefty Grove and Johnny Mize.

(A Williams comment from 1989 at Cooperstown fits here, for making a contrast about Cobb himself. As reported by Phil O'Neill of the *Worcester Telegram & Gazette*, he said, "I talked a lot with Cobb. It's funny, the first thing he said to me was that he never tried to cut (spike) people. . . But then you'd see pictures of him sharpening his spikes.")

Cobb wrote to retired future fellow Hall of Famer Max Carey. As summarized by Christie's, Cobb discussed "the fact that he and other great players such as Lajoie and Wagner should have done something to pass on the secrets of their respective skills to future generations of players. He laments that players of today (1954) do not have the basic skills of hitting, sliding, or base running, and that they don't even know which foot to touch a base with."

In a second letter to Carey that year, he described the burden of responding to fan mail. "My correspondence cannot be organized so some one else can handle the bulk, I have never been one to ruthlessly 'waste paper basket' letters, youngsters for instance seldom enclose addressed envelopes & stamped and there is a certain 'certain class' of smart boys who never, the blood runs true. I find it difficult to toss them aside, I use post cards a lot, stamp bills really amount to considerable, my signature will never be of value for they are not scarce, the balls, & pictures & books, re-wrapping which one must return, bothers so much, enough of this. . . "

In a letter to Danny Goodman, Cobb invited him to Nevada: "we have all the name bands & stars and Reno also." Cobb also mentioned that he had recently turned down four all-expense paid trips, to Georgia and Tennessee, including two that offered him a fee. His reason was, "I am too old to be running around." Also, Cobb asked him to mail something anonymously to his son Jimmy; Cobb told Goodman that he blames his ex-wife for trying to alienate Jimmy from him. Cobb left the envelope open so that Goodman could see what was in it. "I have a purpose in this, his mother has tried very hard to alienate him and I don[']t hear from him as often as [I] should."

In August, Cobb told Burr of the *Brooklyn Eagle*, "The [second] wife and I just like to stick around the house and read magazines." Also, "Once in a while we tune in a game on television. But mostly we read the sport pages." As he had in recent years, he was praising the White Sox for playing "the kind of baseball I like," presumably including by bunting, to get one run at a time.

In the same interview, he praised Campanella as the greatest catcher, "greater today than ever before because he keeps playing with that busted hand. I think Mickey Mantle has a great future if his leg holds up." He added, "But kids of today often quit playing because of injuries when they might be able to work the injury out on the ball field. I was lucky. About the worst thing that happened to me were three broken ribs when I collided with another Detroit outfielder." (In a 1952 letter, reported on by Bob Myers of the AP after getting Cobb's okay to cite it, Cobb had referred to Mantle as "that Mantle" and wrote, "If he doesn't run into physical trouble or the [military] service [in Korea], with Casey's guidance, the indications are very strong that he will be a real star.")

In September, he wrote to former teammate Archie Yelle, "I sure got a tough deal in Placerville[, Calif., where he had been arrested in August for drunk driving and spent several hours in jail before being released on bail, which he forfeited], I suppose you saw it in papers, please believe me they surely gave me a very wrong deal and sometimes I wish I had never been publicly known and carried the name I do. I will tell you about it when I see you, it[']s very difficult not to work up a hate to some of those boys away up in the corner of the state and who is tied up to the local Justice of peace. I was not the only one[,] they took others and my attorney told me two army flyers [pilots] from Maxwell Field [presumably Maxwell-Gunter Air Force Base in Montgomery, Ala.] who had been up to Lake Tahoe, and stuck them the same as I was, I was going to ask for Jury trial as I felt I was treated very wrong, my attorney from Auburn not Placerville stated they had boys that were under obligations and had, had good treatment by the J.P. [justice of the peace] and Jury would be packed and advised me not to ask for Jury trial and the extra expense to me."

Neither 2015 author cited the 1954 arrest for drunk driving (or his 1936 driving-related settlement and speeding ticket); instead, like Rhodes, they noted the 1947 Placerville drunk driving arrest. Hornbaker did find the earlier noted letter to Dr. Elkin after the 1954 arrest in which Cobb told of his drinking.

He wrote to then-Pittsburgh manager Haney, near the end of a 53-101 season. Early on, Cobb stated that he was enclosing a batting pose of young

Pittsburgh slugger Frank Thomas; I saw the first page of the five-page letter where that appeared. The online auctioneer BidAMI.com said this about the letter: "The style is classic Cobb – run-on sentences, a bit rambling with a general disdain for the rules of punctuation. The text is thoroughly legible, however, and presented entirely in his preferred green ink." The text has basically three topics, "advice for Frank Thomas (which is heavily tempered with an urging of secrecy), a consuming sympathy expressed to Haney in having to guide a losing team, and a few pointers in managing."

The auctioneer Lelands had previously offered it for sale. It said that Cobb observed to Haney that Thomas "is in sort of a slump. He has an exaggerated position of hands and bat, so long as he does well never suggest a change but when he gets into a slump then he will be glad to have your suggestion. Drop his hands some not too much, his bat is too far behind his head and too high, in coming from the position as you see into a proper parallel swing the heavy end of the bat has to take a dip and will not be true in swinging. . . Most important is that his hands and elbow should be well away from his body[,] also for true better body balance crouch him a little from his waist up, this boy must have ability, from his record, if he slumps offer these changes in practice and he will appreciate you[r] help also you[r] knowledge, from the position as shown I would say he might have trouble with a ball around his knees, his left elbow if every good except he might elevate it a little more and with more of a crouch and bending over from his waist band with what he has naturally he should be pulled out of a slump and of course possibly even improve."

I did see a copy of the original postscript on the five-page letter. It states, "Again no one is to know this, you are the manager and you should have all credit, [Pittsburgh head scout] George Sisler a fine man, but you must get the credit etc."

In October, he was in South Dakota for pheasant hunting season. He wrote to Goodman that Mrs. Cobb and he first went to Badlands National Park and the Black Hills of South Dakota, where Mount Rushmore is.

In 1955:

Frances Fairbairn Cass (Cobb)

In a letter to a Ralph Holibaugh, Cobb wrote, "I never faked an autograph only thing I ever faked was a bunt to draw 3rd baseman in, then hit through him on next ball. . . "

In signing an item for a George Hipp, Cobb advised him to take a small brush "and put clear shellac over only each signature[.] this will keep ink from fading out." In signing a later item, Cobb thanked him for his courteous return package and advised him to "apply a clear varnish over signature to insure it against possible fade." More notably, in his first letter, Cobb advised Hipp on getting the signatures of some other Hall of Famers. He provided suggested routes for reaching Wagner and Cy Young, who "haven't long to go." Also, "why not grand old Mr. Connie Mack, he can sign his name but that[']s about all." Cobb had just received a letter from one of Mack's three sons in Florida. He suggested Napoleon Lajoie too. "Larry is tough and slow so try him last."

He ordered books from a Mr. Hoag, perhaps Merritt E. Hoag, president of North Georgia College and future long-term trustee of the Cobb Educational Fund. He was seeking a book by neurosurgery pioneer Harvey Cushing, plus one by Sir William Osler entitled *Aequanimitas, with Other Addresses to Medical Students, Nurses and Practitioners of Medicine.* Cobb, in reply to a question from Hoag, noted that his most serious professional interest growing up was to become a surgeon. Also, from meeting surgeons, many have invited him to watch operations, "so I say here I have seen many, needless to add as of today I get a thrill a." [sic] That is how the one page of the letter I saw, its first, ends.

In Chicago, Schalk told a Cobb anecdote soon after himself being elected to the Hall of Fame. In accepting a gift from the Chicago Baseball League and Training School, he said, "Ty Cobb phoned me from his home in Menlo Park, Calif[.], when he learned I had the good fortune to be selected for the Hall of Fame. He talked on and on and finally I said, 'Ty, this isn't a nickel call.' He came right back, 'Oh, you're still trying to tell me what to do, you bantam rooster!'" Schalk was 5'9" and 165 pounds to Cobb's 6'1" and 175. Possibly an inside story is that, as was said by then-Detroit owner Navin at the 1925 banquet in Cobb's honor, "Our scout looked him [Schalk] over and reported him too small to develop into a good big league catcher."

In April, *Newsday* columnist Cannon said Jackie Robinson "plays with a fierce recklessness. Anger is part of his skill. He resembles Ty Cobb more than any man in this generation. There is no compromise for him but this also makes him one of the big attractions of sports."

Also that month, Cobb wrote to McCallum regarding McCallum's apparent raising the possibility of writing a book-length biography of him. Cobb mentioned some of the feelers he himself had received, from Harcourt Brace, Putnam, Scribner's and Simon & Schuster. He added, "I have been urged by friends who seem to have my interest at heart per garbled stories. Many of prominence that have argued with me [said] that it was a duty to have the record clear and that such a book might be appreciated by many. Of course, I refuse to be greatly impressed by my importance." He also noted having received movie inquiries and wrote, "I know enough, dumb as I am, that if I went into this [movies] the first thing they would want – the person playing my part – would be to jump just as hard as he could with spikes in some baseman's face."

He also recalled his 1952 *Life* articles and observed that "most every statement I made has been proven today and been admitted – as we see so often many that are wondering what is wrong with baseball of the present day – for in all the years before the lively ball I can't remember one article that was finding fault with how baseball was being played at that time."

In a letter in May, Cobb invited McCallum to visit him in California or Nevada and offered to have him stay as his guest instead of in a hotel. Also in that letter, Cobb wrote, alluding to McCallum's

John D. McCallum and Cy Young, at Cooperstown in 1955

planned book, "I can not [sic] promise anything and believe me am not playing hard to get, for to be honest I would dread it all." Part of the letter is hard to read, but Cobb seems to have told him that any money received from the book would go to the Cobb Educational Fund.

In late May, Cobb wrote to Spink. There are a number of surviving Cobb letters that include instruction on how to play baseball, and they are relatively dull. This one is the most interesting of the genre that I saw. That is because it gives an idea of what Cobb was like when editing a book:

"Jack McDonald[, of the *San Francisco Call-Bulletin,*] the 'Giant Killer' has just left here, I gave him all I could, subject base stealing hard to outline and define, I gave him lots of high points, he is to do the rest, I will receive what he does and make any corrections, hope will be o.k. for you, I am in your book on outfield play don[']t think I should be too much in book, you should get some of those great present day stars to tell them how to steal etc. the readers might resent these old timer boys telling them how etc. [Cobb sliding and bunting pupil-turned-*Sporting News* base-running expert Bernie] De Vive[i]r[o]s has good ideas to slide and teach, he has too many types of sliding some are bad and conflict to opposite way he has, will confuse the player in learning or using different slides to be decided on the split second, he will be fortunate to get one man out of 20 to work & practice and use the real & proper slide as shown [in] figure 7 on page 39, your book How to Play Baseball, this same slide to other side of bag would be tuck right leg under left and tag bag with the left toe, he is figures 9, 10, 11 & 12 page 40[,] a very difficult slide to learn and occasions to use are not so often, the figures on page 35 might look good to you Taylor or in the book or look good to embryo player, but not right and if De Vive[i]r[o]s is going to teach right sliding then stick to the figure 7 style page 39, DeV— can make himself a good job teaching sliding then scouting also sell his services to other clubs to teach these ideas to their coaches etc., go from one club to another and collect a fee from each, I know DeV— well, see him often out here, he tells me where he got his ideas per page 39 also page 40, do not let him know I disapprove of the other slides, these slides will complicate the ball player also his efforts per results of teaching, DeV— is doing or can do a fine thing in teaching proper fundamentals which the present day star or player have lost or ignored, I do not in any way want my name mentioned or credit given, would like and enjoy trying to see or steer DeV— away from other slides and to only the right ones, so if he would contact me I would try to help him unselfishly.

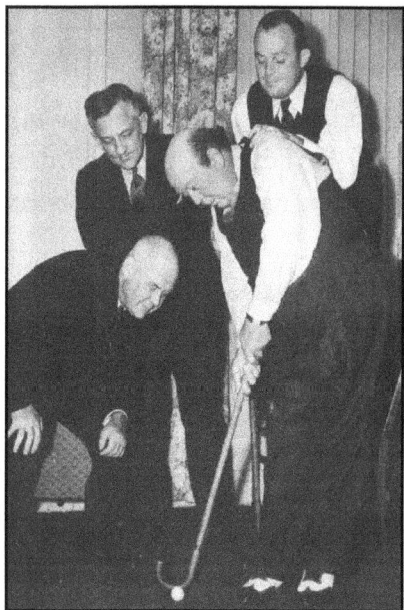

from left to right: Grantland Rice, Gene Fowler, actor Guy Kibbee and Henry McLemore

"The head first slide is out, a base runner jumps high for ball and comes down on the slider's hands, the right way is to give baseman the smallest part of tag – that[']s the toe, at same time body balanced and under control per figure 7 page 39 to get up and advance another base not sprawled flat on his back[,] not being really able to see the bag he is trying to touch with foot etc. you as an old player should see and understand this Taylor."

Proper sliding technique was one of Cobb's favorite subjects. Upon his death, syndicated columnist McLemore recalled being in a hotel with him about a decade earlier, and Cobb giving sliding demonstrations on the rough carpet – "for half an hour." In his mid-20th century history of the Boston and Milwaukee Braves, Harold Kaese told of a retired big leaguer living in Detroit, Bobby Lowe, getting into a heated sliding demonstration with Cobb. It took place in Cobb's home while their respective wives could overhear them.

Also in his letter, Cobb wrote, "I submit to you for your appraisal a most scientific treatment of baseball batting by one [Peter James] Falsey, this is in great detail and of course if some 'bulging brain' ball player could ever think of all this to do, while at bat, with all the action and split second, synchronized thinking and effort then Falsey might have something, but seems to me concentration of mind while the physical effort of swinging the bat at ball is mentioned as the great – must – if you should want Falsey's system in your paper, keep it, if not return it so I can get a few laughs showing to others.

"We have been here about 2 weeks, my [word hard to read] is fine and we both feel so well also away from the throng, plenty of fish now, a record season on all Lake Tahoe predicted by all, building is booming." He also expressed hope that Spink and he would see each other at the Hall of Fame in July. Days later, he wrote to Spink the following, also from Nevada:

"Thought you might like to see the enclosed, X marks the Cobb house on Lake Tahoe, we see snow across Lake year round, yet we have very warm days during summer never rugged winter or summer as to real heat or cold because of altitude. How about a change of address [for his *Sporting News* subscription] up to here above address? Have been boosting sales by buying off stands as I did all last summer."

Cobb then stated that wife Frances (who had rescinded her divorce filing) and he would soon be in Cooperstown and presumably see him there. He first invited Spink and apparently Spink's wife Blanche to Atlanta to "enjoy what we will have, some fine Southern hospitality, am arranging to meet all students that can come to Atlanta" who are Cobb Educational Fund recipients and board members of the fund. "Then if you all would like to motor trip 90 miles, see Royston and the hospital and only house there or more as you wish then by plane or train into New York and on to Cooperstown, this only a thought for you to decide if you would want to

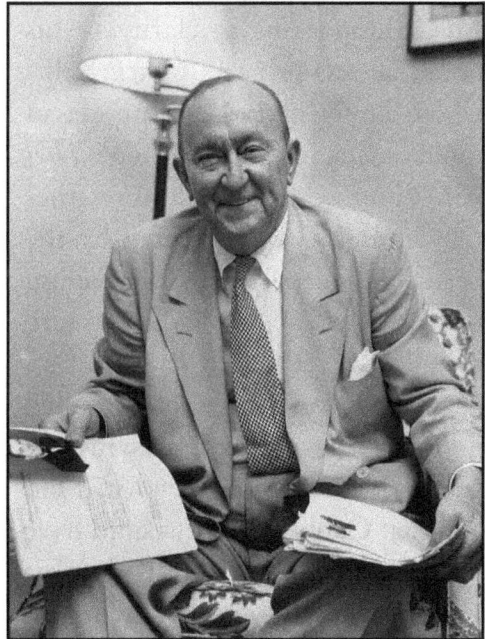

reviewing Cobb Educational Fund applications in 1957

come with us in this, I have written [Coca-Cola Company President] Bob Woodruff 'Coke' – given him my plans and wanted to see him, so I might see him in Atlanta or N.Y. and you could if plans turn out O.K. very well make some 'hay' under perfect circumstances, possibly a 'swish' through Coca-Cola plant Atlanta, but you would really without show of intent get very close to a new deal per advertising etc. we would be only a short time Atlanta and Royston, also we don't need to go to Royston, think this over and give me your present reactions, the Trustees of Educational Fund also students six I believe, this I am going to arrange as I have met only one of the students, be a luncheon at [Atlanta's] Capital City club or Piedmont Driving [C]lub, think will be nice.

"Mr. [Thomas H.] Keating, head of Chevrolet for General Motors, known him longtime [sic] has insisted I at any time or anywhere ask for use of car, getting to Cooperstown from New York City or more nearby point, I might be able to have car etc. think this over and let me hear."

The following detail from 1955 apparently first appeared in McCallum's 1975 book:

McCallum reprinted a pair of Cobb letters from that year. In the first, he began by thanking McCallum for a picture from, as McCallum seems to clarify in his book, actress-princess Grace Kelly, whose family he was in the process of interviewing for his 1957 book *That Kelly Family*. "Like millions of other movie fans, Ty was smitten by the beauty of Princess Grace," McCallum wrote in 1975. Cobb had asked him if he could get her to send him an autographed picture. Cobb recalled knowing her father Jack from his two seasons playing in Philadelphia. I can add that Cobb and Kelly could have chatted at the 1954 Philadelphia

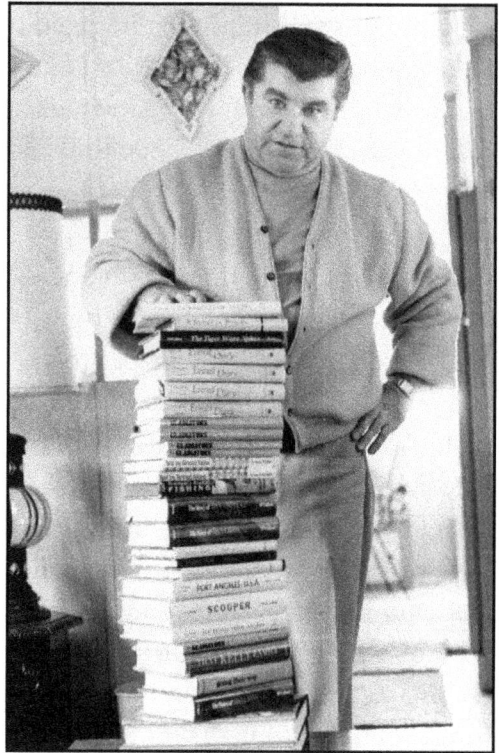

John D. McCallum in the early 1970s

sportswriters' dinner; they are in the group photo reprinted earlier.

In that letter, Cobb rehashed the Keating reference above and raised the possibility of McCallum going in Cobb's car from New York City to Cooperstown; they would indeed go together, with McCallum doing the driving. Days later, Cobb wrote to him the following, after McCallum told him he was seriously thinking of buying a stock that Cobb had told him about during McCallum's stay with him in Nevada. I have modified McCallum's text to match the original version in his papers at Washington State University:

Dear John:

Yours of 7/5/55 received. I hasten to say do not invest in anything I have talked about, I can see where a young fellow can with study and wisdom make himself independent, I see it, but you would have to learn it and at times restrain yourself and hew to certain lines, I could not help or interest myself in your behalf, I have the urge to have my friends participate in what I feel sure of, I have the desire to share and it makes me feel happy, I have in the past under written [sic] losses, it[']s a mistake, I suffer.

Now John the associated Dev. & Research [stock tip] came from a 'big man'[.] I bought 200 shares, I do not like it and am getting out, don[']t know if I lose or what[,] but he is a fellow who hasn[']t the feeling I have, you must remember I did not myself advise you to buy [this stock], I told you of it but stated have your broker give you the dope, the United Corp. is o.k.[,] a good return and utility holding that will in years enhance in value.

If I wanted to tell you of some 3 or 4 or more stocks that would take much money to buy, I could have and in last few days they have done so well but I could not be your financial advisor and feel responsible for I do not gain and would not. I think I told you of Coca[-]Cola[;] well, it has gone up, others have made me so much [money] in one day that it is pitiful, but I could not 'tout' [try to persuade] you. I can stack the chips up high but could not see you take the same chance. Please forget anything I said [about investments], 'your business is your business[.]'

A short excerpt from one of the two remaining paragraphs of the letter appeared earlier; in it, Cobb said he had seen Jimmy Durante perform in Reno and that television personality Dennis Day was at his table. The only other text in the letter rehashed the Keating reference above and again raised the possibility of McCallum going in Cobb's car from New York City to Cooperstown.

Before heading to New York City, Cobb visited Atlanta for a meeting of the Cobb Educational Fund. While there, he appeared on WSB-TV. In a five-minute interview with the station's Ray Moore, he seemed a bit sluggish. Asked if there are any players in current baseball who he likes, he was slow to say, "I like this boy that came from Atlanta [Triple AAA], this Eddie Mathews, and of course the colored boy, Willie Mays. He really is an amazing ballplayer." Later on, Moore asked if any contemporaries were "your kind of a ballplayer," which, when Cobb asked for clarification, Moore characterized as ones who "had the fighting instinct that characterized your play." Cobb did not name anyone.

Instead, he stressed that he admired a player who hustled and hit and fielded before saying, "I wouldn't care if he was a gorilla, I'd like him."

Cobb arrived in New York City at the end of July in advance of the Yankees' old-timers' day. A big chunk of his interview in his hotel room with Carl Lundquist of the United Press was featured earlier, for Cobb's recounting how unjustified the spiker reputation is. About coming to the old-timers' day, he said, "these are the things that mean the most to me, the times, [sic] when we can get together and talk about baseball and to re-live those wonderful games. But when they [cynics] talk about the rough stuff, they forget about some of the things that the good base runners were up against in my time." Then, using the present tense and shouting, he said the following:

"How about that catcher. Who is blocking you off at the plate and he throws his mask right into your path. Or somebody leaves a bat in the way. You hit 'em and you have a broken leg. You avoid 'em and you may be out instead of safe."

clockwise from top left in 1951, at the 75th-anniversary celebration of the National League: Ed Walsh, Cobb and Cy Young. In 1925, when asked to name the greatest pitcher he ever faced, Cobb told sports editor Ed Hughes, "Ed Walsh in his 1908 form. He bothered me more than any twirler I ever faced. He had a spitter and a fast ball, confidence and grit to burn." Cobb added that Young "on his long record over the years might be called the strongest piece of pitching machinery. Walsh was the hardest pitcher for me to outguess in base stealing as well as in pitching."

Then there was a knock at the door and Cobb yelled, "Come in."

Entering were 1955 Hall of Fame inductee Schalk and a 1946 one, pitcher Ed Walsh. "Look at this guy," Cobb cried, pointing to Walsh. "He's 74 years old and hasn't had a sore arm yet. How about that time in 1908 you're pitching for the White Sox and battling us for the pennant and you lose a one-hitter to Addie Joss of Cleveland? That helps us in Detroit to win the pennant. And do you know what Joss did that day?"

"I do," Schalk replied, even though his career began in the following decade. "Joss pitched a perfect game. And there have been only four in major league history. I know because I caught the last one – Charley Robertson's in 1922," against Detroit.

Lundquist ended his article with, "It was time to leave and to let the grizzled gaffers cut up old touches into small hours. But it was an occasion to remember."

Also while Cobb was in the city, veteran Yankees writer Dan Daniel reported some of his less-reported opinions. They included: "Horse racing, with its legal betting, is a menace to the majors. And then there is television, which invites the fans to stay home." As for why he did not think a major league team would be successful in Los Angeles, he said, "They like horse racing out there." As he would explain in 1957, racing is "the toughest competition in the world for baseball. Out here in California, the horses run almost continuously. Down in Los Angeles, the Hollywood and Del Mar (San Diego) tracks run for almost the entire baseball season from May to September. I'd hate to see a club move down there and fail to make it. It won't do baseball any good."

Returning to the chronology of 1955:

As Bak detailed in his 2005 book, Cobb appeared on the game show "I've Got a Secret." The show aired on September 28. Bak's presentation was straightforward. Leerhsen opted to analyze Cobb's demeanor and opine visually on his health. Leerhsen also wrote something subjective: "It is easy to get depressed watching" it. I thought the segment was funny. In explaining his reaction to the segment, he raised a gender-equality objection: namely, that because men are assumed to know more about baseball, that the male panelists had to wear blindfolds.

Then he omitted the key twist, possibly because the twist itself cannot be characterized as "depressing." I wrote up my synopsis before I realized Leerhsen had done one, and Bak too. Actually, I was depressed for a time, because I thought my hour-long effort was in vain. That is because I rehash things in this book only when I have a strong reason too – and it took me weeks after that to discover one: Leerhsen's characterization.

Here is my synopsis:

Garry Moore was hosting the TV game show "I've Got a Secret" as of 1955 when Cobb appeared. The panelists that day were actresses Kitty Carlisle and Jayne Meadows (who I originally thought was Arlene Francis), humorist Henry Morgan and game show host/panelist Bill Cullen. The guests were supposed to guess who has the highest lifetime batting average in baseball history. The men were blindfolded and the women were not. While watching the segment on YouTube, I realized that the men might be stumped, because one of the questions was whether he had played for Philadelphia. He had, and that presumably confused them, because that was only for two seasons of his 24-

year career. (The Philadelphia line of question was, to me, the key twist, a point that Leerhsen did not touch on.) When Moore revealed who Cobb was, apparently Cullen uttered an "Oh, no" while Morgan stuck his head face down on the table and hid it partly with his hands in shame, as if he would never live it down. (Leerhsen omitted that part too.)

To me, the best part was when Moore then rattled off a series of Cobb all-time records and Cobb seemed to relish the moment. That said, it did seem to be getting awkward when Moore went on for 30 seconds but indicated there were many more by saying, "And that's only the beginning of the record." (Leerhsen did not mention both the growing awkwardness and the literal wording of Moore's set-up line, which I think, as a combination, created an opening for what followed.)

Immediately Cullen cut in, "And he spiked a lot of second basemen, too."

Moore then added, "Yes, he was a mean one in his time," and Cobb leaned his head awkwardly sideways while laughing, before getting up as the audience was clapping.

Leerhsen, after concluding his take, wrote, "I wouldn't be surprised if Cobb's appearance on *I've Got a Secret*, or the comment about spiking in particular, made before millions on national television, pushed him closer to the realization that he just *had* to write a book to explode the conventional wisdom about himself, and set the record straight for future generations."

I would not be surprised if readers would tend to agree with me that bluff detector Leerhsen of the *Detroit Free Press*'s Joe S. Jackson just bluffed his way to his next thought.

After all, I can disclose that a Cobb letter to Salsinger three weeks before the show minimized any interest on his part in commissioning a biography. Also, McCallum was working on his, and Cobb wrote to Salsinger that McCallum, a "young fellow," has "been after me," as "this press goes for sports books."

The above and the following was in a long postscript by Cobb in that letter to Salsinger: "As I said I have had several offers for doing a book, I don[']t see at all why such is needed but if I do you will hear from me. I am hesitant, not at all anxious, any relation of facts is always provocation and one is looked upon as trying to alibi[,] to explain away things which in the evening of one[']s life, they surely then can be allowed to tell the truth to correct the record. I have reserved quite a lot that no one knows or have I told of, only to save what hasn[']t heretofore been printed, just in case I ever decided to subscribe to in doing such a book, have had offers Simon & Schuster, Doubleday, Harcourt & Brace, Barnes." Then he mentioned McCallum, whose book was for Barnes.

Also in his postscript, he described McCallum's other planned book, *That*

Kelly Family, of which the actress-princess Grace Kelly was a part. Cobb feared that McCallum "will not do his part in keeping with the Kelly story."

"The Kellys, mother [Margaret] and father [Jack, Sr.,] Irish of course, both very strong character. The Virginia judge, Walter Kelly in vaudeville[,] was one son, John [Jack] Kelly[, Jr.,] the great oarsman[, a three-time Olympic Gold Medal winner,] was refused at last minute to compete" in the Diamond Challenge Sculls on the River Thames in England, "I think, carried a hate, as they claimed he was not a gentleman as he was a brick layer, he raised a son to train and work with for years and he went over and won, [father] Jack Kelly has a very larger contracting business in the east, a millionaire now, his brother wrote two best sellers (books) pictures etc. Grace Kelly is his daughter (pictures [meaning she appears in movies]) and all the Kellys except Grace was and is outstanding athelets [sic] in sports, what a story this can be also it will be out very soon, women[']s magazines already bidding for the strong character Mother Kelly's part as to discipline and a tight rein on some 6 boys."

Cobb did not mention that Margaret was the first coach of women's teams at the University of Pennsylvania, where she instructed in physical education.

In closing his postscript, Cobb wrote, "Pay no attention to my punctuations also written hurriedly and have not corrected."

Cobb's letter to Salsinger may be his last great surviving discourse on his love for the competitive training of dogs and for their use in hunting. In light of what he said was Salsinger's own love for dogs, Cobb enclosed a picture that he thought he may not have, "taken in my back yard in Augusta, Ga. by, I think, one real fine fellow Bill Kuenzel [longtime photographer for the *Detroit News*], the dog you have was a great shooting dog, the one I have was a great, great shooting dog and after 4 years of hunting in a close country as to range etc. I was asked many times to enter him in Field

from left to right sometime in the 1940s:
Bill Kuenzel, Cobb and Harry G. Salsinger

Trials, I did and he adjusted himself to the widest limits and matched or bettered the very best of Field Trial dogs, he was runner up in National Championship and that[']s a story to save and tell you about, this dog [Cobb's Hall] was the top Llewellin setter blood of his day, I have never seen anything like him, he won in Trials also on the bench [as opposed to field trials], he doesn[']t show in this picture his wonderful conformation he has too much long hair on him etc. he had the greatest four bird dog 'nicks' [genes] which is on both sides, dam [mother of a puppy] & sire, in American bird dog (setter) [sic] history."

Also significant about Cobb's letter to Salsinger is that earlier that year, Cobb had made another high-profile appearance in which the spiking issue had come up. It was on the "Where Were You" television series. When host Ken Murray asked if he slid with his spikes in the air on some key plays, he said the notion that he did "gets under my skin because really in my heart I never tried to spike a baseman because the first thing you want to do is to evade his tagging you and I'm supposed to have used a fallaway or fadeaway slide." Also, Cobb volunteered that when a kid calls him "Cobb the spiker" in his presence, that "kind of gets under my skin. I hate for those kids to feel that way because I know it's wrong. I know that I didn't steal bases jumping into fellows. What bases I stole was to evade 'em, to get away from 'em."

Asked what his most embarrassing or funniest moment in baseball was, he said his most embarrassing one was against Washington when he stole third base when the bases were full. "A lot of fans have never heard about this because I was fortunate enough to get back safely to second base."

"What's My Line?" is another game show that Cobb was on while in New York City for his "I've Got a Secret" appearance. Audio or video of that episode apparently does not survive. *Free Press* sports editor Lyall Smith watched it and wrote that Cobb "never was as ill at ease in a baseball uniform as he was before a television camera and audience."

This next story has its roots in an event close to his appearance on the two game shows. A week before the shows, the AP ran the following from New York:

"Myrt Power, a 70-year-old Georgia[-born] grandma with an encyclopedic knowledge of baseball, won $32,000 tonight [about $300,000 today] by rattling off the names of six players who piled up more than 3,000 hits in their careers. Frowning with concentration, the motherly old woman named Cap Anson, Tris Speaker, Honus Wagner, Eddie Collins, Napoleon Lajoie and Paul Waner. Ty Cobb, who holds the record with 4,191 hits in his baseball career, was named by the master of ceremonies."

Myrt Power

The following week, Power covered the World Series for the International News Service. She gave a long analysis of a game between the Yankees and Dodgers at Ebbets Field. For example, she wrote, "I don't even have to look at the book to know them Yankees hold the record for homers. That's their little ol' trademark. But the way my honeys [she was rooting for Brooklyn] are dynamitin' the pitchers, they'll crack those records.

"And didn't my sweetheart Duke Snider [of the Dodgers] come into his own yesterday? He sure enough did. Why, them Yankees were really gettin' a mite cocky, thinkin' they had stopped him. But, [sic] the Duke unloaded a three-run homer to do his bit in knocking the Yankees off but it weren't so much what he did at bat. That was plenty but what he did in the field! Zowie!"

Eight paragraphs later, she wrote, "I got my biggest thrill of the World Series today but it didn't come from the playing on the field, or the homers by my honeys. The thrill came from a kiss smacked full on my lips by that Georgia Peach, Ty Cobb, the greatest hitter of all times [sic]. I'm sittin' quiet as a church mouse in my field box waiting for the umpires to yell 'play ball!' when Cobb and his daughter, Shirley Cobb Beckworth, stroll over. Without as much as a howdy do, Ty plants a kiss on my lips as does Shirley. I felt like I died and went all the way to Heaven. The immortal Ty tells me 'we're neighbors. I live in [grew up in his teens in] Royston, Ga., which is only 20 miles from Buford [where Power lived before moving to Long Island]. It's been a real pleasure meetin' you Myrt.'"

Power concluded her article with, "Wait 'til the home folks in little ole Buford hear about the great Ty Cobb kissing me. These 71 years ain't been lived in vain."

For his part, after a Yankee win in the series, Cobb walked into the Yankee dressing room and grabbed Stengel's hand. "It's the same as it always has been ever since the time of [manager] Miller Huggins and [general manager] Ed Barro[w]," Cobb told reporters. "These fellows just make all the plays well and never beat themselves. They act like champions. I don't think anything will stop them."

Beyond expressing minimal interest in writing a book in his 1955 letter to Salsinger, Cobb wrote at least one other letter that year to that effect. Elderkin of the *Christian Science Monitor* printed parts of it upon Cobb's death. In 1955, Elderkin received two letters from Cobb, the first of which was in reply to a questionnaire that Elderkin had sent him. In the latter letter, Cobb replied as follows to a question from Elderkin about why he had never written an autobiography; Elderkin, in a 1995 article for the same publication, said he had offered to help him with it:

"Relative to your inquiry as to a life story in book form – will say that I have had quite a few offers from several publishers and their representatives. So far I just cannot bring myself to attempt such a task. There are quite a few reasons why I do not care for it.

"First, there have been many plagiaristic stories written, also the usual rainy-day story. Then, there are those not true – simply out of whole cloth. When one writes a book many would say in straightening out the record that he tried to alibi. Then what he has to say is also open to criticism.

"So I am not keen to do a book, though I do have a lingering feeling to correct a lot of stories that were wrong. Also I have kept for myself quite a few experiences and incidents that I have never shared with anyone and which, of course, would be something that had never been written."

From New York, Cobb headed to Washington, D.C., for a Senators-Tigers game to mark the 48th anniversary of Walter Johnson's Senators and big-league debut. Cobb arrived late and the game was interrupted at the end of the first inning to announce his arrival. As reported by the AP, he shook umpire Charley Berry's hand and took a bow. The next day, Cobb spoke at a banquet of D.C.'s Touchdown Club that was being held in honor of the visiting team. At it, he apologetically referred

Clark Griffith and Cobb in 1955 in Washington, D.C. In 1939, three of the Cobbs, Ty, Beverly and Jimmy, had been Griffith's guests one evening at the Columbia Country Club in Chevy Chase, Md.

to himself as "a country boy from Royston, for the [task of] Demosthenian effort." Bob Addie of the *Washington Post* explained, "Cobb was referring to the Athenian orator, Demosthenes, regarded as the model of impassioned reasoning, both for power and finish of style."

"He said testily that 'the youngsters of today are just as good as the oldtimers, except perhaps for a lack of desire in some cases. But they're better fielders because the glove has improved.'"

After the banquet, Tigers manager Bucky Harris said the following about Cobb, reported Hawkins of the *Washington Star*: "He'd cut your heart out." But according to Hawkins, Harris said so in a way that showed "distinct admiration for Ty's tactics."

Possibly also afterward, Senators owner Griffith said, "If I had my pick of all the players I've seen excluding pitchers, I'd take Cobb." Griffith added, "He'd beat the opposition all by himself. He disrupted defenses, distracted pitchers and drove catchers crazy. He could do more things to whip you than any player I've watched." Griffith would die about three months later at age 85.

He testified in his own defense against a rancher and former minor league player who accused him of assaulting him in a fight over a dinner check. The court's ruling would be not guilty. Hornbaker tracked down the original case. As part of an appeal that ended up being denied, the plaintiff, Elbert D. Felts, submitted from Cobb's second wife, Frances, the 24-page bill of particulars from their divorce proceedings noted earlier. Neither Alexander nor Leerhsen mentioned the suit.

I found light notes from Cobb's testimony that made it into a news report. "Cobb provoked an eruption of laughter from the audience in attempting to evade questions as to the amount of money he had." When Felts's attorney, Pierre M. Barceloux, asked Cobb whether he had "stocks and bonds in your possession worth $2,612,631," he replied, "I hope so."

At one point, Barceloux asked Cobb the value of a warehouse that he owned in Twin Falls. Presumably, that was a reference to a Coca-Cola plant and franchise he bought in 1940 for son Herschel. "Cobb told the attorney he would sell it to him for $85,000, and again the spectators laughed." Cobb then volunteered, "Judge, am I out of bounds?" With that, the United Press ended its article. On a more serious note, days earlier when Felts testified, "Cobb was accompanied in court by a nurse, who said the famous baseball star was suffering from a heart condition," the UP reported. That was the second-earliest public report that I found of his having that condition; the next one may not have appeared before 1959. The earliest private report I found was, as noted earlier, his telling Christy Walsh in July 1952 that he had "fibrillation of the heart and followed with two different types of virus flu[,] was in hospital two weeks with heart thing and some 16 days with flu in bed at home." The earliest public report that I found was in 1953, when the AP reported that he had been hospitalized in Twin Falls with "what hospital attendants said was a heart ailment."

In 1956:

The following major diversion zigzags over decades of Cobb's career, and Schalk is included. The story that follows was likely first told before this 1956 version, but my search came up empty. As the story goes, early 20th-century St. Louis Browns manager Fielder Jones told his players, in advance of a series against Detroit, to think of some funny stories to tell Cobb – because keeping him in good humor would help to take the edge off his competitiveness.

In scanning McCallum's 1956 book, that was the story that most jumped out at me. Jones managed in six full seasons in the American League during Cobb's career, with the White Sox from 1905 to 1908 and the Browns in 1916 and 1917. Jones died in 1934, so the time frame for Jones to have discussed that strategy is relatively short. I did find Harry Grayson describing Jones in 1917 as a "'bear' at telling baseball yarns."

Hornbaker found a compelling taking-the-edge-off-Cobb kind of story, from Tris Speaker in a 1939 interview, and paraphrased it briefly. Speaker's full quote, to Charles McMahon of the United Press, was, "I don't think he ever caught on, but we used to try to keep him smiling during the ball game, tell him stories as we passed in the field and josh him along. He was easier to beat that way. Well, you've heard all the stories about he couldn't bear to lose. Well, they're true. Get him sore at you – get in his way on the base line or maybe get a pitch close to his head – and all his aggressiveness came out."

In 1941, Bingay touched on the subject briefly after seeing a *Saturday Evening Post* article on bench jockeying. "The only ballplayer I have ever known who could not be ridden was Ty Cobb. The rougher the boys were to him, the better he played. His batting increased with his rage. Before the close of his great career smart managers tumbled to this and did their best to have their players go out of their way to 'be nice to Cobb.'"

A corollary to Jones's story was told by Schalk, one of the three former big leaguers who attended Cobb's funeral. Apparently before heading to it, he told sports columnist Condon of the *Chicago Tribune*, "As great as the White Sox were in those days, we all had one understanding – never get Ty Cobb mad." Schalk said that the second baseman of the White Sox, Eddie Collins, was "always saying, 'Don't make the Georgia Peach mad.'"

Schalk had made a similar point in 1940. Then former longtime Boston outfielder Duffy Lewis did so in 1945, as part of a Grayson article noted earlier: In a fanning bee that year in a smoke-filled hotel room, Duffy said, "But no other player could carry Cobb's bats. Our instructions were never to speak to Cobb and by all means not to make him mad. And those were the orders of most of the other clubs." Grayson continued quoting Lewis as follows, but this sounds more like a paraphrase: "Steamed up, the fiery genius of the game would tear a club to pieces, and, despite all the warning against teasing the animals, it seems he was riled most of the time."

A newspaper report about the 1907 World Series stated that victorious Cubs catcher Johnny Kling kept up a constant chatter with the younger Tiger batters. For example, "Cobb is said to have lost his temper at one time, and that was just what Kling had been trying to make him do." As it turns out, that story may have been a dud. Detroit 1907 player Germany Schaefer in 1910 told William

Peet of the *Washington Herald* that Kling "never said a word to any of Jennings' players as they came up to the bat, except possibly to me. Ty Cobb and the others will bear me out in this, too."

Hornbaker wrote that as managers, Speaker and Mack "coached their players not to irritate Cobb during a ballgame, convinced that Ty's skills were wholly improved when he was heated. In fact, Tris wanted to keep the Detroit outfielder laughing, and plied him with humor in an attempt to throw him off his game."

The following relates loosely to the above and loosely to Cobb's joking that he had been an "African dodger" at the plate. In his 1949 book *Baseball Personalities*, Jimmy Powers of the *New York Daily News* quoted Mack as telling his own players as of 1925, "Don't get him mad at you. He'll hurt you if he gets mad." Powers printed that quote soon after discussing how Cobb handled pitchers who made him angry. Powers claimed that Cobb had once said of pitchers, "In those days, they were all out to get me. A pitcher would dust me off. If I didn't get my hit that day, they would say that's the way to get me out. I had to put the fear into them because they were trying to put the fear into me."

Powers also wrote, in a combination of restraint and hyperbole, that Cobb "played the game ruthlessly. Once a pitcher tried to dust him off. The ball hit Cobb in the back of the neck. The next time Ty came to bat, his pale blue eyes were round with anger. His thin lips tightened. On the pitch, Cobb laid down a perfect bunt between first base and the pitcher's mound. The first baseman dashed in to make the play while the hurler ran to cover the base. Cobb was out by a good margin, but he didn't stop. About 10 feet from the bag, he hurtled his body in the air, his spikes glistening. He caught the pitcher in the thigh and opened his leg with one slash. That was Cobb's quick retribution for the deliberate beanball."

A year before Powers, Jack Sher had opted purely for hyperbole in his 1948 *Sport* magazine profile: "If a pitcher threw a bean-ball at Cobb, as many of them did, they usually wound up in the showers, nursing their wounds. Ty would bunt down the first-base line. When the pitcher moved over to field the bunt, he collided with 180 pounds of charging, furious bone, muscle, and churning, razor-sharp spikes."

Digressing some more:

Especially in the last years of his life, Cobb was asked about pitchers nowadays throwing at batters. His by-far-meatiest interview on the subject took place in a hospital. A set-up for it is that in 1958, he told Joe Reichler of the AP that pitchers throwing at batters is "as old as baseball itself. It belongs in the game. I don't advocate throwing at a fellow's head. As a matter of fact, it's easier and more effective to throw at his feet. That loosens 'em up. They won't take a toe-hold once they're made to skip rope."

Also in the set-up interview, he laughed when Reichler asked him to comment on the mandating that season of batting helmets in the American League, two years after the National League had done so. He cited old-time players who were great at getting hit, Jennings and Fred Clarke. "I believe the helmet would have made .400 hitters out of some of the boys."

The trumpeted meaty interview was in August 1960, with UPI, as a patient in what is now called Stanford University Medical Center. It was one of his last major ones on any subject. An AP Cobb feature around that time stated that he left the hospital at one point just to watch a Giants home game against the Reds. It also reported that "he was taking treatment and medication for the same ailment that hospitalized him earlier in the year. He declined to divulge what the trouble was, saying only, 'it's a source of poison.'"

The UPI interview came on the heels of the AP one. On the subject of helmets, UPI paraphrased him as saying "that some of the throwing at the heads of players can be attributed to the fact that the players now wear helmets – and thus there is little danger of a serious injury." He also said that beanball was far less prevalent in his day. As noted earlier, in a 1948 letter to Cunningham, he had said "that [Dutch] Leonard and [Carl] Mays and [the white Rube] Foster, possibly following their manager's instructions, did not hesitate to throw at the batter's head. I had two ribs broken by Foster, but this seemed to have been good procedure." A useful point in the 1960 interview that I did not notice him otherwise making was that, in reference to his playing days, "There were very few bean-ball pitchers then."

Then he gave the following rehash of a point that he had made as far back as 1939: "Dutch Leonard and Carl Mays were a couple. When they threw at my head, I would drag a bunt down the first base line. Then when the first baseman came in to field it, the pitcher ran over to cover first. And I would run right over the pitcher. He knew the situation then." (Actually, there is a single play when Cobb did the above to Leonard, and it is in all three of the Cobb biographies. Hornbaker has the best detail on the most notable Mays incident, from 1915. In that one, Cobb headed out to the mound after two pitches that Cobb thought were deliberately aimed close to him. After Cobb returned to the batter's box, Mays's next pitch hit him on the wrist, and Cobb got even by quickly stealing second. Then "two batters later, he bowled into catcher 'Pinch' Thomas to score, sending the audience into a deafening uproar.")

Cobb prefaced his comments above by saying that relative to the brawling that was sometimes now occurring as a result of a beaning, "I don't remember a single incident of fisticuffs caused by the pitcher throwing at the batter in my day." As his proposed cure for the problem, he said the commissioner of baseball should announce that there will be heavy fines for beaning. Also, there should be a sign on the wall of each clubhouse making that point. The umpires, he said, would file reports with the commissioner, for the commissioner to act on.

In 1957:

In February, he participated in a baseball clinic at Stanford University. Because of wet grounds, the clinic was moved inside, and Cobb spoke in the law school auditorium for about an hour, giving pointers and answering questions, sometimes while holding a bat. Rehashing one of his stock lines, he said, "Well, now, they used to say I slid with high spikes. But how else would

Cobb during his 1957 appearance at Stanford University

you get home after a catcher had carefully laid his mask on the base paths in front of home plate and put the bat up there along with it?"

Here are some of the points that he made during his talk:

Batters should sometimes hit the first pitch, because of the element of surprise, especially in a tight game, and they should never swing at a pitch at a count of three balls and no strikes. Also, batters should not be so dependent on signals to determine whether they should take a pitch.

Third base is easier to steal than second, with one reason being that most of the catcher's practice throws go to second base.

Many batting slumps are due to taking too much batting practice. He also repeated one of his standard points, that he asked teammates or his manager to watch his technique when he was hitting well. That way, when he slumped, they could give him better advice.

Asked whether he aimed at a certain spot to land his hits, he said, "No, I'd practice hitting through a certain zone, such as between first and second or between second and short."

In comparing batters now and then, he said current ones are just as good, "but they don't hit as well. Too much emphasis on the long ball."

Later that month, Rosenbaum of the *San Francisco Chronicle* asked Cobb how he spends his time, if he does not golf or fish. "Don't worry, I'm busy enough." He cited the correspondence that he responds to from his two philanthropic endeavors "and I don't mind saying I still get dozens of fan letters every week. I try to answer everything but it's difficult." He told of receiving hundreds of speaking requests each year, but "it takes too much out of a person. I lie out of most requests. . . tell 'em I have another speaking engagement that night. . . and sometimes I really have." (The ellipses are in the original.)

In May, he visited Milwaukee to see his former player, Haney, who had become Milwaukee's manager in June 1956. In 1956, Milwaukee won its first seven games under him, and Cobb had wired him, "You are doing a great job. Give them the works. I always knew you could do it if you had the material. Knock them all off." When he made the May 1957 visit, the team was on its way to a 95-59 record. That would be good enough to win the pennant, and then Milwaukee would win the World Series.

Before touching on the deep coverage of Cobb's visit, I can note one other detailed story about Cobb and Haney or his players, in a prior season.

From 1949 to 1952, Haney had managed the Hollywood Stars/Twinks in the Pacific Coast League. Three weeks after Cobb's visit to Milwaukee in 1957, columnist Bob Kelley of the *Independent* in Long Beach, Calif., recalled several years earlier being in the Twinks' dugout to get a copy of the lineups from Haney. He had seen six or seven Twinks huddling around Haney. "For a moment, I thought they were discussing some inside strategy. Then I saw Haney was holding up a letter and reading it aloud. 'This is from Ty Cobb,' he boasted proudly. 'An old buddy of mine. I use[d] to play for Ty, you know.'"

Kelley continued, "His voice was full of rapture. He treasured the letter he was holding in his hands like a kid would treasure the autograph of Mickey Mantle or Ted Williams." Haney began reading from it before giving it to Kelley. Kelley recalled that it contained advice. Cobb urged Haney to make

from left to right at Milwaukee in 1957: Milwaukee traveling secretary Duffy Lewis,
Milwaukee manager Fred Haney, George McBride and Cobb

more use of the bunt, the sacrifice and the hit and run. Kelley said that he then noticed the Los Angeles players bunting more than they previously had.

The stated hook for Kelley's 1957 column was not Cobb's visit but an article he had seen that panned Haney's team for being bunt-crazy. Sluggers Aaron and Mathews were bunting whenever they got the chance, although, as Kelley loosely paraphrased Cobb, a practice in baseball is to not "employ the 'big guy' for bunting unless you're in the bottom of the ninth in an extremely tight game." Kelley disagreed with what Haney was now doing and concluded, "Evidently Fred Haney still hero-worships Ty Cobb – and his theories of baseball."

On Cobb's advocacy of more bunting, Pittsburgh manager Billy Meyer said in 1952 that a comparison cannot be made between Cobb's era and the current one: "The big players came along" after Cobb retired "and instead of bunting a runner into position to score, the manager sits back and waits for the home run to come," he told sportswriter Jack Hernon of the *Pittsburgh Post-Gazette*. Meyer, who had played in the 1910s, added, "The clubs themselves have moved in that direction by moving in the fences or moving home plate out. The Yankees started this trend."

Meyer continued, "Sure it's marvelous to bunt late in the game for a run, but to do it early is just wasting an out. [Managers] Billy Southworth [in 1948] and Bill McKechnie [in 1939 and 1940] ruined the present[-]day theory by playing for the one run. But they had great pitching and defense at Boston and Cincinnati when they won pennants."

On his 1957 visit to Milwaukee, Cobb visited the team's clubhouse before a game and answered questions from the players. When Bobby Thomson asked if he had really levelled a blast at modern players and how the game had changed, Cobb replied, "Well, I criticized some, but nothing like they made out." Cobb advised, "Take a lead you know you can get back with. Watch the pitcher's foot. That often times is a tipoff to what he's going to do. You know lots of pitchers rear away back with that foot. Sometimes they go so high you can easily steal on him."

Asked whether stealing third is a lot tougher than stealing second, he said, "No. I think it was easier. Don't depend on the third base coach to watch the infielders for you. Do it yourself and gauge your lead. Generally you can take a longer lead off second. And that throw to third sometimes is harder for the catcher to make."

Asked if he was ever picked off first base, he said, "Oh, yes, once in a while."

The one other topic noted in the story, which was by the AP, was the relative frequency of balks.

Cobb's Milwaukee visit also got play a few weeks later, in the *Los Angeles Times*.

Cookie Lavagetto, a Californian who played for Pittsburgh and Brooklyn, with banquet league chum and former amateur golf rival Cobb in 1957 in Palo Alto

Florence Haney, Fred's wife, wrote a letter that the *Times* reprinted at length. The following from it relates to Cobb: "A couple of weeks ago, Ty Cobb called Fred from San Francisco that he was leaving within an hour and would arrive in Milwaukee that night for the game. I don't know when I've seen Fred so happy. He felt complimented that Ty was coming to see him and the club. Cobb stayed three games and was in the clubhouse before games, talking with the boys and answering their questions. They seemed to appreciate the fact that they were listening to one of the greatest. Ray Schalk came over from Chicago to see him, also George McBri[d]e, and then our own Duffy Lewis (traveling secretary). You can imagine the reminiscing that went on about the old days! Ty, you know, was Fred's first manager when he went to Detroit and he always felt he learned more under him than anyone else."

(Possibly from having met Cobb while on Milwaukee, Danny O'Connell, as a Giant in 1960, would receive instruction from him in spring training.)

In June, Cobb told Edwin M. Rumill of the *Christian Science Monitor* the following, about the idea of moving big-league teams to the West Coast: It "would have a lot of competition. Remember there are three major horse tracks around both Los Angeles and San Francisco. Also, it's a great fishing and hunting country, and a lot of folks have come out there from the Midwest on retirement pensions and don't have the money to attend a lot of games." By contrast, "Milwaukee has no race tracks. Neither does Kansas City," where the Philadelphia Athletics had moved and which Cobb had just visited.

In Kansas City, Cobb said this about a variety of quail, bobwhites: "The other morning I woke up in Georgia and I heard a bobwhite for the first time in many, many years." He sighed while saying that and added, "I don't remember ever hearing a more attractive sound."

In July, Cobb wrote Spink from California, "Thanks for letter and pictures, it will be fine for my purpose also have some 25 or 30 others to convince these shake down wolves, in your letter about one [full name unknown] 'Curley' I will tell you, no one else, he is very self centered, I have done lots for him, appearances and visits to hospitals for returned soldiers, many times and some I had to come down from Nevada and then return, he has not as yet responded to my request of a letter of a couple of weeks ago, I am like you, my real weak spot is unjust criticism, it hurts but I try and toss it off, also it reminds me [of] a saying by a noted man when reports would come to him, 'now what great thing have I done to cause my inferior to criticize me.'" Cobb also wrote that he hoped to see Spink in Cooperstown or at a Yankee event for Hall of Famers. He stated that he would be staying at the Ambassador Hotel in New York City.

The day after Cobb wrote that letter, the AP reported that he was packing up his California home and thinking of Georgia, where he was about to return. It said he was recalling "the soft sound of ducks descending on a pond, the faint whirr of quail in a thicket." The move to Georgia did not turn out so peaceful, sports editor Smith of the *Free Press* would write upon Cobb's death.

Smith would recall having spoken to Cobb twice in the last three years of Cobb's life. Citing Cobb's change of plans back in Georgia against building a new house there and instead renting an apartment, Smith wrote that Cobb "was wealthy in memories of his career and in friends. But he was confused and lonely as time began to run out on him. He wanted to live the rest of his days in Georgia. But he didn't want to because he knew he was going to die there, and he didn't like the idea." In the first of those final two chats, Smith recalled hearing from Cobb about the new house idea, and included the ellipses that follow. "I've changed my mind. I'm not going through with it. Why should I stick myself up there on the side of a mountain? I may go out to Arizona and live for a while . . . or back to California . . . mebbe [sic] Lake Tahoe. I just don't know what to do."

In July in Rochester, N.Y., he spoke on the field in advance of a Rochester Red Wings game to fellow old-timers Billy Southworth and Andy High, with *Rochester Democrat and Chronicle* sports editor Pinckney listening in. Players are now devoting too little time to the game off the field, he said: "There's too much entertainment for them, too many things to do before and after a ball game. They just can't wait to jump into their Cadillacs [and] roar away. Golf? There's a good game. But a ball player shouldn't take part in that sport during the season. I know. I had a very unpleasant experience.

"I played golf in the morning of a day a doubleheader was scheduled for Detroit. We were up against Boston, and this was the time when the club wasn't so good. I was in a hitting streak, and it looked to me as though I had a couple of soft pitchers. Know what happened? I went 0-for-8 that day. Couldn't get hold of a pitch. Three times I went out to the pitcher and the rest of the time I just popped up. I couldn't buy a base hit. Right then and there I decided to give up golf while the baseball season was going on."

Modern-day runners, he said, "don't take advantage of their speed" and in his day, he always tried "to find ways to fool the other fellow. It's a mental hazard. If they're worrying about whether you're going or not, they're in big trouble. Once I went down to first base, fell flat on the ground, and pretended I was in agony. I rolled all over, holding my knee. I got up, limped, and rubbed that knee so hard I convinced just about everybody in the park that I was hurt. They let up just for a moment, and on the next pitch I stole second base. I still laugh when I think about that one. See what a mental hazard can do?"

Cobb began to laugh heartily, and Southworth, who was a contemporary of his but mainly in the National League, said, "You never bent over and put your hands on your knees when you were on base. I was told that a man who places his hands on his knees is resting. You never rested."

(Southworth, the manager of the World Series-winning Cardinals in 1942 and 1944, did start his career in the American League. In 1945, he had told sportswriter Lou Smith of the *Cincinnati Enquirer* about a game in which Cobb asked him for a favor. The occasion was a Cleveland home game and Southworth was watching at least part of it from the bullpen. At some point, outfielder Cobb asked him for a pencil and paper, and he used them to figure out his batting average on the spot. One of Southworth's teammates was the illiterate "Shoeless" Joe Jackson, who somehow learned what Cobb had done. Southworth added, "Joe asked if I could figure batting averages. When he found that I could, I spent the rest of the series on mathematics."

Southworth also told Smith that he later summoned up the courage to ask Cobb for a bat. Cobb obliged, which Southworth's teammates were surprised to hear. Cobb invited Southworth to the Detroit dressing room the next day and gave him not one bat, but two. After Cobb did not get a hit that day, Southworth noticed the bats missing from the Cleveland rack, meaning that Cobb had been hunting for a better one.)

Returning a second time to the chronology of 1957:

Cobb's next stop was Cooperstown. On the possible transfer of teams to the West Coast, he said, in New York writer Dan Daniel's presence, "The biggest menace to success for the Giants in San Francisco would be the horses. Both that city and Los Angeles are jammed with patrons of the mutuels." Also, "People out in California don't go for Saturday and Sunday baseball. They like to drive out into the gold country around San Francisco, to Arrowhead [sic] near Los Angeles. They are more fresh air, outdoor barbeque conscious than your New York fans." By contrast, in Milwaukee, "they make $1.5 million [about $8.5 million today] on concessions alone. They had a nasty day when I was there, yet they drew nearly 40,000."

Also, "In San Francisco, citizens are taking pen in hand to write to the editor that they are opposed to spending public funds and increasing the tax rate, by bringing the Giants into town." As far as Los Angeles, he doubted a move there would succeed because its "vast population" is "going to go right on eyes [sic] on meat and grocery costs, and not on baseball schedules."

"I am afraid I have drawn no happy picture of major [league] possibilities in California, and coast sports pages will pillory poor old Ty, but fact is fact."

In August, Haney told sportswriter Cleon Walfoort of the *Milwaukee Journal*, "I haven't had a letter from Cobb since he was in town almost a month ago. When I do hear from him, they're the kind of letters anyone gets from a long[-]time friend and the kind any baseball man would write to another. There's never any idea of Cobb trying to tell me how to run the club. The whole thing is just plain silly." (When he was manager of Pittsburgh in 1955 and then Milwaukee in 1956, Haney said that Cobb was sending him a weekly letter.)

In September, from his new town, Cornelia, Ga., Cobb told Spink various things that author Rhodes repeated, about his new place. Parts he omitted are: "Turkey, deer and squirrel very plentiful on government land as have been planted, etc. per your kindness sending Sporting News, Cornelia, Ga. from now on, sorry about delay answering this but Taylor I really have been on the go far more than two months and am like a 'shot cat,' been back east from Calif. 3 times, leaving Thursday for Calif. and until 25th Sept, then here also to World Series, arranging matters here and in Calif. many details, quite a problem, should I see [now-Hall of Fame Director, formerly of the *St. Louis Star*, Sid C.] Keener I will convey the message that Taylor sends his perfumed regards, kindest regards to Mrs. Spink and best to you old scout. As ever, Ty."

Alexander's book has geographic prose from the letter above; plus, he listened to a taped Cobb interview in Cornelia from early 1958. I can add that second wife Frances visited him, apparently in October; Cobb wrote to Hauck about her being depressed and her menopause in a way that sounds like both contributed to their divorce. In her bill of particulars, in a transcribed phone call with her lawyer, Harlan I. Heward, Cobb told Heward that he had spoken to him and another lawyer of hers "on the mental attitude, the menopause, or whatever it is." (She evidently visited him for two weeks in a later year, in Cave Rock, as cited by Alexander, whose likely source was Maines's 1961 post-mortem letter.)

from left to right at the January 1958 dinner: Del Webb, former Pacific Coast League managers-turned-1957 World Series rivals Stengel and Haney, Cobb and, to be noted later, entertainer-toastmaster George Jessel

In 1958:

In January, more than 1,000 people gathered in the Beverly Hills Hotel to honor Haney for managing Milwaukee to the World Series title. Haney "paid glowing tribute to his longtime idol, Cobb. 'I just wish I knew the baseball Ty has forgotten. He was the first baseball player I ever knew to practice psychology.'" Haney also said, "During the baseball season, his regular letters to me were a great inspiration and help. Without his help, I would never have gotten to first base."

Sports columnist Sam Balter, Jr. of the *Los Angeles Herald and Express* told of having sat next to Cobb on the dais and noticing "the tears which crept into his eyes as Haney described Cobb as his greatest inspiration and finest tutor." Balter said that Cobb had watched some Milwaukee games on television during the season and had sent Haney long letters of analysis.

Several days later, in New Hampshire for the *Manchester Union Leader's*

10th annual baseball dinner, Cobb said he thought the lively ball "has caused people to lessen their interest" in the sport. "Restore the old ball," he urged. He criticized major league baseball's expansion to the West Coast, including because the Dodgers were having to play in Wrigley Field in Los Angeles, "which can accommodate only about 21,000 fans." In addition, it is a "long jump" to the West Coast and "anything can happen on airline flights." Also, according to the United Press, "Cobb said West Coast baseball would have to buck racing in the San Francisco and other areas." On night baseball, he was now citing the greater opportunities it affords to working people to attend games. Because of the physical strain, Cobb traveled to New Hampshire with a longtime Atlanta friend, Clark O'Neill. "Asked to name the greatest active players today, he reeled them off in the following order. 'Musial, Mantle and Williams.' As to the greatest player of all time, he picked Honus Wagner, and said Casey Stengel was the greatest manager of all time."

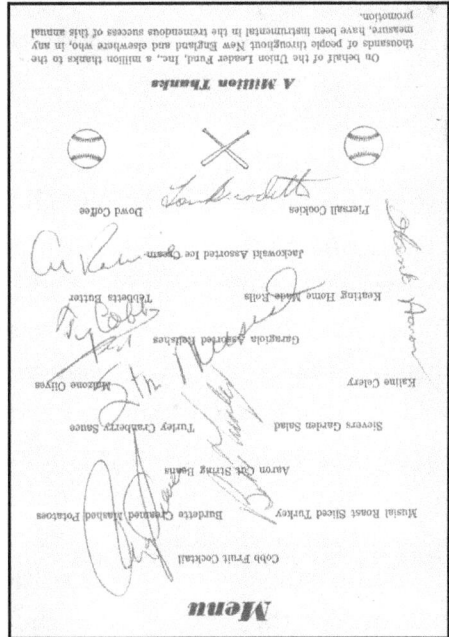

top: an autographed dinner menu from the *Manchester Union Leader*'s 10th baseball dinner in New Hampshire in January 1958, which was mentioned on page 374
bottom: Cobb in Manchester

In May, he wrote to Spink from California, "I am out here since April 14 income tax, a tax case hearing not government but a state thing trying to shake me down as a legal resident here, when I have been a resident of Nevada since 1939, having fully complied in every legal way, so please sympathize with me along with many others, you no doubt know Calif. is a tough, all wrong, shakedown state as to these matters."

Back in April 1957, Cobb had written to Ken Johnson of Carson City, Nev., presumably a former state senator who was the state's top lefty golfer earlier in the decade. He wanted Johnson to attest to his being in Nevada in parts of various years by writing on his official stationery of "the very many times we saw each other both at my house" and his and on the streets of Carson City. In the letter, Cobb indicated that in 1940, he had changed his bank account, driver's license and voting registration to Nevada, as per advice from one or more lawyers.

Also in his May letter to Spink, he wrote, "I have been at my place in Nevada most of [the] time, opening house for the summer, I have seen only two games opening, Brooklyn and first game St. Louis Cardinals. Taylor you know I cannot express myself or opinions, it would not be proper as to what I hope for." If the Giants finish in sixth or seventh place in their eight-team league, "it will be interesting to see fan reaction and I mean confidentially San F– fan reaction, I understand they have lots of tickets sold, the team is surely doing their part to qualify, but out here the fans are wise also can be tough, I would say per tickets sold the Giants will do well this year financially, next year could be the real test, they have a bad condition per parking, lots of squaling [sic] now – already, the inclement weather not now, later it will come as always, July & August, the boys on paper are doing their part – now, home runs are cheap here and of course Los Angeles, it[']s a very different game today, I sincerely hope it all will turn out for the betterment of the game, your last paragraph, I need not tell you of conditions – you know – anyone attending a night game in San F– most all will have overcoats, sweaters and blankets, I have seen it this way many times in past."

He continued, "Please do not quote me but if you do state the Giants are much better than last year, are hustling and so far, showing good power at bat, drawing well, Dodgers with injuries, loss of Campy [Campanella] – and not in peak of condition, but will be dangerous when they get going, Taylor I don[']t want these friends and people out here on my neck besides I could guess wrong, I am returning to Cornelia in a few days, for awhile then to Glenbrook Nevada for summer. Best to all, as ever, Ty" In a P.S., he wrote, "You force me to write and try to answer your letter, I cannot fail you in this."

In June, Burlington, N.C., resident Buddy Lindsey happened to be in Cornelia and phoned Cobb from his motel. Lindsey was a former American Legion baseball coach who was tutored at Duke University by a former top contemporary pitcher of Cobb's who was briefly his teammate, Jack Coombs. Cobb invited Lindsey to his place. Lindsey told a reporter that Cobb "told me he had just finished three miles of roadwork [walking] and was in about the worst physical condition of his life – at 71 years!"

Upon his arrival, Lindsey met Cobb's "lovely stenographer" and then spoke baseball with Cobb for three hours. "Mr. Cobb showed me a record of his batting averages compiled by one of his loyal fans. The record included all the teams he played against and all the pitchers used." Cobb told why he hit better against certain pitchers than others and recited his Walter Johnson story.

In Detroit for old-timers' day, he was the last former player to be introduced. He "kept advising all of the old-timers who preceded him to 'take it easy when you go out there, your legs aren't what they used to be,'" wrote *Free Press* sports editor Smith. Even older old-timers Crawford and Davy Jones "negotiated the trip from dugout to home plate without trouble. Then when Ty was called by a thunderous ovation, he tripped over the warm-up pitching rubber and almost fell. 'That's what I get for worrying about the other guys,' he quipped later."

In July, soon after returning from Detroit, where he had seen a Boston series, Cobb praised the physical conditioning of Williams, who was approaching age 40. Cobb advised him to both get plenty of rest and plenty of exercise.

In August, Cobb visited Yankee Stadium and saw Whitey Ford pitch a 2-0 shutout. About 30 minutes after the game, Cobb, Stengel and some reporters gathered in the Yankees' "plush press club," UPI reported. "The drinks were flowing fast but 72-year-old Ty said he could give a play-by-play of the game from memory and there was no one willing to bet him a glass of [Yankee co-owner] Dan Topping's bourbon on the subject."

"That's a mighty clever pitcher you got there, Casey," Cobb told him. "That fellow is what we used to call an artist." He likened Ford to a fellow left-handed star of the early 20th century who Stengel had overlapped with but in a different league, Eddie Plank. Plank "invented a style of pitching – in-and-out-to-the-spots – because he didn't have the overpowering fast ball of a lot of other pitchers had [sic]." As Stengel rose to leave, Cobb grasped him by the coat sleeve and said, "your left-fielder [Norm Siebern], he's going to be one of the great ones. Not this year because he needs the experience. But next year he's going to be one of the greatest who ever played." Stengel replied with a huge smile and said, "You didn't disappoint me. I knew you'd know."

While in New York City, Cobb praised, as worthy of being stars in his day, Mantle, Williams, Musial, Mays, Ford, Alvin Dark, Aaron and Mathews. That said, wrote Joe Reichler of the AP, "he adds that the old timers were more aggressive, and had more initiative, will to win and devotion to their work."

Cobb told him, "I still insist there is room for more inside baseball, such as the bunt, the hit-and-run and the stolen base. These tactics have been almost completely discarded." Also, "I was always ready to steal a base, even when we were ahead by five or six runs. That was just to let the pitcher know I'd run anytime. Consequently, in a tight game, if I got on base, the pitcher became nervous. His attention was distracted from the batter. Don't you think that helped the fellow at the plate? We won many a ball game that way."

The next stories, from St. Louis sources, relate to 1958, and were possibly not told until 1978, 1998 and 1971, respectively.

The first is from Musial in 1978. In a Florida spring training feature, Musial told Will Grimsley of the AP of an occasion in 1958 when Cobb had just seen him play and wanted to have breakfast with him the next day. Not only did he accept, but he brought teammate Red Schoendienst.

Musial told of ordering a cup of coffee and adding two spoonsful of sugar and a lot of cream. Cobb replied that it was bad for him to add both and said he should choose just one. After discussing baseball topics such as hitting techniques and training routines, Cobb asked Musial if he drank. He answered in the affirmative, and when Cobb pressed him, Musial said he has a social drink occasionally.

When Cobb wondered if it was wine, Musial said it sometimes is, but not necessarily. Later Cobb asked him how many years he still intended to play, and Musial said maybe two. Cobb advised him to have wine every day because it is a good stimulant and will prolong his career.

"From that day on, I never used cream in my coffee," Musial told Grimsley. "I began drinking a little wine for my stomach's sake. You know what, I didn't just play two more years. I played five." In the foreword to Schoendienst's 1998 book *Red: A Baseball Life*, Musial rehashed parts of the story, and also said

Musial and Red Schoendienst in 1957

that their meet-up had been in New York City.

In his main text, Schoendienst recalled asking Cobb how to get out of a batting slump. "He said his secret to break out if he was in a rut was to bunt the ball a few times. He said bunting forced you to keep your eye on the ball until it [the bat] hit the ball, and that's probably the mistake you were making that put you in a slump, not watching the ball all the way until it hit the bat."

Cobb had also made this subtle point. Sometimes when bunting to advance a runner, Schoendienst must have wished instead that he had been able to swing fully at the pitch. Cobb said that comes from having seen the pitch so well, and seeing the ball so well is the key to getting out of a slump.

The following story about 1958 appears in Broeg of the *St. Louis Post-Dispatch*'s 1971 book *Superstars of Baseball: Their Lives, Their Loves, Their Laughs,*

Their Laments. Broeg recalled being with Cobb and fellow Hall of Famer Frankie Frisch at the Hall of Fame. Frisch supposedly invited Cobb to tell him about the time that he spiked a third baseman. Broeg wrote, "Almost like a school girl fluttering her lids, Cobb coyly demurred and – it was amusing to hear a man long in the tooth use the diminutive [grammatically; in this case, addressing Frisch as Frankie instead of Frank] in referring to another past middle age – Ty would say sweetly, 'Oh, now, Frankie, I wasn't nearly as rough as everyone said.'"

Later in August, he wrote to Spink from Cave Rock of having traveled recently to Cooperstown and New York City. "These trips

from left to right at Cooperstown in 1959:
Bill Terry, Mel Ott, Frankie Frisch and Cobb

take a lot out of me, tension and a terribly persistent aftermath, sulpha drugs, of Flu case, the heat here has not helped me, I am not organically sick, it[']s just a terrible weak, blah! blah!! feeling, I put things off, I lead the league at procrastinating, I ask you to forgive me, Taylor there is nothing you could do or say to me that would ever shake me loose from my friendship and feelings toward you, you must bear with me, I have no stenographer, strange impossible [to] get one here, several industries have them all, I am swamped with unanswered mail, I am down & feel so defeated and that[']s bad, there is nothing you have ever asked of me that I would not do, there was no reason that I have had not [been] replying before this [to your most recent letter] except I have been on the go and much fagged out plus lots of people dropping in on while here, if you only knew my tension and how low I feel, you would understand, I feel when I get to cooler climate, I will feel better, all my stationery is packed so please bear with this.

"Thanks for the record books you sent me, now as to what you want me to attest to per the record book how about this and if not strong enough go ahead and change, you know well it's O.K. with me, I feel honored you should ask me." He then wrote, "This unusual pocket size book of baseball records is invaluable to every fan when it comes to settling any difference of opinions as so many baseball lovers usually have." After signing his name, he added, "Change it again, I say, to what you think best."

In November from Cave Rock, Cobb wrote to him, "Reporting that I am now in residence from this time until snow drives me out and that from January 1 inclusive to April 1 my intent is to rent a furnished ranch type house, modest, two bed rooms etc. outside of Phoenix Ariz – Scottsdale and then back here, am giving up building a house in Cornelia, Ga. after purchasing 76 acres and a wonderful site, landscaping, drilling a well and all architects plans, reason cold as hell last winter and hot as hell along with terrific humidity and no physical outlet, golf, riding or what not, so now can I inflict you and someone in your organization to see that I have a change of address from Menlo Park, Calif. to above, viz Glenbrook, Douglas Co. Nevada, for I am missing your paper to here, and have to pick them up on local stands, I just have to have the Sporting News to keep up per real coverage baseball wise oh! yes football and soon basketball, I have not been too well though not sick and abed, I am an incipient prospect for diabetes – reason no exercise at all for 2 1/2 years, a fine case of tension, hope you never have it, then inactivity, result overplus of sugar in urine, treatments, a couple or three shots of insulin also oral medication, again I seem to win a clearance to negative sugar and within a week, so now it[']s care and diet, also sugar or diabetes is easy to control." He continued, "Now you are up to date 'Sailor' no that[']s your expression you are full admiral in my book, my very kindest to you & all yours. As ever, Ty" In a P.S., he wrote, "Stocks?? hope you have had some and have not sold – yes soon if you can per capital gains, I have some – not sold – can't – only thing I can do is give to Educational Fund – no capital gains – can charge off – 30% – ."

Leerhsen's book refers to Cobb's taking of insulin, while Hornbaker's cites his high blood sugar. Alexander has by far the best account of the progression of his medical treatments, including diabetes, and how he was coping with the tremendous pain, apparently from the spread of his prostate cancer. Cobb's November 1958 letter above adds to that by showing his analysis of why he had become a diabetic. On his death certificate, which Alexander likely saw via the National Baseball Hall of Fame Library but which he vaguely referred to, "A[r]teriosclerotic Heart Disease with Atrial Fibrillation" is the first ongoing condition listed as giving rise to "Cardio circulatory collapse," his immediate cause of death. A second ongoing condition listed is "Diabetes Mellitus mild." Listed separately from those two conditions as significant but not related directly to his death is his having "Carcinoma of the Prostate with diffuse metastasis."

Cobb's take on his medical state in the above letter to Spink could be the best surviving example of him making a doctor-like assessment; in an interview in 1924 in Toronto, he had said, "If I had my time over again I would probably be a surgeon instead of a baseball player." In the same interview, he said that while he was satisfied with baseball, he has "only one sentimental regret. That is the fact that I shall not have done any real good to humanity when I retire. I suppose everybody will have forgotten me in a few years' time."

Those thoughts, possibly the most significant direct Cobb quote that I am the apparent finder of, plausibly explain why he would become so emotional in speaking of his philanthropy in the 1950s. Beyond giving baseball tips, he may have been looking all his life to make a substantive difference in the lives of total strangers – as his dad had as a state senator and county superintendent of schools.

One oddity from 1958 is that a Jewish newspaper publisher in Charlotte, Harry Golden, who was now a popular author, weighed in on Cobb in the manner of a social historian. He did so after seeing Furman Bisher's up-close Cobb feature in the *Saturday Evening Post.*

Cobb's story, Golden wrote, "now belongs to the essayist or the social philosopher; and batting averages and other statistics are no longer

Furman Bisher and "Shoeless" Joe Jackson in 1949

pertinent." Then Golden sailed into the theme that the United States is a country of immigrants "and it would have surprised him no end [sic] if he had known that thousands of immigrant boys on the Lower East Side of New York and in Little Italy, were his devoted followers." They were aspiring to the "Anglo-Saxon ideal."

Golden recalled having corresponded with the California Cobb. Golden said that the correspondence began when Golden sent notes to him from James Brander Matthews, the nation's first professor of dramatic literature, who was based at Columbia University. Golden had attended a lecture of his in 1920; Matthews died in 1929. Matthews spoke about "competition" as a major talent. Matthews said that had Cobb entered politics, he would have become President of the United States. Or, had he entered banking or some other field, he would have been a leader in that one too.

Golden said that "nearly forty years later Ty Cobb is still being asked whom he spiked at second base and in what inning." I stumbled across Golden's writings on Cobb before discovering that Stump's 1994 biography accurately reflects, in its opening blurbs, what Golden attributed to Matthews in the paragraph above. Golden rehashed his 1958 column two months after Cobb's death and called him "the best ballplayer that ever lived."

(A point worth contradicting Matthews on is, say, his potential in the area of public speaking. Leerhsen hit on this point too in writing that Cobb "always felt ill at ease when required to speak in public." I can cite the following:

"Tyrus Raymond Cobb is no silver tongued orator and Ty is the first to admit it," Ward of the *Oakland Tribune* wrote in 1948. Ward added, however, "It is to Ty's credit that he never turns down a request by a toast-master to 'say a few words.' Usually he starts out reminding his listeners he isn't much of a public speaker. Invariably he proves the point before he sits down to tumultuous applause." Ward said that Cobb did improve as a speaker in his presence in 1945 when he spoke to wounded veterans at the Mare Island naval hospital in Vallejo, Calif. En route to the hospital by bus, "Cobb took me aside and said: 'Don't call on me, please. I'm not much of a talker. Oh, I'll drift around the wards and say hello to the boys. But I wouldn't know what to say if I had to stand on the stage. Promise?'" Ward said he promised.

After speeches by other former players, Cobb told Ward that he in fact wanted to speak and did so "for 15 minutes without faltering. He spoke from the heart to a lot of crippled and sick young men who drank in every word. He spoke of courage and the will to win – and the determination never to quit." Ward said he had heard Cobb several times since and that that was his best talk.)

Cobb wrote to Stengel in December to salute him on winning the World Series over Milwaukee. The year before, Haney's Milwaukee team had beaten the Yankees, a result that Cobb had presumably rooted for. Coming back to win the 1958 series, after being down three games to one, "has to be your high water mark in your very wonderful career," Cobb told Stengel. Also, "boy you pulled them up, shook them together and came through so grandly, I caught you on the bench at times T.V. once when [Yankee pitcher Don] Larsen was staggering, I saw the old boy fighting, shaking his fists, advising, encouraging, etc. Casey I like that kind of fight & spirit, I say to you that to you alone belongs the credit for winning this last series. I mean this from my heart, I enjoy telling you this because you are a battler for the game and you do belong to that inner circle of those of baseball that really has the right spirit. . . "

Also in the letter, besides lamenting the death of Speaker weeks earlier, he wrote that the batting stance of Yankee shortstop Tony Kubek should have been corrected; Kubek had just 1 hit in 21 at-bats in the series.

In a letter from Nevada to former teammate Archie Yelle and his wife, he said he started looking at a place to live in Scottsdale, Ariz., in the winter "on account of snows[;] also this altitude of near 7000 ft. has bothered me some." The possible new place, which he was at for a few days, resulted in a "great improvement, no short breath etc. also it[']s a most unusual spot in every way, warm days nice, crisp and very invigorating at night, I plan to go, also the major clubs, Phoenix, Giants, Scottsdale, Red Sox, Mesa close by Cubs in training etc. all kinds of activities, horse back, golf etc. I plan to stay close and get some exercise as I need it, but entertainment I will be as quiet as can [sic], I am going for health benefits." Yelle and his wife had stopped by his Cave Rock residence on a day that Cobb had left on another trip, and had left some ducks. Cobb had gone on a deer hunt in October and was planning a duck one too.

In 1959:

In January from Cave Rock, he wrote to Hauck that his breathing was ideal in Scottsdale, but bad in Nevada, and that he was heading back to Arizona.

In March, his diabetes may have appeared for the first time in an article. Soon after, as he told Hauck, and as Hornbaker cited more fully, he was in a hospital for at least 13 days. In June, for health reasons, he was unable to go to Ogden, Utah, for an annual youth game. Besides acknowledging being named a lifetime honorary director of it, he wrote to Al Warden of the *Ogden Standard-Examiner*, "Youth baseball programs are just what the doctor ordered for young Americans." In addition, he sized up a few major league teams and provided the following medical update: "I am coming along well each day with my daily dose of insulin and am becoming quite good at inserting the needle."

As of April, he had moved to Phoenix, and was treating himself to hot mineral baths and massages, he wrote to Hauck. Also, he was now eating three times a day, not his usual two, and happy with a Mrs. Morrow, his housekeeper.

In May, he was the focus of a question-and-answer feature in *American Legion Magazine*. In one answer, he cited his research on mostly 19th-century pitcher Kid Nichols, who won a total of 360 games over a 16-year span and pitched 530 complete games. "A tremendous record! Yet how many times do we hear Nichols' name mentioned today? That is what I mean by research."

On improving attendance, he called for "some of the colorful promotion that the colleges use in exploiting their football teams." Baseball needs to be "more interesting to fans in order to compete with television, movies, opera, and the various outdoor forms of recreation that are growing in popularity with the shorter work week and longer vacations now in vogue. Night baseball – especially for the large industrial cities – was a step in that direction."

The heretofore uncited *American Legion Magazine* article relates directly to Cobb's book. That is because article writer Jimmy Jones was said by the following source to have started the ball rolling toward it. In a letter auctioned in 2012 by Robert Edward Auctions, Jones wrote to John Evangelist Walsh of Prentice-Hall that he, Jones, broached the idea of a Cobb autobiography while interviewing Cobb for that article. In response, Cobb supposedly indicated that he would be conducive to a book with Jones as his collaborator.

In his own five-page letter to Jones, Cobb stated, in part, "I come from a small town in Georgia, I have never rated myself high, innately I happen to be on the modest side. . . now there are a lot of things that need correcting. I do not mean an alibi book, but in certain instances I now feel an urge to correct the record in the evening of my life. . . there are some things, no one has been told, before, my lazy youth, during baseball and all, I have reserved this to and for myself in case I ever wanted to use it, I do think a meeting is more productive, where I can state my desires as to the quality of a book, briefly to do the best book on a ballplayer that to date has been done. . . Sincerely[,] Ty Cobb."

The one possible revelation in that letter is about his "lazy youth." That said, a reasonable guess is that he was referring to not taking baseball seriously enough in his pre-Detroit years. As noted earlier, while playing for Augusta, he was more concerned in one game with peanut taffy (popcorn is in some later versions) than catching a fly ball. That led to his being benched.

In July, after moving out of Phoenix, and before going to Cooperstown, he was in New York City. "Right now he is campaigning for a speed-up in play by the elimination of four thrown balls on an intentional pass," wrote Jack Cuddy of UPI. "'Just have the pitcher notify the umpire he is passing the batter,' he says, 'and let the umpire send the batter to first base. Why go through the time-wasting motions of throwing four balls?'" In 2017, the major leagues made that change. Cuddy also reported, "One reason for his stop-off was a conference with Fred Corcoran, well-known golf executive and business manager of several professional athletes. Corcoran is arranging for the sale of Cobb's life story to a publisher and to a movie company [the idea of a movie was a non-starter to Cobb, so maybe he was floating it to leverage a more lucrative book deal]. Corcoran and Ty are long-time friends." Otherwise, I did not come across any subsequent story of Corcoran helping Cobb on his book project or anything to do with selling movie rights. But it is possible to speculate that Corcoran played a key role in relation to the book: en route to Rome for the Summer Olympics in 1960, Cobb met again with him around New York City.

Days later, he returned to Detroit for what would be the last time. "The journey to Briggs Stadium is one of reluctance now. Not because Cobb doesn't like baseball any more nor because he doesn't appreciate what it has done for him," wrote Bob Pille of the *Free Press*. The *Detroit News* ran a photo of him pointing outside his window at the Pick Fort Shelby hotel and asking where the Hammond Building is. "Informed that it had been torn down, he sighed, 'That's where I used to get my check the first and 15th of every month.'"

"I've got to get out of here before the kids cut me off," Cobb told Pille in a tone "not unkindly but with explanation. 'I'm 72½ now,' says Cobb. 'Things bother me that didn't. I like to sign autographs for them, but I can't stand the jamming, the poking, the shoving any more.'" He also told of having been "on the go for seven days now" all across the country. Part of his jaunt was to attend the annual Hall of Fame ceremonies. He said he was visiting Detroit for business purposes. Pille also wrote that from his hotel, Cobb "was calling for late stock market quotations before the game. He was calling again after. That is the financier Cobb."

Cobb also spoke some baseball to Pille. "They say baseball today is reeking with psychology," he said, placing emphasis on "reeking."

"'But do they use it?' he asks, growling." For example, "Does a base-runner ever keep the pitcher jittery? Does a man ever slide, put on a great show with an injured leg, then steal on the next pitch when the opposition relaxes just the smallest bit? Does a man steal in the ninth when his team has a big lead, making the other side jumpy the next day when the score is tied and they know he can steal the bases that now is important?"

Pille added, "Cobb's tone tells you it doesn't happen."

One loose end from Cobb's July visit to New York City appeared about a week after its supposed occurrence. Feature columnist Robert Sylvester of the *New York Daily News* had been invited to Lawton Carver's restaurant to potentially run into Cobb and some other well-known people. When Sylvester saw Cobb and asked him about DiMaggio, he replied, "Joe DiMaggio? Wonderful. I always told Joe he should have exercised during the winter. That is why he came down lame, his legs went. He should have kept his muscles warm in the winter." Sylvester's report squares well with previous ones on the subject. Back in 1949, Cobb had attributed DiMaggio's leg problems to a "restful" attitude: "Instead of resting, he should come to San Francisco to hustle a truck, run up mountains or pull in commercial fish."

To fill in some context:

In the first year of DiMaggio's retirement, 1952, Cobb in *Life* called him "perhaps the outstanding example of how modern baseball players neglect to train and keep themselves in condition." Later that year, DiMaggio told Leslie Lieber of the *New York Herald Tribune*, "I don't know what would have become of me if I had ever practiced Ty Cobb's custom of winter-long training. Maybe Cobb was afraid of gaining too much weight, I don't know. As far as I'm concerned, I needed rest in the winter and I did what was best for me."

In the interim between Cobb's article and DiMaggio's comment, *Newsday* columnist Cannon had written, "It is Ty Cobb's claim that Winter-time indolence shortened Joe DiMaggio's career. But during the off seasons of '50 and '51 DiMaggio took up golf and walked more than he ever did. 'And I never was in worse shape,' DiMaggio disclosed." Also in the interim, Nap Rucker told the *Atlanta Constitution* that in the article, "Ty shouldn't have accused Joe DiMaggio of being lazy. I don't believe Ty realized that Joe had a delicate bone condition that made it necessary for him to husband his strength."

Of less relevance is a legs comparison in 1957 by veteran Yankees writer Dan Daniel. About star legs in baseball, Daniel had written the following: "It might be said that Mantle has the worst conditioned legs of any truly great batter of the past generation. Babe Ruth had pipe stems hardly suited to carry that heavy frame of his. He was ripped quite often, but had a rare physical gift. He healed fast. Joe DiMaggio's legs were faultless, but that [bone] spur in his left foot was a tremendous handicap. Ty Cobb's underpinning was matchless. It was the Georgia Peach who did the cutting with those flashing, sharp spikes of his. His ruthless style saved his own legs."

Sylvester told one other story from Cobb's visit to the restaurant. Cobb said the following about Yankees' general manager George M. Weiss, a future Hall of Fame inductee, whose team was in the midst of its one mediocre season that decade: "Why do you fellows knock George Weiss? He's a very tender man. He would do anything for me and I would for him. You knock him because he's a proud man. Doesn't anybody understand pride anymore?"

Interactions decades earlier between Cobb and Weiss help explain why Cobb would have had an interest in defending him.

Weiss was one of Cobb's closer friends in baseball and would be named an honorary pallbearer for his funeral. Back in 1916, as noted by Hornbaker, Weiss was the owner of the independent New Haven team that Cobb played for one day until Cannonball Redding entered the game as the opposing pitcher.

I came across two Cobb letters to Weiss from 1918, from right before Cobb headed to Europe for the Great War. In one, Cobb asked if he had received bats that he had sent him. "Sorry I could not get more but the 'Fans' raided me for souvenirs. Also let me know if you want to figure on any Exhibition [sic] games" in the first part of October, "as it will probably be, if I play, the last games on this soil as I will be out of the game for good on my return." I am not sure what Cobb meant by that.

In the other, he apologized to Weiss for not being able to see him on a recent trip to Hartford. Cobb said he had thought "of a cotton trade and wanted to be at a board [presumably the New York Board of Trade] so I could close it out this morning as I can['t] have these things open when I am going away."

Cobb and Walter Johnson became stockholders in that team in 1921, around the time a banquet was held in New Haven in honor of Cobb and New Haven's manager, now-former big-league pitcher Chief Bender. Cobb coordinated with Weiss the hiring of Bender's successor, former longtime Detroit teammate and retired pitcher Wild Bill Donovan. In 1923, Cobb thanked Weiss for informing him by telephone that he would be reimbursing him for shares that he once held in the club. "I want to go on record as saying that by this action you have rounded out fifteen years of fair dealing," Cobb wrote.

The most colorful Cobb-Weiss story apparently originated in McCallum's 1975 book, of Cobb enlisting Weiss in trickery against owner Navin to help him obtain a higher salary. The three biographies passed on it. As literally written, and in light of how above-board the Cobb-Weiss relationship was, it sounds highly inflated.

During a bargaining session in 1925 at the Vanderbilt Hotel in New York City, on some number of occasions when Navin made him an offer, "Cobb would promptly go to a telephone and call Weiss's room" at the same hotel. "He would tell George the proposed figure, and ask if he could meet it. George, who could no more have matched the offer than he could have bought the New Haven Railroad, would promptly name a higher figure, which Cobb would then repeat for Navin's benefit." Cobb ended up getting the higher salary he was striving for, "and that night Ty and George celebrated his success by doing up Manhattan in ribbons."

Returning a second time to 1959:

Apparently during his most recent visit to the Hall of Fame, he met a college student from upstate

from left to right in New York in 1957: Del Webb, George M. Weiss and Cobb

New York, Marie Quinn. He ended up sending her detailed prose about his health; none of it, however, is arguably as profound as what he wrote in November 1958 to Spink. Some of the following quotations and paraphrases from his 1959 and 1960s letters to Quinn are from Sotheby's, which auctioned them in 2010. I have modified those renderings to reflect what I suspect was Cobb's use of his frequent run-on sentence style.

In the first of those letters, he asked that she send any replies to his letters to a male friend of his, apparently the postmaster in Menlo Park, Evan "Doc" Morris. "I have a secty. cook & housekeeper not the usual domestic but her duties are very important to me. . . she sees all my mail. . . you are a woman, while young I daresay you know women and their ways, I have a job keeping her at a distance." Three weeks later, the need for that arrangement changed when Cobb wrote that his house manager had suddenly left him. In that later letter, he wrote "it is not the right that prevails today, no the wrong way seems to be so popular,

from left to right in 1958 or 1959: Cobb, National League President Warren Giles and Dodgers manager Walter Alston

but I say to you, right & honesty prevails in the end."

As of September, he was suggesting that they meet in New York after his upcoming visit to Boston. He offered to take her "to a real nice place for dinner so we can have a quiet time and learn a little more of each other, ideals, principals [sic] etc." He also said that a chaperone could join them. Weeks later, he reported that after losing another female housekeeper, that he was now determined to hire a male. "I think now I have a gem, he does it all and seems so interested. Between he and my 'Jap Gardener' I feel now am set and mind free." Quinn and Cobb spoke on the phone multiple times; in a letter, he stated that "you must call me collect, no more using your money." After declaring that, he asked that she "say a few prayers for me" and in his postscript, as per her request, he was sending her two autographed pictures of him.

Also stemming from the trip to Cooperstown, Cobb wrote to postmaster Morris to ask him to repackage any Quinn letter to him, so that his housekeeper would not notice it. Also, about his taking insulin, Cobb wrote, "I can get a 'jag on now' [get drunk] at no cost, I at times during the day can weave all over the place, a little food rectifies and very soon am normal again, it[']s weird and naturally am unused to it."

In September, he went to Boston for a B'nai B'rith sports dinner, and columnist Bill McSweeny of the *Boston Daily Record* praised his gentility. Hornbaker made use of his coverage of a post-dinner airport chat between

Cobb and Jesse Owens, in which Cobb had his arms around Owens and patted him on the back. The crumbs that Hornbaker omitted are even better, beyond Cobb's parting hug that I also noted much earlier. Besides McSweeny's praise of Cobb, McSweeny wrote that Cobb had referred to him as his "roomie" for apparently staying with him over 48 hours before the dinner. McSweeny wrote, "All your life you hear about a guy, stories, statistics, knocks and boasts. Then the time comes when you live with the legend and see him with his shoes off, a tired man, 72 years old, sitting, as he says, 'in the evening of my life.'"

Also, McSweeny noted to Cobb his diabetes and that he should not travel and instead get lots of rest. "'No,' he said [in response], 'But you have a responsibility to baseball and to the people who were your fans, to your friends. On nights like this, I'm very tired. But I'm Ty Cobb.'" Another leftover from the interview was told earlier, on his financial support of indigent former players.

Another highlight from the visit was in Kaese's write-up in the *Boston Globe*. "Cobb sat in his hotel suite overlooking Copley sq. [sic], clad in pajamas, eating fruit salad, and listening to Joe Casey of Wakefield – who once caught a few games for him in Detroit [41 from 1909 to 1911] – recite poetry."

"Sounds like Kipling," said Cobb.

"It is Kipling," replied Casey. Kipling was Rudyard Kipling, whose poems were famous in the late Victorian Era, when Cobb was growing up. He was the first English language writer to win the Nobel Prize in Literature, in 1907.

Later that month, when Cobb checked into Emory University Hospital, Dr. Hugh Wood, his physician, said, "I haven't seen him since 1952 when he was last in for a routine checkup." As noted earlier, Cobb had a number of health problems in 1952, including fibrillation of the heart.

the first two pages of a January 1960 letter from Cobb to Marie Quinn; the remaining pages are on the following page

TYRUS R. COBB
ROYSTON, GEORGIA   3

call his office girl, the
female bitch that in
her position figures she
is Boss & running the
doctor, takes care no
doubt of her friends. I
wanted like to only talk
on phone to doctor, she
says to me, this is his no
call day, you can't. I
say this is an emergency
she answers me. I told
you that you can't period
so there I was utterly
helpless, I did at most
in distress and I do
not want to be undiplo-
matic and call another
doctor who doesn't
know the Emery line
of treatment for me.
I had to sit, and lie in

TYRUS R. COBB
ROYSTON, GEORGIA   4

bed and walk about, as
I could not stay still
in one place say, I took
one gulp of orange juice,
hit my stomach
and vomited before I
could get to the sink,
I was stomach sick, so
could take nothing, later
hours, my doctor away
in right came and
gave me a hypo and
knocked me out, thats
what I had Sister Marie.
I do not know whether
it was caused by a
poison of milk or
soup, had to be one as
its only thing I had
for three days. as I am

TYRUS R. COBB
ROYSTON, GEORGIA   5

also having some dental
work and —. No Chew.
So I had rather be in
hell with my back.
broke than that again.
am much better today,
last night I made up my
mind, get away from
here, had a servant (Korean)
just a crack house boy
& driver, no cook at
all and hired him as
so recommended, with
me sick he was taking
things away, and caught
him working into my
pockets & money and
as I knew when finally
I took him to task
he quit, so again

TYRUS R. COBB
ROYSTON, GEORGIA   6

was alone, well I reasoned
why stay here, it finally
dawned on me to leave at
once, go to my hospital in
Royston & with every
attention and long time
friends, wait there until
I go to N.Y. Jan 24th Etc.
as I will have to come
back to Emory Feb 1st
and Emory is only
2 hours from Royston,
I can run down and
see my doctors there Etc.
So I finish with dentist
tomorrow, leave for
Tahoe for Sunday &
monday for bank business
on monday, return quick

TYRUS R. COBB
ROYSTON, GEORGIA   7

here, pack my things and
catch jet for Atlanta, Ga.
then up to Royston and
into my hospital.
you can reach me Cobb
Memorial Hospital, Royston
Ga, after Wednesday next
until I come to N.Y.
This is all for now.
Best to you, Sincerely
Ty

Dr. Stewart D. Brown, Sr., a close friend of Cobb's, said Cobb had been suffering from a back injury. Brown said the injury stemmed from his playing days. Brown was presumably referring to a longer-term spine one, to be briefly noted later, as distinct from the bursitis of the right shoulder suffered while hunting goats. The following day, Wood said that reports that Cobb was "rushed" to the hospital erroneously made it seem as if his condition was "critical:"

"'It was nothing like that,' said Wood. 'He's here for a routine checkup, and our preliminary examination shows nothing seriously wrong.'" Wood repeated the line that the injury stemmed from his playing career. (Maines's August 1961 letter, quoted earlier, revealed that it was a hunting accident in late 1959 near Lake Tahoe that led Cobb to decide to have a complete medical and physical examination.)

A week later, Reichler of the AP interviewed Cobb by phone. "'I'm all right,' the voice assured [from Emory University Hospital]. 'I'm feeling 100 per cent. I've had more X-rays and tests in the past few days than I've ever had in my life. The doctors say I should be out of here soon.'" Privately, Cobb was saying something different. In a letter to Quinn that month, he wrote, "I have had an operation it was decided and arranged quickly not as emergency but per my decision to have it done" and over with "as I had had enough of pain. . . I sure had the red carpet treatment here per my friend Dr. Wood."

George H. Maines
circa 1965

In 1960:

A few days into the year, he wrote to Maines from Emory University Hospital, "I know you mean well for me, but the enclosed [that you sent me, which is unstated] is concretely an example of well meaning efforts on your part, but it loads me up with obligations[.] I am a slave to acknowledging etc. this is only one of so many that forces me to write to acknowledge & explain, I have a mass of letters to answer per my hospital stay & findings." Cobb then described the Cobb Educational Fund and how "there are so many all over the country, that channel in to me 'One' – such hopes, I can not cope with it, causes a burden & creates tension in my case. Would you take time out and write this anxious mother and explain my part of what I am trying to do is limited in members[, 36 per year he informed Maines earlier,] also applications are to be of Georgia, etc."

Fortunately for posterity, Maines's 1961 letter provides a compelling explanation of what Cobb was referring to. Referring to his time with Cobb in November or December 1959, Maines wrote, "I was so anxious to have the world know the good deeds Ty had done" with his money. Maines contacted one of his own acquaintances, columnist Vincent X. Flaherty at the *Los Angeles Examiner*. That apparently in turn led to Cobb and Maines sending a paragraph to nationally known entertainment columnist Louella O. Parsons. Maines said the paragraph that they sent described his aid to students and old-time players. "Louella ran a story about Ty, and as a result he got letters from many people all over the continent, – [sic] some he gave to me to answer."

In a version of her column in an Indiana newspaper, Parsons wrote, "Ty Cobb, baseball immortal, is in Em[o]ry University Hospital in his Hometown, Atlanta, Ga. according to George Maines, former Hearst man[.] Cobb, who is worth $3,000,000 [about $24 million today], has set up a foundation which will help young students through college and also help baseball players down on their luck." The latter part of that was wrong, as Cobb's assistance to former players was ad hoc.

Also in his letter to Maines, Cobb said his back pain was now such that he is "having to go higher in pain killer potency. I sleep an hour or so then pains awaken me, I take the medicine, read or walk around or write as I am now doing with you the hour 12 o[']clock, I will tire then to bed for another hour or so, then up again, I do manage during night and next day to accumulate a six hour or more sleep[.] as I might have told you they have pinpointed the cause and infection that works on the

Cobb and (Jewish) pitcher Larry Sherry at the B'nai B'rith dinner in New York City in 1960

nerves and hence muscles drawing & pulling." He was headed to New York later that month and, in the letter, stated that he would need to return to the hospital afterward for more tests with an eye to a "more or less simple operation."

Cobb told Maines that the above "is in confidence for we do not wish to have stories in papers causing many to speculate and my kin alarmed without cause – per cancer – hope you understand, also with bushels of mail. We will announce at proper time, in fact the doctors are now most sure it['] not a drastic case but they in their profession have to be absolutely sure and that will be determined Feb. 1st or 2nd."

He was also exploring whether to make Georgia his official residence "as I won[']t file my permanent will in Calif. and I hear of tricky doings by the racket lawyer outfit in Nev. after one is gone etc."

Later that month, his "sharp pain all the time he was here," as described by New York columnist Joe Williams after an early 1960 Cobb visit to Manhattan, may account for some of his more snappish lines in a long interview with sports reporter Pat Parrish. The interview with Parrish took place just after Cobb, at a dinner of the New York Chapter of the Baseball Writers' Association, had received an award for "Player of the Year" of 1911. Earlier on that trip, he had received an award at a New York B'nai B'rith sport dinner as one of nine "Men of the Age" in various sports. Hornbaker cited the following sentences from the Parrish interview early on in his book: "Why is it that everybody has to have an angle. Just say it the way it happened. I played baseball for a long time and I gave it everything I had. . . everything."

I found the interview before realizing that Hornbaker had cited part of it. It turns out that the three sentences above were not said consecutively; the first came long before the other two. In the original, there is a different, albeit similar sentence immediately before the second one that Hornbaker cited. Addressing Parrish, Cobb said, "I hope you haven't come up here looking for an angle or something."

Some of Cobb's strongest emotion, which Hornbaker passed up on, appeared after Cobb said, "Why is it that everybody has to have an angle?" Here goes:

"They said I called [fellow future Hall of Famer] Wagner a name and he crammed the ball in my mouth when I slid into second base. Do you think I would have done such a thing?

Cobb and Bobby Jones at the B'nai B'rith dinner. Red Grange and Jesse Owens are behind them.

"Why, I was more of a gentleman than to call a man I respected as Wagner such a name."

Digressing to context for that:

A version with a similar tone appeared in a 1943 feature by sports editor Grayson and then his 1944 book *They Played the Game: The Story of Baseball Greats.*

Elsewhere in his book, Hornbaker described a version that had been attested to in 1944 by Ed McAuley of the *Cleveland News.* In it, McAuley said that Wagner, in 1943, had told him that on the play with Cobb, which took place in the 1909 World Series, "I guess I must have accidentally tagged him in the mouth." Stump's 1994

1909 Pirates World Series champs (over the Tigers) George Gibson (now manager) and Wagner (now a coach) with Cobb at Paso Robles, Calif., in 1933

book, incidentally, accurately captures Cobb's point of view on the above and also states that Wagner denied that Cobb had instigated anything. Since accidents happen in baseball, this was presumably an example of one. A larger point relating to Stump is that he cannot be said to have categorically tried to present Cobb in the worst possible light in that book. After all, on such an instance of importance to Cobb, he conveyed it in an optimally pro-Cobb way.

In 1950, Cobb thanked Salsinger in writing for a *Sporting News* article that challenged the accuracy of the Wagner story. Cobb said it was among "quite a few" stories that are "hearsay or even manufactured" and which have "placed me in a false light, things foreign to my nature and makeup, some not hurtful to me and yet even so[,] they hurt because they were not true, one could think me thin skinned over some of these."

Before re-analyzing the Wagner story, he cited for Salsinger's knowledge a whopper version of his collision with Durocher, which appeared on page 224: "For instance, the Durocher thing where he shouldered me at short on my way to third on a potential three[-]base hit, knocking me on my 'can' and I was thrown out, first by the time Durocher was in the league, I knew enough and big enough [sic] not to let such happen[;] again if true I would have been entitled to third for interference."

He then told Salsinger that the following was a canard, "my calling Wagner a Kraut head and what I would do when I came down and his tagging me in the mouth with loss of teeth etc. why no ball player had greater reverence for Wagner, I was only 23 years of age at the time and he was a veteran and I would have been run out of the league, I seldom if ever slid to second or third except a fadeaway or fall away slide and you can[']t do either without the foot on the ground and one at that [sic] to tag [the] bag with, first and home was [sic] only places I would slide straight, to get there quickest way and home when with all their armor they would block one off and yes how about the bat and mask laid in the line in front of plate."

Returning to his 1960 interview with Parrish:

Asked if he often told the opposition that he was going to steal and would then carry out the threat, Cobb replied, "That's not the way you do things, not at all. I never in my life told anyone I was going to steal a base. I'm always made out to be a louse. Cobb was always the louse. Some guy was just after a story always." When Parrish asked if he would set the record straight in his book, he replied, "I may and I may not. Why should I tell you anyway?" Only then did he say, "I hope you haven't come up here looking for an angle or something."

At the time of my research, a search of the Internet and of Google Books showed no prior hits for Cobb saying, "I'm always made out to be a louse." That could be the top quote to explain Cobb's bitterness toward his doomed legacy. It would have to compete against another louse quote from Cobb that began the article; I did find hits for it on the Internet, but only to the original newspaper report in 1960: "I don't believe the Lord would have been so kind to me if I had been such a louse." Considering that Cobb was said to have invoked religion more often toward the end of his life, that might be an even better quote than "I'm always made out to be a louse."

Cobb stalwart Parker of the *New York Mirror* attended the sportswriters dinner and wrote soon after about Cobb's book being in the works: "Can Ty Cobb have lost any of his skill at contract signing time since he retired from baseball when, ill though he is, he is playing two publishing houses against each other from his hospital bed [presumably Doubleday and Prentice-Hall], to drive the best bargain possible for his life story?"

From seeing a draft, Cobb's daughter Shirley recalled telling her dad that it contained slang that she never heard him use. She told that to author Rhodes, and without crediting either, Leerhsen wrote, "No one commented on the fact that in its pages Cobb sounded more like a jaded sportswriter than an old ballplayer." On that point, Alderton of the *Lansing State Journal* wrote that "reading it you find phrases that contemporaries easily recognize as words of the times." And veteran sportswriter Wally Willis of the *Oakland Tribune* declared, "Put together by Al Stump, who has often been criticized for attacks on sports figures, the book becomes one of the most readable sports histories in years. The charm of unsophisticated language, always in the first person, is retained, with only the southern tones [of Cobb's style of speech] gone."

Helping to refute part of that last point is Leerhsen's citing of the following as far-fetched stylistically, right after his "jaded sportswriter" sentence: "No, I didn't once attack [teammate] Nap Rucker, the pitcher, in the bathroom and try to throw him out of the tub in which he was relaxing. That phony fable has dogged me for more than half a century and I doubt there are enough fans to fill a broom closet who don't believe it happened – which it never did. I don't know who first concocted that particular piece of Limburger, but it has an odor I seem to associate with certain New York writers – never exactly *simpatico* to me – who've made certain it appeared in every language but the Sanskrit."

In turn, that is a hook to move onto something else very colorful – Rucker stories about Cobb – including the overlooked-or-devalued bathtub story:

In 1913, Rucker told veteran baseball writer Harold Webster "H. W." Lanigan the following, in what, appropriately, sounds like a journalist's rewrite:

"As I was returning to my native state at the end of the 1910 season, imagine my surprise when I read in the Southern papers that Cobb and I were going to man two demon flying autos in a big race at Augusta. 'It must be the bunk,' I said to myself as the train was scurrying southward. I had not been approached on the matter and it was not only all Greek to me, but I didn't see a chance of the promoters getting me in one of those ninety-miles-per-hour cars without knocking me down and chloroforming me [rendering me unconscious].

"When I got off the train at Augusta, Ty was one of the first souls I bumped into. 'Yes, it goes, Nap,' he confided in me. 'We are in on a 50-50 basis and you'll pull down dollar for dollar with me. It's a big boost and it will be the easiest money you ever made in your life.'

"'But Ty, I don't know how to drive,' I said.

"'Hell, neither do I,' was Ty's comeback. But what differ[e]nce does that make? We can ride on the seat alongside of the speed king and leave it to me to have the papers up North refer to you and I as a pair of Bob Burmans [Burman, a world record racecar driver, would die in a race crash in 1916; Maines was Burman's press agent in 1915-16] and Barney Oldfields.

"Cobb is the same hustler [money-wise] off the field as on it. He's after the money, too, all the time and every fall when he books a show for me in some Georgia town he always acts as my manager and sees that I get just as much as he pulls down. So he's a boomer and a manager after my own heart."

Rucker told Lanigan two other long stories about Cobb, one of which was given the subhead, "TY DOESN'T LIKE JOSHING." In the other story, apparently referring to Detroit's 1906 spring training at Augusta, Rucker worked out with the Detroit team before reporting to his own team, Brooklyn. "Ty had it doped out that [new Tiger outfielder] Davy Jones was the Tiger he had to displace if he were to become a regular, and the day [manager] Jennings began putting his players over the jumps Ty told me that if I did any pitching to him in any of the practice games to slip up the pill in the groove so he could slap it out of the lot." The rest of that story has more to do with Cobb's skill as a batter than anything humorous.

Arthur Daley

The bathtub episode, as reported by Daley in the *New York Times* in 1949, took place when they were teammates on Augusta, and rooming together. After pitching, Rucker had the habit of heading to his hotel room at a leisurely pace, because "his restless, impatient and energetic room-mate always raced to the hotel for his bath and the pitcher had to wait for him anyway."

One day, Rucker was replaced near the end of a game, so he headed to the hotel. "From force of habit Rucker always had dawdled in the bath because there never had been anyone else waiting." Rucker hurried and exited the bath "and was toweling himself off when an angry voice curled around the half-opened door, upbraiding Rucker for his slowness." Rucker answered with some meaningless words.

"Suddenly and furiously the roomie sprang at him. Blind with rage he reached for Nap's throat. The pitcher was rocked back by the initial surprise but he was the stronger of the two. He finally held his attacker off at arm's length and spoke." Rucker supposedly asked Cobb if he had gone crazy.

Then Cobb, after calming down, said, "I got to be first – all the time."

Alexander and Hornbaker did not mention the above story; Leerhsen did so only in the passing reference one page ago. In 1956, Daley would win a Pulitzer Prize, the first sportswriter to do so.

In a 1951 interview with sportswriter Guy Tiller of the *Atlanta Constitution*, Rucker told the following story. "I got knocked out in the early innings one day. So I went on home to the room I shared with Ty. I was in the tub when Ty came in bristling. He blew a fuse at me. Told me to get out of that gol-durned [sic] tub. That I couldn't take a bath before he did. That he had to be first in everything, all the time."

Tiller added, "Nap admits that thereafter Cobb and his fiery temper had priority on the tub."

On another matter, Rucker opined to Tiller on whether players were taking care of themselves between games. He said, "It's unfair to compare kids today with Cobb. Boys have a lot of other interests now that weren't available to us. So you can't blame them too much for those school busses and those convertibles and those pretty young girls who take up so much of their time.

"I imagine us old-timers would have done the same thing if we had had the chance. That is, all of us except Cobb." Earlier in the interview, Rucker had said that modern players "don't practice enough, and when they do they ride up to practice in convertibles. They've got better instruction and play with better equipment. But, compared to fellows like Cobb, they are sissies."

Coverage of the 1960 dinner may have inspired Stump, in his 1961 article, to pile on detail about Cobb's notorious driving reputation. I do not know if Stump was aware of Frances's bill of particulars; in it, she stated that while she was sleeping one day, Cobb literally drove his car into their house.

One newspaper titled Leonard Lyons's syndicated dinner column "The Lyons Den: Ty Cobb is One Terrible Driver." To write it, Lyons recycled himself, taking material from a 1941 column that was featured earlier. Another item in the column involved pitcher Lefty Grove and cigars, with Grove as the source.

His column also covered Cobb's drinking. He recalled the 75th anniversary dinner in 1951 to mark the founding of the National League; Lyons had brought his son George to meet Cobb. As he was introducing George, Cobb supposedly accepted a glass of whiskey and told George that he never touched whiskey or a cigarette until he was 38, thus around 1925. Cobb then advised George against partaking in either, at least until age 38, because after that age, neither will matter. (Cobb did claim in interviews in 1915 and 1924, as noted earlier, that while he smoked cigarettes, he never inhaled.)

Stump portrayed Cobb's driving as follows. To suddenly visit the now-defunct Riverside casino in snowy weather, Cobb decided that they should each take cars in case one breaks down; Stump's one had chains. "Tiring of my creeping pace, he gunned the Imperial around me in one big skid. I caught a glimpse of an angry face under a big Stetson hat and a waving fist. He was doing a good thirty miles per hour when he'd gained twenty-five yards on me, fishtailing right and left, but straightening as he slid out of sight in the thick sleet.

"Suicide wasn't in my contract." After six more miles, Stump "saw taillights to the left. Pulling up, I found Ty's car swung sideways and buried, nose down, in a snowbank, the hind wheels two feet in the air. Twenty yards away was a sheer drop-off into a canyon."

Also at the 1960 dinner, as reported by Lyons, then-famous entertainer-toastmaster George Jessel "was puzzled when Cobb's introduction brought cheers from other ballplayers: 'Why cheers? Cobb spiked every ballplayer in this room.'" In 1958, Lyons had quoted Jessel nearly identically for his introduction of Cobb at the dinner in Haney's honor.

Cobb was possibly irritated in New York City because Quinn did not visit him there. As Cobb wrote to her, "I am coming a long ways back & there for scheduled and arranged plans and honors, you are in a stone[']s throw. . . you be sensible, and be your good common sense self, and don[']t be piling complications on me when really I am the one in stress." Sotheby's noted its unintentionally ironic postscript: "I am not feeling so hot, as usual,

from left to right in 1953: George Jessel, Senator Joseph McCarthy and Jimmy Durante

and yet I have to pitch Marie and do my part[;] also I do not complain."

In an earlier letter that month to her, he had complained extensively. "I have been in torment and I mean hell, was constant acute pain all over my back and legs." He complained of "phony doctors" treating him and their "heartless commercial side." He also had a new servant, a Korean, who is a "crack [illegal drug] house boy & driver" who he caught "working into my pockets & money" for which "I took him to task." (The following also would explain his greater irritability than usual: When Daley of the *Times* interviewed him in New York City on that visit, most of the time "he sat in a cradle of pillows on the sofa of his hotel suite, wincing occasionally whenever pain stabbed him in the back.")

In February, Cobb wrote to financial advisor Hauck about his back pain and "a raw infection from testes or prostate," leading to no appetite and little sleep. Ten days later, Cobb wrote to Quinn, "This is laying it on the line . . . I am not well, also deeply in the evening of my years to live, so am very serious, I have quite a bit to offer to you in material ways, salary, travel, security, open doors, all if you come with me. . . you would be paid well, and yet you are not be a servant, you will [not?] wear a uniform or apron and meet my friends on a common level and yet you will administer to my every service, drive car, shop, keep house, use type writer which I have, help me, and yet Marie not in any way, you will be expected to fill any sex exactions, only if you desire, and yet I am not so sure at my age I can qualify, you are to enjoy my social life, you might meet some person, you feel you would like to marry, just tell me, you will have the freedom of the house, I will help you, your job is to help me, I will help you honey to get married to one of your choosing, and with me in circulation you have a chance, not up there in Windham [her place of residence in upstate New York]. . . that's it, you are to get $7200.00 for the year [about $58,000 today], you are getting too much, so only for a year, I might do more for you in the future, I do not promise, this is it – you have a wonderful chance, to grace my home and meet my friends, I will not ever marry again, even to the Queen of sheba, I really loved one woman [Frances Cass], that's enough, now divorced poor girl, 4 times since after menoupause, [sic] on her knees, crying, asking me. . . I want no more of that, she was a wonderful person, want you to come and be nice to me."

from left to right at an old-timers' party in Arizona in 1959, on St. Patrick's Day: Cobb, O'Doul, Rudy York and Jimmie Foxx. A story that I seem to be the discoverer of is that O'Doul and Dizzy Dean "almost got run down" later that day at Scottsdale Stadium "by a frightened team of horses pulling a stagecoach." Before the game, when a band began to play, "the horses reared up and then headed for Dean and O'Doul, who had their backs to the plugs [horses]. They turned around just in time to get out of the way of the moving stagecoach, which had been used to transport some of the 'Oldtimers' to the ballpark," wrote *Mesa Tribune* sports editor Tom Diskin.

In March, a prospective donor to his scholarship fund wanted him to first send a signed baseball. Cobb sent him a National League ball, saying it was the most convenient one he could find, and added, "hope this doesn't make any difference."

In March and April, he was in Scottsdale to see some spring training games. Emmons Byrne of the *Oakland Tribune* wrote one day, "Baseball's greatest living immortal" is "recuperating in the Arizona sun from a recent operation. So far as baseball is concerned he can take it or leave it. Outside of his remark about [the great fielding of San Francisco third baseman Jim] Davenport and greeting old ball players like Hank Sauer, his conversation was mostly about the stock market." Gillooly of the *Boston Daily Record* wrote, "He came here in his limousine but the fellow he hired to drive him went too fast and had too little respect for the white lines. So, half-way along from Georgia to Arizona, he fired his chauffeur, made him sit in the back seat and took over the controls himself." Cobb was lodging "at the expensive and exclusive Camelback Inn, at the base of the mountain of the same name."

Red Sox coach Rudy York, who as a player had chatted with Cobb in 1939 about their respective dogs, mainly grew up in Georgia. Also in that earlier chat, they had discussed quail hunting in Florida. York and teammate Bobo Newsom had told Cobb that while the quantity of quail there is plentiful, that hunting there was murder on the dogs. "Snakes will kill a dog a day," they reportedly both told him. On this new occasion, Cobb and York "talked turkey and pheasant and partridge for 30 minutes before Cobb switched to a topic which is still his favorite subject. Namely hitting." Cobb complimented him for having been "a helluva batter," while calling his batting style strange. "Didn't look like you were going to hit much at all. Lazy-like up there at the plate. Then, blast, you put your bat to the ball at the last instant and it was always a line drive. Yes, you could hit that ball." York had hit 277 home runs.

York said one should get to know pitchers like they were one's brothers and Cobb said in agreement, "And that's what has made Ted Williams such a great hitter, knowing pitchers." (But back in 1951, as he had more or less said to UPI in 1946, Cobb told the AP's Newland that the then-slumping Williams "cannot be classed as 'a great hitter' unless he can hit to all fields.") Gillooly added, "Cobb said it was better to study rival pitchers and their deliveries and their motions rather than to waste too much time on stance and grip and swing."

In writing up his own interview with Cobb, sports editor Frank Gianelli of the *Arizona Republic* stated, "Cobb was known as one of the most vicious competitors the game has ever known. Pictures of his flying spikes and the stories of his pugnacious attitude are legend." Gianelli wrote that after sitting next to Cobb during a Boston-Chicago Cubs game. "Cobb gets especially critical of batters who don't 'take charge' at the plate. 'That's his territory up there – why doesn't he step up where he can hit the ball?' he bellowed at one stand-back lad. 'Look,' he said, 'from where he's standing, he can't get the fat part of the bat over the plate.'" Gianelli added, "And sure enough, the batter was bamboozled on outside breaking pitches."

In a later article, Gillooly told of Cobb and now-Boston general manager Bucky Harris spending a few hours together at the Pink Pony restaurant in Scottsdale. Referring to a Cobb letter to Boston's Jensen that urged him not to retire, Harris told Gillooly, "Must have been a sharp letter, he [Cobb] quoted me a few excerpts from it." Cobb's paraphrase of the letter appeared earlier.

On a different day in Scottsdale, he sat behind home plate, "the better to second-guess the hitters and pitchers – his favorite pastime," wrote *Los Angeles*

Times sports editor Paul Zimmerman. When the Cubs' Ernie Banks came to the plate, Cobb said, "I don't think he likes to have them pitch 'em in here." As he said that, Cobb "swept his hand across his stomach, a huge diamond flashing."

When Ted Williams came to the plate, Cobb shook his head. "'If I were him,' said the Georgia Peach, 'I'd get into perfect condition this spring for one great season, and then quit. It should be a matter of pride with him to have a big final year.'"

"'I'm down here recuperating,' said Ty as he got up from his seat, 'so I don't usually stay for all of the game.'" He added that he was hoping to be on hand for the season opener in San Francisco, as he waved goodbye. (There is one final Cobb-Williams story of note. Later that year, to no avail, Cobb would urge Corcoran to advise Williams as follows: "With the fine year he's having, it would be a

Cobb and Ted Williams in 1959 in Scottsdale

shame to see Ted retire. With his swing and coordination he can play for at least two more years. All he has to do is keep in shape throughout the winter months." Grayson of the NEA got that from Corcoran, who Cobb spoke to around New York City before heading to Rome for the Summer Olympics.)

Days later, Rumill of the *Christian Science Monitor* wrote, "Almost every day Ty Cobb urges a youngster to consider baseball as a profession. 'Why not?' he said as he sat in Scottsdale Stadium and watched the Red Sox play. 'Where can a young man make such money and have such a good time in the bargain? When he travels, he travels first class and lives in the best hotels. And work, to a ball player, should be play.'

"Isn't that a wonderful thing, that pension? Some of those old-time ball players sure could have used $500 a month [about $4,000 today] in later years." He also said, "They criticize baseball people for luring boys away from school and college, but no one ever considers that travel is educating." He added, "A boy can educate himself with books while he's riding around the country."

A few days after that, *Cleveland Plain Dealer* sports editor Gordon Cobbledick reported from Tucson that Indians slugger Rocky Colavito "was polite and cool to the aged tourist who volunteered a criticism of his batting form up in Scottsdale the other day. It wasn't until a teammate asked, 'What was Cobb tellin' you?' that the Rock [sic] became aware his tutor was Ty Cobb, greatest batsman of them all." (On the Web site of Getty Images, if you look for Cobb images with Ted Williams, three of the four accurate matches show Cobb with a name tag. Presumably, the Colavito episode helped inspire it. Also, in April, the Tigers traded Harvey Kuenn for Colavito, and Cobb wrote two weeks later to Tigers general manager Bill DeWitt the following: DeWitt should have a "loose & easy good fellowship talk with him [Colavito], don[']t talk of his homeruns [sic] or the obligations of such.")

From Scottsdale, he referred to a recent reply by Quinn. "In your letter you spoke of keeping my letter as it indicates a contract, well it works both ways, how about giving me firm assurance." As summarized by Sotheby's, "Cobb's letters continue in this vein for another three months, as he promises Marie a trip to Rome to see the Olympics and assures her 'there will be no "extra curricular" things.' But Marie evidently informed him that her responsibility of nursing a sick parent would once more delay her trip" to visit him.

In a May letter that I saw, he wrote from California that the state is too troublesome, and he cited "the terrific traffic." Nevada would be better because "it[']s quiet, boat ride, and easy tempo in my place there on Lake, which I like so much, the decks are cleared for business matters, yes unanswered letters, that[']s all, to Tahoe, top talent entertainers, out for dinner, glorious surroundings, or stay at home, real comfort & quiet." Also, he said he had placed an advertisement in the Reno newspaper for someone to help around the house. Cobb wanted Quinn to take the job: "if you should change your mind, to stay on, this is one fine job to have, hope you do not disappoint me, things businesswise fine with me." In a margin near his signature, he wrote, "Personally pain wise my days not so good, nerves & sick at stomach, their medicines."

The ad read, "WANT Housekeeper and cook. Must be able to drive auto and do shopping. Someone who really would like good position. Live in. Home on Lake Tahoe near Cave Rock. Must be qualified or do not apply. Write: T. R. Cobb, Glenbrook, Nevada."

Possibly the last subject about his baseball career to pop up in its most extensive form close to his death is this offbeat one: interaction with Tigers trainers in the last six years of his Detroit career. Alderton of the *Lansing State Journal* touched on the subject in 1960. His hook for doing so was the retirement of Michigan State University's longtime trainer, English-born John G. "Jack" Heppinstall.

"Jack's contact with Cobb was made through Jimmy Dugan, the Tigers' regular trainer at the time." Dugan, a boxer on the side who had previously been a trainer for the New York and Boston American League teams, began with the Tigers in 1921. It had been the custom for the Tigers' regular one to work in East Lansing, on the campus of Michigan State, during the football season. "Dugan and Jack quickly became fast friends, and he prevailed upon Jack to visit him at Detroit during the baseball season.

"'He took me to the clubhouse with him,' Jack related, 'and introduced me to everybody, Cobb included. Ty looked me over, and laughingly said, 'Well, what do you know, a professor from the college campus! You know how to rub a man down?'

"Jack said that he did. Cobb quickly shed his clothes, stretched out on the rub table and said: 'All right, give me a college-educated rubdown.'"

Alderton added, "Jack must have filled the order for ever [sic] after that when he visited the stadium with his friend Jimmy."

"He'd kid that my 'college-educated' rubdown was a lot better than Jimmy's, and have fun with Jimmy about it," Heppinstall said. "Cobb had a superb body – finely muscled, and tuned like a fiddle. He took the best of care of it, too." (In 1932, Salsinger wrote that Cobb had had a masseur work on his legs every other week, after being advised so as a way to extend his career, in 1920 in San Francisco by local trainer Dennis Carroll.)

Heppinstall also recalled sitting with Dugan on the bench before games, when "Cobb made it a point of giving opponents the razzberry, individually and collectively." When opposing players went down a tunnel and through the Tigers' dugout, "Cobb would be there waiting, and he'd take 'em apart as they appeared. Some of the names he called those guys! I'll never know why they took it. I guess some of them didn't, because I heard stories that once in a while there would be a fist fight under the stands. Cobb, you could quickly see, was scared of nobody."

He praised Cobb, who he said always called him the "professor," for treating him well, such as by thanking him. Heppinstall said Dugan told him the following story, about Cobb being superstitious about his clothes.

John G. "Jack" Heppinstall in 1923

"If he had a good day, he'd wear the same clothes game after game – sometimes for a week – afraid he would break his luck. Then when he had a bad day, he'd throw all the soiled clothes out of the locker and holler for fresh ones from head to toe."

Harry Tuthill, the Detroit trainer from 1908 through 1919, appears in bit roles in some Cobb biographies. Cited earlier was a recollection from Cobb about having had Tuthill as a roommate. Dugan, the trainer from 1921 to 1926 (and to 1931), is absent from the biographies. Dugan had been working as a hockey trainer in Michigan when he got the following break: After serving with former Detroit pitcher Wild Bill Donovan when Donovan managed Providence of the Eastern League in 1913 and 1914, Donovan brought him along when he became manager of the New York Yankees in 1915.

Dugan was the Tigers' "liniment and bandage man," the *Free Press* said upon his release in 1931. He had been "kneading the aching muscles of athletes for nearly a score of years." Tripp paraphrased the 1966 book *The Glory of Their Times* to describe the work of the Tigers' trainer during Sam Crawford's long career with the team, which ran through 1918. In the book, Crawford said, "We had a trainer, but all he ever did was give you a rubdown with something we called 'Go Fast.' He'd take a jar of Vaseline and a bottle of Tabasco sauce – you know how hot that is – mix them together, and rub you down with that. Boy, it made you feel like you were on fire! That would *really* start you sweating. Now they have medical doctors and whirlpool baths and who knows what else."

clockwise from top left in 1922: Fred Haney, Jimmy Dugan and Bobby Veach

My favorite story in this book that has nothing directly to do with Cobb brings together Tuthill and Dugan. In 1915, Bozeman Bulger of the *New York Evening World* wrote, "There is a war brewing between members of the 'Baseball Trainers' Union.' Jimmy Dugan, new man for the Yanks, is exhibiting a clipping in which Harry Tuthill, former trainer of the Giants and the Tigers [actually he was still with the latter], declares that Dugan has not enough class for the job.

"'I may not have as much class as Tuthill,' says Jimmy, 'but I own my own home, drive my own automobile and rubbed the Providence club into the pennant.'"

Returning a second time to 1960:

In June, as Hornbaker mentioned, the *Sporting News* wrote about the state of Cobb's effort to settle on a biographer. Earlier that month, in a letter to the Ty R. Cobb who was sports editor of the *Nevada State Journal*, he wrote, "my publisher is Doubleday. Collaborator arrives night of

in 1924: Charley Gehringer and Dugan

June 9th – he will be here at my place, will do by tape, framing questions & answers, a conversational procedure[,] my part reciting from very early youth on to my retirement, select from all this what they think might be usable, then final composition continuity, polishing up which I insist. Doubleday and myself will decide what[']s to be."

Leerhsen printed close to the above while omitting the following, including even in his endnotes who the recipient "friend," as Leerhsen called him, was. I can add that Tyrus the sports editor had informed Ty about a subscription bill that his newspaper wanted to be paid. "Tell these yokels not to present me with such offside matters, it is such as this that adds to our tension, most Cobbs like to be people of honor," the ballplayer's opening sentence reads. Near the end, he wrote, "I am getting old Ty. Finding myself getting 'old age edgy' of course I have a couple of diluments [a catch-all term for chemicals in health-related preparations, including potentially toxic ones] which doesn't help me."

A week later, he attended the annual Hall of Fame game in Cooperstown for the last time. On a hotel patio afterward, he said, "The heat chased me from the stands in the sixth inning but I saw enough of [the Cubs' Dick] Drott to know he can be a top-notch pitcher if [he] has a mind to be."

In saying that to Gene Levy, sports editor of the *Oneonta Star*, he sensed that he was about to be asked to compare old-time players to today. So he quickly added, "now don't try to trap me into putting unnecessary fuel into that fire."

Prior to the game, Cobb was on the field "administering a generous dose of the well[-]known Cobb advice and wit to admiring ballplayers," Levy also related. "'Just keep that low and even swing,' he lectured now-Cleveland outfielder Kuenn, 'and you'll win yourself a peck more batting titles.' Then mimicking Vic Power's unique one-handed practice stroke, he set the Negro first baseman to gig[g]ling with the statement: 'Man, you colored boys can sure whack that ball.'"

As alluded to earlier, a doctor who treated Cobb in the summer of 1960, Joseph E. Hardison, wrote about his experience in 1981, in the *Journal of the American Medical Association*. "Mr. Cobb was 73 years old and in pain from metastatic cancer of the prostate. He was not in a good humor. I introduced myself and got no further. Mr. Cobb informed me he would have none of my pestering and poking. I was to give him something for pain right then.

"*Suddenly, there was the roar of the crowd. I was on the mound (I was a pitcher in high school) [sic] facing the Georgia Peach, the greatest baseball player who ever lived, poised on his toes, hands wide apart on the bat, crowding the plate, and murder in his eyes.*

"I told Mr. Cobb I couldn't give him anything for pain until I had talked to and examined him.

"*Mr. Cobb bunted my best fastball down the first base line, pulling the first baseman off the bag, leaving me to cover and face an awesome display of speed, sparks and spikes flying down the line. I was seized with fear for I knew without a doubt that Ty Cobb, with steel flashing, was going to slide into first base.*

"Mr. Cobb told me I was a rank incompetent amateur and I was to give him something for pain immediately. He was wrong – I was not an amateur. I had been issued uniforms with my name on them and was being paid $200 a month. I was not an amateur – I was a professional in my rookie year. I stood my ground, spikes or no spikes, and asked Mr. Cobb again to cooperate with me.

"With disdain Mr. Cobb telephoned and told his private physician he had sent a boy to do a man's job. The attending [sic] told me he understood my position, but he knew Mr. Cobb very well and assured me he would be a different person when free of pain – and so he was. He let me examine him. He talked with me about Babe Ruth, Lou Gehrig, and Walter Johnson. He told me the only player he ever intentionally tried to harm was a pitcher that threw at his head! He signed a baseball for me. We became friends."

The above was the rare decades-later story that I found Hornbaker citing. He paraphrased it in two sentences and attributed it to the *New York Times*; Red Smith of the *Times* wrote a column that quoted Hardison's article extensively. My quotes from the article reflect the medical journal's original punctuation.

After mentioning some biographical points about Ty and Ty Jr., Hardison concluded, "Ty Cobb died in the summer of 1961. It was some time later before I realized I should not have insisted on a complete history and physical examination before relieving his pain. It has taken me 20 years to admit it."

Returning a third time to 1960:

In August, Harry Golden of the *Carolina Israelite* wrote in the *Philadelphia Inquirer* that he recently attended a panel discussion "in which several fairly intelligent men" said "that television is an admirable workshop for writers. This is nothing more than a canard." Golden explained himself. "First of all great playwrights don't emanate from workshops" in the television field that produce scripts. Why should "this multimillion-dollar medium be considered as a primary stage for something better? Why can't it be good in and of itself? It reminds me of the people who say that baseball is a game that makes better citizens. Ty Cobb effectively ruined that argument. All Ty Cobb wanted was to win."

Over the summer, Cobb went to Rome for the Olympics. I found no detailed newspaper reporting on his trip after his departure from New York; the only insights that I found are on postcards. As he wrote to friend Arthur Downey and similarly to Hauck, "just saw track & field events of Olympics at Rome." Alexander wrote, without providing an attribution, that longtime friend Dr. Brown went with him to Rome. Also according to Alexander, Brown was with him for roughly the first 10 days of what sounds like a roughly 18-day trip, before having to return to the United States. Brown conveyed that Cobb had held up well enough in the crowds and the summer heat to be left alone.

Earlier in the year, Cobb told Quinn that "the Olympics are really out of this world. I have seen one, Los Angeles [the 1932 summer games,] and said then no matter where future Olympics are held I would go." He had covered track and field events at the 1932 games for William Randolph Hearst's International News Service. In part one of his four-part series, he said he had not missed an important meet since moving to California (and in 1939, the United Press would state that he had not missed a San Francisco meet in five years). He also wrote in part one, "I saw the intercollegiates at Berkeley, the Olympic finals at Palo Alto and now the marvelous privilege of witnessing the greatest athletes in the world in grim but sportsmanlike action for Olympic laurels is mine [sic]. I don't think I ever became so excited in my life as I did on the day in Palo Alto when Bill Graber, the pole vaulter of University of Southern California, cleared the bar at better than 14 feet 4 inches for a new world's record."

Later in his article, he wrote, "Those pole vaulters, falling from heights of from 13 feet to more than 14[,] strike me as being heroes among heroes because of the terrific punishment they must take in all parts of thei[r] body when they come down to earth like a plummet. Because I was a bit of a runner myself in my younger years, and studied its technique, that sport, too, interests me greatly. I like the sprints, but it is my belief that the real test comes in the 400, 800 and 1500 meters. There it not merely is a matter of luck in the getaway and speed on the paths, but it calls for stamina and heart and lungs and muscles and all that a man can give. Those are races not decided upon the flukish luck of a start – o[r] the lack of it – but upon sheer athletic merit."

In a subsequent article, he compared sprinting and base running. "In these track events, the runners line up and are braced for the getaway. They can go only in one direction – forward. They are tensed at all moments. Alertness is not really vital, except for concentrated attention upon the crack of the pistol." In baseball, by contrast, the runner "must be relaxed in a muscular way. He must be ready to advance or to race back to the bag in safety. His eyes, ears and all of his senses must be alert to the absolute degree."

Returning a fourth time to 1960:

Noted earlier was coverage of his August stay at Stanford Hospital, including his AP and UPI interviews, and his leaving it to see a Reds-Giants game.

In September, he was at Yankee Stadium for an important Yankees' series in the pennant race. Mantle, "aided by a batting tip from the great Ty Cobb about an hour before Saturday's game against Baltimore, smashed a home run in his first time at bat." Before the game, "Cobb huddled with Mantle for some ten minutes in the Yankee clubhouse and again later in the Yankee dugout," the AP also reported. "'Mickey is a great hitter,' said Cobb later, 'and he needs no help from me. But I thought he was doing something fundamentally wrong at the plate last night and it should be pointed out to him. He probably had no idea he was doing it. The trouble with Mickey, as I saw it, was that he was standing too stiff and erect and he had his left elbow down too low. All I said to him was 'why not lean over the plate a little, Mickey, and make them come into the strike zone with the pitch. Then you'll be able to pull the ball.'"

After the chat, Mantle shagged fly balls, while Cobb, talking to reporters, "leaned forward on the bench, shoulders rounded, head bowed, extended fists clenching an invisible bat. 'Like this,' he said, 'with his arms away from his body. Make the pitchers come into the strike zone. Make them cry!'" conveyed Dick Young of the *New York Daily News*. According to the AP, Cobb explained that the last time he had seen the switch-hitting Mantle, while batting lefty he had been holding his right elbow higher and was doing well. Cobb then recalled,

"I used to ask Hugh Jennings (manager of the Detroit Tigers) and Bill Donovan, one of our pitchers, to watch me when I was hitting well. Then, when I wasn't hitting, they knew what I was doing wrong and they'd tell me. You have to have someone tell you when you're doing something wrong because 99 times out of 100 the batter is the last one to know it."

To the side is a dugout image from that series, which ran in the *Sporting News*. Dan Daniel wrote an accompanying story and stated that Cobb "looked very good."

Upon Cobb's death, Mantle would tell the AP, "He used to come see me in the dugout when

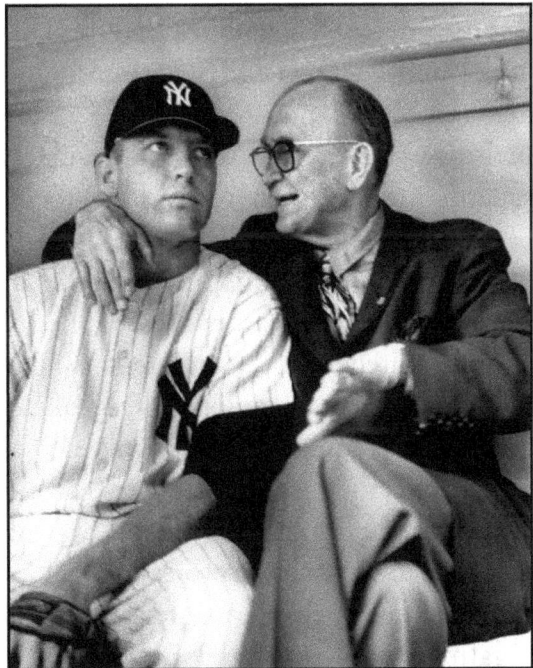

Mickey Mantle and Cobb at Yankee Stadium in September 1960. A candidate for the best dugout visitor photograph in baseball history.

he visited New York and give me some batting tips. He would say, 'Come here, kid, let me show you what you're doing wrong.' He'd tell me I was standing too close or too far away from the plate. He must have helped me two or three times."

At one point in the chat, according to Young, Cobb told Mantle, "I know you didn't do anything to help win that game last night, and they booed you." Then Cobb raised his voice and snapped, "Don't let those — bother you!" Mantle then assured him that they don't. After that, Cobb spoke so low to Mantle for the next five minutes that Young could not hear them. A root of the booing of Mantle, as posited in 1958 by Yankees broadcaster Mel Allen, is that he could

Cobb and Roger Maris

not match the fan favorite that he succeeded in center field, DiMaggio. Plus, as of 1960, he was being compared to newly excelling teammate Roger Maris.

Daniel's *Sporting News* write-up from the New York visit contains some gems. But the quotes from Cobb, as reported first by colleague Williams of the *New York World-Telegram and Sun*, sound more authentic, so that is what appears here. Cobb had most recently seen a game in San Francisco, and he was now praising Orlando Cepeda over teammate Willie Mays. If Cepeda is not Mays' superior now, "he soon will be." (To the AP a few weeks earlier, Cobb had said Mays is "quite a ballplayer, but he'd be better off if he'd get his rear closer to the plate." Through Giants media relations manager Liam Connolly in 2017, Mays said that, like Aaron, he could not recall getting any letters from Cobb.)

About pitchers, Cobb had told Williams, "All of them want to be cuties. Even strong-arm youngsters just breaking in. Instead of making the most of their natural equipment by firing the ball past the hitter, or breaking off a sharp curve, they are obsessed with getting a corner of the plate. They seem to think there's a law against pitching any other way.

"I hate to sound like a professional old[-]timer, but in my day a pitcher with a fast ball, curve, change up and control had it made. It wasn't until the pitcher bega[n] to lose his stuff that he became a cutie. Walter Johnson waited 10-12 years to throw me a curve."

Cobb did concede that conditions are different for pitchers today. "Night ball, along with air travel which has led to more schedule breaks, makes it

tough on the players, dulls their physical edge and saps their stamina. But that's all the more reason for pitchers to take care of their arms. They think nothing of wearing sleeveless sports shirts after a game.

Left handers drive from the park with bare arms swinging in the breeze. Now in my day. . ."

Williams explained to his readers, "Tyrus Raymond suddenly pulled up short" by uttering, "say, I am beginning to sound like an old fuddy duddy, at that."

Joe Williams

Dan Daniel

In 1961:

In January, in a column for John N. Wheeler's syndicate, Ward Morehouse told of having visited Cobb in his hospital room. Cobb "circled the room as he talked, and once sprang up from his chair to show me how quickly he could move." That said, about his future activities, he said, "I know I've got to slow up the tempo." Morehouse wrote that Cobb "doesn't remember being taken by car from Cornelia to Atlanta several weeks ago. He couldn't move at all without severe pain. He has had a series of ailments, ranging from diabetes to bursitis. He was taking cobalt treatments for a while, but those have stopped. He still has to have insulin every day. He said most of the pain has disappeared." Cobb told him, "The only pain I now have is in my tail bone and that's due to a fall I had when I was at Lake Tahoe. I contracted bursitis while hunting goats in Idaho. My low point really was when I came back to this hospital a short time ago." On baseball, he told Morehouse, "Fans are displeased when a star is taken from a minor league to play higher up at a time when he is needed where he is."

Soon after, UPI called Cobb back at his home in Cornelia. "I'm fine – just fine," he said. "Oh, I've been ailing off and on for the past couple of years – and I had a siege of trouble about six weeks ago. But I'm really feeling fine now." As Morehouse had conveyed in part, he was planning to go to Mexico, Phoenix for spring training and San Francisco for opening day. He was also planning to be in Los Angeles as Spink's guest on opening day of its new American League team. Then, back in Cornelia, he had a "plan to build a new house. Does that sound like a schedule of a sick man?" UPI also reported, "Cobb has been undergoing treatment off and on for several years for an injury he picked up more than 50 years ago in his high school playing days."

About his most recent notable medical treatment, he said, "I had a sort of rough go of it there at Emory [University] Hospital in Atlanta about six weeks ago, but they've got some pretty good doctors there – and they've got me back in pretty good shape." He told of taking daily walks and having a full-time nurse, and to UPI also "insisted that he had hired the nurse on doctor's orders to have someone around to see that he took his insulin for his diabetes, and for other routine matters. 'I don't really need a nurse,' Cobb said. 'But my doctor is a pretty insistent fellow and since he's a good guy, I decided to do as he said.'"

Days later, the AP said "he now has practically everything under control, is relaxed and hearty. He boasts that he is now well within the 178 to 188 playing weight of his prime and like[s] nothing better than to take a brisk walk among the mountain scenery. He also takes frequent drives through the countryside and keeps abreast [of] affairs with his television." Finally, he plans to build "a small, comfortable white cedar house. He is living in an apartment now."

In late January, Cobb sent a letter of regret to the organizer of a California dinner in Haney's honor; a line that he suggested be read in his name was, "I come awful close to a love for you a fine fellow, great ability, player and manager, and am proud of your accomplishments." He would see Haney on his final two U.S. trips. The first was in March, to Arizona, for spring training and an annual old-timers' party; his leaving the party early because of a sudden illness "marred" the celebration, wrote sports editor Gianelli of the *Arizona Republic*. "He's a very sick man these days." Upon Cobb's death, he would write, "Ty saw a few practice games, took a few bows, but mostly he stayed in his hotel room with California writer Al Stump, who has just completed what probably is the last biography of baseball's most illustrious player while he still was able to relate his deeds." Also, at the Adams Hotel in Phoenix, Cobb "fainted on the table while he was getting a massage," ex-big leaguer Nagle said upon Cobb's death.

A week after the party, Cobb wrote to Hauck from Scottsdale, "getting plenty of sleep, but the days and early evenings, too many fans and baseball people, drop [in on] me unexpected – and they never know when to leave."

In April to California friend Arthur Downey, he wrote, "I am going to build a small house." That was wishful thinking, because in the same letter he showed how dependent he was on others: "I have a man with me now to do driving, housework, shopping and errands, I do not do anything unless he cannot."

Five days later, Cobb wrote to medical student Rex Teeslink at Tulane University, his soon-to-be end-of-life companion. Leftovers from the letter that Leerhsen did not cite are pretty good. After giving medical detail, Cobb wrote, "By the way[,] your school term is approaching and so don[']t make any plans until we have a talk. Hope you fine progress, get all out of school you can and remember life is short, time is fleeting, the rest of the world will not wait for you." On May 22, Cobb dictated to a nurse a letter that I partially saw. He was responding to one from Teeslink, and the postscript reads, "The help of the nurse is to save my nerves[.]"

As noted earlier, Leigh Montville, for his 1992 *Sports Illustrated* article, spoke to Teeslink. I can add the perspective of an Emory University Hospital female nurse, Betty Jo Parsons; two observations of hers, as noted below, appear in Bak's 1994 and 2005 books. The *Constitution's* Lee Walburn featured her at length in 1962. Walburn began with this quote from her: "Ty Cobb wasn't all mean, just as he wasn't all good. He was, I believe, mostly misunderstood and lonely . . . [sic] and distrustful of others. If he could have made himself believe people liked him just for himself, not for his fame and wealth, he would have been happy."

Cobb with Augusta children at the 1926 rally
in his defense against gambling allegations

Parsons also said, "Ty Cobb was cantankerous, I know, but to see him run his snarled old fingers through the hair of an innocent child, you found it hard to believe." Apparently she was referring to her own children, because at the end of the article, she said, "Most of all I prefer to remember how he would take my children on his knee and entertain them." (Upon Cobb's death, *San Francisco Chronicle* sports editor Rosenbaum told a story with a similar ring: "There was another side to Ty Cobb. One summer day, he had a little-boy caddie who had trouble packing Ty's big golf bag. During the last nine Ty would hit his ball, then pick up the bag AND the boy and carry both to the next shot.")

Parsons said that she got to know him well because many times, "unable to fight off the intense pain with sleep, he would talk to me as I worked. That way I came to know a great deal of what went on in this complex man's mind." Bak quoted or paraphrased this next chunk: "More than anything else, Ty Cobb wanted to be remembered. The shrine planned [although never followed through on] by the state of Georgia would have pleased him although he probably wouldn't have admitted it. He acted as if he didn't care whether the world remembered Ty Cobb for a minute. But he cared. He cared so much."

I can insert another run of Parsons's comments:

She said that a fellow nurse named Walton, who lasted six weeks with Cobb, and she probably were his longest-serving ones. "That's because we didn't pamper him and we let him believe he was getting his way most of the time."

A mood swing story she recalled is: "Once my husband and I went out of town for a few days and I didn't get back on the day Cobb thought we were. When I next saw him he was in a state of fury and said some pretty strong things. I got just as mad. But he stopped suddenly and said quietly, 'I'm sorry. I feared something had happened to you and your family.'"

She also said, "He liked to hear himself talk. Half his waking moments were spent on the telephone talking to his stock broker or some acquaintance from the good old days. He was an old man, but his mind was sharp and alert, although it wandered occasionally. Considering his illness and the amount of alcohol he consumed in his life, his body was still in strong shape." She said one trick he had "was to put his false teeth in a glass of whiskey and many a naive nurse thought it was only denture cleaner." (Cobb told Morehouse that he had been allowed in the hospital to have highballs. In 1960, he had told Quinn about his "new and <u>gleaming</u> set of 'china clippers'[;] no more rabbitt [sic] chewing for me or soups, me [sic] for the red meat and strength it gives.")

A few nights a week, Cobb and Parsons and her husband would go out for dinner. "He always insisted that I have dessert. Then he would have to sample it. It was against the rules for him to order dessert, but I guess he felt this wasn't violating the rules."

Parsons got to see Stump working with Cobb. In his 2005 book, Bak quoted this next part. She said that Stump's 1961 article "was very one-sided. Like so many people he seemed to shut his eyes to anything that reflected good on Ty."

Bak stopped at that point and omitted what came next: "But whether you liked him or not, Stump had guts and patience. He had as much as Cobb himself, who often accused Stump of being nothing but money-hungry."

There is also an October 1961 Stump letter to Hall of Fame Director Keener. Alexander quoted it with respect to Cobb's health, as follows: "I had a very sick and difficult man on my hands." Also, "Ty's family and ex-friends backed clear away from him." Alexander added that Stump "came to feel that he was a combination 'nurse, keeper and whipping boy. . . . at no time was it easy.'" Leerhsen quoted from it for its claim on how well the 1961 book had sold. The Hall of Fame was unable to locate the letter in early 2017. Alexander also cited it in the introduction he wrote for the University of Nebraska 1993 reprint of the book – and which bounced MacArthur's introduction from the original.

Wood's apparent last update of Cobb's condition, prior to his final stay in the hospital, was in May 1961. On that occasion, hospital spokesmen said he was in "satisfactory" condition. UPI reported that he was being tested for "chronic conditions of diabetes and arthritis," with Wood quoted as saying "a man with that condition and his age just needs a checkup now and then."

Only upon Cobb's death would the cancer be reported; the three biographies did not make that point. In its second-day story after Cobb's death, the AP spoke with Wood, who was now disclosing that Cobb had been treated since December 1959 for cancer of the prostate gland that had spread to his pelvic bones and vertebrae. "Wood said the hospital and doctors were not allowed to reveal the diagnosis until Cobb's death. 'In addition,' the physician reported, Cobb 'had diabetes and chronic heart disease. While his general condition had deteriorated during the past two weeks, the end came rather suddenly.'"

In his syndicated column marking Cobb's death, former *Constitution* executive editor McGill presented possibly the best summary of Cobb's recent medical history. "Doctors marveled at him. He would not quit. He had cancer of the prostate and diabetes. His physician would keep him in the hospital for a few weeks and greatly improve his condition. And then, without notice, he would put on his clothes and leave. He would go out and try to find whatever it was he sought from life and then illness would drive him back.

"Last December the twin diseases began to gain. Now and then he would come back in something of a diabetic coma. Not too many weeks before he died he returned to his distressed doctors in really bad condition." McGill's next sentences are a bookend to a squeeze play on one of Leerhsen's most pointed critiques of Stump. In San Diego, as noted earlier, *San Diego Union* sports editor Jack Murphy was quoting future Cobb honorary pallbearer Spink as saying, "A week ago he was lying in that hospital – waiting to die and knowing it was coming – and he had a million dollars' worth of securities beside his bed. On top of the piles of securities was a pistol. I don't know how he got that stuff into the hospital, but he did."

In his syndicated column the same day as Murphy's one, McGill wrote, "He brought with him more than a million dollars worth of negotiable bonds. These he placed on a table by his bed. He then placed a pistol on top of them, undressed and delivered himself into the care of the nurse and the medics.

"'Ty,' said Dr. Hugh Wood, his chief physician, indicating the bonds, 'these things might be knocked on the floor. I'll just put them in the hospital safe.'

"'All right,' said the sick man, fighting to hold onto consciousness in the face of the diabetic trauma, 'maybe that would be best.'"

Here are other angles of note that were touched on upon Cobb's death:

Cobb stalwart Parker of the *New York Mirror* wrote, "No fiercer competitor ever participated in baseball. Ty Cobb was so irascible he couldn't get anyone to room with him [an erroneous claim]. But when life left his cancer-ridden body Monday, after all the fight had gone out of him, and he took up residence in Valhalla [the hall of the worthy dead in Norse mythology], there must have been a mighty scramble among the other immortals for the honor of occupying the niche next to No. 1."

Dan Parker circa 1960

Earlier in his piece, Parker wrote, "Cobb's reputation for taking sadistic delight in spiking opposing players when sliding into a base, his razor-sharp steel cleats carried high, followed him long after he left the diamond and he was angered whenever the matter was brought up by a fan or writer, not aware that this was a worse sore spot with him than any of those he caused with his wicked spurs." Parker then garbled what Cobb had said about the number of players who he had intentionally spiked over the years – in a way that would have shocked Cobb – by saying Frank Baker was the only such player.

In a different article, Tom Yawkey, the nephew of former Tiger owner William "Bill" Yawkey, declared, "Much of my early interest in baseball was aroused by meeting and knowing Ty at a very young age and there is no doubt in my mind that he was the greatest all-around ball player of all time." Tom owned the Red Sox from 1933 to 1977. In his book, Leerhsen related how thrilled Tom was to see Cobb run the bases and that that excited him more than Ruth's home runs. Other details worth adding are that Tom recalled being "a good friend and hunting companion" of his. In covering Cobb's death, the *Boston Globe* printed a picture of Tom and him from a 1927 hunt in Wyoming. Tom had accompanied Cobb, Speaker and Garland Buckeye on it.

Tom also told the *Globe* that in his youth, Cobb "would introduce me to the new players on the Tigers and to the visiting stars. Even if he hadn't been a superstar, Ty still would have been my idol because of these kindnesses. He would come out to my uncle's house for dinner and he'd treat me like an equal."

Days after Cobb's funeral, H. I. Phillips wrote in a syndicated column, "They say an old-timer, lingering at the grave of Ty Cobb long after most mourners had left, explained, 'I still think he may get up and tie the score.'"

A writer for the *Springfield Union* in Massachusetts observed, "Cobb outlived the other superstars of his time – Wagner, Speaker, Lajoie, Johnson, Mathewson and Ruth, though the latter [Ruth] reached the heights somewhat later on – to become one of the last of baseball's 'old guard.'"

Veteran sportswriter Biederman of the *Pittsburgh Press* said that Cobb, as a result of his long friendship with George M. Weiss, had written the then-Yankee general manager the following just before the 1960 World Series:

"I've noted [sic] the Pirates will hit the cripple anytime, whether men are on base or not. And, if the first pitch is a strike, they will swing, too." The cripple is a pitch on which a batter has an edge over the pitcher in the count and thus may be inclined to not swing at the next one. In that World Series, Bill Mazeroski hit the series-winning home run on a one ball, no strike count, showing "Ty was on the right track."

A week after Cobb's death, Elderkin of the *Christian Science Monitor* mentioned the upcoming book with Stump. Haney, who had been sent advance proofs by Cobb, "rates it must reading," Elderkin wrote.

A month after his death, the U.S. House of Representatives was considering legislation that would increase the penalties for persons who peddle dirty books and photographs that end up in the hands of children. One problem with such legislation, said Francis E. Walter (D-Pa.), chairman of a subcommittee looking into the matter, is that judges cannot be forced to impose stricter penalties. Beyond that, courts had yet to reach a consensus on what constitutes obscenity.

"Walter said the controversial book 'Lady Chatterl[e]y's Lover' was a good example," UPI reported. "The Postoffice [sic] banned it from the mails but the courts upset the ruling."

"'I read it myself,' Walter told a congressional hearing, 'and if it isn't obscene, I'm Ty Cobb.'"

In October in the *New York Herald Tribune*, longtime reviewer John K. Hutchens noted a slew of factual errors in Cobb's new book with Stump that show that "in his last innings his [Cobb's] memory was slipping." After reciting some errors, he wrote, "But as all Hot Stove League members are aware, that is one of the joys of baseball literature: the filing of exceptions [legalistic argumentation], especially on the part of graybeards."

In January 1962, veteran cartoonist-baseball reporter Clem Boddington wrote an article on Cobb for *Sir!* magazine. Hornbaker cited a 1960 *Sporting News* article that named Boddington as the forthcoming co-author of Cobb's Doubleday book. Quoted from earlier was a Cobb letter previewing their first get-together. Leerhsen erroneously wrote that that meeting was with Stump.

Boddington's article is underwhelming, considering his access to Cobb and having likely met him at least as far back as the 1920s. The most interesting aspect of the article to me was his negative characterizations. Perhaps he was jaded if his experience with Cobb in 1960 went that badly. Early on in his piece, he called Cobb "a man of violent temper, whom many abhorred as a cad." Soon after, he called Cobb a "cantankerous perfectionist." Much later, he referred to Cobb's "flinty but commanding personality and razor-sharp mind and reflexes" and seemingly paraphrased Dan Daniel's Cobb obituary in the *New York World-Telegram and Sun*, as follows in the next sentence only: Cobb, Boddington wrote, "possessed a memory like an elephant and never forgave a real or fancied wrong." Boddington also observed Cobb as "always with a chip on his shoulder and full of self-importance."

ex-big leaguers Mickey
Cochrane and Ray Schalk
right after the funeral

Near the end of his article, he wrote, "Only three members of the baseball world were among the mourners when baseball's legendary figure was laid to rest." Stump had written in his recent article, "From all of major-league baseball, three men, and three men only [meaning former players], attended his funeral." Leerhsen said Stump's thought was misleading: "In fact, there *were* very few baseball people there – just four [the fourth was Hall of Fame Director Keener; Boddington erroneously omitted Rucker from his list] – but that was because Charlie Cobb and her children had announced that it was a private service meant only for family and close friends."

Stump's article in 1961 had outraged Cobb supporters exponentially more. More in the footnote-to-history category along with Boddington's article was a brush fire that resulted after a 1963 book was published by syndicated columnist Quentin Reynolds. Referring back to the *Sport* magazine dinner that he had attended in 1950, Reynolds wrote, "When the affair was over, he [Cobb] and several dozen other present and former players, managers, team owners, and writers retired to Toots Shor's saloon on West Fifty-first Street. Every year that was the night that Toots never closed, and anyone who tried to pick up a check would get his wrist broken.

"It was Joe DiMaggio who introduced me to Cobb, and I'll admit that for some moments I just stared at him in awe. Cobb was in a good mood and was even gracious enough to say that he had read some of my books. I replied by telling him how he had inspired me to start writing short stories. I reminded him of the day in Philadelphia when he dropped the fly ball [in a game Reynolds had attended]. It was the wrong thing to do.

"'You lousy bastard,' he spat at me, 'I never dropped a fly ball in my life!'"

"Toots and DiMaggio moved quickly between us. They knew Cobb.

"I saw him around a few times after that, and found him to be a weird, filthy-mouthed, tight-fisted drunk. Ball players of his era, I discovered, respected him as a player, but they despised him as a cruel and humorless man. When he died in 1961 it was reported that he left an estate of twelve million dollars. Not publicized [actually with far different facts the following was, by the *San Diego Union* and columnist McGill,] was the fact that the nurse who found him dead in his hospital bed found a million dollars' worth of negotiable securities and a Luger pistol in his bed. He was trying his best to take it with him. While baseball people are notoriously sentimental and loyal, only three of them attended his funeral."

Also in his book, Reynolds wrote that drafting a future article in response to the game in which Cobb dropped the ball, near the end of Cobb's career, "started me on a career of sorts as a short-story writer." He ended with, "I can never write Cobb off. He dropped that ball and gave me a real break."

In 1961, the *Richmond Times-Dispatch* was among several newspapers that ran parts of the Cobb-Stump book as a serial. In 1963, Chauncey Durden was still its sports editor when it reprinted nearly all of the above from Reynolds. According to Durden, Reynolds had done a "real hatchet job on Cobb's memory." In addition, he called Reynolds's book "a *tour de force* in name-dropping." Durden observed, "What happened at Shor's that night may have happened just as Reynolds described it. We were at the dinner which preceded Reynolds's meeting with Cobb. At that dinner we found Cobb, even then suffering from cancer, diabetes, a chronic heart ailment and a severe arthritic condition, gracious, charming and sober." Actually, the notion that Cobb was ill or in pain as of 1950, beyond the joint condition bursitis, seems overstated.

Durden also wrote, "Cobb may have been guilty of many things, but on his testimony Reynolds would be a poor witness about Cobb's character." Also, Durden pointed out that Reynolds wrote in his book that the game took place in 1932; Cobb's last game had been in 1928. (Reynolds had forgotten that five years had elapsed between his article in 1933 and the end of Cobb's career. The article, "Legs Last Just So Long," appeared in *Collier's*.) In addition, Durden wrote, Reynolds had wrongly written in his book that at the time of the game in 1928, his Philadelphia Athletics team was in last place; in reality, it had been in second place. Durden also challenged the accuracy of Reynolds's claim that he had seen Cobb on a few occasions after 1950.

Another Durden criticism of the Reynolds book referred to a landmark Supreme Court libel decision in 1955 in which Reynolds won $175,000, about $1.5 million today, against popular columnist Pegler. Durden claimed that the lawyer who won that case for Reynolds, Louis Nizer, "would tear to shreds Reynolds' testimony against Cobb."

Another pointed post-mortem was by Kaese of the *Globe* in 1970. He wrote,

"By his own admission, the fiery Cobb armed himself with a revolver (off the field) [sic], because he was infuriating teammates, rival players and fans with his rambunctious actions, and feared for his life."

To end on a happier note, a story worth carrying over from 1960 is a tribute on the bright side of his growing old. Early that year, then-*Globe* columnist Red Smith began a column as follows:

Yogi Berra and Casey Stengel

"When somebody asked Yogi Berra how he thought Ty Cobb would do against today's pitchers in the American League, Yogi said Cobb would be lucky if he hit .250. It seemed impossible that he could be serious; after all, Cobb's lifetime average for 24 major league seasons was .367.

"'Yeah,' Mr. Berra said, 'but he must be 70 years old.'"

One of Berra's most famous quotes is "I never said most of the things I said." That could be said to be true in this instance. That is because former big-leaguer Lefty O'Doul, in the 1966 book *The Glory of Their Times*, recalled having uttered the story at a dinner around 1960. O'Doul is the more credible originator of the quote, because he knew Cobb so much better. Back in 1954, sports editor Murphy of the *San Diego Union* had reported, and I was able to confirm, that a similar version had been told in 1953 by then-veteran Pacific Coast League manager O'Doul. Murphy referred to the 1953 version as an "oft-told tale, but worth repeating."

Harry Heilmann and Cobb in 1941

But O'Doul's version is not necessarily the earliest. Povich of the *Washington Post*, in 1951, attributed the quip to the recently deceased Harry Heilmann, a former teammate and posthumous Hall of Fame inductee who was born in San Francisco.

"The late Harry Heilmann had a stock answer when asked what he thought

Ty Cobb might hit against present-day pitching. 'Oh, about .320,' Heilmann would say. 'Is that all?' [w]ould be the usual rejoinder. 'Well,' Heilmann would add, '.320 is pretty good for a man of his age. Remember, Cobb is in his sixties.'"

In 1952, book publisher-humor columnist Bennett Cerf would write, "Somebody asked Vernon 'Lefty' Gomez, onetime pitching star of the Yankees, and a natural wit, what he thought Ty Cobb would bat against the kind of flinging prevalent in the major leagues today. 'Lefty' (also known as 'El Goofo') [sic] pondered momentarily, then hazarded, 'I'd say about .320.' 'That's low?' asked the interrogator in surprise. 'Yep,' grinned Gomez. 'Ya gotta remember Cobb's now over sixty years old!'"

An earlier boast was made in 1937. That year, the NEA reported, "Oscar Vitt believes that Ty Cobb would have hit .500 had he got a whack at the lively ball." Then, in 1942, in a widely printed column, Hugh Fullerton, Jr., of the AP presumably misquoted Vitt as saying, "If Ty Cobb were playing today, he would steal 150 bases a season." In 1940, Salsinger quoted New York writer Dan Daniel to that effect. The earliest proximate version of the quip that I found is from Salsinger, who wrote in 1939, "Ty Cobb, although he is more than 50 years old, could return to base ball today and hit better than .500, just by popping fly balls between the infielders and outfielders."

Years after Cobb's death, a candidate for the most overlooked great source of colorful yet seemingly reliable Cobb detail is Corcoran's 1965 memoirs. Some references to it appeared earlier. Another I can add here is, "Ty Cobb is the only millionaire I ever met who wore a rusty paper clip for a tie clasp until I replaced it." The clip that Corcoran gave Cobb was one of thousands that the Electric Boat Co., reorganized as the General Dynamics Corp., produced to mark its launch of the first nuclear-powered submarine, the USS Nautilus, in 1954. Corcoran gave it to him on a Sunday visit by Cobb to his home in Mamaroneck, N.Y. "He thanked me, and put the souvenir clip in his pocket. A couple of months later, I had a letter from Ty asking if I had another one of those tie clasps. He had given his away to a friend who had admired it."

To get to Corcoran's home, Cobb wanted to take a train, but Corcoran insisted on sending a car to take him instead. "This was an extravagance and Cobb hated extravagance, but I wouldn't listen to his arguments. It was simpler to do it my way." On another occasion, Cobb invited Corcoran to the New York Stock Exchange, to watch it in action. Once inside, the executive of the exchange invited them into his office. While in the office, Cobb asked the executive if he knew the daily high of Coca-Cola's stock on March 18 of that year. After the executive provided the answer, Cobb, on his feet, "slapped the desk angrily."

Cobb said the brokerage firm from which he bought 300 shares that day had cheated him out of 1/8 of a point. After stating that, Cobb "held up his confirmation slip" and "was pounding furiously on the desk, his voice bouncing off the walls. The New York Stock Exchange representative pushed himself back and raised his hands in the time-honored posture of peace lovers the world over." The executive assured Cobb that he would look into it. "But old Ty was breathing fire now. 'I want action right now!' he snarled."

Corcoran added, "Like an old Detroit Tiger stalking his prey, Cobb started around the desk after the Exchange official who was circling to his right as adroitly as [mid-20th century featherweight boxer] Willie Pep[,who was known for his elusiveness]. They had made a complete circuit of the mahogany with Ty shouting and pounding when a couple of guards materialized and led us firmly and courteously out of the building. I made a mental note right then: Never go visiting with Ty Cobb without telephoning ahead to make sure you have a reservation."

Corcoran ended his Cobb chapter by stating, "Perhaps the oddest facet in his many-sided character was the religious fervor which gripped Cobb in his twilight years. While he was having dinner with me and several others in Lawton Carver's restaurant in 1960 [presumably Lawton Carver's Cafe, a successor to the restaurant that Carver sold in 1957], an argument broke out between Carver and me over some trivial issue. Carver let go a verbal blast that was beautifully embroidered with profanity. This brought a swift rebuke from Cobb, who launched into a

Lawton
Carver
circa 1952

lengthy lecture, demanding to know if Carver believed in God and if he prayed regularly." (In a 1959 letter to former Detroit-turned-hockey trainer Tommy Daly, Cobb asked, in light of the death of a mutual friend, likely Dan Howley, "if you <u>do pray</u>??" Cobb added, "I pray a lot and Dan is in my prayers.")

A second-hand epilogue that Corcoran related occurred days later. Through a friend, Cobb invited Carver to visit his room at the Roosevelt Hotel. Carver did and conveyed that the room "was littered with medical supplies of one kind or another. Cobb, he said, looked tired and old, his eyes ravaged with pain of sleepless nights." At one point, Cobb closed the blinds and, although Carver knows religious text by heart, Cobb "delivered a long and blunt sermon, his arms folded in front of him across a book" like a preacher. The sermon ended with his saying that Carver should quit fighting with people and using blasphemous words. With that, Cobb handed Carver the book *We Believe in Prayer*, "which was a collection of thumbnail morality essays by famous people." He had autographed the flyleaf as follows: "To Lawton from Ty Cobb."

13. *And By the Way*

Alexander's book is silent on whether Stump had a relationship with Cobb prior to working on his 1961 book. So is Hornbaker's; it merely noted one Stump-Cobb overlap prior to 1960: an error that Stump made about Cobb in a 1946 article. Leerhsen wrote, "Cobb probably first heard the name Al Stump in late 1959 or very early 1960." Also, "Cobb didn't have the energy to vet Stump's credentials." Finally, he cast Cobb as being easily duped: Stump "was charming, handsome, and smooth."

One of the best-known fraternal organizations in the United States of America is the Elks. The Elks, like many large membership groups, communicates with its members via a magazine. Its magazine, founded in 1922, invites outside submissions to fill some of its pages. Being geared toward men, sports is one of its favorite subjects. If you were to stumble across the magazine in 1955, and the month of August in particular, you would find some relatively ho-hum pieces. There are five bylined articles, in chronological order, as follows: "Ontario," "In the Shadow of the Babe," "For Elks Who Travel," "Rod and Gun" and, fittingly, "In the Doghouse."

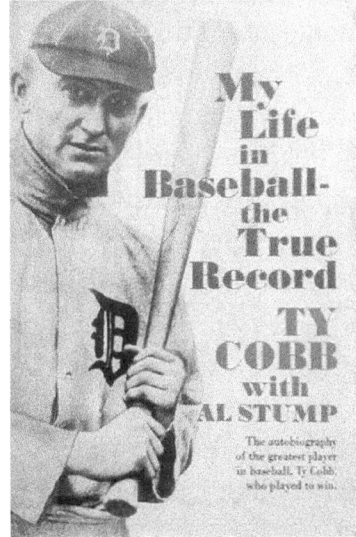

"In the Shadow of the Babe" might sound as if it could be related to Ruth. If so, and the answer was indeed yes, the byline credit for it was to Stump. In his article, Stump did a lot of current baseball name-dropping, but a stretch of it reads as if somebody from days of yore may have been pulling the strings. In paragraph number seven, Stump wrote, "As no previous season has better shown, the home run is not the spicing on America's sport cake. It has become the whole blinking pastry."

In paragraph ten is the first direct quote in the entire article. Rather than quoting anyone from present-day baseball, Stump decided to cite Tyrus Raymond Cobb, as follows:

"It's no wonder that Ty Cobb recently exploded to this writer, 'They used to say pitching was 75 percent of the game. Well, I'd call it 25 per cent! Baseball's lost all its science and gone fence-ball crazy!'"

Next paragraph: "Cobb points to one typical three-day, 33-game week-end round of contests in the two big leagues. Seventy-seven homers, or 12.6 per cent of all hits garnered, decided 72 per cent of the games. One hundred seventy-nine pitchers – an average of one every 3.4 innings – trudged off and on the mounds. Thunder, thunder, everywhere, and not a storm cellar in sight."

Next paragraph: "Still, if there are those who mourn the passing of the clever game, the drag-bunt, hit-and-run, multiple-steal and sacrifice, the example of the Red Sox's Norm Zauchin illustrates why these folk are far in the minority. At this time a year ago, Zauchin was unknown outside of Louisville, Ky., where he played a minor-league first base. But, and overnight, three 400-footers in one game on May 27 shot Zauchin into the headlines. Not even Ted Williams ever did better and Williams never has driven home ten runs in nine innings. At the season's turn, his batting average was a weak .268. But Zauchin was pressing Mickey Mantle of the Yankees for the American League homer lead, with 17, and the Boston fans were delirious."

Guess who is back in the next stanza: "Many another instance (far too many, growl Ty Cobb School of Thought members) of sub-par batsmen becoming the hero of millions because of home run phobia could be cited. Ralph Kiner had a modest lifetime average of .281 at Pittsburgh. Yet he earned from $65,000 to $90,000 a season [an average of about $700,000 today] for leading the NL homer derby seven times. Kiner it was who coined the too-truism that, 'Singles hitters drive Model-T's, home run hitters drive big cars.' If the big hits are delivered in Kinerian numbers – 351 was his total as of this season's start – the car must contain gold doorknobs, TV and a stock market ticker."

Pirates part-owner Crosby and Kiner

Stump then quotes Kiner on who could break Ruth's mark of 60 homers in a season. Kiner responds by naming Eddie Mathews, Duke Snider and Ted Kluszewski. When Stump wonders why he left out Willie Mays, Kiner responds in a Cobb-sounding way: "Mays is too good a singles and doubles hitter to qualify."

The article then takes an extended non-Cobb turn in discussing how Ruth managed to set the record in 1927 and how some later players approached it, including with the help of outfield fences moved in. On cue at that latter point, you know who is back.

"'It makes me sick,' Ty Cobb rises again to object. 'They can't beat the Babe fair, so these bums are trying to do it foul.'" Stump then states, "Shrinking the arena merely is one dodge now practiced. Last season Commissioner Ford Frick reprimanded Durocher and ordered him to stop giving $100 bonuses [about $900 today] to his Giants sluggers for each homer they delivered. Cleveland's Al Rosen – 43 homers in 1953 – was caught with nails in his bat [in 1954]. Rosen blandly explained that they were there to keep it from chipping."

from left to right in 1954: Mickey Vernon, Cobb and Al Rosen

Soon after, Stump focuses the narrative on paragraph-long comments provided by Kluszewski, then Rosen, Snider, Mays and Mathews, on the possibility of their breaking Ruth's record.

Immediately after that, Stump writes, "If the candidates appear none too eager to name themselves as the somebody, maybe it's because they privately agree with Ty Cobb. 'This superman,' Cobb adds, 'also will be playing in parks so small he can spit over the fence – never forget that. And what then? Will he really have broken Babe's record? Not in my book. It'll be a phony title and the public will know it.'" The article ended after two subsequent paragraphs.

The Elks being a successful organization, its magazine was still around in September 1960 when it printed the following four bylined pieces: "Ty Cobb, 1960," "Rod and Gun," "The Best Quarterback I Ever Saw" and "Elks Home Workshop."

If you guessed that the author credited for "Ty Cobb, 1960" is Stump, you are right. It begins, "OUT WEST, when they barbecue a steer and invite a thousand fans to a jamboree kicking off the big-league season, it takes bad news, indeed, to dampen the festive feeling. But last April a collective sigh of disappointment arose in San Francisco when the word was passed: Ty Cobb, the guest of honor, would not appear. 'Ty's been ill, you know – just had an operation,' Dizzy Dean told the crowd.

"But then a shout went up outside and a long, black limousine pulled [up] under the hotel marquee and – very slowly – out climbed the 73-year-old Georgia Peach.

"He paused for a moment in the hot sun, getting his bearings, and a bystander moved forward, to render help. Cobb waved him away.

"Thirty-two years after his last ball game, Tyrus Raymond Cobb hasn't changed a whit – he still loves the limelight as much as ever, yet he dwells in it only upon the terms he dictates."

Stump then recalls Cobb as a law unto himself through an "embattled career" in which he set the all-time marks for games played, hits, runs, stolen bases, batting championships and lifetime average. Such feats, he adds, likely explain why Cobb is deemed the "all-time king of the diamond" in more than 90 percent of the polls on the subject.

The article then goes deeper into Cobb's statistical feats for a few paragraphs. Stump perks it up after that by quoting journalist-screenplay writer Gene Fowler, who appeared earlier for lumping Cobb among the worst car drivers.

One day, Cobb was driving Fowler and others past an airport when an arriving plane dipped directly in front of them, just above the pavement. Cobb was heading straight at the plane while the passengers were screaming for him to stop. Cobb, though, felt he had the right-of-way. According to Fowler, "The plane roared past, missing us by inches. All the time, Ty never stopped talking. About his batting average – how he could improve it." A Cobb golfing-airplane story appeared much earlier, as told by sports editor Rosenbaum of the *San Francisco Chronicle* upon Cobb's death.

Then Stump recalls some of Cobb's playing highlights that included confrontations with opposing players. He moves on to some of Cobb's routine when staying in his "baronial Atherton, California home." For example, Cobb wakes up at 8 a.m. and, for breakfast, usually has scrambled eggs with garlic. "Despite physical disabilities, he continues to drive himself where he wants to get, in a long, black limousine fitted out with special push-buttons." Stump then mentions one of Cobb's car accidents that I noted earlier.

Stump continues by praising Cobb's hearing as excellent and that from the stands, his eyes are good enough to recognize any current outfielder according to his running style. But, he adds, Cobb has diabetes and often startles visitors by having to stop a conversation in order to "jab himself with an insulin needle." Cobb's health had been sturdy until the most recent spring, when he underwent surgery for athletic injuries stemming from his youth and that plagued him during his entire big-league career. (If referring to Cobb's spine, as distinct from his back, the only reports I found of such an injury referred to it as having occurred during his playing career.) "Few people know that Cobb made all those records while wearing a special pelvic supporter." In addition, Stump makes this likely reference to Cobb's prostate cancer: During the operation, "various enlarged veins of the groin area were surgically treated. A long rest was prescribed.

"Ty snorted in disdain, and within a month of the operation, his doctors were wringing their hands." That is because when spring training opened, he drove around 1,000 miles from Atherton to Arizona to be at the camps of the San Francisco Giants, the Red Sox and the Indians.

Stump then describes how active Cobb was during that trip, and notes how he was keeping busy with his philanthropic endeavors. He also notes that Cobb succeeded in his investments long before his Coca-Cola one, in "cotton shares, General Motors, Amco [a car made by American Motors Inc.] and other [stock] issues which prospered greatly."

On Cobb as skimping on money, Stump quotes O'Doul as saying, "Ty tight? Why, he's the biggest check-grabber I know. Ty is a generous, sentimental, wonderful guy beneath his tough exterior."

(Joe Judge, in his 1947 recollection at the University Club in Washington, D.C., had given the following reason for Cobb's reaching out to him at the recent old-timers' day at Yankee Stadium: "I believe Cobb realized there were a lot of fellows among us who had little use for him. I think Ty was a little

Cobb with fellow lefty golfer Lefty O'Doul at a San Francisco tournament in 1932

lonely. Cobb was picking up all the checks and tipping handsomely. In fact, in one spot where we ate he tipped a waiter $1,000 [about $11,000 today] but that was a mistake." A member of their party noticed the error and Cobb lowered the tip to $10, about $110 today. Judge added that former Cobb teammate Al Simmons could not understand Cobb's check-grabbing and recalled "when we [Simmons and Cobb in 1927 and possibly 1928] were rooming together and you threatened to fight me over a $1 laundry bill."

Right after old-timers' day, Judge had told Morris Siegel of the *Washington Post* that at a dinner where Cobb treated everyone, "he kept saying, 'No one but old Ty will pay for this because it's so great seeing all of you guys again.'" Judge noted the contrast to an earlier Cobb, "who was a pinch-penny if one ever lived." Judge also told Siegel that in making up with him, Cobb "put his arm around me and there were tears in his eyes when he said, 'Joe, you and the rest of the gang hated my guts when we were playing, but let's forget it now. Just being with the gang again has done something to me I can't describe.'")

Alvin J. "Al" Stump

Stump also turns to stories from Cobb's youth, especially on how his desire for a baseball career led to friction with his father. He has Cobb telling how he adjusted to the big leagues, including how, being a lefty batter, he improved against lefty pitchers. Stump describes the essence of his stance: "Instead of planting his feet well apart, flat and firm, Cobb stood with his feet close together, and up on his toes. He crouched over. His hands held the bat handle in a sliding grip, enabling him to shift his hold instantly with any pitch."

The next topic is Cobb's disdain for the modern-day stress on home runs, followed by Stump's description of Cobb's home in California. Stump states that Cobb still frequently travels to his Nevada home. Stump then names some of the visitors to Cobb's California home, including supposedly DiMaggio and Ted Williams, and a portrait artist who abandoned making the portrait because, according to Stump, "Cobb hopped around so much."

During the Williams visit to Cobb's home in Atherton, Cobb upbraided him "for allowing his waistline to expand and not hitting to all fields. But there is a deep friendship between them. Williams, in turn, needled Cobb during the visit," including about his spiking of Baker. At one point, possibly during that visit, the phone rang, "and it was a New York publisher calling to discuss 'The Ty Cobb Story,' a forthcoming book covering the Georgia Peach's life."

Stump's above writing, to the effect that Williams and Cobb had a deep friendship, would be erroneously contradicted by none other than Stump in his 1994 book. In it, as noted earlier, he would claim they had a falling out.

Stump continues by describing Cobb's recent visit to Candlestick Park to see the Giants and how Cobb quickly figured out the signals that Giant coaches were giving to their baserunners. Then he discusses a visit by Jackie Jensen to Cobb's home and gives detail about some of Cobb's contract negotiations as a player. Cobb's salary is the next topic, followed by some of his base-running highlights, such as becoming the all-time stolen base leader. Then he quotes Dizzy Dean on Cobb's drive to succeed. After noting Cobb's praise of some modern-day players, Alvin Dark, Phil Rizzuto, Eddie Stanky and Nellie Fox, for being "quick-and-mean" old-fashioned type players, he prints a recollection from Grantland Rice.

The piece ended with a visit back in March by a 9-year-old boy who was just beginning to play Little League ball. Cobb spoke with him for about an hour. Afterward, the father asked the son what Cobb had told him.

"'He said,' the lad answered, 'never to give in to anything.'"

With that the article closed.

As a fitting end to this section, consider the following:

Alexander omitted a line that is in Maines's 1961 letter that referred to what Cobb thought of Stump. Cobb told Maines that he had selected Stump "because Al writes what I want written, and does not pad nor add something just to make up a story." Maines continued, "Ty explained that this would be *his* story and would be for the kids, too. He once said he wished I would contact General Motors and have them get out copies for the children of America to read."

Postscript (or Introduction)

Hall of Famer Tyrus Raymond "Ty" Cobb has been the main focus of about a dozen books or scholarly articles that contain significant detail or insightful analysis touching on his racism. Among them are some heavily researched books, two of which were published in 2015 at about the same time; the most important prior one was in 1984. One of the 2015 biographies, Charles Leerhsen's Simon & Schuster one, so drastically reassessed Cobb's racism, by going back to square zero (if not racially favorable territory), that Leerhsen was inviting a challenge.

While several reviewers cited flaws of logic in Leerhsen's strong pro-Cobb spin, no one was able to refute him. Apparently the only other such effort prior to mine is Steven Tripp's 2016 Rowman & Littlefield self-described "social and cultural history" of Cobb. Tripp chipped away, but mainly at the margins.

I can claim special qualification to have weighed in on Cobb. I am the horse's mouth on Adrian "Cap" Anson, the Hall of Famer most often blamed for the drawing and instituting of organized baseball's "color line." Its implementation helped eliminate blacks from and then keep them out of the professional levels of the sport, with few exceptions, between the late 19th century and 1946.

Without having read through Leerhsen's book for its racism analysis, I wrote a long racism analysis essay in June 2016. In it, I went beyond the racism content in my 2006 Anson biography on claims that Anson played a major role in both drawing and instituting the color line. My organizing theme was focusing on the line between fact and speculation. So, I am on record as pulling no punches in pointing out the flawed use of facts and argumentation on someone with notoriety, loosely speaking, in the ballpark of Cobb.

I am by nature more inclined to stress research over analysis. My four 19th-century books were based on having read through the vast majority of surviving relevant newspapers, in original form or microfilm. I personally did as much of the research as possible, especially with the benefit of living near the Library of Congress. To fill gaps, I liberally borrowed microfilm on interlibrary loan and visited libraries in other states, or found people to do lookups for me. In a few cases, I persuaded the Library of Congress to buy some runs of microfilm, most notably the *Pittsburgh Chronicle Telegraph*.

The nation's preeminent library, it has by far the largest collection of U.S. newspapers. That said, you will rarely find the following point being made about the baseball book genre: Anyone without easy access to the Library of Congress is at a giant disadvantage in doing definitive research on sweeps of baseball history. Often overlooked, beyond having access to perform research, is having access to double-check one's research.

The new-fangled alternative in researching a book is to primarily do so using full-text databases. An unheralded limitation is that they are unwieldy when search terms cannot be logically narrowed, if one would like to fully account for writing on a particular subject. Also, as I already knew from researching my earlier books, the databases can be faulty for their optical character recognition or, at least in earlier 19th-century runs I examined, lacking entire pages. That said, such databases offer an excellent shortcut. Combined with the Library of Congress's newspaper and book holdings, I was able to accumulate an overwhelming majority of what is in this book in about six months.

My spark was an error in a July 2016 online article in *Rolling Stone* and, to a lesser degree, that I then noticed in 2013 in the *New York Times*. The subject in both was baseball players who had reportedly been members of the Ku Klux Klan. *Rolling Stone*, recently disgraced for its false University of Virginia rape story that it stood by for so long, did correct its article by removing Cobb as an alleged member of the Klan. When I shared that fact with a University of Virginia professor, he expressed surprise at *Rolling Stone*'s having actually made a correction.

But it did not remove Anson and replace him with Hornsby despite my checking with the one noteworthy book or article writer who has apparently claimed that Anson was a Klansman. *Rolling Stone* did not respond to my updated refutations. I can only speculate how it differentiated between a Cobb correction request and an Anson one.

The professor who made the error on Anson, Tony Collins, is based in Great Britain. After I contacted him, Collins confirmed my suspicion that his source was an online article from 2008 quoting 91-year-old Marvin Miller, a former director of the Major League Baseball Players Association. Miller had singled out Hall of Famers Tris Speaker and Anson as having been reported Klan members. I told *Rolling Stone* that Miller misspoke and should have said Speaker and Hornsby. (It is also possible that Miller was misquoted.)

In July 2016, I checked with 2016 author Tripp, to see if he might want to write an article about Cobb's racism to complement one that I could write about Anson. Tripp declined, saying that he was onto his next subject. That was my last contact with a Cobb author prior to this book's publication.

Despite my criticism of Leerhsen, we presented our disliked subjects in the context of their times, in a way that may be considered overly sympathetic – apologetic – to them. It is good that there are places in the literary world where one can find an offset for the far more frequent excesses, in racial argumentation, on the negative side of Cobb and Anson. Such excesses are often overlooked by fellow historians or popular writers because they have a soft spot for prose that exudes a moral repugnance toward racism, regardless of whether an author exuding such repugnance is making solid arguments. Also, the safe thing to do is to go with the flow.

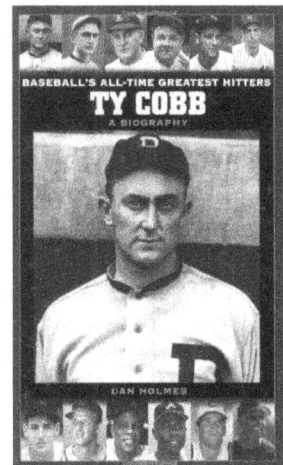

Leerhsen challenged convention by softening the tone of at least one prior biographer, 2004 one Dan Holmes, with regard to Cobb's fights. Leerhsen wrote, "Still, the anecdotal evidence – references in newspapers and popular literature – suggest that fisticuffs were once an everyday way to settle disputes or assert one's alpha male status."

Holmes had written, "Indeed, Cobb owns blame for being a short-tempered, high-strung, impulsive man, but he also was a man of his era. In Cobb's time, baseball was played by tough men who were willing to scrap, claw, and fight to succeed. Cobb stood out in that era for his tremendous ability and success, as well as for the veracity of his feuds and on-field play. But he was by no means the only player to be involved in such episodes."

I challenged convention for Anson by adding context to Anson's use of racial slurs in his 1900 ghostwritten autobiography. Quoting Kevern Verney's 2003 *African Americans and US Popular Culture*, I wrote, "In the early years of the twentieth century[,] books in the top ten best-seller list routinely referred to African Americans as 'niggers,' 'darkies' or 'jigaboos.'" To add context to Anson's book for its criticism of the work habits of the Chicago team's longtime mascot, Clarence Duval, I quoted Joe Feagin and Hernàn Vera's book *White Racism: The Basics*, as follows: "Even the famous American work ethic is sometimes overlaid with racialized images; whites tend to have an almost obsessive concern about the work ethic of black Americans."

14. *Cobb, Finally Finished Off*

The reader may be surprised that just three years after twin lengthy biographies of Cobb, someone could come along and write a far-longer book and so much quicker, with a focus on just what was missed or muffed. The ease with which I was able to do this, besides the proliferation of newspaper databases and my Washington, D.C., location, is due to the imbalance in prior books in presenting mainly the years of his playing career.

I also happen to like assimilating column inches soaked up by the game's greatest print media figures. Cobb is the third such one that I am either the definitive biographer of or, in Cobb's case, merely his post-career expert (32+ years of his life).

My prior expertise was on the bluff-and-gruff Anson and happy-go-lucky and witty Mike "King" Kelly. Anson, I argued in my 2006 *Cap Anson 4: Bigger Than Babe Ruth: Captain Anson of Chicago*, drew the most interesting print coverage in the sport over a long playing and post-career. He played from 1871 to 1897, with the coverage being great over the last half of his playing career and moderately interesting after that. Kelly, I also argued in that book, drew the most interesting print coverage over a short span, when Chicago sold him to Boston in 1887 for a then-record $10,000, about $250,000 in today's dollars. He played from 1878 to 1893, but his 1894 minor league season right before his death, done as mostly a publicity stunt, was extraordinary too.

In comparing Ruth and Anson, I wrote that Ruth "drew a huge amount of coverage in print" and that Anson "attracted far wittier coverage." I did not explicitly account for Cobb in my 2006 book and now can do so. In his playing career, Cobb was by far the least quotable of the four, although he had a chance to show leadership personality as his team's player-manager from 1921 to 1926, when he became the go-to guy in weighing in on how his team was doing.

Despite not being personally popular either, Anson as Chicago's captain-manager from 1879 to 1897 was easy to make fun of – because he had a penchant for bluster. When his team underachieved especially in the late 1880s, the coverage sometimes featured full-blown Victorian Era humor, including in cartoon images, to an extent unparalleled in baseball history.

Kelly was personally popular and exuded half-seriousness on the field. Both traits were opposites to Cobb, despite their sharing a daring style of play.

Within seasons, Cobb's seriousness led to mostly one-dimensional coverage: all action, few interesting quotes. As for what he had become without action as of 1941, sports editor Art Cohn of the *Oakland Tribune* called him "as interesting and colorful in private life as a dull gray wall."

Anson and Ruth had stable family lives in their retirement, while Cobb's then-22-year first marriage began publicly falling apart in 1931. In addition, two of his three sons preceded him in death.

Ruth and Cobb roughly mirrored each other in their sporting interests in their retirement, with golf being number one. Ruth arguably felt the more crushing single disappointment, having hoped to be a major league manager.

Anson loved golf too, plus opened a billiard and pool hall, was elected city clerk of Chicago and owned a semi-pro team. Then, after going bankrupt, he began a roughly 10-year vaudeville career. He kept active until the day he suddenly died, his only big emotional setback being his wife's death in 1916. Despite having so much more money, Ruth and Cobb healthwise had far sadder final years. Cobb had minimal companionship in his last ones, but stoically endured great pain to still travel long distances within a year of his death.

Cobb's retirement-era activities in and of themselves hardly produced interesting coverage, with two great exceptions. One is that soon after retiring, he began commenting negatively on changes in the game, and kept that up for the rest of his life. Anson had done the same too, especially as part of his vaudeville routine, but also told lighter stories about baseball in his day. The other exception is that Cobb made himself relevant by informally advising some major leaguers, especially Joe DiMaggio starting in the 1930s and Ted Williams after World War II, as a substitute for holding a salaried position in the sport.

Separate from Cobb's ongoing comments about changes in the game and his help to particular players, journalists helped him come across as interesting by sharing their own recollections and commentary about his career. Some sought out or overheard contemporaries of his talk about it.

Unlike Anson and Ruth, what is arguably most interesting about Cobb's post-career is something that was not apparent to the wider public: his expressing himself in personal letters. Cobb's willingness to contest Cunningham of the *Boston Herald* on casting his persona helps him soar past Anson and Ruth as having the meatiest-to-analyze post-career; Kelly never got to experience one, as he died in an offseason while still an active player.

No matter how much he might try to persuade by using his intellect, Cobb could never shake the image of having been so aggressive a player as to have been a spiker. Meanwhile, Ruth retained his huge personal popularity without a hitch and was the consummate "happy warrior." Cobb's great solace was reminding people that he received the most votes for induction into the National Baseball Hall of Fame, when its first vote was announced in 1936.

When I started out, I figured that Cobb could not hold a candle to Ruth, in personal popularity. It is worth opining as well that since he had a far longer post-career, Cobb was mentioned in some negative way in many more articles than Ruth was.

The full stories of Anson and Kelly have been much simpler to present; the basic narratives were written by David L. Fleitz and Marty Appel. Fleitz's, though, is too dark a take on Anson, while Appel's and my Kelly one complement each other. On overlapping subjects across my prior books, my writing is generally at least either more accurate or the fuller picture; for example, on the alleged impact of Anson's racism and the extent of Kelly's tricky play.

In those two books, *Cap Anson 4* and *Cap Anson 2* for short, I featured persons that Anson or Kelly had associations with; pure narrative writers tend to stray far less from the main subject. While the latter style can have appeal to a general reader, such a focus shortchanged, in the cases of Anson and Kelly, some of their most notable relationships. For example, theater agent and fellow Boston Elk George W. Floyd was Kelly's most important behind-the-scenes person in some of his key professional, including baseball, dealings. Floyd appears 0 times in Appel's book and 67 times in mine. I am likely the most overlooked recent baseball biographer, by the failure of authors to use either of two free resources to identify books on their topics: the worldwide library holdings database, WorldCat for short, and Library of Congress subject headings. A 2012 HarperCollins Irish-in-baseball book with a special focus on Kelly missed my Kelly one. A 2014 John Wiley & Sons scholarly reference book that contains an essay on 117 baseball ones through 1920 has no trace of my Anson, Kelly and 1890s Orioles ones and otherwise no major omissions.

Rich aspects of Ruth were brought to light and in many respects the last anecdotal word was presented when Robert Creamer spoke to former teammates and contemporaries for his 1974 *Babe: The Legend Comes to Life*. To try to approximate the truth, Creamer got to ask questions of first-hand observers of Ruth, but, of course, not of Ruth himself. No such book was ever written on Cobb, but *Ty Cobb Unleashed* could be the "reality show" inverse to Creamer's: it both quotes Cobb extensively, along with proponents, detractors and neutral observers. Plus, the vast majority in it was said while the main character, a big-time letter writer, was still alive and thus potentially able to weigh in.

A complement to this book, at baseballguru.com, is a compilation of comments made by Cobb contemporaries. They were curated by Cobb aficionado Bill Burgess, who died in 2014. Without having to type a Web address, if you Google "Fred Haney" "George McBride" "Fred Corcoran", the lone "hit" may still be the relevant link. As of this writing, the comments are overwhelmingly favorable but authoritative in being from news reports or books.

My book performs a unique compilation of sorts, by tracking Cobb's sharing of advice with, especially, big-league stars from the 1930s through 1960. Another unique aspect stems from having wallowed in the humor of Victorian Era coverage of Anson and Kelly, much of it crafted by journalists. I have similarly stressed colorful angles on Cobb. For example, I am the first Cobb author to have investigated a variety of entertaining parts of Stump's 1961 article and 1994 book and identified their factual bases.

In great contrast to Anson and Kelly, chronicling Ruth and now Cobb can be said to have been a group effort, with, in Cobb's case, mere articles of the modern day constituting some of the most important writing. I think that anyone keeping tabs on Cobb literature will conclude that *Ty Cobb Unleashed* fills a huge need. A comparison was needed of the 2015 biographies, for claims of stop-the-presses racial content and analysis in one, and general definitiveness in the other. For the 99+ percent of people who could care less about looking at a book on Cobb, mine performs an unrelated public service: showing how technically flawed a mainstream nonfiction book can be. Given their exclusive or near-exclusive focus on evaluating books for their substance and readability, traditional news outlets and newsy blogs should at least occasionally assess big-time publishers for the technical quality of their recent books. As has been noted for decades, those publishers are under little pressure to shape up. A relatively new trend, for example, is for endnotes to be whittled down.

Now available for consideration as part of any such assessment is an award-winning, *New York Times* niche list bestseller, with target-rich examples that are there for the taking.

TIME OUT! · · · · · · - By Jeff Keate

"I know! I know! It's nothing compared to the way
Ty Cobb slammed into a base!"

Below are some of the meatier topics in the movie "Cobb" that are addressed in *Ty Cobb Unleashed*, along with the page numbers in which the topics are touched on in some way. In the genre of Cobb biography, an asterisk indicates that the detail is making its most credible appearance, as a substantiation or refutation, in this book. For example, even if a movie detail below appeared in Al Stump's 1961 article or 1994 book, an asterisk appears if my book uniquely contains (at least loose) credible support for it.

One overall aside: it is not necessarily clear in the movie and in Stump's 1961 article and/or 1994 book which Cobb behaviors took place while drunk (or in great pain) versus while sober. By contrast, as noted on page 135, Cobb's second wife, Frances Fairbairn Cass, was alleging in her 1954 bill of particulars if particular acts of his were done while drunk.

One other source worth consulting, especially for its close analysis of Stump's credibility and its full endnoting, is William R. "Ron" Cobb's 2010 (currently Web-accessible) article "The Georgia Peach: Stumped by the Storyteller."

*Acting up in a Nevada casino and being escorted into its lobby (he at least got into "furious arguments" with dealers in Reno, according to the *Nevada State Journal* sports editor by the same name, 293)

Age quip about what Cobb's batting average would be if he were still playing, 450-51; *I found no examples, however, of Cobb uttering it himself, as in the movie

As a baseball lifer (as if he had no interests besides baseball) (*starkly refuted by Harvey Breitt of the *New York Times*, who instead applied the label to Rogers Hornsby, 349)

The Georgia Peach, Stumped by the Storyteller

William R. "Ron" Cobb, Phys 66, MS NE 67, PhD NE 70

Ron Cobb's historical research aims to debunk many of the myths surrounding baseball legend Ty Cobb (no relation to the author), who is often portrayed as a violent and unstable figure. The author contends that Cobb's bad reputation was largely due to a 1961 biography released after his death, and presents evidence that the wildest stories were fabricated his biographer, Al Stump.

from *Georgia Tech Alumni Magazine* in 2014; distant Cobb cousin William R. "Ron" Cobb issued his 2010 article in 2014 as a mini-book. The Simon & Schuster book should have credited Cobb's 2010 article and 2014 book along the lines in the blurb above and not obtusely, as it did in heaping Mr. Cobb with merely general praise. Omitting specific myth-debunking credit may have misled glowing reviewers and, in turn, award judges in their weighing of 2015 authors. Simon & Schuster's maximizing of its book's potential to garner myth-debunking credit likely helped it soar past Sports Publishing's roughly equally significant 2015 Cobb biography.

As curser (as of the 1950s), 134, 149-50, 294

As a racist (unsubstantiated after the early 1940s):
  *as supporter of institutional racism, 1, 3, 6, 8, 14, 24-25, 27-28, 30, 37, 143, 146 (in caption) and blacks (the most extensive discussions other than in the opening chapters), 103-12, 139-54, 211-14

As anti-Semitic (*unsubstantiated beyond a narrow slice); see remarks on Jews in the book publishing and movie industries, 24, 333, 359-60

As jealous of Babe Ruth or boosting himself relative to Ruth, such as for being the first player elected to the National Baseball Hall of Fame, 368 (*but also writing a kind, substantive letter to the dying Ruth, 302)

As not knowing Stump prior to 1960 work on book (*refuted by Stump's flattering interview of Cobb for his 1955 *Elks Magazine* article, 453-55)

As a deliberate spiker (the incidents actually seem to be relatively few), 71-74

*As a spikes filer, including in open view of the opposition, 69-71

*Encountering bad feelings among fellow former players at a reunion (*but unlike in the movie, Cobb made a generous adjustment, in an incident in 1947 in conjunction with old-timers' day at Yankee Stadium), 457-58

Firing a gun near Stump (*John D. McCallum, in some context in 1972, apparently told of himself having had Cobb throw knives around him), 65

*Having had a gun (before it apparently went into storage) in Emory University Hospital, 58-59, 445, 449 (*but with no indication of firing it in the hospital, as depicted in the movie)

> Cobb ★★ '94 Tommy Lee Jones. Baseball legend Ty Cobb pressures biographer Al Stump to whitewash the sordid details of his life. (2:08) (TMC) 2:35 a.m. 46972843 (CC) (S) (R)

from left to right in (actually) 1968: Melvin Durslag, actor Gary Owens, Stump and East Los Angeles community newspaper editor Alberto Diaz. Durslag and Stump were *Los Angeles Herald-Examiner* colleagues who were receiving awards from the Greater Los Angeles Press Club. Leerhsen interviewed Durslag, who told him that Stump had made up quotes in some of his writings, and worse. Durslag died in 2016 at the age of 95.

The best broad analysis of "Cobb" and the truth is in Hal Erickson's 2002 *The Baseball Filmography, 1915 through 2001*. In the Cobb book genre, Bak's 2005 one has the most to say; Leerhsen's contains a few lines on this angle. Erickson, Bak and Leerhsen all drove wedges between Stump's writings and director Ron Shelton's exercise of editorial license.

Cobb's 1961 book with Stump states that Cobb was in a chemical warfare training accident in 1918. It allegedly took place at Hanlon Field, near Chaumont, France. Cobb and others were exposed to an unspecified poisonous gas in an airtight chamber where some of those present, including Cobb and pitcher-turned-Cincinnati manager Christy Mathewson, missed the signal to snap their protective mask into position. As a result, "sixteen men were stretched on the ground after the training exercise and eight of them died." Cobb's book also states, "I can recall Mathewson saying, 'Ty, when we were in there, I got a good dose of that stuff. I feel terrible.' He was wheezing and blowing out congested matter." For a few weeks straddling October-November 1918, Cobb was at an active training site, the Chemical Warfare Service (CWS) Technical Division's gas training school around Chaumont. After World War II, the CWS was renamed the Chemical Corps.

Captains Christy Mathewson and Cobb in 1918

Leerhsen wrote, "Al Stump's Cobb 'autobiography,' *My Life in Baseball*, says that eight men died as a result of the accident, but there is nothing to corroborate that. We do know [based on the 1961 book] that several [eight other] soldiers became ill. Cobb himself was laid up [showed effects] for about a week ['weeks' is in the book], Mathewson somewhat longer [Mathewson biographer Michael Hartley, in examining his personal military records at Keystone College in Pennsylvania, found Mathewson receiving and heeding an order to report to the 28th Division Pennsylvania National Guard headquarters at Heudicourt for gas officer duty around the time that Hartley estimated the accident allegedly occurred], and when the ex-pitcher died of tuberculosis seven years later at the age of forty-five, it was widely assumed that his susceptibility to lung disease could be traced to the toxic classrooms of [should be near] Chaumont."

The clearest refutation of the 1961 book comes from fellow player-enlistee Branch Rickey. Rickey attained the rank of major in the CWS, while Cobb and Mathewson reached the lower one of captain. Of Mathewson's health problems, Rickey wrote in his 1965 *The American Diamond*, "It was reported that he had been gassed at a gas chamber during training at Choignes, France [just outside of Chaumont]. That is not true. I went through the exact training with Matty and was with him immediately afterward. He had no mishap after the final field-training exposure. In fact, Matty took part in an impromptu broad-jump contest and out-leaped everyone in our group who cared to try, and by a comfortable margin. He was then thirty-eight years old." In 1920, Matty's wife Jane had theorized that he contracted tuberculosis due to a bout of influenza (Hartley found the influenza in Matty's official military service record on the adjoining page) upon his arrival in France, and inhalation of gas while demonstrating lethal gas shells to students during his post-Hanlon Field service in the 28th Division. The first hard cold that he suffered back home "settled into a cough he could not shake off."

I could not confirm that Mathewson suffered gas exposure during his service at Hanlon Field. Plus, while scouring a U.S. depository of CWS administrative records, the National Archives in College Park, Md., I looked at some Army, non-CWS hospitalization-related files and did not find any hospitalization being ascribed to gas exposure.

After my visit I learned of Thomas I. Faith's 2014 book *The U.S. Chemical Warfare Service in War and Peace*. Not only is his book's highest overall praise, archivally, to the College Park location, but Faith states that field hospital illness and death reports could have been error-ridden, "given that during World War I, physicians in uniform who had never encountered a chemical warfare patient before 1918 had to decide if a soldier had been gassed or merely suffered from a cough or conjunctivitis [pink eye]."

Two months after Mathewson's death, Major General Amos A. Fries, the second head of the CWS, was said by the *St. Louis Post-Dispatch* to be "of the opinion that war gas did not cause or hasten tuberculosis [in cases such as Mathewson's, whose doctor said he died of tuberculous pneumonia], but in fact actually prevented it." Fries cited statistical studies and testimony to that effect in 1923 by the-then clinical director of tuberculosis of the Veterans' Bureau, Dr. Albert P. Francine. In 1928, one year before retiring from military service, Fries was in Honolulu to inspect a gas regiment. A reporter for the *Honolulu Advertiser* was present in Fries's hotel room afterward when he said, "the only chance Captain Mathewson had had of being gassed was limited to a whiff or two of innocuous gas that he might have received while in training."

One source for probing Cobb's claim, the National Personnel Records Center of the National Archives in St. Louis, suffered a fire in 1973. About 80 percent of its Army records, for those discharged from 1912 to 1960, were lost. That said, while the St. Louis site does have plenty of descriptive "morning reports" for Army entities tagged with unit numbers, the gas school, as a "technical division," apparently did not subdivide that way. On the one hand, the reference service of the U.S. Army Center of Military History informed me that all non-combat field organizations in World War I, including the gas school, prepared morning reports. On the other hand, the National Archives in St. Louis told me that it can search for a morning report only if tied to a unit number.

Consistent with the school's status as a technical division, Mathewson's service record contains the word "casual" next to his CWS tenure at Hanlon Field. While the St. Louis location of the National Archives does not have the adjacent document, the Miller Library at Keystone College in Pennsylvania does – because his widow Jane donated material to it in 1967. In World War I, as confirmed by the U.S. Army Center of Military History, "casual" denotes an active duty soldier not attached to a specific unit. "CASUAL" also appears in Rickey's CWS records at the St. Louis location, as does the shorthand "MAJ CWS CAS" (major Chemical Warfare Service casual).

Kip A. Lindberg, director of the U.S. Army Chemical Corps Museum, has so far compiled 305 fatalities in the CWS during the Great War. Most died of influenza. Although he has not analyzed Hanlon Field, a comparison can be made to three contemporaneously reported CWS deaths, related to gas production or testing, that he found at the Edgewood Arsenal (now part of the Aberdeen Proving Ground in Maryland and, as of 1918, the largest U.S. poison gas production and testing facility) and one CWS one at the American University Experimental Station in Washington, D.C. It is improbable for there to have been eight deaths at Hanlon Field from one exercise versus a total of four CWS production or testing ones at the two homeland sites. Lindberg said it is possible that the Hanlon Field casualties were non-CWS, visiting Army trainees. Another possibility is that the eight died later: over weeks, months or years.

Other than the claim in Cobb and Stump's 1961 book and the refutation in Rickey's 1965 one, the only other accident prose that I came across from someone in the CWS is from a second lieutenant, John O. Thoen. In the gap in 1961 between publication of the book and Stump's article, Thoen sent the Chemical Corps Historical Office a short essay on his time at Hanlon Field. In the essay, Thoen said his knowledge was limited because his work was administrative and, as he implied, was not closely related to the school's operations. He had no recollection that Rickey had been at Hanlon Field.

On the alleged gas accident, Thoen wrote, "Maybe Christy Mathewson was gassed and later died as a result but if that was so there were enough admirers of his that would have commented on the accident. This story[,] too, may be perfectly true but nothing in my memory confirms it."

He also said he knew nothing of a "gas chamber" that Cobb alleged but indicated that "tear gas" was the type of gas used in training exercises. I obtained Thoen's essay from Jeffery K. Smart, command historian of the U.S. Army Research, Development and Engineering Command. On the type of gas chambers that were used for gas mask training, Smart e-mailed me that they were "small buildings with closed windows and doors." On whether indeed tear gas had been used, Smart replied, "Tear gas was probably chlorine which could be deadly in certain situations."

In his essay, Thoen told the following second-hand story about Cobb. After the November 11 armistice, "he went to the field headquarters office and called someone in New York who had been instrumental in getting his commission and told him he wanted to get back at once and wanted quick arrangements made. He was gone the next day." While conceivable, Cobb did not return to the United States until December, when he sailed back on the Leviathan.

He also wrote, "So far as Cobb is concerned (and he was from my youth my idol as a ball player), there was nothing valiant about his conduct at Hanlon Field. When the new masks were adopted[,] training classes were held to develop speed of application. The men were gathered in a group and tear gas was released. Masks were to be adjusted within a few seconds. I was watching the show and saw a man running and asked another spectator what about that, and was told that was Ty Cobb, he could run faster than he could put the mask on. I am not sure that is true because I was too far away to identify him."

Thoen also reacted to the claim in the 1961 book that Cobb had "'accelerated training' in gas defense before he was shipped to Hanlon Field and that he was assigned to the 'Gas & Flame' division as instructor and that he had some awful dumb culls to train." He wrote, "As I remember Cobb never finished his own training at Hanlon Field." Cobb and Stump had written, "The doughboys who came our way largely were hard cases and rejects from other services. The theory was that they would listen to well-known sports personalities – and to some extent it was effective. Those that gave us trouble and didn't heed orders didn't last long, for we weren't fooling around with simulated death when we entered those gas chambers. The stuff we turned loose was the [real] McCoy and meant to train a man to be on *qui vive* [alert] – or else."

In striving to make sense of baseball history, professors sometimes get carried away with their theories. While their peers may tend to admire such daring, the average person probably is less enthralled by intellectual calisthenics.

This appendix was sparked in April when I saw history professor Edmund F. Wehrle's new book *Breaking Babe Ruth: Baseball's Campaign Against Its Biggest Star*. Wehrle theorizes that for various reasons having nothing to do with qualifications, Ruth was denied the chance to manage a major league team.

I found two punchy 1948 columns on Ruth and managing by Harry G. Salsinger, sports editor of the *Detroit News* since 1909. One ran six months before Ruth's death. The other ran days after the death and then in a long Salsinger section in the 1948 *Sporting News* book *The Real Babe Ruth* written mostly by longtime Yankees writer Dan Daniel. Wehrle called it "Daniel's book" and said it "avoided reality and controversy," thus nullifying Salsinger. On top of that, Wehrle's book weakly overlaps with Salsinger's lines of argument.

About Ruth's failure to manage in the big leagues, Salsinger wrote in his first column, "There is no question that base ball is indebted to Ruth but whether this debt would have been cancelled by making him manager is a mute [sic] question. Ruth retired as the most popular figure in the history of base ball and he has lost none of his popularity with the passing years. Had he been made manager he would have lost much of the luster that he acquired as a player for we can recall no ranking star of the game who had fewer managerial qualifications than Ruth." Later in that column, Salsinger wrote, "Some of the most illustrious players in history were failures as managers."

Wehrle wrote, "Certainly there was precedent for a star player-manager. Since 1921 [to 1926], Ty Cobb had managed the Tigers while remaining an active player" on his team. "In May of 1925, the St. Louis Cardinals appointed star hitter Rogers Hornsby as player-manager. As part of the deal, arrangements were made to sell Hornsby a sizeable portion of shares in the Cardinals team."

In his later column, Salsinger dramatized Ruth's flaws. One may relate to his often addressing other people as "Kid": "Then there was the matter of names. Ruth never remembered any. What would happen when a waiver list came through? Ruth would not know one name from another. What about signs? He never remembered them. When he was hitting home runs he did not have to remember signs and, later on, he did not bother to remember them."

Wehrle did allude to the following allegation that Salsinger mentioned: "His ignorance of signs caused the clubhouse row with [Brooklyn captain-shortstop] Leo Durocher, when [in 1938] Ruth was hired as coach of the Brooklyn Dodgers. Durocher accused him of kicking away a game by not remembering the signs."

On a different front, Wehrle and Salsinger both touched on whether Ruth could have been manager of the Tigers in 1934. Wehrle wrote, "When Frank Navin, owner of the Detroit Tigers, requested an interview, Ruth, on his way to a barnstorming tour of Hawaii, delayed." Wehrle added, "Meeting with Navin, Ruth claimed, would have required breaking barnstorming contracts."

Salsinger wrote that Ruth called at 3 a.m. from San Francisco and demanded a "yes or no" on whether he was wanted as manager. "Navin, irritated at being awakened at 3 o'clock in the morning, and more irritated at Ruth's brusque ultimatum, answered: 'Since you put it that way, the answer is—NO!'"

Worth thinking about is whether Ruth, as manager, would have adequately instructed his players and otherwise disciplined them. Without explaining if he meant strategy in his own play or in that of others, Wehrle called the mid-1920s Ruth an "excellent strategist who rarely made a fielding error."

In 1926, at the end of Cobb's six years as player-manager, Salsinger wrote, "Cobb could never succeed as a manager. Nature, gifting him so generously and splendidly for play, probably never intended him to lead others. His brain was supremely filled to direct Cobb, the individual, but there was only one Cobb for that brain to direct. Other bodies could not function as his, [and] could not follow the rapid twists of thought."

Wehrle argued that baseball officials, feeling that Ruth's "freewheeling ways," such as his pro-labor actions, "needed to be curbed," "thus launched an offensive against Ruth that lasted several decades. Dramatic moves such as suspensions combined with a low-level campaign to infantilize the Babe. Quickly that campaign forced Ruth into a corner." He concluded, "The Babe was essentially forced out of the game and blackballed from future management positions."

Salsinger's second column had opened as follows: "Babe Ruth had his heart set on managing a major league ball club and the fact that he never got the opportunity made club owners the targets of much bitter criticism and abuse. Ruth was called the forgotten man of base ball [especially in a 1938 United Press poll/resulting article – not mentioned by Wehrle – in which 49 percent of sports editors answered "no" to, "Do you think Babe Ruth should be given a chance to manage a major league ball club?"; 25 percent said "yes," but many of the "yes" voters said he should first manage a minor league club; and the rest answered maybe or were noncommittal] and the owners were accused of being a mercenary lot of flint-hearted ingrates who used a man as long as he could pile up profits for them, then ruthlessly tossed him aside like a wornout garment."

Salsinger added, "It never occurred to the critics to inquire into the Babe's qualifications for managing a ball club." Several sentences later, he opined, "The club owners would have been more than happy to bid for his services as manager if they were convinced that the Babe had any of the qualifications."

Articles (in Chronological Order)
* Notable article not previously cited by a Cobb article or book writer and not
mentioned in Myron J. Smith, *Baseball: A Comprehensive Bibliography* book series
** In Smith bibliography but not previously mined in an article or book

Robbins, I. M., "The Economic Aspects of the Negro Problem: VIII. The Problem
    from the Negro's Point of View," *International Socialist Review* 10 (July 1909),
    p. 58.

Foreman, Howell, "When Ty Cobb Was a Boy," *Baseball Magazine* 8 (March 1912),
    p. 2.

Anonymous, "Ty Cobb Twice; a Unique Photograph," *Popular Mechanics* 18
    (July 1912), pp. 48-49.

Anonymous, "Trapshooting – The Sport Alluring," *Baseball Magazine* 16
    (February 1915), p. 101.

Evans, Billy, "Speed and the Base-Runner," *St. Nicholas* 42 (July 1915), p. 821.

McLinn, George (presumably), "Yes, That Was a Funny One," *American Shooter* 1
    (January 1, 1916), p. 36.

*McLinn, George, "Trying To Tie Ty," *American Shooter 1* (January 15, 1916)

Lane, F. C., "A Day with Ty Cobb," *Baseball Magazine* 16 (April 1916), p. 58.

*Fullerton Sr., Hugh, "Ty Cobb Says, If Going Stale, Drink," *Liberty* 5
    (September 20, 1924), p. 41.

*Dreiser, Theodore, "The Most Successful Ball-Player of Them All," *Hearst's
    International* 47 (February 1925). The original is hard to find; I saw a reprint in
    the *Madera Tribune (Calif.)* of March 2, 1925.

*Cobb, Ty, "The Baseball Riddle," *American Legion Magazine* 10 (April 1931)

Reynolds, Quentin, "Legs Last Just So Long," *Collier's* 92 (July 29, 1933)

DiMaggio, Joe, "What Your Boos and Jeers Do to Me," *Liberty* 15
    (August 27, 1938), p. 9.

Reynolds, Quentin, "Ty Cobb's Dream Team," *Collier's* 103 (June 17, 1939),
    pp. 19 and 61.

Reynolds, Quentin, "Pop-Off Kid," *Collier's* 103 (August 5, 1939), p. 14.

Mann, Arthur, "Baseball's Ugly Duckling – Durable Durocher," *Saturday Evening
    Post* 212 (August 19, 1939), p. 15.

*McLemore, Henry, "Ty Cobb Picks Baseball's Fightin'est Team," *Look* 4
    (March 26, 1940)

Anonymous, "Highest Paid Sportswriter, Bill Cunningham Goes to Boston Herald,"
    Life 10 (April 14, 1941), p. 76.

Frank, Stanley, "Rough Riders of the Dugouts," *Saturday Evening Post* 213
    (May 17, 1941), as cited by Malcolm Bingay, *Detroit Free Press*, May 17, 1941

Sarazen, Gene with Arch Murray, "Seventy-Two Hells," *Saturday Evening Post* 213
    (June 7, 1941), p. 114.

Baer, Arthur "Bugs", "The Crambury Tiger," *Collier's* 110 (July 11, 1942), p. 19.

Durocher, Leo, "Nice Guys Finish Last!" *Cosmopolitan* 124 (April 1948), p. 111.

Sher, Jack, "Ty Cobb, the Georgia Peach," *Sport* 5 (November 1948), pp. 56 and 59.

Frank, Stanley, "You Don't Lose Pennants That Way," *Saturday Evening Post* 223
   (August 19, 1950), p. 132.

Graham, Frank, "One for the Book," *Sport* 10 (May 1951), pp. 29 and 87.

McGill, Ralph, "The Multimillionaire Nobody Knows," *Saturday Evening Post* 223
   (May 5, 1951), pp. 27 and 138.

Parker, Dan, "Let's Stop Babying Our Ball Players," *Sport* 10 (June 1951),
   pp. 81 and 83.

Cobb, Ty, and Ernest C. Havemann, "They Don't Play Baseball Any More,"
   Life 32 (March 17, 1952)

Cobb, Ty, and Ernest C. Havemann, "Tricks That Won Me Ball Games," *Life* 32
   (March 24, 1952), pp. 64, 66, 74 and 78-80.

Hornsby, Rogers, "It's Still Baseball, Cobb!" *Look* 26 (June 17, 1952), p. 61.

*Cooke, Bob, "Ty Cobb Strikes Out," *Pageant* 7 (July 1952), pp. 101-05.

Williams, Ted as told to Joe Reichler and Joe Trimble, "This Is My Last Year"
   (Part Two), *Saturday Evening Post* 226 (April 17, 1954), pp. 25 and 147-48.

*Stump, Al, "In the Shadow of the Babe," *Elks Magazine* 34 (August 1955)

Harris, Bucky as told to Stanley Frank, "Ballplayers Are as Good as Ever,"
   Saturday Evening Post 228 (February 11, 1956), p. 80.

Sullivan, Ed, "My Story" Part 1, *Collier's* 138 (September 14, 1956), p. 20.

Mathewson, Tracy, "Ty Cobb, Hardest Hunter of All," *Southern Outdoors* 5
   (March-April 1957)

Bisher, Furman, "A Visit with Ty Cobb," *Saturday Evening Post* 230 (June 14, 1958)

*Jones, Jimmy, "Ty Cobb Answers Some Questions About Baseball: And Raises
   Some Questions About the Game," *American Legion Magazine* 66 (May 1959)

*Stump, Al, "Ty Cobb, 1960," *Elks Magazine* 39 (September 1960)

Stump, Al, "Ty Cobb's Wild, 10-Month Fight to Live," *True: The Man's Magazine* 42
   (December 1961)

*Boddington, Clem, "The Two Faces of Ty Cobb," *Sir!* 18 (January 1962)

Elderkin, Phil, "Use Heavier Bat with Thick Handle is DiMag's Advice,"
   Baseball Digest 27 (October 1968), pp. 66.

Hardison MD, Joseph E., "An Intern Meets Ty Cobb," *Journal of the American
   Medical Association* 246 (October 23, 1981), p. 1886.

**Stump, Al, "Bobby & Ty: From One Legend to Another: Bobby Jones Introduced
   Ty Cobb to Golf, But for the Georgia Peach, It Was the Pits," *Golf* 32
   (April 1990)

Montville, Leigh, "The Last Remains of a Legend," *Sports Illustrated* 77
   (October 27, 1992). Also, a comment by Furman Bisher to Montville is similar
   to Bisher's "blow in any direction" 1994 one on page 50. The article did not
   touch on Cobb's racism, an angle that Bisher broached in 1995.

**Cobb, Ty R., "The Other Side of Cobb," *Nevada* 54 (September-October 1994),
   p. 91.

Gurtowski, Richard, "Remembering Baseball Hall of Famers Who Served in the
   Chemical Corps," *Army Chemical Review* PB 3-05-2 (July-December 2005)

Stinson, Jim, "Cobb Not the Monster He's Portrayed to Be," *Sports Collectors
   Digest* 33 (May 5, 2006) (SCD's cover that week stated, "Ty: Pariah or Peach?")

Schear, Abe J. (interview with Jimmy Lanier), "I Remember Ty Cobb," *Baseball Digest* 35 (January 2007) (newsletter of Arnall Golden Gregory LLP)

Cobb, William R. (Ron), "The Georgia Peach: Stumped by the Storyteller," *National Pastime* 30 (2010), in part citing Doug Roberts, *National Pastime* 16 (1996), "Ty Cobb Did Not Commit Murder."

Anonymous, "Ty Cobb: A Terrible Beauty" (review), *Kirkus Reviews* 83 (March 2, 2015)

Rogers III, C. Paul, "War on The Basepaths" (review), *Nine* 24 (Fall 2015-Spring 2016) (not cited in the main text and not published until December 2017. Rogers, an academic and lawyer, interpreted, in a more-unfavorable-to-Cobb way than I did, Hornbaker's "the jury is still out" tone on Cobb's racism.)

Witherspoon, Kevin B., "Ty Cobb: A Terrible Beauty" (review), *Sport History Review* 47 (November 2016)

Ringel, Paul, "Gil Hodges: A Hall of Fame Life" (review), *Historian* 79 (Spring 2017), p. 153.

Welky, David, Leerhsen/Tripp (joint review), *Journal of Sport History* 44 (Fall 2017)

Internet-based Articles (in Chronological Order)

Zacharias, Patricia, "Ty Cobb, the Greatest Tiger of Them All," *DetroitNews*.com, January 18, 1996; accessed November 26, 2017, at http://blogs.detroitnews.com/history/1996/01/18/ty-cobb-the-greatest-tiger-of-them-all/

Fricks, Wesley, "Ty Was Not a Racist," BleacherReport.com, August 2, 2008; accessed November 29, 2016, at http://bleacherreport.com/articles/43506-ty-cobb-was-not-a-racist

Ashwill, Gary, "Ty Cobb in Cuba, 1910," August 14, 2008; accessed August 25, 2017 (a correction of a slew of modern-day articles and books that claim that Petway threw out Cobb three times one day on steal attempts), at http://agatetype.typepad.com/agate_type/2008/08/ty-cobb-in-cuba.html

Fricks, Wesley, "Ty Cobb, Hall of Famer, Betrayed by Writers for 50 Years. Player's Legacy Ruined," BleacherReport.com, July 17, 2011; accessed November 29, 2016, at http://bleacherreport.com/articles/770355-ty-cobb-hall-of-famer-betrayed-by-writers-for-50-years-ruined-players-legacy

Stolley, Karl, Allen Brizee and Joshua M. Paiz, "Overview and Contradictions," Purdue Online Writing Lab, last edited October 10, 2014; accessed November 27, 2016, at https://owl.english.purdue.edu/owl/resource/589/01/

Kaplan, Ron, "Corn on the Cobb?" June 2, 2015; accessed May 14, 2017, at http://www.ronkaplansbaseballbookshelf.com/2015/06/02/corn-on-the-cobb/

Mooney, Jacob McArthur, review, "Ty Cobb Was No One's Antihero," Deadspin, June 11, 2015; accessed November 29, 2016, at http://deadspin.com/ty-cobb-was-no-ones-antihero-1710623356

Flowers, Mark, review, "The Much-Maligned Ty Cobb: A New Biography for Sports Fans: Adult Books 4 Teens," *School Library Journal* (online only), July 2, 2015; accessed November 29, 2016, at http://www.slj.com/2015/07/collection-development/adult-books-for-teens/the-much-maligned-ty-cobb-a-new-biography-for-sports-fans/#_ (a now-defunct link)

Holmes, Dan, "These Tigers' Managers Were Ejected the Most Times," April 12, 2016; accessed November 27, 2016, at https://www.detroitathletic.com/blog/2016/04/12/these-detroit-tigers-managers-were-ejected-the-most-times/

Morris, Tim, review, "Ty Cobb," April 12, 2016; accessed November 29, 2016, at https://www.uta.edu/english/tim/lection/160412.html

Appel, Marty, "Baseball Books on the 'New York Times' Best Sellers List," October 13, 2016; accessed in 2017 at a now-defunct link; it is now accessible at http://www.appelpr.com/?page_id=3173

Smith, Robert G., review, "Leerhsen, Charles. Ty Cobb: A Terrible Beauty. New York: Simon & Schuster, 2016," *Saber and Scroll* 6 (Spring-Summer 2017), p. 123; accessed in 2017 at a now-defunct link; it is now accessible at https://saberandscroll.weebly.com/blog-ii/archives/04-2017

Books (in Alphabetical Order)

Alexander, Charles C., *Ty Cobb* (New York: Oxford University, 1984), pp. 5-6, 11, 13, 43, 50, 57, 67-68, 80-81, 88, 99, 113, 119, 127, 130, 173, 182, 184, 189, 195, 205, 215-16, 218, 220-24, 228-23 and 235-37. Amazon.com's inside-the-book search tool for it is superior to the Google Books one.

——————————, *Spoke: A Biography of Tris Speaker* (Dallas: Southern Methodist University, 2007), p. 215 (Speaker-Hornsby Klan prose).

Bak, Richard, *Cobb Would Have Caught It: The Golden Age of Baseball in Detroit* (Detroit: Wayne State University, 1991), pp. 168, 170 and 193.

——————————, *Ty Cobb: His Tumultuous Life and Times* (Dallas: Taylor, 1994), pp. 6-7, 49, 113, 165, 168, 171, 173 and 176.

——————————, *Peach: Ty Cobb in his Time and Ours* (Ann Arbor, Mich.: Sports Media Group, 2005), pp. 16, 18-19, 181, 184-85, 188, 195-96, 198 and 204.

Bartell, Dick, and Norman L. Macht, *Rowdy Richard: A Firsthand Account of the National League Baseball Wars of the 1930s and the Men Who Fought Them* (Uklah, Calif.: North Atlantic Books, 1987), p. 125.

Ben Cramer, Richard, *Joe DiMaggio: The Hero's Life* (New York: Simon and Schuster, 2000), p. 123.

Beveridge, Albert J., *The Young Man and the World* (New York: D. Appleton and Company, 1905), p. 101, quoted on page 117 of Charles Leerhsen, *Ty Cobb: A Terrible Beauty.*

Brasch, James D., and Joseph Sigman, *Hemingway's Library: A Composite Record* (New York: Garland, 1981), p. 233.

Broeg, Bob, *Superstars of Baseball: Their Lives, Their Loves, Their Laughs, Their Laments* (St. Louis: The Sporting News, 1971), pp. 62-63.

Bruns, Roger, *Negro Leagues Baseball* (Santa Barbara, Calif.: Greenwood Press, 2012), p. 71.

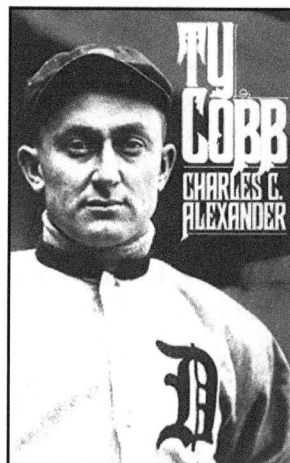

Bryant, Howard, *Henry Aaron: Baseball's Last Hero* (New York: Pantheon, 2010), pp. 451-52 (not cited in main text).

Cobb, Herschel, *Heart of a Tiger: Growing Up with My Grandfather, Ty Cobb* (Toronto: ECW Press, 2013). I do not cite it because its insights are on aspects of the Georgia Peach that are largely outside the scope of my book: interactions with other generations of his family, especially grandchildren. It does contain first-hand negative observations of Stump from author-grandson Herschel, some of which Tripp cited.

Cobb, Ty (with help from John N. Wheeler), *Busting 'Em, and Other Big League Stories* (New York: Edward J. Clode, 1914)

——— and William R. Cobb, *My Twenty Years in Baseball* (Mineola, N.Y.: Dover, 2009)

——— and Al Stump, *My Life in Baseball: The True Record* (Garden City, N.Y.: Doubleday, 1961). See the entry below for online search limitations.

——— and Al Stump, *My Life in Baseball: The True Record* (Lincoln, Neb.: University of Nebraska, 1993), pp. xi-xii. The Google Books version has some hidden pages. Amazon's can offset gaps but the underlying pages are less visible.

Collins, Tony, *Sport in Capitalist Society: A Short History* (New York: Routledge, 2013), p. 71.

Cooper, Brian E., *Ray Schalk: A Baseball Biography* (Jefferson, N.C.: McFarland & Co., 2009), p. 224.

Corcoran, Fred, and Bud Harvey, *Unplayable Lies* (New York: Duell, Sloan and Pearce, 1965), pp. 136, 144-47, 150 and 152-53.

Creamer, Robert W., *Babe: The Legend Comes to Life* (New York: Simon and Schuster, 1974), p. 320.

D'Amore, Jonathan, *Rogers Hornsby: A Biography* (Westport, Conn.: Greenwood Press, 2004), p. 133.

Darnell, Tim, *The Crackers: Early Days of Atlanta Baseball* (Athens, Ga.: Hill Street Press, 2005), p. 92.

Dempsey, Jack, and Bob Considine, *Dempsey by the Man Himself as Told to Bob Considine and Bill Slocum* (New York: Simon and Schuster, 1960), p. 217.

Dickson, Paul, *Leo Durocher: Baseball's Prodigal Son* (New York: Bloomsbury, 2017), pp. 3 and 27-29 (in both review copy and official eBook version of March 2017).

DiMaggio, Joe, *Lucky to be a Yankee* (New York: Rudolph Field, 1946), p. 184.

Durocher, Leo, and Edward Linn, *Nice Guys Finish Last* (New York: Simon and Schuster, 1975), pp. 49-50.

Elliott, Charles Newton, *A Biography of the "Boss": Robert Winship Woodruff* (No Place Identified, R. W. Woodruff, 1979), pp. 206-07.

Erickson, Hal, *The Baseball Filmography, 1915 through 2001* (Jefferson, N.C.: McFarland & Co., 2002), pp. 115-30.

Faith, Thomas I., *The U.S. Chemical Warfare Service in War and Peace* (Champaign, Ill.: University of Illinois, 2014), p. 66.

Feagin, Joe, and Hernàn Vera, *White Racism: The Basics* (New York: Routledge, 1995), p. 150.

Fleitz, David L., *Cap Anson: The Grand Old Man of Baseball* (Jefferson, N.C.: McFarland & Co., 2005), pp. 4 and 6.

Ford, Henry, *The Case Against the Little White Slaver, Volumes I, II, and III* (Detroit: Henry Ford, 1914), p. 65.

Gay, Timothy M., *Tris Speaker: The Rough-and-Tumble Life of a Baseball Legend* (Lincoln, Neb.: University of Nebraska, 2005), p. 260.

Graham, Frank, *New York Yankees: An Informal History* (New York: Putnam, 1943), pp. 142-43.

Grayson, Harry, *They Played the Game: The Story of Baseball Greats* (New York: A.S. Barnes, 1944), pp. 4-5.

Hartley, Michael, *Christy Mathewson: A Biography* (Jefferson, N.C.: McFarland & Co., 2004), pp. 139-40.

Hochwalt, Albert Frederick "A. F.", *The Modern Setter* (Dayton, Ohio: A. F. Hochwalt Co., 1919), pp. 138-39.

Holmes, Dan, *Ty Cobb: A Biography* (Westport, Conn.: Greenwood Press, 2004), p. xxi.

Holtzman, Jerome, *No Cheering in the Press Box* (New York: Holt, Rinehart and Winston, 1973), p. 186.

Holway, John, *Voices from the Great Black Baseball Leagues: Revised Edition* (Mineola, N.Y.: Dover, 2010 mild revision of 1975 original), p. 207.

Honig, Donald, *Baseball When the Grass Was Real: Baseball from the Twenties to the Forties Told by the Men Who Played It* (New York: Coward, McCann & Geoghegan, 1975), p. 41.

——————, *The Man in the Dugout: Fifteen Big League Managers Speak Their Minds* (Chicago: Follett, 1977), p. 152.

Hornbaker, Tim, *War On the Basepaths: The Definitive Biography of Ty Cobb* (New York: Sports Publishing, 2015). As of this writing, the Google Books version has too many hidden pages and no page numbering, and the print edition has no index. The full-text search solution? Buy it on Kindle for around $11.

Kaese, Harold, and R. G. Lynch, *The Milwaukee Braves* (New York: Putnam, 1954), p. 75.

Klima, John, *Bushville Wins!: The Wild Saga of the 1957 Milwaukee Braves and the Screwballs, Sluggers, and Beer Swiggers who Canned the New York Yankees and Changed Baseball* (New York: Thomas Dunne Books, 2012), pp. 54-56 and 144.

Leerhsen, Charles, *Ty Cobb: A Terrible Beauty* (New York: Simon & Schuster, 2015). In Google Books or on Amazon.com, you can type in word strings that I quote in order to, at minimum, find most page number equivalents in the print edition.

Lieb, Fred, *Baseball As I Have Known It* (New York: Coward, McCann & Geoghegan, 1977), pp. 57-58 and 186 (page 186 has the Cobb-Ruth lodging story that is on page 84 of my book. Lieb told a similar version on page 54 of Holtzman's book).

Lyons, Jeffrey, *Stories My Father Told Me, Notes from "The Lyons Den"* (New York: Abbeville Press, 2011), p. 32 (not cited in main text).

McCallum, John D., *The Tiger Wore Spikes: An Informal Biography of Ty Cobb* (New York: A. S. Barnes, 1956), pp. 11, 23, 51 and 98-99.

——————, *The Coit Fishing Pole Club Beginner's Book of Fishing* (Englewood Cliffs, N.J.: Prentice-Hall, 1958), p. 88.

——————, *Ty Cobb* (New York: Praeger, 1975), pp. xii, 4, 85, 129-30, 138, 156-57, 164-65 and 167.

McEvoy, J. P., *Charlie Would Have Loved This* (New York: Duell, Sloan and Pearce, 1956), p. 85.

McNary, Kyle P., *Ted "Double Duty" Radcliffe: 36 Years of Pitching & Catching in Baseball's Negro Leagues* (Minneapolis: McNary Publishing, 1994), p. 46.

Macht, Norman L., *Connie Mack: The Turbulent and Triumphant Years, 1915-1931* (Lincoln, Neb.: University of Nebraska, 2012), pp. 443-46.

Mathews, Eddie, and Bob Buege, *Eddie Mathews and the National Pastime* (Milwaukee: Douglas American Sports Publications, 1994), p. 125.

Metro, Charlie, and Thomas L. Altherr, *Safe by a Mile* (Lincoln, Neb.: University of Nebraska, 2002), pp. 145-46.

Nowlin, Bill, and Jim Prime, *Ted Williams: the Pursuit of Perfection* (Champaign, Ill.: Sports Publishing, 2002), pp. 205-06 (Leigh Montville's Joe Lindia story on Cobb/Williams).

Organized Baseball, Hearings of the Subcommittee on the Study of Monopoly Power of the Committee of the Judiciary, 82d Congress, 1st sess. (Washington, D.C.: U.S. Government Printing Office, 1952), July 31, 1951, pp. 4, 21 and 1083.

Ownby, Ted, *Subduing Satan: Religion, Recreation, and Manhood in the Rural South, 1865-1920* (Chapel Hill, N.C.: University of North Carolina, 1993), p. 12, quoted on page 120 of Charles Leerhsen, *Ty Cobb: A Terrible Beauty*.

Positano, Dr. Rock G., and John Positano, *Dinner with DiMaggio: Memories of an American Hero* (New York: Simon & Schuster, 2017), p. 144.

Powers, Jimmy, *Baseball Personalities: The Most Colorful Figures of All Time* (New York: R. Field, 1949), pp. 80-82.

Rapoport, Ron (ed.), *The Lost Journalism of Ring Lardner* (Lincoln, Neb.: University of Nebraska, 2017), p. 41.

Reeder, Red, *Born at Reveille* (New York: Duell, Sloan and Pearce, 1966), pp. 144-45.

Reynolds, Quentin, *By Quentin Reynolds* (New York: McGraw-Hill, 1963), p. 103.

Rhodes, Don, *Ty Cobb: Safe at Home* (Guilford, Conn.: Lyons Press, 2008), pp. 26-27, 66-67, 132-34, 136, 141-42, 153 and 162.

Rice, Grantland, *The Tumult and the Shouting: My Life in Sport* (New York: A. S. Barnes, 1954), pp. 19 and 29.

Rickey, Branch, *The American Diamond: A Documentary of the Game of Baseball* (New York: Simon & Schuster, 1965), p. 19.

Ritter, Lawrence S., *The Glory of Their Times: The Story of the Early Days of Baseball Told by the Men Who Played It* (New York: Macmillan, 1966)

Robinson, Jackie, *My Own Story, As Told to Wendell Smith* (New York: Greenberg, 1948)

Rosenberg, Howard W., *Cap Anson 2: The Theatrical and Kingly Mike Kelly: U.S. Team Sport's First Media Sensation and Baseball's Original Casey at the Bat* (Arlington, Va.: Tile Books, 2004)

—————————— , *Cap Anson 3: Muggsy John McGraw and the Tricksters: Baseball's Fun Age of Rule Bending* (Arlington, Va.: Tile Books, 2005), pp. 205-06, 217 (Leerhsen misquoted a 1950 Lieb book; see page 482) and 346.

—————————— , *Cap Anson 4: Bigger Than Babe Ruth: Captain Anson of Chicago* (Arlington, Va.: Tile Books, 2005), pp. 7-14 and 40.

Runyon Jr., Damon, *Father's Footsteps: The Story of Damon Runyon by his Son* (New York: Random House, 1953/1954)

Ruth, George Herman, and Ford Frick, *Babe Ruth's Own Book of Baseball* (New York: Putnam, 1928), pp. 112 and 231-32.

Sarazen, Gene, *The Golf Clinic* (Chicago: Ziff-Davis Pub. Co., 1949), p. 10.

Schacht, Al, *My Own Particular Screwball: An Informal Biography* (Garden City, N.Y.: Doubleday, 1955), pp. 137-38.

Schoendienst, Red, and Rob Rains, *Red: A Baseball Life* (Champaign, Ill.: Sports Publishing, 1998), pp. viii-ix and 56.

Shannon, Mike, *Diamond Classics: Essays on 100 of the Best Baseball Books Ever Published* (Jefferson, N.C.: McFarland & Co., 1989), p. 381.

Smith, Myron J., *Baseball: A Comprehensive Bibliography: Supplement 2 (1992 Through 1997)* (Jefferson, N.C.: McFarland & Co., 1998), p. 180.

Stanton, Tom, *Ty and the Babe: Baseball's Fiercest Rivals: A Surprising Friendship and the 1941 Has-Beens Golf Championship* (New York: Thomas Dunne Books/St. Martin's Press, 2007), p. 55.

Stern, Travis W., *From the Ball Fields to Broadway: Performative Identities of Professional Baseball Players on the Nineteenth and Twentieth Century American Stage*; Ph.D. Dissertation (Urbana, Ill.: University of Illinois, 2011), pp. 24-25.

Stern, William, *Favorite Baseball Stories* (Garden City, N.Y.: Doubleday, 1949), p. 243.

Stump, Al, *Cobb: A Biography*/(cover title) *Cobb: The Life and Times of the Meanest Man Who Ever Played Baseball: A Biography* (Chapel Hill, N.C.: Algonquin Books, 1994), pp. vii, 2, 25, 72-73, 180-81, 190, 199, 254, 358, 402 and 418-20.

Trembanis, Sarah L., *The Set-Up Men: Race, Culture and Resistance in Black Baseball* (Jefferson, N.C.: McFarland & Co., 2014), p. 29.

Tripp, Steven Elliott, *Ty Cobb, Baseball, and American Manhood: A Red-Blooded Sport for Red-Blooded Men* (Lanham, Md.: Rowman & Littlefield, 2016), pp. 21, 136-37, 140-42, 147, 149-50, 153, 180 and 395.

Tullius, John, *I'd Rather Be a Yankee: An Oral History of America's Most Loved and Most Hated Baseball Team* (New York: Macmillan, 1986), pp. 159-60.

Verney, Kevern, *African Americans and US Popular Culture* (New York: Routledge, 2003), p. 9.

Vlasich, James A., *A Legend for the Legendary: The Origin of the Baseball Hall of Fame* (Bowling Green Ohio: Bowling Green University Popular Press, 1990), pp. 72-73 and 238.

neither 2015 author noted the 1994 cover title. Hornbaker fully omitted whether Cobb was "mean." Leerhsen cited the term five times: (1) in a dismissal that I rebut on page 53; (2) as downplayed by Teeslink (see my pages 56-57); (3) as uttered on "I've Got a Secret" (see my page 388); (4) in skewing page 141 of Fred Lieb's 1950 *The Baseball Story* (by applying only to McGraw a decades-later roast of the 1890s Orioles; it is in *Cap Anson 3*); and (5) as used by Connie Mack; Leerhsen said at the time, he may have been "fake-mad."

Wagenheim, Kal, *Babe Ruth: His Life and Legend* (New York: Praeger, 1974), p. 37;
an October 2012 analysis by Franklin Hughes on the Web site of the Jim Crow
Museum of Racist Memorabilia of Ferris State University, posted at
https://ferris.edu/HTMLS/news/jimcrow/question/2012/october.htm, tipped
me off to Cobb and Ruth having played variations of African Dodger.

Wehrle, Edmund F., *Breaking Babe Ruth: Baseball's Campaign Against Its Biggest Star*
(Columbia, Mo.: University of Missouri, 2018), pp. 117, 209, 221, 228 and
236-37.

Williams, Ted, and John Underwood, *My Turn at Bat: The Story of My Life*
(New York: Simon & Schuster, 1969), p. 125 (observation about Austen Lake).
——————————————————, *The Science of Hitting* (New York:
Simon & Schuster, 1970), p. 40.

Articles in Books (in Alphabetical Order)

Andrews, Steve, "Making It Home: Cap Anson, Fleet Walker, and the Romance
of the National Pastime," in Gerald C. Wood and Andrew Hazucha, *Northsiders:
Essays on the History and Culture of the Chicago Cubs* (Jefferson, N.C.:
McFarland & Co., 2008), pp. 74-75 and 83.

Brown, Sterling A., "Athletics and the Arts," in E. Franklin Frazier, *The Integration of
the Negro into American Society* (Washington, D.C.: Howard University, 1951),
p. 119.

Strmic-Pawl, Hephzibah, "Racism," in Charles A. Gallagher and Cameron D.
Lippard, *Race and Racism in the United States: An Encyclopedia of the American
Mosaic Volume 3* (Santa Barbara, Calif.: Greenwood Press, 2014), p. 1018.

Letters (in Chronological Order) (those not referred to in news coverage; if cited in
news coverage, they appear under the "Print Media Endnotes" starting on page 491)

Cobb to Erwin Manley, July 21, 1904, at a link in November 2016 that has
disappeared; it can be bought as part of an eBook, which can be found by doing a
Google search for "tyrus-cobb-s-letters-to-erwin-manley-1904-1907"

Cobb to George Craig, January 24, 1908, 2007 SCP Auctions (Crawford).

Cobb to George Craig, no date, 1908, James Spence Authentication (U. of Georgia).

Archibald "Archie" Butt to Clara Butt, May 31, 1911, in Archibald Willingham
Butt, *Taft and Roosevelt: The Intimate Letters of Archie Butt, Volume 2*
(Garden City, N.Y.: Doubleday, Doran & Co., 1930), pp. 668-69.

Cobb to Fred Hall, January 3, 1915, James Spence Authentication.

Cobb to Fred Hall, undated, 1915, James Spence Authentication.

Cobb to Fred Hall, January 27, 1916, eBay.

Cobb to George (presumably) Weiss, September 12, 1918, James Spence
Authentication (bats receiving question).

Cobb to George (presumably) Weiss, undated, 1918, James Spence Authentication
(apology, Board of Trade reference).

Cobb to Helene Champlain, May 30, 1922, James Spence Authentication.

Cobb to Orin Champlain, October 12, 1922, James Spence Authentication.

Cobb to George Weiss, February 11, 1923, 2017 Hunt Auctions.

Cobb to Helene Champlain, March 6, 1923, James Spence Authentication.

Cobb to D. Peirson Ricks, May 29, 1923, James Spence Authentication.

Cobb to Harry G. Salsinger, November 14, 1923, James Spence Authentication.

Cobb to James "Deacon" McGuire, undated, 1925, James Spence Authentication.

Cobb to Christy Walsh, March 9, 1925, 2012 Nate D. Sanders Auctions.

Cobb to Christy Walsh, March 20, 1926, 2012 Heritage Auctions.

Cobb to Kenesaw Mountain Landis, July 4, 1927, James Spence Authentication.

Cobb to George H. Maines, March 7, 1928, National Baseball Hall of Fame Library (NBHOF Library).

Cobb to George H. Maines, June 14, 1929, James Spence Authentication.

Cobb to Clyde "Zeb" Milan, undated, 1929, 2012 Heritage Auctions.

Cobb to Manley Miner, August 6, 1935, NBHOF Library.

Cobb to Steve O'Neill, undated, 1936, in the *Brooklyn Eagle* of March 22, 1936.

Cobb to (first name unstated) Centurba, August 14, 1936, James Spence Authentication (Cobb's advice not to be "hot headed").

Cobb to Alexander Cleland, August 18, 1938, as excerpted on Sotheby's Web site from a 2007 auction.

Cobb to Alexander Cleland, September 24, 1938, as excerpted on Sotheby's Web site from a 2007 auction.

Cobb to Jack W. Tingey, October 28, 1938, 2003 Leland Little Auctions as fleshed out by James Spence Authentication.

Cobb to Alexander Cleland, April 29, 1939, James Spence Authentication.

Cobb to Hayward "Tom" Binney, June 29, 1939, 2013 Love of the Game Auctions auction.

Cobb to Charlotte "Charlie" Cobb, undated, presumably between 1931 and 1939, 2013 Profiles in History auction catalog.

Cobb to Hyman Pearlstone, July 14, 1940, 2016 Heritage Auctions.

Cobb to Stanley Gray, November 19, 1940, James Spence Authentication.

Cobb to Hayward "Tom" Binney, May 27, 1941, 2013 Heritage Auctions.

Cobb to Joseph "Joe" Hauck, May 27, 1944, Joseph Hauck Papers, Bancroft Library, University of California at Berkeley.

Cobb to Otto H. Sherlitz, June 1, 1944, 2006 Robert Edward Auctions catalog.

Cobb to Ernest J. Lanigan, April 21, 1945, in Charles Einstein (ed.), *The Fireside Book of Baseball* (New York: Simon & Schuster, 1956), p. 48.

Cobb to Manley Miner, January 27, 1946, NBHOF Library.

Cobb to Hayward "Tom" Binney, January 29, 1946, 2013 Heritage Auctions. Another stock-advice letter is dated April 27, 1936, 2013 Heritage Auctions.

Cobb to Joe Fisher, April 29, 1947, James Spence Authentication.

Cobb to Joseph "Joe" Hauck, May 20, 1947, Joseph Hauck Papers, Bancroft Library, University of California at Berkeley (diagnosis of faulty gallbladder, plus dietary and exercise adjustments).

Cobb to Jack McGrath, August 20, 1947, NBHOF Library (lost 28 pounds after gallbladder diagnosis).

Cobb to Joseph "Joe" Hauck, October 16, 1947, Joseph Hauck Papers, Bancroft Library, University of California at Berkeley (Del Webb/old timers' day).

Cobb to Babe Ruth, November 19, 1947, BabeRuthCentral.com.

Cobb to Helene Champlain, undated, 1948, 2012 Robert Edward Auctions catalog ("found your gloves").

Ernest Hemingway to Lillian Ross, July 2, 1948, transcribed in Ernest Hemingway and Carlos Baker (editor), *Ernest Hemingway, Selected Letters, 1917-1961* (New York: Scribner, 1981), p. 647.

Cobb to Helene Champlain, August 10, 1948, James Spence Authentication (vine on patio, dog pictures, Stoddard and Creel books).

Cobb to Helene Champlain, November 30, 1948, 2011 Huggins & Scott auction ("am here alone"/Beveridge and Farley books).

Cobb to Helene Champlain, December 6, 1948, 2012 Robert Edward Auctions catalog (Tom McClure).

Cobb to Helene Champlain, January 21, 1949, 2005 Sotheby's auction.

Cobb to Harry G. Salsinger, February 6, 1949, 2014 Profiles in History auction catalog.

Cobb to Joseph "Joe" Hauck, September 27, 1949, Joseph Hauck Papers, Bancroft Library, University of California at Berkeley (New York photographers giving Cobb and his new wife "hell." Hornbaker quoted the letter for his praise of her, with a notable error: omitting an ellipsis before the phrase "she is a wonder.").

Cobb to Harry G. Salsinger, February 28, 1950, 2014 Profiles in History auction catalog (thanks for "your appraisal and defense of me").

Cobb to (first name unstated) Bissell, March 6, 1950, James Spence Authentication.

Cobb to Harry G. Salsinger, July 12, 1950, 2014 Profiles in History auction catalog (kudos for *Sporting News* article rebutting intent-to-injure Honus Wagner story).

Cobb to Joseph "Joe" Hauck, July 28, 1950, Joseph Hauck Papers, Bancroft Library, University of California at Berkeley (beating Vitt at rummy).

Cobb to Joseph "Joe" Hauck, August 1, 1951, Joseph Hauck Papers, Bancroft Library, University of California at Berkeley. (After telephoning him after his testimony, Cobb asked him "to watch San F_ [sic] News and Call-Bulletin for anything 'the boys' should comment on, those who are so friendly & nice when they want something and to one[']s face and so quick to give one a left foot boot when they see an opportunity to say something at one[']s expense, when they know it[']s the truth, and only to build themselves up in their paper to the old California readers, yes and only on the basis of a small part of what was said and fully explained." Also, "I sure want to see the boys['] comments for I 'know' most of them. It is fine here, Frances caught a fish while I was away.")

Cobb to Clyde "Zeb" Milan, August 2, 1951, 2012 Heritage Auctions.

Frederick M. "Fred" Vinson to Sherman "Shay" Minton, August 6, 1951, available at an obscure Web link; an easy way to find it, presumably as the first search result in Google, is to type "Fred Vinson" and "Ty Cobb."

Cobb to Albert "Happy" Chandler, August 16, 1951, James Spence Authentication.

Cobb to Harry C. Byrd, October 31, 1951, University of Maryland Archives.

Cobb to George "Stoney" McLinn, November 26, 1951, NBHOF Library.

Cobb to Joseph "Joe" Hauck, Wednesday (undated, presumed 1952), Joseph Hauck Papers, Bancroft Library, University of California at Berkeley (the source for Cobb writing, "no 'spirits' for some time").

Cobb to Irving Vaughan, April 12, 1952, as excerpted on Sotheby's Web site from a 2010 auction.

Cobb to Stan Musial, April 28, 1952, 2013 Heritage Auctions auction.

Cobb to Christy Walsh, July 12, 1952, Sporting News Archives (includes cutting back on golf).

Cobb to George "Stoney" McLinn, October 28, 1952, 2014 Profiles in History auction catalog.

Cobb to Russell P. "Red" Reeder, Jr., October 30, 1952, NBHOF Library.

Cobb to Lou (last name unstated), December 17, 1952, James Spence Authentication. Lou, someone who Cobb knew, had committed a social faux pas during Cobb's most recent visit to Detroit. Cobb's tactfulness in the seven-page letter to be tactful in dishing out criticism is interesting, but lacks fuller context.

Cobb to Harry G. Salsinger, December 20, 1952, 2014 Profiles in History auction catalog.

Cobb to Harry G. Salsinger, date apparently not in public domain, 1953, referred to in Bak's 1994 *Ty Cobb: His Tumultuous Life and Times* on pages 165 and 168. Bak saw a letter in which Cobb spoke of being always hurt deep by portrayals of him as a dirty player. The one other letter from Cobb to Salsinger that Bak found that I cite, about "those Jewish boys" in either or both publishing and the movie industry, is on page 181 of his 2005 *Peach: Ty Cobb in his Time and Ours.*

Cobb to Gil Hodges, January 25, 1953, 2012 Heritage Auctions auction.

Hodges to Cobb, (undated) 1953, quoted in Mort Zachter, *Gil Hodges: A Hall of Fame Life* (Lincoln, Neb.: University of Nebraska, 2015), pp. 128-29, citing the letter as displayed in "The Glory Days: New York Baseball, 1947-1957," a 2007 exhibit at the Museum of the City of New York from the collection of Jerry Stern.

Cobb to Ronald (a boy, last name unknown), May 12, 1953, 2016 Iconic auction.

Cobb to Danny Goodman, May 15, 1953, NBHOF Library.

Cobb to Leroy Jacobsen, May 16, 1953, NBHOF Library.

Cobb to Joe (presumably) Clements, June 19, 1953, James Spence Authentication. In 2010 in the *Atlanta Journal-Constitution*, William R. (Ron) Cobb said he has originals of copies of 25 letters between Cobb and Clements that overlap with Clements's work in the 1950s as a radio announcer in Twin Falls. A highlight of the two letters that I saw that relates to my book is a food one: Cobb said he wants "only locally raised garlic usually sold in bulk not packaged, don[']t get California or any other kind." In the *Journal-Constitution*, reporter Bill Banks provided later detail; namely, that Cobb sent a check to Clements for famed Idaho garlic and did not receive any for three months. As paraphrased by Banks, "The Peach [sic] responded with a 2 1/2-page flourish, flashing at times his legendary temper during a rather impressive exposition on the nature of friendship." Banks also wrote, "Clements finally replies, apologizing profusely (sometimes in all caps), explaining that Cobb's original letter had been misplaced during a recent move. Clements writes, 'I must admit that you are equally as skilled with the pen as you were on the ball field. . . You've taken me to task as only an artist can.'" In a letter the following month, Cobb wrote Clements some especially kind words.

Cobb to Harry G. Salsinger, June 22, 1953, 2014 Profiles in History auction catalog.

Cobb to Gordon Oldham, June 18, 1953, 2014 Heritage Auctions.

Cobb to Christy Walsh, September 17, 1953, 2012 Heritage Auctions.

Cobb to Eddie Mathews, September 17, 1953, 2017 Lelands.com auction.

Cobb to Joe Clements, October 24, 1953, 2011 Robert Edward Auctions catalog. This letter is the best source that I found for Cobb's mention of the first of two South Dakota pheasant hunting trips in 1953. He mentioned the latter trip, after the fact, in a September 7, 1954, letter noted later.

Cobb to Max Carey, (undated) 1954, 1993 Christie's auction.

Cobb to Koozma J. Tarasoff, January 16, 1954, in "Letters from Ty Cobb," *Saskatchewan History* 47 (Fall 1995), p. 38.

Cobb to Max Carey, April 25, 1954, 2012 Robert Edward Auctions catalog.

Cobb to Danny Goodman, July 31, 1954, NBHOF Library.

Cobb to Dr. Daniel C. Elkin, August 21, 1954, in Jerry Atkins, *The Ty Cobb Educational Foundation Through Fifty Years* (Athens, Ga.: Five Points Press, 2007), p. 58 (as referenced by Hornbaker).

Cobb to Archie Yelle, September 7, 1954, 2013 RRAuction (includes a pheasant hunting plans reference).

Cobb to Fred Haney, September 14, 1954, as excerpted on the Lelands.com Web site from a 2004 auction; the first page is from a 2006 BidAMI.com auction.

Cobb to Danny Goodman, October 27, 1954, NBHOF Library.

Cobb to Ralph Holibaugh, undated, 1955, 2016 Hunt Auctions.

Cobb to Geraldine Cass Sutton, January 26, 1955, 2014 Profiles in History auction catalog.

Cobb to J. G. Taylor Spink, February 15, 1955, Sporting News Archives.

Cobb to (first name unstated, possibly Merritt E.) Hoag, February 21, 1955, James Spence Authentication.

Cobb to Phil Elderkin, March 7, 1955, 2013 Profiles in History auction.

Cobb to George Hipp, March 7, 1955, James Spence Authentication.

Cobb to Danny Goodman, March 14, 1955, 2008 BidAMI.com auction.

Cobb to Danny Goodman, March 23, 1955, NBHOF Library.

Cobb to George Hipp, March 25, 1955, James Spence Authentication.

Cobb to John D. McCallum, April 17, 1955, Manuscripts, Archives and Special Collections (MASC), Washington State University Libraries.

Cobb to John D. McCallum, May 2, 1955, MASC, Washington State University Libraries.

Cobb to J. G. Taylor Spink, May 30, 1955, Sporting News Archives.

Cobb to J. G. Taylor Spink, June 3, 1955, Sporting News Archives.

Cobb to John D. McCallum, July 3, 1955, MASC, Washington State University Libraries.

Cobb to John D. McCallum, July 7, 1955, MASC, Washington State University Libraries.

Cobb to Harry G. Salsinger, September 4, 1955, 2006 Lelands.com auction.

Cobb to unnamed person, undated (most likely 1956), James Spence Authentication (John McCallum-related).

Cobb to Joseph "Joe" Hauck, January 3, 1957, Joseph Hauck Papers, Bancroft Library, University of California at Berkeley (memory faulty).

Cobb to Jack McGrath, March 28, 1957, NBHOF Library.

Cobb to Ken Johnson, April 3, 1957, 2005 Robert Edward Auctions catalog. Cobb sent a similar request on June 30, 1957, to Clements, wanting him to write of Cobb's passing time in Twin Falls. 2013 Love of the Game Auctions.

Cobb to J. G. Taylor Spink, July 12, 1957, Sporting News Archives.

Cobb to J. G. Taylor Spink, September 2, 1957, Sporting News Archives.

Cobb to Joseph "Joe" Hauck, October 26, 1957, Joseph Hauck Papers, Bancroft Library, University of California at Berkeley (besides Frances's visit, Cobb using the word "colored," although, for that reference, Cobb's letter is not cited specifically in the main text).

Cobb to J. G. Taylor Spink, May 4, 1958, Sporting News Archives.

Cobb to J. G. Taylor Spink, August 16, 1958, Sporting News Archives.

Cobb to Joseph "Joe" Hauck, October 31, 1958, Joseph Hauck Papers, Bancroft Library, University of California at Berkeley (Cobb's deer and duck hunting).

Cobb to Mrs. C. B. Hooton, November 6, 1958, NBHOF Library.

Cobb to J. G. Taylor Spink, November 20, 1958, Sporting News Archives.

Cobb to Casey Stengel, December (date unclear), 1958, 2005 Heritage Auctions.

Cobb to Archie Yelle, December 26, 1958, 2011 Heritage Auctions.

Cobb to Joseph "Joe" Hauck, January 4, 1959, Joseph Hauck Papers, Bancroft Library, University of California at Berkeley.

Cobb to Tommy Daly, February 9, 1959, as provided by Sandra Somerville.

Cobb to Joseph "Joe" Hauck, April 4, 1959, Joseph Hauck Papers, Bancroft Library, University of California at Berkeley (health updates captured by Hornbaker).

Cobb to Joseph "Joe" Hauck, April 14, 1959, Joseph Hauck Papers, Bancroft Library, University of California at Berkeley (his writing of 75+ letters, mineral baths, food, housekeeper).

Cobb to Joseph "Joe" Hauck, June 30, 1959, Joseph Hauck Papers, Bancroft Library, University of California at Berkeley (moving out of Phoenix).

Cobb to Marie Quinn, August (date unclear), 1959, 2010 Sotheby's excerpt.

Cobb to Evan "Doc" Morris, August 15, 1959, 2014 CollectAuctions.com.

Cobb to Quinn, September 15, 1959, as transcribed by iCollector.com, based on its being offered by Nate D. Sanders Auctions in 2011.

Cobb to Quinn, October 14, 1959, 2010 Sotheby's excerpt (Jap Gardener).

Jimmy Jones to John Evangelist Walsh, November 13, 1959, as excerpted on Robert Edward Auctions' Web site from a 2012 REA catalog.

Cobb to John Evangelist Walsh, November 28, 1959, as excerpted on Robert Edward Auctions' Web site from a 2012 REA catalog.

Cobb to Quinn, December (undated) 1959, as transcribed by iCollector.com, based on its being offered by Nate D. Sanders Auctions in 2011 (his operation).

Cobb to George H. Maines, January 4, 1960, James Spence Authentication.

Cobb to Quinn, January 7, 1960, 2011 Nate D. Sanders Auctions.

Cobb to Quinn, January 13, 1960, 2010 Sotheby's excerpt (but I also cite parts of full letter for its "hellish pain" and new teeth references).

Cobb to Jackie Jensen, February 9, 1960, as excerpted on the Christie's Web site from a 2006 auction.

Cobb to Joseph "Joe" Hauck, February 19, 1960, Joseph Hauck Papers, Bancroft Library, University of California at Berkeley.

Cobb to Quinn, February 29, 1960, 2010 Sotheby's excerpt.

Cobb to Quinn, March (undated) 1960, 2010 Sotheby's excerpt.

Cobb to William Lengfelder, March 23, 1960, 2006 Sotheby's auction.

Cobb to Quinn, undated, references April 12, 1960, 2011 Nate D. Sanders Auctions (has 1932 Olympics reference).

Cobb to Danny Goodman, April 20, 1960, 2008 BidAMI.com auction.

Cobb to Bill DeWitt, May 4, 1960, 2006 eBay.com.

Cobb to Quinn, May 21, 1960, Christie's 2016 auction.

Cobb to Tyrus Richard "Ty R." Cobb, June 8, 1960, T. W. (Ty) Cobb Jr.

Cobb to Arthur Downey, presumably September (undated) 1960, NBHOF Library.

Cobb to Joseph "Joe" Hauck, September 11, 1960, Joseph Hauck Papers, Bancroft Library, University of California at Berkeley.

Cobb to Joseph "Joe" Hauck, January 26, 1961, Joseph Hauck Papers, Bancroft Library, University of California at Berkeley.

Cobb to (first name unstated) LeJeune, January 28, 1961, 2010 Heritage Auctions (letter of regret for Haney dinner).

Cobb to Joseph "Joe" Hauck, March 26, 1961, Joseph Hauck Papers, Bancroft Library, University of California at Berkeley.

Cobb to Danny Goodman, April 16, 1961, NBHOF Library.

Cobb to Arthur Downey, April 16, 1961, NBHOF Library.

Danny Goodman to Cobb, April 20, 1961, NBHOF Library.

Cobb to Charles Rex Teeslink, April 21, 1961, 2009 Heritage Auctions.

Cobb to Charles Rex Teeslink, May 22, 1961, 2009 Heritage Auctions.

George H. Maines to Rowan D. Spraker, Sr., August 5, 1961, NBHOF Library (includes Jimmy Durante detail).

Alvin J. "Al" Stump to Sid C. Keener, October 21, 1961, attributed to the NBHOF Library (quoted in Alexander book and 1993 reprint of Cobb-Stump 1961 one).

Russell P. "Red" Reeder, Jr., to Ken Smith, November 8, 1971, NBHOF Library.

Audio Interviews

Apparently unnamed NBC Blue radio network interviewer (working with program host Tom Manning), June 12, 1939, at Cooperstown, Library of Congress, Motion Picture, Broadcasting and Recorded Sound Division

Mutual Radio's Bob Wolff, circa 1950 at a hotel in Washington, D.C., Library of Congress, Motion Picture, Broadcasting and Recorded Sound Division

Video Interviews (in Chronological Order)

Unnamed interviewer and unidentified dog, "Cobb speaks on the sport – outtakes," Fox Movietone News Story 5-335, filmed on February 28, 1930, Magruder, Ga., accessed at http://mirc.sc.edu/islandora/object/usc%3A22721

Ken Murray for United Television Programs, Inc., "Where Were You. January 29, 1936?" copyright December 30, 1954, and aired in February 1955, Library of Congress, Motion Picture, Broadcasting and Recorded Sound Division

Ray Moore of WSB-TV Atlanta, "A Talk with Baseball Great Ty Cobb," undated 1955, uploaded by the University of Georgia as a permanent link after the author's query, at http://dbsmaint.galib.uga.edu/cgi/news?query=id%3Awsbn43665&_cc=1

Douglas Cooper and George O'Brien interview of James A. Farley, January 1, 1973, aired on about 30 radio stations including WNYC, Douglas P. Cooper Distinguished Contemporaries Collection, accessed at http://www.wnyc.org/story/james-farley

Bob Stevens interview of Bob Rosburg, undated 2007, uploaded January 9, 2008, accessed at https://www.youtube.com/watch?v=BTGEafVA_lM

Telephone interviews (by the author)

Civil War Bummer, March 7, 2017

James L. Copeland, son of Ernest "Ernie" Copeland, August 1, 2017 (source of speculation on how Cobb and his father met)

Sherry Waterman, daughter of Jolene "Jo" Mosher, August 4, 2017

E-mails

Valerie Komor, October 27, 2017 (no evidence of Stump AP best story award)

Kip A. Lindberg, December 27, 2017 and April 5, 2018 (CWS casualties)

Christine Fish, assistant to the registrar of the University of Washington, March 2, 2018 (1935-39 general studies major Stump did not graduate)

Jeffery K. Smart, March 23, 2018 (supplier of/clarifier of Thoen 1961 CWS essay)

U.S. Army Center of Military History, March 27 and April 11, 2018 (WWI)

Legal Documents (other than archival Mathewson and Rickey CWS ones)

W. R. Turvey v. Tyrus R. Cobb, March 11, 1936, Case No. 47415, Superior Court of the State of California in and for the County of Santa Clara

Bill of Particulars, October 6, 1955, Frances F. Cobb v. Tyrus R. Cobb, Case No. 1807, First Judicial District Court of Nevada, in and for the County of Douglas, pp. 2, 4, 10, 12-13 and 15-17 (a piggyback off of Hornbaker: obtained from the Superior Court of California, County of Butte, as part of Elbert D. Felts v. Tyrus R. Cobb, Case No. 29889, 1954-56)

Frances F. Cobb v. Tyrus R. Cobb, May 11, 1956, Case No. 1807, First Judicial District Court of Nevada, in and for the County of Douglas

In the Matter of the Appeal of Tyrus R. Cobb before the State Board of Equalization of the State of California, March 26, 1959, p. 282, also accessed at https://www.boe.ca.gov/legal/pdf/59-sbe-014.pdf

Certificate of Death, Tyrus Raymond Cobb, July 17, 1961, NBHOF Library

from 1919: U. S. A. stands for U.S. Army; Tracy Mathewson likely was the photographer

Richard Gurtowski wrote of Cobb in a Cobb-Christy Mathewson-Rickey (and others) article in 2005 on ballplayers in the Chemical Warfare Service, "With his expert eye for distance and his experience with hunting and guns, he would have been better-suited for the Field Artillery Corps."

Ty Cobb, greatest living baseball player and ex-captain U. S. A., hunting near his home in Atlanta. The Georgia Peach has not lost his cunning, for out of forty birds at which he shot he had a batting average of 1000 per cent.

Tracy Mathewson

Print Media Endnotes

(The references that follow are to news reports that I cite. I give added explanation of the context only if the detail is not presented within a yearly chronology and within those chronologies is not easy to deduce. One convenient device that I use anyway in my books is to liberally cite reporters, which may be of help in locating particular reports:)

Augusta Chronicle, April 1, 1906, citing

TYRUS COBB, HUNTSMAN

Detroit Free Press, March 18, 1906 ("red hot fanatics")

Detroit Free Press, April 1, 1906 (acquittal/ "knows the ways of the negro")

Detroit News, January 3, 1907 (Cobb's "very 'nerve' that is so galling")

Detroit Times, January 5, 1907 (letter to Frank Dean re: weight) (Dean appears on page 30 of Cobb and Stump's 1961 book for getting him free passes for the Detroit Opera House, which helped him conquer loneliness in his early years in Detroit.)

Detroit News, February 10, 1907 (clarification of letter to Frank Dean)

Detroit Free Press, March 17, 1907 (Schmidt and groundskeeper's friend fights)

Detroit News, March 17, 1907 (Schmidt and groundskeeper's friend fights)

Detroit Times, March 18, 1907 (not cited in

Cobb in the Blue Ridge Mountains in the offseason of 1906-07, as printed in the *Detroit News*

this book's main text: Paul H. Bruske's coverage of the fight was marginal except for the line, "Then Charlie Schmidt and Tyrus took issue on the race question and mauled each other for a while.")

Pittsburgh Press, October 14, 1907 (Johnny Kling's chatter)

Detroit News, November 18, 1907 (Bingay on Cobb's legs/in pain/Dixie Demon)

Oakland Tribune, December 8, 1907 ("learning new fancy steps")

St. Louis Post-Dispatch, March 22, 1908 (what is a Southern gentleman?)

Scranton Republican, April 21, 1908 (Schmidt downplaying Cobb as lucky)

Salt Lake Herald, May 24, 1908 (Jennings on Cobb/Kelly)

Detroit Free Press, June 7, 1908 (asphalt worker Fred E. Collins)

Washington Post, June 9, 1908 ("I wouldn't stand that from any man.")

Flint Journal (Mich.), June 9, 1908 (Cobb not impressed with a Negro's rights)

Detroit Free Press, June 10, 1908 ("Up here they don't understand me")

Indianapolis News, June 20, 1908 (Cobb on Fred Collins settlement)

Inter Ocean (Chicago), July 1, 1908

Boston Globe, August 3, 1908

Salt Lake Telegram, September 18, 1908 (on picking cotton/mammy story)

St. Louis Post-Dispatch, October 23, 1908 (James Crusinberry)

St. Louis Post-Dispatch, October 23, 1908 (tumble at Georgia State Fair)

Pittsburgh Post, October 26, 1908 ("Ty will put in the winter hunting")

Boston Globe, November 13, 1908 (a report from Columbus, Ga., that ran in many newspapers: Mrs. Cobb's barnstorming consent secured)

Detroit Free Press, March 21, 1909 (Joe Jackson on Cobb's new Georgia land)

Detroit Times, March 30, 1909 (Paul H. Bruske: Cobb and the black waiter)

Atlanta Constitution, March 30, 1909

St. Louis Post-Dispatch, May 9, 1909 (S. Carlisle Martin)

Atlanta Constitution, May 24, 1909 (S. Carlisle Martin)

Eau Claire Leader (Wis.), June 24, 1909 (interview with his wife)

Chicago Tribune, August 29, 1909 ("a law unto himself")

Detroit News, September 4, 1909 (Salsinger: Cobb on race of the Cuban players)

Detroit News Tribune, September 5, 1909 (Bingay describing Cobb as "a law unto himself;" plus "always seeking knowledge," "a bundle of nerves" and "comes closer to the athletic ideal." A "bundle of nerves" description of Cobb, presumably also penned by Bingay, appeared in the *Detroit News* on September 30, 1907.)

Pittsburgh Post-Gazette, October 8, 1909

Oshkosh Northwestern (Wis.), October 8, 1909 (Taft meets Cobb at Augusta)

Akron Beacon Journal, October 13, 1909 (Amanda Cobb interview)

Charlotte Observer, October 22, 1909 (174 pounds)

Charlotte Observer, October 31, 1909 (Colonel Cobb)

Charlotte News, November 1, 1909 (Charlotte visit/Cobb's leg injuries)

Winston-Salem Journal, November 3, 1909

Evening Statesman (Walla Walla, Wash.), November 5, 1909 (Taft: Cobb "victim of a damnable conspiracy")

Cheboygan Democrat (Mich.), April 1, 1910

Detroit Times, May 3, 1910, citing the *Chicago Examiner* (Hugh Fullerton: Cobb on smoking)

Boston Globe, May 25, 1910 (Taft and Sherman at game; Cobb visited U.S. Capitol)

Detroit Free Press, August 7, 1910 (black fan drew Cobb's ire)

Boston Globe, August 9, 1910 (open letter with four intervening sentences)

Detroit News, September 12, 1910 (Cobb no longer smoking cigars every day)

Washington Herald, October 10, 1910 (William Peet: Schaefer on Kling)

Detroit Times, November 4, 1910 (Navin telegram to nix Cobb-Rucker race)

Washington Herald, November 10, 1910 (Cobb's delivery to Gabby Street)

Sporting Life, December 3, 1910 (Paul Bruske)

Macon Telegraph, December 19, 1910 (Cuba trip analysis)

Augusta Chronicle, December 21, 1910 (Cobb laughing at *Macon Telegraph* report)

Pittsburgh Press, February 28, 1911 (Corbett was interlocutor)

Brooklyn Eagle, April 9, 1911

Washington Post, May 21, 1911 (Glen Echo)

Washington Post, May 25, 1911 (Glen Echo)

Washington Post, May 26, 1911 (Glen Echo)

Washington Post, May 27, 1911 (Glen Echo)

Washington Post, June 1, 1911 (Cobb and Lively visit to Taft)

Washington Times, June 2, 1911 (Bob Thayer)

Boston American, June 18, 1911, quoted in Ron Rapoport (ed.), *The Lost Journalism of Ring Lardner* (Lincoln, Neb.: University of Nebraska, 2017), p. 41.

Shreveport Times (La.), July 24, 1911 (Tip Wright: likened to John Pierpont "J. P." Morgan)

Escanaba Press (Mich.), August 11, 1911 (Cobb and Jackson compared)

Evening World (N.Y.), August 12, 1911 (Bozeman Bulger)

Detroit Free Press, August 20, 1911 (speeding arrest)

Atlanta Constitution, August 26, 1911 (to-be-minstrel report)

New York Sun, August 27, 1911 (African Dodger balls background)

Denver Post, November 19, 1911 (to complete in Vanderbilt and Savannah trophy races)

Pittsburgh Press, December 17, 1911 (Cobb-Moriarty "battle royal")

Fort Wayne News (Ind.), December 23, 1911 (on acting: "I can't stand the strain.")

Detroit News, December 27, 1911 (Salsinger: on Cobb re: "very slender ankles")

Washington Star, December 28, 1911 ("very slender ankles")

Pittsburgh Press, December 28, 1911 (Moriarty and he "the best of chums")

St. Louis Post-Dispatch, December 31, 1911 ("very slender ankles")

St. Louis Post-Dispatch, January 4, 1912 (John E. "Ed" Wray on "very slender ankles")

Detroit Free Press, January 22, 1912 (E. A. "Eddie" Batchelor and Cobb salvation quote)

Altoona Tribune (Pa.), January 25, 1912 (Billy Hamilton)

Detroit Times, February 19, 1912 (Cobb's address to group for needy children)

Brooklyn Eagle, February 21, 1912 (iceboating)

Evening Journal (Wilmington, Del.), February 26, 1912 (Ty Cobb, Ty Cobb and Ty Cobb)

Salina Journal (Kan.), April 25, 1912 (*Popular Mechanics*-related)

Washington Post, May 19, 1912 (congressional support letter)

New York Times, May 19, 1912 ("players are subjected to abuse each afternoon")

New York Sun, May 20, 1912

New York Sun, May 22, 1912

Washington Times, May 22, 1912 (Grantland Rice: "His one drawback is a lightning temper.")

Macon Telegraph, May 24, 1912, in part referring to *New York Sun*, May 20, 1912

Pittston Gazette (Pa.), June 10, 1912 (bought a share of a Detroit sporting goods chain)

Rocky Mountain News, June 24, 1912 (Amanda Cobb interview)

Denver Post, June 27, 1912 (Amanda Cobb interview)

Los Angeles Times, July 26, 1912 (belated report of Amanda Cobb interview)

Pittsburgh Press, August 5, 1912 (United Press re: Louis Scott de Burgh sermon)

Lexington Leader (Ky.), September 15, 1912 (minstrelsy-related: "My wife won't let me.")

Detroit News, October 10, 1912 (Cobb is Woodrow Wilson Club vice president)

St. Louis Post-Dispatch, October 27, 1912 (Corbett has appendicitis)

Evening Journal (Wilmington, Del.), October 29, 1912 (cotton expertise)

Santa Fe New Mexican, December 11, 1912 (minstrelsy)

El Paso Herald, December 13, 1912 (minstrelsy)

Bourbon News (Paris, Ky.), December 31, 1912 (background on *Lexington Leader* news editor)

Detroit Free Press, February 25, 1913 (bird dog story found by Hornbaker)

Indianapolis Star, March 2, 1913 (H. W. Lanigan: Rucker on Cobb)

Pittsburgh Post, April 24, 1913 (Caruso)

Atlanta Constitution, April 27, 1913 (on coffee/buttermilk/ale)

Cambridge Chronicle (Mass.), May 3, 1913 (background on "The Floral Bower")

Detroit Times, May 9, 1913 (Ralph L. Yonker: Cobb's black spectacles) (Alexander, on his page 113, wrote that Cobb had caught a cold on that trip from Ann Arbor.)

El Paso Herald, May 31, 1913 (Griffith quip on Cobb)

Washington Post, July 11, 1913 (St. Louis-Washington African Dodger contest)

St. Louis Star, July 16, 1913

Omaha Bee (Neb.), July 19, 1913 (Walter Johnson as joke addition to carnival event)

New York Times, August 5, 1913

Tampa Tribune, September 29, 1913

Augusta Chronicle, November 13, 1913 (official starter at Georgia-Carolina state fair)

News and Observer (Raleigh, N.C.), March 1, 1914 (Dr. Frank C. Atchison on Cobb as a future politician)

Brooklyn Eagle, March 18, 1914 (Rice criticizing Cobb)

Detroit News, March 20, 1914 (off-the-wall Wally Schang-Cobb story)

Detroit Free Press, March 27, 1914 (E. A. Batchelor)

Shreveport Times (La.), March 28, 1914 (on Cobb honor in Jackson, Miss.)

Shreveport Times (La.), April 2, 1914, possibly quoting a Mississippi newspaper (rug expert feature)

Anaconda Standard (Mont.), May 15, 1914 (alluded to by Leerhsen: Cobb telling about his temper. The article is under the byline of pitcher Christy Mathewson.)

Seattle Times, June 6, 1914 (Herbert "Hype" Igoe on his legs)

Chicago Defender, June 20, 1914 (African Dodger)

Macon Telegraph, June 25, 1914

Macon Telegraph, June 28, 1914

Evening World (N.Y.), March 1, 1915 (Jimmy Dugan comparing himself to Harry Tuthill)

Baltimore Sun, March 8, 1915 ("armful of bats")

New Orleans Item, March 28, 1915 (the *Akron Beacon Journal* of April 7, 1915, is one of a variety of newspapers that ran the condensed version containing rewrites of the *Item*'s prose)

Town Talk (Alexandria, La.), April 1, 1915 (Annie Kincaid Dent)

Grand Forks Herald (N.D.), April 9, 1915 (a report from Cincinnati: Cobb on suffrage)

Augusta Chronicle, June 11, 1915 (on Cobb and James M. Barrett)

St. Louis Post-Dispatch, June 17, 1915 (baseball supplies to France)

Evening Public Ledger (Pa.), July 9, 1915 (Rice on Cobb/Johnny Evers)

New Castle Herald (Pa.), July 14, 1915 (cotton futures suit)

Independent (Monessen, Pa.), August 16, 1915 (has done some trapshooting)

Detroit Times, August 21, 1915 (Cobb on lynching of Leo Frank)

Asheville Gazette-News (N.C.), September 9, 1915 (George Fitch)

Sporting Life, September 9, 1915 (James M. Barrett: feature)

Boston Post, September 19, 1915 (John M. Austin: Cobb on liquor and smoking)

Richmond Times-Dispatch, September 27, 1915 (alfalfa)

New York Sun, November 1, 1915 (Cobb on football)

Charleston Evening Post (S.C.), November 19, 1915 (Barrett-Cobb duck hunt)

Cobb and George Stallings, as printed in *American Shooter* in 1916

Detroit Times, December 24, 1915 (co-bought hunting preserve)

New York Sun, January 7, 1916 ("no nip for me")

Pittsburgh Press, May 5, 1916 (Arthur "Bugs" Baer)

St. Louis Times, June 28, 1916

St. Louis Star, July 3, 1916

St. Louis Star, July 4, 1916

El Paso Herald, July 7, 1916

Detroit News, August 1, 1916 (Cobb's letter to collegians)

Marion Star (Ohio), August 7, 1916 (Charles Evans Hughes)

Washington Times, August 18, 1916 (visit with Wilson)

New York Tribune, September 2, 1916 (Cobb on Wilson)

Hartford Courant, October 7, 1916 (Cannonball Redding)

Norwich Bulletin (Conn.), October 9, 1916 (Cannonball Redding)

Hartford Courant, October 9, 1916 (Cannonball Redding)

Wichita Eagle, December 13, 1916 (son of national pointer champion added to Cobb's kennel)

Arkansas Gazette (Little Rock), December 13, 1916 (Arthur "Bugs" Baer)

Oregonian (Portland), January 1, 1917 (Harry Grayson on Fielder Jones)

Rochester Democrat and Chronicle, January 2, 1917 (livestock sales)

Washington Times, January 16, 1917 (Clancy bio)

Arkansas Gazette (Little Rock), April 7, 1917 (Arthur "Bugs" Baer)

Los Angeles Herald, April 17, 1917 (Veiock of INS poem; I combined lines to save space)

Honolulu Star-Bulletin, May 25, 1917, quoting the *St. Louis Globe-Democrat* (John B. Sheridan interview). I did not find it in the *Globe-Democrat.*

Omaha World-Herald, November 6, 1917 (Sandy Griswold's Crawford interview)

Washington Post, November 11, 1917 (Robert Hill on prohibition in D.C.)

Nashville Tennessean, December 19, 1917 (does occasional clay pigeon shooting)

Indianapolis Star, January 4, 1918 (Nig Clarke)

Evening News (Harrisburg), May 22, 1918 (Paul Purman)

Des Moines Register, July 7, 1918 (headline from retelling of 1913 bird dog story)

Fort Wayne Sentinel (Ind.), September 21, 1918 (Corbett interview of Cobb)

Evening Review (Liverpool, Ohio), June 14, 1919

Ogden Standard-Examiner (Utah), August 4, 1920 (Pat Harrison)

Concord Times (N.C.), August 5, 1920 (Cox/Roosevelt)

Sacramento Union, August 8, 1920 (Lambert St. Clair: Harrison/Cobb)

Richmond Register (Ky.), September 9, 1920 (DNC Chairman George White)

San Francisco Chronicle, October 24, 1920

Los Angeles Times, October 27, 1920

Evening News (Wilkes-Barre), November 9, 1920 (Mrs. Mathewson theorizes)

New York Tribune, December 19, 1920 (William J. "Bill" Macbeth)

St. Louis Post-Dispatch, January 5, 1921 (Cobb on fisticuffs, Herzog)

Oregon Journal (Portland), January 16, 1921 (New Haven stockholder)

Detroit Free Press, February 3, 1921 (Detroit banquet in his honor)

Macon Telegraph, February 9, 1921 (New Haven banquet)

St. Louis Post-Dispatch, March 21, 1921 (Robert W. Edgren: Cobb on bird dogs)

Detroit News, April 19, 1921 (Charlie Cobb interview)

Baltimore Sun, October 2, 1921 (Maines initiative re: Schacht and Altrock)

Milwaukee Journal, October 27, 1921 (visit to Cobb family home)

Buffalo News, December 5, 1921 (Maines initiative re: Schacht and Altrock)

Flint Journal (Mich.), December 27, 1921 (Donovan/New Haven/Cobb)

News-Herald (Franklin, Pa.), February 7, 1922 (1922 weight)

Greenville News (S.C.), March 21, 1922 (1922 weight)

Detroit Times, May 2, 1922 (Cobb protest letter on Robertson perfect game)

Detroit Free Press, May 3, 1922 (Ban Johnson absolved Robertson)

Brooklyn Eagle, July 20, 1922 (he told the AP that he now needs more sleep. This, from the *Detroit News* of August 6, 1922, does not square with my main text: "For the last 10 years I have religiously figured on 10 hours' sleep and usually I get more.")

The Repository (Canton, Ohio), July 30, 1922 (Frank G. Menke)

Springfield Republican (Mass.), August 17, 1922 (Rice)

Evansville Courier (Ind.), December 6, 1922 (Tuthill boxing lessons)

Brooklyn Eagle, January 26, 1923

Detroit News, March 21, 1923 (Charles D. Carr interview)

Detroit Free Press, May 26, 1923 (Cobb's safety advice)

Ogden Standard-Examiner (Utah), November 13, 1923 (NEA feature)

Detroit News, March 27, 1924 (Salsinger: Robert L. Wynn)

Detroit News, April 6, 1924 (Salsinger: spring training stories)

Greensboro News (N.C.), April 8, 1924 (Robert L. Wynn)

Detroit Free Press, April 24, 1924

Detroit News, May 11, 1924 (Salsinger: presentation-of-20-books-to-Cobb detail)

Washington Star, May 11, 1924 (D.C. dinner in his honor)

News-Herald (Franklin, Pa.), May 13, 1924 (Clancy ad)

Pittsburgh Courier, May 24, 1924 (W. Rollo Wilson)

Toronto Star, July 24, 1924 (Cobb as nonsurgeon, doing good for humanity)

New York Herald Tribune, July 27, 1924 (Frank F. Dole: Cobb on dogs)

New York Mirror, July 29, 1924 (Gene Fowler on Maines/Schacht/Altrock)

Ottawa Journal, November 3, 1924 (Jack Miner and Cobb)

Bridgeport Telegram (Conn.), November 24, 1924 (Salsinger serial/umpires)

Detroit Times, December 14, 1924 (Cobb's letter printed re: serial plans)

Baltimore Sun, December 16, 1924 (Salsinger serial/fights)

Baltimore Sun, December 17, 1924 (Salsinger serial/erudition)

Baltimore Sun, December 18, 1924 (Salsinger serial/psychological examiner)

Baltimore Sun, December 20, 1924 (Salsinger serial/temperament and "literally wept")

Winnipeg Tribune, December 26, 1924 (Salsinger serial/dogs)

Times Signal (Zanesville, Ohio), December 27, 1924 (Speaker won poll)

Pittsburgh Post-Gazette, January 22, 1925 (Salsinger serial/moods/food/"Down South")

Charlotte Observer, February 8, 1925

Atlanta Constitution, February 22, 1925 (Julian Griffin: Mathewson potpourri)

Detroit Times, February 28, 1925 (arrest headline cited)

Pittsburgh Post, March 1, 1925 (arrest; Cobb's specific denial of allegations)

Detroit News, March 1, 1925 (arrest; headline cited on front-page story)

Madera Tribune (Calif.), March 2, 1925 (Theodore Dreiser)

Detroit News, March 3, 1925 (follow-up arrest story not cited in main text; it had the front-page headline, "ATLANTA SURVIVES COBB EARTHQUAKE: Manages to Bear Up Under Peach's Rumblings.")

Winnipeg Tribune, March 4, 1925 (Davis J. Walsh: Cobb on players' eating)

Pittsburgh Post, March 6, 1925 (William Peet)

Bluefield Telegraph (W.V.), March 15, 1925 (1925 weight)

News-Herald (Franklin, Pa.), April 16, 1925 (Jack Miner on Cobb)

New York Telegram, July 1, 1925

Sunday Courier (Harrisburg), July 5, 1925 (Ed Hughes)

Detroit News, August 30, 1925 (banquet)

Pittsburgh Post, August 31, 1925 (AP: Cobb's banquet remarks)

Detroit Free Press, August 31, 1925 (Navin on Schalk; Baer banquet speaker)

Macon Telegraph, September 1, 1925

Detroit Free Press, October 8, 1925 (AP re: doctor on Mathewson's cause of death)

Asbury Park Press (N.J.), October 29, 1925 (Cobb/Barrow/Howley)

Rockford Register (Ill.), December 6, 1925 (Morris Ackerman)

St. Louis Post-Dispatch, December 6, 1925 (CWS's Fries on Mathewson/WWI gas)

Pittsburgh Press, December 16, 1925 (Cobb's serial: daily ideas testing/"rather stormy" baseball career)

Pittsburgh Press, December 28, 1925 (Cobb's serial: not "evenly balanced")

Pittsburgh Press, January 10, 1926 (Cobb's serial quoted on African Dodger/fighting back with spikes)

Pittsburgh Press, January 13, 1926 (Cobb's serial: "hard knocks"/"rough kidding"/nagging)

Atlanta Constitution, February 22, 1926 (AP Augusta: larceny at Cobb house)

Springfield Republican (Mass.), May 12, 1926 (batting tips, kudos to Gehrig)

Brooklyn Eagle, July 26, 1926 (Griffith complaint: Cobb's dilatory tactics)

Boston Herald, August 1, 1926

Baltimore News, August 18, 1926

Washington Times, August 19, 1926

Gaffney Leader (S.C.), October 2, 1926 (in Wyoming)

Detroit News, November 4, 1926 (Salsinger on Cobb's managing tenure)

Pittsburgh Press, November 6, 1926 (Billy Evans)

Springfield Sunday Union and Republican (Mass.), November 7, 1926 (Amanda Cobb)

Lansing State Journal, November 19, 1926 (Alderton re: Cobb/Navin/Moriarty)

Cleveland Plain Dealer, November 23, 1926 (Henry P. Edwards)

Macon Telegraph, December 18, 1926 (AP birthday feature)

St. Louis Star, December 22, 1926 (Cobb's gambling scandal tears)

Atlanta Constitution, December 23, 1926 (special to re: gambling scandal)

Atlanta Constitution, December 23, 1926 (AP re: gambling scandal)

Anniston Star (Ala.), December 23, 1926 (UP re: gambling scandal)

Pittsburgh Courier, January 1, 1927 (W. Rollo Wilson)

Ottawa Journal, January 4, 1927 (Dr. R. D. Sloane defense of Cobb)

Pittsburgh Courier, January 29, 1927 (Mable Ridley)

Macon Telegraph, February 19, 1927

San Diego Tribune, February 23, 1927 (AP story on Cobb turkey photo)

Tampa Tribune, March 3, 1927 (letter to Billy Sunday)

Lansing State Journal, March 4, 1927

Nashville Tennessean, April 16, 1927

Detroit News, May 11, 1927 (Alexander George Washington Rivers)

Reading Times (Pa.), June 23, 1927 (AP white table wine)

News-Review (Roseburg, Ore.), June 23, 1927 (AP white table wine)

Oakland Tribune, September 7, 1927 (Gehrig on Cobb)

San Diego Union, October 9, 1927 (book-opening Cobb whoppers)

Charleston Evening Post (S.C.), October 24, 1927 (AP Wyoming: not cited in main text: Cobb bagged two bear one day)

Oakland Tribune, October 30, 1927 (pitcher's tale from Mack serial)

New York Herald Tribune, March 3, 1928 (Rud Rennie: Cobb and John McGraw)

Nashville Tennessean, March 9, 1928 (AP re: Cobb Augusta/1928 weight)

New York Herald Tribune, March 9, 1928 (Rud Rennie: Cobb and O'Doul)

Macon Telegraph, March 10, 1928 (AP Augusta: Torkas/Cobb)

Detroit Times, May 4, 1928 (Rivers interview)

Louisville Courier-Journal, May 9, 1928 (in Old Gold cigarette advertisement)

New York Sun, June 7, 1928 (Durocher on Cobb)

Springfield Republican (Mass.), June 8, 1928, in part citing *New York Sun*, June 7, 1928 (Durocher on Cobb)

Honolulu Advertiser, July 31, 1928 (Major Gen. Fries on Mathewson/WWI gas)

Brooklyn Eagle, August 20, 1928 (Harold C. Burr: Durocher interview)

Los Angeles Times, September 21, 1928

Chicago Tribune, September 23, 1928 (Alexander Rivers/Westbrook Pegler)

Boston Herald, September 30, 1928 (Carl Watson)

Arizona Daily Star, December 14, 1928 (AP's Newland re: Cobb/Japan)

Cincinnati Enquirer, January 3, 1929 (AP re: Hornsby/Ku Klux Klan)

Pittsburgh Press, January 10, 1929 (UP re: Boston Finance Commission)

Pittsburgh Press, March 26, 1929 (Cobb Shakespeare)

Monroe News-Star (La.), April 25, 1929 (AP's Eddie Brietz)

Evening News (Wilkes-Barre), June 15, 1929 (AP's Davis J. Walsh)

Louisville Courier-Journal, June 30, 1929 (A. F. Hochwalt)

Reading Times (Pa.), July 24, 1929 (AP Paris)

Tampa Tribune, September 25, 1929 (AP re: Simmons was a roommate)

New York Times, October 3, 1929 (Cobb: feelings on baseball after trip to Europe)

Winnipeg Tribune, October 11, 1929 (Walter Trumbull)

Detroit Free Press, October 20, 1929 (support of John W. Smith)

The Repository (Canton, Ohio), November 18, 1929 (Royal S. Copeland)

Warren Times Mirror (Pa.), December 12, 1929 (recounting trip)

Asbury Park Press (N.J.), January 22, 1930 (movies of Europe)

Boston Globe, February 9, 1930 (Durocher goat-getting)

Casper Tribune (Wyo.), February 17, 1930 (Arthur "Bugs" Baer)

Detroit Free Press, April 3, 1930 (AP re: criticizing Bobby Jones)

Cincinnati Enquirer, May 11, 1930

Brooklyn Eagle, June 29, 1930 (AP re: pro-history reading)

Wellington Leader (Tex.), July 24, 1930 (Cobb/Mack mutual admiration)

Brooklyn Eagle, July 30, 1930 (AP re: baseball interest on decline)

Modesto News-Herald (Calif.), September 20, 1930 (Jackson Hole)

Detroit Free Press, October 3, 1930 (Bingay on Gabby Street)

Oshkosh Northwestern (Wis.), December 15, 1930 (wild goose)

Brooklyn Eagle, December 28, 1930 (winter sport coordinator)

Sandusky Register (Ohio), December 28, 1930 (AP birthday interview)

Louisville Courier-Journal, January 3, 1931 (A. F. Hochwalt: Ty Cobb Cup)

Augusta Chronicle, January 27, 1931 (aerial golf)

Augusta Chronicle, February 15, 1931 (recent hunting trip)

Augusta Chronicle, February 23, 1931 (Augusta publicity campaign)

Oakland Tribune, February 26, 1931 (AP retirement story/includes bird dogs)

Lincoln Evening Journal (Neb.), April 1, 1931 (Rice)

Clarion-Ledger (Jackson, Miss.), April 16, 1931 (AP re: divorce)

Chicago Tribune, April 16, 1931 (AP re: divorce)

Detroit Free Press, April 17, 1931 (Alfred Lombard sticking gun in Cobb's ribs)

Dayton Daily News, April 18, 1931 (Robert W. Edgren: Cobb on India/Africa)

Cincinnati Enquirer, April 26, 1931 (Jack Ryder/*American Legion Magazine*)

Democrat-American (Sallisaw, Okla.), June 11, 1931

Riverside Daily Press (Calif.), September 10, 1931

St. Louis Post-Dispatch, September 24, 1931 (AP interview with Street)

Fremont Messenger (Ohio), October 2, 1931 (INS re: Cobb visit to San Quentin)

St. Louis Post-Dispatch, October 2, 1931

Gettysburg Times, October 15, 1931 (AP re: Johnson/Street on Cobb)

Oakland Tribune, October 15, 1931 (Bob Shand on Cobb/Nick Williams)

Detroit Free Press, December 4, 1931 (Dugan released)

Cincinnati Enquirer, February 23, 1932 (AP interview in Chicago)

Baltimore Sun, February 25, 1932 (AP interview in Chicago)

Lincoln State Journal (Neb.), March 9, 1932 (Salsinger on trainer Carroll)

Detroit Free Press, June 2, 1932 (Tuthill on Moriarty/Cobb)

New York Sun, June 3, 1932, in part apparently citing an unnamed newspaper (Sam Murphy: George Moriarty and Cobb)

Eugene Guard (Ore.), June 17, 1932

Atlanta Constitution, July 24, 1932

Evening Tribune (San Diego), August 2 and 4-6, 1932 (Cobb on Olympics)

New York Daily News, August 14, 1932 (Paul Gallico: leg scars/competitive golfer)

Chicago Defender, December 10, 1932 (Cannonball Redding)

Oakland Tribune, January 27, 1933 (Walter Mails on Cobb)

New Orleans States, April 23, 1933 (Maines feature; includes his publicity work for Bob Burman and his *New York Daily Mirror* tenure)

Detroit Free Press, July 11, 1933 (Bingay on luck)

Detroit Free Press, July 16, 1933 (Bingay on Cobb/Armour/Jennings)

Roseburg News (Ore.), July 21, 1933 (Arthur "Bugs" Baer)

New York Mirror, December 20, 1933 (Dan Parker on Ty/Ty Jr.)

Greenville News (S.C.), December 23, 1933 (Dan Parker on Ty/Ty Jr.)

Brooklyn Eagle, January 23, 1934 (Harold C. Burr: Cobb on his possible professions)

San Bernardino County Sun, February 6, 1934 (AP re: Cobb on regrets)

Augusta Chronicle, February 7, 1934 (AP re: Cobb on regrets)

Philadelphia Inquirer, February 8, 1934 (James C. Isaminger on Cobb's regrets)

Reno Evening Gazette, February 12, 1934 (AP's Newland re: Street banquet)

Oakland Tribune, February 15, 1934 (Cobb on California weather)

Sporting News, February 15, 1934 (Bill Dooley of *Philadelphia Record*; I looked in the *Record* on microfilm too and did not find prose on subject)

Oregonian (Portland), March 4, 1934 (David W. Hazen: extensive Cobb interview/Jimmy Collins all-time 3B)

Detroit Free Press, April 2, 1934 (Cobb/Marberry feud)

Santa Cruz Sentinel, April 4, 1934 (Oakland opening day)

Indianapolis Star, May 26, 1934 (Cobb letter clarifying regrets)

Detroit Times, August 23, 1934 (keeps in shape golfing and riding)

Oakland Tribune, October 30, 1934 (supporting Frank F. Merriam)

The Times (Shreveport, La.), January 5, 1935 (AP's Brian Bell)

Richmond Item (Ind.), February 8, 1935 (Joe E. Brown/"Alibi Ike" offer)

Oakland Tribune, March 12, 1935 (boxing/boxing commissioner Goodwin)

Detroit Times, April 8, 1935 (Bud Shaver: Cochrane on Cobb)

Oakland Tribune, June 27, 1935 (Alan Ward on ham at dinner party)

Detroit News, July 31, 1935 (Salsinger: Cobb's avenging of dust-off pitchers)

Oakland Tribune, August 30, 1935 (Cobb hit a pedestrian, then exonerated)

Detroit Free Press, September 8, 1935 (Bingay on Cobb's personality)

Chicago Tribune, September 13, 1935 (Ward re: DiMaggio/Cobb)

Brooklyn Eagle, September 22, 1935 (AP "gone softie" interview)

Hartford Courant, December 30, 1935 (Rice: Ruth vs. Cobb as drawing card)

New Castle News (Pa.), January 29, 1936 (Walter Johns on Cobb/Schang)

Los Angeles Times, February 9, 1936 (Chief Meyers on Cobb)

Boston Herald, February 14, 1936 (Eddie Collins on Meyers/Cobb)

Arizona Republic, February 19, 1936 (UP re: San Mateo supervisor petition)

Nashville Tennessean, March 8, 1936 (Blinkey Horn on Cobb/Dizzy Dean)

Springfield Republican (Mass.), April 15, 1936 (Rice: "types who are naturally nervous")

Detroit Free Press, May 4, 1936 (AP re: Vitt on Cobb)

Greenville News (S.C.), June 16, 1936 (not cited in this book's main text: AP re: Cobb on DiMaggio)

Chicago Defender, July 11, 1936 (Alfred J. Roy)

Cleveland Call and Post, August 27, 1936 (Speaker/Jesse Owens)

Los Angeles Times, September 15, 1936 (how Cobb signs autographs)

Greenville News (S.C.), September 16, 1936 (Cobb letter)

Greenville News (S.C.), September 19, 1936 (Cobb letter update)

Spokane Chronicle (Wash.), October 2, 1936 (headline on AP re: Cobb food)

Bee (Danville, Va.), October 2, 1936 (headline on AP re: Cobb food)

Amarillo Globe-Times (Tex.), October 21, 1936

Clarion-Ledger (Jackson, Miss.), October 23, 1936 (current weight)

Oakland Tribune, November 6, 1936 (speeding ticket)

Vernal Express (Vt.), November 26, 1936 (Hugh Bradley on weight)

Greenville News (S.C.), December 9, 1936 (newer Cobb letter)

Spartanburg Herald (S.C.), December 10, 1936 (AP update on Cobb cook search)

Lincoln Star (Neb.), January 26, 1937 (INS's Harold Heroux)

Oakland Tribune, February 4, 1937 (Art Cohn on Cobb/Bartell)

New York World-Telegram, March 20, 1937 (DiMaggio on Cobb)

Brooklyn Eagle, March 23, 1937 (Frank Reil: DiMaggio on Cobb)

Riverside Daily Press (Calif.), April 26, 1937 (golf win at Del Monte)

Oakland Tribune, June 16, 1937 (Cohn: Cobb on Negroes with rhythm)

Oregonian (Portland), July 4, 1937 (David W. Hazen's nine favorite interviews)

Los Angeles Times, July 23, 1937

Oregonian (Portland), August 29, 1937 (David W. Hazen citing Brian Bell)

Oakland Tribune, September 15, 1937 (AP's Eddie Brietz citing Bell)

San Bernardino Sun, October 16, 1937 (UP re: Cobb and deer)

Ottawa Journal, November 11, 1937 ("Bradley" on Cobb/Eddie Shore)

Muncie Evening Press (Ind.), December 8, 1937 (NEA: Vitt says Cobb would have hit .500 against lively ball)

New Journal and Guide (Norfolk, Va.), January 22, 1938

Sporting News, March 5, 1938 (Dan Daniel on interviewing Cobb/Hornsby)

Nevada State Journal (Reno), March 18, 1938 (Bill Veeck, Sr. on spike filing; Bill Bailey was his byline)

Boston Globe, March 25, 1938 (Rice)

Evening News (Wilkes-Barre, Pa.), April 21, 1938 (Cobb advising DiMaggio article reprint)

Lansing State Journal, April 29, 1938

Decatur Herald (Ill.), May 11, 1938 (AP re: Barrow's regret re: Cobb)

San Francisco Chronicle, May 26, 1938 (Harry B. Smith/Cobb)

Greenville News (S.C.), July 24, 1938 (AP on Charles H. Spencer)

St. Louis Star-Times, September 15, 1938 (ordering golf clubs)

San Francisco Chronicle, September 17, 1938

Chicago Defender, September 27, 1938 (Al Monroe)

Dayton Herald, December 16, 1938 (UP poll of sports editors re: should Ruth be given the opportunity to manage)

Iowa City Press-Citizen, December 23, 1938 (NEA's Harry Grayson: Haney on Cobb, Cobb letter to Haney)

Arizona Republic, December 25, 1938 (AP: Fred Corcoran on Cobb)

Tampa Tribune, January 5, 1939 (NEA's Grayson re: Bartell on Cobb)

Tampa Tribune, January 6, 1939 (AP's Eddie Brietz on Cobb/Bartell)

San Francisco Examiner, February 3, 1939

Oakland Tribune, February 6, 1939

Oakland Tribune, February 8, 1939

Arizona Republic, February 13, 1939 (AP's Middleton on Cobb/Lazzeri)

Oakland Tribune, March 9, 1939 (Pacific Association track and field meet)

Santa Ana Register (Calif.), March 10, 1939 (UP: Cobb and SF track meets)

Detroit Times, March 29, 1939 (Bob Murphy: Jones on Cobb/Crawford)

News-Herald (Franklin, Pa.), April 8, 1939 (NEA's Grayson re: Croke on Cobb)

Lansing State Journal, April 20, 1939 (Alderton on Cobb/Gehringer)

Detroit News, May 9, 1939 (Salsinger: Cobb could hit more than .500 today)

New York Mirror, May 22, 1939 (Dan Parker on Cobb's golfing)

Detroit Free Press, June 12, 1939 (Cobb talking hunting and shooting)

Detroit News, June 12, 1939 (Cobb talking hunting and shooting)

Detroit Times, June 12, 1939 (Cobb talking hunting and shooting)

New York Herald Tribune, June 14, 1939 (Jesse Abramson)

Arizona Republic, June 14, 1939 (UP's George Kirksey)

Washington Star, June 14, 1939

New York World-Telegram, June 14, 1939 (James A. Burchard)

New York Herald Tribune, June 14, 1939 (Fred Hawthorne)

Rochester Democrat and Chronicle, June 14, 1939 (INS's Bob Considine: includes Cobb re: Dutch Leonard/Carl Mays)

Boston Herald, June 16, 1939 (Arthur Sampson)

Brooklyn Eagle, June 18, 1939

Baltimore American, June 18, 1939 (Cobb, Harrison, Merle Thorpe and Rodger Pippen golfed/three Cobbs were Griffith's guests at the Columbia Country Club)

Oakland Tribune, June 30, 1939 (Cohn second-hand: Cobb on his move)

Santa Ana Register (Calif.), July 1, 1939 (NEA: Cobb on taking stealing risk)

Springfield Republican (Mass.), July 2, 1939 (Spencer Abbott/Durocher)

Cleveland Plain Dealer, July 2, 1939 (Ted Lyons tale on Cobb)

Atlanta Constitution, July 5, 1939 (Kenneth Stambaugh letter on Cobb)

Elwood Call-Leader (Ind.), July 7, 1939 (UP's Speaker interview, includes stocks)

Charleston Evening Post (S.C.), August 2, 1939 (AP re: Barrow on Speaker/Cobb)

San Luis Obispo Telegram-Tribune (Calif.), August 3, 1939 (UP: Speaker denies making DiMaggio comparison)

Philadelphia Inquirer, August 5, 1939 (Rice)

Philadelphia Inquirer, January 7, 1940 (Klem on Cobb)

Courier News (Blytheville, Ark.), January 15, 1940 (Mathewson on bird dogs)

Cincinnati Enquirer, January 27, 1940 (AP re: Crosby Pro-Amateur)

Atlanta Constitution, January 30, 1940 (Johnston on Cobb)

Nevada State Journal (Reno), February 8, 1940 (sports editor Cobb on Cobb)

San Francisco Chronicle, March 11, 1940 (Will Connolly on Cobb's conditioning)

Washington Post, March 23, 1940 (Bob Considine interview with DiMaggio)

Philadelphia Inquirer, March 31, 1940 (James C. Isaminger: Cobb's wine cellar)

Chicago Tribune, April 24, 1940 (Ed Sullivan on Cobb)

St. Louis Post-Dispatch, July 28, 1940

Detroit News, September 20, 1940 (Salsinger: Daniel says Cobb would steal 150 bases if still playing; I did not find it in the *Sporting News* or Daniel's newspaper)

Sporting News, November 21, 1940 (Schalk: don't get Cobb mad/Cobb's entitled-to-the-plate-as-much-as-you-are story)

Greenville News (S.C.), December 23, 1940 (Cobb food)

Ames Daily Tribune (Iowa), January 18, 1941 (UP's McLemore: Cobb says widen home plate)

Cincinnati Enquirer, February 23, 1941 (Bernie Boland to INS re: Cobb trickery)

Washington Post, March 13, 1941 (Leonard Lyons syndicated column)

Milwaukee Journal, March 23, 1941 (Brick Owens on Cobb racecar driving)

Pittsburgh Press, April 2, 1941 (Vitt/DiMaggio)

Boston Herald, April 5, 1941 (Cunningham on Cobb golfing)

Wilmington Morning News (N.C.), April 14, 1941 (Arthur "Bugs" Baer)

Los Angeles Times, May 2, 1941 (lefty golfer tournament in Pasadena)

Los Angeles Times, May 13, 1941 (AP: Cobb/Arnold Sharkey suit)

San Bernardino Sun, May 16, 1941 (AP: Cobb/Sharkey settlement)

Detroit Free Press, May 17, 1941 (Bingay on bench jockeying)

Oakland Tribune, May 18, 1941 (Ward: Cobb invitational golf tournament)

Cincinnati Enquirer, June 15, 1941 (INS's Considine on Cobb/Ruth)

Detroit News, June 22, 1941 (John Walter: Cobb's cigarette habits)

Boston Herald, June 23, 1941 (Cunningham on Rice/Nig Clarke)

Washington Post, June 24, 1941 (AP re: Pat Harrison death)

Boston Herald, June 25, 1941 (Arthur Sampson)

Altoona Tribune (Pa.), June 25, 1941 (Whitney Martin observing Cobb rolling cigarettes (not cited in main text)).

Christian Science Monitor, June 25, 1941 (Edwin M. Rumill: Berg on Cobb)

Detroit Free Press, July 30, 1941

Hearne Democrat (Tex.), August 4, 1941 (Cayce Moore on spiking)

New York World-Telegram, August 14, 1941 (Joe Williams re: Cobb/Ehmke)

Oakland Tribune, August 22, 1941 (Cohn: Cobb simile to a "dull gray wall")

Lincoln Star (Neb.), September 26, 1941 (INS: Cobb on Durocher)

Bakersfield Californian, January 26, 1942 (lefty golfer association)

San Bernardino Sun, February 1, 1942 (Idaho deer shooting fine)

Poughkeepsie Eagle-News (N.Y.), February 7, 1942 (AP's Martin re: Cobb on golf)

Alton Telegraph (Ill.), February 18, 1942 (Vitt quip re: if Cobb still playing)

Sporting News, February 26, 1942 (Ward Morehouse of *New York Sun*; I looked in the *Sun* on microfilm too and did not find it there) (includes "a little fat now")

Cincinnati Enquirer, March 8, 1942 (UP: Lobert on MacArthur)

San Francisco Chronicle, March 20, 1942 (Kreling as golfing acquaintance)

Atlanta Constitution, March 30, 1942

Sporting News, April 2, 1942 (Salsinger on Cobb not arguing with umpires)

Omaha World-Herald, April 3, 1942

Detroit Free Press, May 10, 1942 (Cobb on Harry Tuthill)

Washington Star, May 16, 1942 (batting tips to Keller and Rolfe)

Baltimore News-Post, May 18, 1942 (Cobb is guest of Rodger H. Pippen)

Shamokin News-Dispatch (Pa.), May 22, 1942 (E.V. Durling)

Greenville News (S.C.), May 22, 1942 (Latimer: Cobb on war effort)

Greenville News (S.C.), May 23, 1942 (Latimer on Cobb golfing with Rice)

Greenville News (S.C.), June 4, 1942 (Cobb visited Jackson)

Index-Journal (Greenwood, S.C.), June 8, 1942 (AP on Brian Bell's death)

Oakland Tribune, July 6, 1942, in part citing Arthur "Bugs" Baer, "The Crambury Tiger," *Collier's* 110 (July 11, 1942), p. 19.

Post-Register (Idaho Falls), July 24, 1942 (fishing party)

Boston Herald, August 13, 1942 (Cunningham on Cobb as "orneriest cuss")

Greenville News (S.C.), August 26, 1942 (Cobb food)

Los Angeles Times, November 9, 1942 (Henry McLemore/horse interview)

Greenville News (S.C.), December 23, 1942 (Cobb's Christmas greetings)

Des Moines Register, January 9, 1943 (UP's Tommy Devine: Bluege on Cobb)

Hutchinson News (Kan.), February 24, 1943 (Rickey's DiMaggio superlative)

Philadelphia Inquirer, March 8, 1943

St. Louis Star-Times, March 9, 1943

Boston Herald, March 11, 1943 (Eddie Collins on Cobb/Crawford)

Shamokin News-Dispatch (Pa.), March 26, 1943 (NEA's Grayson feature)

Evening Independent (Massillon, Ohio), June 10, 1943 (Dillon Graham)

Morning Advocate (Baton Rouge), October 6, 1943 (AP mildly rewording Robert F. Hyland in *Sporting News*, August 13, 1942)

Clarion-Ledger (Jackson, Miss.), October 10, 1943 (INS's Arthur "Bugs" Baer)

Cleveland News, April 4, 1944 (Ed McAuley: Del Baker/Peckinpaugh/Wagner, and cited in the *Sporting News* of April 13, 1944)

Decatur Herald and Review (Ill.), June 4, 1944 (*Famous Slugger Year Book 1944*)

Sacramento Bee, August 2, 1944

San Francisco Chronicle, August 3, 1944

Pantagraph (Bloomington, Ill.), August 7, 1944 (Cobb's poison ivy)

Reno Evening Gazette, August 26, 1944

Medford Mail Tribune (Ore.), December 5, 1944 (UP's Frank H. Bartholomew re: Cobb on Eddie Collins)

Oakland Tribune, January 11, 1945 (Vitt at Letterman General Hospital)

Oakland Tribune, February 14, 1945 (Mare Island naval hospital visit)

Detroit News, February 25, 1945 (Salsinger: Durocher/Ruth/missing signals)

Detroit News, April 15, 1945 (Salsinger: California Athletic Commission)

Cincinnati Enquirer, April 25, 1945 (interview with Southworth)

Piqua Daily Call (Ohio), May 8, 1945 (Grayson re: Lewis/Grimes on Cobb)

Detroit News, August 17, 1945 (fishing, boating and running; minimal golf)

Detroit Free Press, August 23, 1945 (Bingay: Cobb and Mack a strange pair)

Detroit Free Press, August 23, 1945 (Lyall Smith: Cobb on base stealing)

Des Moines Register, August 25, 1945 (Sec Taylor interview with Cobb, but omitting Cobb on his entertainment preferences until July 21, 1961)

News-Herald (Franklin, Pa.), August 30, 1945 (Grayson interview with Cobb)

New York Times, September 2, 1945 (Arthur Daley interview)

Oakland Tribune, September 14, 1945 (Vitt's visit to Lake Tahoe)

Des Moines Register, October 4, 1945 (pheasant hunting)

Oakland Tribune, November 16, 1945 (AP re: new hospital)

Boston Herald, April 8, 1946 (Cunningham on Cobb's racial views)

Big Spring Herald (Tex.), April 21, 1946 (Tommy Hart: Byron Nelson on Cobb; the 1944 interview, by the AP's Whitney Martin, appeared in, for example, the *Morning Herald (Hagerstown, Md.)* of October 28, 1944)

Beatrice Daily Sun (Neb.), April 28, 1946 (Brown has Cobb's last uniform)

Detroit News, June 7, 1946 (acute tracheal bronchitis)

Lansing State Journal, June 14, 1946 (AP interview; cites "intense reading interest")

Detroit News, August 22, 1946 (Ernest "Ernie" Copeland)

Boston Globe, September 7, 1946 (Kaese's Woodall story about Cobb alluded to)

Boston Traveler, September 9, 1946 (the Binneys' quiz win/biographical sketch)

Boston Herald, September 28, 1946 (Cunningham on Cobb's racial views)

Detroit Free Press, October 24, 1946 (criticism of Ted Williams in World Series)

Detroit News, November 12, 1946 (golfing again three to four times a week)

Greenville News (S.C.), February 15, 1947

Washington Star, March 8, 1947 (AP on final divorce proceedings; includes Cobb's quips)

New York Herald Tribune, March 13, 1947

Indianapolis Star, March 19, 1947 (Westbrook Pegler)

Tucson Daily Citizen, June 4, 1947 (Arthur "Bugs" Baer)

San Mateo Times (Calif.), July 15, 1947 (drunk driving arrest at Placerville)

Sacramento Bee, July 18, 1947

Harrisburg Telegraph, August 20, 1947 (Rice re: Cobb/Nig Clarke)

Detroit News, August 26, 1947 (Salsinger: Cobb and umpires)

Detroit News, August 27, 1947 (Salsinger: criticism of some blacks in majors)

Sporting News, September 17, 1947 ("Ebony Ty Cobb")

Detroit News, September 19, 1947 (Salsinger: Babe Ruth's praise of Cobb)

Arizona Republic, September 27, 1947 (flying with Webb)

Evening News (Harrisburg), October 2, 1947 (INS's Lawton Carver on Cobb/Schang)

Idaho Statesman (Boise), October 2, 1947 (INS's Bob Considine)

Washington Post, October 5, 1947 (Morris Siegel: Joe Judge on Cobb)

Miami News, October 12, 1947 (AP's Martin on Cobb-Ted Williams meeting)

Washington Star, November 19, 1947 (Burton Hawkins: Joe Judge and Bucky Harris on Cobb/Al Simmons as 1927 and/or 1928 roommate)

Oakland Tribune, February 5, 1948 (Ward: Cobb as a public speaker)

Oakland Tribune, February 6, 1948 (Ward: Cobb's genteel remark)

Boston Herald, February 6, 1948 (Cronin on overhearing Cobb/Collins)

Detroit Times, February 14, 1948 (Arthur "Bugs" Baer excerpting Cobb's letter)

Detroit News, February 15, 1948 (Salsinger on Ruth as prospective manager)

Detroit News, March 9, 1948 (Salsinger: Joe McCarthy not recognizing Cobb)

Chicago Tribune, March 24, 1948 (AP Boston: Cobb in hospital)

St. Louis Post-Dispatch, March 24, 1948 (AP: Cobb on Williams LF hitting)

Boston Globe, March 25, 1948 (Cobb to Kaese on Baker spiking)

Detroit Free Press, March 28, 1948 (Cobb's bursitis)

Boston Herald, April 9, 1948 (Cunningham on Cobb/Williams + Cobb/golf)

Beatrice Daily Sun (Neb.), April 15, 1948 (NEA's Grayson Cobb interview)

Tucson Daily Citizen, May 1, 1948

Boston Herald, August 2, 1948 (Cunningham, featuring Cobb's rebuttal)

Baltimore News-Post, August 17, 1948 (Rodger H. Pippen: Ruth reminscences)

Detroit News, August 22, 1948 (Salsinger on Ruth as prospective manager)

New York Times, September 19, 1948 (Cobb plays golf occasionally)

Springfield Union (Mass.), October 12, 1948 (Considine on Cobb/Robinson)

Berkshire Eagle (Pittsfield, Mass.), October 15, 1948

New York Times, November 10, 1948 (Arthur Daley: Cobb spiked catchers)

St. Louis Post-Dispatch, November 17, 1948

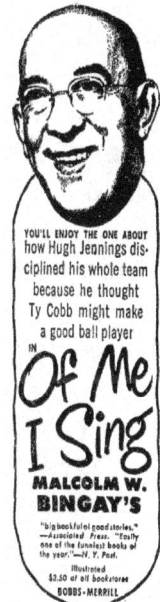

San Francisco Chronicle, January 23, 1949 (Connolly: Cobb on overmanaging (includes platooning) and diet/weight)

Reno Gazette-Journal, February 26, 1949 ("fear of God" into rival fielders)

Greenville News (S.C.), March 16, 1949 (185 pounds)

New York Times, April 26, 1949 (Arthur Daley: "got to be first" story)

Times-Picayune (New Orleans), May 14, 1949 (Cobb's heckling article)

Newark Star-Ledger, May 24, 1949 (James P. Sinnott on Cobb/Dykes)

Washington Post, July 3, 1949 (Shirley Povich re: Stengel on Cobb)

Detroit Free Press, July 19, 1949 (Ben Hogan)

San Francisco Chronicle, September 10, 1949 (Rosenbaum on "Parkey" Sharkey)

Baltimore News-Post, September 16, 1949 (Pippen with Cobb in Chicago)

Baltimore News-Post, September 17, 1949 (Pippen with Cobb in Buffalo)

Hartford Courant, September 17, 1949 (AP: Pippen broke marriage-to-be story)

Post-Standard (Syracuse), October 5, 1949 (Westbrook Pegler)

Sporting News, October 12, 1949 (Ward Morehouse)

Los Angeles Times, October 12, 1949 (Art Rosenbaum: Cobb on DiMaggio conditioning)

Chicago Defender, October 15, 1949 (Lucius Harper)

Greenville News (S.C.), October 16, 1949

Cincinnati Enquirer, November 9, 1949 (INS's Considine on Baer/Cobb)

Bakersfield Californian, November 19, 1949 (Arthur "Bugs" Baer)

Sporting News, December 7, 1949 (Jim McGee: Cobb on early rising/MVP awards)

Waco News Tribune (Tex.), January 3, 1950 (Brown & Bigelow calendar)

Arkansas Gazette (Little Rock), January 5, 1950 (Cobb and new wife/Buck Weaver praise)

Brooklyn Eagle, January 20, 1950 (*Sport* dinner)

Boston Herald, January 21, 1950 (*Sport* dinner)

Oil City Derrick (Pa.), January 24, 1950 (Ed Sullivan re: Cobb's DiMaggio superlative)

Brooklyn Eagle, January 25, 1950 (Rickey on Cobb/Robinson)

Pittsburgh Courier, January 28, 1950 (Albert R. Perkins on Robinson/Cobb)

New York Herald Tribune, January 29, 1950 (foreword for Boddington book)

Cincinnati Enquirer, April 12, 1950 (AP Dallas on Cobb radio profanity)

Courier-News (Bridgewater, N.J.), April 26, 1950 (Cy Perkins NEA column)

Sporting News, May 24, 1950 (Salsinger on Cobb relaxation tips to DiMaggio)

Miami Daily News, June 11, 1950 (Cullen Cain: Jimmy Dykes on Cobb)

Times-Picayune (New Orleans), June 28, 1950 (Christy Walsh/Brown & Bigelow)

Los Angeles Times, July 4, 1950 (Eddie Bracken's future Cobb movie)

Boston Globe, August 17, 1950 (Kaese: Joe Sewell on Cobb)

Atlanta Constitution, August 26, 1950 (Bisher interview with Brown)

Atlanta Constitution, August 27, 1950 (Bisher interview with Cunningham)

Atlanta Constitution, August 30, 1950 (Bisher interview/Bob Cobb)

Miami Daily News, September 1, 1950 (McGill: bird dog and poker stories)

Sporting News, September 20, 1950 (J. G. Taylor Spink: Earnshaw on Cobb)

Los Angeles Times, October 1, 1950 (supporting Warren's re-election)

San Francisco Chronicle, January 14, 1951 (Connolly: Pinelli/Cobb)

Wilmington Morning News (N.C.), February 5, 1951 (AP's Whitney Martin)

Milwaukee Journal, February 6, 1951 (George McBride on Street/Cobb)

Greenville News (S.C.), February 7, 1951 (food and football)

Los Angeles Times, March 10, 1951 (Braven Dyer re: Cobb on Johnson)

Washington Star, March 11, 1951 (Hawkins: Clyde Milan and Joe Engel)

Boston Herald, April 2, 1951 (Cunningham re: Cobb to Schacht)

Los Angeles Times, April 23, 1951 (Dick Hyland on Cobb's legs)

Cincinnati Enquirer, May 13, 1951 (INS's Considine re: Musial on Cobb)

Capital Journal (Salem, Ore.), May 21, 1951 (AP's Newland re: Cobb on Williams, and Chudley picture)

Detroit Free Press, May 22, 1951

Anniston Star (Ala.), June 5, 1951 (NEA's Grayson re: Cobb on Williams)

Asbury Park Press (N.J.), June 15, 1951 (AP re: Cobb on Williams; two earlier AP stories were in the *Troy Record (N.Y.)* and *The News (Newport, R.I.)*, both on May 29, 1951) (the June 15 and *Troy Record* versions say that Cobb's tips were left in advance for Williams on the road).

New York Times, June 24, 1951 (Arthur Daley re: Cobb on Williams)

Washington Star, June 28, 1951 (Corcoran re: Cobb's advice to Williams)

Los Angeles Times, July 10, 1951 (Frank Finch on Cobb/Heilmann)

Des Moines Register, July 23, 1951 (Crawford reconciling with Cobb)

Lansing State Journal, July 31, 1951 (AP's Arthur L. Edson re: testimony)

Los Angeles Times, July 31, 1951 (AP re: Rep. Hillings/Cobb exchange; but page 21 of the hearings transcript has fuller text that I cite)

Shamokin News-Dispatch (Pa.), August 10, 1951 (NEA: Speaker on Cobb)

Eugene Guard (Ore.), August 15, 1951

Atlanta Constitution, August 26, 1951 (Guy Tiller interview with Rucker)

Washington Post, September 9, 1951 (Shirley Povich re: Heilmann on Cobb)

New York Herald Tribune, October 9, 1951 (Smith: DiMaggio on Cobb)

Boston Globe, October 9, 1951

San Francisco Chronicle, October 17, 1951 (Art Rosenbaum: the two Ty Cobbs)

Wilmington Morning News (N.C.), November 12, 1951 (INS re: Maines re: minor league commissioner)

Great Falls Tribune (Mont.), November 20, 1951 (UP: hunting arrest)

Washington Post, December 16, 1951 (AP Twin Falls: Cobb advising team)

Boston American, December 21, 1951 (Cobb advising Williams on golf)

Ogden Standard-Examiner (Utah), December 27, 1951, citing the *San Francisco Call-Bulletin* (Jack McDonald re: Cobb on DiMaggio)

Santa Fe New Mexican, December 29, 1951 (Wheeler on quail hunting)

San Mateo Times (Calif.), January 1, 1952 (Cobb on Nevada residency)

St. Clair Chronicle (Mo.), January 10, 1952 (Rice on Cobb/Jackson)

Washington Star, January 19, 1952 (AP's Newland re: Cobb pro-integration)

Lexington Leader (Ky.), January 21, 1952 (Westbrook Pegler)

Detroit Free Press, Febuary 1, 1952 (Bingay)

Charleston Daily Mail (W.V.), February 3, 1952 (Mrs. William Christian)

Greenville News (S.C.), February 4, 1952 (mammy/food)

Brooklyn Eagle, February 4, 1952 (Tommy Holmes)

Sporting News, February 6, 1952 (Jack McDonald re: Cobb on integration)

Miami Daily News, February 9, 1952 (Cullen Cain: Williams on golf)

Atlanta Daily World, February 10, 1952 (Dean Gordon Blaine Hancock)

Healdsburg Tribune (Calif.), February 21, 1952 (Magic Valley stockholder)

San Francisco Call-Bulletin, February 25, 1952 (Cobb: I'm a "dumbbell")

Times-Picayune (New Orleans), March 10, 1952 (Branch Rickey)

New York Daily News, March 14, 1952 (Hornsby's praise of Cobb)

New York Daily News, March 14, 1952 (Dick Young: Robinson on Cobb)

Salt Lake Tribune, March 15, 1952 (extended version of Dick Young column of *New York Daily News* of March 14, 1952)

Richmond Times-Dispatch, March 16, 1952 (Chauncey Durden)

Washington Star, March 16, 1952 (Hawkins: Griffith on Cobb as senile)

Arkansas Gazette (Little Rock), March 16, 1952 (AP's Reichler re: hazing)

Pittsburgh Post-Gazette, March 17, 1952 (Jack Hernon: Kiner/Meyer on Cobb)

Newsday, March 17, 1952 (Jimmy Cannon: Luke Sewell on Cobb)

Aberdeen Daily News (S.D.), March 19, 1952 (Robert C. Ruark)

Daily Republic (Mitchell, S.D.), March 20, 1952 (AP's Herb Altschull re: National Geographic Society on Cobb's Fuzzy-Wuzzies blind spot)

Panana City News-Herald (Fla.), March 21, 1952 (AP: Rizzuto as "Little Ty")

Washington Post, March 23, 1952 (Povich: Griffith's apology note)

Washington Post, March 23, 1952 (Stengel and Milan to AP's Jack Hand)

New York Herald Tribune, March 23, 1952 (Bob Cooke)

Daily Worker, March 23, 1952 (Lester Rodney)

Akron Beacon Journal, March 24, 1952 (regular editorial)

New York Mirror, March 25, 1952 (Dan Parker)

Daily Worker, March 26, 1952, in part quoting *New York Mirror*, March 25, 1952 (Lester Rodney)

Ogden Standard-Examiner (Utah), March 26, 1952 (Stanley Woodward)

Detroit Free Press, March 27, 1952 (Malcolm Bingay: "America's success. . . "/ Cobb and umpires)

Pittsburgh Press, March 27, 1952 (Lester J. Biederman)

Florence Morning News (S.C.), March 27, 1952 (Joe Molony)

Boston Herald, March 29, 1952 (Bill Cunningham)

Chicago Tribune, March 30, 1952 (Irving Vaughan)

Healdsburg Tribune (Calif.), April 3, 1952 (Magic Valley honorary president)

Santa Fe New Mexican, April 4, 1952 (Wheeler on *Life*/cotton/champagne)

Washington Post, April 5, 1952, in part referring to *Daily Worker*, March 23 and March 26, 1952. I use the *Daily Worker*'s punctuation.

Newsday, April 5, 1952 (Jimmy Cannon on Cobb/DiMaggio)

High Point Enterprise (N.C.), April 9, 1952 (Rickey's banquet story on Cobb)

Washington Post, April 14, 1952 (Walter Winchell)

Washington Post, April 14, 1952 (Griffith/"American Forum of the Air," supplemented by transcript found in snippet form on Google Books)

New York Mirror, April 15, 1952 (Parker: "horned toads"/Russians-related defenses)

Atlanta Constitution, April 20, 1952 (Neal interview with Nap Rucker)

Reno Gazette-Journal, April 24, 1952 (AP Sacramento: tax investigation)

Pittsburgh Press, April 24, 1952 (Cobb letter to Kiner (the full original))

Naugatuck News (Conn.), May 3, 1952 (NEA's Grayson re: Cobb letter)

San Francisco Chronicle, May 10, 1952 (Cobb for Sen. Knowland's re-election)

New York Times, May 11, 1952 (Harvey Breitt's interview with Hornsby)

Sporting News, May 14, 1952 (J. G. Taylor Spink)

St. Petersburg Times (Fla.), May 14, 1952 (Bill Beck on Havemann/Cobb)

San Francisco Examiner, May 15, 1952 (Herb Caen: Ty Jr.'s health)

Miami Daily News, May 24, 1952 (Cullen Cain: Ehmke on Cobb)

Detroit Times, May 31, 1952 (Baer reprinting all of Cobb's 1948 letter)

Detroit News, June 3, 1952 (Salsinger: Cobb and Hornsby both wrong)

San Francisco Chronicle, June 6, 1952 (Bill Leiser on Hornsby's *Look* article)

New York Amsterdam News, June 7, 1952

San Francisco Chronicle, June 7, 1952 (Cobb judge at a high school game)

New York Post, June 11, 1952 (Milton Gross on Hornsby/Paige)

New York Post, June 13, 1952 (slurs in Brooklyn series in St. Louis?)

Bedford Gazette (Pa.), June 14, 1952 (Bennett Cerf on Gomez/Cobb)

New York Times, June 15, 1952 (Arthur Daley on Cobb/Johnson)

New York Herald Tribune, June 15, 1952 (Leslie Lieber: DiMaggio on Cobb)

San Francisco Examiner, June 18, 1952 (Cobb: don't smoke until age 21)

Miami Daily News, July 12, 1952 (Cain: Cobb throwing dirt in 2B's eyes)

St. Louis Post-Dispatch, July 13, 1952

St. Louis Globe-Democrat, July 13, 1952 (Cobb visit and Steve O'Neill story)

New York Mirror, July 15, 1952 (Cobb letter via Rathbone/Laurie to Parker)

Sporting News, July 23, 1952 (visit to St. Louis/Ozarks; Musial's comments)

Daily Notes (Canonsburg, Pa.), September 18, 1952 (UP Moscow: Russian magazine)

Philadelphia Inquirer, October 11, 1952 (Ollie Crawford's spiking quip)

Daily Nonpareil (Council Bluffs, Iowa), October 30, 1952 (NEA: Cobb on spike sharpening)

New York Mirror, November 24, 1952 (Parker on Cobb/Boddington)
Los Angeles Times, December 1, 1952 (AP's Myers: Cobb on Stengel/Mantle)
Richmond Times-Dispatch, December 8, 1952 (Williamsburg/duck hunting)
Richmond Times-Dispatch, December 9, 1952 (baseball observations)
Lexington Leader (Ky.), December 9, 1952 (bidding)
Lexington Herald (Ky.), December 10, 1952 (interview)
Lexington Herald (Ky.), December 11, 1952 (Kiwanis speech)
Detroit Free Press, December 12, 1952 (195 pounds)
Detroit Free Press, December 15, 1952 (commissioning Roy C. Gamble)
Cincinnati Enquirer, February 1, 1953 (letter to Kahn's re: ham)
El Paso Herald-Post, February 6, 1953 (INS re: Cobb on amateur baseball)
Los Angeles Times, February 10, 1953 (Cobb/Leonard Goldstein)
News-Herald (Franklin, Pa.), February 17, 1953 (NEA re: Cobb/Goldstein)
Sporting News, February 25, 1953 (Prescott Sullivan: Cobb on Collins)
Washington Star, March 4, 1953 (Hawkins: Milan/Cobb's stealing "advice")
Los Angeles Times, March 15, 1953
Los Angeles Times, March 17, 1953 (photo with DiMaggio/comedians)
Reno Evening Gazette, April 29, 1953 (AP Twin Falls: hospitalized there)
Beaumont Journal (Tex.), May 14, 1953 (NEA's McCallum on Little League BB)
Newsday, June 4, 1953 (Jimmy Cannon re: Cobb/Ruth and Cobb/Dugan)
San Francisco Chronicle, June 19, 1953 (Cobb judge at a high school game)
Brooklyn Eagle, July 30, 1953
Hartford Courant, July 31, 1953 (AP Chicago: interview at Wrigley Field)
Los Angeles Times, August 4, 1953 (in Lucky Strike cigarette advertisement)
Pittsburgh Courier, August 8, 1953
Chicago Tribune, August 18, 1953
San Luis Obispo Telegram-Tribune (Calif.), August 19, 1953 (UP's Bartholomew re: Chudley/75-mile radius) Because of a space crunch in the opening chapter, I moved text here. Besides Russ Newland, the only other reporter who I found mentioning Chudley by name was Frank H. Bartholomew, a neighbor of Cobb in another of his homes, in Cave Rock, Nev., near Lake Tahoe. Bartholomew in 1955 would become president of the United Press, soon after that to become UPI.
Rochester Democrat and Chronicle, August 25, 1953 (Walter E. Hastings: Cobb/Kiner)
San Diego Union, October 16, 1953 (Fannin/O'Doul batting average quip)
Anniston Star (Ala.), October 16, 1953 (donating $100,000 for hospital)
Cleveland Plain Dealer, December 1, 1953
Lansing State Journal, January 8, 1954 (Alderton on Cobb/Crawford)
San Diego Union, January 14, 1954 (Fannin/O'Doul batting average quip)
Brooklyn Eagle, January 15, 1954
Evening Bulletin (Philadelphia), January 27, 1954 (sportswriters' dinner)
Pittsburgh Courier, January 30, 1954 (helping Arthur Lee Simpkins)

Greensboro News, January 31, 1954 (INS's Considine on MacArthur/BB)

Homewood-Flossmoor Star (Ill.), February 16, 1954 (Mack on Cobb)

Boston Herald, March 2, 1954 (Bill Cunningham re: ballplayer legs)

Joplin Globe (Mo.), March 7, 1954 (AP's Newland re: William J. Croke)

Chicago Defender, March 27, 1954 (Grimm/Cobb/Aaron)

Salina Journal (Kan.), March 31, 1954 (Red Ormsby on Cobb)

Miami Daily News, May 1, 1954 (Cain: Maines has no excuse for Cobb)

Chicago Tribune, July 14, 1954 (Stan Coveleski on Cobb)

Boston American, August 13, 1954 (Austen Lake on refusing invitations)

Brooklyn Eagle, August 16, 1954

Reno Evening Gazette, August 25, 1954 (Placerville drunkenness bail forfeit)

Reno Evening Gazette, August 25, 1954 (Cobb at Dennis Day performance)

New York Times, December 8, 1954 (Arthur Daley re: Stengel on Cobb)

Star-Democrat (Easton, Md.), December 10, 1954 (spiking of Baker)

Reno Evening Gazette, January 8, 1955 (Cass's first divorce filing)

Daily Chronicle (Centralia, Wash.), January 12, 1955 (Newland was a Mason)

Sporting News, February 9, 1955 (Bill Perry's Frank Baker article)

San Bernardino Sun, February 16, 1955 (Wheeler: Cobb hunting tale)

Southtown Economist (Chicago, Ill.), February 27, 1955 (Schalk on Cobb)

Baltimore American, February 27, 1955; *Detroit Times*, March 2, 1955 (Cobb letter to Pippen supporting Crawford for Hall of Fame)

Marshfield News-Herald (Wis.), March 12, 1955 (AP: Schacht on Cobb)

Christian Science Monitor, March 24, 1955 (Phil Elderkin: Cobb's letter)

Newsday, April 7, 1955 (Jimmy Cannon on Robinson/Cobb)

Bend Bulletin (Ore.), April 29, 1955 (sale of Bend, Ore., Coca-Cola plant)

Detroit News, June 7, 1955 (Salsinger: one Cobb argument with umpires)

Atlanta Constitution, July 21, 1955 (Atlanta visit)

Nevada State Journal (Reno), July 31, 1955 (UP's Carl Lundquist)

New York World-Telegram and Sun, August 1, 1955 (Dan Daniel)

Detroit Free Press, August 2, 1955 (Lyall Smith)

Independent (Long Beach, Calif.), August 3, 1955 (Leonard Lyons interview)

Washington Post, August 3, 1955 (Bob Addie on Cobb visit to D.C.)

Washington Star, August 3, 1955 (Hawkins on Cobb visit to D.C.)

Philadelphia Inquirer, August 3, 1955 (AP: Cobb late to game)

Arizona Republic, August 14, 1955 (INS's Considine on Baer/Cobb)

Plain Speaker (Hazleton, Pa.), September 21, 1955 (AP: Myrt Power)

Detroit News, September 25, 1955 (Haney: Cobb sending me a weekly letter)

Detroit Times, September 29, 1955 (Cobb to Luke Sewell: home run quip)

Hartford Courant, September 30, 1955 (Cobb on World Series Yankees)

Boston American, October 2, 1955 (INS Myrt Power column)

Courier-Post (Camden, N.J.), November 10, 1955 (UP: Felts trial: Cobb's nurse)

Chicago Tribune, November 16, 1955 (bill of particulars) (not cited in main text)

Baltimore Sun, November 16, 1955 (AP: Cass on Cobb)

Reno Evening Gazette, November 16, 1955 (Cobb on whiskey pouring)

San Bernardino Sun, November 16, 1955 (UP: Felts trial: colorful testimony)

Corpus Christi Times (Tex.), November 17, 1955 (AP: Felts suit verdict)

Nevada State Journal (Reno), November 18, 1955 (UP: Cass on Cobb)

Los Angeles Times, January 19, 1956 (Jim Scott on McCallum book)

Detroit News, February 29, 1956 (Bernie deViveiros had been taught by Cobb)

Chicago Tribune, January 24, 1956 (David Condon: Charley Root on Cobb)

Janesville Gazette (Wis.), June 23, 1956 (Cobb telegram to Fred Haney)

Detroit News, September 30, 1956 (Haney: Cobb sending me a weekly letter)

Chicago Tribune, January 7, 1957 (David Condon: Robinson vs. Cobb)

Los Angeles Times, February 5, 1957 (Frank Finch's interview with Crawford)

San Mateo Times (Calif.), February 11, 1957 (clinic at Stanford)

Independent (Long Beach, Calif.), February 11, 1957 (clinic at Stanford)

The News (Newport, R.I.), February 19, 1957 (Dan Daniel on Mantle/Ruth/ DiMaggio/Cobb legs: the *New York World-Telegram and Sun* of that date lopped off those thoughts from bottom of article)

Detroit News, March 3, 1957 (not cited in his book's main text: During spring training in Florida, Salsinger wrote that Duke Snider had been quoted as saying, "If Babe Ruth were playing today he'd be just another homerun [sic] hitter. Ty Cobb? They never would have heard of him if Jackie Robinson had been around." Salsinger wrote that "when the present[-]day player attempts to belittle the type of game played in the so-called dead ball era, he generally makes himself ridiculous.")

Sporting News, April 3, 1957 (Harry T. Brundidge interview with Cobb)

Sporting News, April 10, 1957 (Brundidge interview with Williams)

San Bernardino Sun, April 13, 1957 (John N. Wheeler on racecars/champagne/ frogs' legs)

Detroit Free Press, April 14, 1957 (Art Rosenbaum of the *San Francisco Chronicle* wrote a feature for the *Free Press* that later ran in shorter form in the *Chronicle*)

Bee (Danville, Va.), May 30, 1957 (AP: Cobb talking to Milwaukee players)

Kansas City Star, June 9, 1957 (Rickey on Cobb, Cobb and bobwhites)

Christian Science Monitor, June 13, 1957 (Edwin M. Rumill)

Independent (Long Beach, Calif.), June 19, 1957, possibly referring to Grayson's June 16, 1957, NEA column in the *Racine (Wis.) Sunday Bulletin* (Bob Kelley)

Los Angeles Times, June 21, 1957 (Florence Haney on Cobb)

Salisbury Times (Md.), July 13, 1957 (AP: ducks, Cobb on California expansion)

Rochester Democrat and Chronicle, July 19, 1957

Milwaukee Journal, July 21, 1957 (Bob Wolf on Mathews/Cobb)

New York World-Telegram and Sun, July 23, 1957 (Dan Daniel column)

Pittsburgh Press, July 24, 1957 (the Scripps-Howard version of Daniel's *World-Telegram and Sun* column (and mildly different from his column of July 23)

Pittsburgh Press, July 24, 1957 (Chester L. Smith on Cobb/Crawford feud)

Plain Speaker (Hazleton, Pa.), July 24, 1957 (Grayson: Cobb on Mathews)

Progress-Index (Petersburg, Pa.), July 25, 1957 (to Grayson: "I was the original African dodger")

Milwaukee Journal, August 4, 1957 (Cleon Walfoort: Haney on letters)

Detroit Free Press, August 28, 1957 (Cobb recalls Strouthers and Croke)

Ogden Standard-Examiner (Utah), October 13, 1957 (advice to Ben Hogan)

Los Angeles Times, October 24, 1957 (Jeane Hoffman: Goodman on Cobb)

Los Angeles Times, January 9, 1958

Los Angeles Herald and Express, January 9, 1958

Los Angeles Herald and Express, January 11, 1958 (Sam Balter, Jr.)

Courier-News (Bridgewater, N.J.), January 16, 1958 (UP: Cobb in N.H.)

Manchester Union Leader (N.H.), January 19, 1958

Philadelphia Inquirer, January 22, 1958 (Leonard Lyons re: George Jessel)

Tampa Bay Times, March 16, 1958 (*Parade Magazine*: living long advice)

Boston Globe, March 31, 1958 (Ted Ashby: eating lamb chops & roast lamb)

New York Times, June 1, 1958 (Mel Allen on booing of Mickey Mantle)

Carolina Israelite (Charlotte), June 1, 1958 (Harry Golden)

Daily Times-News (Burlington, N.C.), June 17, 1958 (Buddy Lindsey)

Detroit Free Press, June 29, 1958

Washington Post, July 10, 1958 (UPI: Cobb on Williams)

Miami News-Record (Okla.), August 12, 1958 (UPI: Cobb/Stengel hanging out)

Daily Times-News (Burlington, N.C.), August 14, 1958 (Reichler interview)

Pittsburgh Press, September 26, 1958 (Durocher on Cobb incident)

Times-Picayune (New Orleans), November 12, 1958 (UPI: Cobb/George Koster on residency)

Pasadena Independent (Calif.), November 13, 1958 (UPI: Cobb on residency)

Reno Evening Gazette, January 12, 1959 (Nevada license plates)

Detroit Free Press, March 12, 1959 (Cobb has diabetes)

Boston American, March 19, 1959 (Austen Lake: Cobb/Williams)

Mesa Tribune (Ariz.), March 19, 1959 (Tom Diskin: O'Doul/Dean)

San Mateo Times (Calif.), March 26, 1959 (California residency ruling)

Ogden Standard-Examiner (Utah), June 5, 1959 (Cobb illness; cannot visit)

Boston Daily Record, July 22, 1959 (UPI's Jack Cuddy interview)

Detroit Free Press, July 24, 1959

Detroit News, July 24, 1959 (Cobb visit to see Clancy, his hotel pointing photo)

Morning Herald (Uniontown, Pa.), July 27, 1959 (Sylvester of *New York Daily News*)

Boston Globe, September 21, 1959 (Kaese interview)

Boston Daily Record, September 22, 1959 (Bill McSweeny)

Wilmington Morning News (N.C.), December 8, 1959 (UPI: Drs. Wood/Brown)

Daily Times-News (Burlington, N.C.), December 17, 1959 (AP's Joe Reichler interview)

Anderson Daily Bulletin (Ind.), December 19, 1959 (Louella O. Parsons)

Boston Globe, January 10, 1960 (Red Smith: Berra on Cobb)

New York World-Telegram and Sun, January 25, 1960 (B'nai B'rith NY dinner)

New York World-Telegram and Sun, January 27, 1960 (Joe Williams: Cobb on throwing arm/Paul Krichell 1912 play at home plate)

New York Times, January 31, 1960 (Arthur Daley)

New York World-Telegram and Sun, February 1, 1960 (Joe Williams re: Cobb's constant sharp pain)

Battle Creek Examiner (Mich.), February 1, 1960 (AP: dinner background)

Plain Speaker (Hazleton, Pa.), February 2, 1960 (NEA: Pat Parrish interview)

Richmond Times-Dispatch, February 3, 1960 (Chauncey Durden's Frank O'Rourke interview plus (not relevant until writing upon Cobb's death) dinner coverage)

Daily News-Texan (Grand Prairie, Tex.), February 7, 1960 (Leonard Lyons)

Sunday Gazette Mail (Charleston, W.V.), February 7, 1960 (Wheeler lunch)

New York Mirror, February 10, 1960

Oakland Tribune, March 8, 1960

Greenville News (S.C.), March 8, 1960 (UPI Phoenix: Cobb and O'Connell)

Boston Daily Record, March 10, 1960 (John Gillooly: drinking milk, Scotch)

Arizona Republic, March 13, 1960

Boston Daily Record, March 16, 1960 (John Gillooly: Cobb on Jackie Jensen)

Lansing State Journal, March 16, 1960 (Alderton on Cobb/Jimmy Dugan)

Los Angeles Times, March 25, 1960

Christian Science Monitor, March 29, 1960

Cleveland Plain Dealer, April 2, 1960

Reno Evening Gazette, May 25 and May 30, 1960 (housekeeper and cook classified ad)

San Mateo Times (Calif.), June 2, 1960 (PG&E gas and light bill)

Sporting News, June 22, 1960 (Boddington as book collaborator)

Oneonta Star (N.Y.), June 29, 1960

Los Angeles Times, July 13, 1960 (Frank Finch: Greg Mulleavy on Cobb)

Philadelphia Inquirer, August 1, 1960 (Harry Golden)

Lexington Leader (Ky.), August 24, 1960 (AP at Stanford Hospital; includes Mays)

Tyrone Daily Herald (Pa.), August 26, 1960 (UPI interview at Stanford Hospital; the 1939 interview was with the INS's Bob Considine, as printed, for example, in the *Rochester Democrat and Chronicle* of June 14, 1939)

Baltimore Sun, August 30, 1960 (member of Dick Nixon Sports Committee)

Plain Speaker (Hazleton, Pa.), September 10, 1960 (NEA's Grayson: Cobb to Corcoran re: Williams)

New York World-Telegram and Sun, September 16, 1960 (Joe Williams)

The State (Columbia, S.C.), September 18, 1960 (AP re: Cobb and Mantle)

New York Daily News, September 18, 1960 (Dick Young)

Sporting News, September 28, 1960 (Dan Daniel)

Miami Daily News (Fla.), January 8, 1961 (Ward Morehouse's syndicated feature)

New York Mirror, January 12, 1961 (Parker on Durocher incident)

Philadelphia Inquirer, January 15, 1961 (UPI interview)

Bridgeport Post (Conn.), January 17, 1961 (AP health/travel update)

Arizona Republic, March 18, 1961 (Gianelli: Cobb at Scottsdale)

Denton Record-Chronicle (Tex.), March 21, 1961 (AP: DiMaggio on Cobb and contract signing)

Battle Creek Enquirer (Mich.), May 18, 1961 (UPI re: medical update)

Advocate (Baton Rouge), May 21, 1961 (NEA: Donie Bush on Cobb)

Arizona Republic, July 18, 1961 (Gianelli on Cobb/Stump visit in March)

Augusta Chronicle, July 18, 1961 (Tom Yawkey/Rogers Hornsby on Cobb)

Boston Globe, July 18, 1961 (Arthur Siegel)

Boston Globe, July 18, 1961 (Davy Jones/Frank Baker on Cobb)

Boston Traveler, July 18, 1961 (Yawkey's "much of my early interest" quote)

Boston Globe, July 18, 1961 ("always a poor loser"/but didn't antagonize umpires)

Charleston Daily Mail (W.V.), July 18, 1961 (AP: Frank Walker on Cobb)

Chicago Tribune, July 18, 1961 (David Condon: Schalk interview)

Dallas Morning News, July 18, 1961 (AP interview with Wood)

Detroit Free Press, July 18, 1961 (Lyall Smith/Dr. Charles S. Kennedy)

Hartford Courant, July 18, 1961 (AP: Mantle on Cobb)

Los Angeles Times, July 18, 1961 (Goodman on Cobb's largesse)

Mexia Daily News (Tex.), July 18, 1961 (AP: Croke's nixing of bargain sale)

New York Post, July 18, 1961 (Milton Gross)

New York Times, July 18, 1961

Oneonta Star (N.Y.), July 18, 1961 (Gene Levy: Cobb "sissies" comment)

San Diego Union, July 18, 1961 (Jerry Magee)

San Diego Union, July 18, 1961 (Jack Murphy)

San Francisco Chronicle, July 18, 1961 (Art Rosenbaum: Corr/young caddy stories)

San Francisco News-Call Bulletin, July 18, 1961 (McDonald on Cobb/Crawford)

Washington Post, July 18, 1961 (UPI)

Atlanta Constitution, July 19, 1961 (Ralph McGill)

Boston Globe, July 19, 1961 (AP re: McDonald on Cobb/Crawford)

Bridgeport Post (Conn.), July 19, 1961 (UPI's Hal Wood)

Guardian (Manchester) (UK), July 19, 1961

Louisville Courier-Journal, July 19, 1961

New York Mirror, July 19, 1961

Press Democrat (Santa Rosa, Calif.), July 19, 1961 (Jack Hanley: James Crusinberry and Mays-Cobb photograph)

San Francisco Chronicle, July 19, 1961 (Art Rosenbaum: all of his Cobb

reminiscences except for the one below that he conveyed on July 20)
San Francisco Chronicle, July 20, 1961 (Art Rosenbaum: Cobb on perpetuity)
New York World-Telegram and Sun, July 20, 1961 (Dan Daniel: Cobb had memory of an elephant)
Washington Post, July 20, 1961 (Bob Addie)
Corpus Christi Times (Tex.), July 20, 1961 (Emil Tagliabue)
Des Moines Register, July 21, 1961 (Sec Taylor)
Philadelphia Daily News, July 21, 1961 (Larry Merchant)
Boston Daily Record, July 21, 1961 (John Gillooly)
Kokomo Tribune (Ind.), July 21, 1961 (AP: "probably was the most disliked")
Asbury Park Press (N.J.), July 22, 1961 (Ralph McGill's syndicated column)
Las Vegas Sun, July 22, 1961 (Jimmy Cannon)
Detroit Free Press, July 23, 1961 (E. A. Batchelor)
Press Democrat (Santa Rosa, Calif.), July 23, 1961 (Nagle: spiking/fainting)
Springfield Union (Mass.), July 23, 1961
San Bernardino Sun-Telegram, July 23, 1961
Augusta Chronicle, July 23, 1961 (Earl L. Bell)
Rochester Democrat and Chronicle, July 23, 1961 (Paul Pinckney: Keener on Cobb)
Pittsburgh Press, July 24, 1961
Salem News (Ohio), July 26, 1961 (H. I. Phillips)
Christian Science Monitor, July 27, 1961 (Phil Elderkin on Cobb letter)
Lebanon Daily News (Pa.), July 28, 1961 (Henry McLemore)
Pittsburgh Courier, July 29, 1961 (Larry Brown 1925 signing rumor)
Philadelphia Tribune, August 1, 1961 (Cobb pro-racial freedom)
Indianapolis Star, August 24, 1961 (UPI: congressional debate Cobb quip)
Reading Eagle (Pa.), September 8, 1961 (Pegler reprinting Considine)
Post-Standard (Syracuse), September 20, 1961 (Golden 1958 column rehash)
Lansing State Journal, September 22, 1961 (Alderton on 1961 book)
Los Angeles Times, September 29, 1961 (interview with Stump)
New York Herald Tribune, October 1, 1961 (John K. Hutchens)
St. Louis Post-Dispatch, October 1, 1961 (Bob Broeg)
Oakland Tribune, October 4, 1961 (Wally Willis)
Boston Record American, November 27, 1961 (Considine re: Cobb/Carver)
Sporting News, December 6, 1961 (McDonald on Cobb/Crawford/Stump)
Boston Globe, December 24, 1961 (Kaese on Cobb-Stump book)
Sporting News, January 3, 1962 (Stewart D. Brown to Spink re: gun)
Las Vegas Daily Optic (East Las Vegas, N.M.), January 24, 1962 (UPI: Rickey on Robinson as "Ty Cobb-ish")
Kansas City Times, February 26, 1962 (Oldfield bad driver in city traffic)
San Francisco Chronicle, May 10, 1962 (Charles McCabe: Nixon on Cobb)
Atlanta Constitution, September 2, 1962 (Lee Walburn: nurse Betty Jo Parsons)
Lansing State Journal, November 13, 1962 (Alderton on Cobb/Navin)

Virginian-Pilot (Norfolk, Va.), February 18, 1963 (Ed Brandt: Pippen feature)

Boston Globe, May 9, 1963 (Kaese on Woodall/Cobb)

Atlanta Constitution, May 24, 1963 (Jesse Outlar: friend Ernest Tomlinson)

Richmond Times-Dispatch, August 3, 1963 (Chauncey Durden on Reynolds)

Augusta Chronicle, May 31, 1964 (Earl L. Bell)

Detroit Free Press, November 2, 1965 (Edwin A. Lahey on Cobb revolver)

Alton Telegraph (Ill.), January 8, 1966 (Considine on Baer/Cobb)

Abilene Reporter-News (Tex.), May 1, 1966 (Ralph McGill) (an April 30, 1966, column of his in the *Atlanta Constitution* is a shortened version of his syndicated one, including by omitting the bird dog story.)

Arizona Republic, October 26, 1967 (George H. Maines interview)

New York Times, March 4, 1969 (Daley: Williams on Cobb)

La Crosse Tribune (Wis.), March 21, 1969 (NEA's Berkow talks to Jim Cobb)

Mattoon Journal-Gazette (Ill.), June 30, 1969 (Jimmy Cobb to Berkow)

Reno Evening Gazette, September 24, 1969 (AP re: Arnold Sharkey's funeral)

Washington Star, August 30, 1970 (Buck Leonard: roommates Walker and Cobb)

Boston Globe, September 10, 1970 (Kaese on Cobb revolver)

Record-Eagle (Traverse City, Mich.), October 27, 1970 (detail on Maines)

Chicago Tribune, July 27, 1972 (David Condon on Durocher/Cobb)

Seattle Times, December 10, 1972 (Don Duncan: McCallum interview)

Lowell Sun, February 25, 1973 (AP: Sammy Barnes on Cobb)

Atlanta Constitution, April 4, 1974 (Furman Bisher on Aaron/Cobb)

Times Herald (Port Huron, Mich.), February 3, 1975 (Ernest "Ernie" Copeland)

Los Angeles Times, September 28, 1977 (Skip Bayless: Cobb's children)

Anniston Star (Ala.), March 13, 1978 (AP's Will Grimsley: Musial on Cobb)

State Journal-Register (Springfield, Ill.), December 26, 1981 (Red Smith of *New York Times* news service re: Hardison on Cobb)

Los Angeles Times, October 14, 1984 (Ross Newhan: Jack Morris on Cobb)

Detroit Free Press, April 14, 1985 (Mark Kram: Gehringer on Cobb)

Los Angeles Times, August 4-5, 1985 (advertisement and Stump article)

Reno Gazette-Journal, September 7, 1985 (Tyrus Richard Cobb's memories)

Fort Myers News-Press (Fla.), September 10, 1985 (AP's Harry Atkins: Harrison Gailey on Cobb)

San Francisco Chronicle, June 14, 1987 (Art Spander on Rosburg/Cobb)

New York Times, March 31, 1989 (Frank Rich "Cobb" review)

Worcester Telegram & Gazette (Mass.), July 30, 1989 (O'Neill: Williams on Cobb)

Los Angeles Times, July 7, 1990 (Jack McDonald)

Los Angeles Times, December 7, 1990 (AP story on Cobb letter to Hodges)

Detroit Free Press, January 17, 1991 (Betzold: Forester on Cobb spike sharpening)

Los Angeles Times, July 7, 1994 (Jim Murray: DiMaggio on Cobb)

Detroit Free Press, September 23, 1994 (Ernie Harwell: DiMaggio on Cobb)

Dallas Morning News, December 9, 1994 (Bisher interview)

Arizona Republic, December 29, 1994 (AP's Harry Atkins: Bak interview: Bak "refuting" sharp-spikening myth)

Christian Science Monitor, January 13, 1995 (Phil Elderkin)

Atlanta Journal-Constitution, February 12, 1995 (Furman Bisher)

Reno Gazette-Journal, April 28, 1995 (Ty Cobb sports editor interview)

New York Times, June 16, 1996 (Rita Reif on Cobb/Farley)

Philadelphia Daily News, February 22, 2001 (Joe E. Brown owns Cobb uniform)

St. Louis Post-Dispatch, September 2, 2001 (Radcliffe on Cobb)

Augusta Chronicle, May 21, 2004 (re: Alex Rivers in Wesley Fricks letter)

Augusta Chronicle, August 25, 2004 (Bak on cutting Cobb slack)

Detroit Free Press, August 10, 2005 (Bak, with a general focus)

Detroit Free Press, August 17, 2005 (Bak, with a racism focus)

Baltimore Sun, April 6, 2008 (Allen Barra: one of his Rhodes book reviews)

Atlanta Journal-Constitution, August 4, 2010 (Bill Banks)

New York Times, April 17, 2013 (Tyler Kepner: Bob Wolff interview on tape)

New York Times, April 8, 2015 (Sam Roberts obituary of John E. Walsh)

Boston Globe, May 10, 2015 (Barra: review of Leerhsen's book)

New York Times, May 26, 2015 (online) and May 31, 2015 (in print) (John Williams: review of Leerhsen's book)

New York Post, May 31, 2015 (Alex Rivers firstborn-son naming detail)

New York Times, June 1, 2015 (Richard Sandomir: Leerhsen book feature)

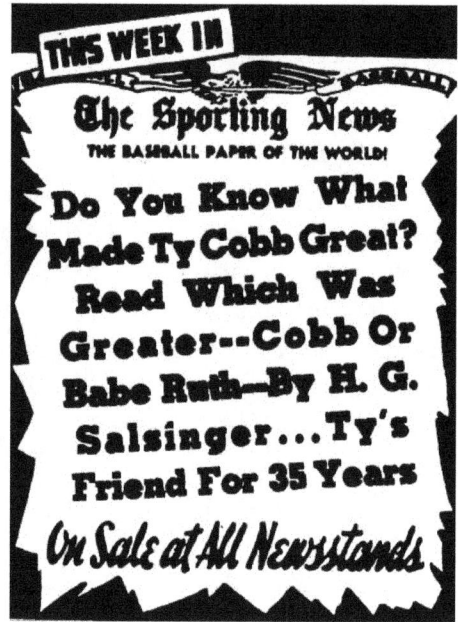

THIS WEEK IN

The Sporting News
THE BASEBALL PAPER OF THE WORLD!

Do You Know What Made Ty Cobb Great? Read Which Was Greater--Cobb Or Babe Ruth--By H. G. Salsinger...Ty's Friend For 35 Years

On Sale at All Newsstands

The following is an exception to the newspaper reference scheme above. These five endnotes correspond to the presentation on pages 206-07 of Clark Griffith delaying tactics on the mound in the chronology of 1926, based on Cobb's alluding to Griffith being hypocritical on the subject. They are in the order that information is presented, with each citation string corresponding to a successive paragraph:

Boston Journal, July 12, 1899 and September 18, 1900; *Brooklyn Eagle*, July 30, 1899.

Washington Post, June 9, 1895; *Chicago Tribune*, May 10, 1896.

Chicago Chronicle, May 18, 1898; *Chicago Record*, June 11, 1898.

Chicago Times-Herald, June 21, 1899; *Chicago Chronicle*, July 22, 1899, referring to the Chicago-Boston series of July 11-13, 1899.

Chicago Times-Herald, July 23, 1899; *Chicago Record*, August 24, 1899.

Cobb with Ossie Vitt in 1952, at a *San Francisco Examiner* baseball clinic

(cover) *Los Angeles Examiner* Photographs Collection, 1920-1961, USC Libraries
(frontispiece) AP Images
(first preliminary quotes page) MSNBC.com: footage@nbcuni.com did not respond to multiple clearance requests, and is a fair use exception

148 James Spence Authentication

153 CivilWarBummer.com

158 Louisville Slugger Museum & Factory

182 James Spence Authentication

195 National Baseball Hall of Fame Library

199 Rose Library, Emory University

200 MIRC, University of South Carolina

203-06 *Boston Herald* (feature by H. F. Manchester)

210 (top) *Times-Leader (Wilkes-Barre)*

213 (latter 1910s) Detroit Public Library/(mid-1920s) *Detroit News*

224 (article) *Times-Leader (Wilkes-Barre)*

227 MIRC, University of South Carolina

228 MIRC, University of South Carolina

229 MEARSOnlineAuctions.com

231 MIRC, University of South Carolina

233 Lelands.com

236 Rose Library, Emory University

238 MIRC, University of South Carolina

240 *Eugene Register-Guard (Ore.)*

246 MEARSOnlineAuctions.com

247 James Spence Authentication

250 unknown AP member (could be defunct)/*Boston Globe*

251 *Times-Leader (Wilkes-Barre)*

252 James Spence Authentication/Baltimore News-American Collection, University of Maryland Libraries

256 (top) National Baseball Hall of Fame Library

269 Burton Historical Collection, Detroit Public Library

272 Baltimore News-American Collection, University of Maryland Libraries

277 Kay Smith (confirmed by Terence Smith)

281 (headline) *Times-Leader (Wilkes-Barre)*

287 James Spence Authentication

298 (Ruth-Cobb) James Spence Authentication

299 (Corsicana) AP Images

300 *Boston Herald*

303 unknown AP member (could be defunct)

306 (headline*) Troy Record*

312 *Boston Herald*

317 (envelope) James Spence Authentication

318 (wedding party) Rose Library, Emory University

324 (both) Bill Mark images, via Rich Bogovich and Kid Nichols descendants

325 (1951 American League) James Spence Authentication

329 unknown AP member (could be defunct)/*Eugene Register-Guard (Ore.)*

334 Franklin D. Roosevelt Presidential Library & Museum

337 Reuther Library, Archives of Labor and Urban Affairs, Wayne State University

338 AP Images

339 British Pathe

340 British Pathe

344 HLC Properties, Ltd.

363 The Topps Company, Inc./National Baseball Hall of Fame Library

364 MEARSOnlineAuctions.com

369 Goldin Auctions/Linda Maines

371 James Spence Authentication

372 unknown AP member (could be defunct)

373 (group) Special Collections Research Center, Paley Library, Temple University

374 James Spence Authentication

379 Huggins and Scott Auctions

381 John D. McCallum Papers (Cage 799), Manuscripts, Archives, and Special Collections, Washington State University Libraries

383 National Baseball Hall of Fame Library

384 John D. McCallum Papers (Cage 799), Manuscripts, Archives, and Special Collections, Washington State University Libraries

386 National Baseball Hall of Fame Library

389 *Detroit News*

392 *Washington Star* collection of the *Washington Post*, D.C. Public Library

397 National Baseball Hall of Fame Library

399 MEARSOnlineAuctions.com

404 unknown AP member (could be defunct)

405 (top) James Spence Authentication

419-20 NateD.SandersAuctions.com

423 National Baseball Hall of Fame Library

427 (ball) James Spence Authentication

429 Del Mar Thoroughbred Club

434 Michigan State University Archives

443 MIRC, University of South Carolina

450 (bottom) Detroit Historical Society

454 HLC Properties, Ltd.

458 Jo Mosher, via Sherry Waterman

462 Louisville Slugger Museum & Factory

468 Sherry Waterman

471 Archives, Miller Library, Keystone College

507 *Detroit News*

520 *Detroit News*

539 Bancroft Library, University of California, Berkeley

542 Caxton Press, Caldwell, Idaho (Walter H. Nagle as told to Bryson Reinhardt, *Five Straight Errors on Ladies' Day*, 1965)

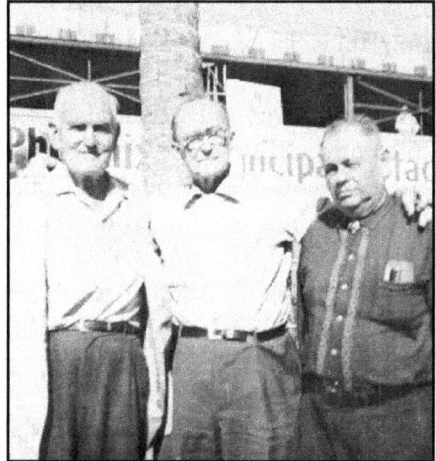

from left to right in March 1961 in Phoenix: Walter H. Nagle; Cobb; and Nagle chum Homer Shirrell, Captain USN (ret.)

Graphics from the defunct original *Sporting News* or its archives (20 (bottom), 134, 144, 183, 293, 323, 355, 357, 377, 417 and 439) were likely taken by hard-to-identify freelancers; 144 and 439 are via MEARSOnlineAuctions.com.

Grand Central Hotel, New York City,
February 1951

National League President Ford Frick,
Unveiling 75th Anniversary Plaque

Georgia Peach

George Sisler

Rogers Hornsby

Tris Speaker

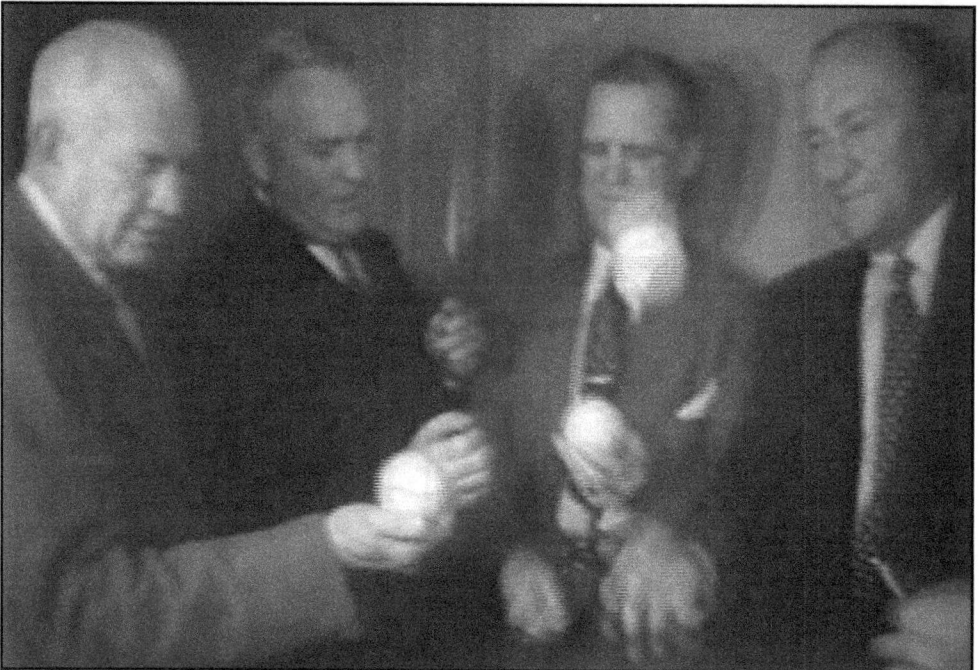